ENGLISH RECUSANT LITERATURE
1558–1640

Selected and Edited by
D. M. ROGERS

Volume 333

MATTHEW KELLISON
A Survey of the New Religion
1605

MATTHEW KELLISON

A Survey of the New Religion

1605

The Scolar Press

1977

ISBN 0 85967 362 6

*Published and printed in Great Britain by
The Scolar Press Limited, 59-61 East Parade,
Ilkley, Yorkshire and
39 Great Russell Street,
London WC1*

NOTE

Reproduced (original size) from a copy in the library of the Abbey, Fort Augustus, by permission of the Prior.

References: Allison and Rogers 430; STC 14913.

A SVRVEY OF THE NEW RELIGION, DETECTING MANY GROSSE ABSVRDITIES WHICH IT IMPLIETH.

Set forth by Matthevv Kellison,
Doctor and Professor of Diuinitie.

DIVIDED INTO EIGHT BOOKES.

Nevvly augmented by the Author.

Nunquid colligunt de spinis vuas, aut de tribulis ficus? Math. 7.
Do men gather grapes of thornes, or figges of thistles?

Vltra non proficient, insipientia enim eorum manifesta erit omnibus. 2. Tim. 3.
They shal prosper no further: for their follie shal be manifest to al.

Printed at Doway by LAVRENCE KELLAM,
at the signe of the holie Lambe.

M. DC. V.

Approbatio.

VISIS *trium S. Theologiæ Doctorum Anglorum testimonijs, quibus testantur hunc librum cui titulus:* A Suruey of the new Religion, *à R*[do] *D. Matthæo Kellisono S. Theologiæ Doctore & professore conscriptũ, nihil continere, quod fidei aut bonis moribus aduersetur; sed plurima, quæ ad fidem Catholicam stabiliendam, & Sectariorum errores profligandos faciunt; dignum censui, quem & ego calculo meo approbarem.*

Actum Duaci 23. Aprilis. *1605.*

Georgius Coluenerius S. Theologiæ Licentiatus ac Professor: & librorum in Academia Duacena visitator.

IN this edition, are added an Epistle of the author to the Honorable Lordes of the priuie Counsel: one chapter in the first booke: one chapter in the last booke: a table of the contents of al the bookes and chapters: the other table is renewed and augmented: and diuers other things in sundrie places for the clerer explication, and more ample proofe or disproofe of pointes handled before.

TO THE MOST HIGHE, AND MIGHTIE PRINCE, IAMES BY THE GRACE OF GOD, KING OF GREAT BRITANIE, FRANCE, and Ireland, Defender of the Faith.

OVR Majeſtie wil meruaile peraduẽture (moſt dread Soueraigne) how a prieſt, whoſe very name hath now ſo longe time, beene ſo odious in your Realme of great Britanie dareth be ſo bold, as to appeare in the preſence of ſo migh- tie a Prince, ſitting in a throne of Majeſtie and terrour, crowned with a Diademe of greater glorie then hitherto hath ſtoode vpon the king of England his head, and holding in his victorious hand a new Scepter, by which he commandeth al the Britaigne Ilandes, and like a Neptune, is Lord of the Ocean ſea, which honour was reſerued for your Royal Majeſtie, King IAMES of great Britanie France and Ireland.

2. And it may ſeeme ſtrange vnto your Highnes, to ſee one of my coate and condition amidſt the congratulations of al the Princes of Europe, ſaluting your Majeſtie with ſo long a Proeme: & euen then when their honourable Legates, haue ſo great and ſo important affaires, to communicate to your Majeſtie from their Lordes and Maiſters, to intrude into your chamber of Preſence, ſo rude a Meſſenger, and euil-

ſpoken Legate of myne, who ſpeaketh only by ſignes of written wordes, and demandeth audience in his maiſters name, who is fayne to ſend becauſe he dares not come: not that he doubteth of your Graces clemencie, or his owne innocencie, but becauſe ſuch as he is, hauing bene for ſo long a time, forbidden al acceſſe both to their prince and countrie, he dareth not approch ſo nere vnto your gracious preſence, though he be aſſured, that you are as milde a Prince, as mightie: and now as mightie, as anie Prince of Europe.

3. Yea I may be thought peraducture, to want both face and forhead, who nether bluſh, nor am abaſhed, to preſent ſo great a Prince with ſo litle a preſent, as is a booke of paper il printed, becauſe in a ſtrange countrie, & as il indighted, becauſe by one who hath liued longer out of his countrie then in it: and euen at that time alſo, when al the Princes of the Chriſtian world, preſent your Highnes with the rareſt and richeſt guiftes, that ſea and land can afforde.

4. But if it ſhal pleaſe your Highnes, to giue eare to your loweſt ſubiect, he wil not doubt but to cleare him ſelfe of al theſe three inciuilities, which may be ſuppoſed to haue bene by him committed, and he wil count it no ſmal fauour, to be permitted to ſpeake for him ſelfe, before ſo potẽt a Prince, and dareth auouch it to be no diſhonour for your Highnes, to ſtoupe to ſo low a ſubiect: becauſe Princes, who by aſcending can mount no higher, as being in temporal Iuriſdiction next vnto God, by condeſcending to their ſubiectes, do ariſe in greatnes, becauſe therin only, they are greater then them ſelues, in ouercomming them ſelues.

5. And from the firſt the Emperour Adrian wil excuſe me, who commended vnto Minutius his Proconſul of Aſia, as a thing of importance, *Ne nomen condemnaretur ſed crimen: that the name should not be condemned but the crime.* For ſayth Tertullian, againſt them that hated Chriſtians, in whom they could find no other thing to hate, but the name Chriſtian,

Tertullian Apolig. c. 3.

which

which they should haue loued: *Si nominis odiũ est, quis nominis reatus? quæ accusatio vocabulorum? nisi aut barbarum quid sonet, aut infaustum, aut maledicũ, aut impudicum. If the name be hated vvhat is the guilt of the name? vvhat accusatiõ is there of vvordes? vnlesse they sound of barbarisme, or vnluckines, or maledictiõ, or vnchastnes.* And therfore if Priesthood be no offence, the name Priest is deuoid of harme, & if Priesthood be no treasõ, a Priest in that he is a Priest, can be no traitour: vnlesse we wil accoũt Christ and his Apostles traytours, who were Priestes, and the first Priestes of the new law, & esteme after the same maner, of the ancient Priestes both of England, and other countries, whom Kinges & Emperours haue honored as their worthie, and haue loued as their most faithful subiectes, who were so far frõ being enemies to the crowne, that from their handes al christian kinges almost, haue hitherto receaued their Consecration, Crownes, and Scepters.

6. As for the second supposed, or rather presumed inciuilitie, that is so far from deterring me at this time, that I think now to be the verie time, when the Legates of the Kinges of earth, in their Lordes & Maisters name, wish your Maiestie a long and a prosperous Reigne, to salute you from the great Monarch of heauen, whose Legate I am, in that I am a Priest: though a miserable sinner, in that I am a man: and your Maiesties lowest subiect, in that I am an English man. Nether can I think, that the Legate of the great king of heauẽ, whose Legacie you shal vnderstand anone (your Highnes wil pardon such high speaches, because it is the maner of Legates to vse them, for their Maisters honour) shal be denied audience of your so gracious Majestie, when the Ambassadours of the Kinges of earth, vvho are but his Viceroyes, Lieutenantes, and Tenantes at wil, are heard with so fauourable a countenance, and such attentiue eares. And if I were neuer so base, yet is now the time of Coronation, when it is lawful for your basest subiect, to congratulate your new and high dignitie,

 and

and when the poorest man in the Realme, hath as good leaue to crie *Viue le Roy*, God saue King Iames, as any Noble man or Pere of your Realme.

7. Nether is the third obstacle any obstacle at al: because although my present be smal and your Personage great, yet to accept of a subiectes good wil is not to diminish, but to agrandize your greatnes: because in that, you are greater then your selfe, and likest the greatest, who tooke in as good part the widowes mite, as the richest offring. But yet I would not haue your Majestie to esteeme of this booke, only as of a bare bundel of papers: because I present you withal, that humble hart, and sincere affection, which a subiect can beare, or owe vnto his Soueraigne, and with my affection, I offer my selfe as your Majesties most lowlie and faithful seruant: which is a guift so great, be the giuer neuer so vile, that the great king of heauen requireth, yea desireth no more at our handes, but esteemeth that we giue al, when we giue our selues, and that we giue no litle, when we giue our al, be it neuer so litle. Nether is my present it selfe to be misprised, nether can it of such a Prince, because the booke is not my present, it is but the boxe, the present is that which it conteineth.

8. And if your Maiestie demand of me what that is? I answere: not gold, nor Iuorie of *India*, nor rich and orient pearle, for with such treasures your Albion, like and *India*, aboundeth: but it is that which is more worth, and which your *India* only wanteth: and what is that? It is Religion: the worship of God, the saluation of your soule, the safetie of your subiects, the health of the body of the Realme of which you are the head, the strength of your kingdome, the peace of your people, and the richest pearle of your crowne. This is the subiect of my discourse, these are the contentes of this booke, and this is my guifte and present, which amongest so many guiftes that by so many and so mightie Princes are presented vnto your Hignes, I offer with al humilitie, hoping

ping, yea persuading my selfe, that such a guift as Religion, can not but be grateful vnto that Prince, who is the defender of the Faith, and protector of Religion.

9. And because this vnhappie age hath bene more fruitful then profitable, in deuising of religions, in so much that, al is not gold that glistereth, so now al is not religiō, which is called so: lest I may be thought to offer counterfet for currant, and heresie for true religion: it is the Catholique Religion (most noble Prince) which I present, and which this booke conteyneth, and by many argumentes as occasion serueth, not only proueth, but also conuinceth to be the only sincere, & true Christian Religion: and vnmasking the new religion by a seuere, yet sincere examination, declareth it to be nothing else but errour & heresie, though vnder the painted face of a reformed religion, it hath deceaued some part of the world, and especially your litle world, great Britanie: which the Poet chose rather to cal a world by it selfe, separated from the greater world, then a part or parcel of it, because like a *microcosmos* & litle world, it conteineth compendiously, and in a lesser roome (which also is a grace) al commodities and perfections, which in the greater are dispersed But because I am more in examining & refuting the new religion, then in confirming the olde (for the good corne groweth easily, when the weedes are extirpated) I intitle it *A Suruey of the nevv Religion.*

10. And if your Maiestie demand of me, why I dedicate such a booke vnto you? I can not want an answer, because I can not wāt a reason. Flauius Vegetius wil tel your Highnes, that it hath bene euer the custome, to dedicate bookes to Kinges & Emperours (as he him selfe did to Valentinian the Emperour) because (sayth he) nether is anie thing wel begune, vnles after God the King fauour it, nether do anie thinges beseeme Kinges better, then bookes: who as they gouerne al, so if it were possible, should know al. For as in the head *In prol. l. de remilit.*

head which guideth the whole bodie, are al the sences, so a Prince the head of the people, should be indewed with al sciences: & as the Sunne, because it illuminateth the planets which vnder it rule, & guide the inferior world, is replenished with more light then they, so the King who is the Sunne of his owne world & kingdome, from whom not only the people, but inferiour princes also, are to receaue their light and direction, should be illuminated vvith a greater light & knowledge, then anie of his subiectes: and therfore Cirus vvas vvont to say, that he is not vvorthie an Empire, who is not better and wiser then the rest: vvhich also in effect king Salomon surnamed wise affirmed, vvhen he gaue that holsome counsaile to his felow Kinges: *Si delectamini sedibus, & sceptris ô Reges populi, diligite sapientiam, vt in perpetuum regnetis: If you be delighted in thrones, & scepters, ô Kinges, loue you vvisdome, that you may raigne for euer.* And to signifie this by an embleme, God him selfe gaue his people for their first king, no other then Saule, who vvas higher then the rest of the people, by the head and shoulders. And seeing that your Maiestie is not only a King, but a learned king also, as by manie monumentes of your rare vvit, & learning, vvhich euen the learnedst do admire, doth plainly appeare: to whom ought I of dutie to consecrate this my worke, but to such a King, vvho for his authoritie, can protect it, and for his wisdome, can iudge of it. Yea the verie subiect of my booke which is Religion, semed to require of right no other Patron, then your most excellent Maiestie, who by office and title, are the protector of Religion, the champion of the Church, & defendor of the Faith.

Sap. 6. — *1. Reg. 10.*

11. This common congratulation also not onlie of your owne litle world, but also of al the Christian world, this vniuersal ioy, these triumphes, these bonfyers, which the french man calleth *feux de ioy*, haue moued and stirred me vp, to shew some signe also of my affection & ioy, wherwith my hart is so ful, that

ful, that my tongue can not be silent. Al reioice (most gracious Prince) at your Coronation, as though it concerned al, and the hope which is generallie conceaued of your graces bountie, hath not only passed your seas, but the alpes also. The world admires the sweete prouidence of the Almightie towardes your Majestie, who euen from your infancie, hath protected you from manie imminent dangers, as though he had reserued you (as no doubt he did) for the crowne of England. The world expected ether ciuil warres, or foraine inuasions, after the death of her Majestie of late memorie, because the Heire apparant was not named, and though al men had their eyes, and expectations, and desires also, fixed on your Highnes person, yet they feared that which they desired, and hoped not without feare: and yet conscience directing your Nobles, and God gouuerning their conscience, vvithout any bloud shed, vvithout contradiction, yea vvith great applause of al, your Highnes is placed peaceably in your Regal throne: &, vvhich is rare, England vvas so inamoured with your Princely vertues, & so moued by your vndoubted title, that she sent for you, as for her louing spouse, and hath betrothed her selfe so fast vnto you, that the death of your person, can not dissolue this mariage: because her mariage with your person, is the spousage with your noble posteritie. These great fauours and benedictions of the Almightie towardes your Maiestie, make the world to thinke, that God hath culled you out for some good purpose, and that your Highnes to shew your selfe grateful vnto him, wil imploy your selfe in some honorable seruice for that church and fayth, of which you are called the Defendour: in so much that if the general voice grounded only on the great expectation, which commonly is conceaued of you, were as true as common, I should not neede at this tyme, to be the suppliant for the freedom, and libertie of your distressed catholiques.

Publike prayer in Rome for his Maiestie by the Pope his cōmandement.

12. And although your Catholique subiectes at home,

haue not yet obteined ſo great a benefit, yet ſo rich hopes, & ſo firme confidence, do they repoſe in your Graces bountie, that from the firſt day of your raigne, they hoped, that your Maieſtie wil proue an other Moyſes, who ſhal deliuer your realmes and kingdomes, from a worſe then Egiptian captiuitie, I meane hereſie, which makes the vnderſtranding a ſlaue to errour, vnder a ſhow of veritie, yea that you wil be vnto them an other Ioſue, who ſhal bring them to their land of promiſe, the Catholique church, which is the land of al gods promiſes, and that after a long famine more then Iewiſh or Saguntine, not of body but of ſoule, you ſhal be an other Ioſeph, who ſhal ſtore vs by your wiſdome and authoritie, with the ſpititual prouiſion of the true word of God, true faith and ſacramentes, by which the ſoule is nouriſhed. Yea that you wil be an other Canſtantine to appeaſe the boyſterous ſtorme of a long perſecution, and to repaire the ruines of the Catholique faith & church, of your realmes of England, Scotland, and Ireland.

13. And I alſo armed with the ſame hope, & biddē by your bountie, & conſtrained by neceſſitie to be bold: in the name of al your Catholique ſubiectes, of whom I am the leaſt: in the name of the catholique church, of which I am a mēber & you a defēdour, in the name of al catholique Princes, yea of al the chriſtian world, which hath conceaued ſuch an expectation of your gracious goodnes: in the name of the great king of heauen & earth, by whom you raigne, and by whom you were preſerued and reſerued for this croune & ſcepter: moſt humbly do beſeech, that it would pleaſe your Maieſtie, to caſt a gracious regard vpon the great afflictiō of your loyal, natural, and moſt ancient ſubiectes, the Catholiques of your realme, and to bend your moſt compaſſionate eares, to their humble & ſuppliant petition, vvho deſire nether landes, nor liuinges, nor offices, nor pardon for offences, but libertie for their cōſciences, whoſe reſtraint they count more greeuons,

then

then imprisonment, yea death of their bodies: and not to contristate them vvith a heauie repulse, at this tyme especially, vvhen euen theeues and murderers, are pardoned so graciously.

14. Our zeale tovvards Christ, & his Church, the loue of our Religion, the desire of the saluation of your Maiesties person our Lord and Leege, of your louing Spouse our most gracious Queene, of your Royal children our noble Lordes, of your Kingdom also our deare countrie, moueth vs to desire your Highnes, to restore vvholly that religion, which your glorious predecessours maintained with crowne, scepter, & sworde, as for the defence therof, they vvere al sworne at their sacred Coronation. But if it shal not stand vvith your graces pleasure, to graunt vs so much, vve moste humblye desire on our knees, libertie only of our conscience & religion, which the nature of both requireth. Nether (as we hope) wil your Maiestie condemne vs of to great presumption, for demanding that, which hath bene so long denyed vs, because there is no prescription against consciēce, when conscience is inforced: and your princely prudence wel perceaueth, that necessitie on our part is importune, bountie on your part imboldeneth, and the religion on your most noble progenitours part, for which we plead promiseth a gracious graunt.

15. For if it much skilleth, from what tree the graffe or fruite is taken, why shal it not much importe, to come of a catholique race? true it must be, which the Poet sayth:

Fortes creantur fortibus, & bonis,
Est in iuuencis, est in equis, Patrum Hor Flac.
Virtus, nec imbellem feroces,
Progenerant Aquilæ columbam.

I graunt that Religion is supernatural, and is not transfused with flesh and bloud, but infused by God, with consent of our wil, and operation of grace: but yet children are naturally bent, to like of that, in which their parentes haue excelled. And truly, for zeale towards the Catholique religion, almost al the noble kinges of Scotland, vvhich vvere your Highnes progenitours, are most famous: as the Valiant and noble Malcolmus, and the blessed S. Marguerit his spouse, king Dauid who builded 15. Abbeyes, & erected 4. Bishoprikes, Iames the fourth your great grandfather, surnamed Protectour of the faith, Iames the fift your grandfather, a moste iust king, and liberal to the poore: to omit diuers others not only of Scotland, but also of England, yea and Fraunce also, and namelie that warlike and most Catholique howse of Guise, to which you are allyed: but of al, your glorious mother is most renowmed: who, as for her goodly personage, she deserued to be spouse to a king of Fraunce, and for her Princely qualities and Roial bloud, was worthy a double croune in earth: so for her zeale in religion, and more then manly Fortitude shewed for the defence of the same at her death, she deserued the theird crowne in Heauen, called *Aureola Martyrum.*

Histoire abbregée par Dauid chambre. He vvas therfore called Rex pauperum. King of the poore.

16. Is is possible then, that your most excellent Maiestie, beholding such rare vertue in your mother, should not desire it in your selfe? or that you should not loue to liue in that religion, for which she loued to dye? I haue heard of some that were belonging to her, and entertained by her, when she was rather detained, then entertained in England, that she spent many howers in prayer, shed many teares of sorow, gaue great almes of charitie, and vsed diuers meanes of prouidence, that your Maiestie might be made a Catholique: & amōgst others she deuised the meanes, that you should be baptized, and confirmed by a Catholique Bishop. That ranne stil in her mynd, that was deepest in her hart, & oftenest in her mouth, for that she fetchetd many a sigh, & sighed out many a wish: & that also, by her last wil & Testament, she cōmended to your Maiestie, when, going to the stage to acte that bloudie Tragedie

Nic. Burne in his preface to K. Iames the sixt.

Tragedie, which she perfourmed so happilie: she commanded her man *Meluin*, to desire your Grace, in so gracious a mothers name, to serue god religiously, to defend the Catholique faith manfully, and to gouerne your kingdom peaceably: and as liuing for this she shed many teares, so dying no doubt, she offered no litle part of her innocent bloud; which as it cryeth vengeance before God against her enemies, so like a pleasing sacrifice (as we hope) it crieth for conuersion of your Maiestie, and your kingdomes, to that religion, for which it was shed. So that as sainct Ambrose sayd once to sainct *Monica*, who was alwayes praying, weeping, and wishing for saint Augustine her sonne his conuersion, who then was a Manichee: *Filius tantarum lachrymarum perire non potest*, I may say of your Highnes: to wit, that the sonne of such a mother, and Prince of such a Princesse, and inheritour of such vertues, such examples, such teares, such wishes, can neuer perish, that is can not but be a Catholique. This her zeale towardes religion, these her desires and wishes, these her prayers, and teares, and aboue al, her glorious Martyrdome, wil euer be before your graces eyes, to moue your hart, if not to admit wholy the Catholique religion, at least to permit it, at least not to persecute it, which she loued her selfe so wel, and wished to your Highnes, so hartelie.

lib. Cōcert. Ecclesia. Anglica.

17. And truely (most gracious Liege) such is our repose in your goodnes, that if there were no other motiues, then your glorious mothers example, your Catholique subiectes miserie, and your owne innate clemencie, we would not at al despaire of a graunt, of our petition: but seing that, the thing we request, concerneth not only our good, but your graces honour also, and the true felicitie of your kingdome, we hope cōfidently, not to suffer a repulse in that, in which your Highnes also hath a part, & for which, not only we are humble suppliantes, but your selfe also, to your selfe, and for your selfe, are an Intercessour.

18 And first, the graunt of our petition, shal be most honorable for your most Excellent Maiestie. King Lucius was the first king christian of our countrie, and the first king, that laboured in the conuertion of it, with Pope Eleutherius, by whose counsail, and preachers which se sent, he extirpated idolatrie and planted christian religion: and for this glorious facte, his name and fame, is, and euer shal be, most renowmed, both in heauen and earth. King Ethelbert was the second king, who by the meanes of Pope Gregoirie (by popes alwayes countries haue beene conuerted) & twelue Monkes of sainct Benedictes order, the second tyme restored this countrie again, vnto the same christian, and catholique religion, the which by the inuasion of the Saxons, was againe becom idolatrical, and pagane; and he is no lesse glorious, before God and men, for so honorable an enterprise. But if your Highnes shal be the third king, who shal againe reduce this countrie to the same aũcient religion, you shal be as much more glorious, and your name as much more renowmed, as heresie is worse then paganisme, & more hardly extinguished. VVilliam the Conquerour, from whom your Maiestie is worthilie descended, is reckened amongst the worthies of the world, and written in the list, and catalogue of the most warlike kinges, for that famouse conquest which he made of your litle world. But if your highnes shal get the conquest of heresie, your honour shal be as far more greater then his, as the conquest of mens soules & myndes, is more glorious, then subdewing of bodyes. In such a conquest, the warre is Christes, the victorie is his and yours, the crowne yours only, not in earth only, but in heauen also.

Beda. lib. 1 hist. Eccles. Gent. Angl cap. 4.

l. 1. hist. Ecc. gent. Aug. c. 23

Th 2. 2. q. 10. a. 6.

19. You haue the occasion offered (o mightie Prince) by which you may make your name and fame immortal, let not such an opportunitie passe: if you can atchieue so glorious a conquest, as you can if you wil (because the body of your Realme wil follow the wil of their head) you shal be

more

more glorious, then al the kinges of England before you. If it pleaſe your Maieſtie, to ſet before your eyes, thoſe glorious champions of the church, Conſtantine, Theodoſius, Pepine, Charles, al ſurnamed great, more glorious for their victories ouer hereſie and idolatrie, then for conqueſtes of countries, more renowmed for propagating the auncient catholique religion (for is was not Lutheraniſme nor Caluiniſme which they promoted) then for enlarging their dominions: you wil eaſilie perceaue, that it is much greater honour, four your Highnes to conſort with them, rather then with Conſtantius, and Valens, thoſe Arian Emperours, enemies to that church, which they defended, & enriched, & Leo Iſauricus, & Conſtantinus Copronymus, thoſe infamous Imagebreakers. And if you pleaſe to calle to mind the catalogue of the noble kinges of England, Lucius, Ethelbert, Egbert, Oſwald, Oſwine, Alfred, and many others before the conqueſt, with Vvilliam the Conquerour, and ſo many Henries, Edwardes, and Richardes, after the conqueſt, al your noble predeceſſours: ſo mightie in force, ſo rich in treaſure, ſo noble of byrth, ſo fortunate in warres, ſo couragious in fyght, ſo glorious in victories, ſo wiſe in gouernment, ſo iuſt in puniſhing, ſo merciful in pardoning, ſo vpright in life, ſo zealous in religion; who built ſo many goodly Monaſteries, erected ſo ſtately Churches, founded ſo learned Colleges, enacted ſo holſome Lawes, and wiſe ſtatutes, and got ſo many, and ſo ſtraunge victories in Fraunce, & other countries, euen vnto Paleſtine: your Princelie wiſdom, wil eaſilie ſee, that greater wil be your honour to ioyne your ſelfe to theſe worthies, then to ſtand ſo nakedly accompanyed, with three only of your predeceſſours, who haue protected the new religion, and ruined what they haue builded: wherof the firſt was not wholly for the new religion, becauſe by Parlament, he enacted ſix catholique articles, and at his death founded a Maſſe for his ſoule: the ſecond was ſo young, that he was he was rather ouerruled then ruled, the last was but a woman: and though they wanted not guiftes of nature, which might beseeme princely authoritie, yet for persecuting the Catholique fayth, & following other pathes then their predecessours had troden, their names are not eternized with that immortal fame, which their predecessours haue purchased by their religious actes.

20. Secondly (redoubted Prince) the Catholique religion vvil be greater securitie, for your temporale state. For if your Highnes dare relye vpon them, who by religion, may disobey your lawes and ordinances (as I haue in my sixt booke demonstrated) much more may you put your trust and confidence, in your Catholique subiectes, whom conscience and religion, byndeth to obedience. For they are taught by religion, that authoritie is of God, and that in conscience they are subiect vnto it, and bound to obey kinges, though otherwise difficile and hard to please, not only for feare, but for conscience also. And this obedience they giue not only to christian, but also to pagan kinges, such as al were, when S. Peter, and S. Paul commaunded vs to obey them. *Vvee are taught* (sayd S. Policarpe to the Proconsul) *to giue to higher povvers that honour vvhich is devve to them, and not hurtful to vs. Vvee* (sayd Tertulian to the Ethnikes) *pray for the Emperour, and reuerence him next to God, and more then vve do your Goddes.* To be breefe, (as I should be with a king, if the matter did not enforce me to be longer then I should be) giue vs (sayth S Austin) such Iudges, such Magistrates, such Souldiours, such Subiectes, as our religion requireth, and Princes shal raigne securely, and their Kingdomes shal flourish more happilie, then Platoes common welth.

Cal. l. 3. Inst. c. 19. ¶ 14. l. 4. c. 10. ¶ 5. 25. 27.

1. Pet, 2. Rom. 13.

Ex Eus.

Apol c. 3. & lib. con. Scap.

Epist. 5. ad Marcellin.

21. And because religion, good, or bad, beareth a great sway in the rule of mans life; the professours of the newe religion, must needes be more prone to disobedience, and rebellion, then wee; because religion, which serueth for a

bridle

bridle to vs, is a ſpurre to them. Vvherfore by Catholiques, al your predeceſſours haue beene ſerued with great fidelitie, both in warre and peace: & your glorious mother, if ſhe were liuing in earth, as ſhe is better liuing in heauen, would not let to witnes, what affection ſhe hath found amongſt the Engliſh Catholiques, and would warrant your Grace, that they wil neuer be falſe to the Sonne, who haue been ſo true to the Mother. But if your Highnes doubt of our fidelitie, we wil bynd our ſelues by corporal oath, to obey your lawes in al temporal cauſes, & to defend your Royal Perſon, your deare Spouſe our gracious Queene, and your towardlie children, our noble Lordes, with the laſt droppe of our bloud: and this our oath we ſhal be contented to diuulge to al the Princes of Europe, yea al the Chriſtian worlde.

22. And as your Grace may accounte of vs as of your ſureſt, ſo not of your feweſt nor weakeſt ſubiectes: for not withſtanding this long perſecution, we are ſo many, that as Tertulian ſayd to the Paganes, of the Chriſtianes of his tyme: we fil your Courtes, your Vniuerſities, your Cities, your Townes, your Villages, yea priſons, not for theftes or murders, but for Religion: only we haue left the Temples to the miniſters, becauſe in them is practiſed and preached a Religion, which our conſciences can not brooke. Yea a greatter part are we, then any particular ſect in your Maieſties realme, and we are linked in Religion to al Catholique Princes and countries about you, who wil be more louing neighbours, if they ſee that we their brethern, fynd this deſired fauour at your Graces handes: and the nobleſt & mightieſt of them, wilbe more deſirous to ioyne in mariadge with your Royal poſteritie: whereby how your Kingdom ſhalbe ſtrengthned, and your dominions enlarged, your Princely wiſdome eaſilie perceueth, and you haue an example in the noble Houſe of Auſtria. Your noble brother of France that now raigneth, may be a preſidēt in this matter, who though he was once an ene-

Apolog. c. 37.

mie to the Catholique religion, yet findeth more faythful correspondence in his Catholique subiectes, then in al the rest: and by permitting both, in some good sorte contenteth both, and serueth him selfe of both.

23. Thirdly (most gracious Soueraigne) to admit the Catholique religion, or at least to permit it, is your greatest safetie for your conscience. For as you are a Prince, so are you a Christian Prince, and therfore a champion, and (as the
Cap. 49.
Prophet Esaie sayth) a *Foster-father of the Church*: and as the French Kinges euen from Clodoueus, the first Christian King of that Realme, haue beene called *Christianissimi*, for
Genebrar. l. 3. Chron.
their good offices towardes the Catholique Church: and the kinges of Spaine, from Ferdinand, yea from Alphonsus, yea
Baron. to. 9. Annal.
as some thinke, from Ricaredus, for extirpating Arianisme, and propagating the Christian fayth, are surnamed Catholi-
Geneb. l. 4. Chron.
que: so the kinges of England, from king Henrie the Eight,
Sleid. l. 3.
your Graces great vncle, for his Catholique and lerned
Georg. Lilius in Chr. Angl.
booke written against Luther, and other his most honorable seruices, which he once performed for the Catholique Church, are called *Defenders of the Faith*, that is, the Catholique faith. VVherfore your Maiestie, first because you are a Christian King, Secondly because you are a *Defender of the faith*, are to see that the right worship of God, and the true Christian Religion be practised in your Realme. This the honour of God, vnder whom you raigne; this the good of his Church, whose Champion you are; this the saluation of your people, whose King you are; this the spiritual health of the body of the realme, vvhose head you are requireth. For if in any countrie it be true, that the people changeth with the King, in England it is most true, as we haue seene by diuerse changes of religion, in this vnhappie age: and so, in your Maiestie it lyeth, to saue or not to saue your people, which so admireth your authoritie, & Princely vertues, that your vvil is their lavv, and your lavv their rule of religion.

24. And

24. And vvhere can your Grace find a securer hauen, for the saluation of your selfe, and your subiectes, then the Catholique Church? In which so many Martyrs haue dyed, so many Doctors haue taught and preached, so many virgins haue liued in flesh like Angels, and so many Sainctes haue wrought so strange and wonderful miracles: by which so many heresies haue beene condemned, so many Councels called, so many Ecclesiastical lawes enacted, and such goodly order and discipline established. For which so many Monasteries, Churches, Colledges, Vniuersities, and Hospitalles, haue bene builded and founded. In which so many Emperours, Kinges, and Princes haue liued, raigned, dyed, and (as it is to be hoped also) haue bene saued: and against which, so many cruel persequutors, in vaine haue raysed forces, and vsed tormentes, and so many heretikes haue raged and railed: which is descended from the Apostles, and can proue a continual succession of her Pastors, and religion, from them vnto this day. VVheras the new Church began but yesterday, and her preachers with her, who also can not proue their mission, nor distinguish them selues from false Prophets: whose doctrin hath al the markes of heresie, and is rather Antichristian then Christian, plucking at Christs Diuinitie, spoiling him of many honourable titles, to wit, Redeemer, spiritual Phisitian, Lawgiuer, Æternal Priest, Iudge of the quicke and dead, equalizing euery Christian with him, making him an ignorant, desperate, and damned man: which hath neither Priest, nor Sacrifice, nor in effect any Sacrament, no prayer, not so much as our Lords prayer, no, not a sermon, according to their doctrine, nor any of the essential partes of religion: which is blasphemous in many pointes against God, iniurious to State and authoritie, fauourable to vice, and bending to Atheisme: al which pointes I haue proued in this booke.

25. But if your Maiesties pleasure, or leisure be not such,

as by perusing this booke, to informe your selfe, which is most likely to be the true Christian Religion, if it shal please your Highnes, to command a conference or disputation, which hath euer bene the vsual meanes to determine cōtro-
3. Reg. 18. uersies, (as appeareth by the disputation of Helias with Baals
Io. 8. Act. Ptophetes, of Christ with the Iewes, of S. Paul vvith Iewes
9. 17. 18. 19. and Gentils, and of the ancient Doctors in Councels, and
20. Aug. ep. out of Councels, with Ethnikes and heretikes) your Maiestie
41. Ruf. l. hist. shal find diuers of your Catholique subiectes, both at home and abrode, vvho vvil present them selues at such a disputation, if you shal but please to command.

26. Lastly suppose your Highnes should persecute the Catholique religion (as God forbid, so glorious a Prince should receiue so fovvle a disgrace) besides the dishonour wherwith your noble crowne and name should be obscured, besides that you can not persecute this religion, but you must make vvarre against your noble progenitors, euen your glorious Mother, you should sooner make a conquest of al the countries about you, then extirpate this Religion? whose nature is to gather greater spiritual force, vvhen greatest furie is armed against it.

27. This Palmetree (ô Mightie Prince) the more it is pressed, the higher it grovveth; this Camomile more it is troden, the thicker it springeth forth. This Vvalnuttree, the more it is beatē the more fruteful it waxeth: this Corne by threshing, is seuered from the chaffe: this Gold by a fierie persecution, becometh purer and brighter: This Arke by a raging deluge, mounteth the higher: These Israelites the more they are oppressed the more they multiply, killing of Catholiques (most clement Prince) is but cutting of boughes, from that tree
Psal. 79. which reacheth from sea to sea, and this cutting is but lopping, the tree aftervvards in height is taller, and in boughes fuller, and this spilling of Catholiques bloud, is but watering of Christs Vinyard, in vvhich for one Catholique

cut of,

cut of, many an hundred do ſpringe vp in the place. Thoſe Neroes, Domitians, Diocletians, and Maximinians, can beare witnes of this, of which the laſt two, hauing gathered great force, and prouided al the engines and inſtrumentes of crueltie, that a cruel hart could deuiſe, made ful account of a conqueſt of the Chriſtian race, and engraued this their preſumed victorie in marble pillers in Spaine, with this Inſcription: *Diocleſian, Iouius, Maximin, Herculius, Cæſſ. Aug. amplificato per Orientem & Occidentem Imperio Rom. & nomine Chriſtianorum deleto, qui Remp. euertebant.* But they counted their chickins, before they were hatcht, triumphed before the victorie, gaue a blaze before their light went out, and exalted their hartes before their ruine: depriuing them ſelues of their Empire, for the diſgrace, which they conceaued in ſuch a foyle, and dying a death ſo miſerable, that it ſeemed the beginning of their Hel. And thoſe your Predeceſſors, who haue perſecuted the litle flocke of the Catholiques of your realme of England, would aſſure your grace, if they were liuing, that this litle part of the Catholique Church, foloweth the nature of the whole: becauſe notwithſtanding ſo many confiſcations of their goods, ſo many confininges imprisonnementes and baniſhmentes of their perſons, ſo many tortures and deathes of their bodyes, Catholiques and Catholique Prieſtes, are mo at this preſent in your realme, then they were fourtie yeares ſince. It muſt be true which S. Leo auoucheth: *Non minuitur perſecutionibus Eccleſia, ſed augetur* &c. *The Church by perſecutions is not dimished but augmented: and alvvayes our Lords fielde is clad vvith a farre richer harueſt, vvhileſt the graynes vvhich fal, ſpring forth againe more multiplied.* And the reaſon is, becauſe that muſt be performed, which Chriſt promiſed: *Portæ inferi non præualebunt aduerſus illam: the gates of hel shal not preuale againſt her.* Her enemies are dead, rotten & forgotten, ſhe ſtandeth ſure vpon a rocke, alwayes the more glorious, the more ſhe is aſſaulted.

Euſ. l. 8. c. 13. 25. 26. 29. Zon. 3 par. Annal. Sur to. 6. die 10. Decemb. Aldus Man. poſt Schol. in comm. Caſ. Bar. ann. 304.

Ser. in nat. Apoſt.

Mat. 16.

28. But I craue pardon most humbly of your gracious Clemencie, for my tedious petition. The miserie of our state, and rhe importance of our humble supplication, required a longer, but your rare Clemencie and humanitie (which hath already wonne the hartes of your people) demanded a shorter. VVherfore I most desire your Highnes, humbly to imagin, that in this petitiō, your Catholique subiectes are not alone; your noble Progenitors and Predecessors, your most glorious Mother, al the Catholique princes, to whom you are allyed, and their Catholique countries, which border vpon yours, the whole Church of God, the Saintes of your realmes, the bloud of Martyrs shed in the same and for the same, the miserie of your most ancient subiectes, your Highnes honour and securitie, both for the temporal and spiritual state of your kingdomes, demand this also with vs. Yea this your owne selfe, so gracious a Lord towardes al, requireth of your selfe: wherfore vsing no other intercessor, then your selfe, we desire your Grace to harken to your selfe, which if it shal please you to do, we make no doubt of our most humble petition.
Prou. 21. In the meane tyme we shal pray to him, who hath the hartes of Kinges in his hand, to bend your compassionate hart towardes your Catholique subiectes, & so to rule it & inspire it, that you may be a King according to his hart: that you vnder him may raygne long & prosperously in the Realme of Britanie: & he by you in his holie Church: & that so your Maiestie may raigne vnder him here for a time, as you may raigne with him herafter for al eternitie.

Your Highnes most humble and obedient subiect

MATTHEW KELLISON.

TO THE RIGHT HONORABLE LORDES, THE LORDES OF HIS MAIESTIES PRIVIE COVNSEL.

PLATO the Diuine Philosopher (Right Honorable and my very good Lordes) estemed that common welth most happie, in vvhich, either a Philosopher raigned, or the King professed Philosophie: giuing vs therby to vnderstand, that such a prince is most vvorthy his Crown and Scepter, in vvhom vvisdom conspireth with power, and Mars and Pallas do symbolize together. For if it be true which experience teacheth, and the vvise Lawier Baldus insinuateth, that to the effectuating of euery thing, knowledge, wil, & power are required: much more shal the same three things be requisit in so great a matter, as is the orderly gouernment of a Kingdome. Where if knowledge in a King be not to direct, wil to folow direction, and power to put in execution, nothing shal be brought to passe worthy the dignitie of a king or the good of a commonwelth. For if the Prince be only vvise in deuising Lawes, but not willing to enacte them, or if he be willing to enact, but not able to put in execution, his knowledge is but mere speculation, his wil is without effect, and al is in vaine. But as knowledge, vvisdom, and prudence in a Prince is the first, so is it the principal, because the first and chiefest point in gouernment, is to know the common wealth: otherwise wil without vvisdom is vvilful, and power, vvithout knowledge hovv to vse it, vvere as a sword in a madmans hand Which the vvise king Salomon vvel knowing, demanded of the Almightie wisdom and princely prudence most especially: & the same before al other thinges he counselleth al kinges to seke for, if they dilight in Diademes Thrones and Scepters. And as prudence is the Prince of al moral vertues, because it directeth them and guideth them to their end, so ought Princely prudence to be the Prince of al pruden-

l. Multam. C. Si quis alteri vel sibi.

3. thinges required in a king.

Cic. l. de orat.

2. Reg 3.

Sap 6.

Princely prudence. prudences, because the prudence of the Subiect directeth but one, that of the Prince directeth many. And vvhere the Prince is indewed with such prudence, there the King is a Philosopher, and a Philopher is the King, and the kingdome is most happie.

2. This benediction wished by Plato, is lately to our great good happe, fallen vpon England: vvhere now a Philosopher raigneth & the King is a Philopher. VVho for his rare wisdome is an other Salomon, and for his princely prudence in gouernment (vvhich in his booke to the noble Prince, his sonne and worthy image of such a parten, he hath made known to the vvorld) semeth, and is in dede as he semeth, an other Solon, Licurgus or Numa Pompilius. But because a King is to gouerne, not him selfe only, & his owne priuat appetites, but holdeth the bridle also, by vvhich he curbeth ruleth and reyneth the wilde vntamed, and vnbrideled affections of al his subiectes: his knowledge and Princely prudence, ought to be as great as if the wittes of al his subiectes were assembled together, and put in one head: that so the members of the ciuil & politique body may be directed and gouerned by the eye and insight of this head, and that the subiectes like lesser starres, from him as from a Sunne, may borrow their light and direction.

The reason of great prudēce in a King.

The necessites of Counsellers. 3. And for as much as no one man, can see al thinges, though he had as many eyes as Argus (because mans witte by nature is to narow to reach so farre and farre of, and by the ouer greedy desire of knowledge in our first parentes, is endarkned now by ignorance) he standeth in nede of Counselers, if not as eyes to see by, at least as glasses to represent to his eyes. Whetfore Moyses though indewed with heauenly vvisdom instilled from aboue, yet vsed the aduise of Iethro, yea and of the Seuentie two Ancients also, to vvhom the graue Consistorie of the Zanedrin succeded. The Romaines also had their Senators: The Assirians, Medes, Persians, and Groians had their Counsellers, without vvhose verdit no matter of moment vvas concluded: vvhose examples the kinges of Spaine, England, France, Scotland, and other Christian Kingdomes haue imbraced: in so much, that now you shal as soone find a King without subiectes, as without Counsellers. Only God is so wise, that he neither vseth neither nedeth any helpe of Counsellers in the gouernment of the Empire of the world, though in execution of the law and order, vvhich him selfe only setteth down he vseth rather the concurrence then the ayde of creatures, and secondarie causes. And although it may seme smal honour to a King, to aske counsel

Exod. 18. Num. 11. Galat. l.4.c. 49. Baron. to. 1. Annal an. 33.

D. Tho. 1. p. q. 22. a. 3.

God hath no Counsellers.

Counsel of his Subiectes, yet is it no disgrace to the head to vse the shoulders for supporters, yea the handes and feete also as inferior ministers, to excute that wich the head shal determine. For although the King be wiser then his Counsellers, yet may they also see some thing wich he marketh not: and so they may assist him, who by him selfe knoweth not al, and yet had neede to know al by him selfe or others, because he iudgeth al *Mammea* Quene mother to the Emperour Seuerus, told him that in changing his sentence so often by the aduise of his Senate, the Emperour and the Empire grew more & more contemptible? Be it so (sayd Seuerus) but I am sure more strong and durable. And certes, as it is a felicitie in a Prince not to be commanded, so is it a miserie, not to be wel counselled. I agree with Homer no moe kinges but one: but yet I adde also, the moe counsellers the better, and that, the king is wisest who wil not be wise alone: because, *there health is, where are many counsailes*. And therfore some kinges haue thought it better to leaue their sonnes vnlerned then lerned, imagining that so they would more easily giue eare to counsel: but both are better, that is wisdome to iudge, lest the king by counsel be abused, and humilitie to folow counsel, when good counsel is giuen. I grant it is a goodly thing, and almost diuine, as resembling the Souueraintie of the diuine Maiestie, to sit in a throne of Maiestie, and with a diademe on head, and scepter in hand, to command and to be obeyed, yea feared and reuerenced; but yet because kinges though they be aboue, yet are not out of the ranke of mortal men, and are not so much kinges for them selues as for their subiectes profit, and haue a king aboue them, to whom as Viceroyes, they are to render a strict account, for their good or euil gouernment; I saye that to be a King is as great a seruitude as Soueraigntie and as great a charge as honour, and his Princely Throne is rather a place of labour then ease, and his diademe as ful of cares, as pearles and pretious stones, and wayeth much more then the gold and stones of which it is compacted, Yea as much, as is the charge of so many subiectes which it vndertaketh. VVherfore Princes especially, haue nede of counsellers to beare some part of their so great a burden: lest falling vnder so great a waight, they ruine both them selues and their subiects.

No dishonour to a King to vse Cousellers.

Lamprid. in vita Seueri.

Prou. 14.

4. Al which his Maiestie, our souueraigne Lord, wisely waying and considering, hath made choise of and established your Honours for his sage and secret Counsellers, wel knowing that as many

 lightes

lightes put together do make a greater, so many wittes vnited do giue a greater insight in matters to be resolued, whether they be lesser wherin counsel is not to be contemned, or greater as gouuernment of knigdomes, wherin it is necessarily required: for if the King ruleth not as becometh his office and person, not him selfe only but his people also perish, and he like a *Phaeton* is ruined with the chariot, which he should haue ruled: as may appear to euidently by the ruful falles & ruines of so many solewise Roboames, who haue ruined them selues and others, because they would not take Counsel of others.

Counsellers charge. 5. But as the next honour to a king, is to be Counseller to a king, so is it the next, and peraduenture not the next, but a greater charge. For first of al, great must be the wisdom and no lesse the experience of them, by whose aduise and counsel a king must be directed, and especially in great Britanie, where the kingdome is a world, and this King so sage and wise, as appeareth by the aforesaid booke, called the kingly guift, furnished with so witty sentēces and holsome preceptes of gouuernment. The holie Sceipture speaketh not to Counsellers as counsellers but rather to priuat persons: *In many thinges be thou as ignorāt & giue eare with silence, & presume not to speake in the middest of great men* But rather they are to harken vnto that of Dauid. *I speake of thy testimonies in the sight of Kinges*. Secondly that the graue aduise of Counsellers may cary credit, & no sooner touch then take, he must procure by vertue, an opinion of vertue, especially Iustice, Temperance, & other vertues which tender the common good. Far as S. Ambrose saythe: *How can be be esteemed in counsel superior, who is in life inferior*. Wherfore the Athenians knowing what a disgrace vice is to sage and witty Counsel, when one of vicious life had spoken wisely and profitably for the common wealth, they imbraced the Counsel but fathered it on an other. *Is ordo* (sayth Cicero speaking of Senatours) *Vitio vacato, cæteris specimen esto*. *Be that order deuoid of vice, be it an example to others*. Lastly as the King ought to respect more the common good of his Realme and the safetie of his people (because in that he is discerned from a Tyrant) then his owne particular: so shoud the Counseller in al his aduises ayme chiefly at that, as the butte of his intentions, remembring always, that worthy speach of a worthy Senator: *Salus populi suprema lex esto: the chiefest law be the health of the people*. But as in man there are two partes, the soule and the bodie: and consequently two healthes also, the one of the soule the other of the body: so are there in a Common wealth two different states, the one spi-

[Margin notes: Βασιλικὸν δῶρον. — Eccles. 21. Psal. 118. — What vertue is required — l. 2. Offic. 8. — An example. — l. 3. de leg. — Ar. l. 8. Polit. c. 8. — They must tender the cōmon good. — Cicero l. 2. de Rep.]

one spiritual the other temporal; the one is called the Church, which ruleth the soules, the other a Kingdome, that ruleth the bodyes, and temporal causes; and the health of this is ciuil peace and order, the end is temporal prosperitie, the health of the other is Grace and Religion, the end is æternal fælicitie. And therfore the Spiritual health of the people, is as much to be preferred before the temporal good, as the soule surpasseth the bodie, the church the common wealth, Religion pollicie, heauen earth, and æternal tẽporal fælicitie And therfore to a christian counseller, the principal marke, at which he is to ayme, must be the spiritual health of the people, which is true faith and Religion.

States in a Kingdome. The temporal state yeeldeth to the spiritual

6. And this is the cause (Right Honourable) why, hauing dedicated this booke, vnto his most Excellent Maiestie in the first Edition, and hearing that is was not taken in euil part, and hauing good occasiõ also to print it again, partly to correct faultes escaped in printing, partely to adde some chapters, and here and there some few lines for fuller proofe & a clearer explication of that which before in some few places was spoken more compendiously, partly to satisfie the desire of many, who requested a new printe because the former bookes were to few in number; I haue presumed so much of your Humanitie, as to adde an Epistle to your Honours in this second edition: not to instruct your wisdomes, but only to put you in mynd of a farther charge then commonly is thought to appertain vnto your office. For commonly that King or Counseller, is counted fully to haue performed his dutie, if preuenting ciuil discord, and forrein inuasion, he so minister iustice, that malefactors be punished, & the iniuried recompensed. And as for Religion and spiritual health of the people, manie do thinke it belongeth only to Bishops and Clergie men, and not to the King nor Counsel. But wise Princes and Counsellers that looke better in to their charge fynd it clere, that though they be not rulers of the Church in matters of faith, yet they ought to be promotors, mainteyners, and defenders of Religion. For as euerie member is bound in his degree, to seke and conserue the health of the whole body, so a king being most excellent, is as much more bond, as God hath made him more able, to defẽd and promote by his temporal authoritie, the spiritual health & good of the Church And therfore to this al Christian kinges are sworne at their Sacring, & Coronatiõ. The Frẽch king at his coronatiõ promiseth to the Archbishop of Rhemes by a solemne oath, to minister iustice to his people, to conserue them

The cause of this Epistle.

Ambr. ep. 33. Greg orat. 17. ad Theod. Kinges and Cousẽlers must defend Religion. To this they are sworne. Girard li 3. del Estat p. 242.

 in the

Belfor. in vita Philip Augusti. Amb. Moral l.11. Conc. Tol 5. c. 2. 3 4 5. Conc. Tol 6 c. 16. 17. 18. Sur. in vit. S. Tho. Cantuar. Stovv in vit. Henr. 4. Liu l.1. Dion. Caß. l. 2. Val. Max l.1. c. 1. Romulus his lavv.

in the vnion of the Catholique Church, and to extirpat and chase out those, who by this Church shal be censured as heretiques. The King of Spaine taketh in effect the selfe same oath, as appeareth by the histories of Spaine. The like doth the King of England promise to the Archbishop of Canturburie vpon the Altar at westminster, where he sweareth that he wil defend the Catholique Church and her priueledges, that he Wil honour her Bishops and Priestes, & minister iustice vnto his people. Yea the Pagans them selues could see that this maner of care of Religion was belonging to the Prince. And therfore Romulus annexed the care of the Temple, Sacrifices, & Ceremonies vnto Regalitie. And Rome was no sooner built, but Religion was established and conserued by ciuil authoritie. And seing that your Honours are christian counsellers to a christian King: that Religion and worship of God which he is boũd to manteine by authoritie, you are to further by aduise and counsel. And therfore Romulus made this law for counsellers: *Sacra patres custodiunto: Let the fathers of the Senate kepe watchfully the Sacred Ceremonies.*

l. 6 Eth. 2. l 2. hist. c. 2. In Apol.

7 But now wheras in a macheuellians eye it may seme good pollicie to preferre temporal state before Religion, when it standeth with commoditie, neuertheles in time the end wil proue, that that is neuer gained, which is il gotten, and that the common wealth rather tottereth then standeth, which is not supported by Religion, as I could proue by many a politique and wordly wise Hieroboam. Aristotle counted it absurd that the ciuil power should dominier ouer the Goddes, that is ouer religion. And Eusebius recounteth as a thing ridiculous, that the number of the goddes in Rome, was limited by the Senat, and that therfore Christ could not be receaued as God amongst them, because it seemed not to stand with pollicie, to addmitte him as God, who was already allowed of by the peoples voice, before the Senates decree. In so much that as Tertullian obserued, God then could not be allowed to be God, vnles it pleased man to be fauourable vnto him. And next vnto this in absurditie it is, that Religiõ can not be admitted vnles it please the state, nor no further then it may stand with state; because Religion should march before, pollicie should come after, and by Religion should be squared out, not Religion by pollicie. Neither is the Prince or Counseller to feare lest by giuing the precedence to Religion, state, be to much debased. For as Grace destroyeth not but perfiteth, and debaseth not but eleuateth nature, as faith ruineth not reason but leadeth

The King & State must be directed by Religion.

it be-it beyond reaſon: ſo Religion is neuer contrarie to ſtate & true pollicie, but cōfirmeth it and directeth it, yea and perfecteth it alſo: nether is the King the leſſe abſolute, becauſe he foloweth the preſcript of Religion, but then eſpecially he raigneth, when by Religion God raigneth in him & he vnder God, and ſo is not one of thoſe *which raigne but not of God.* Cicero ſaith that: *Sublata aduerſus deos pietate, illa virtus iuſtitiæ erga homines tollatur neceſſe eſt:* Pietie towatds God being taken away, the vertue of iuſtice, towards men muſt needes be aboliſhed. And I may adde, that Religion towards God being taken away, loyaltie towards the King and felicitie amongſt the ſubiectes, wil not long remaine, becauſe they wil neuer be truſtie to men, who want Religion, wich maketh them true to God. *l. 1. de Nat. Deor.*

8. This booke (Right honourable Lordes) wil make playne vnto your wiſdomes, which is that religion that is the health & ſaluation of the Realme, and it wil demonſtrat by many argumentes and demonſtrations, that the new Religion now current in England by authoritie, can not be this ſpiritual health, which you are to ſeeke for, but that the ancient, Catholique, & Romaine faith as hitherto it hath bene generally receued of al Chriſtian Kinges and kingdomes, & perſecuted by wicked Emperors and heretikes, for the true Chriſtian Religion, is the only Religion, by which the King and kingdome may be ſaued. And can your Lordſhippes being men of ſuch wiſdom, inſight, and iudgement, imagin any ſecure ſtay for ſaluation, in that Religion, whoſe Founders and Preachers could neuer yet diſtinguiſh them ſelues from falſe apoſtles, becauſe they could neuer alleage more for them ſelues, then the authoritie of their owne priuate ſpirite, wreſting and framing the texte of holie Sripture to that wich they fancie: wich hath euer bene the only argument & Achilles, for al maner of hereſies: VVhich hath al the markes of Hereſie, derogateth ſo much from Chriſt, wanteth almoſt al the eſſential partes of Religion, is blaſphemous againſt God, iniurious to Prince, law, ſtate, and tribunal, and ſo fauourable to al vice and Atheiſme, as by this *Suruey* your Honours wil eaſily diſcouer? And if ther were no other thing in it but noueltie, that me thinke ſhould be ſufficient to bring it in diſcredit with ſo wiſe Counſellers. Noueltie in al gouernement law & true pollice is odio9, in ſo much that Plato would not permit ſo much as the change of tunes and ſonges: and the people called Ephori ſeuerly puniſhed their Muſitians for adding or changing of a ſtring in their inſtruments: & the Locrians made a law, that whoſoeuer would

The improbabilitie of the nevv Religō.

Noueltie odious.

l. 2. de leg.

 propoſe

propose any new law, should present him selfe before the magistrate, which a rope about his necke But especially in Religion noueltie is to be condemned, for as Cicero sayd of the common welth, so say I of Religion, that we haue receiued it from our Ancesters, yea from Christ and his Apostles, as a Picture, to which if you adde ether lyne or colour, al his changed: yea as Aristotle sayd, that the essenses and natures of thinges are like numbers, so say I of Religion. For as if you adde or subtract from any nūber, it is no more the same, but an other number: so if you adde new articles of Religion, or detract from the old, it is no more the same, but an other, and consequently not the true Religion, because there is but one, and that one is euer the same. And the reason is because Christ planted his Church vpon a rock so firmly, that the very gates of Hel and forces of the diuel, shal neuer preuail against it, and so we are not to looke for any innouations nor down falles of Religion. And therfore seing that this new Religion is but a new deuise, an apish imitation, not so good as new turning of an old coate (for who euer heard of this Religion but only in condemned heretikes? who euer wrote of Churches builded for it, or of the seruice or ministerie or disciplin Ecclesiastical obserued in it?) it can not possibly be the stable Church & Religion of Christ. But suppose that this Religion flourished in the Apostles tyme (though no ancient monument of it, was euer seene, felt, or heard) either this Church fel, or it fel not? If it fel, the gates of hel preuailed against it, and so it was not the Church which Christ founded so assuredly vpon a rocke; if it fel not, where was it or in what new world did it flourish vntil Luthers dayes? It was, they say, but it was not to be seene. But if it were not to be seene, then was it neuer the Church of Christ, because that is built not only on a rocke, but is placed also as a Citie on an hil, and a Tabernacle in the Sunne, so high, that it euer hath bene conspicuous: else could it not haue bene so cruelly persecuted by the euil, nor so gloriously enriched ad beautified by the good Kinges and Emperours, nether could it haue bene a place of refuge and recourse for true faith & saluation. And seing that the Romain Church hath euer flowrished from the beginning, notwithstanding so many persecutions, schismes, and heresies, and hath alwayes continued glorious and conspicuous, euen in the enemyes eye, often assaulted but neuer beaten down, that must needes be the Church of Christ, or else he neuer had any Church at al, & in that only can be found the true faith and Religiō, the spiritual health of the people, which Kinges & Counsellers are to fur-

Li. 4. de Rep. *Noueltie discrediteth the nevv Religiō.* *An example* *The reason.* *Mat. 16.* *Refutation of the nevv Religion.* *Mat. 5.* *Psal 18.* *Chrys. ho. 4. de verbis Isaiæ vidi Dom.* *Proofe of the old Religion*

to further. Wherfore (my Lordes) your owne doctors are enforced to confesse, that once our Church was the true Church of Christ, though afterwards (as they say) it fel. But if it was the true Church, then stil it is, & if it once stood, thẽ certes it standeth stil, for els hel gates had preuailed: yea they say that it is stil the true Church, & so of late it was grãted, yea so much Caluin him selfe cõfesseth: but yet it is now corrupted (as they say) and couered with errors & heresies. But let vs take what is granted. Is it stil the true Church? then are they heretiques who haue left it, & builded Church against Church, & altar against altar: because going forth, and breaking out, is a marke of an heretike, as in this booke is declared. *li. 2. c. 1.* Is it stil the true Church? then are her preachers the true Pastors, because the Church can no more be without Pastors, *See the first* then a body whithout a head: and so the true Church and true Pastors must euer go together: *booke, chap. 4.* and consequently your ministers are vsurpers, who intrude them selues into the true Pastors roomes & preach without commission. Is it stil the true Church? then out of it, neither King nor kingdome nor Counseller can fynd saluation. *li. 2. c. 4.* Is it stil the true Church, then is it not ouergrown with heresies. *li 8. c. 8.* It it stil the true Church? then can it not erre in matters of fayth, because anie one heresie seuereth from the true Church, *See the 2. booke, chap. 4.* & as it chãgeth numbers, so doth it Churches. But perhaps they wil say our Church hath of later yeares admitted new pointes of Religion; which yet they can not proue. For let thẽ take any point of our Religiõ, be it Purgatorie, prayer to Saintes worship of Images, free wil, or the Real presence, & let them name the tyme vvhen it began, and if I proue it not more ancient then the tyme they assigne, vnlesse they grant it begune with the Apostles by whom Christian Religion was reueled, I wil yeeld them the victorie. For although some Ecclesiastical lawes & Ceremonies, heue bene added, as the Church deemed requisit for tymes & persons, & although some bookes of holie Scripture haue bene defined to be Canonical, which before were not so Canonically, & commonly knowne, & although some pointes of Religion, in Councels haue bene more explaned, yet shal our aduersaries neuer proue, that our Church did adde new pointes of faith, or diminishe the nũber of old. And so your wisdomes do easily see, what reason you haue to suggest vnto his most excellẽt Maiestie, either to admitte againe the ancient Catholique Religion, which hitherto hath bene the Religion not only of England, but of al Christian kingdomes also, or at least to permitte euerie one, there to seeke his saluation, where he persuadeth him selfe to find it.

9. But

9. But peraduenture your Honours wil alleage, that notvvithstanding the probabilitie produced for the Ancient Catholique Religion, yet it standeth not with your present State, and so can neither be admitted nor permitted. Alas (my Lordes) and if it were so, yet you know, and I haue already proued, that state must yeld to Religion as to a higher pollicie, vnto which it is subordinate. And I may truly auouch also, that our Religion is no enemie to state, as appeareth by so many states and kingdomes, which stil are & euer haue bene manteined by it, but is the piller and vpholder of Christian states, and of al honest pollicie. For that our Religion commandeth to honour our Prince, such as we al acknowledge most willingly King Iames to be: it teacheth vs also, not for fear only, but for conscience to obey him and his lawes in al temporal and ciuil matters, and so to giue to God and his holy Church what belongeth to them, that we forget not to yeld to Cæsar what apperteineth to him. And besides Religion, nature vrgeth vs to folow nature, that is to be kind to our countrie, & not like vngrateful byrds, to stayne the nest wherin we were hatched, nor as monstrous members to seke the destruction of that body, of which we are partes and members. what then (Good my Lordes) is the cause why we are holden in such a iealous supiscio? Is it peraduéture some strange or sauage nature, into which our Religion hath changed vs by a metamorphosis? we are men as others are, & we are as much English men as who are most, & we are more anciét Subiectes then any which his Maiestie hath, by whom al the ancient Christian kinges of Englãd haue bene serued most faithfully, both in peace and warre, at home and abroad. Or is it the freindship which we haue with forrein Princes, who being Catholiques as we are, do tender our case as their owne, and thinke them selues not to liue at ease, when they see vs their brethern vexed with so long and so sore a persecution? But alas, is there any force of freindship comparable to the natural affection which we beare to our countrie? Zopirus the faithful seruant of Darius, knowing it to be as incredible as it seemed impossible, that any Subiecte should be false vnto his natural King and countrie, was faine to cut of both nose, lippes, & eares, and to father al this iniurie vpon his King Darius, dispairing otherwise to winne credit in seruice against his countrie. And now by this generale peace, which this peaceable king hath made, al occasions of ielousies and suspicions are taken away. For if we would contemne Religion, and put of al natural loue towards our countrie, with whom now should

Cath Religiõ a freind to State.

Mat. 22. Rom. 13. 1. Pet. 2. See the sixt booke.

Religion and nature vrge vs to loue our King and Countrie.

The peace made freeth Catholiques from al suspition.

Iustin. l. 1. hist. in fine.

we conspire against either king or countries? vvith the Spanyard? he is now your freind, by an assured and desired league. VVith the French? He now of an old enemie, is become no new nor late freind. With the Pope, who of late hath bene holden for so great an enemie. He not as a freind only, but as a Father loueth our King, who so soone almost as his Maiestie was proclaimed, commanded publique prayer in Rome for his Maiesties prosperous succese, and by many signes and offices, hath giuen no smal tokens of his exceeding good wil and affection to his Maiesties person. Or is it because our Religion is contrarie to yours? you tolerate, or hitherto vvinck at diuers Religions in the Realme, which wil hardly subscribe to the Protestants religion, and so you may permitte ours also, being the Religion of al yours and our forfathers. As for our loyaltie, I trust our actes deserue, your H. H. good opinion: because no subiectes of his Maiestie did euer more desire to see this crowne vpon his head then Catholiques, and none shewed moe signes of hartie ioy then they at his wished coronation. Certes if hartes had windowes, as Socrates wished, or were penetrable by sight, as christal is, that their secrets might be discouered, I would not doubt but that your H. H. should see, which now iustly you may beleue, as true affection & loyaltie in the Catholiques hartes, as any subiects can beare to their Soueraigne. But peraduenture your Honours do feare least by libertie of conscience the number of Catholiques would increase, and their forces with their number, and so might seeke to domineer who now are kept vnder. To this also we haue an answere, and that, as your Honours will perceue, most reasonnable. For first, if your Honours esteme of your own Religion as the truer, you must counte it also the stronger, bicause the true Religion, is *an immaculate law, conuerting soules*, and Religion hath euer been to hard for superstition, and the true faith of Christe, hath euer had the maistrie ouer al sortes of heresies: and so to feare least the Catholique Religion (which hetherto hath vanquished al heresies) should get the vpper hand of the Religion by you established, it especially being now so backed and seconded by authoritie, is to doubt of the veritie of your own Religion, but bee it that in tyme by reason of the secunditie of our Religion, both Catholiques and Catholique Religion would encrease, yet besides that Religion byndeth vs to obedience to our Prince, such order by his Maiestie & your Honors might be takẽ not only with vs but with the Pope him selfe & Catholique Princes, that though our Religiõ should encrease

Psalm. 18.

ũ and we

and we with our Religion, yet nether your forces should be dimini shed, nor your state impeached, nor preiudiced. And you haue a President in Fraunce to assure you of your state: bicause there the Catholiques are in number so many, and in force so mightie, that the partie of your Religion is not an handfull vnto them, and yet such is the Catholiques modestie, and respect vnto the Princes Edicte of libertie of conscience, that your partie is nether iniuried nor molested, much lesse oppressed by them, & much lesse should it bee in England where it is so fauoured by your state and authoritie. Why then, most honorable Lordes, al occasions, and iust feare to the contrarie being taken away, may not our consciences & Religion enioy some freedom and libertie, or at least toleration?

10. Truly (Right Honourable Lordes) now thinges are come vnto that passe, that although in former tymes, when you had not stricken this so firme a league with Catholique Princes abroad, you might in some sorte cloke so seuere procedings, against the Catholique subiectes: bearing the world in hand (how iustly God knoweth) that Catholiques plotted treasons, conspiracies and inuasions, with those Catholique Princes, who of iust compassion releeued vs, and consequently that we were not executed for Religion, but for treacherie & treason: & although then you might perswade the late Queene frayle and fearfull by sexe, & some forrain Princes also, vnto this so sinister an opinion: yet now we can not but conceiue better hope, of better & more gentle dealinges: partly because now for a Queene we haue a King, so wise, iust and moderate in al his actions, who like an other Alexander the great, alwayes keepeth one eare open for the accuseds cause: partly because by this late peace & vnion, which his Maiestie hath contriued, al occasions of such suspicions and pretences are cut of. So that now if stil you continew the execution of your so sharpe and eagre lawes, as your predecessors haue done before you, you shal giue occasion to his Maiestie, and al the Christian world, to say and see that it is Religion only against which you arme your furie, from which notwithstanding you haue hitherto disclaimed, as frō a barbarous crueltie: & so your former pretences wil grow to be, suspected, & your future seueritie wil be farre more odious; and not your selues only, but his Maiestie also, (whose name, as yet renowmed, in so infamous a persecution must be vsed) shall be much dishonoured, and we the persecuted shal be as farre more couragious, in our wonted suffering, as our cause herafter shal be so much more glorious, by how

Catholiques hope.

The reason.

by how much it is more freed, euen from al pretence and colour of al treacherie and treaſon.

11. Pardon me (my Lordes) if I ſeeme ſome what vehement, it is a publique cauſe, and a general calamitie of my Catholique brethren, for which I plead: neither let it ſeme ſtrange vnto you, that leauing now the King, I haue recourſe vnto his Counſel, becauſe the world is ſo wel perſwaded of this ſo amiable a Prince, & Catholiques haue already found him ſo gracious and fauourable, that al now is thought to conſiſt in your Honours, and that what ſoeuer ſeueritie is vſed againſt them, doth either al procede from you, & not from the King at al, or if from him, not from him as from his owne diſpoſition, but as from his Counſelers ſuggeſtion. It can not be vnknown to your wiſdomes, what a long and ſeuere perſecution we haue endured, and our quartered & mangled bodyes, which ſo lately remained on your gates, poles, and bridges, and your priſons, from which this ſo clement and compaſſionate Prince hath freed manie; & the diſtraction and diſſipation of Catholiques goods not yet reſtored, yea your ſeuere Lawes which as yet remaine in Vigour, are ſufficient and to to lamentable witneſſes of the ſame, and ſufficient motiues as we hope of a more gentle proceding. But we are not to rubbe olde ſores, leſt we make new woundes, but fougiuing and forgetting, and deſiring God alſo to forgiue what ſo euer is paſt, wee moſt humbly ſupplicate, & beſech your Honours, that as you reſpect the honour of his Maieſtie, & your own alſo, as you tender the common ſpiritual good and ſaluation of the Realme, & as you meane to diſcharge your office honourably before God and men: you wil vouchſafe to worke the meanes with his moſt Excellent Maieſtie, already ſo wel enclined to his Catholique Subiectes, that the Catholique Religion may be permitted vnto them, who can be induced to no other, it hauing ſo euident markes of the true Chriſtian Religion, and being deliuered to them by ſo renowmed Prelates, embraced, cheriſed & maintened by ſo noble predeceſſors, leſt by conſtraining their cõſciences, you ruine their ſoules, & anſwere for them alſo at that day, when euerie one, & eſpecially counſellers, & men of place and dignitie, shal haue ynough to anſwer for their owne: that ſo (my Lordes) as in his Maieſties line the vnion of the noble houſes of Yorke & Lancaſter is ſtil continued, and by this peaceable Salomon, ſo general a peace is contracted, and the coniunction alſo of the two Realmes of England & Scotland is expected: ſo by his authoritie and your counſel, the Catholique Religion,

The Kinges fauour to Catholiques.

gion, in which only vnion in faith consisted, may be admitted, or at least permitted, that we with the rest of of our felow subiectes may liue peaccably & amiably as members of one body, vnder the rule & gouernment of this our one so glorious head, & that so these Realmes & kingdomes thus vnited, may be as farre more strong at home, and terrible abroade, as vertue and force vnited, is greater then the same dispersed.

But now my Paper telleth me that I haue vsed to much of it for an epistle, & my epistle blusheth to haue presumed to play the Counseller euen to Counsellers them selues, and would neuer dare to appeare before so graue an assembly, did not that wise King Alphonsus giue some hart and courage, who being demaunded whom he deemed, the best and sincerest counsellers, answered, the dead; meaning bookes and Epistles, which because they haue nether hartes to feare nor faces to blush, do neuer alter their intended purpose, nor breake of their discourse for hope of fauour or feare of disfauour, but freely and sincerly vtter the Authours conceipt of euery mannes bounden dutie. And though the Authour may perchaunce haue erred in making his Epistle speake some one thing or other, which might haue been concealed, yet he hopeth not to haue offended, because he meant but well: that is, good to his Countrie, Zeale to the common cause, loyal dutie to the Prince, and due respect to his priuie Counsel, and libertie, if it may bee, of conscience, for his afflicted Brethern.

Your Honours humble seruant.

MATTHEVV KELLISON.

TO THE CHRISTIAN READER.

The inanimate & vnreaſonable creatures (*Gẽtle Reader*) becauſe they haue neither ſufficiẽt knowledge to direct them ſelues to their end, neither wil to moue them ſelues vnto it, are by the prouident gouernour & menager of al, indewed with natural inclinations, propenſions, or inſtincts, by which they are caried euery one directly to their end, as though they knewe it, and deſired it. For as the arrowe, though it know not the marke, yet, becauſe it is directed by one that knoweth it, flyeth as directly to it, as if it knewe it, and as ſwiftely, as if it were in loue with it: ſo theſe creatures although they know not their end, yet becauſe they are directed by natural propenſions, and indiſtincts, which God, who wel knoweth it, hath put into them, ayme alwayes at their conuenient places, endes, and perfections, as if they not only knew them, but alſo moſt earneſtly deſired them.

Inſtincts of nature direct vnreaſonnable creatures.

A ſimilitude.

2. The heauens, as we ſee, do moue ſo vniformely, as though by common conſent they were aggreed, to be the neuer erring dials, which meaſure our actions, and diſtinguish our tymes, and ſeaſons. The Sunne riſeth at a iuſt tyme, as if he were mans cocke, to cal him vp to his worke, and his candle alſo to giue him light by which he may ſee to worke: & he ſetteth alſo at his tyme, putting man in mynd, that then it is tyme for him, to take his reſt, and to ceaſe from labour. The Moone in her change, is vnchangeable, and conſtant in her inconſtancie, and both the Sunne and Moone, are ſo ſure moderators of tymes and ſeaſons, that winter and ſommer, ſpring, & the fal of the leafe, neuer change their order; not that theſe planets know their tyme, but becauſe they are moued by one that knoweth.

3. Brute beaſtes as ſoone as they are able to nible vpon the graſſe, can chooſe the hearbs, which are moſt cõuenient for them, as though

they were cunning herbistes, & you shall seeldome or neuer see them dye of surfitting, or mistaking one hearbe for another: not that they know the vertues of Simples, but because God hath giuen them an instinct of Nature, to take that which is agreable to Nature. The byrdes of the ayre keepe a certaine, and a most conuenient tyme for breeding, & building; and their nestes they build as artificially, as if they were carpenters by occupation, & their young ones they feed with that discretion, as if they were experte nurces. The spider wil not yeeld to the fisher, who as cōingly weaueth his webbe, & placeth it as craftilie to catch the flye, as he doth his net to take the heedles fishes. The Bee when the winde riseth, taketh claye in his mouth, lest the wind haue to great force ouer his litle body. I wil say nothing of the so wel ordered common welthes of Bees & Antes, nor of the strange operations, of other liuing creatures, because of them I am to treat in diuers places of my booke. Plantes and trees, seldome, or neuer deceiue the husband man, but after the dead of winter (al which tyme they also seemed dead) they send forth, first theyr leaues, and afterwardes their bloomes, as messengers to fortel the fruites, which for his labour in pruning them, they meane to bestow vpon him. And neuer shal you see them bud in the middest of winter, but in the spring only, when the ayre is so warme, that their young ones can take no harme: not that they know the most conuenient tyme, but because God who knowes it, hath engrauen such an inclination in them.

4. But more bountifully hath the Almightie dealt with man, then with any other corporall creatures, because he is more noble thē them al, & is an abridgement of al: for to him he hath giuen vnderstanding to know his God, his good, his end, and felicitie, and a will also, to desire and pursue the same. And lest his vnderstanding should banguer, in approuing falshood, for truth and veritie, he hath engraued in it a natural propension to veritie, and lest his wil should, embrace euil, and badde for good, she also hath the like inclination to good. In so much that as the eye seeth nothing but light or colours, and the eare heareth nothing but sound, so the vnderstanding aymeth only at truth, and the wil desireth nothing else but good: and as the eye can not perceiue sound, nor the eare colours, so the vnderstanding can not giue his assent to a knowen vntruth, and the wil can not affect euil, as euil. Hence it is that we can not with hart thinke that the crow is white, or the swanne blacke, because this is a knowen

Mā knoweth his end and good.

Mans vnderstanding assenteth only to truthe.

vntruth

vntruth, and where neither the truth nor falsehood is apparant, there we doubt, and suspend our iudgement, which is the cause why we neither iudge the sandes of the sea, nor the starres of the skye, to be euen or odde in number, because we haue no more reason to thinke the one, then the other. The wil in like maner can not affect a knowen euil, as euil, because her obiecte is good, and therfore Dionisius Areopagita sayd, that no man intendeth euil as euil, but euen then when he embraceth vice, which is the the greatest euil, he aymeth at some apparant good of pleasure, or profit, which he imagineth in that euil. Wherfore al knowen goods, such as knowledge, vertue, & felicitie are, euery man desireth, & loueth euen in his enemie whom he hateth, though he like not of the difficulties, which are to be deuoured, before he attaine vnto them.

lib. de diuinis nom. c. 4.

Mans wil affecteth only good.

5. Who now would thinke that man, ether should or could approue errors and heresies, for true doctrine, & falle in loue with vice in which is no true goodnes to be liked? But nothing is so good which may not be abused. God hath giuen man freewil, not to sinne, but to merit, which if he had not, his weldoing would deserue no god amercie, & his euil deeds should be worthy no blame, because they who of necessitie do otherwise then beseemes them, are rather to be pitied, then blamed And yet from hence proceedeth al iniquitie, from whence vertue, merit, and laudable actions should haue had their source and beginning. He hath grafted in our nature passions of loue, feare, anger, and such like, that by loue we might imbrace good, by feare auoid euil, and by anger chastice vice and euil: and yet whilest we giue passions the head & bridle, passions rule, reason is ouerruled, man is ouerthrown, and ruined by that, by which he should haue stoode. He hath imprinted in vs a natural loue, & liking of beatitude, in so much that no man is so barbarous, who, if you aske him whether he wil be happy or no, can, or wil say, no, with hart & mynd. Wherfore S. Austin saith, that the Iester, who promised that he would tel euerie one the thing which his hart desired, had hit the nayle on the head, if he had sayd, *Omnes beati esse vultis, miseri esse non vultis: you wil al be happie, miserable you wil not be*: & yet whilest by this natural propension, we seeke for felicitie in honours, riches & pleasures where it is not, and not in God, where it is, that is made our bane which should haue beene our good.

The benefit of free wil.

The abuse.

Passions.

The abuse of them.

Al men desire felicitie.

l. 11. de Trin. c. 12.

The abuse of the loue of it.

6. And so God hath bountifully bestowed on vs vnderstanding, wholly bent to truth, & ouly to truth, and yet by abuse, that is made

The abuse of the vnderstāding prone to truth. the fountaine of al errours, which should haue bene the ofspring of verities. For whilest like Æsops dog, we snatch at the shadow, in steed of the flesh, that is, seeke after truth in those thinges in which is no truth at al, but only a show and shadow, we make our natural propension which we haue to truth, a cause of our errour, which should haue bene our best direction, and with as great a vehemencie we embrace our errours, as we are propense and prone to truth, euen as that dog, the more greedily leaped at the shadow, the more desirous he was of the flesh. *The source of superstition & heresie.* And hence proceede idolatries, superstitions, sectes, and heresies, to which we would neuer giue so obstinate an assent, did we not imagin some truth to be, where only is deceite and errour. *The abuse of the wils procliuitie to good.* He hath giuen vs also a will, wholy bent to good, and altogether auerted from euil: and yet whilest with those foolish byrdes, we pecke at *Zeuxis* painted grapes, that is seeke after good in pleasures, riches, & honours, where is but a painted hewe of good, we embrace vice our greatest euil, in steed of our greatest good, & so much the more greedily, by how much we are more inclined to good. *The fountain of al vice.* And hence proceede fornications, aduouteries, theftes, and murders, which we would neuer desire so vehemently, did we not apprehend in them, good, that is, pleasure or profit. So that the banquets of our wil, proceed only from mistaking of badde for good, & the errours of our vnderstanding, procede not from any prones which we haue to vntruthes, but from mistaking of apparant, for true verities.

7. And this is the cause (most gentle Reader) why I haue made so exacte a Suruey of the new Religion, because I know thy vnderstanding to be so naturally inclined to truth, and so auerted from al vntruthes and errours, that to lay open vnto thy vew, the manifold & grosse absurdities, which it implyeth, is to refute them, and to make them knowne vnto thee, is to dissuade thee from them. For truly I find many pointes of this Religiō, so opposit to light of reason, that I dare auouch, that no man can be either Lutheran or Caluinist, vnlesse he want wit, or hauing wit, enter not into consideration, or be caryed away with passion, or partial affection. I wil not deny but that many a good wit may be found amongst the Professours of this Religion, but yet I say, that these good wittes, if they layed aside passion and partialitie, and would vouchsafe to enter into due consideration, could be neither Lutherans nor Caluinists, because to euident vntruthes the vnderstanding can giue no assent nor approbation.

8. And

8. And vvhat more euident vntruth then Lutheranisme or Caluinisme? First of al their preachers can say no more for proofe of their authoritie or doctrin, then Simon Magus, Ebion, Cerinthus, Basilides, Nestorius, Eutiches, Vvicleph, or any other Heretike could haue sayd, and euerie false prophet hereafter may say, preach he neuer so absurdely, as I haue demonstrated in the first booke most euidently. For neither can they proue their mission to be ordinarie by succession, nor extraordinarie by miracle: & so if you giue eare to them, you must bynd your selfe to harken to al false prophets, who wil say & sweare that they are sent from Christ, & if you put them to the proofe of their mission, they wil say you are partial, in reiecting them, and receiuing Luther and Caluin, who can not proue their mission. But no man can with any showe of reason admitte al false Prophetes, because they teach playne contraries, ergo he can haue no reason to receiue Luther and Caluin, as the true messengers and ministers of Christ: and consequently, he can not in hart receiue them, because the vnderstanding can not approue a thing, for vvhich it hath no probable reason.

The absurditie of the nevv religion.

The first argument.

Al heretikes say as much for them selues, as these of our time.

9. Secondly their doctrin, if it be wel considered, is as euidently false, as that vertue is vice, or black is vvhite, but the vnderstanding (as is already proued) can not approue manifest falsehood and euident vntruthes, ergo no man of vnderstanding and consideration can admitte Luthers and Caluins doctrin. Now that their doctrin is euidently false, I can both euidently, and also easily proue. For to a Christian it is euident, supposing the veritie of Scripture, that heresie is errour and falsehood, but in the second booke I haue demonstrated, that al the markes of heresie agree as fitly to this new doctrin, as to Arianisme or any old heresies, ergo to a Christian it is euident, that this new doctrine is errour, and consequently it can not be approued by a Christian of iudgement and consideration, because the vnderstanding can not giue assent to an open vntruth.

The second argument.

Al the markes of heretikes agree to these nevv preachers.

10. It is euident also to a Christian, that Antichristian doctrin, vvhich is dishonorable and repugnant to Christ, can not be true, but Lutheranisme and Caluinisme is altogether opposit to Christ, because it pulleth at his Diuinitie, & maketh him nether Redemer, nor spiritual Phisitian, nor Lavv maker, nor eternal Priest according to Melchisedechs order, nor Iudge of the quicke & the dead, but rather æqualizeth euerie Christian to him in grace and sanctitie, and maketh him ignorant, fayneth him also to haue despaired, yea bringeth him to hel & dãnation, & litle esteemeth manie thinges, which were much

The third.

Their doctrin is antichristian.

† beloued

beloued of him, or belonging to him? al vvhich the third booke conuinceth, ergo a Christian of vvitte and consideration, can not in hart brooke such a religion.

The fourth. 11 In like maner to a Christian, yea to euery man that beleueth that there is a God & relgion, it is euident that Religion can not stand without Priestes, Sacramentes and prayer: but it is euident also, that in the newe religion, none of these essential partes of religion can be found, especially according to the doctrine of the same Religion, as the fourth booke maketh manifest, ergo a Christian of vvit and dewe consideration, can not approue it for true Religion.

The fifth. 12. Againe as euident it is, that the new religion is absurd, as that God is not the author of sinne, and the only sinner, that he is not vnreasonable, cruel or tyrannical, for according to the reformed doctrine, al these blasphemies are verified of God, as the fifth booke teacheth, ergo the reformed doctrine is euidently absurde.

The sixth. 13 Likewise it is euident to reason, that al lawful authoritie is of God, that Princes lawes binde, that their tribunals are iust and lawful, and that correspondence betwixt the Prince and Subiectes, and betwixt one subiect and an other is necessarie to vphold societie, to vvhich God and nature encline vs, vvhich is proued in the sixth booke: but the reformed doctrine despoileth Princes of authoritie, bringeth their lawes and tribunals in contempte, and ruineth al Societie, as is euidently also proued in the same booke, ergo a man of common sense and iudgement, who entereth into a dewe consideration, can not with hart admit of this religion.

The seuenth and eight. 14. Vice & Atheisme, by light of reason, are euidently knowne to be repugnant to reason, vvherfore seing that this new religion leadeth to al vice, and Atheisme, and that by many pointes, and principles of the doctrine of the same, as in the seuenth and eight bookes is demonstrated, it is an euident absurditie, euidently repugnant to reason, and consequently can not be approued by a man of reason and consideration, because the vnderstanding can no more assent vnto an euident vntruth, then can the wil affecte and like of euil, as I haue already proued.

The authors desire. 15. Wherfore (most gentle Reader) if thou be a Catholique, and vouchsaffe to peruse this booke, I hope thou shalt be more confirmed: if thou be a folower or professor of the new doctrin, when thou seest the fowle absurditie thereof, and the clere veritie of the Catholique, I hope thou wilt reiecte thyn erronious opinions, and imbrace

brace the only true Catholique Religion. And if this my desire haue successe in anie, the prayse is al dew to God, who is principal agent: the defects or faultes are myn, his vnweldie instrument. If anie reape cõmoditie by my laboures, I count them very wel bestowed, & it is the reward I looked for. If some that may wil not, yet they are not lost, *quia aliquid est voluisse*, it is something to haue desired to do good.

16. If the stile please thee not, refuse not gold because it is il fashioned, and remember, that though the author be thy countriman by byrth, yet he is more a stranger then an Englishman by education. If I seme to speake to sharpely some tymes, it is not for any tooth against anie person, but for hatred of heresie. And if thou take this my impolished vvorke in good worth, thou wilt giue me the occasion and courage to take in hand an other, in vvhich I shal explane (as I haue in part already) certaine pointes of the Catholique Religiõ (to wit Indulgences, Merite, Satisfaction, vvorship of Saintes, Images, and Reliques, with many such other) vvhich seme to the deceiued, to imply iniurie to Christ, or absurditie, as I haue discouered the grosse errors of the new Religion. *his excuse.*

17. But now for a Vale & frendly farewel, I besech thee to take this counsaile at my handes. Build not vpon that, not so flattering as false opinion, wherwith many vse to comforte them selues, that thou maiest be saued in any religion. The second booke wil assure thee, that vvithout a true and intier faith, it is impossible to please God, and that out of the true Church, there is no saluation. As God is but one, the truth but one, so his Religion, Church, and worship is but one. This Church and Religion is not to be found amongst the reformers, because they haue al the markes of heresie: It is only to be found amongst the Catholiques, who are nicknamed Papistes, as thou myest see in the second booke, and in some chapters of the first, and by the other bookes euidently demostrated. *His counsaile to the reader.*

18. The Catholique Church then is the hauen of securitie, and the porte of saluation, to which thou must repayre, the arke wherin Noe lodgeth & his familie, that is Christ and his faithful people, it is the barne vvhere the good corne is layed vp, til the vvinowing day, it is the folde of Christes sheepe, the piller of truth, the treasurehouse of Christs Graces, the shoppe of spiritual negotiation, the land of promise, the paradise of the second Adam, the temple of the second Salomon, the mystical body of Christ, the terrestrial heauen of those that hope to be blessed, the only vvay to life euerlasting. If then thou *The Catholique Church is the only place of saftie and hapines.*

desire to be free from tempests, and contrarie vvindes of disagreing heresies, direct thy ship and saile to this quiet hauen, if thou wilt not make shipwrake of thy soule, fly to this porte of saluation, if thou wilt not be drowned in the deluge of sinne or Infidelitie, haue recourse vnto this Arke, out of which none can escape damnation: if thou wilt be of Christes chosen corne, repose thy selfe in this his barne, which is the only place of purging from the chaffe, if thou wilt be one of Christs flocke, be in this folde, that thou mayest be fed with his shepe: if thou wilt be sure of the truth, kepe thy standing vpon the piller of truth: if thou wilt be enriched with Christs spiritual treasures, this is the treasure house of al his graces. if thou wilt traffique for heauen, and heauenly merchandise, enter the shop of Christ his Church, the only place of merite, and Christian negotiation: if thou vvilt be partaker of Christs promises, dwel in the land of al his promises: If thou vvilt enioy true felicitie, enter into this paradise of the second Adam: if thou wilt honour God with true Sacrifice and worship, this is the only Temple, out of vvhich nether prayers, nor oblations, not sacrifices are pleasing: If thou wilt receue any influence, and motion from Christ the Head, incorporate thy selfe to the Church his mystical body: and if thou vvilt be partaker of his spirite, which is the soule and life of this body, dismember not thy selfe, but endeuour to be a liuely member: if thou wilt enioy the blisse of Angels in the vpper heauen, enter first into this lower heauen, out of vvhich is no hope to ascend to the higher: if thou vvilt attaine to life euerlasting, passe by the Church, for it is the only vvay: If thou wilt be one of the Church triumphant, be first one of the Church militant: and if thou wilt haue God for thy father, take his Church for thy mother. Nothing more dangerous then to liue out of this Church, & no surer damnation, then to dye out of this Church. Be not carelesse therfore in seeking out this Church, & vvhen thou hast found it differre not thy greatest affaire, a matter of most importance, because theron dependeth, not a temporal state of thy bodie, but eternal saluation or damnation, both of body and soule. Farewel, and pray for him that prayeth and laboreth for thee, that thou mayst do wel. Iul. 18. an Dom. 1603.

Extreme danger to liue out of this Church. assured damnation to dye out of it.

MATTHEVV KELLISON.

A table of the particular contents of these eight bookes: and of euerie chapter therof.

THE first booke conteineth a Suruey of the groundes, on which the pretending reformers of Religion seme to build, and maintaine their doctrine: and proueth that they haue no sufficient fundation at al, but such as openeth the way to al Heretikes & Heresies.

Chap. 1.

The preachers of the new religion can not proue them selues to be sent from Christ, vvhich vvere absolutly necessarie: els none may geue eare vnto them, vnles they wil harken also to al false Prophetes and Preachers.

Chap. 2.

As pretense of bare & onlie Scripture is a special ground of this new religion, so is it of al other heresies, seruing them al, as much as these of our time: and therfore is not a cōuenient ground of Religion.

Chap. 3.

Much lesse is the priuate spirite (vvhich these men make supreme iudge in vnderstanding Scripture) a ground of faith or Religion; but in dede bringeth in al heresies, and serueth al Heretikes, that haue bene, or may be.

Chap. 4.

By refusing the ancient Fathers & Councels, for vnderstanding and expounding holie Scriptures, the pretended reformers geue entrance to al Heretikes.

Chap. 5.

These new preachers haue no probable meanes to induce a reasonable man to their religion: and therfore vvhosoeuer wil credite them, may as wel credite anie other Heretike, teach he neuer so absurde and phantastical paradoxes.

Chap. 6.

In that they haue no visible Iudge in matters of Religion, they open the way to al Heretikes. Who may preach vvhat they list, hauing no Iudge to controle them.

Chap. 7.

These new pretended christians know no end in beleuing: and therfore vvhosoeuer receiueth their Religion, shal neuer be setled, but alwayes seeking and yet alwayes to seeke.

THE

THE second booke contayneth a Suruey of the markes of Heretikes. Which are proued to agree so fitly to the professors of this new Religion, that if euer there were anie Heretikes, these are Heretikes. Chap. 1.

Breaking out of that Church, vvhich is commonly counted the true Christian Church, is the first marke, & agreeth euidently to the pretended reformers. Chap. 2.

Later standing and noueltie is an other marke of Heretikes, and agreeth to the pretended Gospellers of this time, as fitly as euer to anie heretikes of former times.

Chap. 3.

A particular name taken either from the Maister & beginner of a Sect, or of the particular doctrin, or some particular accident, is an other marke, and agreeth to these new preachers, who can not be knowen by the common names of Catholique or Christian.

Chap. 4.

Renewing of old condemned heresies is a fourth marke: and agreeth also to these of our time, shewing them to be heretikes: and that also for errors long since condemned.

Chap. 5.

Want of Succession is a most notorious marke of Heretikes & false prophets: and agreeth most euidently to the pretended Gospelers of this time. Chap. 6.

Dissension in doctrin, from their owne first maisters or pretended reformers, and diuision into manie Sectes, one contrarie to an other in substantial points of faith, is an other marck: & is most clere in these young Maisters lately sprong out of Martin Luther.

Chap. 7.

To be a seueral congregation, of some particular place, or of smale continuance of time, is an other special marke of Heretikes: & agreeth to the new reformers, who neither haue possessed al ages and countries, nor yet one hundreth yeares, nor euer anie one whole kingdome or countrie.

Chap. 8.

To be condemned for Heretikes by that Church, which is cōmonly counted the true christian Church, as these of our time be, is an other sure marke, that they are Heretikes.

THE

THE third booke contayneth a Suruey of the new doctrin concerning Christ. where is clerly proued, that these new maisters are rather Antichristianes then Christianes.

Chap. 1.

Their doctrin spoyleth Christ of his Diuinitie, wherby they shew them selues not to be sincere Christians.

Chap. 2.

Their doctrin, that by Christs redemption no law bindeth, no sinne hurteth, so one beleue that he shal be saued, maketh Christ an absurde Redemer. *Chap.* 3.

If their doctrin were true, that none is, nor can be truly iust, but so imputed only, and that in dede the iustest man is a damnable sinner, that is, the slaue of the diuel, then Christ were no Redemer at al.

Chap. 4.

In that they teach, that Christ doth not heale, but only couer the wound of sinne, they make him no spiritual Phisitian.

Chap. 5.

The new Gospellers, Luther expresly, Caluin by consequence of doctrin, teach that Christ is not a Lawmaker.

Chap. 6.

Lest they should be forced to confesse, that the Masse is a proper Sacrifice, they denie that Christ is an eternal Priest, according to the order of Melchisedech. *Chap.* 7.

Seing those that beleue not are already iudged, and by the new Gospellers doctrin, no other sine is imputed to a beleeuer, no reward of good vvorkes, because they say there is no merite, neither anie discussing of vvorkes, good or badde, for they say there is no difference, they take from Christ the whole office of a Iudge.

Chap. 8.

In that they teach, that euerie beleuer is reputed iust, by the selfe same iustice, by vvhich Christ is iust, they make euerie one reputed as iust as Christ him selfe. *Chap.* 9.

Most of the new maisters, namely Luther, Caluin, Beza and others say, that Christ vvas ignorant of some things.

Chap. 10.

Caluin and his disciples affirme, that Christ feared the sentence of damnation, and for the time despayred of his owne saluation.

Chap. 11.

Chap. 11.

Caluin and his folowers ſay, that Chriſt ſuffered the paines of hel in his ſoule. and ſo make him companion of the damned.

Chap. 12.

The new Goſpellers can not indure the honour of ſuch perſons & things, as belong moſt ſpecially to Chriſt, by which & al the former derogations from him, is manifeſt, that they are no ſincere Chriſtians.

THE fourth booke contayneth a general Suruey of the new reformers religion and worſhip of God, vvherin is proued, that either they haue no religion at al, or a graceles religion.

Chap. 1.

Forſomuch as Prieſts and Religion went alwayes together, the new Goſpellers admitting no Prieſts nor Prieſthood, haue therfore no religion.

Chap. 2.

Likewiſe denying & reiecting al proper Sacrifice, as they do, they can not poſſibly haue anie true Religion.

Chap. 3.

Some Proteſtants denying more, ſome fewer of the ſeuen Sacramēts, they al detract ſo much therby from Religion, as they diminiſh the number, and valure of Sacraments, which neceſſarily alwayes goe with Religion.

Chap. 4.

Holding that Sacramēts are bare ſignes, only to diſtinguiſh Chriſtianes from Infidels, & denying that any grace at al is geuen by them, they make Sacraments of ſmal importance, and therby ſhew their owne graceles religion.

Chap. 5.

The Proteſtants of England granting only two Sacraments in name, but denying the effectes of them both, neither confeſſing that ſinne is forgeuen by Baptiſme, nor Chriſt to be really preſent in the Euchariſt: and ſo in effect haue no Sacraments at al.

Chap. 6.

According to Proteſtantes doctrin there ſhould be no prayer at al vſed, no not our Lordes prayer, for that (as they ſay) it neither ſatiſfieth nor meriteth anie thing, & repugneth with diuers other pointes of their aſſertions, nor yet anie ſermon by their opinions.

THE

THE fifth booke contayneth a Suruey of the new Maisters doctrin concerning God. Where is declared that they are most impious and iniurious to the Diuine Maiestie.

Chap. 1.

They make God the author of al sinne and wickednes.

Chap. 2.

God were not only a sinner, but the onlie sinner, and men nor diuels no sinners at al, if Protestants doctrin were true.

Chap. 3.

God were an vnreasonable Prince, if the Commandements, vvhich he geueth, were vnpossible to be kept, as Protestants teach they are.

Chap. 4.

Yea God were a cruel Tyrant, in condemning men to euerlasting damnation, for not obseruing his commandments, if the same were vnpossible to be obserued.

Chap. 5.

By these false and horrible opinions of God, they frame to them selues such a God, as in dede is not: & so adore an Idol of their owne imagination, in steede of our Lord God.

THE sixth booke conteyneth a Suruey of the Protestants doctrin concerning Kings & Princes. Shewing how they spoile al Princes of authoritie, and bring their lawes in contempt.

Chap. 1.

In that they teach, that no Prince, nor Superior can bind anie subiect in conscience, to kepe his law or commandment, they both diminish the Princes authoritie, & take away the chiefest obligation from subiects, vvarranting them, in respect of sinne or conscience, to disobey, yea to rebel, if they list and be strong ynough.

Chap. 2.

By this doctrin, that Princes lawes bind not in conscience, Iudges & Iudgement Seates are only respected for temporal feare, not for the offence of God.

Chap. 3.

Likewise by this doctrine al lawes lose their force, and are in respect of conscience, but as consailes, which the subiects may choose vvhether they wil obserue or no, and so are easily contemned.

Chap. 4.

If lawes did not bind in conſcience, Princes ſhould haue no other but temporal confidence in their ſubiects Subiects would ſtil feare oppreſſion, & tyrannie, and ech man vvould ſuſpect others: & ſo al mutual truſt would decay, and al ciuil ſocietie periſh.

THE ſeuenth booke conteyneth a Suruey of the new doctrin concerning maners. Where is declared, that it maketh way to al vices and ſinnes. *Chap. 1.*

By preaching againſt the hope of heauen, & feare of hel, which are moſt frequent in holie Scriptures, and al the Fathers, they bring in al ſlouthfulnes to vertue, and prones to ſinne.

Chap. 2.

The doctrin, that only faith iuſtifieth, doth alſo make vvay to vice, and taketh away the care of doing good vvorkes, as nothing worth. *Chap. 3*

But eſpecially by that falſe perſwaſion, that euerie one muſt aſſure him ſelfe, that he is elected, and that he ſhal be ſaued, it leadeth to extreme preſumption, and looſeth the bridle to al iniquitie.

Chap. 4.

In ſaying as they do, that faith maketh no ſinne to be imputed, they geue leaue to al that ſo beleue, to commit al ſinne & wickednes.

Chap. 5.

Againe teaching that al mens actions are mortal ſinnes, they bring their folowers to vtter deſpaire of doing wel, vvherby they are induced into al vice. *Chap. 6.*

The ſame deſperate occaſion of running into al vice is geuen, by their falſe doctrin, that man hath no freewil, but doth of neceſſitie and conſtrant, whatſoeuer he doth.

Chap. 7.

Auouching that Gods commandments are impoſſible brideth the ſame deſperations. *Chap. 8.*

Likwiſe in ſaying that Chriſt hath fryed al men, that they nede not kepe the commandments nor lawes, openeth the gate to al vice.

Chap. 9.

Alſo in making God the author & worker of al ſinne, they take away al feare of ſinning, and embolden men neuer to reſiſt anie tentation.

Chap. 10.

Chap. 10.

Againe by denying the obligation of lawes, and freewil; and by saying that al actions, euen the best are mortal sinnes, yet that no sinne is imputed to him that beleueth, and that God is the author of sinne, they say in effect that there is neither vertue nor vice in mens actions.

Chap. 11.

It foloweth also of the forsaid groundes, that none nedeth to make anie conscience of sinne. Which being taken away, they that hope to auoid the eye of the Magistrate, or are able to resist his authoritie, neither yet feare Gods punishment, so they beleue to be saued, may sinne without feare.

Chap. 12.

In particular the forsaide opinions set open the gate to pride.

Chap. 13.

Also to idlenes, yea by their onlie faith, and assurance of saluation, they make idlenes the perfection of Christian life.

Chap. 14.

Their doctrin is so opposite to virginitie, that it also impugneth vidual yea and coniugal chastitie.

Chap. 15.

Finally, this new doctrin by exacting an impossible beleefe of a sinner, that he is iust, before he be iustified, for this beliefe they say is the cause of iustification, & so must goe before, holdeth him so fast in sinne, that being once fallen he can neuer rise againe.

THE eight booke conteyneth a Suruey of the new doctrin, declaring how it leadeth to Atheisme. Which is an vglie monster, not only as it denieth God in plaine termes, but also as it lightly esteemeth of Religion & seruice of God; preferring worldlie estate before Gods seruice. Both vvhich sortes the heresies of this time do bride.

Chap. 1.

Notwithstanding it is euident by manie arguments, that there is a God, Maker & Maister of al other things, yet the Protestants doctrin teacheth and describeth God to be such a one, as he neither is nor can be: as to be the author of sinne, vnreasonable, cruel, tyrannical, so that a reasonable man wil rather thinck there is no God at al, then such a God.

Chap. 2.

The forsaid doctrin & false conceipt of Gods goodnes & mercie taketh away the vertue of Religion,& al affection to serue God,which prepareth the way to thinck there is no God.

Chap. 3.

By contemning the Churches authoritie, for declaring and defining vvhich Bookes are Canonical Scripture, and the word of God, they take away a chiefe ground of al Religion, and so bring in Atheisme.

Chap. 4.

In that they admire some Bookes of holie Scripture, yet reiect others, hauing as assured proofe for al as for anie, they bring al in doubt, and so open the way to contemne al Scripture, and our whole Religion.

Chap 5.

Their dissention of doctrine in chiefe points of Religiō, geueth direct occasion to denie al their new assertions, and so if there were not a certayne doctrin besides, and before theirs, it would lead men of discourse to denie al Religion, and to professe Atheisme.

Chap. 6.

The vvant of one visible head, to kepe vnitie in Religion, alloweth euerie one to be of what pretended Religion he wil, and not finding one more probable then an other, he may by the same libertie be of none at al.

Chap. 7.

Denial of Christs real presence in the blessed Sacrament, which is the greatest Sacrament, & the only Sacrifice of Christian Religion, and is clerly proued by the very letter of holie Scriptures, maketh the way to denie al other Mysteries also, and so to depriue the vvorld of the onlie true Religion, and to bring al to Atheisme.

Chap. 8.

The last chapter recapitulateth the chiefest things proued, and disproued in this vvhole booke: shewing how deformed, and deforming the congregation of the nevv pretending Reformers is: with a clere and euident proofe, that the Catholique Romain Church is the only true Church and that out of the same there is no saluation. Exhorting therfore the christian reader, to liue & dye a member therof.

FINIS.

THE FIRST BOOKE CONTEINETH A SVRVEY OF THE GROVNDES AND FVNDATION OF THE NEW RELIGION.

The first chapter examineth the mission of the preachers, of this nevv religion, and shevveth, that they can not proue them selues, to be sent from Christ, & that consequently vve can not giue eare vnto them, vnles vve vvil harken also to al false prophetes.

HARDLY shal we finde a subiect so disloyal, or priuate man so imprudent, vvho vvil arrogate vnto him selfe the honourable office of an Ambassadour, to deale betvvixt Prince and Prince, in denouncing vvarre, or offering peace, or in establishing a nevv league, or renewing an olde, vnles he haue authoritie from his Prince, in vvhose name he dealeth, and can by letters of credit, or other tokens make an euident remonstrance of his legantine povver and commission. For if he go vnsent, he abuseth his Princes name, and if he can not shevv his comission, he runneth on a sleeueles arrande. If this be so (as experience teacheth vs that it is so, and reason telleth vs that it must be so) and that betvvixt man & man, vve haue no reason to think Almightie God to be so deuoid of Princelie prudence, as to send his Apostles and preachers, to denounce his vvil, & to impert his minde to his people, and not to giue them vvithal, letters patentes of their comission: or to be so vnreasonable, as to binde vs to giue credit, or audience to such Ambassadours, vvho can only bragge of their embassage, but can not by any probable proofes, acertaine vs of it. For so vve might imbrace

Vvhat is requisit in an Ambassadour.

Preachers & Pastors must be sent.

Moyses vvas sent. a false preacher & Apostle, vvhen in dede vve haue a lewd and lying prophet by the hand.

Exo 3. 2. This Moyses vvel knovving, neuer dreamed of that great embassage, in vvhich he vvas sent from God to Pharao, to deale for the deliuerie of the oppressed Israelites, vntil God had called him, and tolde him that he intended to send him: knovving that if he should haue gone vnsent, he should haue abused his Lord and maisters name. *Aaron vvas sent.* Aaron also durst not aduenture vpon priestlie function, before that Moyses by Gods commandement, had consecrated him. Whose example *Exod. 28.* S. Paul proposeth vnto al Pastors, as necessarie to be folowed, saying: *Leuit. 8.* *Nec quisquam sumit sibi honorem, sed qui vocatur à Deo tanquam Aaron: Neither* *Heb. 5.* *doth any man take vnto him selfe honour, but he vvho is called of God as Aaron* *The Prophets sent.* *vvas.* The prophets likewise, presumed not to tel vnto the people Gods mynd and wil, nor to fortel the thinges to come, of which he would *Angels sent.* haue his people forewarned, without an expresse commandement *Psal. 103.* from him, as may appeare by the proeme and beginning of their pro- *Greg ho 34.* phecies. And those immortal creatures, which are by nature spirites, *Dan. 10.* are by office called Angels, because they are sent from God, as his le- *Luc. 1.* gates, & Ambassadors, for so much the greeke word ἄγγελοι implyeth, *S. Iohn Baptist sent.* from vvhich our English vvord *Angel*, is deriued. Wherfore the Angel that came to Daniel, declareth vnto him his commission, before he *Malach. 3.* telleth him his message. *Daniel*, saith he, *sta in gradu tuo, nunc enim missus* *Luc. 1.* *sum ad te: Daniel stand in thy place, for novv I am sent vnto thee.* And S. Luke *Ciril. lib in Io.* describing that great ambassage of the Archangel Gabriel, vnto the *c. 17.* blessed virgin Marie, saith that he was, *Sent from God into a citie of Galilie,* *Beda in c. 1.* *vvhich vvas called Nazareth, vnto a virgin despoused vnto a man, vvhose name* *Mar.* *vvas Ioseph.* In like maner S. Iohn Baptist the Precursor of Christ, and *Ioan. 1.* more then a prophet of God, who not only foretolde the Messias, but *Theoph. in c. 3.* also poynted him out with his finger, is called an *Angel*, not because *Luc.* he was an Angel by nature, as Origen imagined, but because he vvas an Angel by office, as being sent to make the way and to prepare it for the Messias. Wherfore S. Iohn the Euangelist reciting the prayses of S. Iohn Baptist saith, that he was *a man sent from God.* And Theophilact explicating these wordes of S. Luke: *Factū est verbum Domini ad Ioannem: the vvord of God vvas made to Iohn*: by the word, saith he, vnderstand thou the commandement of God, that thou mayst learne that he did not rashly, without vocation, intrude him selfe to giue testimonie of *Christ sent* Christ, but moued by the diuine Spirit and commandement of God.

Ioan. 8. 12. 3. Yea Christ him selfe would not vndertake the office & function of a Mes-

of a Messias, & Mediator, before he vvas sent by his Father: *For I*, saith he, *came not of my selfe but he sent me*, and therfore he saith his doctrine is not his ovvne, but his Fathers, because although he preached the same, yet for that he preached it in his Fathers name vvho sent him, he calleth it his Fathers doctrine. And as Christ was sent from his Father, so were his Apostles from him, else had not their name agreed to their person, because the word Apostle cometh of the greek word ἀπόςολ☉ which signifieth a messenger or Ambassador. And if they had not bene sent, they could not haue preached, because as faith and religion is reuealed only by God, so none can haue authoritie to preache it but frō God, according to that of S. Paul: *hovv shal they preach vnles they be sent.*

Ioa. 7. *Aug. trac. 29* *The Apostles sent.* *Io. 20.* *Matt. 16.* *Rom. 10.*

4. And as it is proper to al true Apostles, not to presume to preach before they be sent, so is it as common to al false Prophetes to runne before they be sent, and to preach their owne fancies vvithout mission, or commission: vvho therfore in diuers places of Scripture are said to come, but neuer to be sent. *Al they* (saith Christ) *vvho came before me are theeues and robbers.* Where you must note that he saith not, al they vvho vvere sent, because Moyses and the Prophetes vvere sent before him, and yet vvere neither theeues nor robbers, but he sayth, *al they that came before me, are theeues and robbers*, that is vvho came of their ovvne heades neither sent nor commanded, because they stole authoritie from God, and arrogated that vnto them selues, which he neuer gaue them, vsing and abusing his name, & crying that the Lord saith so, whem he neuer sayed so, nor ment so. Which kinde of theefe is specially noted with this marke of comming. *A theefe doth not come but to steale and kil.* The like maner of speach vseth S. Paul, saying: *If he that cometh shal preach vnto you any other Christ.* To be briefe he that can not lye, because he is the prime and first veritie, and vvil not lye, because he is goodnes it selfe, giueth vs this marke to knovv a false Prophet by: *Bevvare* (sayth he) *of false Prophets.* But vvhat marke doest thou giue vs, ô Lord, to knovv them by, that vve may take hede of them? *VVho come*, sayth he, *vnto you in the garmentes of sheepe, but invvardly are rauening vvolues.* Wherfore God by Hieremie complaineth, that the false Prophets ran before he sent them, preached before he spake vnto them, and deuised lyes of their ovvne inuentions. So that if any preachers come only, that is, come vnsent, they are theeues, that steale authoritie which vvas neuer giuen them, and they are false Prophets, vvhich runne on their ovvne heades before they be sent, and preach their ovvne deuises, before they haue commission.

False Prophets run vnsent. *Scripture saith that they come but not that they are sent.* *Theoph. & Beda in c. 10. Ioan.* *Aug tra 45. in Ioan.* *Maldonatus in Io. c. 10.* *Ioa. 10.* *2. Cor. 11.* *Mat. 7.* *Hier. c. 13. & 24*

The nevv preachers must shevv their mission.

5. If then our new reformers and Prophetes of the Lord (as they cal them selues) be sent from God (as they say they be) to reforme the Church not only in maners, but also in faith & religion, let them tel vs their mission, & shew vs their commission, & we wil reuerence them as the messengers, and respect them as the Ambassadors and Angels of God. But if they come on their owne heades, or can not giue vs assurance that they are sent from God, they must pardon vs, if we giue not eare vnto them: for if they be not sent, they haue no authoritie to deale with vs, and if they can not proue their mission, we haue no warrant to deale with them.

Else they are not to be credited.

The reason.

Missions ordinarie, extraordinarie.

6. Two maner of missions, which God vseth in sending preachers vnto vs, I find in holy writte, which also haue bene practised in the Church of God, the one ordinarie, the other extraordinarie. The extraordinarie mission is made immediatly from God, the ordinarie mission God maketh by meanes of some other, vvhom he hath sent immediatly from him selfe. For as God ordinarily doth nothing immediatly by him selfe, but by meanes of second causes, causing light by the Sunne, and heate by the fire, producing fruites by trees, and men and beastes by some of their owne kinde: yet he doth not so tye him selfe vnto his creatures, but that some times extraordinarily he worketh by him selfe, without any concurrence of them: as he did when with a word, or touch, he restored health, which ordinarily he doth by phisitions, and second causes: so likwise ordinarily God sendeth Pastors and preachers, and giueth them authoritie by others, yet somtimes also extraordinarily he sendeth them immediatly from him selfe.

Examples
1. Tim. 4.
2. Tim. 13.
Act. 6. 1. 4.

7. As for example: Moyses and Aaron in the old law were sent immediatly from God, to recal his people out of Ægipt, and to rule and gouerne them in matters of religion, but the high Priestes which succeded Aaron, and were consecrated by him, and his successors, were sent by an ordinarie mission. In like maner in the new law, S. Peter and the rest of the Apostles were called and sent extraordinarily & immediatly from Christ: but they vvhich succeeded the Apostles, and were ordained by them by imposition of handes & other ceremonies, were sent by an ordinarie mission, because our Sauiour Christ vvhen he instituted his Apostles, did also appoint a continual order, by which orthers should succede them in their offices, vvhich was imposition of handes, by a Bishop lawfully consecrated: and so the Bishops which now are, may truly affirme that they are sent from Christ to rule & gouerne his Chuch, because they are cōsecrated & instituted, by the order

Imposition of handes.

χειροτονία.

Hier. in c. 58. Isaiæ.

vvhich

which Christ hath appointed, and they succede the Apostles, whom Christ immediatly sent to preach, teach, and minister Sacramentes.

8. Now betwixt these two missions, this amongst others, is one difference: that an extraordinarie mission must be proued by miracles, or plaine prophecies, els euerie one may bragge that he is sent extraordinarily, and no man shal controle him: but an ordinarie mission needeth no such proofe: and therfore he vvho is sent by an ordinarie mission, if he can shew that he was instituted, by the ordinarie meanes which Christ hath left in his Church, & that he succeedeth them, who were counted lawful Pastors and preachers, he giueth sufficient testimonie of his ordinarie mission, and commission.

Extraordinarie missiō proued by miracles.

Ordinarie proued by succession.

9. If then our new preachers be sent by an ordinarie mission, let them shew their succession, and tel vs the pedegree of their predecessors, that vve may see who were Bishops before them, and who consecrated and instituted them, and who gaue them commission and authoritie, to entermeddle in the rule and gouernemēt of the Church. For so Christ ordinarily sendeth preachers and Pastors to his Church. Thus Tertullian vrged the heretikes of his time. *Let them*, saith he, *shevv vs the origin of their Churches, let them vnfolde the order of their Bishopes, vvhich by successors, so runneth on from the beginning, that the first Bishop haue for his author and predecessor some one of the Apostles or apostolical men, vvhich liued in the Apostles time, &c. As the Church of the Smyrneans doth register Polycarpe placed by S. Iohn, as the Church of the Romaines hath Clemēt ordained by S. Peter. &c.* To this proofe S. Austin putteth the heretikes of his age: *Number*, saith he, *the priestes, euen from Peters seate, and looke vvhich to vvhich succeded in the order of those Fathers.* And in an other place he saith, that this succession of Priestes, is the thing *vvhich holdeth him in the Catholique Church*: because he knew, that there is the true Church, where is the true religion, there true religion, where true Pastors to teach it, and there true Pastors, where one succedeth to an other by an ordinarie succession. Wherfore S. Ciprian by this succesion excludeth Nouatian, for, saith he, *Cornelius succeding immediatly to Fabianus Pope, and possessing the place of Peter, there is no place for Nouatianus.* And in an other place he maketh the like argument: *Ecclesia*, saith he, *si apud Nouatianum est, apud Cornelium non fuit, si verò apud Cornelium fuit, qui Fabiano Episcopo legitima ordinatione successit, & quem, preter Sacerdotij honorem, martyrio quoque Dominus glorificauit, Nouatianus in Ecclesia non est, nec Episcopus computari potest, qui Euangelica & Apostolica traditione contempta, nemini succedens, a seipso ortus est.* If the Church be vvith Nouatian, it was not vvith Cornelius, but if it vvas

lib presc. c. 32.

Psal. con. part Don. tom. 7. lib. cont. ep. fundamenti.

Ep. ad Antonianum de Cornel and Nouat.

l. 1 ep. 6. ad Magnum seu ep. 77.

with Cornelius, who ſucceded by lawful ordination to Fabian the Biſhop, and whom our Lord beſides the honour of Prieſthood, glorified with Martyrdom. Nouatian is not in the Church, neither can he be counted a Biſhop, who contemning the Euangelical and Apoſtolical Tradition, ſucceeding to none, began of him ſelſe. And ſo we muſt vrge our new reformers, to declare vnto vs the pedegrees of their anceſters, and to ſhevv vvho be the predeceſſors, to whom they be ſucceſſors, if they wil haue vs to admit them, as the miniſters of God, ſent by an ordinarie miſſion. But this they can neuer do: for who, I pray you, was the immediate predeceſſor of Luther and Caluin? or who he that made the firſt Superintendent in England? I am ſure and al the world, yea they them ſelues, wil witneſſe, that they are no ſucceſſors to the Catholique Biſhopes and Paſtors, becauſe they degenerate from them altogether, and they were faine to contemne and diſobey them, before they could open their mouthes in pulpites. Yea our Paſtors were ſo farre from ordaining them, or inſtituting them, & giuing them authoritie, that they cried out againſt them, as new ſtartuppes, and condemned them for heretikes, Antipaſtors, and new yea falſe Apoſtles. Neither can they deriue them ſelues from any other lawful paſtors: for before they them ſelues tooke vpon them the name and office of Paſtors, there were none at the time of their riſing, but our Catholique Paſtors. Yea as in the next booke is proued, they can not deriue their deſcent from ancient heretikes, becauſe in al pointes they agree not with any of them: and if they could, yet were not that ſufficient, for they were counted and condemned for arrant heretikes, vvho intruded them ſelues as theſe men do, into the true Paſtors offices, and were them ſelues as theſe men are, the firſt of their families, ſucceding to no predeceſſors. They wil ſay peraduenture that their firſt Biſhops, Prieſts, and preachers, were ordained by ours, before they departed from vs, and that they ordaining others, ſtil continued the ſucceſſion. But this euaſion is not ſufficient. For firſt of al, either our Paſtors were lawful or vnlawful; if lawful, then are theyrs vnlavvful, who preached againſt the commandement of ours, yea then are they vſurpers who thruſt out their lawful Paſtors, and ſetled them ſelues in their roomes. If vnlawful, then do they abſurdly chalenge ſucceſſion from them: becauſe none can ſuccede lavvfully to vnlawful predeceſſors, if they haue no other title but from them. Secondly although ſome of their Apoſtates were made Prieſtes and Paſtors by our Biſhops: yet al were not ſuch, Luther and Caluin the firſt founders and

The nevv preachers are not ſent ordinarily.

ders and many others were no Bishops, and so could not ordaine Priestes and Pastors, and they which were true Bishops amongst them, vsed not the matter and forme of ordination, but only by a letter of the Prince, Superintendent or magistrate, constituted their inferior ministers, with as litle solemnitie as they make their Aldermen yea Constables, and Cryers of the market. And if they had truly ordained their ministers, as their Apostat Bishops might haue done if they had vsed the forme and matter of order, because power of consecrating and ordering, which diuines cal *Potestas ordinis* is neuer abolished, yet besides order, Iurisdiction and mission from a lawful Pastor is also required, for, as S. Paul sayth, *Quomodo prædicabunt nisi mittantur? hovv shal they preach vnles they be sent?* And seing that our Pastors were so farre from sending thẽ, that they forbad them al pulpits & preaching, from them they could not haue their mission: and so they can not prooue their or dinarie mission. To say as Luther and Brentius did, that it is sufficient to approue their mission, that they haue commission from the Prince or Magistrate, is to confound Priestes and Princes, magistrates and ministers, yea the Church and common welth: because if they may make ministers and giue authoritie to preach, then them selues may play the partes of ministers. And although we read that by Apostles and Bishops, and by imposition of their hands, Pastors and preachers haue bene appointed, yet neuer was there any such authoritie giuen to Princes or magistrates, and neuer was there any such practise vnlesse it were amongst heretikes as it was in Tertulian. Yea in the old testament Amarias the high Priest menaged matters of religion, and Zabadias medled only with vvarre: and Ozias vvas stricken vvith a Lepresie for vndertaking priestly function: and in the new law of grace, Christ commended his Church to S. Peter and the Apostles, but neuer to Princes and to Magistrats at vnto Superiors, but only as vnto defenders, fauourers, and foster fathers.

Rom. 10. Com. Ep. ad Gal. Ex Hosio li. cont. Brent.

Act. 13. 14. Tit. 1. & 1. Tim. 4. 2. Tim. 1. l. presc. c. 41.

2. Par. 19 & 26.

10 Here they find them selues much pressed, and knovv not, I dare say, vvhat to answere: but they vvil play smale play rather then sit out, and vvil make hard shift rather then no shift, and shape a misshapen answer rather then no answere. And vvhat is that? they say that the Apostles vvhich were the first Bishops & Pastors, had for the tyme their lawful successors, but at the length the Church failed and the Pastors vvith it, and vvith them the succession decaied: but afterward Luther and Caluin reuiued this dead Church againe, and restored the Pastors: And so, say they, vve succede the Apostles and their immediate successors

Ioan. 20. 21. Act. 14. Ephes. 4. Mat. vlt. Isa. 49.

The reformers ansvver that the Church fel &c.

successors, but by interruption of manie hundred yeares.

A poore answer. *Tert. li. 1. Prescr. c. 29.*

11. But this God knoweth is a poore shift, and a stale shift. For this was the answer of the heretikes in Tertulians time, against whom he vseth no other argument then the absurditie which foloweth so absurde an answere. Then (saith he) truth which was imprisoned, expected Marcionites her redemers, and in the meane time Pastors preached falsly, and the Christians beleued erroniously, manie thousandes were wrongly baptized, so manie workes of faith ministred amisse, so manie Chrismes were euil wrought, so manie Preisthoodes & ministeries not rightly done, so manie martyrdomes al in vaine. The like may be said against Luther, Zuinglius, Caluine, & other new Apostles of this time. Is the Church failed before your comming? then she expected manie hũdred yeares for you in particular, then al ministerie in the Church was al this while vvrong, preaching and teaching vvas false, they vvho boare the name of true Pastors vvere not so, that societie which was dispersed throughout the world, & was counted the only Christian Church, and was persecuted for the same by the diuel & his ministers, was a synagogue of the diuel, established & vpholden by the diuel, and so one diuel persecuted an other: al martyrdomes in that Church were in vaine, al actes of religion were superstitious, al Councels vvhich vvere gathered in this Church, al Pastors that ruled in it, al Doctors that wrote and taught in it and for it, deceiued, and were deceiued. Happie then vvas the day in vvhich Luther leaped out of his Monasterie, disobeied the Pope & Church: & hauing gotten a yoke felovv, out of a cloyster of professed & vowed virgins, deuised a new religion, to cloake his villanie. And could not Christ al that while, find out a man fit to restore his Church from death to life: was there no *Ambrose*, no *Austin*, no *Hierome*, no *Gregorie* fit for such a purpose? and vvas Luther the onlie man, vvho for learning and vertue (though he vvere an apostata) vvas according to God his hart and liking, whom God vvished for, and expected so long? Tertulian thinketh it as absurd to say, that Christ sent new Apostles, as that he was borne againe, and descended againe from heauen, dyed, and rose againe, because (sayth he) these two go together. And therfore to say, that the Church fel and vvas again restored by nevv Apostles, is to say, that Christ is again descended, and dyed, and rose again to send vs new Apostles. But if I demonstrate that the true Church can not die, not euer decay, then is their Church a bastard synagogue, which, as they say, once florishing in the Apostles time, & a smale time after, then died for no litle time, but

The absurditie vvhich folovveth an absurde answer.

lib prescr.

The nevv Church is a bastard church.

for

for some hundredes of yeares: or else they must of necessitie shew a succession of their church and Religion, from age to age, and of their pastours, from pastour to pastour: and if they can not, they are not sent by an ordinarie mission, because they succed to no predecessours, but are the first of their families. This I haue demonstrated in the second booke, as the reader may see, if he please to turne ouer a few leaues, & so here I may suppose it, and supposing conclude, that they are not sent by an ordinarie mission, because they succed to none.

That the church cā not faile, is proued in the next booke chap. 5.

Another answer for their ordinarie mission, to wit, that they had a succession of Pastours inuisible. chap. 5.

12. But if this answer wil not serue (as a blind man may see that it doth not) then they haue an other in store: and what is that? they say forsooth, that they are true successours to the Apostles, and that they haue their predecessours vvho beleeued as they do, ruled the Church, ministred & receaued Sacrements, but secretly, and inuisibly, because their church it selfe, was al that time inuisible. And so if you demaund of them, who were their predecessours? they wil answer, that they had predecessours, but they were inuisible. This is an other blind shift of theirs, which I shal refute in the next booke at large. Here only I demaund, whether this inuisible Church was inuisible to them selues, or to papistes only and paynimes, who were not of their religion? If it were inuisible to them selues, how can they tel that there was anie religion, like to theirs before their time, or that there were anie pastours of their kinde? for that which was inuisible vnto them, could not be seene of them, & so we are no more to beleeue them, in saying that they had a Church and pastours before Luthers tyme, then a blynde man that wil determine of coulours. If they say it was inuisible only to papistes and paganes, and others which were not of their Church: then as it is like, Luther and Caluin who were members of that Church, knew wel the pastours to whom they succeeded, and of whom they receaued authoritie. Let them tel vs then who they were, else we can not receaue them as ministers of God sent by on ordinarie mission, because they can not shew vs their predecessours, to whom they succeeded. Thus I haue plainlie proued that these men are not sent by an ordinarie mission, because they succeed to none who were their predecessours. What now can they saie why we should not reiect them as false prophetes, who run before they be sent, and preach before they be called to that function?

The refutation of it.

13 They wil say, as often tymes they do, that they were sent immediatly from Christ, by an extraordinarie mission. But then we must put them also to the proofe of this their missiō. And first of al in saying

An other answer.

Christ sēdeth no preachers but by succession. that they are sent extraordinarilie, they bewraie them selues to be those Apostles which runne vnsent, because it is manifest in scripture, that Christ appointing Apostles, ordained a succession of pastours to the end. For as he instituted a visible Church, which is neuer to faile or falle (as shal be in the next booke demonstrated) so did he appoint perpetual gouernours and pastours to gouerne & rule this Church in a visible manner, as there also shal be proued: else should that visible and goodlie mystical bodie of Christ, haue bene left headlesse with out a visible head: and because the same pastours could not alwaies liue to gouerne the Church visiblie, it followeth that Christ instituted a succession of them, and consequently that Christ sendeth none to rule in his Church, but by succession to some others, by whom they were ordained and instituted: and therfore he that enters into the gouernement of the Church and not by this entrie, and dore of succession, he is a theefe that seeketh windowes, corners, & bywaies, as them selues do, who because they meane no good, dare not enter into the house, as honest men do, by the ordinarie waie. Let not then the reformers brag of their extraordinarie mission, because Christ hauing instituded a perpetual succession of ordinarie pastours, meaneth not to send any extraordinarie preachers, rather they maie be ashamed of their monstrouse natiuities: for they are like vnto those heretikes of whom Optatus speaketh *Qui de se nasci voluerunt: VVhich vvould be borne of them selues.* They are like to Victor the Donatist, who as Optatus affirmeth, was a sonne without a father, and a disciple without a maister. They are not vnlike Nouatian, who as S. Cipriane auerreth *Nemini succedens, à seipso ortus est. Succeding to no man, began of him selfe.*

Ephes. 4. Chap. 5. *He is a theefe that ēters not by succession.* *The mōstrous birthes of the nevv preachers.* *l. 1. cont. Par.* *l. 2. cont. Par.* *l. 1. ep. 6.*

14. But let vs giue them leaue to saie at least that they vvere sent extraordinairilie, that so we maie see better how they can proue their extraordinarie mission, and how we can disproue the same. First I demaund of them vvhere they read in scriptures that after Christ had established a succession of pastours to gouerne his Church to the end, he vvould send somtymes extraordinarie ministers, to put them out of office, & to enter into the gouerment of the Church to reforme al absurde abuses? for if they can not bring scripture for this, they are not to be credited, & that by their ovvne confession. But I knowe they can not alleage any one lyne of scripture for that purpose, and I am sure, & they are not ignorant, that Christ sayd he builded his Church vpon a rocke so that it should not neede the repairing of these new masons, & established a kingdom, & consequently gouernours, which

Ephes. 4. *No scripture foretelleth extraordinarie preachers.* *Mat. 16.* *The Constancie of the church.*

vvhich should continew for euer, and so should neede no innouation: vvhich point here after shal be more amplie proued. *Dan. 2. Second booke. chap. 5.*

15. But suppose that our sauiour had foretolde the fal, & ruine of his Church & ordinarie pastours, & had fore vvarned vs of new Apostles & pastours to be sent to make a reformation: yet seeing that God hath also vvarned vs of false prophetes, vvho vvil falselie prophecie in his name, whereas he sent them not, & who shal deuine & foretel lyes and vanities, saying that the lord sayd so, and seeing that the Apostle commaundeth vs verie straitly to take heede of false prophetes, which come in sheepes fleeces, yea in coates of true pastours, bearing the name of pastours, & alleaging scriptures for a cloke to their heresies, as true pastours do for their true doctrine; yea sithence that Christ him selfe biddeth vs to beware of false prophetes, who come in the garmentes of innocent sheepe, but inwardlie are rauening wolues: that is (as Vincentius Lyrinensis expoundeth) who inuest them selues in the goodlie garmentes of the Prophetes and Apostles testimonies, but inwardly, if you vnmaske them by expounding the testimonies which they alleage, you shal espie rauening vvolues vnder sheepes & sheepeherdes coates, and byting, yea deuouring heresies, coucred verie cominglie vvith the sayinges of the Prophetes & Apostles: seing that I say we haue such warning of false prophetes, vve haue good reason to suspect these reformers for such kinde of cattle, & vve haue no reason to harken vnto them as vnto true prophetes, vnles they can proue their extraordinarie mission, by extraordinarie signes & tokens of prophecies, or miracles, & so can giue vs a note to distinguish them from the false prophetes, vvhose comming is so often and so plainlie foretolde. Otherwise if it be sufficiēt that they can say the are sent extraordinarilie, then do we open the gappe to false prophtes, who when they come, wil not let to say, yea and to sweare as much, and so they can not be excluded if these men be admitted. Yea we make God most vnreasonable, to thinke that he wil send extraordinarie messengers & yet giue them no letters of credit, nor extraordinary signes or tokens of their embassie. For in so doing he should ether cause them to rōne on a sleeules arrande, or else he should bynd vs to giue eare vnto them who can proue their commission no better, then false prophetes can, of whom not withstanding he commandeth vs to beware. *Hier. 6. 14. 2. Cor 11 Gal. 1. 2. Tim. 3. & 4. Rom 16. Math. 7. l cont. prophanas hæresum nouitates c. 37 Good reason to suspect the nevv preachers for false prophets.*

16. This Moyses wel perceauing, vvould not take vpon him that great Embassage, vntil that God had promised him the guift of vvorking miracles, by which he might proue his mission. *Non credent mihi* *Exod. 4.*

 (saith

Moyses mission proued by miracles.

(saith he) *neque audient vocem meam, sed dicent non apparuit tibi Dominus: They vvil not beleue me, nor giue eare vnto my voice, but vvil say, God did not appeare vnto thee.* As if he had said: thou saiest, o lord, that thou meanest to send me into Ægipt, vnto the tyrant Pharao, to deliuer thy people from his tyrannie, but how shal I make it knowne ether vnto him, or vnto thy people, that thou in deede dost send me? my bare word wil not be taken, because they vvil say I am a stranger vnto them, & for any thing vvhich they know, may come as vvel in my owne name, yea in the deuils name, as God his name. This seemed to God so reasonable an excuse, that he gaue him by & by the guift of vvorking miracles, by vvhich he might proue his extraordinarie mission. For he said vnto Moyses, *Vvhat is that vvhich thou hast in thy hand?* Moyses answered, *a rodde*: and God said, cast it on the ground: and it vvas tourned into a serpent. And this saith God I do that they may beleeue that I appeared vnto thee. Wherfore when after his coming into Ægipt, he had vvrought so straung miracles, & admirable vvorkes, the Israelites beleeued that he vvas sent to deliuer them, & accordingly they followed him, though Pharaos hart vvas so obdured, that al those miracles could nether breake, nor mollifie it, he by his free vvil resisting gods graces, & forcible callinges

The reason.

Vvhy made not Luther the same excuse?

Exod. 4.

Mal. 3. Mar. 1. Luc. 1.

Saint Ihon Baptists mission is proued by extraordinarie signes.

17 In like maner, S. Ihon Baptistes mission, vvas proued not only by the prophecie of Malachie, but also by his miraculous natiuitie, & the testimonie of an Angel; although he came not to preach any new doctrine, but only to exhort the people to penance, vvhich before by other prophetes had beene inculcated: and to poynt out the Messias vvith his finger, vvhom al the prophetes had fortould so plainlie, that when Christ appeared, it was almost euident, that he vvas the man on vvhom had ronne so longe a beadrolle of prophecies and predictions. The Messias also him selfe Christ IESVS, because he succeeded to none, but came vvith extraordinairie autoritie, sent immediatly from his father, proued his mission by so manifest workes & miracles, that he said his workes did testifie, from whom he was sent, and the people also confessed that he could not haue wrought such wonders, if he had not beene of God. And although Christ had sufficiently by miracles and prophecies, which ranne of him, proued that he was the Messias: Yet he thought not that sufficient for the proofe of the mission of his Apostles, but because they were sent immediatly from him, and were successours to none (for to Christ they were only vicegerentes) he gaue them also power to worke miracles, by which they might

Christe proueth his mission by miracles.

Io. 7. 9. 10. 11.

So do the Apostles.

might proue their mission and *confirme their doctrine vvith signes that folloved.* Now then if our ghospel-spillers be sent by an extraordinarie mission, immediatly from God, let them shew vs some miracles for proofe of their extraordinarie commission, or else were we more thē madde to credit them, being forewarned that false prophetes shal come, from whom these men can not distinguish them selues, vnlesse they can shew vs some manifest prophecies, or worke some wonders amongst vs. To say that they preach nothing but the word of God, and that the spirit inwardly hath moued & excited them to preach, is not sufficient, because that is to make bare scripture and the priuat spirit vmpiers in religion, which in the two next chapters is refuted, & to say so, is to say no more then al heretikes may say, & so, if for so saying, without any miracles, vve admit their preaching, we can exclude no false prophets.

Math. 26.

The nevv preachers are vrged to shevv their miracles.

18. Let Luther then the first man of this new familie, vvho as he & his say, is sent by God extraordinarilie, to reforme the Christian world, & to make vs new-no christians, let him, I say, shew his miracles, if he wil haue any audience: for else vve may iustly feare least he be one of those false prophetes, of whom before hand God hath warned vs. In deed, I graunt, that he on a time, to shew him selfe a true prophet, auouched verie boldy that after two yeares preaching, he would be the death of al Popes, and would banish Cardinalls, Monkes, Nunnes, masses, and bells out of the christian world. But Luther is gone long since, and yet Popes raigne, Cardinalls flourish, Monkes and Nunnes possesse their olde monasteries, sauing in England, and some few other corners: masses also are not only said but sounge solemnlie, and bells do ringe stil, and the world doth ring of bells He caused also to be engrauen vppon his tombe this verse in Latine *Pestis eram viuens, moriens, ero mors tua, Papa.*

VVilest here I liued, I vvas thy plague, and dying (Pope) Ile be thy death.

Luthers vaine prophecie.

So Cocleus vvrites. also Lindan in his dialogue, & Surius An 1538.

Surius Ann. 1546 & Lindanus sup.

But yet Popes liue, and may treade vppon Luthers graue, stil Popes raigne, & thoughe they be excluded from England, Germanie, Scotland, and some few other places, yet do they exercise their authoritie stil, and as much as euer, in Italie, Spayne, France and other countryes, and haue by the Benedictins, Dominicanes, Iesuites, Augustines, and Franciscanes meanes, and industrious laboures, extended their iurisdiction to the Indies and other new found landes and countreys. Likewise the same Luther in his railing booke against king Henry the eight thus againe prophecieth: *Dogmata mea stabiit & Papa cadet:*

Lopes l. 1. c. 2. Gen. l. 4 cron. anno Christi 1492 Gōzal, 2. p. hist. de la Chine. c. 24. l. 3. hist. gen. c. 28.

l. cont. Regem Angl. *An other of his proud and fonde prophecies.*

cadet: Viderit Deus, vter primo fessus defecerit, Papa, an Lutherus. My opinions (saith he) *shal stand, and the Pope shal falle, let God looke to it, vvhether the Pope vvearied out, or Luther shall first fayle.* And yet vve see that Popes liue and raigne, & Luther is dead & descended to hel, and his doctrine decaieth more and more, and many are now vvearie of it, and see more and more into his absurdities. On a tyme also this man of God, this great Patriarche and fift Euangelist, this second Elias, and eight vvise man, to get him selfe a name, assaied what he could do, in dispossessing of a deuil, but it vvould not be, & the reason I thinke vvas, because one deuil vvil not, or can not, cast out an other: yea the deuil so scarred Luther for attempting so great a matter, that the dores being shut by the deuil, the man of God vvas fayne to breake the windowes least the deuil should teare him in peeces. But peraduenture he vvil bragge of his natiuitie. In deede that vvas straunge, for although he was not borne by miracle, as S. Ihon Baptist vvas, yet some are of opinion, that he is descended eyther by father or mother from the deuil him selfe, vvho vvas *incubus* to his mother, or *succubus* to his father.

His vaine attempt to cast out a deuil. *Staphilus Apol. 2 Genebr. chron. l. 4. an. Crist. 1536.* *His euil successe.* *His Natiuitie.*

Font. in trac. sacr. de statu rel. *Belsec. c. 13.* *Caluins pretended miracle.*

19. Ihon Caluine also an other patriarch of the new Church, made the like attemptes, but they had the like successe. He agreed on a tyme, for a peece of money, vvith a man, to fayne him selfe first sicke, & after dead, and he coniured his wife to weepe and lament the death of her husband, that by her teares and lamentations, the iest might seeme more probable. The sicke man was cõmended at euerie preach, to be praied for, afterward the man fayned him selfe to be dead, his vvife crieth out, Caluine goeth a vvalking vvith a great troupe, and passing by the sicke mans house, demaunded, as one altogeather ignorant of the matter, vvhat vvas the cause of those cryes and lamentations, and answer being made that one vvas dead, he entreth in, falleth downe on his knees, praieth to God to shew his power, in raising the dead to life, and therin to glorifie his seruaunt Caluine, that the world might know, that he vvas the man, vvhom God had culled out to be the only man, vvho should reforme & repaire the Church of Christ. And hauing ended his praier, he takes the man by the hand & commaundes him in God his name to arise. But the man after much calling not arising, his wife calleth on him also, & rubbes him on the side, to signifie that now vvas the tyme to rise: but he nether could answere nor moue, but by God his iuste iudgment (vvho nether vvil nor can worke a miracle, to maintaine a falshoode) was stone-deade and as colde as claye: & so the ieste was tourned into good earnest, and the com-

The successe of his miracle.

the comedie into a tragedie: vvhich his vvife perceauing, cried out on Caluin, & called him a coosening knaue, & murderer of her husband: but Caluine departeth vvith a flea in his eare, saying, that ouermuch greefe had operessed the vvife, & depriued her of her vvittes.

20. Wherfore since that the nouellers can vvorke no miracles, raise no dead men, dispossesse no deuills, foretel no future thinges, heale no diseased, not so much as a lame dogge, to proue their authoritie, what reason haue we to harken vnto them? And if we giue eare vnto them: who may not chalenge audience at our handes? For suppose some brainsicke Brownist, some brother of the familie of loue, or some other, if it may be, more phantastical, should preach the dreames of his drowsie head, & vayne conceiptes of his idle brayne, calling them new points of religion, and reformations of the olde, might he not alleage some scripture for euery fancie of his, though neuer so vayne, & make a shew also of proofe, if he expoũd it as he please? might he not discanon bookes of scripture vvhich seeme to stand in his vvaie? and being demanded by vvhat autoritie he taketh al this vpon him, might he not say that he is sent from Christ immediatlie? And being further requested to shew some miracles, as extraordinarie signes to proue an extraordinarie mission, might he not easilie answer, and that out of scripture also, that miracles are for infidells, and that Luther & Caluin are accepted of, vvho neuer could so much as heale a halting dogge, and therfore that he & his preaching can not be refused, if they & theirs be admitted?

If the nevv preachers be admitted vvithout miracles, no heretikes can be reiected

21. And so we see, that if we accept of the reformers of this time, as the true Apostles, ministers, & messengers of God, not vvithstanding that they can nether shew succession for their ordinary, nor miracles for their extraordinary mission, we open the gappe to al false Apostles, and heretikes whatsoeuer: the dore is open for them, they maie enter in thicke, and threefolde into the ministerie, and can not be excluded, if these new reformers be receaued, without playne and palpable partialitie. And so thou seest, gentle reader, that in England, & other places, where this new doctrine hath taken roote, they haue no probable assurance of their religion by the authoritie of their preachers, because they can say no more for proofe of their authoritie, then can the false Apostles.

22. Sithence therfore thou art warranted that the Church & succession of her pastours, shal neuer falle nor fayle, and art forewarned also, that false prophetes shal come and say they are sent, when God neuer

No false prophets can be reiected if the

nevv prechers be admitted. neuer ſent them at al, how canſt thou hang thy ſaluatiō, on theſe new miniſters, whom thou canſt not diſtinguiſh from falſe prophetes, becauſe they can ſhew no more probabilitie of their ordinarie or extraordinarie miſſion, then they did, & to whom thou canſt not giue eare, but thou muſt harken alſo by the ſame reaſon vnto al falſe prophetes who can ſay as much for them ſelues as thy preachers can do, and therfore can not be reiected if theſe be receaued, with out playne partialitie.

The ſecond chapter shevveth, hovv the Reformers grounding their Religion on bare ſcripture, do ſet the gate open vnto al heretikes and hereſies.

HE deuil hath alwaies played the ape, euen from the beginning: for after that he perceaued, that he could not be God in deede, to vvhich dignitie by climing thoughts he had ambitiouſly aſpired, he endeuoured by al meanes poſſible, ſo to bring his intentes to paſſe, that he might at leaſt go for a God, & be taken for a God; and therfore like an ape he hath euer imitated God ſo neerly, that he would be honoured and ſerued in the ſame faſhion and manner as he ſaw the true God vvas vvorſhipped. God is ſerued vvith ſacrifice as with a ſeruice dew vnto diuine Majeſtie, the deuil vvas euer honoured amongſt the paganes vvith his Hecatombs, & Sacrifices, euen by the Emperours of the vvorld, God hath his prieſts, the deuil his flamins, God hath his Sacraments, the deuil his expiations, & ceremonies; God hath his Baptiſme, his Euchariſt, his Nonnes, & the deuil hath his waſhings, his oblation of bread, & his veſtal virgins, & as God promiſeth a heauen to his ſeruantes & vvorſhippers, ſo doth the deuil promiſe his Eliſian feelds, and threatneth his ſtigiane lake. And euen as the deuil by Idolatours hath imitated Gods ſacrifice, ſacramentes, and manner of vvorſhippe, ſo by heretikes, he hath alwaies affected, to be as like as may be, to Chriſt and his Apoſtles, in citation and allegation of ſcripture. Vvherfore Vincentius Lyrinenſis, noteth it to haue beene the practiſe of heretikes the mēbers of the deuil, to alleage ſcriptures againſt the true chriſtians and

The deuil playes the Ape.

Tert. l. preſc. cap. 40.

Tert. ibid.

Heretikes are apes alſo.

cont. proph. c. 37.

and members of Christ, as once the deuil their head, against Christ IESVS our head, wrested a place of scripture, to proue that he must needs cast him selfe headlong from the pinnacle of the temple, to proue him selfe the sonne of God.

The custome of heretikes to alleage scripture. Mat. 6.

2. Marcion (as VVitnesseth Tertullian) to proue that the vvorld (which he imagined to be of an euil nature) vvas created of an euil God, vsed that place of Sainct Matthew: *Non potest arbor bona malos fructus facere: A good tree can not bring forth euil fruites.* Valentinus, as the same autour relateth, to perswade the world, that Christs body was framed of the substance of the heauens, and consequently was no true flesh, nor truly conceaued and borne of the Virgin Marie, but rather passed through her wombe as through a pipe, taking no substaunce of her: alleaged S. Pauls wordes, who comparing the first Adam, from whom we fetch our carnal pedegree, with the second Adam Christ IESVS, from whom we are descended spiritually, vseth these words: *The first man of earth earthly, the second man from heauen heauenly*: Not knowing, or not willing to know, that Christ is called heauenly, ether in respect of his diuinitie and diuine person, or because he was not earthly, that is subiect to sinne, vvhich proceedeth from earthly and terrene desires, or because his body, by right, vvas from the first moment of his conception, celestial, that is glorious, as are the bodies of the blessed (which therfore saint Paul calleth also spiritual) and afterwarde was the first body that rose to that glorie to which it euer had good right, because a glorious soule, such as Christs was from the first infusion of it in to the body, required as dew a glorious body: but Christ would haue his body to want this dew, whilest he liued with vs, that he might suffer for vs, which he could not haue done in a glorified body. The Arians to proue God the Sonne, inferiour to his father, and not cõsubstantial, nor coæqual vnto him, brought his owne words against him: *the father is greater then I*: omitting many pregnant places which auouch the sonne to be consubstantial, and æqual vnto him, to which places, this also is not contrarie, because it proueth only that Christ as man, is inferiour to his father. The Nestoriãs by those places by which we proue two natures in Christ, the one humaine, the other diuine, proued two persons in Christ. The Eutichianes by the same places of scripture, by which Catholiques do proue that in Christ was but one person, endeuoured to proue that in Christ was but one nature. And it hath bene the propertie of al heretikes, to make no bones of scriptures, but prodigally to spend them, and to lauish them out, to proue

l. præsc. c. 51. So did Marcion. Mat. 7. l. de carne Christi c. 10. So did Valentinus. 1. Cor. 15. Hovv Christe is called heuenly. ibidem. Io. 14. August. l. 1. Trin. c. 7.

Supra. therby their heresies, were they neuer so phantastical. *Hic fortasse* (saith Vincentius Lyrinensis) *aliquis interroget, an & hæretici diuinæ scripturæ testimonijs vtantur? Vtuntur plané & vehementer quidem, nam videas eos volare per singula quæque diuinæ legis volumina: Here perchaunce some vvil demaund vvhether that heretikes do vse the testimonies of holy scripture? they vse them assuredly and that vehemently, for you shal see them flye through euery volume of the heauenly lavv.* Read (sayth he) *the vvorkes of Paulus Samosatenus, of Priscilianus, Iouinianus, or Eunomists, and thou shalt find an infinite heap of examples, almost no page omitted, vvhich is not dyed and coloured vvith sentences of the olde & nevv Testamēt. remember* (saith Hilarius) *that there is no heretike vvhich doth not fayn that his blasphemies, vvhich he preacheth are according vnto Scriptures* And S. Austine is of opinion, that heresies proceede from no other fountaine, then scriptures wrongly expounded, and crookedly wrested: *Non aliunde natæ sunt hæreses, nisi dum scripturæ bonæ, intelliguntur non bene: From no other source heresies do proceede, but whilest good scriptures, are euilly vnderstood.*

Orat. 2. cont. Const.

Tract. 18. in Ioa.

3. But yet herein, these heretiques are liberal of that which is none of their owne, and like Æsops crow, they proudly decke them selues with other byrds fethers. For what right or title haue they to scriptures, of which they are so prodigal? or how came they to get the possession of scriptures? truly as theeues take possession of other mens goods. For Catholiques haue had the scriptures in their keeping tyme out of mynde, as al histories, al councels, and ancient tradition, wil witnesse for vs: and so at least by prescription, Catholiques are the true and lawful possessours of scripturs. Yea histories, and the ancient bookes of the fathers, who from the first age alleaged scriptures, are arguments that we are the lawful heires to the Apostles, concerning the inheritaunce of scripture, because as hereafter shal be proued, we only are successours to the ancient fathers, and Apostles them selues. And seing that such arguments would cast them in law, if the controuersie were but about a peece of ground, I see no reason, but that if the reformers of this tyme, and the Catholiques should put this case to any indifferent iudge, to wit, whether they or Catholiques are the lawful possessours of scripture, the iudge must needes giue sentence for the Catholique partie, which was the first possessour, and possessour, euen from the Apostles, of holy scripture. Yea the Reformers of this age, Luther, and Caluin, when they began to preach, receiued not the Bible of any of their prædecessours, because before Luther, ther were no Lutherans, nether were there Caluinists before Caluine,

Heretikes haue no right to scriptures. Catholiques are the true ovvners. Their right and title is proued. Second booke chap. 5.

Caluine; but they found the Bible in the Catholique and Romain Church, which euer had the custodie of this treasure, and out of this Church they tooke the Bible, else had they neuer come to the know-ledge of it: and seing that they tooke it, with out the lawful owners leaue, it must needs follow, that they are theeues, and no lawful pos-sessours, and consequently, haue no right to vse it, especially against the right owner. Wherfore if they wil fight with vs, with no other weapons then scriptures, we must first put them to the proofe of their title, least we admit them to scriptures, who haue no right vnto them, and permit them to vse our owne weapon, to cut our owne throats. And seing that they cannot proue them selues lawful possessours of scripture, nether are we bound to dispute with them by scripture, ne-ther haue they any right, or reason, to alleage scripture against vs. But yet at I haue declared, heretikes fingers itche, and are neuer wel but when they are fingring of Scriptures, and their tongues are neuer so glibbe, as when they are sauced with textes of scripture. *Heretikes vse to alleage scri-pturs.*

4 And why thinke you, do they so willingly alleage scripture, & decide al by the bare letter of scripture? Many reasons ther are why they do so. For first their guiltie conscience vrgeth them thereunto. For as the fowle and beautilesse mayde, perceuing her defect and vvante of natural beautie, is fayne to vse extrinsecal colours, to make a shevv of beautie, wher indeed is none; so the heretikes, ether doub-ting in conscience of the veritie of their opinions, or at least not able othervvise to defende them from errour, are constrained to vse scrip-tures, as colours, to make at least a show of veritie, where indeede no veritie is to be found. Fos as S. Ambrose sayth, impietie seeing au-thoritie to be esteemed: couereth her selfe with the veale of scrip-ture: that vvheras by her selfe she is not acceptable, by scripture she may seeme most commendable. Wherfore Vincentius Lyrinensis sayeth, that heretikes herein are like to sluttes, vvho perfume vvith sweete odours & pouders, those things vvhich of them selues are stin-king, or to those nurses who anointe the cuppe brimmes with hony, to make heedles children to drinke down the bitter potion: or to those Apothecaries, who vppon the boxes, vvhich conteine poison, vvrite the names of soueraine restauratiues: for so heretikes vvith the sweet odours of scriptures, persume the ordurs of their heresies, & vvith the svveet hony of Gods vvord, vvhich tasted to Dauid lik the hony combe, deceue the vnheedy and make them drinke poison in their golden cupps, & applying scripture to their poisonful doctrine, they *And vvhy. The first rea-son. A similitude Amb. in c. vlt. ad Tit. c. 36. Heretikes fit ly compared. Psal. 118.*

make the simple to buy of them deadly poison, in steed of holsome medecins, that is heresies, in steed of true faith and religion.

It is not enough to alleage the letter of scripture. 5. Let not then our Reformers bragge so much of scripture, nether let them thinke to cary away the bucklers, because they alleage scripture for euery thing, and let not the simple people thinke them selues secure, because their minister proueth vvhat he preacheth by scripture, because euery heretike doth the same, & the deuil him selfe hath alleaged scripture, and vvould haue proued, that Christ must cast him selfe headlong from the pinnacle, if he might haue had that libertie, which al heretikes do take, that is to expoũd scripture as he pleaseth. Vvherfore Tertulian refuseth flatly, to dispute with heretikes by bare scripture, and countes it but lippe-labour. And good reason had he, because ether they wil deny scripture, when they can not drawe it to their byas, or they wil expound it as they list, if it may abide glossing, and so they shape not their doctrine according to scripture, but rather scripture according to their doctrine. and so they are like to that Tyrant, who stretched forth thẽ that were to short for his iron bed, ant cut them shorter, that were to longe: framing them, according to his bed, not his bed according to them. Yea it is so vsual a thing amongst them, to discanon bookes of scripture, or to dismember and mayme them, if they stand in their way, that ther is almost no part of scripture, which by one heretike or other, hath not beene reiected or mangled.

The deuil did so. Mat. 4. Li. præscrip. c. 19. Tertulian refuseth to dispute by the bare letter. His reason. Castro v. Scriptura. Sixtus l. 7. 8. Bibl.

Vvhy Marciõ vvas called the mouse of Pontus. 6. Marcion was so coning in this point, that Tertulian calleth him *mus Ponticus, the mouse of Põtus*, for gnawing of scriptures. Cerdon denyed S. Matthewes Ghospel, because it settes dovvne the genealogie of Christ, vvhich could not stand vvith his heresie, that avouched that Christ had no true flesh, and that he vvas not truly borne. The Ebionits refused saint Pauls Epistles, because they reiect the Iewish ceremonies, vvhich those heretikes allovved of. And vvhy did Martin Luther the Archeretike of this age, disallovv of S. Iames Epistle, but because it is so opposit to his solafidian iustice? other vvise vvhat more certaintie hath he of S. Pauls Epistles, then of that of S. Iames, especially he hauing no knovvledge nether of the one nor the other, but by the Romain and Catholique church, vvhich esteemeth of both alike: S. Austin vvas so far from doubting of the veritie of this Epistle of S. Iames, that he affirmeth it to haue beene vvritten of purpose, against certain heretikes, vvho misconstred S. Pauls Epistles, as Luther and Caluin do. Vvhy doth Luther discanon Iob? Vvhy iesteth he at Eccle-

Li. 1. contra Marcionem. Tert. l. præscr. c. 51. Iren. l. 1. c. 8. Epiph. her. 30. Prefat. in Euang. Cocl. in vita. l. de operibus c. 14.

Ecclesiastes? Vvhy contemneth he al the glospells but Saint Ihons, the epistle to the Hebrewes, and that of Iudas? Vvhy doth not Caluin like of Ecclesiasticus, Iudith, and the Machabees, but because that these bookes are opposite to some point or other of their doctrine?

See the 8. booke chap. 4.

7 What meruеil then, if we refuse to decide controuersies with them, by bare scripture, who if wee bring a place of scripture, against them, wil deny it to be scripture, though al the world say contrarie? And although they admit some bookes of scripture, yet those they so admit, that they wil haue the bare letter, or ioined with their volũtarie exposition, to be the iudge of controuersies, that so they may make scriptures to speake as they liste, and to giue that sentence which pleaseth them: & this is an other reason, why they would haue the bare letter of scripture to be Iudge. For bare scripture is of a waxie nature, and is as plyable to admit diuers expositions, as waxe is to take diuers impressions. Which is the cause, why heretikes out of scripture so easilie can excogitate, and deuise euen contrarie heresies. Luther therfore calleth scripture the booke of heretikes, an other compared scripture to Æsops fables, because you may as diuersly interpret scripture, as you may moralize those fables. Others calle scripture a nose of waxe, because it may be wrested and wried euery waye: which comparisons although they be odious, and litle beseeming the maiestie of scripture, yet are they true, if by scripture you vnderstand the bare letter of scripture, without an assured interpretour, as the reformers do. For the bare letter of scripture, is so ambiguous, & may haue so many senses and meanings, that it may be applyed to what you wil, and may be, and already hath bene vsed, for the proofe of the most absurd heresies that euer were.

The bare letter is pliable to many senses.

Ex Hosio li. 3 contra Brent.

Ex Alano copo dial. 6. c. 9.

Some call scripture a nose of vvaxe.

8 But whilest they alleage the bare letter of scripture for confirmation of their doctrine, wel may they so delude the vnlerned, but men of learning and intelligence, are wel assured, that the bare letter is no more scripture, then the body of a man is a man. For as the soule is the life of the body, and that which maketh a man: so the sense is the life of the word, and that which giueth scripture life, essence, and being. Wherfore sainct Hierom sayth, that *The ghospel is not in the vvord but in the sense, not in the barke, but in the sappe, not in the leaues of the vvords, but in the roote of the meaning*. Let not therfore our reformers vaunt in their pulpits, that they trye their doctrine by the touchstone of scripture, nether let them insult ouer Catholiques, as though they relyed only on mens decrees, and Popes Bulles, for if they giue vs the letter of

The bare letter is no scripture.

A similitude

The sense is the life of the vvorde.

Com. ad Gal.

Catholiques estimation of scripture. scripture, with the true meaning, which is the formal cause and life of the word, we wil reuerence it as the word of God, and preferre it before al the decrees and writinges of Pope and Church: but take the true sense from it, and it is no more scripture, then is a man without a *A similitude* soule, because, as the same body, may be the liuing body of a man, and a dead carcas also, so the same letter with the true meaning, is the word of God, with a false meaning, it is the word of the deuil. As for *Io. 14.* example, those words of our Sauiour: *The father is greater then I*, taken in the right sense, that is, according to Christes humain nature, are *The same letter may be the vvord of God and of the deuil.* the true word of God, but taken in the meaning of the Arians, who imagined Christ a creature, inferiour euen in person to his father, they are no word of God but of the deuil, vnlesse you wil graunt heresie to be the word of God. The reason of this is, because words, are *The reason.* wordes, in that they are signes of the myndes meaning, and do explicate her inward conceipt, and consequently that is Gods word which explicateth his meaniug, and diuine conceipt; but if it explicate the mynd of the deuil or of his ministers, such as al heretikes are, then is it not the word of God, but rather of the deuil.

9 Wherfore when the letter of scripture is ioyned with the right meaning, then do wee graunt though men wrote it, that it is the word of God, because it explicateth his meaning, who spake vnto the holy writers in that meaning, and directed their hartes and handes in the *Isa. 1.* writing of the same. In so much that God sayth, to Esaie: *Behold I haue* *Heb. 1.* *put my vvords in thy mouth* And S. Paul saith that God *diuersly and by diuers* *Scripture is the vvord of God.* *meanes spake in tymes past vnto our forfathers in the Prophets*, that is in the mouth of the prophets, putting in their mouthes, that which they were to speake, and directing their handes to write it. For as the vi- *A similitude* tal spirit of man frameth his wordes in his mouth, and giueth them their meaning, so the words of the prophets, and other holy writers, *Psal. 44.* were framed in their mouthes by the spirit of God. Which is the very *Præfat. in Mat. 1.* cause why diuines saye, that God was the principal speaker, and writer of scripture, and that the Prophet, Apostle, or Euangelist, was *Li 7 conf. c. vlt. l. 18. Ciuit. c. 38.* his instrument, and as it were the pen, mouth, and tongue of God, in that he was guided and directed by him, and his holy spirit. Wherfore Dauid who was one of these writers sayth, that *His tongue is the penne* *Hom. 10. in Hexam.* *or quil of him that vvriteth svviftly*: and S. Gregorie, and S. Austine affirme scripture to bee the *Venerable stile of* the holy ghost, and S. Basil sayth, that not only the sense of scripture, but also euery word aud tittle is inspired by the holy ghost.

10 Whe-

10 Wherein a difference is put betwixt scripture and definitions of the Church, Pope, or Councels. Because these are assisted by the holy ghost, only that they may define the truth, and so the sense of a Councels definition confirmed by the Pope, is of the holy ghost, but it is not necessarie that euery word or reason in a Councel proceed from the holy spirit of God, and therfore diuines say that in a Councel, that thing only is necessarilie to be beleeued, vvhich the Councel of set purpose intended to define. But as for other thinges vvhich are spoken incidently, and as for reasons vvhich the Councel alleageth, they are not of that credit, although vvithout euident cause they are not to be reiected. And this is the cause vvhy the ancient fathers do way & ponder euery word & tittle of scripture, which interpretours of the Councels, Canons, or Definitions, do not. Vvherfore (as I sayd) let them not charge vs vvith cõtempt of scripture, for our opinion & estimation of scripture is most venerable, if it be in deede scripture, yea we auouch that in it selfe it is of far greater authority thẽ is the church or her definitions, because though God assist both, yet after a more noble manner he assisteth holy vvriters in vvriting of scripture, because he assisteth them infaillibly, not only for the sense and veritie, but also for euery vvord vvhich they vvrite, and euery reason and whatsoeuer is in scripture, vvheras he assisteth the Pope and Councel infallibly, only for the sence and veritie of that vvhich they intend to define, but nether for euery vvord, nor for euerie reason, nor for euerie thing, vvhich is incidently spoken, as is already declared. And yet vve say also, that although scripture of it selfe be greater then the Church, and independent of her, because not from her, but from God it hath authoritie and veritie, yet the Church is better knovvne to vs then scripture, & therfore though she make not scripture, yet of her we are to learne vvhich is scripture, & vvhat is the meaning therof: which is no more disgrace to scripture, then that S. Ihon and the Apostles should giue testimonie of Christ, because they were better knowen then he, though his authoritie in it selfe, was greater then theirs, and not depending of them. Yea the reformers, euerie one in particular, be he a cobler, is according to their doctrine, to iudge by his priuate spirit, which is scripture, and what is the meaning of scripture, which seemeth to haue more difficultie, then that the church, and her common spirit, which Christ promised her, should chalenge vnto her such authoritie. Giue vs therfore true scripture, and we wil reuerence it as the word of God, but corrupt this scripture, by putting a false sense and

A difference betvvixt scripture & Coũcels.

VVhy fathers vvaye euery vvord of scripture.

Hovv God assisteth the vvriters of scripture.

Hovv scripture dependeth of the church.

See the 3. cha. follovving.

Io. 14. 15.

and ſignification to the letter, as the reformers do, and then we wil not acknowledge it for the word of God, becauſe it explicateth not his mind and meaning, but rather we deteſt it, aboue al other wordes and writinges whatſoeuer, becauſe in that it beareth the name of the word of God, and yet is not, it is the moſt pernicious word that is. For as the ſowreſt vineger cometh of the beſt wine, ſo the moſt pernicious word, is the letter of ſcripture corrupted, and miſinterpreted.

Scripture euilly interpreted is the vvorſt vvorde

A ſimilitude.

If then our aduerſaries wil haue ſcripture, to be iudge in cōtrouerſies of religion, let them alleage true ſcripture, that is the letter, with the true meaning, of which not euery priuate ſpirit, but the cōmon ſpirit of the church muſt be iudge, as ſhal heareafter be proued. But if they wil make the bare letter to be iudge, we deny firſt that the bare letter is ſcripture, and then we auouch, that the bare letter is no good rule nor lawful iudge of religion, becauſe the letter of ſcripture, may haue diuers ſenſes, & may ſerue euery heretike, for his purpoſe; as before is declared, and ſo can be no rule nor iudge, which both muſt be aſſured, and certaine.

The bare letter is no certaine rule.

The firſt anſvver is, that Scripture is eaſie.

11. To this they anſwer that ſcripture is ſo eaſie, that the meaning is euident to euery one that hath eyes to ſee it, & ſo he may as eaſilie ſee the conformitie of their religion vnto the rule of ſcripture. For as when the meaſure is known, it is euident how long the cloth is which is meaſured by it, ſo ſcripture, as they ſay, being eaſie, it is moſt euident when religion is true, bicauſe it is euident when it is agreable, and conformable to the aſſured, and knowne meaſure of ſcripture, by which al religions are to be ſquared out and meaſured.

12 But that ſcripture is not eaſie to be vnderſtood, it is eaſily to be proued, and ſo this anſwere is as eaſilie to be reiected. For firſt ſcripture her ſelfe, confeſſeth her owne obſcuritie. For S. Peter in his epiſtle which is a part of ſcripture, auoucheth that in S. Pauls epiſtles, which our reformers wil not deny to be an other part of ſcripture, *are certain hard things, hard to be vnderſtood, vvhich the vnlearned and vnſtable deprave, as alſo the reſt of the ſcriptures, to their ovvne perditiō.* And S. Auſtin ſaith plainly, that thoſe hard thinges are his commendations of faith, which the ignorant euen from the Apoſtles tyme did ſo miſconſter, as though his meaning had bene, that only faith, without charitie and good workes doth iuſtifie. The Eunuch could not vnderſtand Eſaie without an interpretour, Dauid cryeth for vnderſtanding at Gods hands, before he dareth aduenture to ſearch the law: the Apoſtles could not vnderſtand ſcripturs, til Chriſt opened their ſenſe and eyes of vnderſtanding, and yet our

2. Pet. 3. Scriptnre hard.

lib. de fid. & op. c. 14.

Act. 18.

Pſal. 118.

Luc. 24

yet our reformers are so eagle-eyed, that they can see clearly, and that at the first sight, into the darkest and obscurest place of scripture. The ancient fathers affirme that scripturs are obscure, and amongest them S. Hierome sayth, that the beginning of Genesis, and the end of Ezechiel, in tymes past, was not permitted to be read of any, til he were thirtie yeares of age: and why, but for the obscuritie which might rather deceue, then direct the younger sorte? S. Austin that great light of the Church, and miraculous vvitte, vvho vvhen he vvas but tvventie yeares of age vnderstood the predicamentes of Aristotle at the first sight, thought nether so highly of him selfe, nor so basely of scripturs, as to thinke him selfe able by reach of wit, to attain vnto the profound sence and meaning of them, but rather though he had studied them moe dayes & nightes then our ministers haue done dayes only, yea or houres, and had written more for the interpreting of scripturs then euer they read, yet saieth he: *So great is the profunditie of them, that I might euery day make profit in them, if I should vvith greatest leisure, greatest studie, and a better vvitt, endeuour to come vnto the knovvledg of them only, and that from my tender youth vnto crooked olde age.* And in his bookes which he wrote vpon Gen., in his tractes vpon S. Ihon, & diuers other partes of scripture, he moueth many doubtes and difficulties: and yet Luther sayth that scripturs are more playn and easie then al the fathers commentaries. Petrus Lombardus commonly called the maister of sentences, S. Thomas & other diuines armed vvith philosophie, and furnished with the schoole literature, apply notvvithstanding al their wittes to the explicating of the first chapter of Genesis, and the creation of the world in the first six dayes, as also S. Basil, S. Ambrose & others do. And yet Luther boldly affirmeth, that no part of scripture is to be called or counted obscure. S. Gregorie Nazianzen and S. Basil studied scriptures for thirtene yeares together, and yet durst not swerue a iotte from the interpretation of the auncient fathers. S. Hierom notwithstanding that he was so wel seene in the Greeke and Hebrew tongue, and other both prophane and sacred literature, yet went he as far as Alexandria to conferre with Didimus. Who also running after a cursorie manner ouer al the bookes of scripture, fyndeth such difficultie in euery one, as though he vnderstood this only in scripture that he vnderstandeth not scripture, or as though this only in scripture were easie to be vnderstood, that scripture is not easie, & ending with the Apocalipse thus he concludeth: *Apocalypsis Ioannis tot habet sacramenta quot verba, parum dixi pro merito voluminis, laus omnis inferior est,*

Ep. ad Paul.

l. 4. conf. c. 16

Ep. 3. ad Volus

Præfat. assert.

l. 2. d 12. & p. 1. q. 65.

in Hexamer.

l. de seruo arbit

Ruff. l. 11. c. 9.

Ep. 65. 103.

Al scripture is hard to S. Hierome.

Al scripture is hard to S. Hierome.

in verbis singulis multiplices latent intelligentiæ : The Apocalipse of Ihon hath as many sacraments as vvords, I haue sayed litle for the merit of the volume, al prayse is inferiour, in euerie vvord there lye hidden many senses and meaninges. And yet Luther and Caluin, and commonly Puritanes and Protestants, auouch scripture to be so facile and perspicuous, that by the owne light you may see it, and see into it, and neede no more helpe of an interpretour, then of a candle to see the sunne, when it shineth in the midde-daye.

But easie to our heretikes,

VVhy then disagree they? VVhy retaine they a lecture of diuinitie.

13 But if this doctrine be true, why is ther such contention amongst the reformers for the true explication of scripture? Why did the Fathers, and why do the reformers make so large commentaries vppon scripture? Why retayne they a diuinitie lesson in Oxford and other vniuersities, especially now that they haue turned the Bible into the vulgare tongue, which being done, by the priuate spirit of the minister at the first sight, it is easilie vnderstood: If this be true, then certainly had the auncient fathers very dul pates, who with al their studie, industrie, prayer, fasting, solitude, tongues, philosophie, and sanctitie of life, could not attaine to that knowledge of scripture in a long lifes tyme, which a minister by and by getteth at the first opening of the Bible.

Experience teacheth scriptur to be harde.

14 But tel me in good sadnes: are you in iest or earnest when you say that scripture is easie? When you read the first chap. of Gen. the prophecies, especially of Daniel, the Psalmes of Dauid, Iobes witty sayinges, Salomons Prouerbes and Canticles, sainct Paules epistles, S. Ihons Apocalipse, do you finde no difficultie? I can not thinke it, because euen experience teacheth that nothing is more euidẽt, then that scripture is not euident. For first the very letter and phrase of scripture is obscure and ambiguous. Secondly many speeches in scripture are prophetical, many parabolical, many metaphorical, which commonly are ful of obscuritie. Thirdly it is proper to scripture to haue many senses vnder one letter, as the literal sence which the holy writer first intended, and this sense some tymes is signified by proper words, some tymes metaphorical, yea sometymes also this literal sense vnder one letter, is diuers. Sometymes the sense is spiritual, which is that which the thinges vnder the letter do signifie: as for example those words of S. Paul: *Abraham had tvvo sonnes one of the handmayd another of the free vvoman,* literally do signifie Abrahames two sonnes, because, that, the letter importeth, and that first is intended, but these two sonnes were figures of the old and new Testament, or the two peoples which liued vnder

Three causes of the difficultie of scripture.

The literal sense.

The spiritual sense.

Gal. 4.

An example.

vnder those Testaments, and so this is the spiritual signification of those words, which they not immediatly, but by meanes of those two sonnes do signifie. And this spiritual sence is ether moral, or tropological, when it tendeth to manners, or allegorical, which tendeth to fayth or the Church, or anagogical, which tendeth to heauen or life euerlasting. Wherfore this worde, Hierusalem, literally signifieth the citie so called, morally, the soule of man which God inhabiteth by good life or the deuil by bad, allegorically, the Church militant, and anagogically, heauen, and the Church triumphant. Now who is he that dareth promise to tel vs infaillibly, when a place of scripture is to be vnderstood literally, or spiritually, and in what literal or spiritual meaning? Sainct Hierom affirmeth, that Apollinaris, Tertulian, and Lactantius, and other Millenarians, imagined after the resurrection, a reedification of the Temple and terrestrial Hierusalem, and that Christ in it should raigne for a thousand yeares, and we that tyme should liue in al corporal pleasurs, because they vnderstood certaine places of scripture literally and properly, which should haue been vnderstood spiritually and metaphorically. And contrariwise the same father ascribeth Origens errours in the exposition of the beginning of Genesis to no other cause, thē that he imagined that the sayd chapter ought to be vnderstood metaphorically & spiritually, which should haue beene interpreted historically, properlie, and literallie. And what man in his witte, can thinke it so easie to hit alwayes of the right sense, where the senses are so diuerse, and in which so many learned men haue banguered.

The spiritual sense, moral, allegorical anagogical.

In c. 36. Ezec.

Ep. ad Paul.

15 Truly when I consider with my selfe how euident a thing it is that scriptures are hard and obscure, I meruaile how our reformers can perswade them selues that scriptures are easie. and some tymes I am induced to thinke that when they say so, they speake not as they thinke: but yet when I cal to mynd another opinion of theirs, which is, that the true meaning of scripture is that, which euerie ones priuate spirit imagineth, I see it to bee as easie to interpret scripture, as to imagin, which is most easie, because the imagination is free, & can as wel imagin Chimeraes as true obiectes. As for example, if that were the true meaning of Aristotle, which euery one would imagin, then were it an easie matter for euery cobler to vnderstand Aristotle, were he in Greek or Latin, because he can imagin what it pleaseth him with great facilitie. And this if I be not deceaued, is the cāse why now euery sister of the lord whom S. Paul cōmaunded to be silent in the Church, wil needs

The reason vvhy scripture seemeth easie to heretikes.

An example.

The cause of vvomens boldnes vvith scripture.

 be a biblist

a bibliste & an interpretour of Scripture. For if that be the true sense of scripture which the priuate spirit imagineth, if she haue the spirit (as why should she not as wel as the minister especially it being a receaued doctrine amongst them that euery one by his priuate spirit can iudge of scripture) why may not she comment vppon the scripture, and mount also into the pulpit, there to preach the doctrine of her spirit. But o fancies, o Luciferian pride, to which heresie leadeth, euen the frayle and imperfect Sexe, which nature seemeth to haue debarred from pulpits. This pride Tertulian espyed in the heretical women of

Lib. præs.

his tyme. *Ipsæ mulieres hereticæ quam sunt procaces quæ docere audent, contendere exorcismis agere, curationes repromittere, forsitan & tingere: Euen the heretical vvomen hovv malapert are they, vvhich dare be so bold as to teach, and to take vpon them to exorcise, and to promise miraculous cures, yea perhaps to baptize.* And vvheras Apprentices are bound seauen yeares to an occupation, to learne only a mechanical trade, the art and science of expounding scripture, which is the highest science that is, seemeth to these subtile wittes so easie, that as Saind Hierome obserued in some of his tyme, euery cobler, euery olde trot, and doting foole, can with out a Doctour fynd out the secret meaning of scripture, and teach before they be taught.

Heretikes make mecanical artes harder then scripture.

ep. ad paulin.

16 But let them say and beleeue if they can or wil, that scripture is easie, the experience and reason which I haue alleaged wil proue the contrarie. And truly if hony be hidden in the combe, marow in the bone, and pretiouse stones in the sea: if gold be gotten with labour out of the bowels and secret vaines of the earth, and roses be hedged in with pricking thornes, if nature hath hidden al perfection and natural sciences, & vealed them with such obscuritie, that without great industrie they can not be discouered, good reason vvas there that the mystical meanings and sacred senses of scripture, should be vealed with an obscure letter, and couered with many ænigmatical speeches.

nature hideth perfectiō, and selles it for labour.

17 For first by reason of this difficultie the study of scripture asketh a mans wholle life, and so keeping him occupied, distracteth him from prophane, idle, and euil occupations. Secondly the difficultie of scriptur makes a man to haue a better esteeme & higher conceipt of the same, because things easily learned are easilie contemned; & knowlege hardly gotten is highly prized. And therfore as S. Austin noteth, the holy ghost in scripture hath prouided easie things to satisfie our hunger, & obscure places also, to take away lothsomnes. Because our vnderstanding with easie things only, would be soone cloyed, & with obscuritie

The first reason vvhy God vvould haue Scripture hard

The second reason.

li. 2. doct. Christ. c. 6.

obscuritie only, would easilie be deterred. Thirdly this difficultie imprinteth in our memorie the word of God more deeply. For as the iron is more hard to receaue impression then wax or vvater, yet keepeth it more firmly, so that which we learne hardly, we forget not easilie. Fourthly it controleth our high-clyming and deepe searching wittes and maketh vs to acknowledge the weaknes of our intellectual eyesight, which if it be so dimme, that it can no more susteyne the blazing spendour of natural verities, then can the night crowes eyes the beames of the sunne, much lesse can it behold (vnlesse it be by a glimse and glimmering) the splendent rayes of supernatural verities, reuealed through the darke veale of holy scripture. Fiftly this difficultie increaseth merit and desert, when so constantly we beleeue those verities which in scripture are rather vealed then reuealed. Sixthly this difficultie preserueth scripture from prophanation, and is the cause why euerie one can not babble of scripture as they do of easie thinges, and as the heretiques of this tyme do, because they imagin scripture to be easie. Seauenthly it hides our sacred mysteries from prophane infidells, who are no more worthy of this diuine knowledge then are the beastly swine of preciouse pearles. Eightly as Ciril or rather Origin very wel obserueth, these obscure phrases and figures, wherin the diuine veritie is clad, are as it were a seemly habit, which graceth the word of God, and makes it seeme the better vnto our weakish eyes. For more are we delighted to see the veritie of the sacred Eucharist, vnder the figure of Manna, and of the Sacrament of Baptisme, in that shadow of the red sea, then if we sawe the same set forth to our vew, in bare wordes though neuer so playn.

The third. *A similitude* *The fourth.* *The fifte.* *Sixte.* *The Seuenth.* *Orig. li. 1. in Leuit.* *The eight.*

18 But now let vs see what our ghospellers can saye to this experience, and reason, by which I haue proued scriptures to be hard and difficile? It is true, sayth Luther, scriptures are in many places hard, but where they treat of thinges necessarie to saluation, there are they playn and perspicuouse. Is it true (Luther) that some partes of scripture are hard? then must thou eate that word of thine in which thou saydst. *Ego de tota scriptura dico, nullam eius partem obscuram dici volo. I say of al scripture, I vvil haue no part of it called obscure.* And wilt thou stand to it, that where scripture treateth of thinges necessarie to saluation, there it is plain and easie? I aske then of thee, whether the doctrine of Baptisme be not necessarie to saluation? And if thou say yea, then is some part of scripture, which treateth of thinges necessarie, hard and difficile, for otherwise Caluin vvould neuer

The first answere of heretikes. *The refutation of it.* *Præfat asser. art. l. de seruo arbit.*

Io. 3. *Harm. ibid.* haue cauilled so much about those wordes of Christ: *Vnlesse a man be borne againe of vvater and the holy ghoste.* Is not the doctrine of the blessed Sacrament necessary to be beleeued? And yet vvho seeth not, how many diuerse expositions the ghospellers haue deuised vppon those few words, *This is my bodie*? *Mat. 26.* *Luc. 22.* Is not the doctrine of iustification necessarie? And yet it is so obscurely set downe in scripture, that Osiander auoucheth, that amongst the cōfessionistes, there are twentie different opinions about the formal cause of iustification, & euery one is deduced out of scripture. *Bel. l. 1. de Euch. c. 28.* *Ex Bel. to. 1. l. 2. de Iustif, initio to. 1. l. 3. c. 1. de verbi dei interpret.* At least they wil graunt me that the doctrine and fayth of the blessed Trinitie and of Christes diuinitie, and humanitie, is of necessitie to be beleeued: & yet the Ebionites, Arrianes, Nestorians, Eutichians, Valentinians, Monothelites, and Appollinaristes, who held diuerse heresies concerning the Trinitie and Incarnation, proued them al to their thinking, out of scripture. Vvhich is a signe that scripture is not easie: for where al is playne, al men commonly aggree, and if scripture where it speaketh of those mysteries, were perspicuouse, they would neuer hauebanguered so grossely in expounding them.

The second ansvver. 19 But rather then my aduersarie wil stand out, he wilbe content to play smale play. If, sayth he thou be a good Grāmarian, al wil seeme easie vnto thee. *The refutation.* And was not I pray thee S. Austin who read Rhetorike in Millan, was not S. Hierom, who was excellent in al the three tongues, a grammarian? They were, they were, and yet they confessed as I haue declared, that scriptures were ful of difficultie. *Supra.* Yea in England our ministers haue the Bible in English, and so haue no neede of any helpe of Grammer, and yet can they not aggree about the scriptures meaning. Yea in al sciences, it is one thing to be a grammarian another thing to attayne to the knowledge of the science: for many a schoole maister in England can constrew Aristotle, which yet can not vnderstand him, and if grammer were sufficient, then after grammer, we should neede no studie, nether in diuinitie nor philosphie, nor any other science: And to vse no other argument then experience, let our grammarians in England after they haue constrewed the psalmes, tel me whether they do yet vnderstand the psalmes?

Another ansvver. 20 But my aduersary wil shew that he is not tongue-tyed and therfore wil not be put to silence. If (sayeth he) you confer one place vvith another, one wil explicate another. This is another starting hole vvhich he hath found out. *The refutation.* But this also, is but a poore shifte. For although one place conferred vvith another, many tymes giueth a great

great light to both, yet doth it not so allwayes fal out. For diuerse haue conferred the same places, and yet haue gathered diuerse meaninges: yea somtymes conference of places augmenteth the difficultie, and maketh a show of contradiction, which before appeared not. As for example, that of Genesis: *It is not good that man be alone*, conferred with that of S. Paule to the Corinthians: *It is good that a man touche not a woman*, seemeth to imply a plaine contradiction. That also of Genesis: *Encrease and multiplie*, seemeth quite contrarie to that of our Sauiour: *Happie are the barrein which haue not borne children*. Moyses also sayeth that *God tempted Abraham*, and yet S. Iames sayeth, *God tempteth no man*. And Christe commaundeth that, *soe our lighte shine before men that they may see our good workes*: And in the next Chapter, hee biddeth vs *Take heede, that vvee doe not our iustice before men to bee seene of them*. S. Paule describinge his vocation, vision, and conuersion, sayeth, *that his companie heard a voice, but savve no body*: and yet afterwrarde he sayth, that *they savve a lighte but hearde no voice*. In his Epistle also to the hebrewes he sayeth, *that in the Arke vvas a golden pott of Manna, Aarons rod & the tables*: And yet in the third booke of Kinges wee reade that in the Arke *vvas nothinge else but the tables of the lavve*. To bee breife, S. Marke, S. Luke, and S. Iohn, say the woemen came to Christes monument in the morninge, S Mathewe, in the Eueninge. Soe that Collation of places, manie tymes augments the difficultie, and maketh a contradiction to arise, vvhere none before appeared.

Gen. 2. 1. Cor. 7. Gen. 1. Luc. 23. Gen. 22. Iac. 1. Mat. 5. Mat. 6. Act. 9. Act. 22. Heb. 9. 3. Reg. 3. Mar. 16. Luc. 24. Io. 20. Mat. 28.

21. Nowe gentle reader thou wouldst think that this man were satisfied, or else that his mouth were stopped, but yet he desireth one answere more, and if that vvil not serue, he wil ether yeeld or hold his peace. If you pray to God (sayth he) to illuminate you, he wil reveal the meaning of scripture vnto you, or if you haue the spirit, & be not carnal but spiritual, or if you be prædestinate, you shal find al as playne in scripture, as the kinges high way. This answere is so poore, that it wel argueth that our aduersarie is put to an harde shift and to a last reply: because in this answere hee declareth *ignotum per ignotius*, *an vnknovven thing by that vvhich is more vnknovven*. As for example, I vvould haue him to assure vs whether that wee expound scripture rightly or vvrongly, & hee telleth vs that if we praye as vvee ought to do, or if wee bee of the electe, or if wee bee spiritual men, wee shal easiilie find out the meaning of holy scripture. And seing that nothing is more vncertayne then whether wee praye as wee ought to do, vvhether vvee bee electe or no, or vvhether wee bee true

The fourth answver.

The refutation.

bee true ſpiritual men or no: by this rule vvee ſhal neuer bee aſſured of the true ſenſe of ſcripture. And vvere not I praye you S. Auſtin, S. Hierom, and other Fathers before mentioned, the elect Saintes of God? was it not like that if any prayed aright, that they did ſo? vvere not they liker to bee ſpiritual men, then our fleſhly ghoſpellers, whom their vviues can not content? Or can the reformers aſſure vs that they them ſelues are electe, that they praye iuſte as thy ought to do, that they are ſpiritual menne, vvho haue the right ſpirit of interpreting ſcripture? It followeth therfore, vvhich I intended to proue, that if vve beleeue the reformers, becauſe they alleage ſcriptures according to their owne expoſition, vvee muſt of neceſſitie giue eare vnto al falſe prophetes, vvho can, and haue already, & herafter vvil alleage ſcripture for vvhat ſoeuer they ſhal preach: and ſo if theſe Reformers be admitted, no heretikes nor hereſies can be excluded or reiected. Which concluſion, although it neceſſarily proceedeth from the premiſes, which before are layed dovvne, yet to helpe the readers memorie, I vvil laye them dovvne again breefly, that out of them he maye gather the intended concluſion more eaſily.

22 Thou muſt therfore (gentle reader) cal to mynd which before is proued: to wit that it hath alwayes bene the manner of heretikes, though they had no right thervnto (the Romain church being euer the right owner) to alleage Scripture, therby to grace their hereſies: and that they might ſay what they liſted, and frame Scripture to their doctrine, and not their doctrine to Scripture: if Scripture chanced to be ſo plaine againſt them that it could not bee gloſſed, they would flatly deny that parte, if it were ambiguous, they would expound it as they liſted to make it ſpeake as they wiſhed: litle caring that the church and fathers, other wiſe expounded: Which Scripture though with ſuch a meaning it was in deed no Scripture, yet the bare letter and name ſufficed for their purpoſe. And ſeing that Luther, Caluin, and al the packe of our new preachers, can ſay no more nor bring any other proofe for their doctrine, if we admit & receue them, wee can reiect no heretike at al, ether of former, or preſent, or future tymes. For what can luther and Caluin alleage which olde heretikes, haue not hertofore alleaged? Luther and Caluin alleage ſcripture: ſo did they. If Scriptures were playne againſt old heretikes, they plainly denyed them: So do luther and caluin. If Scripture were ambiguous, they expounded it to their own aduantage: So did luther & caluin, & no better nor no other proofe can they bring. Wherfore if we receiue Lu-

A repetition of that vvich before is ſayd,

ue Luther, Caluin, or any of the new preachers, we open the way to al heretikes that euer were or shal be: because where the same proofe is alleaged, the same credit must be giuen, vnles we wil be partial. And for as much as we can not giue credit to them al, because they teach contraries, yea & contradictions, our best wil be to giue eare to none of them al, but rather to listen to the cōmon receiued, that is, the Romane Church, who as she hath euer had the custody of the book of Scripture, so is it most like that she best knoweth the meaning of it, hauing this book from the Apostles, and with it, the Apostles and their Successours interpretation.

The third Chapter treateth of the priuat spirit. vvhich the pretended Reformers haue made supreme iudge in earth, in the interpretation of scripture: vvherby, as it is proued, the vvay is opened to al heretikes, and none can be excluded, if these nevv Reformers be admitted to determine of religion by the priuat spirit.

SELFE-loue (sayth one) is as good as guilding, which maketh that to seme goodly, wherin our selues be parties. For as guidling maketh al to seme gold, be it but stone or wood vnderneath: So selfeloue maketh to our selues, euen our selues, and al our actions to seme comelie and semely, be they neuer so absurd and vnsemely. *Suum cuique pulchrum* (sayth the latin prouerbe) to which is answearable in English: Euerie man as he likes, quoth the goodman to his cow. To Pan, his owne pipe and piping sounded more melodiously then Apollo his harpe and harping. Euery mayd thinketh her selfe of al to be the fayrest, or if she acknowledge any one defect in beautie, she thinks that to be counteruayld in many other perfections. Euery mother deems her owne children the best fauoured, to euery henne her owne chickenes are most pleasing, yea euery owle & crow thinketh her own youngone fayrer & better fethered, then the white doue, hauke, or Eagle. Artizanes prayse most their owne workmanship, Poets price their owne poemes at the highest rate, and euery scholar thinketh his own witte most pregnant, and euery doctor preferreth his owne books and vvritinges before al other. Yea al men by nature

Selfe loue.

A similitude

The blindnes of selfe loue.

Examples.

nature not ruled by reason, nor corrected by grace, fal most willingly in loue with their ovvn conceipts, and the broods and young ones of their owne deuising wittes. The reason herof is, ovvne selfe, to vvhich, as euery one is more neere, then to an other, so is he most addicted and affected. For to our selues we are one, to others we are only vnited, and so first we like our selues, and our owne doings, next of al, those and their actions, who are nearest and most vnited vnto vs. Wherfore although, in that God is chiefest good & goodnesse it selfe, he should by al reason be first and best beloued, yet because he is not so neere vnto vs, as we are to our selues, we giue the maydenhead and prime of our affection vnto our selues. This S. Bernarde in his book which he made of the loue of God obserued long since. *Imprimis* (sayeth he) *diligit homo seipsum propter se, caro quippe est & nihil sapere valet, cum que se videt per se non posse subsistere, Deum sibi quasi necessarium incipit diligere, at veró cum Deum cœperit, occasione propriæ necessitatis, colere & diligere, Deus illi dulcescit, & sic gustando quam suauis est Dominus, transit ad tertium gradum & diligit Deum propter se: First of al man loueth him selfe for him selfe, because he is flesh, and can like of nothing but him selfe, and vvhen he seeth that of him selfe he can not stand he beginneth to loue God as a thing necessarie vnto him: but vvhen he beginneth to loue God vpon occasion of his ovvne necessitie, then God beginneth to vvax svveet vnto him, and so by tasting hovv svveet God is, he passeth to the third degree and loueth God for him selfe.* And as we loue our selues and our own thinges best, so doth this selfe loue blinde vs & hide from our ovvne eyes our owne defectes. Wherfore Demosthenes was vvont to say, that it is a most easie thing to deceiue our selues, for while we desire especially to haue our owne actions liked, we easily persuade our selues, that they are to be liked. And therfore Plato counsayleth euery man to flye this vice of selfe loue which the Grecians cal *Philautia*, and not be ashamed to learne of others, especially when they are our betters.

The reason vvhy selfloue is belived. *God should be first and best beloued* *l. de diligendo Deo.* *But we first loue our selues* *Selfe loue hideth our defectes.* *l. 9. de leg. 1. 9*

2. Now if euer any were sick of this disease, it is the heretike, especially of our tyme, who preferreth his owne opinion before the common consent of Fathers, and his owne priuate and particular spirit, before the common spirit of the Church: who though a by general councel, in which al the grauitie, sanctitie, wisdom, and learning of the Church is assembled together, define the contrary, wil neuer change his opinion, but wil prefer his owne particular opinion and priuate spirite, before al councelles, fathers, ages, & Churches: and he but one, vvil stand against al, and he but one, vvil be iudge of al, in interpreting of scripture, and vvil be iudged of none. This intole-

An Heretike especially is sick of selfe-loue. *l. 8. cont. her. c. 2.*

rable

rable pride & self loue of their owne opinions, S. Ireneus auoucheth to be a common disease amongest heretikes. *Vnusquisque* (sayth he) *fictionem quàm à semetipso adinuenit, illam esse sapientiam dicit, seque indubitatè & incontaminatè & sincerè absconditum scire mysterium. Euery one sayeth that his ovvne, vvhich he hath deuised, is vvisdome, and that he vndoubtedly, incontaminatly, and sincerely doth knovv the hidden mysterie.* Arius that famous or rather infamous heretike, not for spoiling Dianaes temple, but for robbing Christ of his diuinitie, vvas so vvise in his ovvne conceipte, that he thought none of the ancient Fathers vvorthie to be compared vvith him. Aetius an other souldiour of Lucifers bande, vvas vvonte to say that he knevv God, as vvel as he knevv him selfe. Manicheus bragged, that he vvas not only an Apostle of Christ, but also a Paraclete. Nestorius eloquent in dede, though not so svvet in vtering, as forvvard to come to the vtteraunce, took such pleasure therin, that he had no minde to read the ancient Fathers.

The pride of Arius.
Nic. l. 8. c. 7. l. 4. c. 22.
Of Aetius.
Theodoret. l. 4. her. fab.
Aug. cont. ep. fund.
of Nestorius.
Socr. l. 2. c. 28.

3. But to leaue the olde, and to come to our nevv borne heretikes, you shal see that in this selfe loue & liking of their ovvne opiniōs, they degenerate not a iotte from their ancetours. Luther seing him selfe oftentimes to be pressed vvith the old fathers authority, preferreth his ovvne priuate opinion before their common sentēce, and decree: & blusheth not a vvhit at the matter. *Nihil curo* (sayth he) *si mille Augustini, mille Cypriani, mille Ecclesiæ contra me sentiant: I care not if a thousand Augustines, a thousand Ciprianes, a thousand Churches thinke othervvise then I do.* And in an other place: *Doctrinam meam* (sayth he) *nolo iudicari à quoquam, nec ab Episcopis, nec ab Angelis omnibus, volo per eam & Angelorum iudex esse: I vvil not haue my doctrine iudged of any, nether of Bishops, nor of al Angells, I vvil by my doctriue be iudge euen of the Angels.* And againe in an other booke of his: *ego* (sayth he) *in hoc libro non contuli, sed asserui, & assero, nec penes vllum, iudicium esse volo, sed omnibus suadeo vt præstent obsequium. I haue not conferred in this booke but I haue affirmed, and I affirme, nether vvil I that any man iudge herof, but I counsayle al to obey myn opinion.* But especially he triumpheth in an other place of the afore saied booke which he wrote against Henry the eight *I oppose* (sayth he) *the Gospel* (but expounded as he pleaseth) *against the sayings of fathers, and Angeles* (as though Angeles vvere in opinion contrary to the Gospel) *Here I stand, here I remane, here I glorie, here I triumphe, here I insulte, against the Papistes, Thomistes, Henricistes, Sophistes, and al the sayings of men, though neuer so holy.* See how this man pleaseth him selfe in his ovvn opinion, & how he preferreth it before al men and Angeles. For although he wil seeme to preferre only the Gospel before them, yet seing that the con-

Luthers Luciferian pride.
Li. cont. Regem Angl.
Prol. lib. cont. statuta Ecclesiæ.
L. de seruo arbitrio.
Intolerable arrogancie.
Luther preferreth him selfe before al Fathers and Angels.

trouersie is not betwixt Scriptures, & Fathers (because the Fathers reuerenced Scriptures more then euer Luther did) but whether Luther or they expoũded Scripture rightly? he in dede preferreth him self before al the Fathers that euer were: & in conceipt triũpheth ouer them al, but before the victorie. Caluin also in this selfe pleasing opinion showeth him self as bragging, & Thrasonical as Luther for his hart, & contendeth with him, who shal stout it most. *Nulla* (sayth he) *Conciliorum Pastorum, Episcoporum nomina, nos impedire debent, quo minus omnes omnium spiritus, ad diuini verbi regulam exigamus: No names of Councels, Pastours, Bishops, ought to hinder vs from examining the spirits of al men, by the diuine vvord.* And in an other chapter of the same book, explicating those words of scripture: *This is my bodie* in a contrary sense to the Lutherans, he sayeth, that he *hauing by diligent meditation examined those vvordes, doth imbrace that sense vvhich the spirit telleth him, and leaning to that* (sayth he) *I dispise the vvisdom of al men, vvhich can be opposed against me.* See, see, the pride of an heretike. may not Luther & euery false prophet say, that he hath vsed diligence, and that the spirit telleth him the contrary? Were not the Fathers as diligẽt, as Caluin, as wise, as learned, and as vertuouse, who expounded those vvordes in their proper sense? No, no, one Caluin in his owne conceipt surpasseth them al, and his opinion and priuat spirit must take the place, and vpper hand of al the Austines, Ambroses, Gregories, Hieromes, of al the Councels, yea and Churches also, although they were thousands in number. Of these mens priuate spirits may be sayed, that of the Poet *Sua cuique Deus fit dira cupido: Euery ones cruel lust is his God. Sibi quisque profecto est Deus: Euery one truly is to him selfe a God.* For these men especially, who preferre their priuat opinions before Fathers, Councells, Churches, yea and Angels also, What do they but adore the idols of their owne imaginations, as their God? Truly these men which are not *sicut cæteri homines, like other men*, are either goddes, or beasts, & that by the sentence of Aristotle, the prince of Philosophers. For if by this philosophers verdict, solitarie men or rather haters of societie, whom the Grecians vse to cal *Misantropi*, be either gods or sauage beastes, vvhat are these men, vvho flying alwayes the company, and common consent of Christians, vvil go alone in al their opinions, and symbolize or sorte them selues with no men. But this it is to leaue the Catholique Church, vvhich vvhen the heretike forsaketh, he biddeth adieu to al Fathers, Councels, Antiquitie, & common consent, vvhich only are to be found in this Church; and must of necessitie stand post alone, and stick to his priuat spirit, and opinion, against

Caluin as Thrasonical.

l. 4. Inst c. 9.

c. 17. & 25.

Mat. 26.

Virg. Aeneid 9.

Ouid. met. 8.

The heretikes priuat opinion and spirit is his God.

He is either a God or a beast.

To leaue the church is to stand post alone.

against al the Christian vvorld. I vvould S. Bernard had bene to deale with these singular spirits; but because he is ridde of such trublesome companions, we wil at least alleage his words, vvhich he once vsed against one Petrus Abailardus, possessed with the same euil spirit, who sayed, that man was not deliuered by Christ from captiuitie of the diuel. *Although* (sayeth he) *the Doctors of the Church thinck the contrary, yet other vvise it seemeth vnto me. VVhat* (sayeth S. Bernard) *shal I deme more intolerable in these vvords, blasphemie, or arrogancie? VVhat more damnable rashnes or impietie? VVere it not more mete that such a mouth should be bobbed & beaten vvith stones, then refuted by reasons? doth he not iustly prouoke al mens hands against him, vvhose hands are against al? Al* (sayeth he) *thinke thus, but I think othervvise. But vvhat dost thou think? vvhat bringest thou better, VVhat more subtilitie doest thou find, vvhat greater secret doest thou boste to haue bene reuealed vnto thee, vvhich hath not bene knovven to so many Saincts, vvhich hath escaped so mayn vvisemen? yet tel vs, vvhat that is, vvhich seemeth true vnto thee, & vnto no man else?* And so forth. If to these vvords of S. Bernard (gentle reader) thou adde Luther or Caluin, in steed of Petrus Abailardus, and putting out his singular opinion, put one of theirs in the place, thou wilt easily perceiue, that these vvords may as wel be vsed against them as him, for they are, no lesse singular then he, as appeareth by their proud asserrions, vvhich I haue alleaged, & may appeare more by their opiniōs of the priuate spirit, which in other places they make the iudge of the meaning of Scriptures, and of al other controuersies of religion. Do not they say stil in effect, that which S. Bernard calleth intolerable and damnable: *I say so, let al the vvorld saye the contrarie?* Do not they prefer their owne exposition of Scripture, before Fathers, Councels, Churches, yea Angels also? Do not their mouthes out of which haue proceded such arrogāt speaches, deserue rather to be beaten vvith stones, then to be refuted by reasons.

Epist. 190

S. Bernards sentence against proud spirites.

Luth. art. 27. 28.

Calu. l. 2. Inst. & l. 4. Inst. c. 9. 17.

4 Behold Englād my deare & fouly deceaued countrie, to what pride these Lucifers haue induced thee. Why didst thou forsake the Romain Church, which vvas euer taken, euen of infidels, for the only Christian societie? Whō diddest thou folow, when thou didst leaue that Church, but only a singular spirit? And vvhereon now doest thou rely, vvheron doest thou ground thy religion? Not vpon Fathers, nor Councels, nor Antiquitie, nor Church, nor common consent, for al these, thy nevv Apostles vvhom thou hast folowed, haue reiected. Doest thou then rely vpon Luther or Caluin, or the new found ministeres? Thou seest by the first chapter, how they can not proue their mission, nor distinguish them selues from false prophets, which are assuredly to come, & are al

A iust complaint.

VVhat England hath gained by leauing of the Church.

ready come. And what reason hadst thou to forsake thy graue and learned forefathers, for these skipiacks, and the common spirit of the Church, for their singular spirits, which are so priuate that thou shalt hardly finde two of them, conspiring in one opinion? Doest thou ground thyself on scripture? Bare scripture, as I haue proued, in the second chapter, is no sure ground vvithout the true sense, and how doest thou know that thou hast the right meaning of scripture? I know thyn answer: My spirit (sayest thou) telleth me so. This then is thy staye, this is thy ground in religion, this is thy last refuge, which thou must needs stick vnto, as I haue declared, when thou leauest the Catholique Church. But is it not intolerable pride, to make thy priuat spirit to be iudge of scripture and sense of scripture? Is not this intolerable arrogancie, to make thy owne priuate spirit iudge of Councels, Fathers, Church and al, and to prefer thyn owne priuat opinion, before their common consent, as though thou being but one, couldst see further into scripture, and that at the first reading, then they al could do, by great studie and labour?

Intolerable pride and as great follie.

5 Thou wilt answere that no lesse is the pride of the Pope, who being but one man wil censure al men, and bynd them al to accorde to his priuate sentence and definition, and consequently, that thou hast as good assurance as Catholiques haue, yea better. Because the Catholique in matters of faith relyeth vpon the priuate spirit of the Pope, thou standest to the censure of thy owne spirit, of wich thou hast better assurance, then hath the Catholique of the spirit of the Pope, because a mans owne spirit is better knowen vnto him, then is the spirit of an other. To this I answere. That we haue not the Popes warrant only for our religion, but we haue first the consent of fathers, which as I shal proue in the next chapter, is an infallible rule because they being appointed our pastours, & we being commanded to obey them if they could al conspire in an errour, we should be led with them into errour, & not they only but God also, who is truth it selfe, should be cause of thy errour. Secōdly we haue the cōsent of the whole Church, for as at this day the Church of the Catholiques, aggreeth in al pointes of religion, so hath it euer done, & neuer did nor could with common consent admit of any heresie, or errour in matters of faith, & religion; & therfore is called the *Piller of truth*. Thirdly we haue general Councels confirmed by the Pope, as for exāple the Councel of Trent, where the grauitie, autoritie, learning & sanctitie of the Church was assembled, to which (although by scripture we were not warrāted of their autoritie) in al

Ephes.
Melchior Canus l. 7. de locis Theol.
1. Tim. 3.

in al sense and reason, we should rather harken, then to any priuate spirit. So that we rely not only on the Pope. Secondly I answer that we haue more assurance of the Popes spirit, then of our owne, or any particular mans spirit in the world. For although some are of opinion that the Pope as a perticular person may be an heretike, yea although that some also affirme, that as a publike person, he may erre. Vnles he vse the counsail of a general Councel: yet more probable it is, that though he vse but his owne ordinarie Councel, he can not erre, in matters of faith, when he defineth & cōmandeth al to stand to his iudgement. Because as I wil proue in the sixt chapter of this booke, he is the successour to S. Peter, to whom, as to his Vicegerent, Christ promised to geue the keyes of opening: and to builde his Church on him, as on a sure rorcke: yea for him, and consequently for his successour (because the Church hath now as much nede of a sure visible head and pastour, as then) Christ prayed that he might not erre, and so we haue more assurance of his spirit, especially when he defineth as a publike person, then of any other particular & priuate spirit, though he be otherwise more learned & more holy also then the pope is. And so it is a reasonable thing, to rely on the Popes spirit, because he is a publike person, and to him as supreme pastour of the church an infallible assistāce is promised, which warrant we haue not of anie other particular or priuate spirit.

Ephes. 4. Mat. 23. Mar. 5. Ioa. 21. Erasmus. in Schol. in ep. Hiero. ad Dam. Occham an Deus potest errare. Gerson 1. part. de potest. Dei. Almain. tract. de pot. Dei. Adrian. in 4 Mat 16. Luc. 22.

6 But what assured stay may be had of a priuate spirit, we shal see anone. Now I wil put a difference herin betwixt these spiritual men, & that absurd heretike Suenkfeldius, least I seeme to do iniurie to my aduersarie, and not to be able to ouercome him, vnlesse I bely him. Suenkfeldius therfore denieth al Sacraments and scripture, and is so spiritual, that he wil liue only of the spirit, and nether of the worde, nor Sacraments. But Luther and Caluin admit, both Sacraments and the worde of scripture, mary yet they wil haue the spirit to giue sentence of scripture, and the meaning of scripture. For if you aske them how they know, that fayth only iustifieth? they wil answer, by scripture. But aske them how they know that which they alleage for that opinion, to be scripture, or that to be the true meaning of scripture, in which they take the scriptures by them alleaged? They wil not say, that by the Fathers, Councells, or Church, they are assured, but by their own priuat spirit. So that although Caluin writeth against the Libertines, for relying only on the spirit, yet at last he falleth into the same labyrinth him selfe. for albeit he wil be iudged by scripture, yet so that his spirit must giue sentence, vvhich is scripture, and vvhat is the meaning

The difference betvvixt Sueukfeldius and Luther and Caluin.

Luc. 22.

meaning therof, he pronounceth the last sentence, from which is no appeal, by his priuat spirit.

Reasons to refute the priuat Spirit. The first.

7. Against this spirit of theirs I could bring many arguments, but of it self it is so phantastical, that these few shal suffice to refute it. First I say, that although God might haue gouerned his Church by interual reuelation of a priuate spirit, which should propose vnto euery one in particular, which is Scripture, & what is the meaning therof, which is true fayth, what is the wil of God, which is the way to saluation, and what are the commandements: neuertheles this were a gouernmēt rather for Angels then for men. For men are visible and haue a visible conuersation, and therfore are to be directed by visible pastours, visible lawes, and rules, and not by an inuisible spirit. For this cause almightie God, who could sanctifie vs as he doth the Angels, without any visible meanes, yet because we are men, he hath alwaies bestowed his graces vpon vs, by sensible signes, & sacraments, and by a visible dispensation of men. Secondly suppose God should gouerne euerie one by his inward spirit, yet this were not sufficient for others, amongst whom we conuerse: for how shal they know my spirit to be of God, and not of the diuel? Wherfore this spirit is not sufficient to gouerne and direct men in a peaceable conuersation: because whilest euery man would brag of his spirit, and none could proue the same vnto others, no more then our spirites in England can: they would fal together by the eares about their spirits, & neuer should be able to part the fray, ot to end the controuersie.

A visible gouernment is necessarie for men.

The second. It is not sufficient to satisfie others.

The third. It is not sufficiēt for a mās ovvne selfe.

Thirdly neitheir is this spirit vnles it be ioined with a plaine reuelatiō (as out spiritual heretikes see by experience that it is not) sufficient for a mans owne selfe to rely on, for the assuraunce & quietnes of his conscience. For I ask of him that thinks him self most assured, how he knoweth that his spirit is of God & not of the diuel? If he answere, that the spirit bringeth with it, a certain firme persuasion, which maketh man to his thinking, assured: I say that this is not sufficient, because euerie heretike, yea euery Turk hath this inward persuasion & Suenkfeldius, who denyed al Sacraments and Scriptures, and would be guided only by the spirir, vvas fully thus persuaded by his spirit, which he also did verily think to be of God If these men thought verily that they had the spirit of God, and yet were deceaued: why may not Caluin, why may not euerie brother, begin to doubt of his spirit? Yea why should we beleeue him on his bare word, to haue the true spirit, vnles he can proue it by miracles, or the authoritie of the Church, to

whom

whom Christ promised this spirit, which he can neuer do. For as for miracles he neuer could rayse a dead lowse from death to life, and to proue his spririt, by the authoritie of the Church, were to proue it conformable to the common spirit of the Christian Church, which he neither can, nor wil do, because he wil be singular. If he proue his spirit by the Scripture he windes him self in a circle, out of which he can neuer get him selfe with honour or honestie. For euen nowe he proued Scripture and the meaning therof by his spirit, and now he proueth his spirit by the Scripture, and if you aske again how he knoweth this to be Scripture, he wil answer, by his spirit, and so wil neuer get out of this circle, but wil stil proue Scripture by his spirit & his spirit, by Scripture, for which kinde of argument the Logicians, wil deride him, & hisse him out of the scoole. For to proue scripture by the spirit, and the spirit by Scripture, when Scripture according to Caluin is not knowen but by the spirit, is to proue the spirit by the spirit, and *idem*, per *idem*. But behold I pray you to what the diuel can persuade man, when he hath blinded his eyes, by depriuing him of the light of fayth. There is nothing so secret vnto man, as is this spirit: because the hart of man is a bottomeles pit, whose depth a mans owne self can not sound, it is a labyrinth into which when you enter, you can hardly finde the way to get out, spirites also are diuerse, & want not in mans hart, places to shrowd and means to tranforme them selues: They wil often times make a shew of the spirit of God, when in dede they are the spirit of the deuil, who long since promised that he would be *a lying spirit in the mouths of al false prophets*: and yet euery brother of the new religion, waranted neither by miracle, nor euident reuelation, nor Church, nor Councel, wil nedes be persuaded, yea and assured also, that his spirit is of God. Fourthly God had bene vnreasonable, if he had giuen vs no other iudge to interpret his lawes, then this secret spirit. For he hath bound vs to a religion which is aboue reason, and often tymes against sense and sensualitie, and this he hath deliuered vnto vs in a booke very obscure and harde to vndestand, and withal he hath obliged vs to the beleef, and obseruation of this lavv and religion, vnder paine of æternal damnation. Now he hath giuen vs no other interpreter of this lawe but our owne priuat spirit, which is so subiect to errour, that he should seme to haue intended and desired our damnation, & to haue giuen vs a lavve not for a rule to direct vs, but for a snare to catch vs, & a pitfal to ruinate vs, because we can not kepe this lawe vnles we vnderstand it, and not keeping it we shal bedamned. Truly better

Ioa. 14. 15. *no Heretike can proue his spirit to be of God.*

Caluin casteth himselfe into a circle.

3. Reg. 22.

The fo[illegible] reason.

For God to rule vs by a priuat spirit vvere vnreasonable.

had princes prouided for their subiectes, then God for his, because princes make plain lawes, and yet lest the subiectes should plead ignoraunce, or complain that they are punished for not keeping a lawe vvhich they vnderstand not, they haue prouided interpreters whose glosses are playne: and yet Christ our lawegiuer according vnto Caluins opinion, hath giuen vs an obscure lavve, and a more obscure interpreter, to wit, the secret and vncertaine spirit, and with alexacteth hel paines of vs, if we obserue not his lawe, in the right sence and meaning. Fiftly if this priuate spirit be admitted for an vmpier in matters of religion, al Hierarchie and order in the Church falleth: for then al are heades, none are fete, al are eyes to direct, none are inferiour members to be directed, al are pastors, nos shepe, al are masters, no schollars. Away then with Bishops, yea and superintendents also: auaunte preachers, we are not tyed to any mens spirit in particular, no not to the Churches spirit in general, because euery man is *Theodidactos* taught of God immediatly by his priuat spirit. It is not true vvhich S. Paule sayth, that Christ *gaue vs some pastors some doctors*, because al are pastors: It is not true that the Scripture affirmeth in many places, which shal herafter be alleaged, that the gouernment of the Church is monarchical, no nor Aristocratical, but rather Democratical and populare, because euery one of the people by his priuate spirit, is supreme iudge, and a supreme head in matters of religion, euery cobler or tinker, if he be a faithful beleeuer, iudgeth al and acknowledgeth no superior: because whilest his spirit iudgeth vvhich is Scripture, and what is the meaning of Scripture, to vvhich al are subiect, he summoneth al to stand to his iudgement, and he wil be adiudged by none: and so vvhilest al are superiors, none are inferiors, yea none are superiors, because a superior can not be without an inferior, and where is no superior nor inferior, there is no subordination, where is no subordination, there is no order, there is confusion, and so where the spirit ruleth, there can not be the true church, which is cōpared to a citie, and to a kingdome also, in both vvhich is a semely order. The Sixt is, that this opinion is against al Councels and practise of the Church. For in the first Councel of the Apostles nothing was done by the priuat spirit, but by common consent of the Apostles, and great inquisition: and the like was the practise in the first foure general Councels, which our aduersaries wil seme to receiue, & in the rest. Yea if the priuate spirit be a sufficient rule of religion, in vaine hitherto haue bene al conferences, disputations, Schooles of diuinitie, and

The fift reason.

This spirit taketh avvay al order and Hierarchie.

Ephes. 4.

Mat. 5. & 13.

Dan. 2.

Act. 15.

tie, and Councels also, both general and particular. Lastly this spirit openeth the vvay vnto al heretikes and heresies, vvhich according to my promise, I shal proue euidently, and lay open manistly. For if that be true sense of Scripture, vvhich the priuat spirit suggesteth, if the reformed new religion be the sincere religion, because it is squared and ruled by Scripture, or rather by Scripture interpreted by the priuat spirit, hen certainly by the same way, that this pretended religion is entered into the world for currant, may al heretikes and heresies, al false prophetes and false apostles, claime frie passage also, and by no equitie can be excluded, if Luther, Caluin and their brotherhood be admitted. For euery lying prophet can alleage Scripture as wel as they, he can bragge of his spirit as wel as they, he can say and sweare also, that he hath the right spirit as wel as they: and seing that the reformers of this age can say no more (for they haue neither miracles, nor other authoritie, to proue their spirit, as already is proued) it foloweth euidently, that if they be admitted and receiued, no false prophet, though neuer so phantastical, can be reiected. *The last reason is, that this spirit openeth the vvay to al heretikes.* *The Conclusion.*

The fourth Chapter demonstrateth, that in reiecting Fathers and Councels, vvhich consist of Fathers, the pretended reformers open the gate, to al heretikes and heresies.

PARRICIDE, and murder of parents, in old tyme was deemed so hainous an offence, & so vnworthy a fact (as being not only contrarie to reason, but also repugnant to nature) that Solon the famouse lavv-maker decreed no lavv against it: not for that he thought it not vvorthy punishment, but because he counted it more barbarouse, and inhumain, then could be by man committed. And in dede mans nature so much abhorred this vnnatural fact, that vntil six hundred yeares after Rome vvas built, no man euer is read of, so vnkinde, as vvho could find in his hart, to imbrevv his handes in his parentes bloud. Lucius Ostius, as some do think, was the first who laying aside al humanitie, against natures propension and natural affection, layed violent hands vpon his father, & depriued him of being, of vvhom he had receiued being. Which fact vvas no soonea cōmitted *Cicero. orat. pro sexto. Roscio Amerino.* *VVhy Solon made no lavv against Parricide.* *Plut. in vita. Romuli.*

 but

but nature abhorred it & the Romaines the most ciuil people, to represent the enormitie of the offence, deuised a punishment, vvhich should not only be a iust paine, but also an Embleme of the fault. They decreed first of al, that the murderer should be sowed vp in a lether sack Secondly that sacked, he should be cast into the vvater. Thirdly vvith him vvere included a cock, a viper, an ape, and a dogge, to acompanie him at his death, vvhose natures he had imitated in his life. He vvas inclosed in a sack and cast into the riuer, that so at one time, he should lose the light of the sunne, vvhich he could not see; the vse of the fyer, vvhich he could not feele, of the aire, in vvhich he was not permitted to breath, of the water in which he swimming was not refreshed, of the earth which he touched not: and so he was depriued at one time the of benefit of the sunne, and fowre elementes, of which al were produced, because he had bene vnkind & vnnatural to him, of vvhom he was begotten. His companiōs at his death were a Cocke, because as this byrd fighteth with his sire, so he hath bene iniuriouse to him that begotte him: A viper, because as this beast eateth him selfe out of his dammes belly, so he ruineth him who gaue him being, an ape, because as he imitateth man in his actions, and somewhat resembleth him in forme of bodie, yet is in dede no man, bus a beast: Fo this vnnatural murderer, caryeth the shape of a man, but in conditions is no man, because he hath cast of al humanitie. And lastly a dog, because this creaturs faythful seruice to his master, vvho only fedde him, may confound this monster, and condemne his treacherie, vvho hath bene so false to his parent, that not only fed him, but also begot him.

Cic. supra. Iuuen. Satyr. 8.

The punishment of parricides.

2. This kind of death some men haue thought not vnfit for heretikes, especially the most malicious, for vvith them who erre not of malice, al men with more gentle dealing, but Arch-heretikes are so vnnatural children to Christ their father, as shal appeare in the third booke, and so vnkind to the Catholique Church their mother, which by the Sacrament of Baptisme regenerated them, and gaue them spiritual being, and do so reuile & miscal the ancient Fathers, of whom they receiued fayth & religion, that they deserue to be depriued at one time, of the heauens and elementes, of which al things are in some sorte produced, who contemne the Church, the Councels, the Fathers, & chief Pastors, of whom & by whom, they receiued their supernatural being, by which they are Christianes. They deserue a cock at their death, because as the cocke fighteth often times with his sire, & abuseth the henne that hatched him, so they contend with ancient Fathers, and as much

A punishmēt not vnfit for Arch heretikes.

much as in them lyeth deflower their mother the Church, which bare them spiritualy; a viper also ought to dye with thē, because like vipers by schismes & heresies, they eate them selues out of the wombe of the Church: an ape must also suffer with them, because as he resēbleth man but is in deede a beast, so they like apes imitate true Christians, bearing the name of Christ, admitting certayne Scriptures and Sacramentes as they do, deuising superintendentes for the Bishops of the Church, ministers for Priestes, tables for Altars, & a prophane Cene & supper, for the sacred Eucharist. And yet in dede are no true christianes but monstrouse infidels & worse then Iewes & Paganes: a dogge also, to make vp the number, they worthily deserue, to put them in mind, that dogges may teach them fidelitie. For dogges though they receiue some times blowes, & commonly no greater benefit, then crustes and bones, yet are so faythful to their masters, that they wil not leaue them to death. Wheras the Arch-heretike is so vngratful & vnfaithful to Christ, & his spouse the Church, that for no other cause then an itching humour of pride, and selfloue, he wil become a Sectmaster, that can only drop a few textes of Scripture, interpreted by his owne spirit, leauing the Church and ancient Fathers, and consequently Christ him selfe, because they euer went together, and who heareth one, heareth the other. But lest I condemne them to the punishment of parricides for contempt of ancient Fathers, before I proue them to be guiltie of the fault, I wil set downe some of their owne sayings by, which shal appeare, what respect they beare, and what kindnes they shew, towards their ancient forfathers.

Heretikes vvorse then Ievves and Paganes. Th 2. 2. q. 10. ar. 6.

Luc. 10.

Heretikes contempt of Fathers.

3 Basilides an infamous heretike, vaunted that he and his only knew the truth, and that al his forfathers were *sues & canes*, *hogges and dogges*, not worthie the margarites of his doctrine. The Valentinians (sayeth Ireneus) if you vrge them with Scriptures, vvhich they can not answer, wil denie them: if you prouoke them to be tryed by tradition, deliuered vnto vs by a successiōn of Priestes and Fathers, *aduersantur traditioni, dicentes: se non solum Presbyteris, sed etiam Apostolis existentes sapientiores, sinceram inuenisse veritatem: they oppose against traditions saying that they being vviser then the Priests and Apostles, haue found out the sincere veritie.* Arius as before I haue rehearsed, thought none of the Fathers comparable vnto him. Nestorius disdained to read their works And our reformers of this age, shew by their vnreuerent, and rayling speaches against the Fathers, that they are descended of the same race of parricides, and reuilers of their ancient fathers.

Ex Epip. her. Basilides contemned Fathers.

Li. 3. c. 2. So did the Valentinians

So did Arius and Nestorius chap. 5.

 4. To

Luther nò lesse contemneth fathers.

4 To beginne therfore with the first patriarch of this new religion Martin Luther, that man not of God (for by his owne cõfession he was so familiar vvith the diuel, that he did eate a bushel of salt vvith him) in his booke against the king of England, hauing called him blokhead, beetlehead, grossehead, dul pate, and such like names, for pressing him *l.2. cont. Reg. Angl. f. 348.* with the authoritie of Fathers, thus he decideth the matter: *Henricus dicta patrũ inducit pro sacrificio missario, &c. Henrie for his massing sacrifice bringeth in the sayinges of Fathers. Here say I, that by this meanes, my sentence is confirmed: for this is it vvhich I sayed, that the Thomistical asses, haue nothing vvhich they can alleage but a multitude of men, and the ancient vse. But I against the sayings of fathers, men, angels, and diuels, put dovvne the Gospel, vvhich is the vvorde of the æternal majestie: here I insult ouer the saings of men, though neuer so holy, so that I care not though a thousand Austines, and Ciprianes, should stand against me.* *Li. de Seruo. Arbitr. apud steph in defen. Apol.* And in an other place hauing reiected Fathers, Councels Scooles and ages, he thus concludeth. *Neither let the multitude, magnitude, latitude, profunditie, miracles, saintitie of the Church, of Saintes moue thee a iote, al of them vvere damned, if they thought as they vvrit.* Thus one Martin Luther braueth them al, & thus this good child reuerenceth, and respecteth his ancient Fathers: for, as I sayed in the last chapter, although he seemeth only to preferre the Scripture, yet seing that they admitted, and alleaged Scripture also, the question is, who hath better skil in expounding Scripture, and if we beleeue this man, al the Fathers might haue gone to schoole to him. *In expos. ar. 64. fol. 178.* Zuinglius wil not be behind Luther in this matter. *They affirme* (sayeth he) *and vve deny, that the masse is a sacrifice.* *Zuinglius not behind Luther.* *Vvho shal be iudge of this controuersie? The sole,* say I, *and the only vvord of God. But by and by thou beginnest to crye, The Fathers, the Fathers haue thus deliuered vnto vs. But I bring to thee not Fathers, nor mothers, but I require the vvord of God.* *Caluin yeeldeth not vnto them.* Caluine desireth to be counted modest, but herein also he could not conteine him self. *Vvhen the aduersaries obiect to me* (sayeth he) *that this vvas the custome, I ansvvere that the old Fathers in this matter vvanted both lavv and example, & vvere caryed avvay into errour, vvhilest they attributed to much to the name of pœnaunce, and the common peoples opinions.* *l.3. Inst. ca. 3. n. 10.* *And again: I am litle moued vvith those things vvhich occurre euery vvhere, in the vvritings of Fathers concerning satisfaction.* *c. 0. n. 11.* *I see truly many of them yea (I vvil speake simply as it is) almost al of them, vvhose bookes are extant, vvere in this matter deceiued, and spoke hardly.* *in Antid. can 3.* And in an other booke of his, he calleth the Fathers of the councel of Trent *hogges & asses.* *l. de votis.* Peter martyr calleth Papistes, Patrologos, not Theologos, for alleaging Fathers. *Peter Martyr.* Doctor Humphrey in the life of Iewel, perceiuing that Iewel had offered to much,

When

when in his sermon, he was content to be tryed by Fathers, sayeth, that he might haue vsed a better defence for him selfe, then the authoritie of Fathers! *Vvho* (sayeth he) *if they teach contrarie, it litle skilleth. For vvhat haue vve to do vvith Fathers, vvith flesh & bloud, or vvhat perteineth it to vs, vvhat the false Synods of Bishops do decree?* Beza calleth Athanasius Satanasius, and the Fathers of the Nicen Councel, blind sophisters, ministers of the beast, and slaues of Antichrist. And although Luther affirmeth that S Gregorie the great, vvas a good Pope, yet Bibliander calleth him in derision, the Patriarch of ceremonies. Melancthon condemneth him, for allovving of the Sacrifice of the masse for the dead. Paulus Vergerius vvrote a booke of the toyes and fables of Gregorie. Horne in his booke against Abbot Fecnam, calleth this saint (to whom we Enghish men owe no lesse then our conuersion from paganisme to christianitie) a blind bussard. Bale the cronicler sayeth, that this Saint, sent Austin the monke to plante in England his Romish religion, but yet (sayeth he) Latimer is much more worthy to be counted Englands Apostle, because Austine brought nothing but mans traditions, masse, crosses, letanies, wheras Latimer with the hooke of truth cut of these superstitions. Whitaker in his booke of reprehension sayeth, that the Fathers for the most part were of opinion that Antichrist is but one particular man, but in that as in many other things they erred. The like respect they beare to general Councels, in which the wisest and grauest Fathers of the Church vvere alvvayes assembled. Luther in his booke of Councels calleth them Sicophants, and flaterers of the Pope, and sayeth, that the Canons of the Councel of Nice, which Constantine reuerenced and honoured with his presence, are *hay, strovv, stickes, and stuble.* Yea in this Councel he findeth a plaine contradiction, as he thinketh, because the Councel forbideth al Eunuches to be promoted to Priesthood, and yet commandeth Priestes to liue chastly. As though only they vvho are gelded could liue chast, and as though there were no meane betwixt wiuing, and gelding. Yea sayeth Luther, if al the decrees of Councels vvere povvred into thee with a pipe, yet vvould they not make thee a christian. Caluin vvil examine al Councels by the vvord, before he wil giue any credit vnto them, and seing that the Faters in Councels examined their decrees by Scripture also, Caluin wil make an examination vpon their examination, and so vvil be Iudge of them al. But lest I vveary the reader with to long a catalogue of reuiling speaches of these contumelious Chammes and parricides, I report me vnto the indifferent

reader,

Doctor Humphredey. Vide eundem in præfat in Orig. Beza. l. cont. Papatum. Bibliander prefat. ep. Zuing. & Oecolūpadus. Melancthon. l. 4. chron. in Hear. 4. P. Vergerius. Horne. Cent. 3. pag 66. 72. Cent. 8. pag. 678. VVhitaker. Heretikes contemne Councels. Luther. Ibidem. l. cont. Regem Angliæ. l. 4. Inst c. 3. sest. 3. Caluin.

reader, vvhether they deserue not the punishment of parricides, who so scoffe, taunt, contemne, and reuile their forfathers. But my meaning was not to condemne them, vpon whom God his sentence must passe, my drift is herby to shew, how much in reuiling Fathers they crack the credit of their religion, & how withal in reiecting this authoritie, they open the gap to al heretikes and heresies. And as concerning the first point, it is wel knowne, that antiquitie was alwayes reuerenced: old age vvas euer respected, old coynes priced, ancient statues admired, old vvriting estemed, & in al artes, the most ancient professors of the same, beare the bel away. In painting Appelles hath the credit aboue al painters, in statuarie works Lycippus: in comedies Plautus & Terence, in Tragedies Seneca: in histories Liuie, Salust, Iustine: in Poetrie, Homer, Virgil, Ouid: in Rhetorick Demosthenes, and Cicero: in Philosophie, Plato, & Aristotle. And shal not the ancient Fathers & Doctors of the Church, vvho by their art professed exposition of Scripture, be reuerenced, and credited in their art before our vnlearned and vpstart ministers? shal antiquitie geue credit to Poetes and painters, and not to Doctors and interpreters of Scripture: What is this but to preferre prophane literature before religion, Philosophie before Faith and Diuinitie, Paganisme before Christianitie, Poetes & painters before Doctors and Fathers of the Church. If any one new should say, that Plato, and Aristotle, were but doltes and Asses, that Appelles was but a blurring painter, that Cicero vvas but a railing Rhetorician, that Virgil & Ouid, were but riming Poets, vvhose eares could abide such contumelies? Think then, indifferent reader, how fowle mouthed the heretiques of this age are, who thus miscal the ancient Fathers, renowmed for their skil in interpreting Scripture, and other learning as appeareth by their learned Commentaries Homelies, and other workes; Think kow arrogant these men are, who preferre themselues before al ancient Fathers, euen in that learning, vvhich vvas their profession, and for vvhich they haue bene for many hundreed yeares, as famouse, as euer Cirero was for eloquence, Aristotle for Philosophie, or Virgil, and Ouid, for Poetrie. But vvhilest they contemne the authoritie of ancient fathers, vvhat great authoritie do they bring, but vpstart and vnlearned ministers: Whilest they reiect the Fathers as men who might erre, are they goods or angels? are not they men as the Fathers were and not woorthie to be their men and seruantes, to cary their bookes after them:

In reiecting Fathers they cracke their credit.

Antiquitietie alvvayes reuerenced.

Fathers for their antiquitie to be reuerenced.

Heretikes are fovvle mouthed.

6 But now according to my promise, I wil declare the first point

by me

by me proposed, to wit, how in reiecting Fathers, they crack their owne credit. For these Fathers vvere learned, graue, wise, glorious in working miracles, and great in bearing of authoritie in the Church of God. Their profession was preaching, teaching & interpreting of Scripture, in which art they are ancient, and famous for many hundred yeares. Some of them were scholars to the Apostles, others succeeded immediatly the Apostles scholars. The new Apostles are new & yong, who beganne but the other day to study, and to interprete Scriptures, and peraduenture many of them would neuer haue bene able to make a sermon, had they not the helpe of the Fathers commentaries and homelies. Let then the indifferent reader be iudge, whether the religion vvhich the Fathers taught and professed, or that vvhich these new Apostles haue deuised, be likest to be true, and vvhether it be not more probable, that they preached and taught according to Scripture, rather then our new and later clerkes. Truly to say that a Luther, a Caluin, Zuinglius, Beza, is herin to be preferred before Austines, Ambroses, Hieromes, Gregories, were much more absurdly spoken, thē if one should preferre the painters of these dayes, before Appelles, or the Phisitions of this age before Galen. More ouer where these Fathers went, there alwaies went religion, where they were Doctors, that was the Church of Christ, where they were Pastors, there vvas alwayes the fold of Christ, of them consisted al the general Councels, by them were the ancient Canons decreed, and old heresies condemned, al the Bishoprikes, and Churches, by them vvere gouerned, and by their meanes erected. They were the men, who in al ages opposed them selues against heretiques, as true Pastors against the rauening wolues, who had only the coate of shepheards. Against them & their people, vvereraysed al the persecutions, as against the only Christianes, their actions, their offices, in Gods Church, their bookes, their miracles, their liues, their deathes, do fil Ecclesiastical histories, the vvriters wherof intending to vvrite the beginning and progres of the Christian Church, writ only of the Romain and Catholique Church, Pastors and Doctors, wherof were the ancient Fathers. So that vvhilest our reformers refuse the authoritie and doctrine of the Fathers, they cut them selues from the Church of Christ, because that and the Fathers (as al histories and monumentes declare) went euer together, and they ioyne in part with al old heretikes, vvhom the Fathers by doctrine and censure, euer condemned, because in one heresie or other they agree with them al, as shal be in the next booke demonstrated,

The comparison betvvix. Fathers and ministers.

It is absurd to say: that the nevv preachers better vnderstand Scriptures, then the Fathres.

The Fathers & the church euer vvente together.

The reformers in reiecting Fathers cut them selues from the Church.

Campian. rat. 5.

monstrated, and they let not to confesse, with Tobie Matthew, that no man can read Fathers and beleue them, and imbrace this new religion. Read Genebrard (gentle reader) and thou shalt see how in the end of euery age he setteth downe a catalogue of al the ancient Fathers, vvho were counted the onlv true pastors, and vvhom the Catholiques vvhich novv liue, professe to folovv (as the heretikes of this age wil confesse) also a list of al the heretikes, vvhom the reformers odore and embrace, as I shal proue hereafter in the second booke. Iudge thou then, vvhether the Church and Christian religion be with these reformers, and reuilers of Fathers, or with the Catholiques vvhom they haue nicknamed Papistes.

The Authoritie of Fathers trubled Luther.

Præfat. l. de abrog. missa priuata.

To. 4. annot. breuiss.

7 This argument of the Fathers authoritie, put Luther many tymes to his shiftes, & sometimes afflicted him, with no litle scruples: but because he had a large conscience, he swallowed them vp and in time digested them al. *Hovv often* (sayeth he) *did my trembling hart beat vvith in me, and reprehending me, obiect against me that most strong arguments? Art thou only vvise? Do so many vvorldes erre? VVere so many ages ignorant? VVhat if thou errest and dravvest so many into errour to be damned vvith thee æternally?* And in an other place. *Doest thou, a sole man, and of no account, take vpon thee so great matters? VVhat if thou being but one man offendest? If God permit such, so many, and al to erre, vvhy may he not permit thee to erre? Hitherto apperteyn those arguments. The Church, the Fathers, the Councels, the custome, the multitudes, and greatnes of vvise men. VVhom do not these billes of argumentes, these thick cloudes, yea these seas of examples ouervvhelme?* And yet again this scruple assaulteh him. *Some* (sayeth he) *vvil say vnto me: The Church so many ages hath so thought and taught, So haue thought and taught al the primitiue Churches, and Doctores most holy men, much more great and more learned then thou. VVho art thou that darest dissent from al these, and obtrude vnto vs a diuerse doctrine?* Thus God moued Luthers hart, vvhich might haue bene a sufficient cal, to haue recalled and reclaimed him: but he being obstinate put this motion by thus: *VVhen satan thus vrgeth, and conspireth vvith flesh, and reason, the conscience is terrified and despaireth. vnles constantly thou returne to thy selfe, and say, vvhether Ciprian, Ambrose, Austin, or Peter, Paule, and Iohn. yea an angel from heauen, teach othervvise yet this I knovv for certain, that I counsayle not men to humane but diuine things.* Art thou sure Luther, vvhen thou hast so many, and so learned Fathers against thee? Darest thou preferre thy owne particular iudgement, before their common consent? Yea (sayeth M. Whitakar) Luther in some case may prefer him selfe before al the Fathers, and a thousand Churches.

To. 5. in Gal.

Luther did not ansvver the authoritie of Fathers.

Churches. For vvhen his doctrine is according to Scripture then is it to giue place to no Fathers. But this is as much to the purpose as the patch beside the hole, because the comparison is not betwixt Fathers and Scriptures, vvhich are to be perferred. For the Fathers allowed and alleaged Scripture euen for those pointes of doctrine for which Luther doth, and al the Luthers in the world can not proue that al the Fathers held any one opinion against Scripture; but the question is vvhether Luther or al the Fathers, did best vnderstand Scripture; and therfore if Luther hold gainst the Fathers in exposition of Scripture, he preferreth him selfe before them al. As for example, Luther alleageth Scripture to disproue frie wil, al the Fathers alleage Scripture to proue it, and Luther expoundeth Scripture one way, they an other, else they could not both alleage Scripture for contrarie doctrine. Wherfore if Luther sayeth that he expoundeth Scripture truly, and therfore careth not for al the Fathers, he preferreth his owne iudgement before them al, and so can not answer that argument grounded in the Fathers authoritie, nor comfort him selfe with this, that he forsooth hath the vvord of God, vvhich is aboue them al. And so Luther must giue vs leaue, to come vpon him with his owne argument, which he shal neuer answer. The Church frō the begining hath taught & expounded Scripture otherwise then thou doest, so many Austines, Ambroses, Ciprianes, Councels, and ages, haue preached otherwise. Are they al deceiued? hast thou only found out the truth? what if thou rather art deluded? Thou art but one, they are many, thou art of late they of ancient standing, thou a sinner, they Saintes: thou some schollar, but they were learned doctors, thou hast a witte, but al their wittes were of a greater reach, thou seest some thing, but so many eyes must needs haue a greater insight; Thou hast studyed Scripture, but they more: thou hast watched at thy booke, but they in nightstudie haue spent more oyle then thou, though thou peraduenture more wine then they, and thou alleagest Scripture for thy doctrine, they for the contrarie. And so their iudgement must be preferred before thine, and consequently theirs shal be the true doctrine, they the true Pastors, theirs the true Church; and so ours now is the true Christian religion, we the right Christianes, who agree with those Fathers, and the Church of vvhich they were Pastors and preachers: and Luther and the reformers, who wil haue no part with the Fathers, are no members of the true Church, because the anciēt fathers & the true Church were neuer yet seperated, but alwayes went together.

See M. Reinolds in his Refut. chap. 3. pag. 47. M. Vvhitakers ansvvere is not to the purpose.

Luther confoūded vvith his ovvne argument.

A comparison of Luther and the Fathers.

In reiecting Fathers the reformers open the gappe to al heretikes.

Vvhat the autoritie of Fathers is.

8. The first point being proued, we wil come to the second, in which I shal proue that in reiecting Fathers, they open the gap to al heretikes, who may say what they wil (as the reformers do) if that authoritie be contemned. But first it shal not be amisse to declare what authoritie the Fathers haue, & whether they haue infallible assistance of God, to expound Scriptures rigthly, for if they haue not, neither are Catholiques assured of their fayth by their authoritie, neither do the heretikes open the gappe to heresies by reiecting their authoritie, which if it be not infallible, may it self also authorise & countenaunce heresie. S. Paul sayeth, that God hath prouided vs of *some Apostles, some Prophets, others Enangelists, others Doctors, & Pastors, to the consummation of Saintes, to the vvorke of the ministerie, vnto the edifying of the body of Christ,* that is, for the instruction of his Church. Where the first place is geuen to Prophets, Apostles and Euangelistes, who wrote the Scripture: in the second place folow Doctors & Pastors, because their office is not to write Scripture, but to interpret it. And the reason is yeelded, why these Doctors are geuen vnto vs, *lest vve should vvauer like children, & be caryed about vvith euery vvind of the doctrine of men.* Now if al the Pastors and Doctors, which we cal Fathers, should or could erre, then were they not appointed to keepe their shepe from wandering, rather should they be the cause of their error, for the sheepe must heare the voice of their Pastors: and so if the Pastors erre, the shepe must erre with them, if they wander, the sheepe who know nothing but by their Pastors, can not keepe the right way. And if thou say, that in case of error, the people must leaue the Pastors, I demand of thee how they shal know when the Pastors erre, who knowe nothing, but by the voice of their Pastors? And suppose they should leaue their Pastors, then is the frame of the body of Christes Church dissolued, and the members are separated from the head, and the Church is a headles body: then do they leaue the salt, by which they should be salted, and preserued from corruption in religion: Then do they leaue the light, by which they should be illuminated. And how then is that true: *Vpon Moyses chair sit the Scribes and Pharisies: do those thinges vvhich they say?*: are the Pastors of the Church of lesse authoritie, then the Pastors of the Synagogue? If they can erre, then is it not true which Christ sayed: *VVhosoeuer heareth you, hearteh me*, vnles you wil say, that Christ also may erre in them, and with them. But our heretikes wil say, that al the Fathers are men. I graunt it, but they are men directed by the Holy Ghost, and Christ was a man, & yet not only as God, but as man also, he could

Ephes. 4.

Ibidem.

Vve must not leaue of pastours.

Matt. 5.

Matt. 19.

Luc. 10.

he could not erre. And the writers of Scripture, as Moyses, and Salomon, and the Prophets of the old law, and the Apostles and Euangelistes in the new law were men, and yet they erred not, nor could not erre, vnles we wil cal Scripture in question. But where (saye they) read you, that the Fathers haue the infallible assistance, in exposition of scripture? Where I read, that they are light, that they are salt, that they are Pastors, to whom vvhen vve harken, vve harken to Christ. Where I read that vve must do vvhat they say, vvhere I read, that the Church can not erre, vvhich must folow her Pastors, vvhere I read, that the Church, vvhich learneth al of her Pastors, is a piller of truth. But some Fathers haue erred. I grant it, but neuer al agreed in one error together: neuer al the Fathers of al ages, yea not of one age (for to these also vve must harken) haue conspired in an vntrutrh. And I demand of our reformers: VVhether they be not men also? And I think they vvil not deny it. If they be men, I aske vvhether they can not erre in expounding Scripture? If they can, then neither they, not others by them haue assurance. If they can not erre, because euery one of them hath the spirit, Then say I, that more probable it is, that so many spirits of the Fathers conspiring in one can not erre, then that no particular & priuat spirit can erre, especially seing that the priuate spirites are diuerse and contrarie, and vve haue no more assurance of one then of an other. Iudge novv (gentle reader) whether that the Catholique religion vvhich is conformable to the Fathers, and Pastors of the Church, be the sincere Christian religion, or rather the religion of the heretikes, which is agreable to no common, but only to a priuat spirit: especially seing that vve haue such vvarrant for the common consent of Fathers, but none at al for the priuat spirit of euery priuate man.

The Fathers vvere men, but such as could not al errre.

Proofes that the Fathers can not al erre.

Mat. 5.
Io. 21.
Mat. 13.

1. Tim. 3.

9. Novv let vs see in a vvord hovv by reiecting this infallible authoritie of Fathers, they leaue no certain rule for exposition of Scripture, and so open the vvay to al heretikes and heresies. For lay avvay Fathers, vvhich vvere in al ages counted the only Pastors, of the Church, the authoritie of Councels is nothing vvorth, for they consisted of Fathers, the authoritie of the Church is of as litle esteeme, because she alvvayes beleeued, as her Pastors did, yea she could not tel vvhat to beleeue, but by their instruction. Scripture therfore is only left and the priuate spirit, & seing those tvvo bare authorities, as before is proued, open the vvay to al heresies, the denyal of the Fathers authoritie must needs do the same. For suppose a nevv heretike, yea a

Hovv by reiecting Fathers, the gap is open to al heretikes.

Yea to the diuel. diuel from hel in the likenes of a man, should preach a nevv heresie, contrarie to the heresies that euer vvere, might he not alleage Scripture for it, expounding it as he pleaseth? And if you demand of him how he knovveth that he expoundeth it aright, might he not say, that his spirit telleth him so? And if you alleage that al that euer taught before him vvere of an other opinion, and gaue an other exposition of Scripture: might he not say, as easily as Luther and Caluin do, that they vvere men, & erred al the packe of them? And so if authoritie of Fathers be reiected, he or any other might say, vvhat he vvould, and no man could controle him. *The conclusion.* Wherfore to conclude, if we giue eare vnto the Gospellers of this tyme, who haue reiected the authoritie of Fathers, & wil consequently iudge al by Scripture, sensed by the priuate spirit, vve must harken to al heretikes, and open a gap and make way to al false Apostles, who can not without manifest partialitie, be excluded and repelled, if these men be admitted.

The fift chapter shevveth, that they haue no probable meanes, to induce a reasonable man vnto their religion, and that therfore, if vve giue credit vnto them, vve must geue credit to al heretikes, preach they neuer so absurd, & phantastical paradoxes.

Our faith is aboue reason, yet credible and not vnreasonable.

T is a common opinion amongst the ancient Fathers and Diuines, that our Fayth being supernatural, can not be demonstrated by reason, as opinions of Philosophers may be, because it aymeth at thinges aboue reason. Philosophie soaring no higher, then reason geueth her leaue, and so in Christian religion, vve ought more to rely on fayth, and authoritie, then reason: and we can not shew our selues more reasonable, then to leaue of reasoning, in thinges aboue reason. But although it be so, that we can not proue our religion by reason, yet we may set it forth with such testimonie of miracles, antiquitie, common consent, and such like motiues, as shal conuince a man of reason, that this religion inuolueth no absurditie against reason, but rather is very probable, and most credibly to be
2. 2. q. 1. a. 6. beleeued. For although, as S. Thomas sayth, our religion be not euidently true, yet is it *euidenter credibilis, euidently credible.* For though in it selfe

it selfe it be obscure, yet hath it bene so credible deliuered vnto vs, by credible signes & tokēs, that no man can with reason thinke it otherwise, then very credidle, if he wel consider, what testimonies may be alleaged for it; vvhich, as Dauid sayed, are *credibilia nimis*, *very credible*, that is so credible, as we can not vvith reason desire greater testimonie, for things aboue reason.

Faith is euidently credible.

Psal. 92.

2. In the beginning God catechised man in this religion, by Angels whom he sent, and by Patriarches & Prophetes whom he inspired, by whom he taught the people, what Sacramentes to vse, what Sacrifices to offer, and other pointes of Religion, such as then men vvere capable of. In the lavv vvritten he deliuered his wil and meaning concerning lavv, and Religion, and the Ceremonies, and Sacramentes belonging thervnto, by his seruant Moyses, to whom he appeared by an Angel in thundering, and other such signes, and by whom he wrought in Ægypt, and in the desert so many miracles, for proofe and confirmation of this Religion. Afterwards, in the law of grace and fulnes of tyme, and tyme of spiritual plenty and riches, as in more ample manner, so with greater testimonies and signes, this fayth vvas deliuered vnto vs. For first our Sauiour proued his mission by al the ancient Prophetes, vvho had fortold his coming, and the maner of his coming, his office, the place & circumstances of his natiuitie, life, and death, vvhich al agreing to him concluded him to be the Messias. Secondly by infinite miracles he proued his authoritie & doctrine, in so much that he sayed, that the vvorkes which he did, gaue testimonie of him, yea the Iewes cōfessed that he could not haue doone so strange thinges, if he had not bene of God. And seing that he vvrought these miracles, to proue him selfe to be the Messias, & his doctrine to be of God, it could not be otherwise, because as God can not deceiue, being *prima veritas*, *the first veritie*, nor be deceiued, being vvisdom it selfe, so can he not geue testimonie of an vntruth by miracles, for then should he be both a lyer, & a deceiuer. The Apostles in like maner, after that in Pentecost they had receiued the Holy Ghost in visible forme and manner, receiued power also to geue this Holy Spirit visibly to others, and to worke miracles also, to proue their mission, & doctrine, in so much that S. Mark sayeth, that *they preached, and God confirmed their doctrine by miracles, and signes that folovved*. Wherfore although the doctrine which they preached vvas out of reasons kenning, yet it vvas made euident by testimonie, and so vvas euidently credible, because if God can not geue testimonie to an vntruth, then in that

In the lavve of nature vve receued religion from Angels, and Patriarchs.

In the lavve vvritten religion vvas taught by Moyses, first taught by Angels.

In the lavve of grace by Christ, and his Apostles.

Io. 9. & 10.

God can not geue testimonie of an vntruth by miracles.

Act. 2.

Mar. vlt.

Hovv faith is euidently credible.

in that he gaue testimonie by miracle of their doctrine, it must nedes folow that it was of God.

The strange planting of our faith proueth our religion. *Iosue 6.* *A fit similitude.*

3 Secondly the strange conquest vvhich the Apostles made of Idolatrie, in despite of al the Philophers, and Tyrants of the world, and the miraculous planting of the Christian fayth, is an argument to proue our religion to be of God, most pregnāt, & a motiue to perswade any reasonable man, most forcible. For as once the Israelites by making a Procession about the walles of Hierico, and sounding of their trumpets (an vnlikely stratageme to surprise such a citie) dismantled the towne and leueled the walles with the ground: so Christ Iesus by the circuit of a few Apostles and disciples, about the world, and by the blastes of their mouthes, which were the golden trumpets, that promulgated the new law, ransaked the citie of Idolatrie, that then was as great almost as the world, made the Romain Empire subiect to Christes Church, and caused the Scepter to yeeld to Christes Crosse, & made Philosopie as an handmayd, to serue and attend vpon the fayth of Christ.

The Conquest vvhich the Apostles made of Idolatrie vvas strange First in respect of the Souldiars vvhich vvere vveake. *1 Cor. 1.* *Poore.* *Luc. 9.* *Base.* *1. Cor. 1.*

4 A strange conquest certes, whether you consider the warryers, or the maner of fight, or the force of the enemie, against vvhom they waged battayle. For as concerning the souldiars, good Lord hovv vnlikely men, to atcheue such a victorie! Warriers should be men of force and strength to make the assault, and to giue the onset, to defend or offend. These were feeble fishers. *Infima mundi elegit Deus: God chose the vveakelings of this vvorld.* Warryers especially the King or General, should haue riches and treasures good store, because armies can neither be leuied nor releeued without money, vvhich therfore is called, *neruus belli, the sinevv or strength of vvarre.* These men vvere poore fishers, who had no other treasure then ragged nettes, and their General Christ Iesus, vvas as poore as they, liuing on almes, & not hauing sometimes that vvhich vvolues and wilde beastes haue, a chamber to lodge in. Warriers, especially if they be the leaders, must be of noble birth, and parentage: for souldiars be hardly led by them, who are base, and nor easily commanded by them, vvho are as meane in qualitie and condition as them selues. These men were fisher men, the basest kind of people, if we beleeue Plutarch, that are to be found: who therfore by their trade are banished humain societie, & conuerse more with fishes then men, and liue more on the water then on the land *Ignobilia & contemptibilia huius mundi elegit Deus: God hath chosen the ignoble and contemptible of this vvorld.* Warriers should be wise and ingenious to lay plottes,

to deuise

to deuise stratagemes, and to vse force of wit, where force of armes wil not serue. These vvere simple fishermen, neuer trayned vp in schooles, and more cunning with a hooke, then vvith a booke: *Stulta huius mundi elegit Deus: God chose the foolish of this vvorld.* Souldiars should be many in number lest the grosse troupes of the aduersarie terrifie them, vvith the sight of the multitude: These were a smal army, and a silly flocke, only tvvelue Capitaines, the tvvelue Apostles, and 72. priuat souldiars, I meane seauentie tvvo Disciples. And yet these vveakelings, were to wrastle with the might of the Romain Empire, These poore beggers vvere to deale vvith them that had the vvelth of the vvorld. These base fishers vvere to contend vvith the nobilitie of the vvorld. These simple soules vvere to encounter vvith the vvisest Philosophers. And these few waged battayle against al nations vpon earth, yea al the diuels in hel, vvho also opposed against them al their hellish forces.

Simple. *1. Cor. 1.* *Fevve.* *Luc. 12.* *The force of the aduersarie.*

5. And as touching the maner of the fight, it made the victorie more incredible. For the enemies came vvith the florish of eloquence, these vvith halfe barbarouse simplicitie: they came armed vvith povver, these vvith infirmitie, *in vvhich vertue is perfited*: they vvith pride, these vvith humilitie: *they shot maledictions, these benedictions:* They layed on blovves, these boare them patiently: they cried, Kil kil, these cryed, Suffer, suffer. A strange maner of figt, vvhere the souldiars ouercame, by putting vp iniuries, not by reuenging, by bearing not by geuing blowes, by laying the body open to the enemyes vveapon, not by closse vvarding or defending. But if these few souldiars so il armed, might haue kept together, they had bene more strong, because force vnited, is greater then the same dispersed, but these few souldiars diuided forces, and one man single went against a whole countrie, yea sometimes many Countries. S. Peter setteth vpon Pontus, Bithinia, Galatia, and Rome it selfe. S. Paul goeth against Illiricus, Cappadocia, Ciprus, S. Iames the elder encountreth with al Spaine. S. Iames the younger with Iurie: S. Thomas with India, S. Matthevv vvith Æthiopia, others vvith other countries, And in fine, thus they conquered the greatest part of the world.

Secondly the Conquest was strange in respect of the maner. *2. Cor. 12.* *1. Cor. 4.* *Force vnited is greater.* *One apostle setteth vpon a vvhole countrie.* *The places to vvhich the Apostle were sent especially.*

6. Now if vve consider in vvhat consisted the victorie, it vvil yet appeare more admirable. This victorie consisted not in surprising of a citie, in vndermining a castle, in burning of villages, in gayning of rauelings, in mayming and killing bodyes, but in extinguishing of

Thirdly in The thing.

idolatrie, in extirpating vice, in subdewing mens vnderstanding, in ouercomming their willes, in curbing & bridling their affections, in planting a new religion, neuer heard of before, which commandeth men to beleue firmely things aboue reason, and to obserue lawes contrarie to sensualitie, vice and pleasure, which by long custome were become almost natural vnto men. And to this they perswaded not a few, but al the world, not fooles but Philosophers, such as Dionisius Areopagita, Iustinus martyr, and others were: not poore men, but Kings, yea and Emperours, such as Philip, and Constantine were, and that in despite of the tyrants in earth, and maugre al the deuils in hel. Yea so firmely they perswaded men vnto this new religion, and new life, that thousandes by and by were ready to suffer al torments, rather then to deny the least article of this new beleefe. Let not any therfore obiect vnto vs, that our Religion is obscure, and that it teacheth thinges aboue reason For although vve can not by reason see the truth, nor proue the truth of religion, yet it can not but be true and of God, because such men as the Apostles were. to such as al the world but they were (that is nusled and perswaded in a contrarie religion) and after so strange a maner, could neuer haue planted so hard a Religion, and that in despite of the Tyrants in earth, and diuels in hel, vnles God had both set them on, and assisted them.

Vvhom the Apostles vanquished.

Hovv firmly they persvvaded men to religion.

Our religion can not but be of God.

Read S. Aust. in the 22 booke of the Citie of God. c. v.

7. Let not then the Atheists of this godles tyme, cal in question the miracles of Christ, and his Saintes, vvrought by them in confirmation of this Religion, & related in the Scripture, & Ecclesiastical Histories, as though they were but old wiues tales, which they tel amongst their maides. Let them not say that neuer miracle was wrought for this religion, by this they shal gaine nothing, I vvil come vpon them vvith that of S. Austine, that such a religion by such, & in such a maner should be planted in the vvorld vvithout miracles, is the greatest miracle of al, and so in denying miracles, wil they, nil they, they graunt a miracle. Deny if thou vvilt our miracles (for vvhich notwithstanding we haue as good, & better histories, then thou hast for the Romain Emperours, Captaynes, Legions, vvarres, & victories) thou canst not deny, but that a few fishermen, obscure, meane, vnlearned, haue turned al the vvorld vpside downe, for this thou seest. Thou canst not deny but that the vvorld is dissvvaded from idolatrie vnto Christianitie, from sensualitie to chastitie, from gluttony to fasting, from riches to volūtarie prouertie, from vsual vice to vnacquainted vertue, from the broad & easy vvay vvhich leadeth to perdition,

Against the Atheistes vvho deny miracles.

l.22.ciuit.c.5.

vnto

vnto the strayt and narrovv vvay, vvhich tendeth to saluation. Thou canst not deny, but that men vnlearned, and impotent, haue done this, vvhom thou canst suspect neither to haue vsed deceit, nor compulsion. Thou canst not deny, but that many Emperors haue resisted these men, & yet they haue gotten the victorie. Let then this religion be neuer so repugnant to sense, neuer so high aboue reason, I beleeue it is of God, I beleeue it is true, else by such men & after such a maner, it could neuer haue bene persvvaded. Yea I vvil boldly say vvith a certain lerned man: *Si error est (Domine) à te decepti sumus: If this vvhich vve beleue be an error, thou (ô lord) hast deceiued vs:* But thou can neither deceiue nor be deceiued, therfore we are assured of our religion.

Rich. de S. Victore. l. 1. Trin. c. 2.

8 God therfore vvho hath alvvayes deliuered fayth vnto vs so credibly, and induced vs vnto it so svvetly, by probable meanes, yea by euident signes and testimonies, if he hath permitted this fayth to decay, or to lye hidden for many hundred yeares, or if corruption and error in religion, hath for long tyme bene taken for sincere religion, then no doubt by them, by vvhom he restoreth this religion agayne, and deliuereth it in the former perfection, by whom he reformeth these errors, vvhich haue gone for truthes, he vvil giue vs probable & credible meanes, by vvhich like reasonable men, vve may be induced vnto this reformation. For if vve haue many hundred yeares, bene taught by our forfathers that there are seuen Sacramentes, that the Sacrament of the Altar is a Sacrifice, and conteyneth Christes body and blood really, that there is Purgatorie, that we haue friewil, that good vvorkes are necessarie, that our euil vvorkes are no vvorkes of God, that payer to Sainctes, and reuerence done to them and their images, is not superstition: then no doubt, if God vvil haue vs to leaue these old opinions, and to imbrace new, he wil in so important a matter as this is, vvhich toucheth saluation and damnation, vse probable and credible meanes to dissvvade vs from our old errors, lest that seing no reason vvhy vve should leaue them, vve persist stil in them, or lest that vve expose our selues to danger of imbracing new heresies, for old religion, as easily we may, if without any reason at al, vve vvil forsake that fayth, in vvhich vve & our greatgrandfathers vvere baptised.

As God plãted religion by credible meanes, so he vvil reforme.

Else vve might persist in olde errors or imbrace nevv.

9. For although fayth be a Theological vertue, and therfore, as Diuines say, consisteth not in a meane betvvixt tvvo extremes in respect of God, vvho is the obiect (because he is *prima veritas*, whom we can not credit to soone nor to much) yet in respect of vs, and the

Faith is a Theological vertue.

Faith in reſpect of vs is placed betvvixte 2. extremities.

meanes by which we come to know God his authoritie, we may exceed in beleeuing, and we may be wanting in beleef. They are deficient and to ſlowe in beleeuing, who when God his mind and wil is propoſed by ſufficient motiues, and to kens, yet wil not giue credit.

VVho are vvanting in beleſe.

This was the fault of the Ievves who were ſo ſlow and hard of beleſe, that though Chriſt by miracles and prophecies had proued him ſelf to be the Meſſias, and his doctrine to be of God, yet they would not beleeue him. This alſo was the fault of the Apoſtles, though not in ſo high a degree, whoſe eyes were ſo blinded with Chriſtes paſſion, that although the ſtone of his ſepulchre was remoued, and that the Angel had affirmed that he was riſen, yet they would not beleue it, who therfore were called *tardi corde ad credendum, ſlovve of hart to beleeue.*

Luc. 24.

VVho are raſh in beleeuing.

They are raſh & to haſtie in beleeuing, who beleeue without ſufficient reaſon or teſtimonie. Such were the Galathians who were to eaſily caryed away from that which was preached vnto them. Wherefore the wiſe man ſayeth, that *he is light of hart vvho beleeueth to quickly.* And in dede if God would haue vs giue oure aſſent where we ſee no reaſon, nor teſtimony ſufficient, he ſhould firſt do vs great iniury, becauſe it is the nature of our vnderſtanding, to be moued at leaſt by probabilitie, or credibilitie. Secondly he ſhould expoſe vs to danger of error, for he that wil beleeue when no probabilitie moueth him, may eaſily fal into an error.

Gal 1.

Eccl. 19.

See the epiſtle to the Reader.

God vvil not haue vs embrace an improbable religion.

Wherfore it may wel be ſuppoſed for certayne, that God wil not haue vs to beleeue any religion, though it be preached in his name, vnles we haue ſome credibilitie or probabilitie to perſwade vs thervnto.

Tvvo vvayes for a Doctor to vvine credit.

10. If then our reformers would haue vs to beleeue, that in theſe and theſe pointes, we and our forfathers haue erred, and that henceforth thus and thus we are to beleue, they muſt at leaſt ſhew vs probabilitie, that we haue bene deceiued, and that they are ſent to put vs into the way. For otherwiſe we being forwarned of falſe Prophets, and commanded alſo to harken vnto our Paſtors, we haue no reaſon to forſake our ancient religion, and to imbrace new opinions, nor to leaue our ancient Paſtors, and to runne after ſtrangers, vnles they can bring ſome probabilitie, yea and that greater then the old Fathers can bring, for that which they haue taught vs.

The firſt is reaſon.

11. Two meanes only I find which a Doctor or preacher can vſe to perſwade his auditors. The firſt is euident reaſon which conuinceth the vnderſtanding of the hearer or ſcholar. And by this meanes religion can not be proued, becauſe reaſon can not reach vnto

mysteries

mysteries of fayth, vvhich are aboue reason. And so the reformers can not conuince vs by reason, that they are sent from God to reforme vs, and that their doctrine is the veritie, because they teach many things aboue reason, as wel as we do: to wit the Trinitie, Incarnation, Resurrection, Fayth, Iustification, and such like: yea (as I shal proue herafter) many thinges also against common sense and reason. Not the first, because they are aboue reason, not the second, because they are against reason. The second meanes to persuade is the authoritie of him vvho teacheth. This meanes Pithagoras is sayed to haue vsed in his schoole, vvho commanded his scholars to silence for the space of two yeares, al which tyme, they might ouly harken, but not aske any questions: and for that tyme they were called *Acostici*. *hearers*. Aftervvards they might aske questions of their Master, but vvhen he had ansvverred they might aske no reason, but must content them selues vvith his authoritie, and count it sufficient, that *Autos ephi* he sayed so.

The second meanes is authoritie.

And. Gel. l. 1. c. 9.

12. Novv, authotitie is vvonne either by vvit and learning, or by vertue, or antiquitie, or number, or office & dignitie. And the reason herof is, because vvise and learned men are likest to see farthest into maters, & so the more vvillingly vve beleue them: vertuouse men are dearest vnto God, & so vve are more easily persvvaded to thinke that God imperteth his mind to them most amply. Truth also is the daughter of time, for that time bringeth truth to light: & therfore we are most prone to beleeue olde men, to whom long time bringeth great experience, & we wel imagine that to be true, which for a long time hath bene holden for true. And because many men see more then one alone, vve count the voice of many men, the voice of God, and we reuerence that for a veritie, which most men haue auerred. And lastly because al authoritie is of God, and men in office are appointed by him to gouerne, we are ready to think that God especially directeth them, who haue charge, not only of them selues, but of others also: which is the very cause why vve vse to reuerence Superiors decrees, vnles we see a manifest absurditie in them. If then the reformers wil haue vs to forsake our old Pastors, and to harken to nevv, if they vvil haue vs abiure old religion & imbrace a new: let them shew vs greater authoritie then that of the ancient Fathers, else vve haue no reason to preferre them and their doctrine, before old Doctors, and old religion. But this they can neuer do, and so they can neuer binde vs in reason to accept of their religion.

By vvhat meanes authoritie is gotten.

The reason.

Rom. 13.

The authoritie of the new ministers and the olde Fathers is vvayed.

For vvit and learning the ministers come shorte.

13 For if we compare them with the old and ancient Fathers, in al the meanes alleaged, by vvhich credit and authoritie is gotten, we shal finde them to come short, by many furlongs in euery one of thẽ. And first for witt and learning, I think neither Luther nor Caluine nor any of them al, vnles their faces be brasen, haue the face to compare with the ancient Fathers. Namely with Gregories, Austins, Ambroses, Basilles, Hieromes, Cirilles, and such like, who wrote more then euer they read, and studied more then euer they loytered, and were in al literature so learned, that the reformers were not worthy to cary their bookes after them. And although Luther and Caluin wanted not altogether learning, yet they came short of these men. And as for their folowers which were neuer trayned vp in our scholes wel may they prattle in Greeke, and florish in a Ciceronian stile, yet solide learning either in Diuinitie or Philosophie they haue not. Let the vniuersities of Oxford & Cambridge (which for Humanitie I preferre before other vniuersities of the new church) or of Basil and other places, let the cõfraternitie of Geneua shew vs a Ballarmine, Baronius, Molin, Suares, Vasques, Bannes, Gregorie of Valence, an Allen, Harding, Sanders, Stapleton, Bristow, Martin, Campian, Reinolds, if they can. What workes haue they set out comparable to the bookes of these Catholique writers? Let an indifferent reader peruse the learnedest bookes of these reformers, and he shal see in them false allegations of Fathers, corruption of Scriptures, of Fathers and Councels, lyes, impostures, affirmations without proofes, wordes without matter: *and almost nothing else.* As for vertue, if they haue any modestie remayning, they wil not (being guiltie of so vicious liues) make any comparison with the former Fathers, who by the cõmon report of al were Saintes, and their writinges, miracles, almes deedes, fastinges, austere penance, prayer, chastitie, mortification, contempt of the world, and such like, wil testifie no lesse.

Sinceritie. scarse anie thing but falshood. Ievvel. Plessis.

In vertue the ministers are not comparable to the olde Fathers.

14 And although they may obiect that many amongest vs also, haue liued viciously, yet we can giue them herin a manifest difference. For first, the first founders of our religion were men of great perfection, as the Apostles, and their successors in the primitiue Church, yea as the planters of religion in euery countrie were. Read S. Bede, & you shal see, that the Religious Monkes, vvhom S. Gregorie sent into our country, to cal vs from Idolatrie, were Saincts, and moued more the King by their holy conuersation, then by their preaching and miracles? And yet euen the first of these nevv families, the preachers of this

A difference betvvixt heretikes and Catholiques, for euil life. The first. l. 1. c. 23. ret 26.

of this reformation, euen Luther and Caluin themselues, were notorious, and infamous for euil life. Luther was an Apostata, he maried a Nonne, he liued beastlike, and dyed accordingly. For after a merry and a moyst supper, he was found dead the next morning in his bedde, with his tongue hāging out of his mouth. Caluin liued like an Epicure, he was giuen to reuenge, and vvas puffed vp vvith pride, and ambition. True it is, he caryed markes on his backe, but not such as S Paul caryed, but such as the minister of iustice noted him withal, for his abominable vice, and as he liued so he dyed, an Herodes death, for lise were his executioners. Secondly althougth many be badde amongest vs, yet I thinke, more among them. Thirdly euil life amongst vs, is a fault of our owne peruerse wil and nature, but amongst them, it is the verie frute of their doctrine, vvhich (as by many argumentes I shal proue hereafter) leadeth & induceth to al dishonestie. Lastly they which amongst vs lead a vicious life, are neuer amended by comming vnto them: which experience hath taught, and proued in some loose Catholiques, who partly for feare, partly for libertie, haue repayred vnto them. But were so farre from being reformed by them, that so long as they conuersed with them, they fel dayly from one vice to an other, and neuer stayed, til they came to the depth of iniquitie. And yet we haue sen ne many wilde Gallantes, loose in life & rioutos in conuersation, who after that they be admitted into our Church ad societie, & instructed in our fayth and religion, do cast of al euil customes, become modest in behauiour, temperat, sober, and who before feared neither sinne, nor God, nor the diuil, waxe scrupulous, and fearful of conscience, and who before could not spare one halfe hower in a day for prayer, thinke now vvhole dayes to short a time. Yea you seme to giue good life vnto vs. For you wil trust our word, more then an obligation of one of your owne sect, and if you see a man milde, modest, chaste, temperate, giuen to prayer, fasting, almesdeeds, vpright in al his actions, and examplair in conuersation, you suspect him for a Papist. Therfore some Catholiques the better to escape your Pursiuantes, fayne them selues in outward shew, & habit, to be roisters, ruffians, and dissolute companions, as though vice vvere the badge of your religion. As for number, we excede them by many countries and ages, in vvhich they neuer liued, and for one new minister, we haue hundreds of ancient Pastors, and learned Fathers. For antiquitie, although they fayne an inuisible Church before Martin Luther, yet, as I haue proued in the first chapter, and shal again herafter, their preachers

Luthers and Caluins life and death.

Turrian. l. 5. de Epist. pont. c 2.

Hol. l. de heres Gen. l 4. cronic.

Bolsec. in vita eius. & Gen. l. 4 an Christi. 1566.

The second difference.

The third.

In the seuenth booke.

The the fourth.

The Catholique religion amendeth euil maners.

Men of good cōscience are suspected to be Catholique.

In number Catholiques exceed heretikes.

For Antiquitie also.

preachers are vpstartes, their doctrine is as young, and vvhereas vve can shew a succession of our religion & Pastors, for the space of sixten hundred years, euen from the Apostles, they can deriue their pedegree no higher, then from Martin Luther. Lastly our Doctors were also Pastors, and bare great offices in the Church of God. And the first of them in our countrie, and in euery countrie, proued their authoritie by miracles, and their successors proued the same by succession. But as yet, the new preachers could neuer proue their authoritie & mission, to be ether extraordinarie, by miracles: or ordinarie, by succession: as is allerady demonstrated in the first chapter. So that for learning, vertue, antiquitie, number, dignitie, by vvhich authoritie is gotten, we and our religion, do carie the price away. What reason then haue men to forsake Catholiques, and their Pastors & preachers, to harken vnto these new Prophets, who neither in learning, nor vertue, nor antiquitie, nor number, nor dignitie, can make anie iust comparison with them?

S. Bede l. 1. c. 35.

For office and dignitie also.

No reason to preferre the nevv preachers.

15. Suppose some one should be wauering, and doubtful in religion, and deliberating with him selfe, whether to folow the old Fathers or new preachers, should make this discourse with him selfe. I haue bene baptized, & brought vp in the Catholique religion, at least so were my forrefathers time out of mind, but of late yeares some haue bene so bold as to auouch, that they were al deceiued, & damned also, vnles ignorance excused them: wherfore seing that without true fayth no man can be saued, it is good that I looke into both the old and new religiō, to see which by al reason I ought to imbrace. But before I giue eare vnto these Reformers, which say that they come to correct old errors, let me see what probabilitie they bring for their pure & reformed religion. First I see they agree not, & yet euery one sayeth, that he teacheth true faith, & reformed religion: & seing that one bringeth no more authoritie thē an other, that is Scripture interpreted by his owne spirit, I see no reason vvhy I should giue credit more to one then to an other, and therfore because I can not giue credit to al, I see no reason vvhy I should credit any of them al. Secondly I am forwarned that false Prophets shal come vnsent, and yet auouch also that they are sent from God, and therfore vnles these men could say more for themselues then they can, I see no reason, vvhich can binde me to giue eare vnto them. They say they are sent from God. So wil false prophets say. And I examining vvhat is their mission, find therein a great defect. For either it is an ordinanarie mission: and then they must shew a succession of

The discourse of one that doubteth of his ouvvn religion

No probabilitie.

For the nevv religion.

Hier. 1. 13. 14. Mat. 7.

sion of Pastors vvhose Roomes they supply, vvhich I see they can not do, because no historie maketh mention either of their Pastors or their Seruice, or practise of their religion: or it is an extraordinarie, by vvhich they are sent immediatly from Christ, and then they must proue it by miracles, else I must by the same reason hearken vnto euery false prophete. Neither doth it suffice to say, that they preach no other doctrine then the Apostles did, and therfore neede no other miracles, then those vvhich vvere vvrought by them, for so euery Archheretique may say, and you can no way controle him, vnlesse you put him to his miracles. But they alleage Scripture for their doctrine; so haue al heretikes done, as is shewed in the second chapter. But heretiques expounded Scriptures amis, these men hit vpon the right meaning. How shal I know that? they say they haue the true spirit in interpreting of Scripture. But how shal I know, or how cā they tel that, seing that nothing is so secret, as is this spirit, as is proued in the third chapter? And did not Arius say, that he interpreted Scriptures by the true spirit, when he alleaged them, to proue that the Sonne was a creature, and neither equal, nor coequal, nor consubstantial to his Father? Yea do not al heretikes say so, do not al the Reformers say so, euen vvhen they hold contrary opinions? I see no reason therfore, not so much as probable, why I should hearken vnto these reformers, vnlesse I wil harken also vnto al the heretikes that euer were, or shal be. Much lesse can I see any reason, why to forsake my ancient Pastors, who made me and my forfathers Christians, and to preferre these pretended reformers before them. For as for learning they surpassed these reformers, and for vertue they excelled, and so were more likely men to see into the sense of Scripture, and veritie of religion, and were fitter instruments for God to vse, and vessels more capable of God his spirit, and reuelations. In antiquitie they are before them by many hundred yeares, in number they are an hundred at least for one: for authoritie they were honorable Prelats, and Bishops of the Church, vvho proued their mission, commission, and authoritie by succession. yea and by miracles also: neither of vvhich proofes the reformers can alleage for their mission, and authoritie. Shal I then leaue such learned men, for such young clerkes: so vertuous men for so vicious, so ancient Pastors for so new, and so late vpstartes: so many For so few: and men of such pastoral dignitie, for them that can not proue their commission, no more then a false prophet can do? Surely I see no reason vvhy I should, and seing that God wil not bind me, to giue credit

No reason to induce a man tole of the nevv religion.

 to them,

God can not in reason or iustice damne a man for not being a Caluinist or Lutheran.

to them, that can bring no probabilitie, for their owne or their Doctors authoritie, I see not how with any shew of iustice, God can at the latter day, cōdemne me for not harkening vnto them: for I might answer with reason, that I saw no reason, why I should harken to them, rather then to euery false prophet, much lesse why I should forsake myn ancient religion for a new, and myn old and graue Fathers for a few yong ministers, who were borne but yesterday.

16. By this, gentle reader, thou mayst see, how little reason men of vnderstanding haue, to giue credit vnto the newe religion. But lest I may seme to parcial, or thou (gentle reader) mayst be to timorous in pronouncing the sentence, let the matter be brought before an indifferent iudge, who is neither of the old, nor the new Religion. In Iosephus his histories, I find an example in the like case of cōtrouersie. The Iewes (sayth he) and the Samaritanes, contended once about the place, where God should be worshipped. The Iewes sayed Hierusalem was the place: The Samaritanes would haue it to be the mount Garizim. The matter vvas brought before a Pagan king, yet a discreet and indifferent Iudge. Prolocutors were appointed on both sides to plead the cause, Sabeus, and Theodosius for the Samaritanes, Andronicus for the Iewes. Andronicus had leaue granted to speake first: who recounteth a succession of the high Priestes from Aaron vnto his tyme, al which time the Iewes vvere counted the true worshippers of God: he declareth the Antiquitie of the Temple of Hierusalem, and of the Sacrifices there offered: he telleth how that place was euer taken for the true place of worship, and that therfore it vvas adorned and enriched, not only by the guifts of their owne kinges, but of strangers also, and namely by the kinges of Asia, and that there was neuer doubt of this, til the Samaritanes made a schisme. After that Andronicus had told this tale, the prolocutors of the Samaritanes beganne to speake, but being demanded to show the like antiquitie, and succession, they could not, but rather were enforced to bewray their infancie, and the reuolt vvhich long after, that God had bene worshipped in Hierusalem, they made from the Iewes. Wherfore the king pronounced sentence for the Iewes, and declared them to be the right worshippers, and the Temple to be the right place, where the Iewish religion was to be exercised.

l. 18. Ant.

Deut. 12.
4. Reg. 15.
Io. 4. Io. l. 11.
Ant. c. 7 8.

Vvhether the Ievves or Samaritanes vvere the true vvorshippers of God.

17. If In like maner before the like Iudge, I for the ancient Catholique religion, & some one of the ministerie for the new religiō, were appointed prolocutors: for whom, thinkest thou (gentle reader) would the sen-

The like controuersie be-

the sentence be pronounced? If I should beginne to shew a succession of our Pastors and religion, by al histories and monuments euen from the Apostles? If I should shew a catalogue out of Ireneus of al the Popes from S. Peter to Eleutherius, out of Optatus vnto Siricius, out of S. Austin vnto Anastasius, our of Eusebius, Genebrard and others, euen vnto these dayes, and that in this succession, by no Historiographer was euer noted any change, or fal in Church or religion? If I should proue out of the same histories that this ancient catholique Church, was that which was persecuted by the euil Emperors, and afterwards enriched by Constantine and other good Kings and princes, that for this Church, Churches and monasteries were builded, that in this Church al the general Councels were holden: that by this Church al heretikes were condemned, that this Church was euen by Paganes counted the only Christian Church, that al ancient Fathers, Doctors, Martyres, and Saintes, were members of this Church, should I not incline the Iudge to my part? If when I had done, some one of the Ministery should rise vp and beginne to tel his tale, and say that al the ancient Christians were deceiued, & liued in error and ignorance, vntil that Luther, or Zuinglius, or Caluin like so many Sunnes appeared in our horizon, that the religion of these men, is the reformed religion, though it was neuer heard of before. And if being by me demanded, how their preachers proued their mission, he could alleage no proofe at al, or being asked how they proued their religion, he should answere, by Scripture sensed by his priuate spirit, which alwayes hath bene the proofe of al heresies; & being commanded by the Iudge to shew (if their Church be Christian) a succession of their Bishopes, preachers, and practise of religion; he should fly vnto an inuisible Church, or say, that the Christian Church decayed quite after the Apostles time, and yet could neither tel the time, nor the occasion of so notorious a fal, nor alleage one historiographer that writeth of so great a mutation in the word: If I should tel the first tale, and he the second (for I see not what better answer he can make) for him selfe: thinkest not thou (gentle reader) that the iudge vvould ansvver, that although he beleeued not at al in Christ, or his religion, yet that it seemed most probable, that Catholiques are the true Christianes, and that their Church is the place of the practise of this religion, as the Temple of Hierusalem was of the Iewish seruice and worship of God. If then there be no probable reason, by which these Reformers can perswade vs to their reformation, there is no reason vvhy we should forsake

tvvipt vs and heretikes.

Iren. l. 3. c. 3. l. 2. cont. Donatist. Epist. 165.

The good ansvvere a Catholique could make.

The slender ansvvere of a minister.

The conclusiō.

our ancient Pastors to folovv them, vnles vve vvil bynd our selues also to harken vnto al false prophetes, preach they neuer so absurde & improbable doctrine, and so open the vvay vnto al heretikes and heresies.

The Sixt Chapiter proueth, that they haue no Iudge in matters of religion, and so do open the vvay to al heretikes, vvho may preach vvhat they list, if there be no iudge to controle them.

AS YET there was neuer sene any societie wel ordered, were it great or smal, but some gouernor or moderator ruled & menaged the same. For many men as they haue many heades, so haue they diuers opinions, and as they are of different complexions and constitutions, so are they of diuerse conceipts and inclinations, and therfore wil neuer agree in one, vnlesse they be directed and commanded by one, or at least by diuerse vvhich agree in one Wherfore we see that euerie kingdom hath his King, euery dukedome a Duke, euery common welth a Migistrate, euery Citie a Maior or Bailife, euery army a General, yea euery village almost hath a constable, euery familie a goodman of the house, euery schole a scholemaister. And shal not the Church of God, the societie of his faythful and chosen seruantes, haue a visible head to direct it, and a Iudge to rule it by lawes, and gouern it by authoritie? Or shal we think that he hath left that societie, which he calleth his spouse, & which he loued so dearly, that he dyed for it, as a kingdom without a King, a Citie without a Maior, an army without a General, a shipp vvithout a Pilot, a fold without a Pastor, or a body without a Head? No, I warrant you he that descended from heauen to earth, to establish this spiritual kingdome, and shed his blood to enrich it, hath wel prouided for the gouernment of the same, and so wel, that therby you shal perceiue the skil and wisdome of the Gouernour.

No societie cã be vvith out head.

Much lesse the Church.

By the effect, it is plain that the Church had euer a head.

2 And truly if by the effect, we may take a scantling of the cause, the goodly order, the fitine peace, & long continuance of the Church, wil beare witnes of a most prudent princes gouuernement. For as diuerse

diuerſe ſtones in a building could neuer haue kept that order as to make a goodly pallace, had not ſome intelligent workman diſpoſed them: ſo this goodlie order and Hierarchie in the Church, could neuer haue bene eſtabliſhed, had not ſome Prince and gouernor put euery ſubiect in his roome and place. And, as many ſtrings or voices can neuer make one muſical harmonie, vnles ſome cunning muſician tune the ſtrings, and giue vnto euery voice his tone: ſo ſhal many people of diuerſe diſpoſitions, nations, ſexes, conditions, (ſuch as are in the Church) neuer liue in peace, free from iarres and diſcords, vnles there be a Superior to tune theſe diuerſe natures, and a head to direct theſe diuerſe membres of the body of the Church. And as the ſheepe vvhich want a Shepheard, can not long keepe together, but are like to wander, and to come in danger of the vvolfe: as an armie can not long vvithſtand the enemie, vnles ſome General appoint, and command euery ſouldiar to his ſtanding, and as the ſhippe is not any long tyme free from ſandes or rockes, vvhen the mariner is abſent: ſo could neuer the Church of Chriſt, eſpecially againſt ſo many violent perſecutions, for ſo long a time haue endured, vnles ſome potent and prudent gouernour, by his lawes, vviſdome, and authoritie, had vpholden, guided, and directed it. And the reaſon is, becauſe in a ſocietie, and eſpecially this of the Church, are diuerſe men, yea diuerſe nations, and diuerſe men haue diuerſe natures, and diuerſe natures, haue diuerſe diſpoſitions, and diuerſe diſpoſitions cauſe diuerſe opinions, and diuerſe opinions, moue contradictions, and contradictions end in factions, and factions make an end of al ſocieties, vnles there be a moderator to preuent them by his vviſdom, or appeaſe them by his authoritie.

A ſimilitude

A ſimilitude

A ſimilitudes to proue a head in the Church.

The reaſon vvhy a head is neceſſary in the Church.

3. A head then is neceſſary in al ſocieties, & not only neceſſary but alſo principal. For although the obedient and complying nature of the ſubiect, doth help much to the maintenance of peace and order, yet the head and Superior moſt of al preuaileth. For as the head is the principal part, ſo doth it beare moſt ſway in the gouernment of the bodie, wich is the cauſe why the body is affected according to the head, and vvhy the ſubiect foloweth the Princes humour. Yea euen as vvhen the head in mans body is intoxicated the vvhole body reeleth, and if the head vvant eyes the body tumbleth into ditches, and falleth into danger: ſo if the head of a ſocietie be inconſtant, the vvhole ſocietie wauereth, if the Superior vvant eyes of circumſpection, the ſubiectes are in danger. Wherfore Philip King of Maced & father to

The head in ſocieteis is principal.

A ſimilitude

Another ſimilitude.

Alexander the great, was wont to say: malle se exercitum ceruorum, cui præesset Leo, quam Leonum cui præesset Ceruus: *That he had rather haue an armie of fearful harts, gouerned by a Lion; then of lions, ruled and commanded by a hart:* insinuating thereby, that as the head in a societie is the principal member, so is he most necessarie & principal in gouernment. If then the Church of Christ be a peaceable, and wel ordered body, it hath a head to guide and rule it.

4. And if we looke into the gouernment of the same, euen from the beginning, we shal find that this goodly common vvelth, neuer vvanted a Prince and gouernour. In the law of nature first of al, Adam our first parent, as he was our common father according vnto flesh, so was he a Prist, and Pastor of the soules of those, vvho liued in his time, and a gouernor of his familie, which vvas descended of him, not only in domestical, ciuil, or temporal, but also in spiritual matters concerning fayth, and religion. For this cause he was indewed with al knowledge and science, that as the first Doctor he might instruct and direct his posteritie; and although by his fal, he lost al infused grace & knowledge yet stil so long as he liued, remained Pastor & supreme head of the Church. Wherfore Theophilus Bishop of Antioch sayeth, that God for no other cause framed Eue out of Adams side, but to demonstrat vnto vs a misterie and figure of the Monarchie of Church: that as Adam vvas head of the same in his tyme, so euer after, there vvas one Pastor chief of al And S. Chrisostom sayeth plainly, that Adam vvas one head giuen vnto al, and his reason is, Because (sayeth he) *God Knevv, that æmulation could not be auoided amongst æquals, vvherfore he vvould haue no popular gouernment but a kingdom.* After Adams death, Seth and others succeded him in the like pastoral authoritie euen vnto Noe. Noe dying, Sem his eldest sonne vndertooke the same charge: and euen vnto Aaron the first high Priest of the Leuitical law, al the heres, males of euery familie (if vve beleue S. Hierom) vvere Priestes, vvho ministred Sacramentes, and offered Sacrifices euery one in his familie. And amongst al the Priests of diuers families, one vvas the supreme Pastor and Iudge of the rest, to vvhom belonged the final sentence in matters of religiō. And this supreme authoritie as it seemeth belonged alwayes vnto the most ancient, to whom al the rest as they were in age inferior, so vvere they subiect in authoritie. As for example, Abraham and Sem vvere Priests at one tyme, because Abraham vvas the eldest sonne of Thare, Sem of Noe, yet because Sem vvas the most ancient, he was the higher Priest, & therfore to him (for the Hebrewes as S. Hie-

The Church had Adam for her first head in the lavv of nature.

l. 2. ad Autol „ „

Ho. 14. 1. Cor.

Adams successours in the supermacie. Seth.

q. heb. q. 7.

Sem & Melchisedech al one.

as S. Hierom vvitnesseth, affirme, that Sem and Melchisedech were al one) Abraham offered tithes, and was blessed of him as of his Superior. Yea it seemeth probable that Melchisedech in his time vvas the high Priest and Supreme head of the Church. Wherfore Theophilus speaking of Melchisedech, vttereth these words: οὗτος ἱερεὺς ἐγένετο πρῶτος πάντων ἱερέων τοῦ θεοῦ τοῦ ὑψίστου *This man vvas a Priest, the first of al the Priestes of God the highest.* Where he can not mean that Melchisedech vvas the first in time and yeares, because Adam, Abel, and Noe before him, and therfore his meaning must be that Melchisedech was the first Priest in dignitie, and the highest of al the Priests of his time. So that euen in the law of nature, that is from Adam to Moyses, there was alwayes an high Priest to rule the Church, and to compose controuersies, that might arise in matters of religion.

Gen. 14.

Supra.

Melchisedech vvas supreme head of the Church.

5. After that, in the lavv writen, the high Priest ruled al in Ecclesiastical affayres, as is playn in the bookes of Exodus and Leuiticus. In Exodus we read hovv Moyses like a spiritual Iudge giueth sentence in causes ecclesiastical, and answereth al doubtes and questions, which arose concerning the obseruation and interpretation of the lavv, and although to ease him selfe he was perswaded to lay part of his charge & burden vpon others shoulders, yet stil he reserueth to him selfe the iudgement of matters concerning the law and ceremonies. And in Deuteronomie vve find that the people vvere commanded, in al difficulties of religion, to haue recourse vnto the Priest of the Leuitical lavv, vvho ruled at that time, and God threatneth that if any be so proud & stubborne as to refuse to obey his sentēce, he shal suffer death by the decree of the Iudge. Wherfore Iosephus in his second booke against Apion sayth, that so the Priestes of that law did dispense, and rule in chiefe matters, that the high Priest had authoritie ouer them. Where a blind man may see that the Synagogue had her Iudge to decide al controuersies in religion. And shal vve imagin that the Church and spouse of Christ, wanteth a head to direct her, and a Iudge to giue her satisfaction in al doubts of religion? No, in the lavv of grace, as God hath bestowed more grace on his Church, then he had done on his Synagogue: so hath he prouided her of a Iudge and gouernor, whom, for his Churches sake, he assisteth more particularly.

In the lavve vvritten vvas also a Supreme head.

Exod. 18.

Deut. 17.

The Synagogue had a head, must more the Church.

6. And first of al Christ him selfe, whilest he liued gouerned this Church him selfe, and in al points played the part of a Supreme Head, High Priest, and Pastor. For he instituted a nevv law, a nevv Sacrifice, & nevv Sacramentes: he ordayned Priestes and ministers, and gaue

Christ the principal and first head of tho Church.

gaue them authoritie to preach, & to minister, and to gouerne in the Church vnder him. And after that he had withdrawem his visible presence from vs, he lefte vs not without an vnder Pastor, but presently after his resurrection, he appointed S. Peter his vice-gerent in earth, that stil the Church might haue à visible iudge, to whom she might repayr in al her difficulties. For after his resurrection he appeareth to his Apostles and singling out S. Peter from the rest, he demandeth of him three times, not only whether he loued him, but also whether more then the rest: and finding in dede that he did so, & that consequently he was the fittest (for the chiefest thing in a Pastor is loue) he maketh choise of him before the rest, and comitteth to him the charge of his sheepe, in so ample maner, that he excepteth none, but giueth him authoritie ouer al both lambes and sheepe, that is lesser and greater Christianes, euen Apostles & Bishops, who al must acknovvledge Peter for their Pastor, if they vvil be the sheepe of Christ. For as S. Bernard noteth, *VVhere there is no distinction, there is no exception*,

Christ ding leaneth S. Peter his Vicaire

Io. 21. Chrys. in hũc loc. Leo. ser. 3. de Assumpt. sua. Greg. l 4. Ep. 32. Theoph. in c. vlt. Io.

Loue is cheefest is a pastor

Amb. in cap. vlt. Lucæ. l. de consid.

7. This supreme authoritie may plainly be proued not only by the maner of the guifte, but also by the promise. For S. Peter hauing made that rare confession: *Thou art Christ the Sonne of the liuing God*: Christ by and by for a recompence of so great a faith, maketh him this promise. *Vpon this rocke vvil I build my Church.* And although our new Scripturistes to despoile Peter of this headship ouer the Church, by the *rocke* vnderstand Christ him selfe, or the faith of Peter, as if Christ had sayed, Thou art Peter and vpon my selfe, or vpon thy faith, I wil build my Church: yet this is a wrested and forced exposition, because the demonstratiue pronowne *hanc*, *this*, must be referred to that vvhich was spoken of immediatly before. And seing that Christ immediatly before named Peter saynig: Thou art Peter, & then immedialy added, *& vpon this rocke I vvil build my Church*, by the *rocke* he must needes vnderstand S. Peter, and neither himselfe nor the faith of Peter, because he had not spoken of them before. And this the Syriake language in which Christ spake, demonstrateth. For as Christ before had told him, that he was Simon the sonne of Ionas, and should herafter be called *Cephas*: so now changing his name, he saith in the Syriak tongue: Thou art *Cephas*, and vpon this *Cephas* I vvil build my Church. As if he had sayd thou art a rocke and vpon this rocke wil I build my Church. For that is the signification of *Cephas*. I graunt that the grecke text is here ambigous, because that changeth the Word which is answerable to

Mat. 16.

Luc l de potest Papæ. Centur. cent. 1. c. 4. Cal. l. 4. c. 6.

Io. 1.

Matt. 16.

Hieron. in c. 2. Gal.

Cephas

Cephas, as also the Vulgate latin text doth. For in greeke it is thus: *Thou art Peter and vpon this Peter:* but yet if our new interpreters would here repaire to the fountaine; that is to the Hebrew in vvhich S. Matthew wrote, and Syriake in which Christ spake, they should easily perceiue, vnles they vvould vvilfully erre, that Peter is the Cephas and rocke, on which Christ promised to builde his Church, and that as the rocke and foundation is the principal part in a building, so Peter is the principal part, and head of the Church. Yea both the greeke & latin text do also proue S. Peters Supremacie. For both *Petros* and *petra* do signifie a rocke, and seing that Christ promiseth to build his Church on that rock, which before he had named, Peter must be this *rocke* and consequently head of the Chnrch. Doctor Rainolds in his Cōference With Maister Hart, admitteth, that Christ, when he sayd *and vpon this rocke I vvil build my Church,* vnderstood Peters person, and yet he sayth, that thence it foloweth not, that Peter is head of the Church, but only that he is a stone, on which the Church is builded. For (saith he) the Church is a spiritual house, of which Christ is the first fundation, the next ranke of stones are the Apostles amongst whom Peter is one, vpon whom with the rest of the Apostles next after Christ, this building relyeth. Whence it foloweth, not that Peter is the head of this Church, but only a principal member as the other Apostles were, who are called 12. fundations. And with this exposition he triumpheth, but before the victorie. For first, although the Greek vvordes *Petros* and *Petra* may sometymes signifie a stone, yet more commonly and properly a rocke, as also the latin vvord doth: and *Lithos* in greeke & lapis in latin are the ordinarie vvordes for a stone. Secondly the Syriake vvord Cephas, vvhich both the greeke and latin do expresse, signifieth a rocke. And so Peter is not only an ordinarie stone of this building, as other Christians are, because the house is not rightly sayed to be built vpon euerie stone, but only vpon the fundation, or lower stones next to the fundation, neither is he only one of the principal stones nere to the fundation, as al the Apostles are, *Ephes.* 2. because they vvere the first preachers and Pastors, but he is also a secondarie rocke next vnto Christ, on vvhich euen the Apostles and *Ep. ad Felicē.* Bishops do rely, as S. Athanasius sayth. For that the vvord Cephas, and petra do signifie: & the singling out of Peter, and the particular promise made to him in the presence of the rest, argueth that Christ promised him more then the rest of the Apostles, else Peters so rare confession, vvhich Christ promised to reward by building his Church vpon him, had receued no more recompence then the other Apoſtles taciturnitie.

L preſc l. 4. Con. Marc. ca. 5. L. 3. c. 3. L. 5. in ep. ad Rom. c. 6 & in matth. de can. nouites. in Ancor. in mat. c. 16. in Anniuers in hymno ep. 55. 79. l de bono patien. l. 2. can. Eu. nom & hom. 20. & 29 de pen. L 4 de Trin ser. De Cath. pet. & pſ. coupart Don. ep. 4. ep. 17. ad Dam. l. con tel. & in c. 60. Iſa. L. 1. Rectrac. c. 21. Trint. l. 8 in luc. c. 9. ſupr. a ho. 55 in matt. Epheſ 2. ep ad Felicem.

8. Laſtly the ancient Fathers alluding to this place do cal S. Peter the rocke on vvhich the Church is builded. So do Tertulian, Hippolitus Martyr, Ireneus, Origines, Epiphanius, Hilarius, Leo, Ambroſe, Ciprian, Baſil, Ciril, Auſtin, Hierom, vvith many others. And ſeing that the very text, and the Interpreters of the ſame, fauour Peters ſupremacie, I refere it to the Readers, yea to M. D. Reinolds Iudgement (if he lay aſide affection, and ſpeake as he thinketh) vvhether the text it ſelfe, and ſo many and ſo ancient and lerned interpreters are to be beleeued, or his bare aſſertion, vvith the ſingular gloſſing of his priuat ſpirit. I grant that S. Auſtin by the *rocke*, hath ſometime vnderſtood Chriſt, becauſe he his the principal rocke, and others vnderſtand the faith of Peter. But yet, S. Auſtin leaueth to his reader to chooſe this or the former opinion, vvhich he (vvith others alleaged) foloweth: and this opinion he had neuer folowed had he attended to the Hebrevv & Syriake, vvhich as before calleth Peter him ſelfe a rocke: as for the others, they differ not from them ſelues, and the Fathers alleaged, becauſe they only meane that the Church is builded vpon Peters faith, as he is a Publique perſon and Paſtor of the Church. For in two ſenſes Peter may be ſayd to be the rocke of the Church, firſt as he is a particular man, and ſo if the Church had beene built vpon him, it muſt haue fallen with him. Secondly as vpon a publique perſon & ſupreme Paſtor, vvho is to haue ſucceſſors, to whom conſtācie in faith is promiſed, by which they ſhal vphold the Church. and ſo the Church dyeth not with Peter, but kepeth her ſtanding vpon ſucceſſors. And becauſe Peter and his ſucceſſors, by their indeficient faith, in vvhich as Supreme Paſtors they ſhal neuer erre, do vphold the Church, therfore the Fathers alleaged ſometimes ſay that the Church is builded on Peter, ſometimes on his faith, as it is the faith of the ſupreme head: vvhich in effect is al one. For if Peter vpholde the Church, by his indeficient faith vvhich he teacheth, then Peter vpholdeth the church, as he hath aſſured faith, & his faith vphold eth the the Church, not howſoeuer but as it is the faith of Peter, and the ſupreme head, whoſe faith eſpecially vvhich he teacheth out of his chaire (that is not as a particular man only, propoſing his opinion; but as a publique Doctor and chiefe Paſtor) defineth and commandeth what al Chriſtians ought to beleeue, ſhal neuer faile; & conſequently the Church vvhich relyeth on his definition, though ſhe may be

ſhaken,

shaken; yet shal neuer be ouerthrowne.

9. And seing that after S. Peters death, the Church hath no lesse nede of a visible Pastor, then before, as Christ left him for his vicegerent, so in him did he appoint a continual succession of his successors, that the Church might alwayes be prouided of a visible Pastor. And therfore as Bishops are the Successors of the other Apostles, so some one must succeed S. Peter, & must haue that Superioritie ouer other Bishops, which S. Peter had ouer the other Apostles. And truly, no man more likely to be this man then the Bishop of Rome. For in the Sea of Rome S. Peter did last of al reside, there he dyed, and there, before his death, he appointed Clemens, who refusing, Linus succeeded, & after him Cletus, after him Anacletus, after him Clemens, & so forth euen vnto Clement the eight, who now in Rome residing, ruleth the Church, not only of Rome but of al the Christian world. Wherfore the Bishops of this Sea were euer called the Vicars of Christ, & Successors of S. Peter, they haue euer called general Councels & cōfirmed the same, they made lawes, to vvhich al Bishops, yea al Christians acknovvledged them selues bond & obliged, they haue excommunicated Bishops and Emperours, whersoeuer they liued, thinking none that are Christianes to be out of their iurisdictiō, they haue taken appellations from al partes, & shewed them selues in al these actions supreme Pastors not of Rome only, but of al the vvorld: and yet vvere neuer counted vsurpers: & therfore sithence that S. Peter must haue a successor, and that needs there must be one visible Iudge vnder Christ, to vvhom in al doubtes we must repayr, the Pope of Rome is likest to be he, or else if any one be more like, then let the aduersarie name him. And if they name any other but him, I vvil auouch that the Church hath bene vvithout a head nere 1600. yeares, for al this while neuer any executed that office but he. S. Hierom I am sure tooke the Bishop of Rome to be the man, for he in a doubt and controuersie of the high Mystery of the Trinity, flyeth to Damasus Bishop of Rome, not that he was more learned then S. Hierom, but because he knew, that for S. Peter, & consequently for his successors, Christ prayed, that he might not erre, but rather confirme his bretheru. *A pastore* (saith he) *pæsidiū ouis flagito: Of my Pastor I demand the helpe devv to a sheepe.* Yea (sayth he) Beatitudini tuę, id est, Cathedrę Petri communione consocior, super illam petram ędificatam Ecclesiam scio, quicunque extra domum hanc agnū comederit, profanus est: To your Blessednes, that is, to the chair of Peter, I am associated by cōmunion, vpon that *rocke* I know the Church

After Peter a head also necessarie,

The B. of Rome S. Peters Successor.

Eges. l. 3 excid. Iren. l. 3. c. 3. Tertul. l. presc. Eus. l. 2. c. 25. & in chron. an. 44. Hierom. de viris Illust. in Petro. Sulp. l. 2. hist. Epiph. her. 27. Doroth in Synop. Aug. l. 2. con. lit. Petil. c. 51.

Pope Victor the Bishops of Asia. Eus. l. 5. c. 24. 25. Bar. an christ. 198.

to be builded, whosoeuer shal eate the lamb out of this house, he is profane. Where he affirmeth that Pope Damasus is the rocke (because he was Peters successor) on which the Church is builded, and that he is profane vvhosoeuer eateth the lambe out of that house and Church, of which Damasus was the head & rocke. S Bernard calleth Eugenius, once his scholar, but then the Bishop of Rome, once his shepe but then his Pastor, by many honourable tytles. For he saith, that he is the great Priest, the chiefe Bishop, and Prince of Bishops, and heire to the Apostles, who in Primacie is Abel, in Gouernment Noe, in Patriachship Abraham, in Order Melchisedech, in dignitie Aaron, in authoritie Moyses, in Iudgement Samuel, in Power Peter, in vnction Christ. S. Gregorie Nazianzen saith, the Romaine Church doth beare authoritie, because that the Emperial seate was seated in Constantinople. Ciril saith that *VVe must, being members, sticke to our head the* Romain Bishop. S. Hierom calleth Damasus Pope, his Pastor and the successor of Peter. S. Austin with the whole Concel of Mileuet hath recourse vnto Innocentius Pope, as vnto their Superior, because, sayth he, God hath placed him in the Apostolical seat: & in an other Epistle, he saith, *that in the Roman Church hath euer florished the principalitie*. Prosper his Scholar sayth, that the Romain Church is *head of the VVorld*. Anselmus Archbishop of Canturburie dedicating his booke to Pope Vrbane, calleth him Lord and Father of the whole Church. S. Ciprian calleth the Romain Church, the mother Church of al, and the chaire of Peter. Anacletus saith that the Romain Church receiued the Primacie of our sauiour, when he sayd to Peter: Thou art Peter, and vpon this rocke etc: which could not be true, if the Roman Bishop were not Peters Successor. Ireneus calleth the Romain Church, the *greatest* Church, to which euerie Church must repaire, by reason of the more powrable Principalitie. Ignatius in his Epistle to the Romanes geueth the Romain Church many glorious titles. By which it is plaine, that the Fathers and the practise of the Church and Councels acknowlege the Romain Bishop for Peters Successor, and the head of the vvhole Church.

l. 2. de Consid. — In cap. de vita sua. — In lib. The sauri. — Ep. ad Damasum. — Ep. 92. ad Innoc. — Ep. 262. — l. de Ingratis. — c. de Incar. — l 1. — l. 1. Ep. l. 4 — Ep. 8. — Ep. 3. — l. 3. c. 3.

The nevv christians are vrged to tel their head of their Church vnder Christ

10. Now then let our new Christians, if they be the Church of Christ, which euer had a visible head, tel vs who is their supreme Iudge, and Pastor? They wil say peraduenture, that Christ him self is their Iudge, and Pastor, and that they neede no other, because as he planted his Church, so stil he ruleth the same. But this shift vvil not serue the turne: for Christ now conuerseth not visibly amongst vs, so

besides

besides him, the visible Church must haue a visible head, as hitherto she hath euer had. And although Christ stil remayneth our High Priest, Doctor, and Pastor, yet he offereth not Sacrifice immediatly, but only by his vnderpriestes, neither doth he teach vs by his owne voice or reuelation, but by Doctors, vvhom S. Paul sayeth, he hath appointed, neither doth he feede vs by his owne hand, but by the hand of inferior pastors, who minister his Sacraments vnto vs, & deliuer his word in the true meaning, by vvhich the soule liueth. Wherfore besids him, the Church being a visible body, must haue a visible head, else we may say of it, as once Epaminondas sayed of a great armie which wanted a General, *Video pulcherimam bestiam, sed sine capite: I see a very fayre beast, but vvithout a head.* And the reason herof is, because a head and Iudge in the Church, is necessary to decide controuersies in religion, vvhich arise almost euery age, yea often in the same age, sith then vve can not now haue accesse to Christ, besides him we must haue a visible Iudge, vvhich Christ him selfe vvel knowing, presently after he had left vs, he appointed S Peter as his vicegerent, as is already proued.

Besides Christ a visible head is necessarie. *Io. 10.* *Heb 5. 6.* *Ps. 109.* *Ephes. 4.* *Mat. 4.*

Vvhy a visible head besides Christ is necessarie.

11. I demand then of al the professors of this new religion, especially of them in England, vvho is their Iudge in controuersies of religion? They can not say that Scripture is this Iudge, because Scripture is but a written lavv, that can not speak, nor interpret her selfe: and therfore if the controuersie be, vvhich is Scripture, or vvhat is the meaning of it, Scripture can giue no sentence: yea I haue demonstrated in the second Chapter that bare Scripture is no sufficient Iudge in any matter of religion. They can not alleage the spirit to be this Iudge, as is euidently proued in the third Chapter: neither wil they confesse that the Pope, Fathers, or Councels are this Iudge, and if they would, al these would condemne them, as is declared in the fourth Chapter. Peraduenture they wil be Iudged by their founders, Luther, Caluin, and such others. But first these agreed not, neither one with an other, nor with them selues: for what one affirmeth an other denyeth, and vvhat one of them taught one yeare, he corrected the next, and if they had agreed, yet were they no sufficient Iudges, because they can not proue their mission, as is proued in the first Chapter, and so are not to be admitted for lawful Iudges, vnles we vvil admitt also al false prophets. Who then is this Iudge, to whom in controuersies they repayr, and by vvhose iudgement they square out their religion.

Vvho is the Iudge in matters of religiō in England? *Bare scripture no sufficient Iudge.* *As is proued.* *The animal spirit is no first Iudge.* *The Pope and Councels in England are reiected.* *The funders of the nevv relegion no lovvful Iugde* *The reason.*

12 They wil say perchance that the Prince is this Iudge. But this is as vnlikely, and as flatte against Scripture, & practise of the Church,

The Prince is not Iudge in these matters.

King Henrie the eight and Q. Elizabeth vvould not meddle in expounding Scripture, though they chalenged the Supremecie in causes ecclesiastical.

2. Par. 19.

The Priests and Princes Office.

2. par. 26.

Io 21. Act. 2. Ephes 4. Is 49. 38 60. Ep. 13.

as any thing can be. And although the late Quene, and her Father before her, did chalenge as dew vnto them authoritie in causes Ecclesiastical, of vvhich I dispute not at this tyme, yet I am sure they would not entermeddle in matters of religion, to geue sentence vvhat is the meaning of Scripture, vvhich bookes are canonical, and vvhat opinions are heretical, and contrary vnto Gods word, no more then they would entermedle in ministring of Sacraments, or peraching of Gods word. For they knew wel ynough what Iosaphat, that good king sayed, that Amarias the high Priest vvas to rule in matters of religion, & Captain Zabadias to menage matters belonging to the Kings office. And Ozias may be a sufficient exãple vnto al Princes, who was strickẽ with a leprie for vsurping the Priests office in incensing. We read in dede that Christ commanded S. Peter to feed his sheepe & to gouerne his Church, Priests also & Pastors haue the same charge cõmitted vnto them: yea the Prophet Isaie sayeth: that Princes are Nurces, Furtherers, fouourers and defenders of the Church, but he neuer calleth them rulers of the Church, nor Iudges in religion. Wherfore S. Ambrose Bishop of Milan vvriting to his sister, sayth that he told Valentinian the Emperour, vvhat belonged to his office in these words: *Truble not thy self, O Emperour, as to think that thou hast any Imperial right to meddle in diuine matters. Extolle not thy self, but if thou vvilt raygne long, be thou subiect to God. It is vvriten: giue to God vvhich belongeth to God, and to Cæsar vvhich belongeth to Cæsar. Vnto the Emperour Pallaces appertaine, vnto the Priest Churches. The charge of the publique vvalles is committed to thee, but not of sacred and holy things.* A sentence vvorthy to be set in a tablet of gold, and to hang about a Princes neck. And truly if Princes vvere Iudges of Religion we must change religion at their pleasures, and so we should haue almost as many religions as Princes.

A VVorthy sentence for al Kings.

The parlament is not Iudge in matters of faith and religion.

Sanderus in l. de Schis. Angelic. Also. Stovv in his. Chronicle.

13 Much lesse can the Parlament be Iudge in Religion, for that consisteth of temporal men, for although in England the Lordes spiritual are ioyned with the temporal, yet are they al ruled by the Prince. And vvhere, I pray you, doth Scripture vvarrant vs, that the Parlament is our Iudge in matters of religion? yea we see that Parlamentes varie in religion, and so they can giue no certain sentence for religion. In France the Parlament is Catholike, & is cõtent to be subiect to the Pope, & in no wise wil medle with matters of religion. In King Henries time, the eight of that name, the Parlament enacted six Catholique Articles. In King Edvvards time the Parlament alowed of an other religiõ, in Queen Maries time of an other, & in Queen Elizabeths time of an other,

an other. If then the same man had liued in al these princes tymes (as many haue doone) and the Parlament be Iudge, he must in conscience, though religion be but one, haue changed fowre times his religion, else had he bene fowre tymes an heretike, & as often a traytour. Yea I thinke if the Parlament vvere demanded to define vvhich bookes of Scripture are canonical, and vvhich is the true meaning, they vvould answer, that such matters belong not to them. But you wil answer, that the Parlament is Iudge vvhen it is conformable to Scripture, as it is at this present, but was not in Queen Maries tyme. Thus they may answer but with how litle reason, it wil easily appeare. For either the Parlament precisely, or the Parlament agreeing with Scripture is this Iudge? If they grant me the first, then must we in conscience change religion as often as the Parlament changeth. If they grant only the second, then is the Parlament no infallible Iudge, yea no Iudge at al: for yet we must haue a Iudge to iudge the Parlament, and to determine vvhen the Parlament foloweth the word of God: else shal we neuer be satisfied. And vvho I pray you is this Iudge?

An absurd answere refuted.

14. Now I see not vvhom they can name, vnles it be my Lord of Canturbury, or the ministerie of England, or of al countries vvhere their religion florisheth. But then I demand of them, first vvhere they read in Scripture, that their Clergie is an infallible Iudge in matters of religion? They wil say, that the Scripture commandeth vs to giue credit to our Pastors. True, but if I deny that they are true pastors, they can not proue them selues to be so, because they can not proue their mission, as in the first chapter is proued most euidently. Secondly, the Clergie of England, since King Henry the eight, hath changed religion diuers tymes, and this new Clergie vvas neuer yet constant in fayth, for one whole yeare together: yea they agree not amongst them selues, and so can be no assured and infallible Iudge. Thirdly either the Clergie of England is Iudge in matters of religion, because it is the Clergie of England, or because it is the Clergie of a vvhole countrie, or because it conspireth with the vniuersal Clergie of their religion. If they grant me the first, then doth it folow that only the Clergie of England is this Iudge, and so al other countries must be subiect to the Inglish Clergie, to which they wil neuer agree. If they grant the second, then euery Clergie of a vvhole countrie is Iudge, and so we shal haue as many religions almost as countries: and although the new Clergies of England, Germany, Scotland, Holland, Geneua, are contrarie ech one to the other, yet the people of euery country must acknowledge them as Iudges,

Neither the nevv Clergie of England, nor of other countries vvhich professe the nevv religion is a fitte Iudge.

The first reason.

The Second.

The third.

as Iudges in religion, and so must imbrace contrarie opinions. If they grant the third, I must desire them to agree al amongst them selues, before we stand to their iudgement. For if this new Clergie be diuided into many Sects, as al the world seeth it is, then seing we haue no more assurance of one Sect, then of an other, we may refuse to be iudged by any of them, especially they them selues refusing to be iudged, one by an other. Yea not al this new Clergie, nor any Sect of the same, can proue their mission, and therfore are not to be admitted for true Pastors and Iudges in Religion, vnles we wil receiue al false Prophets also, and false Apostles.

15 Is there no Iudge then, neither in England, nor in al the new Church of the Gospellers. If there be, let them name him, if they can: if there be none, as it seemeth there is not (for I haue named, and reiected by good reason, al vvhom I think they can name) then is not their Church the Church of Christ, in vvhich, as is before proued, is alwayes resident a visible Iudge to compose controuersies: yea then the Church (vvhich, as I shal proue in the next booke, is a peaceable kingdom) shal be a common vvelth the worst prouided for that euer vvas: it shal be a body without a head, a kingdom vvithout a King or Prince to command, a conuenticle of vvranglers, the worst ordered and the most dissentious societie that euer vvas: to be briefe, the Church militant in earth, shal more resemble that mutinous route of the damned in hel, then the peaceable societie of the Church triumphant in heauen: yea then shal that folow vvhich I intended to proue, to wit, that in the new Church of the Gospellers, there is no meanes to compose and determine controuersies, because vvhere there is no visible Iudge, there euery man may beleeue and preach vvhat he list, and no man can controle him: and if diuers preach contrarie doctrin, they may go together by the eares, and no man shal be to part the fray, because there is no Iudge to take vp the matter betwixt them: and so the gappe is open to al false prophets, vvhose doctrin must go for currant, be it neuer so absurd, because there is no Iudge to giue sentence of the truth or falshood of the same.

Chap. 6.

16. And to make the matter more plaine, suppose that now in Englãd some new preacher should preach a new heresie, yea that many at once should preach contrary opinions, and so fal to variance, there vvould be no meanes to compose these controuersies: because there is no Iudge to take vp the matter, neither is there any way to preuent them, because where there is no Iudge to define, euery man may teach

A supposition.

vvhat

vvhat he list, and vvhere euery one may teach vvhat he vvil, there arise iarres and discords, and vvhere no meanes are to appease them, the societie is ruined: *Because euery kingdom diuided vvith in it selfe, shal be made desolate.* *Luc. 11.*

17. But in this case peraduenture they would cal a Prouincial or general Councel, and so compose matters by common consent. Be it so that they could cal such a councel, and could also, al or the most part agree, yet I see not how we are warrāted to assure our selues that they al can not erre, & that therfore we may rely vpon their sentence, For if they say, they are waranted because they are the true Pastors, I can tel them that this is not so sure, because they can not proue their mission, and demand of them, whether the Catholique Clergie, which is farre greater, and vvhich for fiften hundred yeares before Luther was heard of, was counted the only Clergie, may not haue their voice, and if they may, certainly their voice wil be negatiue, and opposit to these mens affirmatiue. But this is spoken vpon supposition, that they could cal a councel and agree also in the same, for I haue good cause to doubt, that they neither can cal a cōucel, nor would agree in a councel. For if there be no visible supreme Iudge, nor Pastor in their Church, as I haue proued that there is not, vvho should cal this councel and summone al the Clergie to appeare. *A Councel of their Clergie vvould not serue.* *They can not cal a Councel.* *Lut I conc. 51.*

18. Luther and Caluin say, that this belongeth to the Emperour: but seing that this is an Ecclesiastical office concerning religion, it can not appertain vnto a temporal Prince, and now that the Emperour is a Catholique and a Papist as they terme him, I thinke they vvould not obey him if he should summone them to apeare, especially becaule he vvould cal Catholique Bishops, and vvould giue the preeminence to them. But I haue proued already that the Emperour though in the name of the Pope as an assistant, he may by the Churches permission, cal a councel, yet of him selfe he can not meddle in spiritual matters. Wherfore the Councel which the Apostles called, was called without the Emperours authoritie: where then there is no Supreme Pastor (as I haue proued that amongst them is none) vvhosoeuer should take vpon him to cal a councel, should vsurpe, and the others might refuse to obey his cal. *Calu li 4. Inst. c. 3.* *No man amongst them to cal it.* *Not the Emperour.* *The first Coūcel vvithout an Emperour.*

19. Peraduenture they would choose one by common consent, & so al would stand to his arbiterment. But in this also is difficultie, for vvhere there is none to command, who shal cal them together to agree in the election of one man? Yet let vs suppose that they should *They can not Choose a Iudge.*

meet by chaunce, as crowes do in the Pease-field: when they are met, it is not so easie to agree vpon one, & vvhen they haue agreed, it is not easie to agree vnto his sentence. For if he pronounce sentence for the Protestant, the Puritan wil repine, and may say that he hath no warrant for his sentence, who is but a man, constituted by men, and can shew no Scripture to proue that he can not erre.

If they could be vvere not sufficient.

As yet they neuer could.

20. But truly I can not think that in this matter, they vvould euer proceed so farre. For as yet they neuer called a Councel together out of al partes of their Church, and those that vvere called together, for vvant of a Iudge to determine, could neuer agree in any one point of religion Surius relateth how on a time twelue Catholique Doctors and tvvelue Ministers met at Wormatia, to make some attonement betwixt the Confessionistes, but after a litle disputation fiue of the twelue ministers were excommunicated by the rest, and cast out for vvranglers: and so nothing was concluded. Diuerse other assemblies and meetings they haue attempted, but al ended in thundering excommunications, bitter taunts, and infamous libels, and as yet they neuer could agree in any councel vpon any controuersie in religion, & al for vvant of a visible Iudge, & Pastor, to whom al the rest are subiect.

Anno 1554. Gen. Cron. Vanie attempts for a Councel. Stapl l. 4 de prim sed c. 35.

21. And this they haue gotten by leauing the ancient Catholique Church: which acknowledgeth the Bishope of Rome, as S. Peters Successor, and Christes Vicare, and relyeth vpon his sentence as infallible, because Christ prayed for him, that his fayth might not fayle: and because he hath Supreme authoritie (vvhich al Catholique Bishops haue euer acknowledged) he hath called many Councels and determined many controuersies, & vvhilest the Church euer standeth to his Iudgement, vvhich neuer yet was contrary to it selfe, she enioyeth great peace, and vnitie in fayth and Religion. Wheras the Gospellers, because they haue no visible head, could neuer cal Councel, neuer agree vpon any one point of religion, which was before in controuersie, & neuer shal hereafter: because matters of religion are hard, and therfore vvhere there are many heads, there are many opinions, and where are many opinions, there are many contradictions, and so no peace, nor vnitie, because no one supreme visible Iudge to determine.

By leauing the Church, this they haue gotten. Luc. 22.

The cause of Vnitie in the Cath. Church.

VVhy the Gospellers dissent.

22. And as for vvant of a visible Iudge, they can not appease dissensions after they are risen, so can they not preuent them. For if there be no visible Iudge euerie Cockbrain may preach his owne fancies for true fayth, and religion, and no man shal controle him, nor condemne his doctrin, nor forbid his preaching: because if there be

no visible Iudge, no man hath the authoritie, and so the gap is open to al false prophetes, who may enter into the new Church, thike, & threefold, because no man therein is of authoritie to forbid them. Whence it foloweth that if vve accept of the new religion, and incorporate our selues to the new Church, we expose our selues to al false prophetes, vvho may preach what they please, because no man hath authoritie to controle them.

The Conclusion.

The seuenth Chapter auoucheth, that the nevv Christians knovv no end of beleeuing: and consequently if vve receiue their religion, vve shal neuer be setled, but alvvayes vncertain, and alvvayes seeking, and yet alvvayes to seeke.

NO creature so vnable, but it hath some action, no action so vaine but it hath some end præfixed, and no end so bad, but it giueth some contentment: because euery action is a kind of motion, and al motion is for rest, which only is to be found in the end. And therfore no creature resteth til it attaine to the end appointed, & none there is that resteth not, vvhen it hath attainedroit. The heauens for some end, do moue without end, that is for a more æqual distribution of their light and influences. The foure Elementes with no litle hast hasten to their homes and places, where when they are arriued, they take their natural rest, because they haue obtained their end: and byrdes for some end do build their litle pallaces in that forme and fashion; & for some end, the spider also weaueth that his curious web, whose threeds he spinneth out of his owne bowels; but hauing finished that taske, he resteth contented, though he receiue no other recompence then flyes for his labour. To be briefe, al creatures ayme at some intended end, and (as the Philosopher saith) euery Agent worketh for an end: and the reason therof he yeeldeth, because the end is the cause of causes, and that which first exciteth and moueth to operation: and therfore if that were not, either creatures would be idle, hauing no end to moue them, or they should worke in vaine, because to no end or purpose, or they should alwayes be working, without hope of reposing, be-

Al creaturs ayme at some end.

L. 2. Phys. & Th. 1. 2. 4. 1.

The reason.

cause no action ceaseth til it attayne to the end, where only is the place of resting. And to illustrate this discourse by a clere and plaine example. If bearing of fruites were not the end of trees, they would neuer begin to budde, because the end of budding is bearing: or if they should budde, without possibilitie of bearing, they should alwayes be budding, and neuer bearing, and so should budde in vaine also, because to no end nor purpose. Wherfore (to draw this beginiugto my end proposed, if our new Reformers be desirous, that we should admit their doctrin, and beleeue their preaching, they must shew vs some end of beleeuing: because beleeuing is an action, and euerie action is for rest, which only can be found in the end. Or if there be no end of beleeuing amongst them: one of these three thinges must of necessitie folowe: to wit, that either we can not with any reason beleeue them at al, because there is no end to moue vs: or that we shal beleeue them in vaine, because to no end nor purpose: or else we shal bynd our selues to a restles beleeuing, and so shal alwayes be seeking, and yet alwayes to seeke in our faith and beleefe: which must needs breed discontentment in an vnresetled mynd, and contempt also of al religion, when we see no certain stay in any. True it is that we are commanded to seeke, and especcally for true faith and religion, because that is the groundworke of al: but we are promised also to fynd, else should we seek in vaine, because the end of seeking is fynding. We are bidden also to aske, but promise is made withal, that we shal obtain our sute, else should we aske in vaine. Aud we are willed to knocke also, but with a warrant that it shalbe opened, else should we knocke in vaine, because the end of knocking is opening. *But vvhere* (saith Tertulian) *shal vve find an end of asking, knocking, and seeking? VVith Marcion? But Valentinus also biddeth vs seeke vvith him, and vve shal fynd. VVith Valentinus? But Appelles vvil vrge vs vvith the same proposition: and Ebion: and Simon Magus, and euerie one of them, vvil seek to drovv me vnto him.* The like question do I demand of our new Reformers. Where shal we find an end of beleeuing. With Luther, vvho called the B. Sacrament Christ his body, because it is really in the bread and with the bread? But Zuinglius biddeth me seeke with him, affirming that it is called Christes body because it is a figure of it. With Zuinglius? But Caluin addeth to him, that the Eucharist is not a bare signe or figure, because though it contain not Christes body really, yet whilest it stirreth vp faith, which apprehendeth Christ, it conueigheth Christ really vnto vs by a secret conveihance. With Caluin? But his scollars haue sought further,

An Example. *The application.* *Mat 7.* *Ibidem.* *Ibidem.* *L. Presc. c. 10.* *A question, vvhere to find a stay in beleefe.*

further, and haue corrected him in many pointes: and therfore they also wil cal vpon me to seeke vvith them. VVhence it must needs folow that I shal alwayes be seeking, and neuer fynding an end of beleeuing. Thou wilt say, that I may harken to some one of these Sectmastes, and shut myn eares to the rest. But certes this I can not do with any shew of reason. For first euerie one of them, alleageth the same authoritie to drow me vnto him, to wit Scripture sensed by his priuate spirit: and so if for this authoritie, I begin to folow Luther, I must folow Zuinglius also, vvho bringeth the same authoritie: and after Zuinglius, I must runne after Caluin, because he vrging the same argument deserueth the same credit: and so I shal rune my selfe cleane out of breath in running after Sectmasters, and yet shal neuer find that which I seeke for, which is a stay in religion but shal alwayes be to seeke and yet neuer find. Secondly suppose I could cleaue to one only Sectmaster, & seuer my selfe from the rest, yet neither thus can I find any stay or rest in beleeuidg, because he also him selfe is alwayes seeking without any hope of fynding. Luther once affirmed, that faith only was the thing which iustifieth, that euil workes can not hurt, where faith is present: that good vvorkes are not necessarie, but rather pernicious, that they which are laden with sackes of good workes, must lay down such incombrances, if they wil passe the narrow straites to heauen: yea that such are like to the pilgrimes of S. Iames of Compostella, who lading their heades and shoulders with multitudes of shelles, make their pilgrimage more vneasy. And yet in his visitation of Saxonie, he saith, good workes are necessarie, and can not be separated from a true faith. Once also he absolutely denyed friewil, and boldly auouched, that wickeph if sayd truly, when in one of his articles condemned at Constantia, he affirmed most lewdly, that al thinges happen by a fatal destinie. And yet the same Luther in his aforesaid visitation, complayneth much, that some very indiscreetly do babble of friewil, and confesseth plainly, that man hath friewil in external actious, and frie choise and election to do good and auoid euil. He once affirmed Scripture to be more easie, then al the Fathers commentaries: and yet in an other place, he humbly confesseth that neither he nor the wisest nor holyest, can with any modestie, yea not without impudencie, promise to expond the Psalmes in euery part, no not any part of Scripture in al pointes. The like is his inconstancie in his opinion of the number of Sacramentes. For once he sayd: that he must deny seuen Sacramentes, and

Giue eare to one, and giue eara to al.

Luth. in c. 2. Gal l de libert. Christ. l. de Capt bab. ser. in illud: Sic Deus dilexit

L. de visit Saxon.

In assert. art. 36. damnati a leone 10.

L de visit. Sax Præfat. assert. art. damnai, 1. a leone 10. præfat in psalmos.

L. de Capt. Bab.

and falow of three for the tyme. Hade saith for the tyme, because hade vvas not yet sure, whether his spirit might chance so to blow, as to blow away one or two or al those three. Zuinglius and Carolstadius once iumped with Luther, but afterwards they left him in the lurch, and changed as he him selfe had done. How mutable Melancthon was, his diuers editions of his common places wil testifie. How Caluin hath cauilled, changed, and contradicted him selfe, one Westphalus Heshusius, and other Lutheranes protestrantes haue noted very diligently. So that they them selues are so variable and inconstant, that we can haue no more hold of them then of a slippery eele. The reason of this is, the vnceretaintie of the rule, by vvhich they square their doctrin. VVhich rule is the bare letter of Scripture, which is obscure and ambignous, and the priuate spirit, vvhich is secret, and as mutable as the wind, or wethercocke: as is before in the second and third chapters more at large declared. For as if the Seaman would bind him selfe alwayes to sayle towards that coast, to which the wind bloweth, or the Cock standeth, should neuer be assured of his voiage: so they that wil square religion by bare Scripture, and the priuat spirit, as al the Reformers do, shal neuer be assured of their faith or beleefe, because the bare letter of Scripture is pliable to al heresies, and the priuat spirit is as changeable as a chamelion, and as mutable as any Proteus. So that, neither by harkning vnto diuers sect. Masters, nor by cleauing and stiking to any one of them, can we fynd any certain stay in beleefe, faith, and religion. Hence it is no doubt, that many in England vvho runne on lyke blind bayards, neuer looking before them, are doubtful, perplex, and neuer setled in religion, but fal from Puritanisme to Brownisme, from Brownisme to Barowisme, from many religions, to no religion, and so to Atheisme. Vvherfore he that vvil fynd any certainty, and vvil not alwayes be seeking, and consequently neuer fyndnig, he that wil know and see some stay and end in beleeuing, he that wil not be alwayes vnresolued and perplex in religion, let him repayre vnto the Catholique and Romain Church, which (as I shal proue in the next booke) is the only place of peace and vnitie, and the quiet hauen of tranquilitie. And he that wil stand sure and steadfast, let him keepe his standing vpon this piller of truth. The reasons why this Catholique Church is a place of peace, are many. The first is because she is directed by the Holy Ghost, vvhich is the God of peace, and alwayes teacheth the truth, which is but one. Secondly the high Pastor and head of the Church, vvho

A reason of this inconuiscie.

A similitude

Hovv men fal to Atheisme.

In the Romain Church is only staying

Chap. 6.

1. Tim. 3.

The cause of vnitie and stay.

Io, 14. 15.

vvho vnder Christ gouerneth this Church in a visible maner (which Pastor is the Vicare of Christ, and Successor of S. Peter, and no other then the Romain Bishop, as in the former Chapter is proued) is an other cause of this vnitie: because whilest al obey one, who (as before in the former chapter also is proued) can not swerue from the truth, because he is the rock of the Church, for vvhom Christ prayed, that his faith might not faile, al must needes agree in one, because faith and truth is but one. Thirdly the rule and square by vvhich al Catholiques trie their religion, is a third cause of this vnitie, and that is, the definition of the Church, or Scripture expounted by the Church, vvhich rule was alwayes so right, and so vnuariable that our religion squared by it, hath alwayes bene the same. And therfore S. Paul biddeth Timothie to keep the depositum, & faith, vvhich as a treasure is committed vnto him and to the Bishops his Successors, and consequently to the Church, vvhich as Ireneus witnesseth, is diues depositorium *a rich treasure house* of this treasure. And whilest this Church inuenteth no new beleefes, but stil keepeth the old, as an ancient treasure committed to her fidelitie, she maintaineth peace and vnitie amongst vs, because she stil teacheth the same. Wherfore Tertullian saith: that Christ hauing instituted our faith, al nations must seeke for it, til they haue found it, but after that they haue found it, they must seeke no further, but persvvade them selues that no further is to be sought, because no endles seeking is of a certaine thing. And therfore, sayth he, let them looke to it better, vvho are alwayes asking, knocking, and seeking; because they aske there where no body is to grant, and they knock there vvhere none is to open, and they seeke there vvhere no certaintie is to be found. To this counsel I wih and pray, that my countrimen in England would voutsafe to harken and giue eare: for then I perswade my selfe they would more spedely leaue their new preachers and Sect masters, because amongst them shal neuer be fond cetayne stay in religion. For if they harken to one, they must harken to al that come, because al alleaging the same athoritie, vvhich is Scripture sensed by a priuat spirit, must needes be credited alike, & so shal they folow one new preacher after an other, and though they rune them selues out of breath, yet they shal neuer fynd any rest or stay amongst them, as is already proued. Or if euery one wil choose some one sectmaster to sticke vnto, vvhich yet he can not in any reason do, because he that cōmeth after him, vvil alleage as much as he hath dono, & so also must be credited: yet shal he find no stay in religion, because he folowing an vn-

The second.

Mat. 16. *Luc. 22.*

The third.

1. Tim. 6.

L. 3. con. her. c. 4.

Vide vinc lyr. l. con. prophan.

L. prescr. c. 10.

The Autours Consel.

an vncertaine rule, vvhich is Scripture sensed by a priuat spirit, must needs him selfe vvant a stay, as also is proued. Or if he vvil stand post alone, and trust only to him selfe and his owne priuat spirit, yet neither thus can he find an end of beleeuing, because this spirit is diuers and variable also, not only in diuers, but also in the same men, as already is declared. And so he that wil forsake the Catholique and Romain Church, vvhich is the piller of truth, and the hauen of al tranquillitie, and wil listen & giue eare to nevv preachers, or priuat spirits, shal neuer be setled nor resolued in religion, but alwayes doubtful, perplex, variable, alwayes seeking and yet alwayes to seeke, and shal as soone catch a hare with a taber, as find out any end of beleuing amōgst these new preachers and priuate spirits: and so either he can not beleeue them at al, because there is no end of beleeuing to moue him to beleeue, or else he shal bynd him selfe to a restles beleeuing of new preachers and doctrines; which, as it is vayne and to no purpose, because it hath no end, so must it nedes breed a great disgust and discontentment in the mynd of the beleeuer, & leaue him stil vncertaine and vnresolued in religion.

The Conclusion.

1. Tim. 3.

THE

THE SECOND BOOK CONTEINETH A SURVEY OF THE MARKES OF HERETIKES, WHICH ARE PROVED TO AGREE SO fitly to the professors of the nevv religion, that if euer there vvere any heretikes, these are heretikes.

The first Chapter handleth the first marke of an heretike, vvhich is the breach he maketh out of that Church, vvhich is commonly counted the true Christian Church.

HEY say commonly, that although the diuel disguise him self neuer so much, yet by one marke or other, he bewrayeth him selfe. For altough sometymes he inuest him selfe in the habit of a young gallant, or of a mortifyed religious man: yea although in outward showe he transforme him selfe into an Angel of light, yet so it commontly happeneth, that by one marke or other he is discouered. For either his staring eyes, or stinking breath, or horned head, or forked feet, or base voice discryeth this gallant creature, to be not as he seemeth, but as he is in deed, a fowle & deformed feend: euen so the member of the diuel, that shrowdeth him selfe vnder the name of a christian, and wrappeth & pethlap him selfe frō top to toe, in the innocent habit of a Pastor, which is Scripture, and the vvord of God, yet by one marke or other, yea not by one only but by many, he descrieth him selfe to be as he is an heretike.

The diuel by one signe or other be vvrayeth him selfe.

So it hapneth to the heretike

Vincent. Lyrin. l. contra probh. heres. uouit. c. 14.

2\. And the reason is, because the counterfet neuer attayneth vnto the perfection of the currant, and art though she may imitate nature,

yet

yet shal she alwayes be wanting in one thing or other. The counterfet gold of the Alchimistes hath a great resemblance vvith the true gold, but either the sound, or wayght or operation, vvil proue the old prouerbe to be true: that al is not gold that glistereth. *Zeuxis* painted grapes on a boyes head so liuely, that the byrds pecked at them, but yet art came short of nature, for if the boy had been painted as vvel as nature frameth her vvorkes, the byrds would not haue beene so imboldned: yea the grapes vvanted some thing, for at least by pecking, the byrds perceiued, that al is not grapes that seemeth so. Lysippus could in marble stone make so goodly a portrait of a man, that he would shew euery bone, vaine, and wrincle, vvith al proportion, but the vvant of life and motion wel declared, wherein art was enforced to yeeld to nature.

So the heretike be some marke or other is descryed. *The reason.* *Zeuxis.*

3. Wherfore let the heretike counterfeit neuer so coningly, let him vse al the art possible to shew him selfe a sincere and true Christian, yet the counterfeit must come short of the currant, and art must yeeld to nature, and he in one point or other vvil bewray him self to be no true Christian, vvhich he professeth him selfe to be, but a faythles heretike which he would not seeme to be.

The first marke of an hereke is his breach. *A similitude*

4. And the first mark by which he is bewrayed, is the breach he maketh out of the Church and Christian societie. For as the wandring sheepe was once of the fold, and the rebel was once a subiect, and the boovv cut of once liued and florished in the tree: so heretikes especially Arch-heretikes, were for the most part, once sheep of Christes fold, subiectes of his kingdome, and members of his body the Church. Wherfore S. Iohn giueth vs this mark to knovv an heretike by: *Ex nobis*
1. Io. 2. *prodierunt, sed non erant ex nobis: They vvent out from vs, but they vvere not of vs.* That is, they liued amongst vs (for else they could not haue gone

The first exposition.

out) yet so, that they were not worthy our company, and therfore as rotten boowes are soone broken of, so they were soone shaken of, and took occasion to go from vs, vvho before for their euil life in desert were none of vs. Or else, to folow an other exposition, they vvere

The second. *Aug. tract. 3. in ep. Io.*

amongst vs in outvvard shew, because they frequented Sacraments with vs, but they vvere heretikes in mind and so none of vs, and therfore they vvent out from vs. They vvere in the Church but as euil humors in mans body, and therfore were to be expelled, because they were hurtful to the body, & no part of the substance. For commonly heretikes liue some time secret, before they open and disguise them selues, and so before they went out from vs openly, they were none

of vs

of vs secretly. Or else according to an other interpretation: they were once amongst vs, and like true Christianes liued vvith vs, but euen then when they vvere by present fayth and iustice members of our Church, God forsavv by his diuine foresight, that they vvould not continew amongst vs, and therfore they vvent out from vs, because euen then when they were amongst vs, they were none of vs finally, to perseuer with vs: not that God his prescience was the cause, but because he forsaw which was to be, that they which were as yet of our societie, were of their owne frie wil to leaue vs, & so in God his foresight vvere finally none of our company. So that one euident marke of an heretike is, that he maketh, a breach out of the body of the Church, of which he either was, or semed to be a member. *The third.* *Aug. tract. 4. in Io.*

5. The same marke S. Paul giueth vs also to knowe an heretike, when he sayeth, that *Some shal depart from the fayth, and that some are accustumed to forsake the assembly*, and that some *going out from vs, do truble others vvith vvords*. So the first Sacramentaries, I meane the Capharnaites, who vvould not beleeue that Christ could giue his body to be eaten, left Christ and his Apostles, and vvould vvalke no more vvith them. So that going out, or breaking forth of the Church, is a note and marke of an heretike. Wherfore Tertulian sayth, that we must not meruaile nor think the worse of our Church, when some do leaue vs, because (sayeth he) this sheweth vs to be of the true Christian company, according vnto that: *they vvent out from vs, but they vvere not of vs.* Yea he sayth, that al heretikes vvere once Romaines in religion, and therfore now are heretikes, because they separate them selues as Marcion, and Valentinus did, of whom (sayth he) it is certain, that they beleeued once as the Romain Church, vntil vnder Pope Eleutherius they were cast out of the same. And this note is so certaine, that if you runne ouer the catalogue of al the ancient heretikes, you shal find that their heads, at least, were al once members of that societie, which was commonly called and counted Christian, and when they left the same, they were by and by noted for rebels, runagates, and Apostataes. As the Scripture noteth the time and occasion, vvhen the Samaritanes left the Temple of Hierusalem, and vvould vvorship God no more in that place, as the Iewes euer had done. So haue Ecclesiastical histories noted the time, & occasion of the breach of euery Arch-heretike from the Church: and as yet vve vvel remember (it is not so long) the time and occasion of Luthers reuolt from the Catholique and Romain Church. *1. Tim. 4.* *Heb. 10.* *Act. 15.* *Io. 6.* *l. præsc. 3.* *Ibid. c. 30.* *Al Arch-heretikes vvere for the most part once Catholiques.* *3. Reg. 12.* *Euseb.* *Hist. Tripart.* *Geneb.* *Sauder.* *Baron.*

 6. Yea

Alphonsus Castro. Philostr. Pratrolus. in c.1.ep. Gal.

6. Yea him selfe confesseth that once he was a Papist, and that in the highest degree, for these words he once vttered in his commentaries vpon the first Epistle to the Galathians: *Si quisquam alius, certè ego ante lucem Euangelij pie sensi & Zelaui pro Papisticis legibus, & patrum traditionibus, easque magno serio vt sanctas, & earum obseruationem tanquam necessariam ad salutem vrsi, & defendi: If euer any, truly I, before the light of the Gospel* (he meaneth his owne Gospel) *thought holily, and vvas Zealos for the Papistical lavves, and the fathers traditions, and I vrged and defended them, as holie, and their obseruation as necessarie to salutation.* Yea he confesseth how he watched, fasted, prayed, and tamed his body when he was a friar: yea sayeth he: *Tanta erat authoritas Papæ apud me, vt vel in minimo dissentire ab ipso, putarem crimen æterna damnatione dignum: So great vvas the Popes authoritie vvith me, that I thought it a crime vvorthy eternal damnation, to dissent from him in the least point. Yea once,* sayth he, *I vvas so Zealous for the Pope, that I thought Ihon Husse a vvicked heretike, and vvould haue burnt him vvith my ovvne handes.* And as Luther was, so were al the packe of their first fathers, children of our mother the Catholique Church: and sithence they are gone out, they vveare the badge and cognisaunce of heretikes.

Ibidem.

Ibidem.

Their ansvver that our Church vvas corrupted before they left it.

7. They vvil answer peraduenture, that we vvere not the true Church, but were long before metamorphized, and changed into the synagogue of the diuil, and that therfore it was time for them to leaue vs. But if we vvere degenerated, I demand of them, vvhen, vnder vvhat Pope, or Emperour, and in vvhat age, and from vvhat Church did we degenerate, out of vvhat Church did we make a breach? for nothing degenerateth, but from that which it was before. And if they can not tel vs when we begun to degenerate, nor from vvhat Church, then can they not put this marke vpon vs. Yea I shal in this booke proue, that our Church vvhich now is, agreeth with the Church, vvhich in al ages euen from the Apostles, vvas counted the only Christian Church. Neither is it sufficient to say, that we vvere not the true Church, for so Arius, Nestorius, Eutiches, and euery heretike was accustomed to say, vvho notwithstanding because they vvent forth of that Church, which was commonly called and counted the Christian Church, vvere counted heretikes.

The refutatiõ.

Chap. 5.

Euerie heretike may say that it vvas not the true church vvhich they left.

8. Yea although the Church had bene ouergrowne vvith errors, yet can not that excuse them from being heretikes, because in their opinion, the Church may stand with errors, and so they are heretikes, for leauing it as al ready is proued. Caluin confesseth that the Church of the Iewes vvas obscured with many errors, & that yet the prophets

Esaie,

Esaie, Hieremie, Ioel, Abacuc and the rest, would not forsake the Synagogue, nor erect altar against altar, but rather remained in the church to reprehend abuses. Yea he saith, that the Church of the Corinthians, and Galathians, was corrupted in faith and doctrine, and yet S. Paul would not forsake them. To be briefe, he confesseth that the Church ouer vvhich (as he sayth) the Pope tyrannizeth, is stil the true Church, though it be prophaned. Monsieur du plessis also (more famous for his foyle vvhich that learned Bishop and worthy Cardinal Monsieur d'Eureux gaue him, in detecting his false allegations, then for any vertue or solid learning) defining vvhat the Church is, saith that it is a Congregation of the faithful vvhich beleeue in God by Iesus Christ. And explicating this his Definition, he saith, that the formal cause of the Church, and that vvhich giueth it being and essence, is the belefe in Christ, and inuocation of him. And then he addeth, that although the Church be couered vvith a thousand errors, yet if she retain this inuocation of Christ, she remaineth the true Church, euen as a man couered with sores ceaseth not to be a man, so long as he enioyeth one threed of life. Yea (saith he) I wil admit the Romain Church to be the true Church (as he needs must by his former definition, because the Romain Church beleeueth in Christ, & calleth vpon him) so that it be granted me, that she is corrupted, I wil acknowledge her the spouse of Christ, so that it be confessed, that she is also an aduouteresse. And herin they folow their first Patriarch Luther, who once vttered these wordes of the Romain Church: we confesse that there is in Papacie much christian goodnes, yea al christian goodnes, and that from thence it is come to vs: to witte, we confesse in Papacie to be the true Scripture, true Baptisme, the true Sacrament of the Altar, true Keyes for remission of sinners, true Ministerie of the word. etc. I confesse truly that vnder the Pope is true christianitie, and many good men indewed wtih excellent sanctitie. But this confession hangeth them. For if the Romain Church notvvistanding errors (as they say) remaine stil the true Church, then are they heretikes, vvho haue left her, and made a breach from her, ad haue set vp a new Altar and a new Misterie, and a new Synagogue against her.

l. 4 c. 1. & 18 & 19. & c. 2

l. 4. c. 1.

En son traicté de l'Eglise.

Ep. ad duos pastores to. 2. Germ.

9. Sith therfore Luther, Caluin, & the rest haue departed from our Church, vvhich vvas and stil is called the Christian Church, either they are heretikes, or else Arius, Nestorius, yea Simon Magus, Cerinthus, and Ebion were no heretiks.

10. Neither can they instly bragge that many haue left them also,

See the 6. ch. and seuered them selues from their company: for that vvas alwayes the maner of heretikes, not long to continew in one religion, but to diuide them salues into many Sectes. And if they count those heretikes, who goe from them & make new Sectes, then are they al euen the first of them, heretikes, because the first of them vvent out of vs.

11. Wherfore in few words to comprise al, and to conclude which I intended, They can not name the Church, from vvhich we departed, nor the time, nor the occasion. But we tel vvhen they departed, & from vvhat Church, that is the Romain Church, which vvas and is stil commonly counted the true Christian Church. And so it foloweth euidently, that we are stil in the right Church, because there was neuer any other, out of which we could breake forth, they are runne out, we weare the badge of true Christianes, which is neuer to goe out, neuer to forsake that vvhich once we haue professed: they weare the badge and are noted with the marke of heretikes, vvhich is to goe out, and to forsake the common receiued Church. And so if euer there were any heretikes so called, and counted, for breaking forth, and going out, then are these heretikes, and neuer shal be able to hide this marke, goe they neuer so disguisedly.

The Conclusion.

The second Chapter discouereth the second marke of an heretike, vvhich is later standing and noueltie, vvhich also is proued to agree as fitly to the Gospellers of this tyme, as to any heretikes of former tymes.

GOod goeth before bad, truth before falshood, the currant before the counterfet, and nature before art: because euil is but a priuation of the good, & falshood is that vvhich swerueth from the truth, & the counterfet is but resemblance of the currant, and art is but an imitation of nature; and so these come after, those of necessitie must goe before.

2. No meruayle then if religion take the precedence of superstition, and Christian fayth of heresie, which is but a priuation of good, a falsitie swreuing from truth, a conterfet resemblance of currant, and an artificial imitation of Christian sinceritie. Religion vvas planted be-

ted before superstition tooke roote, vertue vvas rooted before vice was sowne, and the seed of true fayth was sowne, before the enemie scattered the euil cockle of heresie: and as the true Apostles liued and preached before Simon Magus, and other false-prophetes his successors: so true fayth vvas sowne, rooted, and come to some height and ripenes, before euer the false Apostles scattered the nettleseed, of their heresies. Yea not only by the Apostles generally in the world, but also by their successors particularly in euery particular country, fayth grew and florished before heresie was sowne, for as Bozius in his fourth booke of the signes of the Church learnedly proueth, the first conuersion of euery country from Paganisme vnto Christianitie, vvas not to heresie, but to the true fayth and Romain religion: and vvhen that was receiued, then heresie being but a corruption of true fayth, as vineger is of wine, began to take place, then the cockle sprong vp after the good corne. And therfore S. Paul giueth vs this marke to know an heretike, and heresie, that they arise after the true religion. *I knovv* (saith he) *that rauening vvolues* (*that is heretikes*) *after my departure shal enter amongst you not sparinge the flocke*. So that after S. Paul had preached and perswaded true fayth, the false prophetes entered, to ruine the spiritual building vvhich he had framed.

Religion before superstition and heresie.

Mat. 13.

In euerie countrie Cath. religion before heresie.

Boz. l. 4.

Act. 20.

3. In like maner the ancient Fathers haue euer noted heretikes and their heresies of later standing and noueltie. *In al things* (sayth Tertulian) *the Veritie goeth before the image, and last of al cometh the similitude.* Yea, sayth, he, it is a folly to thinke, that heresie in doctrin is the first, especially seing that the true religion fortelleth heresies. And in an other place, thus he concludeth: *In summa, si constat id verius quod prius, id prius quod est ab initio, ab initio quod ab Apostolis, pariter vtique constabit, id esse ab Apostolis traditum, quod apud Ecclesias Apostolicas fuerit sacrosanctum. In brieef, if it be manifest, that that is truest, vvhich is first, that first vvhich is from the beginning, that from the beginning, vvhich is from the Apostles, it shal likevvise be manifest that that is deliuered by the Apostles vvhich hath been inuiolably holden in the apostolical Churches.* And in his booke against Praxeas he sayth, that it is adiudged against al heresies, that that is true vvhich is first, that is counterfet vvhich is later. And this he sheweth by a similitude, for (sayeth he) as the wild oliue springeth often tymes out of the sweet oliue nutte, and the wild figtree out of the good figge, so heresies haue growne out of our ground, vvhich yet are not ours, degenerating from the true graine of fayth. Ireneus also subscribeth to Tertulians opinion in these vvords: *Omnes illi valde posteriores sunt quam*

l. præsc. c. 29. 30.

li. 4. aduersus Marcionem.

l. aduers. praxeam.

l. præsc. c. 36.

Episcopi,

l. 5. circa medium. *Episcopi, quibus Apostoli tradiderunt Ecclesias. Al they* (he meaneth heretikes) *are of much later standing then the Bishops, to vvhom the Apostles committed the Churches.* And as heretikes are noted of later standing, so is their doctrin counted to sauour of noueltie. Wherfore Zozomenus (l. 1. c. 14.) sayeth that Arius was not afrayed to affirme, that vvhich neuer any durst auouch, to wit, that God the Sonne vvas created of nothing.

The Cath. Church kepeth the olde. *Vincent l. con. proph. hæresū Nouit. c. 27.* *1. Tim. 6.*

4. And Vincentius Lyrinensis vvriting a booke against heresies, intitleth it: Against prophane nouelties, and vvisely obserueth that the Catholique Church kepeth the old, and deuiseth no new doctrin: to vvhich sense he explicateth those vvordes of S. Paul: *O Timothee depositum custodi O Timothie kepe that vvhich vvas deposed vvith thee, and committed to thy custodie: Depositum custodi* (sayeth he) *non quod à te inuentum, sed quod tibi creditum est, quod accepisti, non quod excogitasti, rem non ingenij, sed doctrinæ, non vsurpationis priuatæ, sed publicæ traditionis, in qua non author esse debes, sed custos, non institutor, sed sectator, aurum accepisti, aurum redde, nolo mihi pro alijs alia subiicias.* Kepe that vvhich is deposed, not vvhich is innented by thee, but vvhich is committed to thee, vvhich thou hast receiued, not vvhich thou hast deuised, a thing not of wit, but of doctrine, not of priuat vsurpation, but of publique tradition, in vvhich thou oughtest not to be an autor, but a keeper, not an institutor but a folower, thou receiuedst gold, restore gold, I wil not haue thee put in one thing for an other.

Faith is stil the same though it be more explicated. 2. 2. q 1. a. 7.

5. Wherein he putteth a playne difference betwixt Catholiques and heretikes; that they sticke to the old, these are euer deuising new doctrin. For although the Church by new Councels and definitions addeth greater explication of her religion, and although by the laborious endeuors of the Doctors of the Church, which in no age are vvāting, many points of our fayth are more illustrated & dilated, yet in substance our fayth is stil one and the same. And therfore Diuines say, that fayth neuer from the beginning hath increased in substance, but only in explication, and that the Church since the time of the Apostles, neuer had new reuelations in the Articles of beleef, and that in general Councels she defineth no new things, but rather those things vvhich before were extant in Scriptures, Fathers, or Tradition, she by her definition, declareth more certainly, and proposeth more plainly to the vew of the world.

A fit similitude.

6. So that as Vincentius Lyrinensis sayth, euen as mans body increaseth by nutrition and augmentation, yet gayneth no new limmes and members, but only getteth more quantitie and strength in the former, so

mer, so Christian fayth by no increase did euer yet gaine nevv Articles, but only hath gotten greater and clearer explication of the former. Vvherfore the same Doctor counsayleth euery preacher and teacher, so to explicate thinges after a new maner, that he preach not nevv doctrin: *Eadem quæ accepisti* (sayeth he) *ita doce, vt cùm dicas nouè, non dicas noua* c. 27. *The same things vvhich thou hast receiued, so do thou teach, that vvhen thou speakest after a nevv maner, thou speake no nevv things.*

7. And the reason vvhy fayth admitteth no nouelttie is this: because God speaketh once, and neuer recalleth or amendeth his word: and in him that prouerb taketh no place: *Secunda consilia meliora, second counsayls are the best.* For God is as vvise and circumspect at the first as at the last, & therfore he hauing once reuealed and planted fayth, that must stand for good, and he that seeketh to change, declareth him selfe a corrupter, not a correcter: and in that he commeth after vvith his deuising vvit to adde, or detract from the olde receiued faith, he bewrayeth him selfe to be of later standing, and so an heretike, and his doctrin to sauour of noueltie, & so to be an heresie. *The reason.* *Iob. 33.* *Psal. 61.*

8. Vvherfore to conclude, sith it is certaine, that Catholiques, vvhom they cal Papists, are of no late standing, nor anie vpstarts, (for I demand vvhen they beganne, and after vvhom they arose?) they can be no heretikes, and seing that it is no lesse certain, that the reformers of this time be al nouellants, and nouellers, vpstarts, and of later standing, arising many hundred yeares after the Romain Church, vvhich vvas euer counted the only true Church (for Luther the first of al this nevv frye and his religion is not yet an hundred yeares old) it is as certaine, that they are heretikes, and their religion heresie, as that Arius, Nestorius, Pelagius, vvere heretikes: and the same Fathers and Scriptures before alleaged, vvhich haue condemned them for heretikes, because of their late standing, can not without plaine partialitie, frie our reformers from the same sentence, who weare the same badge, & are noted vvith the same marke of an heretike, vvhich is later standing. *The conclusion.*

The third Chapter noteth the Reformers vvith an other marke of an heretike, vvhich is a particular name, taken from their Sectmaster.

Psal. 7. Sap. 1. Th 1. p q 57. art 4. The secrecie of the harte.

HE hart of man is a secret closet, of which God only keepeth the key, it is a bottomles pit, which he only who searcheth the hart and reines, can sound to the bottom: in so much that vnles God reueale, or this hart of man vouchsafe to open it selfe, neither diuel nor Angel can discouer the hartes cogitations, much lesse can one man know vvhat an other thinketh. Wherfore, that mē might impert their thoughts one to an other, God hath geuen them a tongue as an Interpreter of the mind, & a messenger of the thoughts, & a mouth also as a trumpet, wherin the tōgue soundeth forth by voice, vvhat the hart thinketh. And because the things which we would speak of, can not by them selues immediately be brought into discourse, the tongue frameth words & giueth names, vvhich goe for the things, that so vvhen vve heare the sound of the word & name, we may vnderstand the thing which is spoken of.

The tongue is the interpretour of the harte. Names God for thinges.

2. Wherfore the new Christians of this time must not meruail, that by their name, as by an infallible marke, I seek to discouer them: for names are Symboles and signes, by which we know the natures of things, together with their proprieties. But what, wil you say, is this name, by which they are conuinced to be heretikes? it is the Surname which they take from their Sect-master, by which they were alwayes more famous, then by their proper names.

By names vve knovv the thinges. The name by vvhich an heretike is knovven.

3 At the first when al Christianes were of one hart and lippe, beleeuing and professing the same names, as Christianes of Christ, brethren for their mutual charitie, faithful in respect of one fayth. But vvhen certain inconstant and deuising heads, would vary from the rest of the faythful incertain pointes of religion, their names changed as they them selues vvere altered, & because they novv beganne to leaue the common receiued fayth, which Christ by him selfe and his Apostles, and their successors had deliuered, they were no more called by the common name of Christianes, but by the name by which their

At first one name vvas common to al Christians. VVhen Christians vvere called by particuler names.

Autour

Autour vvas called, who deuised their religion: and therfore as in fayth they were separated from other Christians, so in names also which explicate the natures of things, they were of necessitie seuered. Simoniās were named of Simon Magus, the Ebionites of Ebion, Marcionites of Marcion, the Manichies of Manicheus, the Arrians of Arrius, Nestorians of Nestorius, Eutichianes of Eutiches, Pelagians of Pelagius, Donatists of Donatus, vvho notvvithstanding before they varyed in religion, and folovved nevv Masters, vvere called only by the common names of Christians, and so the ancient Fathers euer condemned them as heretikes, vvho vvere marked vvith these particular names. *Names of sectemasters.*

4. S. Hierome pronounceth boldly this sentence: *Sicubi audieris eos qui dicuntur Christiani, non à Domino Iesu Christo, sed à quopiam alio nuncupari, vtpote Marcionitas, Valentinianos, Montenses, &c. scito non Ecclesiam Christi, sed Anti-Christi esse Synagogam: If any vvhere thou heare of them vvho are called Christians, yet take their name not of Iesus Christ, but of some other, as for example, if they be called Marcionits, Valentinians, Montanists, &c. Knov thou, that there is not the Church of Christ, but the Synagogue of Anti-Christ.* Iustinus Martyr discrieth heretikes by the same badge and marke: *There are* (sayeth he) *and euer vvere many, vvhich come in the name of Iesus, yet are called by diuers Surnames, as Marcionits, Valentinians, Basilidians, Saturninians euerie one Borovving a name of the first inuentor of their doctrin.* Of such kind of men this is S. Ciprianes opinion: *They vvhich vvere once Christians, novv Nouatians, are novv no more Christians, because* (sayeth he) *primam fidem vestram perfidia posteriori, per nominis appellationem mutastis: you haue changed your former fayth, for a later infidelitie, by the appellation of of your name.* *li. contra Lucifer. in fine.* *Dial. cum Triphone.* *Ep. ad Nouat. hereticum.*

5. And the reason vvhy these Fathers accounted always such nicknamed persons as heretikes, is easily sene; because such as leaue the Church and wil not heare her voice, were always estemed as heretikes, as the Greeke vvord *Heresis* importeth, which signifieth election and separation. And therfore S. Austin and S. Ciprian put this difference betwixt an heretike and a schismatike, that although both do separate them selues from the Church, yet a schismatike only is diuided in vvil, contumacie, and breach of charitie: an heretike in fayth also and opinion, and therfore seing that these diuerse names taken from diuerse Autors, argue such a separation (for if they had stil remained in that Church, vvhich commonly vvas called Christian, and had not folowed newmasters, there had needed no distinction of names from other Christians) it must needs folow, that al such as are distinguished *Mat. 18.* *Li. 2. contra Faust. c. 1.* *Cip. l. 1. ep. 6.*

thus in name from other Christians, are diuided also from them in fayth and religion, and so are no true Christians, but persidious heretikes.

6. I demand now of our Lutheranes, Zuinglìannes, Caluinistes, Osiandrians, Bezists, Brownists, Martinists, & such like new-named Christians of this age, whether they dare stand to the sentence of Iustinus Martyr, S. Cyprian, and S. Hierom in this point? Truly I think they dare not: and I thinke also that they haue good cause: for if that they be heretikes which are surnamed of particular autors (as they plainly affirme) if our new Christianes be so surnamed, as al the world vvil be vvitnes that they are, then must needs folow this conclusion, that they also are heretikes.

The. Conclusion.

7. But to conclude more plainly that which was intended. This marke of an heretike can in no wise agree to Catholiques, but rather to them agreeth the signe of the true Christians. For as in the time of the Arians, they vvere counted true Christians, vvhich vvere called by general names, Christians, and Catholiques, and they vvere esteemed of as heretikes, which had particular names deriued from the autour of their Sect, as Arians, AErians, Eudoxians, and such like: so now vve that are called by the same names of Catholiques and Christians, and by no name taken from other autor, must needs be taken for true Christians, vvho as vve neuer changed name, so neuer changed religion, and the reformers vvho are called Lutheranes, Caluinistes, Zuinglians and such like, of some particular Sect-master or other, must needs be condemned for heretikes.

8. And as before that the ancient heretikes forsooke the common receiued faith, they vvent by the common names of Christians, and Catholiques, and neuer tooke vnto them particular names, before they folowed particular maisters, and imbraced particular doctrines, so before Luther and Caluin reuolted from the Church, they vvent by the common name of Christians, and neuer changed their names, til they changed their religion, neither vvere any Christians called Lutheranes, Caluinistes, or such like, before they relyed vpon new and particular masters.

9. And as the Arians, because they could impose no name of any autour to the Catholique Christians, were fayne to cal them Homousians, of their doctrine, as before them they were called *Psichiki*, that is carnal, for defending second mariages against Tertulian and the Montanistes: so at this time our reformers are fayne to cal Catho-

liques

liques Papistes, for holding the supremacie of the Pope, who is no new autor of any new religion, but ancient Successor of S. Peter, and Vicare of Christ.

10. As for the names of Thomists, & Scotists, they are no names of autors of nevv religion, because al held the same fayth, but of autors of some other new opinions or maners of teaching in Philosophie, and schoole pointes: likevvise the names Benedictins, Dominicanes, Franciscanes, are names deriued from autors of nevv states of life, but not of new faith or religion. So that in vs whom they cal Papistes, is no name which argueth vs to be heretikes In the reformers are particular names of particular autors of new pointes of religion, and so they vveare the caracter of the beast, and are infamous heretikes, if Montanus, Marcion, Arius, vvere worthily called heretikes.

The fourth Chapter discouereth an other marke of an heretike, vvhich is a renouation of old heresies, vvhich argueth these reformers to be heretikes, if euer any vvere iustly so counted.

MANY there are in the world, who finding many absurdities in the new religion, and yet some difficulties also in the old, vvil neither hold altogether with the one nor the other: but comfort them selues vvith a flattering opinion, that a Christian may be saued in al religions, so that he retain the principal articles of Christian beleef. For (say they) if he be firmly grounded in a right fayth of the Incarnation, & Trinitie, perswading him self that God is one in essence and three in persones, and that Christ is one in person, yet subsisting in tvvo natures, that he suffred for man kind, and is the Messias and Sauiour of the vvorld; he is a Christian good ynough, vvhatsoeuer his opinion be in lesse matters, as iustification, merit, Sacraments, and such like: vvhich to them be but petie matters, and not of such importance, as that a mans saluation should depend theron.

Many thinke to be saued in any religion.

2. But this opinion of theirs, vvould they neuer so fayne that it were true, is most vntrue, and as false as flattering. And the reason is,

A false and flattering opinion. because one only opinion in a matter of fayth, obstinately defended against the Churches authoritie, is sufficient to dismember a Christian from the mystical body of Christ his holy Church, in that it depriueth *The reason.* him of infused fayth, vvhich is the glew, yea the sinew that vniteth the *Th. 2. 2. q. 5. a. 3. & 3. p. q. 8. a. 3.* members of this body together. And in dede as yet we neuer heard of an heretike, but he professed some principal parts of Christian faith: as that Christ vvas God and man, or the Reedemer of mankind, or the *One heresie sufficient to dismember vs from the body of the Church.* autour of the law of grace, or some such like: for if he altogether denyed Christ, he was rather an Apostata then an heretike. For he is an heretike, vvho professeth Christ in some sorte, and him selfe also a Christian, yet obstinately denyeth some part of Christian religion: and he is an Apostata, vvho quitte renounceth Christ and his religion. Wherfore vnles vve wil grant, that al heretikes may be saued, we must *Euerie heretike professeth Christ.* needs confesse, that one heresie is sufficient to damne a man perpetually.

3. But in this matter lest my censure seme to rigorous, and my sen- *The differēce betvvixt an heretike and an Apostata.* tence to seuere, I wil alleage Scripture, vvhich can not deceiue vs, if they be rightly vnderstood. Our Sauiour Christ denounceth him to be like an Ethnike and Publicane, vvhich wil not heare the Church, and sayth not, who wil not giue credit vnto her in principal matters, but *Mat. 18.* absolutely he sayeth, if he wil not heare the Church, let him be vnto thee as an Ethnike and Publicane, that is shunne his company as the Iewes did al familiaritie with paganes & publicanes. And again Christ threatneth that he, *vvho beleeueth not shal be damned.* To which agreeth S. Paul saying *that vvithout fayth, it is impossible to please God.* meaning no *Mar. 16.* doubt a vvhole and entier fayth, deuoid of al errors. For else al hereti- *Heb. 11.* kes may be saued, vvho beleue some parts of Christian beleef. Wher- *An intier faith is necessarie.* fore S. Paul amongst the workes of the flesh, that is of a man vvhich foloweth not the spirit of God, but his owne sensualitie and liking, reckeneth not only fornication, drunkennes, murder, and idolatrie, *Gal. 5.* but also dissensions, sectes, and heresies, and against al these workes *Heresie a vvorke of the flesh.* he pronounceth the sentence of damnation: *I fortel you as I haue fortold you, that they vvhich do such things shal not obtein the Kingdom of heauen:* which sentence as he would haue pronounced against one fornication, or *One heresie damneth as one fornication.* murder, so would he against one heresie. To this agreeth Athanasius in his Creed saying, that vnles a Christian Kepe intierly and inuiolately the Catholique fayth, he can not be saued. Which to me seemeth a sufficient argument, that one only heresie is a sufficient matter of cō- *Symb. Atha.* demnation.

4. And

4. And truly if we wil looke backe to ancient tymes, and take a vewe of Ecclesiastical histories and councels, vve shal find, that for some few errors, yea sometymes for one only, & that not in the principal points of our beleef, many haue been accused and condemned for heretikes. Pelagius beleued that there were three diuine persons, æqual, coæqual, and consubstantial: he professed that Christ was God and man, & the Sauiour of the world, and that by his grace we might more easily come to heauen: yet because that he auerred that without this grace we might keep the commandements, and withal, that litle infants were neither conceiued nor borne in original sinne, he was by the common voice of the Church and Christian vvorld, condemned for an heretike. Vigilantius beleued also the Trinitie and Incarnation, and yet for that he condemned, and contemned reliques, vigilles, lighting of candels in the Church, prayer to Saynts, and æqualized matrimony with virginitie, S. Hierom condemneth him euen vnto hel. Iouinian also for making al sinnes, and good vvorkes, equal in demerit and merit, and for putting no difference betwixt the state of Virgins and the Maried, was by the same Doctor condemned for an heretike: to vvhich his sentence al the christian vvorld subscribed.

Heretikes accursed, vvhich yet beleeued in Christ.

Pelagius. Posid. in vita Aug.

Vigilantius.

l. con Vigil.

lib con. Iouin.

5. And no meruaile. For if one heresie depriueth vs of fayth as it doth, because he that beleueth not God, and his Church in one article, beleueth them in none, if fayth be the linke which vniteth vs as members to the mystical body of Christs Church, then one heresie is sufficient to separate vs from the Church, as the very name in Grecke *Heresis* importeth, & consequently one heresie is ynough to damne vs, because out of the Church is no saluation. For as the arme cut of dyeth, and the boow riuen from the tree withereth: so whether by one or many heresies we be separated from Christs mystical body, vvhich he viuificateth by his spirit, we dye and vvither, and remain deuoid of life, sappe, and saluation, because the spirit of God, vvhich is as it were the soule and spirit of this body, imparteth it selfe to none, but those vvho by true fayth are members of this body, and boowes of this tree, vvhich extendeth it selfe, by reaching boowes from sea to sea.

Th. 2. 2. q. 5. a. 3.

A reason vvhy one heresie condemneth.

A fit similitude.

Psal. 79.

6. Wherfore S. Cyprian sayeth, that *vvhosoeuer is separated from the Church, hath no part in Christes promises: he is an alian* (sayeth he) *an enemie, a prophane person, and one that can not haue God for his father, vvho hath not the Church for his mother.* Yea (saith he) *such an one may dye for Christ, he may burne, he may be cast to the vvild beastes, but that death shal be no crovvne of fayth but a pain of infidelitie: such a one may be killed, but he can not be crovvned.*

L. de Vnit. Ecclesiæ.

No Saluation out of the Chuch.

Ibidem.

7. Pacia-

Ep. 2 ad Sympron. 7. Pacianus casteth Nouatian out of the Church, for only denying Confirmation, the Sacrament of Penance, and opposing him self to Pope Cornelius, & telleth him that he can not be saued though he dye for Christ. *Porro* (sayth he) *etiam si passus est aliquid Nouatianus, non tamen etiam occisus, etiam si occisus, non tamen coronatus. Quid ni. Extra Ecclesiæ pacem, extra concordiam, extra eam matrem, cuius portio debet esse qui Martyr est.* But although Nouatian hath suffred something yet he vvas not killed, although he vvere killed, yet not crowned. Why not? Out of the Churches peace, out of her concord, out of that mother, whose portion he must be, that is a Martyr. *Lib. de hæres. ad Quod vult Deum in fine.* Wherfore S. Austin, hauing rehearsed fowre score heresies, saith that there may be manie moe heresies of lesse moment vnknowen to him, and of the least of them this terrible sentence he pronounceth: *quarum aliquam quisquis tenuerit, Christianus Catholicus non erit.* Of vvhich heresies, Whosoeuer shal hold any one, shal not be a Christian Catholique. And I wil adde, that consequently he can not be saued, because out of the Catholique Church is no Saluation, as is already *Supra.* proued in this Chapter, and in the seuenth Chapter folowing. And so a man can not be saued in al faithes and religions, because one heresie cutteth him from the Church out of which is no Saluation, and against *Saluation not possible in al religions.* one heresie, as before, S. Paul would haue pronounced the sentence of damnation, as wel as against one fornication. And so Foxe is a foxe, vvho in his lying historie to shew a continual succession of his visible Church, raketh vp Waldenses, Albigenses, Wiclefists, Lollards, Hus- *Supra. In his protest. to the church of England.* sites and such other damned heretikes, making them members of one Church, to make vp a body of his pretended Church. For first the Church of Christ should be a monstrons body compacted of so many diuers, and so vnlike partes and members, and should be as ridiculous *The first reason. For his church is monstrous.* as the Poets Picture, vvhich had a mans head, a horses neck, a fowles body, and a fishes taile. Secondly if one heresie be sufficient to cut a man cleane from the Church (as I haue proued that it is) then certes these heretiks vvhich so disagreed amongst them selues could not be *Horat. Flac. de art. Poetica the Second reason.* members of one true Church, as neither can our Protestantes, Puritanes, Brownists, & others in England; and therfore though they may be damned, because they haue out them selues from the Romain Church, vvhich this booke proueth to be the true Church, yet can they not possibly al be saued. And so Foxe also is a foxe in compiling a Kalendar of Martyrs, Confessors, and Saints of many and diuers sectes, vvho like Sampsons foxes agreed only in the taile against the Romain Church,

but

but neither in head nor body. For if one heresie be sufficient to cut a man quite of from the Church militant in earth, it must needs cut him also from the Church triumphant in heauen: and so though diuers heretikes may be al damned, and be al members of one damned crue in hel, yet can they not be al saued, neither can they al be Saints and Citizens of one heauen, and consequently are most absurdly & foolishly put in one Kalendar. If then it be so that one error in faith obstinately defended, is sufficient to cut a man from the Church, & to make him an heretike; then certes the Gospellers of this time, must needs be heretikes, and that in the highest degree, who haue renewed almost al the old heresies, and euen those vvhich by the Christian vvorld, were alwayes condemned for damnable errors.

The nevv Christians vvho renevv old heresies must needs be heritikes.

8 For if Simon Magus and his successors were euer heretikes for such and such opinions, if these men wil defend the same opinions, they must needs be condemned for heretikes also, vnles we wil vse plaine & palpable partialitie. Simon Magus sayed, that God was the autor of sinne, whom Cerdon and Marcion, Manicheus, Photinus, and Blastus folowed, & were for this doctrine, by the common voice of the Christian world, adiudged heretikes. And shal not the same sentence passe vpon our reformers, who say not only (as Simon Magus did) that God by a certaine consequence is the autor of sinne, in that he hath giuen man a nature necessarily inclining to sinne, but affirme also that he directly moueth to sinne, yea prouoketh vs, and eggeth vs forward? Shal Manicheus and the others aboue named be heretikes, vvho sayed only, that the euil God was autor of sinne (for they imagined tvvo Gods) & shal our reformers be counted good Christiãs, vvho say that the good and the only God is the cause and Promotor of al lies and wickednes? Certain old heretikes euen in the Apostles time, grounding them selues vpon S. Paules Epistle to the Romaines, which as S. Peter witnesseth, they did wrongly interpret, affirmed only fayth to be sufficient to saluation (which phantasie Simon Magus, and Eunomius also imbraced, and for this they were accursed for heretikes) and shal Luther and Caluin, and their adherentes go for sincere Christians, who teach the selfe same doctrin? Leo the third Emperour, Constantine the fifth, and Leo the fourth with their adherentes called *Iconomachi*, and *Iconoclastæ*, Were condemned as heretikes for denying honour to Images, and for breaking and defacing them; and how can our Gospellers shew their faces amongst Christians, who excede those Image-breakers by many degrees?

Vinc. Lirin. Aug her. 65. Simon Magus heresie. The agreement of the nevv and old heretikes. Bol. l. 2. to. 3. c. 3. Manicheus heresie. Li. de fide & operibus c. 14. 2. Pet. 3. Iren. l. 1. c. 20. Aug her. 54. The old Solifidians. Iut. in c. 2. Gal. Calu. in Antid. sect. 6. can. 11.

The old image breakers. Zonor. vita Leo 3. Paulus Diaconus. Old and nevv Sacramentar. Iren l 8 c.24. Ignat. ep. ad Smyrn. Tho. Vvald l. 2. de Sacram c. 1. B. Gvvit. l. 1. Damasc. l de heres. Ter. l de bap. Vvald to. 2. c. 69. Infra. Soc. l. 4. c. 24. Hier. Prom l. cont. pel. Hiere. l. cont. illos. S. Paul. l. 7. Visib. mon p. 371.

9. Vvith the Simonians, Menandrians, and others in S. Ignatius tyme, yea vvith Berengarians and Vvicleph istes, they deny that in the Eucharist, Christs body is really present: with the Messalians and Ciians, they deny that the Sacraments giue grace, with Iohn Vvicleph they deny that Baptisme, Confirmation, and Order imprint caracters in our soules: with the Pelagians they say that Baptisme is not necessity: and that without it children may be saued, by predestination, or the fayth of their parents: with the Nouatians they deny the Sacrament of Penance: with the Gnosticks, Manichies and Encratites, they say Matrimonie is no Sacrament, no more (sayeth Caluin) then tillage of the ground, yea spinning and carding: Vvith the Manichies they deny friewil: with Aerius the Sacrifice: with Heluidius and Iouinian, they make mariage equal with virginitie. They marie Priests, and despise Reliques with the same Vigilantius, & with Rhetorius they prayse al heresies, & renew them al: and shal they for one heresie be accursed heretikes, & these men who haue raked hel to rake them altogether, be esteemed of, as pure, sincere, and reformed Christians? Shal seueral heresies make them heretikes: and shal not al heresies almost assembled together, be sufficient to make these men heretikes? Truly vnles Apostasie excuse them from heresie (who haue denyed almost al pointes of religion, only Christ remaining to vvhose denyal notwithstanding, as the next booke shal proue, they haue made a great steppe) I can not see why the ancient heretikes, for seueral heresies should be counted heretikes, and these for so many which they haue raked together, go for good Christians: especially seing that any one heresie is sufficient to make an heretike, because euery one seuereth, and separareth from the Church, and her faith and doctrin.

Nothing but Apostolia cā excuse the reformers from heresie. The cōclusion.

10. Certes if these men be no heretikes, the old heretikes were none, if these be no heretikes, neuer as yet were any. If these haue not the marke of an heretike, Simon Magus, Marcion, Cerdon, Pelagius, Wiclif had none: if these be good Christians, al heretikes were so, or if they were noted with the caracter of an heretike, these are so marked, that they shal neuer be able to hide, or wipe away this marke, vntil they abiure heresie, and imbrace vvholly and intierly the Catholique faith vvhich they haue forsaken.

The fifth

The fifth Chapter handleth an other marke of an heretike, vvhich is vvant of succession.

VR aduersaries neither can, nor wil deny, but that our Sauiour Christ and his Apostles, once planted true religion, and established a true Church in the world, in which Pastors and Doctors were appointed, to minister Sacraments, to preach the word of God, and to gouerne and rule in the Church. The Actes of the Apostles witnes no lesse, which set before our eies the beginning and progrese of the primatiue Church, the beginning in Hierusalem, the progres amongst the Gentils. For when Christ dyed the principal fundation and corner stone vvas layed, when the Apostles were confirmed the building went on, and when they by preaching and miracles augmented the number of the first Christianes, then was the building of this Church perfited, and brought to that splendour & perfection, that the Scribes and Pharisies emulated, and enuied the glorie therof, and sought the meanes to ruine this worke of God, but in vaine. For as Gamaliel told them, the work of God no prower can dissolue. Against this Church the diuel raysed a tempest, which began vvith a storme of stones, amongst the Ievves. The Emperours and heretikes haue continued the like to this day. In this Church was called a Councel in Ierusalem, where S. Peter as the head prononnceth sentence, and S. Iames subscribeth and promulgateth.

Ephes. 4. *Act. Apost* *Religion vvas once planted.* *Act. 5.* *Act. 7. c.* *The first Concel.*

2. The first Pastors of this Church were the Apostles. S. Iames was Bishop of Ierusalem, S. Iohn of Ephesus, S. Marke of Alexandria, S. Peter first of Antioch, then of Rome, which were his particular Seates. For he was supreme Bishop also of al the Christian world. And in Antioch Euodius succeded to S. Peter, and after him Ignatius. In Rome after that he had exercised the function of a supreme Pastor, for the space of twentie & fiue yeares (departing notwithstanding some times as busines or persecution enforced him) before his death he appointed Clemens for his successor: but he refusing, Linus and Cletus S. Peters coadiutors, succeded him, and after them S. Clemens accepted of the charge. The other Apostles in other places left their

The Seate of the first Pastors. *Eus. l. 2. c. 15.* *Io. 21.* *Ep. ad Anti.* *Act. 15.* *Gal. 2.* *Epiph. her. 27* *Sand pa. 256.*

scholars to succeed them, yea and placed others in other places, where them selues could not reside: as S. Iohn appointed Policarp at Smyrna. To be briefe, Ecclesiastical histories, from the Apostles, deriue a Christian Church, and succession of Pastors vnto these dayes. So that a true Christian Church was once planted and established.

Tert. l. præs. c. 38.

A Church once planted. That is novv the true Church vvhich is likest the first.

3. Which if it be true, then vndoubtedly, that is now the true Church, they the true Christians, those the true Pastors, that the true faith, which from the first and primatiue Church by a continual succession can be deduced: for the Church is called Apostolical, not only because is was once planted by the Apostles, but also because it is descended from them by succession. And they must be heretikes and bastard Chistians, degenerating from their first institution, who can not shevv this succession, and their Church can not be Apostolical, but apostatical.

Vvhy the Church is called Apostol.

l. præs. c. 20. They are heretikes that can shevv no succession.

4. This argument handleth Tertulian in his booke of Prescriptions, where he sheweth how al particular Churches were first planted by the Apostles, and hovv other Churches from them receiued faith and religion, and (sayeth he) if now you wil know what religion is the true Christiane religion, you must conferre it with some former Church, from vvhich it is descended: because (sayth he) *omne genus ad suam originem censeatur necesse est:* It is necessary that euery kind be valued and esteemed according vnto his source and origine. If you vvil iudge of water, marke the fountain, if you vvil know a mans gentrie, looke how he descendeth from the first of his familie, if you wil informe your selfe of any mans title vnto a lordship, you must consider how the first lord entered into possession, and how he is descended from him. And so if we wil discerne the Christian from the heretike, we must haue an eye vnto the roote and stock, from which he descendeth, for so we shal know whether he be legitimate or baseborne. For if he fetch his pedegree from any other then the Apostles, or those vvhich by succession descended from them, then is he a bastard Christian, and caryeth the marke of an heretike.

Hovv to knovv the true Church. Hovv to knovv an heretike.

An heretike is a bastard

The Romain Church setcheth hir pedegree frõ the Apostlts.

5. The Romaine and Catholique Church which now is, can deriue her Pastors, Religion, & Gouernement, euen from the Apostles, and those whom they appointed Bishops and successors. For if you runne ouer Ecclesiastical histories, you shal find our Church and the practise of our religion to haue florished from the beginning vnto these dayes For they treat almost of nothing else, but of the progresse of our Church, of the persecution vvherevvith it vvas assayled, of the

heretikes

heretikes by vvhom it was molested, of our Bishops, Prelates, Martyrs Virgins Doctors, of our General and Prouincial Councelles, and of the miracles vvhich were vvrought in confirmation of our fayth. In so much that if our matters were not, the historiographers should haue had no subiect to vvorke or write on. Ireneus reckeneth the Popes of Rome from S. Peter vnto Eleutherius, Eusebius vnto Siluester. Optatus vnto Siricius. S Austin vnto Anastasius: others goe farther, and Doctor Sanders our countriman bringeth the succession of our Popes, Bishops, Ceremonies, and Religion vnto Pius Quintus tyme, Genebrard hath doone the like vnto Gregories the thirtenth his tyme, and Cardinal Baronius in nine tomes already set forth, hath most exactly set downe the practise of our religion vnto Ludouicus Pius of France, whose life and death do argue his religion, and in his 10 tome he bringeth it on a 1000 yeares, to Siluester the second, and Otto the Emperour. And if our Church agree with the primatiue Church, if our fayth vary not from the ancient fayth, if our Pastors be descended from the Apostles, and their scholars as al histories and monuments do beare witnesse, then must our Church nedes be the true Church, because it agreeth with the original, and is conformable to the primatiue Church, vvhich as it vvas nerest vnto Christ and his disciples, and vvas persecuted and honoured for the true Church, so was it the true Church, vnlesse we wil say that Christ and his Apostles neuer planted a true Church.

l 2. cont Donatist. ep. 165. Sand l. de visib. mon. Gen. in Chronol. Baron in Annal.

The Romain Church the true Church.

6. This succession vvas counted alwayes a marke of the true Church, which in our Creede vve professe, vve beleue the Apostolical Church, to wit, that which is by succession deriued from the Apostles and planted by them, and the want of it was alwayes esteemed a note to know an heretike by. Wherfore Ireneus sayth that by succession vve confound al heretikes: S. Austin sayth, that it is the thing, vvhich holdeth him in the Catholique Church, because (sayth he) that Church in vvhich is this succession, is the rock against vvhich the gates of hel can not preuail. If therfore our new Christianes vvil discharge them selues of this marke of an heretike, vvhich is vvant of succession, let them shew vs (as Tertulian demanded of the heretikes of his tyme) the catalogue of their Bishops, and the origen of their Church, that if in the same vve find them to be descended from the Apostles, we may acknowledge them as true Christian, if we find that they are not descended from so noble a race, we may shut them out of the Church for heretikes.

Succession a marke of the true Church. Symb. Nic. Supra. Lib. cont. ep. fund c. 4. l. de vtilit. cred. c. 17. ps. cont. part. Donat. l. præsc. c. 32.

Nevv heretikes may some points do renevv old heresies.

7. But I am sure they can shew no succession, because they are the first them selues, and can as soone name their predecessors, as they can find out Lutherancs before Luther, and Caluinistes before Caluin. I wil not deny but that they can deriue some pointes of their doctrin from Simon Magus, and other ancient heretikes: but this succession prouath them also to be heretikes, as is before demonstrated, but a succession from that Church, vvhich was commonly counted Christian, they can not shew: yea they can not shew vs a succession of their doctrin from any ancient heretikes, but are them selues the first of their familie, succeeding to none, but sent and ordayned by them selues, borne prodigiously of them selues, Children without fathers, and scholars without masters. For although they borow their heresies of other heretikes, yet they iumpe vvith no heretikes in al points, but either adde or detract, and so succeed in al points to none.

See the first booke & first chap.

But they agree novv fullye vvith any old heretikes & so are successors to none.

8. Wherfore though sometymes they vaunte that they succede the Apostles, and the primatiue Church, yet some tymes the truth breaketh from them against their wils, as it doth from the diuel, when by coniuration he is compelled to tel the truth, and then they confesse them selues to be the first of their familie: but this confession condemneth them. Oecolampadius they cal the first bishop of Basil, and Caluin the first of Geneua, Latimer the first Apostle of Ingland, and Knoxe of Scotland. And Martin Luther the most anciét of them al is not afrayed to say, that he was the first man that manifested the Gospel, and the truth vnto the world. *Audemus dicere* (sayth he) *à nobis primò diuulgatum esse Christum: Vve dare say that Christ vvas first by vs made knovven vnto the vvorld.*

Oecolampadius called the Apostles of Basil. Caluin Geneua, Latimer of Ingläd Knoxe of Scotband.

In præfat. disp. Lypsia.

9. I let passe that he hath pigges in his belly, & therfore he speaketh in the plural number, but he hath no braynes in his head, nor bloud in his face to blush withal, and therfore he dareth be bold to say, that he is the first man that promulgated the christian law. Art thou the first, thou vaunting compagnion? modestie vvould yeeld at least to the Apostles. So he wil peraduenture, but at least (sayth he) I am the first after them. O monstrous and Luciferian pride, and now not Luther but Lucifer. Art thou the first after the Apostles? Where then vvas the Church al this while? Where were other Pastors and Doctors of of the same? Vvhere were the Austines, Ambroses, Gregories, Hieromes? Vvas there none al this vvhile to haue bene imployed, but God must needs expect til an Apostata fryar leaped out of a Cloister, and maryed with a Nonne, notwithstanding that both had promised chastitie

Luther proudly terme him the first planter of Religiö after Christ.

Luther an other Lucifer.

chastitie before God and man by a solemne vow.

10. But they haue a shift or two by which they think to auoid this argument of succession. The first is this: our doctrin (say they) is Apostolical and vve are the Apostles successors, because vve preach conformable to that doctrin vvhich they haue left in the Gospels and Epistles by them written. *The reformers first ansvver.* But this shift wil not serue, because this is to make bare Scripture Iudge of their doctrin, as al heretikes haue done which notwithstanding (as is in the first booke demonstrated) is no certain rule to square fayth and religion by. *The refutatiō* Wherfore they haue yet an other answer in store, vvhich is this: They grant that the Apostles once planted a true Church, true religion, and established true Pastors: but afterward this Church fayled and degenerated from that it was, into the Synagogue of the diuel, which they cal the Papistical Church, and possessed the world for many hundred yeares, til at length Luther the man of God, builded this Church agayne, renewed the religion, and appointed new Pastors: so (say they) we succede to that Church vvhich the Apostles founded, not by a continual succession, but by an interruption of many hundred yeares. *The second as litle vvorth.* But aske them vvhat yeare of our Lord, vnder vvhat Emperour or Pope, vpon vvhat occasion, this Church fayled, and then they can not giue you a resolute answer. *The refutatiō.*

11. Luther in the Assembly at wormes publikely auouched, that the Church fel in tyme of the Councel of Cōstance, in which Vvicleph vvas condemned. The same Martin, not alwayes myndful of euery word vvhich he hath spoken, in his book intitled against Papacie, sayth, that this Church fayled a thousand yeares after Christ, and his reason is, because the Apocalips sayth, that Satan for a thousand yeares shal be tyed, and so for six hundred yeares he hath bene loose. *Luthers inconstancie about the famed falle of the Church.* *Tom. 7. l cont. Papatum.* In an other place he sayth that S. Gregorie vvas the last good Pope, and that since that tyme the Church and Pastors are degenerated. *l. de Capt. Babyl.* Yea the same man perceiuing how litle agreement is betwixt his religion and that vvhich vvas practised euen in the first age, and tyme of the Apostles, and how vnlike his ministers are to those ancient Pristes and Fathers: he sayth, that the Apostles themselues erred in their Councel holden at Hierusalem, or else (sayth he) we sinne now in eating bloud-pudings which they forbad: not knowing (absurde companion as he was) or not acknowledging, that the precept vvas but for a time to content the Iewes. *Act. 15.* *Luther condemneth the Coūcel of the Apostles.* As for the Councel of Nice vvhich was some 300. yeares after Christ, he auoucheth that the Canons and Articles

of the same

He disalowe the Councel of Nice. Supra. of the same are but *Straw and Stuble.* : which epithetons he giueth also vnto S. Iames his Epistle. Caluin sayth that Bonifacius the Pope, was the first that was made suprem head of the Church, by Phocas the Emperour, and so he thinketh that then the Church first degenerated: yet the same man in his preface to the King of France, sayth that the Church fel not til the tyme of the Councel of Basil. *Also S. Iames Epistle. Caluins inconstancie about the same* Melancthon sayth that Pope Zozimus was the first Anti-christ, and that since, there was neuer any true Bishop of Rome. Foxe our Martyr maker one while saith that the church fel vnder Pope Gregorie the seuenth, an other while vnder Innocentius the third, an other while vnder Bonifacius the eight as the Treatisse of thee three conuersions deduceth out of his lying martyrologe.

This disagreement argueth that the Church neuer fel. 12. But first this disagrement of the tyme of this fal, is a sufficient argument that the Church neuer fel: for if it had fallen (it hauing bene once so famous, so glorious, so conspicuous) the fal therof, with the time, occasion, and other circumstances could not haue bene concealed: and as soone may the sunes fal from heauen be knowen to the world, as the fal of the Church: which is sometimes called a citie on an hil, sometimes a tabernacle placed in the sunne. *Mat. 5. Psal. 18. Mat. 16. 1. Tim. 3.* Secōdly if the Church fel, then certes it was not *builded vpon a rocke but on the sands*: *then is it not a piller of truth* : then did Christ *pray that Peters fayth might not fayle*, that his Father would send *his Holy Spirit to remain with the Apostles for euer* (that is in their successors, for with them in this life he could not remain for euer) and was not heard. *An other argument that the Church fel not.* Then did Christ promise that he would *stay with them for euer*, but performed not what he promised. Then was Christ an vnfaythful Spouse, who betrothed him self to his Church, but seperated him selfe from her many hundred yeares. *Luc. 22. Mat. 28* And then did Daniel vnwisely compare Christes Church vnto a *Kingdom which should neuer be ruined.*

Ser. 2. in Psal. 107. 14. But as S. Austin wel noteth, it is the propertie of them who are not of the Church to say: the Church is not. *They which are not of the Church say it failed.* *Sed illa Ecclesia* (sayth he in the person of the Donatists) *quæ fuit omnium gentium iam non est, periit. Hoc dicunt qui in illa non sunt. O impudentem vocem, illa non est, quia tu in illa non es? vide ne tu ideo non sis, nam illa erit, etiam si tu non sis: But that Church which consisted of al nations now is not, it is perished. So they say who are not in it. O impudent voice, Is not that extant because thou art not in it? Looke lest thou therfore be not, for the Church wil be, although thou be not.* Wherfore S. Bernard who was one of this Church, doubted not but that she should perseuer to the end: *Ser. 9. in Cant.* *Ita est, & tunc, & deinceps, non deficiet genus Christianum, nec num, nec fides de terra, nec charitas de Ecclesia, venerunt flumina, flauerunt venti & impegerunt in eam & non cecidit, eo quòd fundata erat supra petram, petra autem erat Christus: So it is, both then, & afterward, the Christian race shal not fayle, neither fayth from the world, nor charitie from the Church: fluddes haue come windes haue blowen and beaten vpon her, but the Church fel not, because it was founded vpon a rock, and the rock was Christ.* *See page. 74.*

15. The words of Christ must be verified (sayth S. Chrisostome) because heauen and earth shal fayle before Christs words: and what are those words saith he, euen those and no other: *Thou art Peter and vpon this rock wil I build my Church.* This Church sayeth he was impugned, but could not be ouercome, dartes were shotte against it, but could not pearse, engines of warre were vsed to ouerthrow it, but this tower could not be beaten downe: Consider (sayth he) the tyrants, beasts, swords, deaths, dartes, which the diuel prepared against this Church but al in vayne, for the diuel hath emptied his quiuer, and shot al his arrowes, but the Church hath no hurt. The persecutors are now dead rotten, and forgotten, but the Church florisheth. Where is now Claudius, where is Augustus, where are Nero and Tiberius: these are now naked names, for them selues are not extant And thinkest thou, o diuel (sayth he) that thou canst ouerthrow the Church, that art not able to encounter with a young Agnes, a tender Christian mayd, who hath proued stronger then al thy force, and instruments of torments. And if (sayth he) thou couldest not ouercome the Church, when she was young, and had the Iewes and Gentils, Kinges and Emperours against her: thinkest thou now to giue her the foyle or falle? And truly he that sayth that the Church hath fayled, must consequently say with the Atheists, that it was the worke of men not of God, deuised by men to keepe fooles in awe, for if the Church was established by God, then by Gamaliel his rule, it could not by any force of man, be dissolued.

Hom. 1. de Pœnit. *Mat. 16.* *S. Chrisostoms opinion of the stabilitie of the Church.* *Ser. post exilium.* *Act. 5.*

16. Thirdly it is manifest by al histories, general Councels, bookes, of the ancient Fathers extant, and al ancient monumentes, that their Church is nothing at al like the Church, in the first 600, or 300. yeares: and so neither by a continual, nor by a broken succession can they be sayd to succeed the Apostles, and first Christians, as appeareth by the doctrine of the Fathers, and practise of the Church sett downe by Genebrard, & Baronius, and by the histories of Eusebius and others. And this they them selues some tymes confesse. For Luther auoucheth that concerning friewil, the ancient Fathers were al deceyued. And in an other place, he insulteth ouer the Austines, Ciprianes, & al the Fathers,

l. de seruo arb. *l. cont. Regem Angl.*

thers, whose authoritie King Henry the eight had alleaged, for the Sacrifice of the Masse. Caluin as I haue related in my first booke, & fourth chapter, sayeth al the Fathers erred in the matter of penance & satisfaction: which also the Magdeburgians auouch of the Fathers of the fourth age. Yea Caluin also confesseth, that for a thousand and three hundred yeares, al the anciēt Fathers allowed of prayer for the dead: yea he sayth, that al the ancient Fathers except S. Austin, erred a bout friewil. Luther goeth higher: he sayth, that the first Councel of the Apostles erred, as also the Councel of Nice. The same Luther in his shortest Annotations vpon the sixtenth chap. of S. Matthew sayth, that no man must be beleued against Christ, although it were Peter him selfe: where he supposeth that an Apostle may erre. Caluin saith that the name) Apostle) requireth of the Apostles, that they babble not aboue their commandement: and so he supposeth that Apostles may teach errors. Melanthon saith, that from the beginning the ancient writers of the Church, obscured the doctrin of the iustice of fayth. The Magdeburgians complaine of S. Sohn the Euangelist, for allowing of Penance, and voluntarie pouertie: of S. Thomas for hauing the crowne of a Deacon, and for commanding a fast of seuen dayes, and allowing the signe of the Crosse. of S. Andrew also, for præscribing fast: of S. Matthew for allowing of the vowe of Chastitie, and for instituting a colledge of Nunnes, and saying of Masse. They reiect also. S. Iames and S. Iudas Epistles. And Musculus sayth, that whosoeuer was author of S. Iames his Epistle, although he were the brother of Christ, & a piller amongst the Apostles, yet his doctrine can not be any præiudice to the doctrin of onlie sayth. So that either the Church was neuer planted, neuer pure, not in the Apostles tyme, or else the Church of the Reformers, is not Apostolical, because it hath no likenes with the Fathers, and Pastors of the first age, and so neither to them can they succeed, because al the Fathers of the Church, that can be named, yea the Apostles them selues, in their practise and gouernment, euen from the beginning, are contrarie to them in many pointes, and that by their owne confession. This Argument so presseth them, that they dare not stand to this answer, yet they wil play smal play rather then stand out.

l. 1. c. 4. cent. 4. *l. 3. Inst. c. 5.* *l. 2. c. 2. s. 4.* *l. de concilijs.* *Actorum 15.* *l. 4. Inst. c 8.* *Mel. in 1. Cor 3.* *Cent. 1. l. 2. c. 10.* *c. 4. Col. 54.*

17. Luther therfore in his book of notes of the Church, granteth that the Church neuer quite decayed, but only for the most part, and so (sayth he) it decayed euen in the Apostles tyme, for as Christ (sayth he) from the beginning had his Church, so the diuel had his chappel, which

l. de notis Ecclesiæ. *An other answer of the aduersarie.*

which was bigger then the Church, & so there hath been euer a succession of both, but the chappel as it was euer bigger so was it most famous. And this chappel (sayth he) is the Church of the Papists, which is so famous in Ecclesiastical histories.

18. But this shift is pore and ridiculous. For if the Church of the Papists generated from the beginning as Simon Magus did, why were not we called by particular names as al heretikes are? Why was not our autor named? Why is not the tyme & occasion registred? If our Church was euer the greater then was theirs the chappel, for it is against the nature of a chappel to be greater then the Church. If our Church was the greater and most famous, then was ours that societie, which was commonly called the Christian Church, then was our societie that which condemned heresies and called Councels, which was persecuted by Tyrants (and consequently was not the diuels chappel, for he persecuteth not his owne) and fauoured by Constantin and other Christian Emperours, Kings and Princes: for which Monasteries were erected, Churches builded, in which al the ancient Doctors ministred Sacramentes, preached, teached, ruled and gouerned. And where was then Luthers litle flock? What Historiographer wrote the progres of it? What Emperours persecuted it? Vvhat heretikes rayled against it? Vvhat Churches were builded for it? What ministers ruled it? And what was the maner of gouerment in it? If there were no such societie, and no other counted Christian but ours, then either ours was the true Church or else the Church quite fayled, and so they must returne to their former ansvver, wich yet wil not serue their turne, as is already proued.

A poore ansvver.

If the Romain Church changed vvhy chaged it not the name?

Vvhere vvas Luthers Church before Luther?

19. Wherfore if al other fayle, they haue yet an other shift, and that is this. Vve grant, say they, that the Church neuer decayed, but stil stood immoueable vpon the rock, vpon vvhich Christ founded it: but soone after the Apostles time, or peraduenture before they were al dead, this Church became inuisible, and appeared no more openly, but vvas preserued secretly in obscure cornes, til at the length Luther (whom God and his Church al that vvhile expected) brought it to light againe. And al this vvhile (because Ecclesiastical histories conuince them) they confesse that there was a Church commonly called Christian, in vvhich Popes ruled, and Kings and Princes were baptized, but that (say they) vvas not the Church of Christ, but the conuenticle of Papists, and chappel of the diuel, and thus these euil doers fly the light.

A third ansvver of the aduersarie, that the Church vvas inuisible til Luthers tyme.

Mat. 16.

Io. p. 3.

The ansvver serueth them for. 2. purposes.

20. This shift serueth them for two purposes. For first thus they wil frie them selues from al Iudgement-seats. For if you conuent them before Ecclesiastical Iudges, or the whole Church, they wil say that they are not lawful Iudges, and that it is not the true Church, vvhich summoneth them to appeare, and therfore they are not bound to stand to their sentence, who haue al authoritie on their owne side. And if you aske them from whom they had authoritie, they wil say, that they had their predecessors to whom they suceed, and their Church whose fayth they preach, and that from them they haue authoritie, if you then bid them shew some historie or ancient monument of their Church, they wil answer, that it was inuisible and so wil say what they list, and by no Church past or present, shal you be able to controle them, for they haue a Gyges ring to go inuisible by. Secondly if the Church was inuisible, you can not vrge them to shew any continual succession of it from the Apostles. For they wil say, that their Church succeeded the Apostles, and is the same vvhich they planted, but after the Apostles tyme, was neuer senne til Luther pulled away the bushel, vvhich couered this light.

First to auoid al iudgement seats.

Heretikes haue a Gyges ring

Secondly to auoid the argument of succession.

Hovv their Church vvas inuisible.

21. And truly I wil easily grant that their Church before Luther was inuisible. For that vvhich vvas not, could not be senne: but that the true Church was at any tyme inuisible, is altogegether improbable. For vvhen hapned this darkenes I pray you? The Church was once *a citie vpon an hil*, and *a tabernacle placed in the sunne*, how then could it on a sodain come to be inuisible, and no man in the world to note it? Historiographers write of earth-quakes and darknesses: and al the world noted the darknesse which hapned at Christes death: and was there no man to note this darknes vvhich couered the whole face of the earth, and hapned after so conspicuous a light? Aristotle sayth that the same sense iudgeth of the obiect, and priuation: as for example, the eye which beholdeth colours and light, perceiueth also, or at least giueth occasion to the inward sense, called *sensus communis*, to perceiue darkenesse, vvhen the light is gone: vvhy then could not they vvhich had senne the Church florish and shine conspicuously, perceiue also vvhen first she lost her light. And if they perceiued it, how chanceth it, that none euer wrote of so strange an accident. But vvhat should I aske so many questions, where I am sure to find no reasonable answeres? I wil now with one argument make al this darknes of this erronious doctrin, geue place to the light of the truth, to wit, that the true Church can not be inuisible.

Mat. 5.
Psal. 18.
If so conspicuous a Church became inuisible the tyme of that darkenes must needs haue been noted.

22. For

22. For Christ biddeth vs, vvhen our brother wil not harken vnto our admonitions, to complayn of him to the Church. Suppose then that some heretike should preach false doctrin, and being admonished to correct his error, vvould yet remaine obstinate: there is no other remedie but to complayn of him to the Church. And how shal this complaint be made, if the Church can not be found out, as it can not, if it be inuisible? Suppose again some Christian or infidel should beginne to doubt of his fayth, and would fayne be instructed, no doubt his only remedie is, to repayre vnto the Church for a resolution, where only truth is taught, saluation is found; but if the Church be inuisible or decayed, how shal he haue accesse to this Church, vvhich either is not or at least (as they say) is inuisible? Truly if the Church either decayed or was inuisible, then was the world without meanes of saluation for many hundred yeares.

Mat. 18. *The true Church can not be inuisible.* *The first supposition.* *The second.*

23. But let me demand of them how their Church vvas inuisible, vvhich consisteth of men, and is gouerned by men, and mainteined by visible gouerment, visible Sacraments and audible preaching? They liued not alwayes in holes, some tymes they came abrode, and comming abrode and carying the name of Christians, they were by Papists alwayes enforced to frequent Masse and Sacramentes, and to professe their religion, else had they bene excommunicated, and deliuered to secular power: whence it must needs folow, that either Luthers & Caluines Church was neuer before them selues beganne to preach, or that their Church dissembled against cōscience for fifteen hundred yeares.

Hovv vvas their Church inuisible? *If their Church vvas inuisible they vvere dissemblers.*

24 But what do I fight against shadowes, & that which neuer was or neuer was senne? Let me conclude now that which I intended The ghospellers can not deny but that the true Church was once planted, and that therfore, that is now the true Church, which can by succession be deriued from it (for to say that the Church fayled, or was inuisible, is but a vayne imagination) & seeing that Catholiques can by al Histories and monuments shew, that their Church is descended from that, which was in the tyme of the Apostles, theirs is the Church and they are the true Christians; and seing that the reformers can not thus deriue their Church from the Apostles (because before Luthers preaching it was neuer senne heard nor felt) it foloweth that their Church is not Apostolical, but rather apostatical and heretical, and they no true Christians but Heretiks.

The cōclusion. *Successiō proueth the Rom. Church.* *Vvant of successiō argueth our aduersaries to be heretikes.*

The sixt chapter handleth the sixt marke of an hereuike, vvhich is dissension in doctrin; and proueth that peace is a marke of the true Church, and that the dissensious Gospellers, are heretikes if euer any vvere.

ICERO that famous Orator speaking of peace, geueth it this worthy commandation: *Pacis nomen dulce est, res vero ipsa, cum iocunda tum salutaris: The name of peace is svveet, but the thing it selfe is both pleasant and soueraine.* To which opinion of his al men wil easily subcribe, if they enter into consideration of the nature of peace. For what is more pleasant then that which al things desire? & what more healthful and souueraine, then that which preserueth al things?

Peace is so pleasant that al thinges desire it. 2. So pleasant is peace that euen sensles creatures, seme wholly to desire it. *The heauens.* The heauens moue al from the East to the west, caryed with the sway of the first heauen, called *primum mobile*, and yet by their proper motions, at the same tyme they moue also from the west to the East, and some swiftly some slowly, yet vvith such vniformitie and agrement, as though they desired nothing more then peace, and feared nothing more then iarring and disagreeing in their motions. *The Elemētes desire peace.* The Elementes, vvhen they are out of their natural place, do moue speedily, and make great hast to get to their home, because there only they find peace and rest, to which their nature inclineth. *Brute beastes also.* Brute beasts also of one kind, commonly kepe together, and folow one head, as it were with common consent, because one easilier maketh peaceable agreement then many. *Bees flockes & heards.* Bees folow one King (sayeth S. Cyprian) and obey the humming of one master-bee. In al flocks of shepe, there is one Belwether, and in euery heard one is the ring leader, yea, sayth S. Hierome: Cranes folow on in a long order, vvhich they do for loue of peace: *Cranes.* for in folowing diuers heades, they would be more diuided, and lesse vnited. *l 19. Ciu. c. 12.* Yea sayth S. Austin, no Tigre is so cruel, vvhich doth not licke *Tigres.* and like her youngones. No Kite but loueth her brood and seeketh to *The kite also.* conserue her familie in peace: much more doth man, who is indewed with reason, couet and desire peace, seme he otherwise barbarous and deuoid of humanitie.

3. The

3. The Passionate man who fighteth continually against reason to satisfie his passions, seeketh to geue them their desire vvithout contradiction of reason, and consequently coueteth peace: but this is an inordinate peace. The reasonable and vertuous man, vvho seeketh to subdew his passions, & to make them yeeld to reason without repugnance, seeketh an attonement betwixt passion and reason: and this is an orderly peace. The rebellious and mutinous subiectes, who rise in armes against their lavvful Prince, are desirous to enioy their owne wil and to possesse vvhat they desire without resistance, & consequently intẽd a peace: but this is an vniust peace. And although by rebellion they breake common peace, yet that is not because they hate peace, but because they enioy not that peace vvhich they desire. The iust Prince vvho maketh vvarre against iniust vsurpers, euen then vvhen he biddeth warre, aymeth at peace, and intendeth not warre as vvarre, but as a meane to come to peace: and this is a iust peace. Cacus, that barbarous felow, who liued in caues as beastes do, and fed him selfe of the spoyles of others, vvas desirous to enioy his owne desires without molestation, and so desired peace, but a brutish peace. And as peace is most pleasant and therfore desired of al, so is it most soueraine, and therfore preserueth al.

The passionate may desire peace, but inordinate. The reasonable man desireth an orderly peace. Rebelles desire an iniust peace. Aug supra. The iust Prince in vvarre aimeth at peace. Aug. ibidem Cacus desired a brutish peace

4. Peace betwixt the humours and elementarie qualities in mans body, is health; peace betwixt the two repugnãt partes in mans soule, reason and sensualitie, is vertue: peace betwixt God and man is Charitie: betwixt man and man, is frendship: peace and consorte in voices or instruments, is musick: peace and agreement in colours is beautie: peace in the heauens motions, and in the Elemental qualities, is the conseruation of al. Peace is the maintenance of Families, the preseruation of Cities, the establisment of Colleges, the strength of Common Welthes, the force of Kingdomes, & the felicitie of al Societies. Peace vpholdeth heauen, & without it hel is confused, because *euery Kingdom, diuided in it selfe, shal be made desolote*. Peace and vnitie (sayth the Philosopher) maketh natural causes to passe them selues in force and efficacie, because force vnited is stronger then it selfe diuided. You may breake a thousand arrowes one being taken from an other, but in a bundel or sheafe not so. Diuide the greatest riuer which is, and a childe wil passe it, but when the water is vnited, you must haue a shippe or boate to sayle ouer. Lay a coale in one corner of the house, and an other in an other, and you may stand in the middest, and blowe your fingers for colde, but vnite them together, & they wil warme the vvhole

Peace preserueth al things. Frõ peace proceedeth health vertue charitie frendship musicke bevvtie. Conseruation. Peace the maintenance of al Societes. Mat. 12. Marc. 3. Peace addeth force and strength to al things. Examples.

whole house. Oxen diuided, can not draw that weight, vvhich they can vnited. The greatest armie that is, if it be diuided, is soone defeated, but vvhen the forces are vnited, it is inuincible.

5. Moreouer as peace preserueth al thinges, and giueth strength and force to al: so contrariv vise dissension is the bane of al. Dissension or distemperature of humours in mans body, is sicknes: disagreement of reason and sensualitie in the soule, is vice: iarring of voices or instruments, is vngrateful discord: in colours it is deformitie, in porportions, mis shape. Dissension is the vndoing of Families, the dissolution of Colleges, the vveakning of Cities, the ouerthrovv of Armies, the ruine of Kingdomes, & the bane of al Societies. Vvhat Kingdom vvas more likely to haue stood then that of the Angels? Dissension which Lucifer sowed, had almost quite ruined it. What place better fensed, more fertile, and frutful then Paradise? yet dissension betwixt God & man, yea betwixt man and him selfe (for when man disagreed from God, his flesh beganne to resist his spirit, and al creatures before obedient to him, began to rise in armes against, him) banisshed thence the happy inhabitants, and with them al fœlicitie. Who more nere then Cain and Abel? dissension was the death of the one, and the reprobation of the other. Vvho more likely to haue liued louingly together then Abraham and Lot, Ioseph and his brethem? dissension seuered and separated them. Vvhat Kingdomes more strong and potent then those of the Medes, Persians, Chaldies, and Romaines? Read histories and you shal see, that dissenfion vvas the chiefest cause of their ruines. If then the Maxime of the philosopher be true, that one contrarie setteth forth an other, by the destroying nature of dissension, you may easily perceiue how souerain a preseruatiue peace is, & how iust cause, al creaturs haue, so vehemently to desire it.

It had almost ruined the Kingdome of the Angels.

It ruined the happy state of Paradise.

It vvas the death of Abel

It separated Abrahá and Lot, Ioseph & his brethern.

It ruined the Empires of the vvorlde.

6. This Iewel Christ bequeathed to his deare spouse the Church, when soone after his Resurrection, standing in the midst of the Apostles, he sayed to them: *Pax vobis: peace be vvith you.* Of this peace in an other place he maketh mention, where he sayth: *Pacem relinquo vobis, pacem meam do vobis: I leaue peace vnto you, I geue my peace vnto you.* Vvhere, for a legacie he bestoweth on his Church, not Gold and siluer, nor Kingdomes nor possessions (though he permitteth Kings to bestovv these things also vpon her) but that which is more vvorth then al the Diademes, and Scepters in the vvorld, to wit peace, without which, no societie can endure. This peace the Prophet Esaie long since foresaw and fortold, when he sayed: *That the vvolfe and lamb shal dvvel together, and the*

Christ bequeathed his peace to his Church.

Io. 20.

Io. 14.

Isa. 2. 11. 65.

and the Lion, Beare, and Calfe, liue peacebly one vvith an other, and that a litle boy shal driue them to the field. For his meaning is, that in the Church shal be such agreement, at least in matters of Religion; that they who before their conuersion were persecuting Vvolues and Beares, shal liue peacebly with the harmeles lambes and Christians, and that a litle boy, Christ Iesus, the autor of al this peace, shal driue them to field, that is, shal rule & gouerne them. The same Prophet by an other Metaphore describing the same peace saith: *In those dayes the infant from his mothers pappes, shal delight and disport him self, ouer the Aspes hole, vvithout receiuing harme:* That is, such peace shal be in the Church, that the children of Christes Church, shal liue quietly with those, who before they receiued Christian fayth, by heresies, infidelitie, or poysoning maners, like serpents infected others. For as in the Arke of Noe, those beasts which were by nature sauage, so long as they were in the Arke, forgot al crueltie, and liued with the rest most quietly: so how soeuer men before their incorporation and admission into the Church of Christ, were Barbarous in maners, and mutinous in opinions, yet when they are once made mẽbers of the peaceble Kingdom of Christs Church, they lay aside al sectes and factions, and liue quietly together, at least in matters of fayth and religion. Vvherby it plainly appeareth, that in the Church of Christ is peace and vnitie in religion. Which the Apostle also insinuateth saying: *Being careful to kepe vnitie of fayth, in the band of peace, as you are called in one hope of your vocation, one bodie and one spirit, one fayth, one Baptisme, one God and Father of al.* For as there is one God, one Heauen, one Baptisme: so is there but one faith, and that they are the true Christianes, which conspire in the same.

Ibidem. *Gen. 7.* *A similitude* *Ephes. 4.* *One faith only.*

7. And the reason herof is, because the truth is one, neuer disagreeing from it selfe: lyes are many, mutable and contrarie: and therfore seing that the Church is the *piller of truth*, it must needs folovv that where the Church is, there is vnitie, because the truth in which the members of the Church agree, is but one. I wil not deny, but that the Church consisteth of diuers nations, but yet they are so linked in one faith, that in Christ Iesu there is no distinction, betwixt the Barbarous and Grecian, not betwen Iew and Gentile: and although these diuers nations speake diuers languages, yet as Ireneus noteth, these diuers tongues professe one fayth. I grant also that in the Church there are diuers functions & dignities: for there are Popes, Patriarchs, Primates, Archbishops, Bishops, and so forth: and from them the state of the laitie is distinct, and subiect to them: but these diuers orders

The reason is because truth is one. *1. Tim. 3.* *Diuers natures in the Church, but one fayth.* *Rom 10.* *Diuers languages but one professiõ.* *l.1. cont. her. c. 3.*

Diuers functions but one Hierarchie. ders make one Hierarchie. I confesse like wise, that in the Church there are diuers states and orders of religious, as of Augustins, Benedictins, Benardins, Dominicanes, Franciscanes, Iesuits, yet these diuers members make one body, al linked vnder one head Christ Iesus, by one fayth and religion.

Diuers orders & mēbers yet one Church, one bodye.

The vnitie of the Church militant strāger then that of the Triumphant. 8. This vnitie, peace, and agreement in one fayth and religion; vvhich is to be senne in the Church militant in earth, seemeth more admirable then that of the Church triumphant in heauen. And the reason is, because the inhabitans of that happy Kingdome, behold God face to face, and see most euidently that vvhich vve beleeue only, and see not at al; and so their agreement in vnderstanding is not so strange, because the euidence of the verities vvhich they see, inclineth them to one assent. *The reason. In euident thinges al men agree.* For as the Philosopher sayth, the vnderstanding of it selfe is prone to giue assent to veritie and truth, vvhen it is euidently proposed (vvhich is the cause why in things which are euident al men are of the same opinion) and therfore to this proposition: *The vvhole is greater then the halfe*, al men agree, but about the creation of the world, the immortalitie of the soule, the felicitie of man, the substance of the heauens, and such like things, which are not so euident, *In hard thinges they disagree.* there haue bene great disputes and contentions, whence hath risen that diuersitie also of the sectes of Platonists, Peripatetickes, Stoicks, Epicureans, and such like. Vvherfore seing that the happy inhabitants of heauen, do see euidently the Diuine nature, and al the Mysteries which we only beleue, I meruayle not that they al agree in one opinion, because the euidence of these things moueth them to one assent. *That Christiās so agree must needes be of God.* But that so many Christians, of so diuerse countries, and times, so diuersly affected, and disposed, should agree in one fayth and opinion, and thinke, and beleue the same of al the Mysteries of Christian Religion, which they see not, this seemeth most admirable, and so strange that I must needs say: *Exod. 8.* *digitus Dei hic*, *The finger of God is in this matter*, and he it is, that is the cause of this peace, vnitie, and agreement. *Stoius q. 2. prologo.* For seing that the euidence of our Mysteries causeth not this agreement, and and that it can not be the diuel who thus linketh their *The reason.* vnderstandings (because this Religion in al points is repugnant to him, and his designements) it must needs be God, who inspiring into these diuerse nations and natures one light of fayth, maketh them al *l. præsc. c. 28.* to conspire in one belief and opinion. And therfore sayth Tertullian: *Nullus inter multos euentus vnus est exitus, errare non possunt qui ita in vnum conspirant: There is not one end amongest many chances, they can not erre vvho thus*

agree

agree in one. Thus vve proue the translation of the Septuagint to be of God, because those diuers writers, being placed in diuers Celles, and forbidden to conferre, could neuer haue so agreed in the translation of the Bible out of Hebrew into Greeke, as if al their translations had bene copied out of one, had not God directed their vnderstandings, and inspired them alike.

Iustinus orat. paran ad gent.

The proofe of the Translatio of the Septuagint.

9. Sith then amongst the Catholiques only, this vnitie is to be found, they only are the true Church, to which Christ hath bequeathed this peace and vnitie, and they only are conformable to the primatiue Church planted by Christ and his Apostles, for then the Christian world was of one hart and mynd. And for as much as amongst the new Christians of this age, there is nothing but wrangling and dissension & that in principal matters of religion, their Church is the Synagogue of Satan, and they no members of Christs Church, but heretikes, apostates, & members cut of: for by this marke of dissension the ancient heretikes were euer knowen and discried to be heretikes.

Vnitie in faith only amongst Catholiques Vvho therfore are the true Church.

Act. 4.

VVrangling amongst heretikes.

10. Simon Magus the first famous Arch-heretike beganne a sect, but it remained not one for any time, but by and by degenerated into many, and from the Simonians proceeded the Menandrians, Saturnians, Basilidians, Carpocratians, and from them were descended the Gnosticks. From Cerinthus sprong the vnhappy branches of the Ebionits, Marcionits, Cerdonists and such like. The Arians were no sooner hached, but they vvere by & by diuided into Ætians, Eudoxians, Eunomians and diuers others. So variable they were, that Socrates reporteth that they changed their Crede and forme of belief no lesse then nine tymes. The Donatistes likewise were by and by parted into Rogatists, Maximinianists, and Circumcellions. The Nestorians were seuered into Tritheites, Theopaschites, Agnoetians, Seuerites, and such like: The Eutychians into Montophysites, Iacobites, Acephalites, and Theodosians. Vvherfore the ancient Fathers haue obserued that dissension is a marke inseparably fastened vnto heretikes. I lie (sayth Tertulian) if they vary not from their ovvne rules, vvhilest euery one at his pleasure altereth and modifeth (he sayth tuneth) those things vvhich he hath receiued, euen as the first autor framed them at his owne arbitrement, the increase declareth the nature of the beginning and origin? The same is lawful for Valentinus, and for the Marcionits, which was lawful for Marcion: to wit, to deuise new sects and opinions as their sect masters did before them. As Donate (sayth S. Austin) endeuored to diuide Christ that is the Church of

Vvho therfore are the Synagogue of the diuel.

Simon Magus and his Sectes.

Cerinthus & his Sectes.

Arius and his Sectes.

l. 2. c. 32.

The Sectes of the Donatistes and others.

l. præscr. c. 42.

Dissension a marke of an heretike.

l. de agone Christi. c. 4.

 Christ,

Christ, so him, his owne Scholars by dayly hacking and mangling diuided in many peeces.

11. Now that the new Christians of this our last age are in like maner diuided, and consequently of the same paste and kind, it is toto manifest. Luther was the first man who in this last age beat his witte to deuise new faythes & religions, and for a tyme he was folowed by many, but in tyme also, his folowers fel from him, who perceiuing that they had as good authoritie to preach new doctrin as he had (for they could say also that Christ sent them, and they could alleage Scripture for their opinions, if they might interpret it by their priuat spirit (as why may they not as wel as he?) they thought it more honourable to be folowed, then to folow, and to be Masters then scholars, and so leauing Luther in the lurch, they deuised also new doctrines different from his, & became sect masters as wel as he. Zuinglius therfore being wearie of Luthers seruice, whom he had courted so long, & perceiuing Luther would haue denyed the real presence (therby to haue preiudiced the Pope) but that the words of Christ (as he confessed) seemed to plaine, deuised a glosse for those words: *This is my body*, and said that Christ called the bread his body, not becuise it cōteineth his body really as Luther affirmed, but because it is a figure of his body. And as Zuinglius delt with Luther, so did others. For now the Lutheranes are diuided into seuere & moderate Lutherans, & some glorie in Illyricus Flacus, some adore Melancthon, so that now Luther is left of al his Scholars, and not any one remaineth who agreeth with him in al poincts. And as Zuinglius delt vvith Luther so did others vvith him, for from him are descended the Osiandrians, Semiosiandrianes, and Antiosiandrians. Yea out of Zuinglius sprong that vnhappy branch Caluin, who addeth to Zuinglius opinion, that although the Sacrament be but a figure of Christ, yet with it we receiue Christ verily and really, but by fayth: vvhich doctrin hovv it can stand vvith it self, vve shal herafter discourse. And novv these mens Scholars, are diuided into Lutheranes and duble Lutheranes, Zuinglianes, Oecolampadianes, Caluinists, Anabaptists, demi-Lutheranes, Trinitarians, Suenkfeldians, Protestants, Puritanes, Brownists, Martinists, brethren of the familie of loue, and of the damned crew, and I know not how many. And it is a world to see, with what animositie these brethrē write one against an other. Luther writeth seuerly against the Zuinglians, and Sacramentaries: and a litle before his death in steed of a benediction, which this father should haue bestowed vpon these his children, he curseth them

Luthers forsaken of his Schollars.

Mat. 26.

As Carolstadius and others.

chap. 5. Dissention of al the Gospellers.

l. in Zuingl.

Luthers Inuectiue, and malediction of his children.

them to hel: refusing al writing & communication with them, saying that in vayne they beleue the Trinitie, and Incarnation, vnles they beleue also the real presence. To whom the Tugurine Zuinglians, answered that Luther sought his owne honour, not the honour of Christ, that he was obstinate and insolent, and one who vseth to deliuer men vp to Satan, that wil not agree to his opinion. And yet our Sacramentaries in England say, that Luther vvas a man of God, and Caluin, sayth that he taketh Luther for an Apostle, by whose labour especially the truth was restored.

Sur an. 1545.

Apol. Eccl. Angliæ.

Luther no man of God.

12. It were a tedious thing to recount their dissentions, and it is a pitiful thing to behold in steed of one fayth (in vvhich al the world before Luthers preaching conspired) so many faythes and religions. Of such dissension Hilarius complained in these words: *It is dangerous and miserable that novv there are as many faythes as vvilles, and as many doctrines as maners, and as many causes of blasphemies as vices, and that vvheras according as ther is one God, one Lord, and one Baptisme, so one fayth also should be, vve fal from one faith, and vvhilest many faythes are fayned, no fayth remaineth.* And as he thus complayneth of the Arians dissensions, so may we of the dissensions of this age, of which also the very autours of these garboils them selues complaine most lamentably. Luther him selfe sayth, that there is such dissension in the interpretation of Scriptures, that if the world continew we must haue recourse again vnto the trial of Councels, else we shal neuer agree. Cithreus conplaineth that the Euangelical Doctors (he meaneth ministers) are at greater daggers drawing, then any quarelling souldiars. Heshusius confesseth that whither soeuer he turneth his eyes, nothing almost occurreth but dissensions, new increase of errors, and falling of great Doctors from the veritie. So that euen by their owne confessions there is nothing but wrangling and dissension in religion amongst them. And consequently their Church is not the Church of Christ, in which peace and vnitie florisheth: vvhich hath vpholden and shal stil vphold Christes Kingdom against the tyranies of persecutors, and might and slight of the diuel, and al his members: wheras the kingdom of heretikes must nedes fal of it selfe by ciuil discord and dissension.

l. cont. Const.

The Gospellers complain of their ovvn. Dissension

l. cont. Zuing.

Luther by force recurreth to Councels.

Deprauat. conf. Aug.

Ep. de Exorcismo.

13. Wherfore Epiphanius compareth them to the vipers of diuers Kindes, vvhich the Ægyptians vsed to conclude in one place together, without either meate with in or meanes to get out: for as they, vvhen they were almost famished, began with teeth to teare and deuour one an other, til al the rest being consumed, the last hauing nothing left to exercise

In Panario.

Heretikes like Vipers.

A similitude

exercise his teeth on, dyeth for hunger: so heretikes ruine one an other, and one sect deuoureth an other, til at length, the last dyeth of it self by her owne impietie. Others compare them to the Cadmeam brethren vvhich were no sooner borne, but they killed one an other: Others say that they are like Sampsons foxes, which are diuided in the heads, that is in faythes, but yet are linked in the tayles, conspiting al in this intention, to ruine the true Church, but in the meane tyme they ruine their owne, and beating them selues against the rocke of of Christes Church, they do but breake them selues as waues do. Tertullian compareth them vnto waspes, which as Varro witnesseth, are like vnto bees, and singe like bees, but gather neither hony nor vvaxe, and can only sting, and therfore are cast out of the hiue: but being cast out they make their combes by them selues. For so heretikes are baptised like true Christians, cary the name also of Christians, and sing also like them, euer hauing Christ in their mouthes, the Lord, and the Word, but they haue neither the hony of sweet doctrin, nor the waxe of good workes. only they can sting vvith their heresies and blasphemies, the right bees and Christians, and therfore by the chief Pastor, as it vvere the Master bee, they are cast out from the good bees companie, by the censure of excommunication, and being cast out they make their combes, that is sects apart, which they also fil not with waxe or hony, but vvith the poison of heresie.

Heretikes like to the Cadmees.
To Sampsons Foxes.
Li. 4. contra Marcionem.
Var. l. 1. de regist. c. 10. Epip. har. 44.
To VVaspes.
A fit similitude.

14. If therfore some one in England (as there are many such) should doubt of his religion I vvould fayne knovv, to vvhich of al the Churches, Sinagogues and sectes, he should repaire for a resolution? If he demand and where Christ is, where true exposition of Scripture is, where true fayth is to be found? the Protestants vvil say, that it is to be found amongst them, the Puritanes wil assure him that Christ is with them: no, wil the Brownists say, he is with vs. And so the poore man shalbe perplex and doubtful to which partie he shal adioine him selfe: for whilest none of al these Sectes and Sect-Masters can proue their mission, and euery one of them vvil alleage Scripture, and their priuate spirit, and none can say more for his Sect then an other, he shal be in doubt vvhich to folow, because one hath no more reason to induce him then an other, and yet he can not folowe them al because their doctrines and faythes are contrarie. Wherfore he shal do vvel to giue eare to none of them, but rather his best wil be to folow the Counsail of Hilarius: that is to imitate the mariners, vvho after they haue left the hauen and are lanced into the maine Ocean, if they find stormes

If one doubte of his faith, he shal find no satisfaction amongst heretikes.
l. cont. Const. Hilarius counsel in such a case.

stormes and tempestes, returne again to the hauen, as the only place of securitie. For so he hauing left the Catholique Church, and out of it finding nothing but stormes, tempestes, and contrarie vvindes of opinions, should returne again to the same Church, as the only peaceble and quiet hauen; vvhere is no dissension in fayth, but al peace and agreement.

15. But they wil say that amongst vs also are great dissensions, and diuers sects also of Thomists, Scotists, Nominals, Reals, and such like. To which I ansvvere, that this diuersitie of opinions, is not in matters of fayth, but only in certain subtilities of Philosophie, or of Schoole Diuinitie, or other indifferent points of doctrin, not defined by the Church, but left to the frie censure of euery man. But yet these men as herin they shew them selues men, who commonly neuer agree where any difficultie is, so they shew them selues Christians, who, if the Pope or Church define any opinion, are then al ready to yeld and agree: and then you shal see how in Christ Iesus, and his faith there is neither Scotist, nor Thomist, but al good Christians. Vvhich is the cause of the great vnitie in the Church, which must nedes be vvanting in the heretikes Synagogues, who hauing left the Church, and refusing to stand to her censure, haue nothing to make them agree. For neither is bare Scripture, nor the priuat spirit sufficient, neither haue they any visible Iudge as is proued, and so whilest amongst them euery man may beleue as he list, they must needs haue almost as many opinions as heads.

Diuersitie of opiniens amõgst Catholiques it not in matters of faith.

VVhen the Pope or Church defineth them Catholiques agree.

Heretikes haue nothing to hold them in peace and vnitie.

16. Vvherfore to conclude, seing that in the Catholique and Romain Church, is such peace and agreement, that al nations which are members of the same, professe the same fayth and agree al in one religion, that must nedes be the Church to vvhich Christ bequeathed his peace, and for as much as among the Gospellers there is nothing but daggers drovving and vvrangling in religion, that can not be the Church of Christ, who is the author of peace and concord, but rather it is an heretical Synagogue, and they if euer there were any, must needs be heretikes, who were euer noted for vvranglers in religion.

The cõclusion.

The seuenth

The seuenth chapter conteineth the seuenth marke of an heretike, vvhich is to be of a particular Sect.

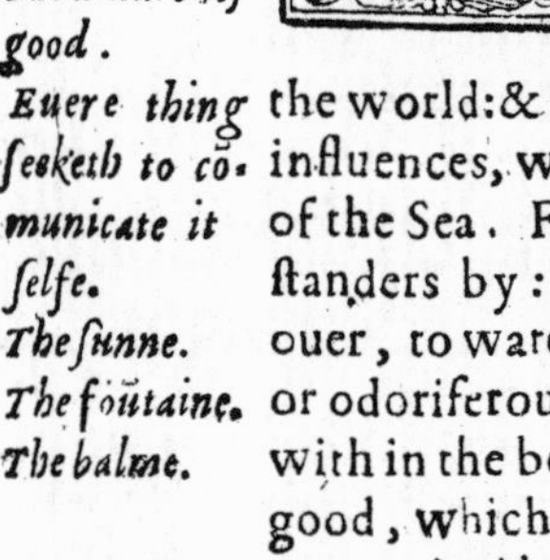

Dionis. l. de diuinis nom. c.4.
The nature ief good.
Euere thing seeketh to cōmunicate it selfe.
The sunne.
The fōutaine.
The balme.

THE nature of good is, not to conteine it selfe with in it selfe, but rather to impert it self, and to make it selfe common vnto others. That goodly Planet and celestial body, the Sunne, which is the light, and eye of the world, and moderator of tymes and seasons, is not content to abound in him self with light, but bestoweth the same bountifully on al partes of the world: & where he can not be liberal in light, he is bountiful in his influences, which reach euen to the bowels of the earth, and bottom of the Sea. Fire vvil neuer be warme alone, but heateth also the standers by: the fountaine wil not only it self be ful, but runneth ouer, to water the fieldes medowes and gardens. The sweete balme or odoriferous ointment, conteineth not it self with in it selfe, no not with in the boxe, but perfumeth al about. To be briefe, there is no good, which is not good to others.

God most bountifully imparteth him selfe.
First by Creation.
Secondly and especially by Incarnation.
Man an abridgement
Hovv God imperted him self to the humain nature of Christ.

2. And herin the riuers imitate their Fountaine, the effectes their cause, & the creatures rather resemble their Creator, then attain vnto his perfection. For he as he is the Fountain of al goodnes, and goodnes it self: so doth he most bountifully impert this his goodnes to others. In the creation of the world, what did he but impert him self by participation vnto al his creatures more or lesse, according to their capacitie? But aboue al, in the Incarnation he hath shewed him self most bountiful, by vvhich he hath communicated him selfe to our nature, not by participation, as he did in creation, but by hypostatical vnion, in substance and person. And because in man, as in a litle world al things are contained (for man hath being with inanimate creatures, life with plantes, feeling with beasts, and reason with angels) he hath in man, in some sorte, imperted him selfe to al creaturs. But especially to the humain nature of Christ he hath declared his bountie, to which he hath in such an admirable sorte vnited his Diuine Person, that the same man Christ Iesus s God and man, omnipotent, immense, infinite, and enriched with al the diuine attributs,

butes, *per communicationem idiomatum*. Wherfore since the tyme of Christes Incarnation in which he so bountifully bestowed him self, God would no more be so sparing of his graces, as to conclude faith and saluation within the confines of Iudea, but he would haue al saued, would be knowne to al by faith, and honoured of al by religion. And therfore now he hath called Iew and Gentile, the Grecian and the Barbarous, and al nations vnder the sunne vnto his Fayth, Church, and Religion.

Since the Incarnatiō God is more liberal
Psal. 75.
He would haue al saued and al to be of his Church.

3. Wherfore this Church almost from the beginning, euen when it was confined within Hierusalem, conteined Parthians, Medes, Persians, Mesopotamians, and as the Scripture sayth, almost al nations vnder the sunne And when the Holy Spirit descended vpon the Apostles and Disciples in firie tongues, and gaue them the guifte also to speake al languages, that was to signifie that the Church of Christ was not to speake English only, or Scotish and Flemish only, but al languages. Wherfore God promised our Sauiour Christ that he would giue him not England only, not Scotland, Flanders, and Germany only, but *al nations for his inheritance*. And he auoucheth that his Church shal *rule from Sea to sea*: and that *al nations shal haue accesse vnto it*. And so accordingly Christ gaue authoritie to his Apostles to preach vnto al nations. Vvherby I gather that the Church of Christ is not to be a particular Sect confined with in any straites & corners of the world, but rather an ample Kingdome, reaching ouer al the world.

Act. 2.
The Church of Christ was Catholique from the beginning.
Ibidem.
Proofes that the Church is Catholique.
Psal. 2.
Psal. 79.
Psal. 81.
Mat. 28.
Marc. 16.

4. And this we professe in our Crede, when we say that we *beleue the holy Catholique* Church. For *Catholique* is as much to say as *Catholon* vniuersal: *Vvhich name* (sayth S. Austin) *holdeth me in the Church*. And why? because he knew it to be a signe of the true Christian Church, which neuer yet agreed to any heretical sect, either of the Manichies (of which once he was) or of the Donatistes, or Pelagians, or any other. And this, sayth S. Austin, is so manifest a marke of the true Church, that heretikes them selues, ambiciously affect the same: but yet if you aske for the Catholique Church, they point to ours, knowing in their conscience that ours only is in deed Catholique. And so S. Austin and Optatus refuted the Church of the Donatists by this argument especially, because it was confined with in the limites of Africa. And Pacianus sayth that so soone as certain singular Sect-masters deuised new religions, and were called by particular names, the true Christians, to distinguish them selues from particular sectes, tooke the name Catholique euen from the beginning (as appeareth

And not a particular sect
Symb. Apost. & Niceph.
Aug. ep 170 l cont. ep fundamenti c. 4.
The name Catholique vvhy it holds. Au. Ibidem. & li de vera rel c. 7. l. de vtil. credendi. c. 7.

R by the

by the Crede which the Apostles made) which name soundeth neither of Marcion, nor Apelles, nor Montanus as he sayth, nor of Luther, nor Caluin may you say. And Tertullian so long as he remained Catholique him self, confessed that the true Church was that which was diffused through out al the world. Yea he sayth, that in his tyme the true Christians notwithstanding the violence of persecution *filled the Paganes cities, Ilands, Castles, Courts, Senats, and only left their temples to them selues*: but no soner was this man become an heretike, but he affirmed most absurdly, that the Church might consist of three persons, though they were of the laitie. Vvhich he did partly because he would make vp a Church of Montanus Prisca and Maximilla, to whom he had vnited him selfe, partly to deliuer him selfe from the name of an heretike, to which he sawe him selfe subiect, because he was now of a particular sect. Pacianus sayth that *Christian* is his name, *Catholique* his surname: by that he is called, by this distinguished from al heretikes. And yet againe he saith, that the Church is a ful body dispersed through al the vvorld, a vine ful of branches which reach from Sea to sea, a house ful of al kinde of vessel: and that al heretikes are no bodyes, but partes, no vines but branches cut of, no whole thing but only parcels peeces and patches, as S. Austin sayd of the Donatistes. Optatus mileuitanus writing to Parmenianus a Donatist, pronounceth this sentence of him and his felowes: *Intelligite vel serò vos esse filios impios*, &c. *Vnderstand you though lately, that you are vvicked children, bovves riuen from the tree, branches cut from the vine, and a riuer separated from the fountaine. For the riuer can not be the source and fountaine, because it is litle*, &c. and a litle before that, he proueth them not to be the Church of Christ, because they were only in Africa. And as the Church filleth al countries, so doth it by succession replenish al ages, as aboue in the fifth chapter is proued. S. Ciril also in the same sense vnderstandeth the name Catholique: *Catholica vocatur*, &c. It is called Catholique, because it is diffused through out the whole world, &c. So that it is sufficiently proued that the Church of Christ is *Catholique* that is, a Societie professing one fayth in al countries, yea and ages also, according to that of Vincentius Lirinensis: *In Ecclesia Catholica tenendum quod vbique, quod semper, quod ab omnibus creditum fuit: In the Catholique Church that is to be holden vvhich euery vvhere, alvvayes, and of al hath been beleeued.* For that (sayth he) the name Catholique importeth.

5. Now let vs see whether the Romain Church and fayth, or rather the Church of the reformers, be the Catholique, and consequently the

Christian

Ibidem. *l. cont. Iudæos c. 12.* *Apol. c. 37.* *l. de exh. cast.* *Supra.* *Ep. 3. ad Sympron. ps 79.* *Aug in ps. 65* *l. 2. cōt. Parm.* *Catech. 18.* *The Church Catholique. Vvhat is Catholique. chap. 3.*

Christian Church, for these two *Catholique* and *Christian* euer went together. And here I require no Diuines, nor Philosophers to be Iudges in this matter, only let me haue men that haue eares or eyes, and I desire no more. For the eye wil easily iudge, vvhether of these two Churches is most like to be Catholique. The Romain Church, which the aduersary calleth Papistical, hath florished in al ages & in the most part of the world, as al histories wil testifie. And now at this day our fayth and Church, one and the same, is diffused through out Spaine, France, Italie, Portugal, and a great part of Flanders and Germanie, yea it reacheth euen to the Indianes and other new found countries, conuerted by the Iesuites Franciscanes & other religious men. And so it is Catholique, because being one and the same, it hath euer possessed al ages, and countries, and stil doth euen to this day.

The Romain Church Catholique.

See the first booke & first chap.

6. As for the reformers Church and faith, I see no signe of a Catholique Church in it. For first it began not an hundred yeares since, as before is demonstrated. Secondly it neuer yet possessed the whole world, nor any great part of it, as the eye wil beare vvitnesse, only it hath gotten entertaynment in certayne partes of the world, as England, Scotland, Holland, and some Cantons of Germanie. Thirdly it is not one Church nor fayth that possesseth al these places, but many, yea scarce one religion filleth one shire or citie. Wherfore although England were al the world, and this age al ages, yet were not their religion Catholique, because it is not one fayth and religion in al the shyres of England, nor al the yeares of this age: for in England are many sectes, and religions, & they also different from the new faythes of other countries: for there is great difference betwixt them, and the Lutheranes in Germanie, Hugonots in France, and Gues in Flanders. Neither is it sufficient for any of them to say, that their fayth is Catholique, because al are inuited to it, and comanded to accept of it, for so euerie sectmaster may say of his religion, and I haue proued that the true Christian fayth, Church, and Religion, is Catholique in that it being one, possesseth al ages, and countries.

The heretikes Church is not Catholique.

In the fifth chapter.

7. Wherfore to conclude, seing that the Church or rather Churches of the reformers neuer possessed al ages and countries, yea neuer one and the same filled any one countrie, it foloweth that their Church is not Catholique and consequently not the true Christian Church, and so they are no true Christians, but heretiques and singular sectmasters, if euer there vvere any: because in that they are of particular sectes, they vveare the same badge vvhich Donatistes, Arians, Nestorians, and

The cōclusion.

ſuch like haue worne before them, and for which they were euer counted, and called heretikes.

The eight Chapter diſcourſeth vpon the eight marke of an heretike: vvhich is to be condemned for an heretike by that Church vvhich vvas commonly counted the true Chriſtian Church.

Similitude.

AS vvhen the ſubiectes beginne to make rebellion, the Prince ſuppreſſeth them or cutteth them of, & whē any ſhepe of the flocke are infected, the good ſhepheard ſeparateth them from the reſt, leſt they infect the vvhole flocke: as the ſurgeon cutteth of the rotten member leſt it corrupt the whole body; & the careful huſbandman plucketh vp the vveedes, leſt they ouergrow the good corne: ſo the ſupreme Paſtor of the Church, when any rebellious heretikes roſe vp againſt the Church, to whom they ought of right to be ſubiect, aſſembled alvvayes his forces together, that is, called General Councels of his Biſhops, and by the cenſure of excommunication ſuppreſſed theſe rebelles, leſt by their ciuil warres they ſhould moleſt the peace of Chriſt his Church, and endeuoured to ſeparate theſe infected ſheepe, leſt they ſhould infect the whole folde of Chriſt, and to cut of theſe rotten and rotting members, leſt they ſhould corrupt the whole body, and to pluck vp theſe noyſome weeds, leſt they might paraduenture ouergrovv the good corne.

Thecauſe vvhy at the firſt there vvere no General Councels.

2. And although in the beginning, by reaſon of perſecution and want of habilitie, the Church could not haue her General Councels, yet euen then the Paſtors of the Church aſſembled them ſelues together in writing, by which they refuted al hereſies, and made the autors Knowne, that others might the better auoid them. But after that the Church had gotten a Conſtantin for her champion, & temporal Princes for her Protectors, then againſt Arius ſhe gathered a Councel at Nice conſiſting of three hundred and eightene Biſhops: by which number as Abraham once ſubdewed fiue Kings, ſo our Sauiour Chriſt by Pope Silueſter his Vicare, at Nice the citie of Victorie (for ſo much the Greek word importeth) by Victor alſo and Vincentius, vvhoſe names are vi-

TheCouncel of Nice againſt Arius.

Athan ep ad Iou & diſp. con. Arin.

are victorious, gotte the victorie of Arius, and the Quartadecimanes and defined against the Arrians, that the Sonne was consubstantial to the Father, and against the Quartadecimanes vvhat day Easter should be kept and obserued. Which being done the excommunication, condemnation, curses, and anathems were thundred out against them: and a Synodical Epistle was written to Pope Siluester, who confirmed the Councels sentence in an other Councel at Rome. The Emperour Constantin reuerencing this sentence as the sentence of Christes Church, banished Arius commanded his bookes to be burned, and him and his to be taken for accursed heretikes; and after a banquet to vvhich he inuited the holy Bishops, he conueighed them home as honorably, a they were called together. So against Macedonius, vvas gathered the second Synode at Constantinople by the authoritie of Pope Damasus, for the defence of the Holy Ghosts Diuinitie. Against Nestorius a general Councel was called at Ephesus by Pope Celestin, vvherin vvas defined that in Christ is but one Person. At Chalcedon by the authoritie of Pope Leo the first in a general Councel, Eutyches was condemned for affirming but one nature in Christ. And the like general consent of the Church in condemnation of the Pelagians, Imagebreakers, Berengarians, Wiclephistes, and such others I could easily alleage out of Ecclesiastical histories, and the Councels them selues. But this may suffice to shew that whensoeuer any preached new doctrin, the Christian world wondered at them, the Church admonished them, and if they refused to obey her, she in General Councels condemned them, and the Emperors & Catholique Princes executed their lawes, vvhich were enacted against heretikes, and then al good Christians shunned them as infected and infecting persons.

Eus. l. 2. de vita const. Socr. l. 6. 7. Constantines reuerence to this Councel. The 2. Sind of Constantinople against Macedonius. Ex Photino l. de 7. Syn. The Ephesin councel against Nestorius ex Euag. l. 1. c. 4. A councel at Calcedon against Euti. Ex Euang l. 2. c. 4. Councels vvere commonly called vvhē nevv heretikes arose.

3. For as Vincentius Lyrinensis sayeth: *Annunciare aliquid Christianis Catholicis præter id quod acceperunt, nusquam licet, nunquam licebit, & anathematizare eos qui annunciant aliquid, præterquam quod semel acceptum est, nunquam non opertuit, nusquam non opertet, nunquam non opertebit: To preach vnto Christians other doctrin then that vvhich they haue already receiued no vvhere is lavvful, and neuer shal be lavvful: and to accurse as heretikes those vvhich preach other doctrin then vvhich before hath been accepted, it vvas euer behoueable, it is euery vvhere behoueable, and euer shal be behoueable.* And whosoeuer readeth the Ecclesiastical histories shal see how alwayes, they were taken for heretikes, vvho were condemned by General Councels, and holden so by that Church vvhich commonly was called Christian. And good reason, for he that wil not obey the Church must be by Christes commande-

l. cont. proph. hæresum nouitatet c. 10. They vvere euer counted heretikes vvho vvere cōdemned by councels of the church vvhich vvas cōmonly called Christian.

mandement, eschewed as an Ethnike and Publicane.

The marke of cō demnation by the Church agreeth to the Gospellers

4. Let now the indifferent reader be Iudge whether this note and marke agreeth not as properly to Luther, Caluin, and their folowers, as euer it did to Arius, Macedonius, Nestorius, Eutiches, and such like, vvho by their owne confession were infamous heretikes. They taught strange doctrines neuer alowed by that Church vvhich was commonly counted Christian: so did Luther and Caluin. At them, vvhen they began to preach, the Christian world vvondered: so did it vvhen these men began. Vvhen they by the Churches admonition could not be reclaimed, the Church by a General Councel, in vvhich the Pope ruled by his Legates, condemned them as heretikes: so when Luther began to preach, Pope Leo the tenth of that name warned him of it, & sent Cardinal Caietan a learned & famouse diuine, to conferre with him, but he being protected by the Duke of Saxonie, though some tymes he fayned that he would submit him selfe, remained obstinate: wherfore a general Councel vvas called at Trent, where by the sentence of the learnedst, grauest, and wisest Prelates of the world (for there were present six Cardinals of which foure were Legates, three Patriarches, 25. Arch-bishops, 168 Bishops, seuen Abbots, seuen Generals of religions, 39. Procurators, and other learned men very many) Luther and al the heretikes and heresies of this age were condemned, euen as Arius and other heretikes in other Councels before had been. But they say that it was not the true Church vvhich condemned them. And might not Arius haue sayed the same? And vvhen I pray you, did the true Church that once vvas, and vvhich condemned Arius, degenerate? Vnder vvhat Pope and Emperour? In vvhat age? in what year of our Lord? vpon vvhat occasion? But this miserable refuge of theirs is already reiected. At least that Church, vvhich vvhen Luther began to preach, vvas commonly counted the only and true Christian Church, condemned them, and so if euer there vvere any heretikes, these men also must be counted so, else the sentence geuen against Arius, by that societie which was commonly connted Christian, must be reuersed, or at least again examined.

The Councel of Trent called against the nevv Gospellers

Their vain obiection.

cap. 5. The cōclusion.

Other markes of heretikes.

5. To these markes may be added others, as want of mission, allegation of bare Scripture, bragging of the priuate spirit, cōtempt of Fathers, wāt of a visible Iudge, of which, I haue spoken in the first booke, for these were the properties of al heretikes, and are as proper to our new reformers, as euer they vvere to any ancient heretikes, as by the same chapters doth appeare most euidently.

THE

THE THIRD BOOKE CONTEINETH A SVRVEY OF DOCTRIN CONCERNING CHRIST: IN WHICH BY MANY poinctes is proued, that the pretended reformers are Antichristians, rather then Christians.

The first Chapter proueth that their doctrin despoileth Christ of his Diuinitie, and that therfore they are no sincere Christians.

EVERY man liketh and loueth that he professeth & wil speake honourably of him whom he foloweth in that profession. The Stoickes commend Zeno, the Platonistes prayse Plato, the Peripaterickes Aristotle, the Epicureans Epicure, the Atheists Diagoras, and euery one reuerenceth & respecteth him, whose doctrin and profession he embraceth. If then the reformers be sincere and real Christians (as they wil seme to be) they must think, and speake of Christ very honourably, & giue that homage to his Person, which his doctrin hath deserued. And as in wordes they seme to do.

The reformers vvil seme to geue much, yea al to Christ.

2. Luther when he first began to preach against Indulgences, merits, satisfaction, good workes, and inherent iustice, affirming that only to beleue, that Christs Iustice is ours, is sufficient to saluation, vsed this for a cloke, that forsooth he gaue al to Christs iustice, & nothing to our workes. Caluin also in the preface of his Institutions which he wrote to the French King, commendeth his owne doctrin for this

Lut. in com. Gal fol. 290.

In præf. Inst. ad Reg. Gall.

for this point especially, that it geueth al honour to Christ, & leaueth nothing to our owne force and habilitie. *And vvhat doth better agree vvith faith (sayth he) then to acknovvledge our selues dispoiled of al vertue, that of God vve may be clothed: deuoid of al good, that of him vve may be filled: bond-seruants of sinne, that of him vve may be made free: blind, that of him vve may be enlightened lame, that of him vve may be made straight, feeble, that of him vve may be vpholden: to take from our selues al matters of glorying, that he alone may be glorious on hygh: and in him vve may glorie.* So that vvhilest they deny good vvorkes to be necessarie and affirme fayth only sufficient, vvhilest they say that we haue no inherēt iustice, but are the best of vs, though Apostles, mortal sinners before God, that our best workes are sinnes, and that we haue no other Iustice then the iustice of Christ apprehended by fayth, and imputed only to vs: vvhilest they deny that we can obserue the commandementes, or haue the power and free wil to do any good, or resist any tentation, they attribute, forsooth al to Christ, and leaue nothing to vs, that he only may be glorified. But by this booke I hope to make better knowne their deep dissimulation, vvho in wordes seme to giue al to Christ, and by their doctrin, do robbe him and despoile him of al his honourable titles.

Hovv they pul at Christes Diuinitie.

l.1.Trin.fo.7. 34.53.l.2.fol. 38.& in dial.

3. And first you shal see how sacrilegiously they plucke and pul at Christes Diuinitie. I wil not here relate the blasphemies of Michael Seruet who yet vvas a brother of this religion, because they wil say, that for such doctrin Caluin caused him to be burned, for he sayed plainly that God the Sonne was not true God, nor coequal with his Father, yea he sayd that God the Father only was God: which doctrine notwithstanding he gathered, or might haue gathered out of Luthers and Caluins vvorkes. Neither wil I say any thing of the heretikes and new Arians of Transiluania, who in this also agree with Seruetus. But Luther the grand Patriarch and new Euangelist must not be omitted: who in his booke against Latomus sayth, that he can not abide the word omousion. *Anima mea* (sayth he) *odit vocabulum* Homousion: *My soule hateth the vvord consubstantial.* So did the Arians hate the same word, & called it *exoticum, strange and vnusual.* But Athanasius gathereth this word out of Scriptures, and ancient Fathers, vvho in that they affirme that the Sonne is begotten of his Father, & coequal vnto him, and one vvith him, affirme also, that he is consubstantial, and of the same substance with his Father, because nothing is equal and coequal to God the Father but God, and nothing is God which is not the same substance with him, because there are not many Gods. And vvhy should

l. cont. latom.

Luther hateth the vvord homousion.

So did the Arians.

Ep. Decr. Conc. Nic.

should Luther hate this word but for the signification, for the sound is no more vngrateful then the sound of other words? If he hate the signification, then is he an Arian, vvho beleueth not that the Sonne is consubstantial, & of the same substance with the Father, & cõsequently he thinketh him not to be God, or else he thinketh that there are many Gods different in substance. The same Luther as diuerse affirme in an edition of his Commentaries vpon Genesis (which I haue not of seen) calleth the Sonne of God the instrument of his Father, by which he created the world, which maner of speach Arius vsed: And seing that the instrument is neuer of so noble a nature, as the principal agent, what is this but to make the Sonne of God, inferior to his Father, and consequently a creature? And this testimonie (as I haue read) Seruetus alleaged against Luthers Scholars in the Alban disputation. Luther also blotted out of the Germain prayer books, those ancient words *Sancta Trinitas Vnus Deus, miserere nobis: Holy Trinitie one God, haue mercy vpon vs.* And vvhy? for some spite belike vvhich he conceiued against Christ Iesus the second Person in Trinitie. For why else did he in his Germain Bibles when he came to the translation of those words of the ninth chapter of Esaie, *Deus fortis, strong God:* leaue out, God? as though Christ were strong but not God. Vvhy did he leaue out quite those words of S. Iohns Epistle, *Tres sunt qui testimonium dant in cælo, Pater, Verbum, & Spiritus Sanctus, & hi tres vnum sunt. There are three vvhich giue testimonie in heauen, the Father, the VVord and Holy Ghost, and these three are one?* *in 1. ed. Gen.* 1. *Io.* 5.

4. The same Luther in his booke of Councels excuseth Eutyches, and Nestorius and accuseth S. Leo and S. Cyril as men vvhich vvere to eagre against them, for (sayth he) as Eutyches sayed so may it wel be sayed, that Christs Diuinitie suffred. O blasphemie! did the Diuinitie of Christ suffer? then was it not true Diuinitie, and consequently Christ was not God, because God as God can not suffer. I may vse here Alamundarus vvitty answere against certain heretical Bishops, that sayd Christs Diuinitie suffred on the crosse: for vvhen he heard that they were come to speake with him, he commanded his man presently after their entraunce to whisper him in the eare, vvhich being done Alamundarus started at the whispering, and semed astonished. The Bishops thinking that his man had told him some euil newes, demanded vvhat it vvas at which he was amazed? My man (sayth he) telleth me that Michael the Archangel is dead. Tush, Tush, (sayd they) that newes can not be true, because Angels can not dye. Can not Angels dye

l. de concil. 2. par. *Luther sayth the Diuinitie suffred.* *Niceph l. 16 hist. c. 35. Baron in Annal. anno Christi 509.* *a vvittie maner of ansvvering.*

gels dye (sayd Alamandarus) and thinke you that Gods Diuinitie could suffer?

Melanthonus Diuinitie of the Some of God.

5. Melancthon in his book of common places, and in diuers other places hath these propositions. *The sonne of God according vnto his diuinitie prayd vnto his father for his Kingdom, glorie, and inheritance The diuine nature of the sonne, vvas obedient to his Father in his Passion.* The like saying hath Beza, yea and Caluin also. Is not this to deny Christs Diuinitie and coæqualitie with his Father? For who but an inferior prayeth. Who but an inferior obeyeth?

Anno 1556. l.cont. Stanc. ep. ad Elect. Ep. 28 tract. pag 994. Beza & Caluins opinion.

Illic. Romn. apud Bel. to. 1. l 3. de Christo in initio Lut ser. de cœna Domini to. 8.

The opinion of the Vbiquetaries.

6. The Lutheran Vbiquetaries also, vvho affirme that the diuine attributes are really communicated vnto Christs humain nature, and that in such sorte, that the humain nature was immense and omnipotent as the Diuinitie was, destroy Christes diuinitie, vvilest they extol his humanitie: for by this doctrin it foloweth that Christs Diuinitie was nothing else but his humaine nature deified and really turned into Diuinitie, and seing that humain nature can not in this maner participate of the Diuinitie, it folovveth that Christ is not true God, because he hath not true Diuinitie. For although by incarnation man was God, and so consequentely immense and omnipotent, by a certain communication, vvhich Diuines cal *communicationem idiomatum*, Yet the humanitie could neuer really be the Diuinitie, nor omnipotencie, nor any other diuine atribute.

Li. cont. Valētinū Gētilem. Caluin sayth, the Father is the principal God.

li. 1. Inst. c. 18. 9. 10. 28. 25. Yea that Christ is not God of God. VVhitiker.

7. And to come to Caluin, he sayth plainly that the name of God agreeth to the Father *per excellentiam by excellencie.* Which if it be so, then God the Sonne is not so Excellent a God as the Father, and consequently no God at al. He also in diuerse places auoucheth that Christ is not God of God, as the Nicen Councel calleth him, he denyeth that by eternal generation God the Sonne hath his essence from his Father, yea (sayth he in the same place) the essence of the Sonne is no more generated then the essence of the Father. To whom in this point subscribeth our countriman M. Whitaker in his booke against Father Campian. O blasphemies! and that of them that wil nedes be counted reformed Christians. Better were it to deny Christ flatly, then to professe his name, and yet vnder hand to disgrace him: for dissembled religion is duble iniquitie. Is not Christ God of God the Father? then is he some other God, hath he not his essence from his Father? Then is he not the Sonne of God, because the Sonne taketh his substance from his Father. Is not the Sonnes essence generated? then is not the Sonne begotten of his Fathers substance, then is he not consubstantial to his Father,

Out of Caluins doctrin is deduced that

ther, but rather of an other nature, and consequently either a creature or an other God. The diuines grant that the essence and Diuinitie absolutely without addition, is not sayed to be generated, for then it should be generated in God the Father also, but yet they affirme that God the Sonne is God of God and begotten of his Father, and that by eternal generation he receiueth without al imperfection his essence from his Father, and consequently that the essence is generated, not absolutely but in the Sonne, else were he not a Sonne nor should be consubstantial to his Father.

Christ is not the sonne of God.

8. The same Caluin accompanyed with diuers others both Caluinists and Lutheranes, affirmeth that Christ according to his Diuinitie was Priest and mediator. To whom Iewel in his booke against D. Harding subscribeth, where he saith that in Christ there were two natures, & that the Humanitie was offered in sacrifice, but the Diuinitie played the Priest & offered vp this sacrifice. See here an other blasphemie. Is Christ Priest according to his Diuinitie? Did his diuine nature offer vnto the Father the sacrifice of the humain nature? then certes Christ was not only as man but also in respect of his Diuinitie, inferior to his Father (for the Priest is inferior to God to whom he offereth sacrifice, because in oblation of a sacrifice he acknowledgeth God the supreme excellēcie) & so was ether a creature or a lesser God, and so no God at al. The ancient Fathers and diuines do grant that the same Iesus Christ was Mediator betwixt God and man, and God also, to whom Mediation was made, by reason of his two natures subsisting in one Person. For a Mediator like a meane, must participate of both extremes, & therfore sith man had offēded, & God was offended, the Mediator must be God & man. For God only could not satisfie, because he could not suffer, man only could not satisfie, because his satisfaction would haue bene lesse then was the iniurie: wherfore it was necessarie, that one who was both God and man, should make this meditation and satisfaction. And so the same Iesus Christ, God and man satisfied, yet not as God but as man, & he as the Person offended, receiued also the satisfaction, not as man, but as God. In like maner the same Christ Iesus was the Priest, the sacrifice, and the God to whom this sacrifice was offered. And so Christ was the Priest yet not as God but as man, for in this only respect Christ had a superior to whom he might offer a sacrifice: Christ also was the sacrifice, but as man, for his humaine nature only suffered. And Christ also was he to whom the sacrifice was offered. but as God, for so he was no lesse offen-

Ep. duabus ad Polon. Pet. Mar. duab. ep. Kem l. de duabus nat. Mel. loc c. de filio. Iewellus a 37

If Christ as Caluin and Others, say was priest according to his Diuinitie thē was he not God.

The Fathers maner of speach.

How Christ was priest. Sacrifice and God to whom sacrifice was offered.

offended, and iniuried by mans sinne, then God the Father. I referre the reader to a booke which one *Ægidius Hunnius* a Lutheran vvrit against Caluin, in which he declareth how Caluin stil expoundeth the old and new Testament in fauoure of the Iewes, as though the places spake not of Christ, and therfore this man calleth his booke, *Caluinus Iudaizans*, *Caluin playing the Ievve*.

Caluinus Iudaizans.

9. Tel me now gentle reader, whether these men (as they say) do attribute al vnto Christ, who as thou hast heard, do despoile him of his greatest titles of honour, that is true God, and Sonne of God? But thou wilt say, that in many places Caluin and others grant that Christ is true God, and the Sonne of God. I wil grant it also, for Caluin in the first booke of his Institutions and thirtenth chapter, indeuoreth to proue Christes Diuinitie, but yet thou seest also how they eate their words, and deny in one place which in an other they affirmed. And so to conclude either they speake thus wittingly of Christ, and so they are no Christians but renouncers of Christ, or of ignorance, & so they are not men to be folovved in so great matters as fayth is, who haue neede them selues to lerne their catechisme, which teacheth how to speake, and beleue of Christ and God.

l. 1. Inst. c. 11.

The Conclusion.

The second chapter shevveth, hovv by their doctrin they make Christ an absurd Redeemer.

MAN once was frie of condition as being created Lord ouer al, and subiect to none but God, vvhose seruice is no seruilitie: he vvas noble of birth as being framed by God his owne hãds of virgin earth, which yet was not stained by sinne: he was happie in state, as being indewed with a body immortal, fried from diseases, death, and distemperature, neither benummed with cold, nor parched with heat, nor pined with hunger, nor molested with thirst: enriched with a soule filled with grace and spiritual treasures, which was prone to vertue, not inclined to vice, neither molested with concupiscence, nor overruled by passion, but ruled by reason, which was ruled by grace. His superior part vvas obedient to God, his inferior part to the superior, sensualitie to reason, the flesh

Mannes felicitie in paradise.

to the

to the spirit, and al creatures to him were buxome and obedient. Besides this inward fœlicitie of soule and body, he was placed in Paradise, where he was enuironed and compassed about with al delightes, and pleasures, and farre from al displeasures.

2. But vvhen by sinne man vvould not be subiect to God, he became a slaue to his owne flesh, passions, and sensualitie, a bondman to sinne, captiue to the diuel, subiect to death and mortalitie, hel, and damnation. And of al this seruile subiection, sinne vvas the cause. For vvhen Adam sinned, and vve in Adam transgressed, vve vvere by and by guiltie of death, vvhich is *the revvard of sinne*, and by sinne vve became slaues to sinne, and concupiscence. For as Christ sayth: *VVhosoeuer sinneth is a slaue to sinne*: and being slaues to sinne, vve vvere slaues to the diuel, vvho hath no authoritie nor provver ouer vs but by sinne: and being slaues to the diuel vve vvere captiues of hel, vvhich is the prison vvhere the diuel holdeth sinners perpetually. And behold here briefly in vvhat bondage, by sinne, the diuel had gotten vs. After that by sinne vve vvere despoiled of grace, if he tempted vs vve could not haue resisted, and if vve had fallen by sinne, vve could not haue risen again by force of nature, & force of grace vve had none, because sinne had depriued vs of it: and so vve vvere slaues to sinne, and the diuel, and captiues also and prisoners of hel, vvhich is devv to sinne: vvherfore S. Paul sayth: that *VVe vvere deteyned captiues, at the diuels pleasure.*

Mannes seruitude after sinne. *The cause of mans seruilitie.* *Rom 6.* *Io. 8.* *1. Io 8.* *2. Pet 2.* *Rom. 6.* *Mans bondage to the diuil..* *Th. 1 2 q. 109. 6. 7.* *1. Tim. 2.*

3. To ransome this prisoner, & to redeme this bondslaue by vvay of æquitie and iustice, it vvas necessarie that a Diuine Person should become man: for God only could not satisfie, because he vvas God, & could be indebted to none: Man only vvas not able to pay so great a ransome, as sinne required: only God & man, vvas a fitte pay-master. For as S. Leo sayth if he had not bene true God, he could not haue giuen vs a remedie, and if he had not bene true man, he could not haue giuen example, yea he could not haue suffered, and so could not haue satisfied.

Mannes Redeemer. *Ser 1. Nat Domini.* *None but a Diuine Person could pay mans rāsom.*

4. And amongst the three Diuine Persons, the second vvas the fittest. For who fitter to be a mediator then the midle Person? Who fitter to be the Sonne of man by incarnatiō, then he who from al eternitie vvas the Sone of God? Who fitter to repaire the image of God in man, then he who was the image of his Father? Vvho fitter to make an amendes for Adames inordinate desire of knowledge then he vvho vvas the wisdome of his Father? Who fitter to abate Adams pride, who would haue been like to God, then he who was in deed the likenes of

none fitter then the second Person vvhy? *Gen. 3.*

God his Father, & yet by incarnation, of purpose became in outward show as vnlike him, as man is to God? Briefly who fitter to appease the storme, then Ionas for whom the storme was raysed? for it was no other then the Sonne of God for whom the storme in heauen was raised, when Lucifer would be like the Highest. It was no other then the same Sonne of God, for whom in paradise that storme arose, when Adam puffed vp with pride, would be like to God in Knowledge of good & euil; for to him is proper the likenes and image of God, vvhich they inordinatly affected.

5. The ancient then of yeares became a child, the Word was mute, God became man, the second and midle Person played the mediator, the Sonne of God became the Sonne of man, and in mans nature which he had taken vpon him, repayred what man had ruined, and destroying sinne by flesh, vvhich by flesh was committed, ouercame the diuel by flesh, by vvhich he had ouercome: and where as with one teare, yea one worde he might haue remdemed vs, he would sheed his bloud for vs, and vvheras one drop had bene sufficient, he powred out al, to shew the greatnesse of his charitie, and the greatnes of our ingratitude, vvhich stil commit sinnes, that cost Christ so dearly, to shew the malice of sinne, whose staine could not be taken out without the bloud of this lamb, and to shewe the greatnes of the ransom, and the price of our redemption.

The great price of our redemption.

6. So great was this price vvhich was payd for vs, that S. Peter sayth *Vve vvere redemed not by gold and siluer, but by the pretious bloud of Christ.* (*1. Pet. 1.*) And S. Paul sayth *that vve vvere bought by a great price:* so great, that Dauid (*1. Cor. 6.*) calleth it *copiosa redemptio, a copious redemption. Prorsus copiosa* (sayth S. (*Psal. 129.*) Bernard) *quia non gutta, sed vnda sanguinis per quinque partes corporis manauit* (*Ser. 22 in Cãt.*) *Copious in deed because not a drop, but a stream of bloud, issued out at fiue partes of his body so rich a price vvas this bloud* (sayth he) *That it vvas sufficient to haue satisfied for the sinne vvhich shed it.* (*Ep. 290.*) So that Christ is our Redemer. *Vvho hath deliuered vs out of the povver of darkenes,* (*Col. 1.*) fried vs from the slauerie of sinne, and the bondage of the diuel. For (as S. Austin sayth) Christ now hath (*Ser. 197. Domin. 1. post Trinitatem.*) tyed the diuel in a chaine, so that he can no farther tempte vs, then we can resist: barke he may, tempt he may, sollicite vs he may, but byte he can none but those, which wilfully cast them selues vvithin his reach.

7. Who now is so vngratful as not to acknowledge this benefit? Vvho wil arrogate vnto him selfe the name of a Christian, and wil not also acknowledge Christ for his Redeemer? Dare now the refor-

mers deny

mers deny Christ the title of a Redeemer? they dare not. Yet by their doctrin they make him a most absurd Redemer and so more dishonour him, then if they had denyed him this title altogether.

8. For they say, that there is no iustice but Christs iustice, no good workes but his workes, no merit but his merit, no satisfaction but his, and consequently, that Christs passion was our iustice, our merit, and our satisfaction. Out of which doctrin they inferre, first that neither there is any inherent iustice or sanctitie in man, neither is there any necessarie at al, because Christs iustice is ours by imputation, and that is sufficient. So (sayth Caluin) and to him subscribeth Luther as shal appeare by their wordes, vvhich shalbe related and refuted in the next chapter, as also in diuers chapters of the seuenth book. Secōdly they gather out of the same doctrin that good workes are not necessarie because Christs workes are ours & they are sufficienr: which doctrin I shal lay open in the same next chapiter. Thirdly hence they inferre also that no lawes, either humaine or diuine, can bind vs in conscience, because Christs Passion was the ransome, which fried vs from al lawes. Fourthly that we are bond to no satisfaction, because Christs satisfaction was sufficient. Fiftly that no sinnes nor euil workes can hurt vs, because Christs iustice being ours, no sinne can make vs sinners, which doctrin, shal be set downe in the same booke. Sixtly that no hel nor iudgement remaineth for vs: because Christs iustice being ours, sinnes can neither be imputed to vs in this life nor punished in the next. And in these pointes they say that Christian libertie consisteth. So that Christ according to these doctors opinions, hath redemed vs from the slauery of sinne, because his iustice being ours no sinne can hurt vs, he hath deliuered vs from the yoke of the law, because no law can bynd vs, he hath deliuered vs from hel and the diuel because howsoeuer we liue, if we belene that Christs iustice is ours, and our satisfaction, and payment, the diuel hath no powre to punish vs in his hellish prison, because Christ hath suffred the payne dew to our sinnes before hand.

The reformers denie inherent iustice in the iust.

l. 5. Inst. c. 11. 2.

Luth. in 2. Gal fol. 298.

The second absurditie.

The third.

The fourth.

The fifth.

The Sixt.

How they say Christ hath redemed vs.

9. Vvherin the discreet reader may easily perceiue what an absurd Redemer they make Christ to be. For if Christ hath redeemed vs from the slauery of sinne, because no sinne can hurt vs, then doth he open vs the gappe to al maner of sinnes & outrages. For who wil care for sinne, that is perswaded, that Christs passion is so imputed to him, that no sinne can hurt him? If Christ hath redemed vs from the yoke of the law, because no law now can bynd vs in conscience; then doth he giue

They make Christ an absurd redemer, in that they make his passion a cause of sinne, & trāsgression.

he giue vs the occasion to transgresse freely, and contemne boldly al maner of lawes and ordinances. If Christ hath deliuerd vs from hel, because he hath payed the punishement dew to sinne, and requireth no other satisfaction at our handes, then doth he in a maner egge vs forward to al vice, from vvhich no man wil absteyne, if feare of hel do not bridle his vnruly appetites, and kepe him in awe. And so Christs passion vvhich was a sacrifice to abolish sinne, is a cause of al sinne, and Christ who came to redeme the world from sinne, filleth the world with sinne, and so is an absurd Redemer, so to redeme vs from sinne, that he inuiteth vs and eggeth vs forwardes vnto sinne.

An example.

10. So they make Christ not vnlike to that father, who seeing the excessiue expences of his prodigal sonne, doth not command him to vse more thriftines, but payeth before hand to al disers, cookes, Inkeepers, and merchantes, al that possibly he can loose at dise, or lauish out in apparel, or consume in banquetting: wherin he doth nothing else but inuite his sonne to al vnthriftines, who needeth neuer to care how he spendeth, when al his debtes are payed before hand. For so the Gospellers say, that Christ perceiuing, that we could not keepe the law, freed vs from al lawes, and seing that we could not auoyd sinne, imputed his owne iustice so vnto vs, that no sinne can hurt vs, and knovving that vve vvere not able to satisfie for sinne, he abode the pain him selfe, and vvould haue none required at our hands. And in so doing, vvhat else hath he doone, but opened the vvide gate to al licencious libertie, vice and iniquitie.

The reasonable opinion vvhich Catholique haue of Christes passion.

11. Hovv farre more reasonable is the opinion of the Catholique Church, vvhich affirmeth that Christes Passion vvas not our formal iustification nor satisfaction, but only the meritorious cause of our redemption and saluation: vvhich deserued for vs at Gods handes grace, by vvhich together vvith our cooperation, we may be redeemed and saued. For as vve fel by our ovvne vvilles into captiuitie: so Christ thought it good, that by our owne willes together vvith his grace (for without his grace, we may fal, but we can not rise again) we should rise vp again, and wind our selues out of the seruitude of sinne, and the tiranie of the diuel. So that Christ hath redemed vs from the seruitude of the law, not that the law bindeth vs not, but because Christ hath taken away the heauinesse of the law, and by his grace vvhich he giueth vs, hath giuen vs force easily to fulfil it, which otherwise would haue tirannised ouer vs, in commanding more then we should haue bene able to haue performed. Christ also hath redemed vs from

A similitude.

Hovv Christ hath redemed vs from the lavve.

vs from captiuitie and bondage of sinne, not because no sinne can be imputed vnto vs, but because his passion hath deserued grace for vs, by vvhich vve may dispose our selues to iustification, vvhich is a resurrection from sinne to nevvnesse of life, and by vvhich vve may auoid sinne vvhensoeuer vve are moued therevnto. Christ also hath freed vs from the tyrannie of the diuel and captiuitie of hel, because he hath procured vs grace, by vvhich vvhen the diuel by him selfe, or the vvorld, or the flesh prouoketh vs, vve may resist, maugre al the force of hel. Christ also hath satisfyed for our sinnes, not because his passion vvithout any cooperation on our part doth suffice, for so, as is proued, the gate vvere opened vnto al iniquitie, but because his passion had obteyned grace for vs, vvithout vvhich vve could not satisfie for the least venial sinne, & by vvhich, if vve cooperate ther vvith, by fasting, almesdeds, prayer, and other vvorkes of pænance, vve may satifie for al our sinnes, and al the paynes devv to our sinnes. *From sinne.* *From the diuel.*

12. So that Christ hath redemed vs from the seruitude and heauy yoke of the law, and yet we must kepe the lavv, and now especially, because the heauinesse therof is taken a way by Christ his grace. Christ hath fried vs from the seruitude of sinne, & yet we must auoide sinne, and now especially, because Christs grace hath giuen force to arise by penance from our former sinful life, and to walke in the way of his commandementes, and newnes of life. Christ also hath deliuered vs from the tyrannie of the diuel, because he hath giuen vs grace to resist him; wherfore we must not yeeld vnto him, but now especially we must stand against him. Christ also hath satisfied for vs, and yet we must satisfie, and now especially because he hath giuen vs grace by vvhich we may do pænance for sinne, and satisfie for the payne. For although that Christ hath payed the price of our redemption, yet would he haue vs to applie it by our cooperation not only in faith (for so he should open the way to al vice) but in pœnance, in obseruation of the conmandementes, and receiuing of the Sacramentes. Wherfore our Redemer him selfe, who fried vs from the yoke of the law, yet commandeth vs to kepe the law *if vve meane to enter into life*; and although he hath satisfied for our sinnes, yet he commandeth his Apostles to preach penance vnto vs, necessarie for remission and satisfaction of our sinnes. *Not vvithstanding that Christ hath redemed vs yea vve must kepe the lavv.* *Auoid sinne.* *Psal. 118.* *Resist the diuel.* *Do pænance.* *Mat. 19.* *Luc. vlt.*

13. And if he had redemed vs in that maner which the Gospellers imagin, and had set vs at that libertie, that no law can bynd vs, nor sinne hurt vs, & that no good workes, nor satisfaction, nor any other *The cõclusion.*

cooperation besides faith, can be required on our part, then had he bene a most absurd Redemer (as I haue already proued) and had rather tumbled vs dovvne into the depth of sinne and damnation, then Redemed vs.

The third Chapter shevveth hovv by their doctrin they make Christ no Redemer at al.

Mat. 7.

Heretikes are disguised vvolues.

VEL did our blessed Sauiour compare heretikes vnto Vvolues wrapped and inuested in sheepe skinnes, vvhose maner hath alvvayes bene vnder prætence of religion, to vtter blasphemie, and then to meane and intend the worst, vvhen they speake fairest. Vvhat I pray you, is so common in our Gospellers mouthes, as that Christ only is our Redemer, and sole Mediator? Vnder which pretence they condemne al honour giuen vnto Sainctes, and abandon al prayer and intercession made to them, as iniurious to Christ & his title of a Redemer. In vvhich truly they seme not vnlike to Iudas, who vvould needs kisse Christ vvhen he meant to betray him; and me thinkes (and vvhat I think I shal proue anone) in this point they resemble the Ievves, vvhich inuested Christ like a King, called him King, and adored him as King, yet in deed derided him as a foole. For so these men cal Christ the Redemer, and rather then they vvil not seme to meane so, they take from the Saincts, the mother, and frends of Christ, al secondarie mediation and intercession, and vvil seme to be so zealous of Christes honour, that they vvil haue none honoured but him: and yet in deede vnder this faire shovv, they cary false hartes, & euen then vvhen they cal him and adore him as a Redemer, they robbe him and despoile him of that honourable title.

Not vnlike to Iudes and the Ievves.

Luthers and Caluins doctrine of imputatiue Iustice.

Lut. in com. Gal fol. 298.

2. Luther in his cōmentaries vpon the second Chapter to the Galathiās sayth plainly, that *Christ apprehended by faith is Christian iustice for vvhō God reputeth vs iust.* Caluin also subscribeth that our iustice cōsisteth *in the imputation of Christes iustice vnto vs.* And because this iustice is extrinsecal and is not inherent in vs, they say that though for Christes sake vve be reputed iust, yet the holiest that is, is a greuous sinner, & al his vorkes are vvorthy nothing else but damnation, vvhich doctrin herafter diuerse

uerse times, and especially in the seuenth booke shalbe related, hence .3.*Inst.c.*
it is also that they say, that our sinnes are only couered with Christes 1.2.
iustice, which is imputed vnto vs, but are not taken away nor extinguished. This they explicate by a similitude: for (say they) as if a man looke through redde glasse, al semeth redde, be it blacke or white, so God beholding vs through Christes iustice, reputeth vs iust though in deed we be sinners. And this, Caluin in his preface of his Institutions auoucheth not to derogate frō Christ, but to make much for his honor, for what (sayth he) is to Christ more honourable then to acknowledge our selues despoiled of al vertue, that of him vve may be clothed, that is, reputed iust for iustice vvhich is imputed vnto vs. But let vs see how honorable this is to Christ.

Aboue in the first chap.

3. I wil not deny but that it is honorable to Christ, and expedient *Th.* 1.2.q.
for vs, to acknowledge that of our selues without Christes grace vve 109.
are sinners and can do litle else but sinne, but to say that notwithstanding Christes grace which he hath bestowed on his iust, and is ready to bestow on al repentant sinners, we are stil sinners, & only reputed iust for Christes iustice, which is by fayth apprehended, & by God imputed vnto vs: is most dishonorable to Christ. For if we haue no other iustice then Christs iustice, which is imputed vnto vs, then haue we no internal sanctitie in vs, then are vve not truly sanctified, then are we stil sinners be we neuer so iust. Caluin and Luther, and al the Lutheranes, and Caluinists haue no other ansvver to this then *concedo totum*: I grant al.

4. Are we then stil truly sinners and not truly iust? then was the first Adam more potent in malice, then the second in grace and sanctitie: for he made vs truly sinners, Christ could not make vs truly iust. Then vvas S. Paul deceiued who sayth, that Christs grace exceeded Adams sinne. Are we stil sinners and not truly sanctified? then hath not Christ verily redemed vs from the seruitude of sinne, *for vvhosoeuer is in sinne, is a slaue to sinne.* If we be not redemed from sinne, then are we not fried from the tyrannie of Satan, whose only title is sinne, by *Rom.* 5.
which he domineereth ouer vs. And seing that hel folovveth sinne, as *Io.* 8.
a iust punishment for such a fault, then are we stil captiues and prisoners of hel, and Christ is no Redemer, who hath neither redemed vs from sinne, nor hel, nor damnation.

Out of their doctrine of imputatiue Iustice follovveth that Christe is no Redeemer.

5. The same Gospellers affirme, that by sinne our nature is so weakened, that not withstanding Christes grace, we can not resist any tēptation of the flesh or diuel, that we can not possibly fulfil the law and

First chap. The conclus. cõmandementes, that we can not do any good worke, but must needs sinne in al our actiõs, as shal appeare by their doctrin & their words in the seuenth booke, which if it be true, then are we not by Christ fried from the diuels tyrannie vvho stil so tyranniseth ouer vs, that vve can resist none of his tentations; then are we stil slaues to our ovvne concupiscence and sensualitie, whose assaults we can not withstand; then are we bondemen of sinne, which so ouerruleth vs, that we can do no other thing but sinne: then are vve not deliuered from hel and damnation, vvhich God hath prouided against sinners. And so the fayrespoken Christians, which cal Christ the sole Mediator and only Redemer, make him no Redemer at al.

The fourth chapter shevveth, hovv by their doctrin they make Christ no spiritual Phisitian.

Mans perfit health of body and soule in paradise.

OD created man in good plight, sound, whole and immortal, bestowing on him a tree of life, vvhose, frute should haue preserued him from diseases, distemperatures, and death of body, & indevving him vvith original iustice, vvhich if he had kept, it had kept him and preserued him in perpetual health of soule. But he not knovving hovv to vse such felicitie, by a surfet vvhich he tooke of the forbidden frute, distempered his body vvith mortalitie, vvhence proceed diseases, infirmities, and death it selfe, & cast him selfe at one tyme into no fevver then fovvre diseases of the soule, vvhich Diuines commonly cal *Vulnera animæ the vvounds of the soule*, vvhich reside also in fovvre partes or faculties of the soule. The vnderstanding vvhose obiect is truth, and vvhose perfection is knovvledge, was obscured vvith ignorance. The wil whose marke at vvhich she aymeth, is good, and vvhose perfection is loue, vvas infected vvith malice. The irascible part vvhose obiect is difficultie, and vvhose glorie is victorie ouer difficulties, vvas vveakned vvith infirmitie: and the concupiscible part, vvhose obiect vvas moderate delight: and vvhose felicitie vvas contentment in the same, vvas galled vvith the itching, and il pleasing sore of concupiscence.

Adams surfet

Four vvoũdes of the soule.

Th.c.2.q. 84. art. 3.

The vnderstã. ding vvoũded vvith errors.

The vvil vvith malice.

The irascible part vvith infirmitie.

The concupis.

2\. And Adam was the man of whom we tooke this infection, vnhappy

vnhappy to him selfe, and vnlucky to vs, who poisoning him selfe infected vs, and running him selfe through, wounded vs. For when this vnhappy wight descended from Hierusalem to Hierico, that is from Paradise the place of peace and pleasure, vnto this vale of misery and changeable world, as mutable as the Moone (vvhich the word Hierico importeth) he fel into the handes of theues, to wit the diuels, who despoiled him of his garment & coate of innocencie, & al supernatural habites and graces, and wounded him euen in natural perfection and facultie, which before by original iustice vvas much confirmed and perfited, and gaue him the fowre wounds afore mentioned, yet so, that they left him halfe a liue: not liuing the supernatural life of grace because sinne had bereued him of it, but yet liuing a natural life, because he had lost no natural perfection, though he was weakened and wounded also in that, because he lost original iustice which gaue no smal force and vigour euen vnto nature, and greater then nature of her selfe could haue had by nature. And whilest, he lay thus spoiled and wounded, the Priest and Leuite passed by him, and gaue him no helping hand, that is the law & the Prophets could tel him the nature of the disease, but could giue him no grace to heale it.

cible vvith inordinat concupiscence.

Adam thus vvounded vs.

Luc. 12.

The parable applyed

Tho. supra

Beda.

Luc. 10.

Ibidem.

3. Wherfore the Samaritane Christ Iesus (who when he vvas so called refused not the name) played the part of a merciful Phisitian, by the oyle of his mercie and vvine of his bloud, vvhich he provvred into his vvounds, to cure him So that if novv Hieremie demand of vs: *Nunquid resina non est in Galaad aut medicus non est ibi! Is there not rosen in Galaad, or is not there a Phisitian?* We can ansvver him quickly: yes Hieremie in Galaad the Church of Christ, vve vvant no rosen, salues, nor medecins, for vve haue seuen Sacramentes, vvhich al giue grace to heale al spiritual vvounds: and vve haue a Phisitian vvhose name is IESVS, vvhich importeth saluation, who came not for the whole but the sicke, not for the iust but for the sinful, and vvho in al respects hath playd al the partes of a good Phisitian.

Io. 8.

Hier. 7.

Luc. 5.

Th. 3. p. q. 1. a. 3

4. Phisitians are more in company with sicke then with the whole, so was this spiritual Phisitian, who one while conuersed with Pharisies, an other while with harlotes, an other while with Publicanes, and alwayes almost with infirme patientes. Phisitians haue their medicins, Christ hath his saluing Sacraments. Phisitians to alure their patients to take the prescribed potions, wil tast of them first them selues, and Christ to make vs patiently to drink downe the bitter potion of persecution and aduersatie, which is soueraine for the soule, first be-

The partes of a phisitian aplied to Christ

Mat. 9.

Mat. 7.

first began him selfe vnto vs, that we might pledge him the more willingly. Phisitians to cure vs do some tymes launce and cut vs, some times they prescribe vs fasting, and some times they let vs bloud: but this Phisitiã in this point far exceedeth them. For they to deminish the disease wil bid vs fast, but wil not fast them selues. Christ fasted for vs fourtie dayes and nightes to recure our surfet. They to ridde vs of superflous humours, or corrupted bloud wil launce our flesh or let vs bloud in a vayne, but wil not lose one drop of their owne bloud for vs, but Christ permitted his owne flesh to be cut in his circuncision, to be torne when the was whipped, and to be perced vvhen he was crucified, and would be let blood euen at the hart, to make a potion for our recouery. Other Phisitians seke to take away our disease, but wil not take it vpon them to ridde vs of it: but Christ hath taken our sinnes vpon him to ease and ridde vs of them. He hath taken our ague to him selfe, to take it from vs, not that he hath taken the malice of our sinnes, but the payne of sinne vpon him, and hath *suffred it in his body vpon the vvood of the crosse.* For as in a corporal ague there is the disease and the paine, and the disease or ague is a distemperature of heate and humours, the paine is not the ague but the effect of it, so in the spiritual ague of the soule which is sinne, there is the malice of sinne, vvhich is the disease, and this Christ could not take vnto him, because he was incapable of sinne, and there is the paine also dew vnto sinne, vvhich is not the ague, but a burning in Purgatorie or hel, if we do not preuent it by other corporal and voluntarie paines & satisfaction. And this Christ tooke vpon him in suffering hunger, thirst, cold, and other paynes which we had deserued, yea suffring death that we might liue, and so by taking vpon him the paine dew to sinne, hath cured the disease of sinne, and hath rid vs of our ague, by abiding the burning of the same. And hetherto we and the Gospelers agree, for they also wil say, that Christ is the Phisitian of our soules, but yet their doctrin is cleane contrarie, and so whilest in words and shew, they seeme to acknowledge him our Phisitian, in doctrine and in deed they make him none at al.

Christ susteined the paine to cure vs.
Mat. 4.
Christ vvas let bloud to make vs a potion.
1. Pet. 2.
In an ague, is the disease & the paine.
In the agaue of Some are thinges the disease, and the paine.
Christe tooke the paine dew to sinne, but not the sinne.

5. For if you remember, Luther, and Caluin are of opinion that we haue no inherent and internal iustice or sanctitie, but are iust only by Christes owne iustice, vvhich (say they) maketh vs reputed iust, but not in dede iust, hideth our sinnes but healeth them not, and couereth our spiritual wounds but cureth thẽ not. Which if it be true, then certes is Christ no true Phisitian, who healeth not but hideth only

See the third. chap of this booke.
Imputatiue iustice makes

only our sores and diseases. O blasphemie, ô ingratitude, ô iniurie, ô sacriledge couered with a pretence of religion! They wil seeme forsooth to attribute much to Christ, who as they say, hath made vs iust by his owne iustice, which he imputeth vnto vs, but whilest they acknowledge no other but Christs iustice imputed to vs, they are enforced to say, that Christ hath not verily sanctified vs, nor verily healed the spiritual sores & maladies of our soule, but hath only couered them and hidden them from the sight of God, by an imputation of his owne iustice, and so he may be a hider and couerer of our wounds, but no healer, nor Phisitian.

Christ no Phisitian.

The Conclusion.

The fifth Chapter shevveth hovv they robbe Christ of the title of a Lavv maker.

IF Moyses for prescribing lawes vnto the Iewes, Licurgus vnto the Lacedemonians, Solon to the Athenians, Romulus to the Romains, Plato to the Magnesians, Trismegistus vnto the Egiptians, and others for geuing lawes vnto their subiects, were so famous and renowmed: Vvhat honour must it be vnto our Sauiour Christ to haue bene the authour of the Christian law, and the lawgiuer vnto the Christians? They præscribed lawes only vnto some certaine people or nation, Christ vnto al nations. Their lawes had for their scope and proiect an external and ciuil peace, Christs law aymeth at an inward peace of the soule in earth, and an æternal peace in heauen? Their lawes forbad only external sinnes, as thefte, murder, adultery, and such like, litle respecting the inward desire and intention, Christes law restraineth euen the inward consent, desire, and dilight. Their lawes forbad not al vice, neither commanded or counsayled al vertues, for Platos lawes permitted wiues to be common, and other vices also: Licurgus his lawes vvere corrected as being toto rigorous, vvhich thing he tooke so heauily and so greeuously that he pined him selfe with abstinence: But Christes law either commandeth or counsayleth al vertues, not only moral but also Theological, and forbiddeth al vices vvhat soeuer. Wherfore Dauid sayth, that *God his lavv is immaculate conuerting soules: immaculate,* because it permitteth no filth of sinne,

Lavvgiuers.

Christ the Lavvgiuer to Christians.

Christ and his Lavv excelleth al other Lavvgiuers and lavves in many pointes.

Chris. ho 4. in Act.

Tertul. in Aptlog.

conuerting soules: because it induceth vs to al maner of vertue. Their lawes were ful so many superstitions and absurd errors, for they com-
August. l. de Ciuit. mended many Gods to be worshipped, and those beasts and serpents, and some of their wisest, denyed Gods prouidence, as Aristotle, some
l. de mundo. his foresight and prescience, as Cicero: some made God the soule of the world, some confined him vvith in the heauens, some held the
Psal. 18. soule to be mortal. But the lavv of Christ *is Praeceptum lucidum, illuminans oculos: a lightsome Precept, illuminating the eyes*: that is illuminating our vnderstanding, the eye of the soule vvith true fayth and knovvledge, and dispersing al clouds of ignorance, errors, and superstition. And no meruaile, because Christ the lavvgiuer vvas the vvisdom of his Fa-
Io. 14. ther, and vvhen he gaue his lavv, he gaue his Spirit vvho *teacheth his Church al Veritie.*

The Sume of the Christian lavv. 2. The lavv of Christ may be reduced to tvvo heades, to vvit, thinges that are to be beleeued, and things vvhich are to be obserued.
VVhat vve beleue. Vve beleue that there is a God, & him vve acknovvledge the only God and Creator and Ruler of al, vvho taketh account of al our actions, and vvil accordingly hereafter revvard vs. And although vve beleeue also thal this one God is three in Persons, and that the second Person vvas incarnate for vs, dyed that vve might liue euer, and rose again for our Resurrection, vvhich things are out of reasons reach, yet are not these or any other of the Mysteries of our beleefe against reason, or
The credibilitie of Christiã religion. vnbeseming the Diuine Maiestie, or repugnant to Philosophie, as Diuines do proue, vvho do so explicate these Mysteries, as nothing appeare repugnant to reason, and so do answere infidels obiections, as that they can conclude nothing euidently against vs. Yea Iustinus
Apol 1. ad Anton. l. 19. ciu. 6. 29. Martyr and S. Austin do shew, how the Platonists and other Philosophers, taught the like vnto many of those Articles vvhich Christians beleeue. And as concerning those thinges vvhich are to be obserued, to wit the precepts of good life, they are reduced vnto two, which
VVhat vve are to do. are the loue of God aboue al thinges, and the loue of our neighbour as our selfe: which are most reasonable, because God is the chiefest good,
VVhat vve ovve to God. and so most of al to be beloued, and our neighbour is like vs in nature, and ordained to the same end to which we are, and so to be belo-
VVhat vve ovve to our neighbour. ued as our selues. To our neighbour therfore we must do as we would be doone vnto, and therfore we must neither kil him, nor robbe him, not iniurie him in goods, life, or other thing, for our selues would not willingly be thus iniuried. And so we are forbidde al sinne against God, and al iniurie against man: yea we giue by our law to God, that

Which

which is dew to God, to wit, supreme honor because he hath supreme excellencie, supreme loue because he is the fountain of al goodnes, we yeeld him gratitude, because he is our best benefactor and redemer, feare because he is our Lord yea our Iudge. To men if they be superiors, we giue reuerence and obedience and that of conscience, to our æquals we owe charitie, to our inferiors we condescend by a complying nature. Vve are forbidden not only to kil, but also to be angry, not only to absteine from adultery and fornication, but also from lasciuious lookes, yea desires, we are bidden not only not to offend our freinds, but also to loue our enemyes. And to induce vs to this, the two things vvhich conteine al common welthes in awe, to wit, paine and reward, are proposed vnto vs: payne in hel, reward in heauen, payne to feare, reward to hope for.

To God vve giue al supremacie.

To men their devve.

Mat. 5.

3. No law more reasonable then this, none so perfect, which teacheth no errour, permitteth no vice, omitteth no good, but either cõmaundeth, or counsayleth it. And seing that Christ is the author of this law which surpasseth al lawes, greater is his honour and renoume then euer was the honour of Plato, Licurgus, yea Moyses or any other. Wherfore the prophet Esaie recounting other titles of honour dew vnto Christ, amongst others calleth him a lavv-maker; *Dominus iudex noster, dominus legifer noster, dominus Rex noster: Our lord is our Iudge, Our lord, our lavv maker, our lord is our King.* If he be our Lavv-maker he may make lawes to bynd vs, if he be our iudge he may pronounce sentence against the transgressors, and if he be our King he may punish vs, yea if he had called him only our King, it had been a sufficient argument to proue him a lavv-maker, because the principal meanes for a king to rule his subiects are his lavves and ordinaunces. Micheas speaking of the promulgation of Christs lavv at Hierusalem in Penthecost, sayeth, *That a lavv shal proceed from Sion & the vvord of God from Hierusalem.* The same Prophecie hath Esaie in the same words, and addeth that *Ilandes shal expect his lavv.* By which it is playne that Christ is a law-maker, who hath prescribed lawes, & therfore when he gaue his Apostles authoritie to baptise and preach, he bad them also to teach the Gentiles to kepe al those thinges, which he had commanded. And yet our Gospellers vvho bragge that they giue al to Christ, despoyle him of this honourable title, and auouch that he was a redemer only but no law-maker.

No Lavv like to the Christian lavv.

No Lavv-maker to Christe.

Isay. 33.

6. 4. c. 4.

c. 2.

c. 4. 2. 42.

Mat. 5.

See the first chap. of this booke.

Luther saith Christ. vvas no Lavv-maker.

4. Luther sayth plainly that *it is the office of the lavv to cõmand, threaten and terrifie, but the office of Christ is only to embrace sinners, vvho haue transgressed the lavv.*

in c. 2 ad Gal.

Ibidem. *the lavv.* Yea sayth he: *If vve make Christ an exactour of the lavv, vve confound Christ and the lavv, and make him the minister of sinne.* Wherefore thus he concludeth with this exhortation: *Quare Christum recte definias, non vt Sophistæ & Iustitiarij qui faciunt eum nouum legislatorem, qui abrogata veteri lege nouam tulerit, illis Christus est exactor & tyrannus: vvherfore define thou Christ a right, not as the Sophists do and the Iustitiaries* (so he calleth Catholiques because they affirme inherent iustice and auouch that, good workes are necessary) *vvho make him a nevv lavv-maker that hath abrogated the old lavv, and enacted a*
Ibidem. *nevv: to them Christ is an exactour and a tyrant.* How then I pray thee wouldst thou haue vs to define Christ? he sayth *that as it is the art of Christians not to care for lavves nor to imagin, that I bynd in conscience so is it an hard art, vvhich*
The arte vvhich Luther teacheth Christians. *I* (sayth he) *my selfe can hardly learne: to define Christ after this manner.* But yet this great Logician, at length giueth vs this definition of Christ: *Christus autem definitiue non est legislator sed propitiator & saluator: But Christ definitiuely is not a lavv-maker, but a propitiatour, and Sauiour.* By vvhich do-
Ibidem. ctrin it is playne, that Luther is of opinion, that Christ came not to
Hovv Luther defineth Christ terrifie vs, to or exact any law at our handes, but only to embrace the transgressors, so that they beleue only that he is their Redemer from
See the seueth booke c. 7. the law, which doctrin how it openeth the gap to vice, I shal herafter declare: here I only note that Luther despoyleth Christ of the title of a Lawmaker, and auoucheth that he neither made law, nor exacteth any law at our hands, which how iniutious it is to Christ, may appeare by the commendation, vvhich is due to Christ and his law.

l. 2. Inst. c. 11. n. 19. 5. Caluin putteth this difference betwixt the old and the new law, that the old promised grace and glorie with this condition if we kepe
Caluins difference betvvixt the old lavv and the nevv. the commandements, but the new law promiseth these things absolutely without that condition. So that Caluin thinketh that glory and saluation is promised by Christ, whether we obserue the law or no, and consequently he thinketh, that no law byndeth vs vnder payne of damnation. Whence it foloweth, that Christ neither exacteth, neither prescribeth any law vnder payne of damnation, and so is no law
Caluin makes Christ no lavv maker. maker. And the same Caluin after that he had discoursed of Christian libertie, which he sayth consisteth in a freedom from al lawes, concludeth thus: *vve conclude that they are exempted* (he speaketh of the faythful)
l. 3. Inst. c. 19. 9. 10. *from al lavves.* Whence it must needs folow that Christ is no Lawmaker for where there is no obligatiō there is no law (as shal be proued hereafter) where no law, there is no Law-maker, and therfore if Christ exacteth no law at our handes, and byndeth vs to none, he can by no right haue the name of a Law-giuer or Law-maker.

6. Let the Prophet Esaie therfore looke how he calleth Christ our *Lavv-maker*, yea let Christ him self correct and amend that saying of his: *Mandatum nouum do vobis, vt diligatis inuicem. I giue you a nevv lavv and commandement, that you loue one an other:* A new lavv (sayth S. Austin) Christ giueth vs, because although it be old, as being commanded in the old lavv, yet it is nevv, either because Christ hath annexed nevv grace vnto it, which in the old law it had not, or because by this grace annexed, it maketh vs nevv creatures, vvho before vvere old by sinne: or else (sayth S. Clement) it is a nevv lav, because Christ hath renevved it. Let him also remember his office better, vvhich (as Luther and Caluin say) is not to prescribe or exact lavves, but to imbrace the trasgressours. He forgot therfore his office, vvhen he bad vs *Keepe the commandementes if vve vvil enter into life:* and vvhen he corrected the olde lavv, commanding vs not only not to kil, but not to be angry, not only to loue our friends, but our enemies also.

c. 33. legifer. *Io. 13.* *l. 3. cont. ep. par. c. 2.* *l. 6. Const. Apost. c. 5. 2.* *Mat 19.* *Mat. 5.*

7. See, see, what open iniurie, against the playne text of Scripture, yea and against al reason also, these men are not afrayed to offer vnto Christ, in taking from him the title and office of a Lavvmaker. For if he could make no lavv, he was inferior to the meanest Prince in the world: vvho established a common vvealth, his Church, but hath no authoritie to command his subiects, who instituted Sacramentes, yet could make no law to bynd vs vnto them, and therfore when he threatneth damnation to them, that vvil not receiue his Baptisme, and protesteth that we shal haue no life, vnlesse *vve eate his flesh* and *drinke his bloud,* we may boldly contemne such peremptorie commandementes, because if Christ be no Law-maker, he could make no law, and where no law is, there is no obligation, and where is no obligation al men are as frie, as they who are Lordlesse and subiect to none.

Open iniurie against Christ. *Io. 3.* *Io. 6.* *The Conclusion.*

The sixt Chapter shevveth hovv they despoile Christ of the title of an eternal Priest, according to the order of Melchisedech.

The necessitie of a priest.

Lmightie God being highly offended, and iustly displeased, that so meane a creature as man, should contemne his commandement, and not care for his displeasure, it was necessary that a Priest should be found out, vvho by some pleasing Sacrifie, should appease this his indignation so iustly conceiued. And many Priestes in deed haue assaied by diuerse sacrifices to pacifie God thus angry, but haue al fayled of their intended purpose. For neither were they of that authoritie, as to be Mediators betvvixt God and man, for such a reconciliation, neither were their Sacrifices of that vvorth, as to make amends for so great a fault.

The insufficiencie of the priest of the old lavv.

2. Wherfore God by his Prophetes complayneth of their insufficiencie, saying that he *is ful, and cloyed vvith the multitudes of their sacrifices,* and telleth them plainly that if *they offer vnto him Holocaustes and vovves of fatlinges he vvil not looke at them.* Because (sayth he) God is not *delighted in such sacrifices.* Yea so insufficient were al the Priestes of the old law, that God by his prophet Ezechiel threatneth, that he wil put them out of office, and in steed of so many he wil giue vs one Priest, and Pastor, Christ IESVS, whom he calleth his seruant Dauid, because as man he descended lineally from Dauid, and in respect of his humaine nature, he was Gods seruant and inferior.

Isa. 1. Amos 5. Psal. 50. cap. 34. Philip. 2.

Christ the preest. Heb. 7.

3. This Priest, Christ IESVS, is the high Priest, and the only high Priest of the new law. For although in the lavv of Moyses it was necessary to haue many high Priestes, because (as S. Paul sayth) their mortalitie would not permit them to liue and remayne alwayes, and because death puts them out of office, it was necessarie that others should succeed them in the same authoritie. And so the first of this ranke and line of Priestes vvas Aaron (for Moyses vvas extraordinary) to whom Eleazarus and others succeded, to the number of fovvrscore and odde: yet in the nevv lavv one christ Iesus is sufficient, vvho though he haue many vicegerentes, vvhich are Bishops and Priestes of the

Ioseph. l. 20. Ant. c. 8. Tol. in c. 18. Ioan.

of the nevv lavv, yet hath he no successors. For no man succedeth to an other, vnles the other either dye, or giue ouer his office: vvherfore seing that our Sauiour Christ, though he dyed yet rose again, neuer to dy agayn, and neuer surrendred or gaue ouer his office, but stil offereth Sacrifice, stil baptiseth, stil ministreth Sacramentes, and ruleth and gouerneth his Church by his vicars and ministeres, he hath no high Priest that succedeth him, but is the sole and only High Priest of the nevv lavv, far exceding al the Pope, Bishops, and Priests that euer vvere.

Christe hath no Successor.

Christ the only high priest.

4. For his priestly authoritie (as diuines say) vvas not grounded vpon a caracter, vvhich other Priestes receiue in the Sacrament of Order, but vpon hypostatical vnion, by vvhich he vvas the Sonne of God: his authoritie extended not it selfe to Christianes only, or them that are baptised, as the Popes & Churches authoritie doth, vvho haue no iurisdiction ouer them that are out of the Church, and vvho neuer were baptized, but also euen vnto Infidels, vvhom he commandeth to receiue fayth, and the Sacrament of Baptisme: by his Priestly povver he instituted Sacraments, established a Church and Pastors, and prescribed a monarchical gouerment, vvhich ordonances the Church obeyeth but can not alter: by his authoritie he could giue grace vvith out Sacraments as he did to S. Mathevv, Marie Magdalen and others: vvheras the Pope Bishops and Priests of the Church giue no grace infallibly but by Sacraments. And this is the Priest vvho for the dignitie of his Person, and the valevv of his Sacrifice, vvas the only Priest vvho could appease Gods vvrath and indignation.

The differences betvvixt the priesthood of Christ, and others.

1. Cor. 5.

Mat. 19.

Luc. 7.

Christ the only preest vvho vvas able to appease God his anger.

5. This Priest must nedes be hard because the dignitie of his Person suffereth no repulse, & the worth of his Sacrifice was vnspeakable, the same that offered the sacrifice, vvas the God vvho vvas angry and & he to whō was offred the Sacrifice. The Priest was more holie, then is the person for vvhom the Sacrifice vvas offered vvas malicious, and the Sacrifie vvas more pleasing to God, then the sinne displeasing. So precious vvas the Sacrifice that if Christ had put the Sacrifice in one ballance, and the sinne in the other, it vvould haue ouer vvayed sinne, as a thing of no vveight, vvhich notvvithstanding is so heauy that it vveyeth dovvn to hel. For if euery operation of Christ be it neuer so litle, because it vvas *Theandreke* that is the operation of God and man, vvas of infinite valevv, by reason of the dignitie of the Person: vvhat shal vve say of that heroical operation of Christs Passion, vvhich vvas an act of singular charitie, couragious fortitude, inuincible patience, perfect

Heb. 5.

Rom. 5.

Iob. 6.

The Valeur and merit of Christes operations.

Io. 15.

Phil. 2.

perfect obedience, and sacred religion, for it vvas a Sacrifice?

Christ offered. 2. Sacrifices. The first at his last Supper. The second on the Crosse. 6. This Priest offered two Sacrifices, the one at his last supper, vnbloudy, the other vpon the Crosse, bloudy, or rather one and the same Sacrifice (in respect of the thing vvhich was offered) after diuers manners, and vnder diuers formes. For in his last supper he offered his sacred body and bloud after an vnbloudy manner, on the crosse he offered the same after a bloudy maner, at his last supper he offered his body, and bloud, vnder an other forme, that is vnder the formes of bread, and wine, on the crosse he offred the same in their owne forme and likenes. *Heb 7. 9.* The bloudy Sacrifice was but once to be offered, because it was so precious that one oblation vvas sufficient. But because it was offered only as a general cause of al grace, & price of our redemption, it vvas conuenient that this general cause, should be determined by more particular causes, and that this price should be more determinately applyed, as by Sacramentes; fayth, and good works: so by the vnbloudy Sacrifice of the Masse. Yea because the Sacrifice of the *The necessitie of the first Sacrifice. See the fourth booke ch 2.* crosse being bloudy, could not be repeated after Christs resurrection, he then being impassible and immortal, it was conuenient that an vnbloudy Sacrifice should also be offered continually in the Church, for the worship of God and exercise of religion, vvhich (as I shal proue in the fourth booke) can not stand without a Sacrifice. By the bloudy Sacrifice Christ was a Priest and high Priest, but neither according vnto the order of Aaron (because that Priesthood by Christs Passion vvas abrogated and was confined whithin the Tribe of Leuie, of vvhich Christ was not) neither according to Melchisedech, because there was no similitude nor agrement in their Sacrifices.

Psal 109. 7. Wherfore seing that our Sauiour was a Priest according to the order of Melchisedech (for God affirmeth it with oth, and the Prophet Dauid, and the Apostle S. Paul auouch it) we must needs haue a *Heb 7.* Sacrifice, by which he resembled his Sacrifice, and was a Priest according to his order. *The Conueniences betvvixt Christ and Melchisedech.* And this S. Paul proueth at large by diuers conueniences which were betwixt these two Priests & their Sacrifices. For as Melchisedech was a King and Priest, and a King of Salem, that is of peace, so was Christ. As Melchisedech hath neither father nor mother recorded in Scripture, so Christ as man had no father, and as God no mother: As Melchisedechs Priesthood descended not by carnal generation, so neither did Christes Priesthood. As Melchisedechs priesthood was æternal, because neither the begining nor ending is set *Ps. 109.* downe in Scripture, so Christs Priesthood hath no end as Dauid affirmeth.

firmeth. As Melchisedechs Priesthood vvas of higher perfection, then the Priesthood of Aaron (for Melchisedech blessed Abraham and in him the whole Tribe of Leuie, vvhich argueth superioritie) so was Christ and his Priesthood farre aboue Aaron and his Priesthood. Lastly as Melchisedech offered a Sacrifice of bread and vvine, so Christ offered his body and bloud in his last supper vnder the formes and accidents of bread and wine. And this last conuenience, is that for which Christ especially is sayd to be according vnto the order of Melchisedech, not that he is of the same order, or that his Sacrifice and Melchisedechs are al one, for Christs Priesthood and Sacrifice farre excelled his Priesthood and his Sacrifice: but because there is most resemblance betvvixt them and their Sacrifices. And this last conuenience S. Paul expressed not, because the Iewes, to whom he wrote, were not capable of so high a Mysterie, yet as the Fathers note he insinuated it, when speaking of Christ whom he had before called *Priest and Bishop according to the order of Melchisedech* he added: *Of vvhom vve haue great speach and inexplicable to vtter, because you are become vveake to heare.*

Gen. 14. Heb. 7.

Christ is a Priest according to Melchisedech by the Sacrifice of the Masse. Heb. 5.

8. This dignitie of an ęternal Priest according to the order of Melchisedech, which the Prophet Dauid and the Apostle S. Paul giue vnto our Sauiour Christ, our Gospellers (who vaunt that they giue al vnto Christ) sacrilegiously take from him For although they grant that Christ offered a Sacrifice on the Crosse, yet that is not sufficient to make him an ęternal Priest, nor according to the order of Melchisedech. And this shal appeare most plainly by this argument. Betwixt a Priest and Sacrifice is a necessary relation, by which one inferreth the other: for as a father can not be without a sonne, nor a maister without a seruant, so neither can a Priest be without a Sacrifice, because a Priests principal office is to offer sacrifices to God. And as no sonne no father, no seruant, no Maister, so no Sacrifice, no Priest. And as a Priest can not be without a Sacrifice, so neither can an æternal Priest be without an æternal Sacrifice. Wherfore if Christ neuer offered other Sacrifice then that of the Crosse, as our aduersaries affirme, thē is he not a perpetual Priest, because he hath no Sacrifice which either by him selfe, or by his ministers is perpetually offered.

Psal. Heb. 57.

Our Gospellers robbe Christ of the title of an æternal priest according to Melchisedech.

A priest and a Sacrifice are correlatiues. Heb. 5.

9 To say that the Sacrifice of the Crosse stil remayneth in effect, because by that vve receiue grace and redemption, and from that our Sacramentes haue their efficacie, is not sufficient. For the effects of this Sacrifice, are no Sacrifice, and the Sacrifice it selfe is not perpetual, because it was but once offered, and so that Sacrifice is not sufficient to

Thee Sacrifice of thee Crosse is not sufficient to make Christe an æternal Priest.

according to Melchisedech. cient to make Christ an æternal Priest. Much lesse can it make Christ a Priest according to the order of Melchisedech, because there is no resemblance betwixt their Sacrifices. If onr aduersaries would grant, as Catholiques do, that Christ in his last supper offered him self as a Sacrifice vnder the forme of bread and wine, I could easily see how Christ is an æternal Priest according to Melchisedechs order, because that Sacrifice is stil offered in the Masse by the handes of Christs ministers, & altogether resembleth Melchisedechs Sacrifice. For though it be not bread and wine, at his was, yet hath it the formes of bread and wine, and is vnbloudy as his was.

That Melchisedech did Sacrifice. 10. But rather then they wil grant this (such is their hatred against the Masse) they wil deny, against plaine Scripture, that Melchisedechs bread and wine was a Sacrifice. Yea against plaine Scripture, because in the booke of Genesis, Moyses recoũteth vnto vs how Melchisedech *brought forth bread & vvine, for he was a Priest of God the highest,* *Gen. 14.* vvhich reason argueth that this bringing forth of bread & wine, vvas an offering of bread and vvine in maner of a Sacrifice: for if this bringing forth was but a prophane distribution of bread & wine amongst Abrahames souldioars, vvhat consequence had bene in that saing: *he brought forth bread and wine, for he was a Priest?* as wel might he haue sayd, because he was a barber: and better and more to the purpose should he haue sayd, because he was a Baker, or an Inkeper, or a good house keeper: vvherfore vnles we wil say that Moyses spake impertinently, we must affirme that his bread & wine was a Sacrifice. And if we hold Christ to be an æternal Priest and that according to Melchisedechs order, vve must acknowledge that Christ stil offereth a Sacrifice in the Church, and that, vnder the formes of bread and wine.

Either the Masse is a Sacrifice or Christ is no æternal priest nor according to Melchisedech. 11. Wherfore seing that our aduersaries wil acknowledge no other Sacrifice then that of the Crosse, they deny Christ to be an æternal Priest, and in that they auouch that Christ neuer offered any Sacrifice vnder the formes of bread and wine, lest they should be enforced to admit the Masse for a Sacrifice, they deny him to be a Priest according to the order of Melchisedech. For although he agree with Melchisedech in that as God, he had no mother, and as man, he had no father, as also in that he was a King and Priest, as he was, yet can he not *Heb. 7.* be an æternal Priest vvithout an æternal Sacrifice, neither according to Melchisedeches order, vnles he haue a Sacrifice like vnto his Sacrifice. *The Conclusion.* But both these pointes our aduersaries deny, because they vvil not admit the Masse, *ergo*, notvvithstanding their bragging that they giue al to Christ,

to Christ, they robbe him and despoyle him of that glorious title of an *Psal. 109.*
æternal Priest according vnto Melchisedeches order, which S. Paul, *Heb. 7.*
and King Dauid giue vnto him, and God him selfe auoucheth, and confirmeth with an oth.

The seuenth chapter shevveth hovv they make him no Iudge of the quicke and the dead.

NOthing more frequent in Scripture, nor more common in the mouthes and hartes of true Christians, then the two Aduentes, or Comminges of Christ. The first Aduent he hath already performed in al humilitie. The second he wil performe in al maiestie and glory: the cause of the first was mercie, of the second iustice. In the first he vvas a meke as a lambe, in the second he wil be *Io. 3.*
as terrible as a Lion. The first was to saue sinners, the second wil be to *Io. 1.*
condemne sinners. In the first he exhorted vs to good, and dehorted vs from euil, in the second he wil reward the good, & punish the euil. *Zach. 9.*
Of the first Aduent prophecied Zacharie saying, *Behold thy King shal come vnto thee iust, and a Sauiour, Poore, and mounted on an asse.* Of the second *c. 7.*
speaketh Daniel vvhen he sayeth, *he savv*, that is for saw, *one coming in clovvds like the Sonne of man, to vvhom the Ancient of dayes gaue Honour, Povver and a Kingdome.* Of the first speaketh Christ him self when he sayth: *God* *Io. 3.*
did not send his Sonne to iudge the vvorld, but that the vvorld might be saued by him: Of the second speaketh the Prophet and Euangelist S. Iohn, vvhen he *Apoc. 1.*
biddeth vs *behold Christ comming in cloudes, and telleth vs that euery eye shal see him, euen they vvho pricked him, and that al the tribes of the earth shal bevvayle themselues vpon him.* And of this Aduent speaketh Christ him selfe de- *Luc. 21.*
scribing his owne comming to Iudgement in a terrible forme, and sayth, that *they then shal see the Sonne of man comming in a cloud vvith great povver and maiestie.*

2. For vvant of vvitte to distinguish these tvvo Aduentes, and to apply them to the same Person at diuers tymes, some imagined that two diuerse Persons were to come, the one called the sonne of Ioseph, who they say shalbe slaine in the battayle of Gog & Magog: the other called the sonne of Dauid, who shal come againe (as they say) the *The cause of the Ievves and others error concerning the comming of Christ.*

Ex Petro Galat l 4. de Arcanis fidei Cath. c. 1.

sonne of Ioseph & shal redeeme Israel, & restore the Israelits to their Kingdome againe. Others hauing their eyes dasled with the splendor of the second Aduent, can not see the first which is base and humble, and therfore say (which is the common voice of the Iewes) that the Messias shal come like a temporal King in glorie and Maiestie, and by force of armes shal restore the Iewes to their former glorie, and because they haue not as yet seene such a Messias, they say that he is not yet come, but stil is expected. But by the Scripturs alleaged it is manifest that one and the selfe same Christ IESVS should come, first to saue the world and after to iudge the same. Vvherfore S. Peter sayth,

Act. 10.

that Christ commanded him & his felovv Apostles *to preach to the People, and to beare vvitnes, that he it is (to vvit vvho before came to redeme vs) vvho is constituted by God the Iudge of the liuing and the dead.* And Christ him self sayth,

Io. 5. Vide Maldon. in c. 5. Io. Act. 17.

that *God the Father iudgeth none (that is in a visible maner) but hath giuen al iudgement to his Sone.* And lest that any should imagin, that Christ only as God is Iudge, but not as man, he addeth, that God the Father *hath giuen him povver to iudge vs because he is the Sonne of man.* And S. Paul sayth, that God hath *appointed a day in vvhich he vvil iudge the vvorld by a man, vvhom he hath raysed from death to life.* So that the same Christ IESVS, who came first in humble maner to cal vs by his grace, & to receiue vs to his mercie, shal come againe in glorie, to giue vs our final sentēce. And God the Father, and God the Holy Ghost shal Iudge vs, as vvel as God the Sonne, yet he only as man and as an vnderiudge shal iudge vs in a visible maner, and in this sense God the Father shal not iudge.

The same Christ cometh tvvise.

Christ the only visible Iudge,

2 Cor 5.

3. This Iudge shal giue sentence vpon al men, because as S. Paul sayth, we must al appeare before the tribunal and Iudgement-seate of Christ. This Iudge in this Iudgement shal exercise the three principal actes of a Iudge, to wit discussion, remuneration, and condemnation. He shal discusse and examin the cause of euery one, and euery circumstance of the same, and therfore by the Prophet Ioel he sayth, that *he vvil dispute vvith vs.* A sore disputation, where the Creator disputeth and the creature ansvvereth, vvhere God that is offended vvil be the iudge and witnes, where the iudge is of such insight, that he seeth farther into the guilties cause, then he him selfe, & is so wachful that no excusing, cloking, or hiding, can deceiue him, so iust, that no bribes can corrupt him, so seuere, that no teares at that day can moue him, so resolute in his sentence, that no repreeue nor appellation can be admitted. This discussion and examination shal be doone in a trise, because it is nothing but a reuelation, and manifestation vnto our consciences,

3. Actes of this Iudge. Discussion of causes. Ioel. 3. A sore disputation.

Hovv quicke this discussion shalbe.

sciences, what euery one hath doone, which shal be so euident, that our selues shal accuse and crye guiltie, before the Iudge condemne vs. This examination and discussion the Iudge shal vse only vvith Christianes, because the cause of their condemnation (they being Christians) is not so manifest: and not with Infidels, because in that they want fayth, the cause of their condemnation is euident, and so no discussion shal be nessary. VVherfore S. Austin sayth: *Ad iudicium non veniunt, nec Pagani, nec Heretici, nec Iudei, quia de illis scriptum est, qui non credit, iam iudicatus est. To Iudgement do come neither Paganes, nor Heretiks, nor Ievves, because of them it is vvritten: he that beleueth not is already iudged*, that is in respect of discussion of his cause, he is already iudged, & nedeth not in the general iudgement any other discussion, for the cause of his exclusion from glorie, because his infidelitie is a cause most euident: yet (as some diuines affirme) for their other sinnes and for the diuersitie of their paynes, their cause also shal be discussed, not that God Knoweth it not without discussion, but because he wil make it known to the world.

VVhose cause shalbe discussed.

Serm. 33. de Sanct.

Io. 3.

Vide Mald in c. 3. Ioan

D. Th. disp 55.

4. The second office of a Iudge which Christ shal exercice, is called the sentēce of remuneration, which after the discussion of their causes and approbation of their merites, he shal pronounce for the elect, in those most confortable words: *Venite benedicti Patris mei, percipite regnum &c. come you blessed of my Father, take possession of the Kingdome, vvhich vvas prepared for you, from the beginning of the vvorld.* The third office and action of a Iudge which Christ shal exercise, is the sentence of condemnation, which after examination of their crimes, God shal pronounce against wicked Christians, and faythles infidels also, because, *he that beleueth not shalbe condemned.* And this sentence shalbe pronounced by the mouth of Christ, & with an audible voice, in those terrible words which the Euangelist also hath set dovvne, *Ite maledicti in ignem aeternum*, &c *Goe you accursed into euerlasting fire, vvhich is praepared for the diuel and his angels.* This is the honourable title & office of Christ, which the Gospellers also confesse in words and professe in their Creed, but in their other doctrin deny it, as I shal euidently demonstrate by their opinions and vvords, which take from Christ the three offices of a Iudge already alleaged.

The sentēce of remuneration

Mar. 25.

The sentēce of condemnatiō.

Mat. 16.

Mat. 25.

5. And first of al to beginne with the last act and office vvhich a Iudge exerciseth, to wit, condemnation, Caluin sayth plainly that *Christ is our Redemer and is not to mount vp into his tribunal seate for the condemnation of a faithful man.* Adde to this that place of Scripture *vvhosoeuer*

l. 2. Inst. c. 16. 18.

Io. 3.

beleueth

beleueth not is already iudged. And thou shalt see that Caluin leaueth none for Christ to condemne, at the latter day And truly herin Caluin speaketh very conformably to his owne doctrin. For he is of opinion that Christ hath so redemed vs that no law can bynd vs, and no sinne can be imputed vnto vs, which if it be so the title of a Redemer and a Iudge are repugnant, and so if Christ be our Redemer after this maner, he can not be our Iudge. For if our redemption importeth a release from al lawes, and such a friedom from sinne, that no sinne can be imputed vnto vs, then certes Christ can not for any sinne, condemne vs at the latter day.

See the fourth booke & fift ch. and seueth booke chap 4.

No faithful man can be cōdēned by their opinion.

6. Secondly they deny al merit, and affirme that al our actions are of them selues mortal sinnes, seme they neuer so good: which is the opinion both of Luther and Caluin, and is commonly receiued of al their scholars: by vvhich doctrin they take away the sentence of remuneration. For if our actions deserue nothing at God his hands, then although he may frankely bestovv vpon his elect, vvhat glorie it pleaseth him, yet can he not be sayd to remunerate and reward their works: for where is no desert, there is no reward, and so though Christ may like a liberal King bestow glorie on them, yet he can not like a Iudge hy sentence of remuneration reward them: and sc Christ loseth an other part of his office.

Li. 3. Inst. c. 8. 9. l. Inst. 6. 57 Lut. l de capt. Bab. c. de bap. & in cap. 2. ad Gal.

No sentēce of remuneration by their doctrin.

7. Tney affirme also that al our sinnes are æqual, and they scoffe at the distinction of mortal and venial sinnes: and in this also Caluin speaketh according to his grounds: for he sayth, that al our actions are vicious, because they procede from a vicious nature corrupted by original sinne, vvhence foloweth, that al our actions are alike defiled, because they procede from the same fountaine of corruption. Which doctrin if it go for true, then doth Christ lose the third part of his office, which is discussion of sinnes and causes. For where there is no distinction betwixt the crimes and offences, there can be no difference in punishement, and vvhere no difference is in punishment, the Iudge must pronounce the same sentence & giue the same iudgement, without al discussion either of the offences or the punishmentes.

Lut. Calu sup. Mel in locis tit de discrim pec. mor. & ven.

No discussion of causes by their doctrin.

8. They auouch also that vve haue no libertie nor frie vvil in our actions, whence it foloweth (as I shal demonstrate in the seuenth booke) that in our actions is neither vertue nor vice, neither meritie nor demerit, and so Christ in his iudgement can exercise none of al the three offices which are before mentioned. For where is no vertue, nor merit, there can be no sentence of remuneration and revvard:

See the seuēth booke c. 7. chap. 10.

ward: where is no vice there can be no sentence of condemnation, & where is no vertue nor vice at al, there can be no difference of workes, either in vertue, or vice, merit, or demerit, and where is no difference of causes, there can be no discussion, as is already proued. And so Christ should be no Iudge at al. For as S. Austin sayth. *If friewil be not, hovv can God iudge the vvorld?* And if we haue not frie wil, why are not brute beastes called to iudgement as wel as we, seing that nothing can excuse their cruelties but want of frie wil?

Epist. 46.

No reason by their doctrin vvhy brut beastes are not arraned and Iudged.

9. Lastly they are not afrayd to auerre, that God and consequently Christ, is the author of al our sinnes, that Iudas his treachery and Dauids adulterie were as much God his vvorke, as S. Paules conuersion, yea Caluin sayth, that God vrgeth vs, eggeth, & enforceth vs to sinne: vvhich doctrin, if it go for currant, Christ can not iustly condemne any, because as Fulgentius sayth: *Deus non est autor eius cuius est vltor: God is not the autor of that of vvhich he is the reuenger, and punisher.* And consequently can not iustly punish sinners, if he be author of their sinnes. For vvith good reason might the condemned persons make exception against his sentence, and stand to it, that by no reason nor iustice God can condemne them for that, in vvhich he had as much part as they, and to vvhich he inforced them. And so thou seest (gentle reader) how these great bosters who bragge they giue al to Christ, despoile him and robbe him of his honourable title of *Iudge of the quicke and the deade,* which they professe in their Creed, but deny in their doctrin.

See the fifth booke & first chap.

l ad Monimū

VVhat the dāned may say for thē selues out of the nevv doctrin.

The cōclusion.

The eight Chapter declareth hovv to no smal iniurie of Christ they make euery Christian, and faythful man, as good and as holy, as he him self is.

LVTHER, Caluin, and al the packe of their adhærents, as in the seuenth booke shalbe related, and in part, in the second and third Chapter of his third booke is already declared, are of opinion, that we are iustified & sanctified by the selfe same iustice, wherevvith Christ him selfe is iust, which is inherent in him, and imputed to vs, and apprehended by vs vvith the reaching hand of faith, and so made our owne. They are afrayed forsooth to

The reformers deny inherent iustice.

grant inhærent iustice, lest they should giue vs occasion to glorie in our owne sanctitie, and so to fal into Pelagianisme, which affirmeth that Christes grace is not necessary. But whilest they feare where they neded not, they feare not where they should, but runne boldly, and desperatly into absurd blasphemie. For Pelagius is not condemned for auouching inherent grace, but for denying that Christs grace was necessarie, either to the obseruing of the law, or to the meriting of eternal glorie, or to the ouercoming of tentations, or auoiding of sinne: and for affirming that man by his owne frie wil without grace might do al these thinges Wherfore to grant inherent grace, by which we are iustified and sanctified, hath no resemblance with Pelagianisme: neither doth it giue vs occasion of pride, for thorgh this grace be in our soules, yet is it the guift of God, and an effect of Christs Passion, and so is his, by guift and merit, because be giueth it, and deserued it for vs, & it is ours only by donation, and possession.

Ex Aug hær. 22. ep. 95. 205. 206 l. de nat. & grat. c. 10. & 18.

Pelagius opinion.

To grant inherēt iustice is no Pelagianisme.

2. But whilest they seeke to auoid Charibdis they fal into Scylla: for if we haue no created inhærent iustice, but are iust only by Christs iustice imputed to vs, then doth it folow, that so soone as we apprehend Christs iustice as our owne, we are at the very first come to a ful point in perfection, and so perfect that vve can proced no farther, because Christs grace is so perfect that it neuer increased: for as the first Adam, was created in perfect growth & stature, so the second Adam was indevved from the first moment of his conception, with perfect sanctifie, and was euen then at his ful pitch, and spiritual growth neuer increasing either in grace or knowledge, but only in body, yeares, and experience. And so if we be iust by his grace imputed to vs, then are we so perfect that as the Beguines & Beguards sayd, we can be no perfecter, and so are al iust alike, and consequently shal al receiue the same glorie as Iouinian the heretike sayed, and shal not differ in glorie as starres do in brightnes, as S. Paul auoucheth.

To vvhat absurdites Imputatiue iustice driueth our aduersaries.

The first that vve are perfect the first moment. that vve are al iust alike.

Christ neuer increased in sanctitie.

1. Cor. 15.

3. Secondly hence it foloweth that we are al as iust as Christ. For if we be iust by his iustice, then is his iustice and ours al one, and so we as iust as he. They wil say, that his iustice in him is inhærent, to vs only it is imputed, & is only so much ours as we apprehend it by faith, and therfore we and he may be iust by one and the same iustice, and yet not iust alike. But this wil not serue their turne: for although this may make some difference in the maner of iustification, yet in iustice and sanctitie it selfe, we are as iust as Christ: because we are iust by his iustice which faith apprehendeth: and seing that faith apprehendeth

The second that vve are as iust as Christ.

Their ansvver

The refutatiō

al Chrial Christes iustice, al is imputed to vs, and so we are as iust as Christ, or at least reputed as iust as he.

4. Let no man then meruaile at Martin Luther, for auouching once in the heat of his sermon, that euery Christian is as holy as our blessed Lady, neither let him think that Bucers mouth ran ouer, whem he sayd that the vilest of the ministerie or faithful is better thē S. Iohn Baptist: no, he must not be scandalized at those bold speaches of some, who as D. Tapper relateth, were not afrayd, nor ashamed to bost that they were as grateful to God as Christ him selfe is. For if we be iust by Christs iustice (which by faith on our part is vvholy of vs apprehended, and wholy by God imputed vnto vs) we either are, or at least are reputed, as iust as he, and consequently are as grateful and acceptable to God as he. O Luceferian pride, ô sacriledge worthy reuenge from heauen. For what is this but to make them selues felovvmates vvith Christ, and consequently to make them selues gods, or him a creature? By Luthers and Caluins leaue, the creature novv may compare vvith the creator, and the redemed with the Redemer, and may boldly say not only as Lucifer did, that he wilbe like the highest, but may adde to his pride and aspire higher then he, affirming boldly that he is already as iust, as holy, and as good as Christ, who is the highest And thus the reader may see how true it is that these men giue al to Christ, who giue so much to them selues, that they wil be as good as he.

Ser. in Nat. Virg.

Luther sayd al are as good as our B. Lady.

cap 3 in Mat.

Bucer that a minister is as good as S. Io. Baptist.

In explic. ar. de iustif.

The reformers are so many Lucifers.

The Conclusion.

The ninth Chapter, shevveth hovv they make Christ ignorant, not knovving vvhat belonged to his office, and hovv therby they bring the nevv testament, and Christian Religion in question.

AS the first man Adam, in the first moment of his life, was creared not a babe, infant, or weakling, but a strong and lustie man, as if he had bene at fortie or fiftie yeares of age, (for then men at that age were most vouthful and lustie) so vvas he indewed with al science and knowlge belonging to his state. For if God gaue him from the beginning, a perfect stature and pitch, & an able body fitte for generation, because he was to be the common father, by whom

Adam the first day vvas a man pecier. l. 4. in p. 1. q. 1.

Adam: Knovvledge Plato in Gratilo. Perier. l. 5. in Gen. q. 1. 3. 4. Molina 1 p in trac. de opere Sex dierum. The second Adam Christ Iesus, vviser.

vvhom mankind should be propagated, no doubt he gaue him also a soule furnished with al natural sciences, because he was the first Doctor, to whom mankind was to goe to schoole, to learne of him as of a Master the secrets of nature, the inuentions of artes, the knowledge of God, & the Mysteries of fayth. Neither is this collection myn only, but is the common opinion of Diuines, which Ecclesiasticus confirmeth, who no litle extolleth the first Adams knowledge. If therfore the first Adam was so vvise and so rich in knowledge, what shal we say of the second Adams knowledge, who vvas the high Priest, and Doctor of the nevv Lavv, and vvas to reueale greater secretes and Mysteries to his Church, then the first Adam should haue manifested vnto his posteritie?

3. Reg. 3. 4. Ecclesiast. 1. Salomons VVisedom. 3. Reg. 4. 10. Mat. 12. The second Salomon Christ Iesus, vviser then the first. Agg. 2. Mat. 12.

2. Salomon also is famous for his profound wisedom, in so much that holy Scripture giueth him this preeminence, that *he vvas vviser then al that vvent before him, or come after him, and excelled al that euer vvere in Hierusalem, and vvas more learned then al the Easterne Sages.* In so much that not only the Queene of Saba, but others also from al parts of the world resorted vnto him, to heare him discourse vpon the natures of beasts, trees, and plantes, euen from the Cedar, to the Isope. If Salomon, King of the Iewes only, who built but a material Temple for God, was indewed with so rare knowledge, vvhat shal we thinke of the second Salomons wisdom, Christ Iesus, who vvas as a spiritual King to rule the whole world, and was to builde a Temple and Church for God to dwel in, no lesse then the Christian world, which was and is farre more glorious then that of Salomons building, for *the glorie of the last Temple, vvas greater then that of the first?* And behold sayth Christ pointing to him selfe, *more then Salomon here.*

Christs Knovvledge. S. Tho. 3 p q. 9 & 10. Caiet. Zuarez. Bart. Medina Ibidem Scholastici in 3. d. 14. Isa 11. Col. 2.

3. Wherfore Diuines with one common consent affirme, that our Sauiour Christ was enriched with the euident and cleare vision of God, by which euen as man he sawe God face to face, and al his diuine attributes, and perfections. Secondly they say, he was endewed with al natural sciences, which are perfections and ornamentes of mans soule. Thirdly they say, that he had a supernatural and infused science, by which he saw clearly the Mysteries of Christian fayth, vvhich we beleue, by vvhich he forsaw al future thinges, euen the day of Iudgement, and penetrated so the harts of men, that he knew euery mās cogitation. And this the Prophet Esaie insinuateth, when he sayth *that the spirit of vvisdome and vnderstanding shal rest vpon him.* To which S. Paul subscribeth when he calleth Christ the *treasure house of Gods vvisdom.*

An

And this knowledge Christ obteyned not by studie and labour, but by infusion euen from the first moment of his conception: and therfore vvhen he was but twelue yeares old, and had neuer bene trayned vp in Schoole or Vniuersitie, he disputed so learnedly with the Doctors, that they were al astonished at his vvisdome. And no meruayle for he was the vvisdome of his Father, and the Word of God, and his humaine nature was the booke in vvhich Gods vvord, vvas as it vvere written, by Incarnation, with an abbreuiation, and so must nedes be the treasure howse of Gods vvisdome, and as it were the Academie of al sciences. This is the opinion which Catholiques haue of their High Priest, chiefe Doctor, and Maister, Christ Iesus.

4. But the Gospellers and nevv Christians of this age haue not so honourable an opinion of him, but rather like proud Disciples they wil correct this their Maister, and accuse him of grosse ignorance. Luther wil stand to it that Christ knew not when the day of Iudgement was to happen, yea that some tymes he was ignorant of other matters. Zuinglius, Bucer and Beza are opinion that Christ profited in knowledge by litle and litle, and knevv not yester day, what he knoweth to day. Wherin they imitate the Gnostickes, and Agnoits and the author of the booke of Christs infancie, which recordeth that Christ went to Schole and learned his A. B. C. Caluin in his iarring Harmonie vpon the Euangelists, explicating those words of S. Luke: *And the child encreased and vvas comforted in spirit.* sayth plainly, and repeateth it tvvise or thrise, that Christ profited not only in apparance, but verily and inwardly, in grace and knowledge, & was ignorant also of many things, euen as other men are, sauing that ignorance in men is a paine of sinne, and a part of original sinne, in Christ it was not so. And in the same booke he sayth, that Christ as man knew not the day of Iudgement, not only because he knevv it not to tel it to others, but also because he could not informe him selfe of the same. The like song Caluin singeth in the same Harmonie hãdling that place, where Christ is sayd to haue prayed to his Father to frie him from the Chalice of his Passion, if it were possible: for there Caluin often repeateth that those wordes issued out of Christes mouth ere he was aware, and that feare & griefe did so perturbate his mynd that he knew not what he sayd, and therfore corrected him selfe by and by. O arrogancie more then Luciferian: Dareth the potte accuse the potter of vvant of skil? or dareth the creature accuse the Creator of ignorance, and the Christian condemne Christ of folye, error, & inconsideration? If he be worthy

Christs knovvledge vvas infused.
Luc. 2.
Io. 7.
Christ as man was the booke in vvhich Gods vvorde was written, and the treasure hovvse of Gods knovvledge.
The Gospellers say that christ was ignorant.
Conc. de Nat. Domini Hom Dom. 1. post Epiph.
Luthers opiniõ of Christs knovvledge.
Iren. l. 1. c. 17.
Amb l. 1. 5. de fide c. 7. liber: in Brew c. 19.
The Gnostikes opinion.
Isid l. 8 etym. c. 5.
Calu. in Har. Luc. 2.
Caluins opinion.

Mat. 5. hel that shal say (*foole*) to his brother, how many helles deserueth Caluin, that in effect, vvith the same contumelious vvordes, myscalleth Christ him selfe.

Caluins obiection. Mar. 13. The ansvver. Hovv Christ knevv not the day of Iudgement. Amb. in 29. Luc. Nazorat. 6 Theol. Hier Chrys. Theophilc. 2. Mat. Hier in c. 2. Mat. Luc. 2. An other obiection. The ansvver. S. Th. 3. p. q. 7. a. 12. Caiet: Zuar. medin v ibide.

5. But say they, Christ him selfe saith, that he knew not the day of iudgement, *ergo*, he was ignorant of it. I grant he semed to say so, but his meaning is to be taken. And the ancient Fathers rather then they would say that Christ was ignorant, would seeke to interpret these wordes, so as they might not seme to derogate to him. Some therfore sayd that he knoweth not that day, because *he vvas ignorant of it in his members*, others say, that he ment only, that he knew it not by humain knowledge, but yet denied not but that he knew it by reuelation: others say that he sayd he knew it not, because it was committed to him in such secret, that he might not reueale it, and so knew it not, to reueale it vnto others: yea some rather then they would make Christ to be ignorant, auouched that those words were foisted in by the Arrianes, to proue Christ to be but a creature, and pure man. They obiect also that S. Luke sayth, that IESVS, *encreased in age, grace, and vvisdome, before God, and men.* But this argument is as easily answered, for some expound those wordes thus: Christ encreased in age verily, and before God and men, but in grace and wisdome only in outward apparence and before men: others say, that he encreased in grace and wisdom, that is in actions of grace and wisdome, because as he came to riper yeares, so he made more remonstrance of his grace, & wisdome, by meritorious operations, & actes of wisdome, which were in dede meritorious, gracious, and wise, and were esteemed such before God and men. Although inwardly they neither augmented Christes grace, nor his wisdom: for as diuines say, at the first he was as holy and wise as at the last, because in his conception as al grace and vvisdom vvas then new because he was the Sonne of God, so al was then infused: and only he had greater and greater experience.

an other obiection of Caluin. Gal. Harin. Mer. 14. The ansvver. Mar. 14.

6. But yet they haue not doone. Either (saith Caluin) Christ knew that it vvas possible to escape death, or he knevve not. If he Knevv, why doubteth he? If he knewe not, then was he ignorant. Thus the diuel laboureth in his members and ministers, to make the vvisdome of God ignorant. To this therfore we must also giue an answer: and that we shal as easily. For Christ knew that it was absolutely possible to auoid death and therfore sayd to his Father: *al thinges are poßible to thee*: he knew also that supposing his Fathers vvil and commandement, he was to dye: yet thus he spake and thus he prayd, to shew him selfe

true

true man, and to declare that according vnto the flesh he feared death, yet absolutly according to the wil of his superior part, he was resolued to die, as appeareth, by those words folowing: *But not as I vvil, but as thou vvilt.* As if he had sayd, as I am flesh and bloud, and according to natural affection I feare death as it is repugnant to nature, and in this respect I would faine espace it, but yet because it is thy wil (ô Father) and is expedient, yea necessary for mankind, I am most willing to dye, & therfore not my wil (that is the desire which as I am flesh and bloud is common to me with other men) but thy wil be done, to which the wil of my superior & reasonable part is alwayes conformable. Which tvvo willes in Christ are not contrarie, because the one feareth death as it is contrarie to nature, and the sensual part: the other imbraceth death as it is the price of mannes redemption, and the obiect of Gods wil, neither doth the latter wil correct the former, but both are right in their kind. For as death is against nature, it is to be feared, and as it is the obiect of fortitude, and the meanes of mannes redemption, it is to be imbraced, and the one sheweth Christ to be a man, the other declareth the force of grace wherewith the weakenes of humain nature is corroborated. And so Christ knew that his Fathers wil was that he should suffer, and his wil also in the reasonable part was resolued: but yet to shew him selfe a man, according to his sensual part he sayd: *if it be possible free me from this chalice.*

Christs vvil alvvayes resolued to dy.

The wil of the Superior part of Christs soule, and the vvil of the inferior part not contrarie.

How death is to be feared, hovv to be desired.

7. Now if you desire a reason vvhy Christ that vndertooke our mortalitie, would none of our ignorance: diuines wil giue you one most euident. Because Christ (say they) vndertooke only those imperfections of our nature, vvhich either were necessarie to declare him selfe a man, or to make satisfaction for our sinnes, or to giue vs example: and because obedience, fasting, prayer, humilitie, pouertie, and such like serued for paternes for vs to imitate, he vvas obedient, he fasted, prayd, humiliated him selfe, and liued poorly: and because also hunger, thirst, cold, heate, mortalitie, vvere necessarie to suffer and to satisfie for vs, he vvas hungry, thirstie, hote, cold, and mortal; and lastly, because nothing more declared that he vvas a man then feare of death, vvhich manes nature abhorreth, he feared, and svvet for feare, not vvater only, but also bloud. But because sinne vvas against the end of redemption which he proposed to him selfe, he would none of that, yea he could not because he vvas the Sonne of God: and for as much as inordinate motions of the flesh serued neither for example, nor satisfaction, yea vvere rather contrarie, he also refused them: and because

Vvhy Christ tooke not our ignorance.

Vvhat imperfections he tooke.

cause ignorance, also is many tymes ioyned with sinne, either as the cause, or effect of sinne (for whosoeuer sinneth, sayth the Philosopher is ignorant and inconsiderate) yea because this was repugnant to the office of a Messias who vvas to instruct the vvhole vvorld in heauenly doctrin, and vvas not necessary to declare him selfe to be man, because feare and other imperfections serued for that purpose sufficiently, yea could not demonstrate him to be man because Angels and diuels may be ignorant: he vvould take no ignorance vpon him.

If Christ had bene ignorant he might haue sinned.

8. But let the heretike blaspheme a while, and let him exceede the diuil his father in blasphemy: if Christ vvere ignorant, he was subiect also to sinne: because he might haue folowed his ignorance. For if the vnderstanding may erre or be inconsiderate, the wil which is directed by the vnderstanding may vvander & swarue from reasons rule and kore, and consequently also may sinne: And so our reformed Christians wil make a deformed Christ of our Messias, vvho being him selfe subiect to sinne (as he is if he can be ignorant or inconsiderate) & consequently hauing neede him selfe of a redemer, wil yet take vpon him to redeeme others, and to saue others, vvho him selfe nedeth a Sauiour. See how basely these men conceiue of Christ, who though they say that they giue al vnto him, yet do make him an ignorant and inconsiderate man: and yet they them selues wil be so eagle-eyed that they can find out al the true meanings of Scripture with a priuate spirit, and know as vvel as the begger his dish, theyr owne iustification and predestination.

Our Gospelers vvil not be ignorant of their predestination nor of Scripture.

The Conclusion.

Io. 14.

To grant Christ to be ignorant, ruineth Scriptur.

Heretikes deceiued and deceiuers.

9. But to come nearer to our purpose, and conclusion, if Christ were ignorant and inconsiderate, then can the truth erre, vvisdom can be deceiued, and the vvay can goe out of the way for *he vvas the vvay the truth, and the life*, and the wisdome of his Father. If Christ can be ignorant, he may be deceiued, if he may be deceiued he may deceiue, (because he may teach according to his error) if he may deceiue, paraduenture he hath deceiued and then paraduenture his preaching, his Gospel, and whatsoeuer he hath taught of Christian religion, is error, and deceipt: and so by litle, and litle, heresie leadeth to Atheisme, and this their blasphemous doctrin, ruineth Christianitie. But fye rather vpon these blasphemers, Christ is the vvisdom of his Father, and so can not be deceiued, he is *prima veritas the prime veritie*, and so can not deceiue, & he is *summum bonum chiefest good*, yea goodnes it selfe, and so vvil not deceiue, and our Gospellers are heretikes, that is deceiued, & deceiuers.

The tenth

The tenth chapter shevveth hovv they make Christ a desperate man, vvho not only feared the iudgement-seate of his father, but also despaired for the tyme, of his ovvne saluation.

THese Reformers haue not yet in their opinion, deformed Christ sufficiently, for not content to haue made him an ignorant man, they auouch also that he feared his Fathers tribunal, and dispaired of his ovvne saluation, & so they vvil make him also a desperate man. Caluin in his Harmonie of the Gospels sayth, that vvhen Christ vvas in his agonie in the garden, it vvas not the feare of death only vvhich made him svveat blood and vvater, but sayth he: *It vvas the terrible iudgement seat of God, and the iudge armed vvith incomprehensible vengeance vvhich he proposed before his eyes, and on the other part our sinnes, vvhich he had taken vpon him pressed him vvith their vveight: so that it vvas no meruail if this bottomlesse pitte and horrible confusion of damnation, did so feircely torment him vvith feare, and anguish.* And a litle after: *death of it selfe could not so haue tormented the soule of the Sonne of God, had it not been that he perceiued that he had to do vvith the iudgement of God.* And again he repeateth this his blasphemie, lest you should think it escaped him vnaduisedly: *Vvhence it folovveth that he feared a greater euil then death, vvhich prouoked him to desire to be exempted from death: vvhich vvas, that proposing before his eyes the vvrath of God, in so much that he presented himselfe before his iudgemēt seate being charged vvith the sinnes of the vvhole vvorlde, it vvas necessary that he should be affrighted & afrayed of the profound bottomles pitte of death.* And with in some fevv lynes after he sayth, that *this deadly svveat could not procede but from an vnaccustomed & horrible feare.* Yea sayth he, to think that this agonie proceded only from feare of death, *vvere to attribute vnto Christ a pusillanimitie, vvhich vve vvould condemne in an ordinarie man.*

In c. 26 Mat. 37. in fine.

Caluin saith christ feared the tribunal Seat aud sentence of God yea damnation.

38.

Ibidem.

2. Here Christian Reader, do not thy eares burne to heare blasphemie so often repeated? and vvil thy Christian zeale permit such disgrace to be offered thy redeemer? vvhat Iohn Caluin, did Christ feare the tribunal seat of his Father? then feared he the Iudges sentence, lest it should be pronoūced against him, then feared he damnation and

The sequel of Caluins doctrin.

Mat. 25. doubted vvhether he should be comprehended in the sentence of *Venite benedicti, come yee blessed of my Father, or Ite maledicti, goe you cursed into fier euerlasting*: then vvas he in a perplexitie and doubt, vvhether he should be placed on the right hand vvith the elect, or on the left hand vvith the reprobate: And so the Sonne of God vvho came to saue others, vvas not sure of his ovvne saluation. Novv therfore if I vvil shevv my selfe a Christian, zealous of Christs honour, or careful of myn ovvne saluation, I must seeke to frie him from this feare of his Fathers sentence: for if he perish (as Caluin sayth he feared lest he should perish eternally) then must vve al perish, because by him only vve looke for saluation.

The securitie of the iust at the later day. Sap. 5. Christ could not feare the later day.

3. The vviseman sayth that at the later day *the iust shal stand in great constancie*, euen then vvhen the sentence shalbe pronoũced, much greater no doubt shal be the constancie of Christ Iesus, the Sonne of God, of vvhom al the Saincts that vvere, haue borovved their fortitude and courage. For he being the natural Sonne of God, knevv ful vvel, that his Father neither vvould, nor could deny his Sonne, and vvas assured that he vvho vvas to sitte in iudgement, and to pronounce the sentence, could not be him selfe arraigned And is it likely that God vvho indevved Christs humaine nature vvith al knovvledge, and reuealed to him al secrets, euen harts cogitations, and the day of dome, which the Angels know not: would kepe this only secret from him, and would not let him know vvhat should become of him selfe at the day of his death? The Diuines with one consent are of opinion, that Christs soule from his conception, receiued the blisse & glorye, which at the day of our particular iudgement, or at our deliuery out of Purgatorie, our soules shal receiue: and they say that to a glorified soule, is dew a glorified body, because the glory of the soule naturally imparteth it selfe vnto the body, & that in Christ, it was no miracle, that his body was so glorious in his transfiguration, but rather it was a miracle that his glorious soule did not make his body also pertaker of that glory from the beginning: but yet this miracle Christ vsed that he might suffer hunger, thirst, cold, and other miseries, which he could not haue done in a glorified body. How then was it possible that Christ should feare his Fathers tribunal, and terrible sentence, vvho vvas already in possession of the glory of his soule, and assured that his glorious soule, should haue at the length, that is after his Passion, a glorified body.

Christ vvas blessed from the beginning. a glorious body is dew to a glorious soule. The trãsfiguration was no miracle. Vvhy Christ would not in this life let his body be partaker of this soules glory. Caluins obiection.

4. But sayth Caluine: Christ had taken vpon him our sinnes, and

therfore

therfore might very wel feare to appeare before his Fathers iudgemēt-seate. This is his diuinitie or rather blasphemie. For if he meane that Christ hath so vndertaken our sinnes, that he verily made them his owne, what more blasphemie could he vtter? For although Illiricus auouched that God the Father so poredly imputed our sinnes to Christ that he made him a sinner, yet Christian tongues abhorre to vtter, and Christian eares do burne to heare such blasphemous speaches. For S. Peter, who sayth that Christ *bare our sinnes*, addeth withal, that *he bare them in his body vpon the wood*, to signifie that he tooke not the malice of our sinnes vpon him (for then he should haue sayd that he bare our sinnes in his soule, because the soule only is the subiect of sinne) but that he suffered the paines dew vnto our sinnes, when he suffered the death of body, vpon the crosse. Yea as when one satisfieth for an others offence, he taketh not the offence vpon him, but is content to abide the punishment, to set his freind at libertie: so Christ our Mediator and Redemer, is sayd to haue taken our sinnes vpon him and to haue satisfied for them, because he hath endured the paynes which were dew vnto them: but as for our sinnes, he was not capable of them, and therfore the same S. Peter in the same place sayth, that Christ *neuer sinned, & that guile or fraude was neuer found in his mouth.* Wherfore though Christ might feare death, & the torments of the crosse, because those he was to suffer for vs, yet had he no cause to feare hel & damnation, because although that punishment was dew vnto our sinnes, yet was not Christ to suffer it, because his passion was sufficient, as in the next chapter shal be proued And this I hope vvil suffice a reasonable man.

The answer.

Illyricus sayd that christ by taking our sinnes on him was a very sinner.

1. Pet 2.

Christ vndertooke the paine dew to sinne but not the sinne.

an example.

Christ feared death but not hel nor damnation.

5. But Iohn Caluin stil cauileth and vvil not be satisfied vvith reason. For sayth he, Christ had bene very effeminate, if for feare of death only he had svvette bloud and vvater, therfore it vvas no lesse then hel and damnation, vvhose feare cast him into such an extraordinarie svveate. See vvhat care Caluin hath left Christ should be counted a covvard: and yet, vvhilest to find out a sufficient cause of such a feare, he sayth that he vvas afrayed of iudgement: he maketh him to feare that vvhich he vvas sure should neuer happen, vvhich is the greatest folly in the vvorld, and argueth the most effeminate, and covvardly hart that can be. I ansvver therfore that the feare of death only, was sufficient to make him sweate vvater and bloud: For if, as Aristotle sayth, abundance of bloud, and distemperature of body, be sufficient to make men sometymes to svveate bloud, vvel may vve conceiue how feare

in cap 2.

Luc. 2.

Caluin maketh Christ a Coward.

The answer.

l. 3. hist animalium c. 19.

distemperature may make a man sweat bloud

Hovv the feare of death only might make Christ svveat bloud. *Christs feare proceded not of impotencie of mynd.*

feare of death in Christ (vvhich must needs be very great, partly because he would haue it so for our sakes, and partly because he would not impart any comforte, or strength, vnto his humaine nature) might cause a distemperature in his body, that it being already extenuat, and emptied of other humours, might sweat blood and water: neither proceded this from any impotencie of mynd: for he that giueth such courage to his Sainctes, could haue taken the same him selfe, but he vvould permit death, and such a death to do al, that such an obiect could do, and he would not giue any ayde vnto the inferior part of his soule, vvhere this passion of feare afflicted him, that he might beginne in the garden the doleful tragedie of his Passion, vvhich he ful, acted afterwards vpon the stage of his Crosse.

Caluin addeth, that Christ despaired also in the garden. *in c. 27. Mat. 11. 46.* *Blasphemie of Caluin.*

6. But Caluin hath not yet cast al his poison: he sayth that Christ not only feared iudgement and damnation, but dispared also of his Saluation. These are his vvords vvhich with the other before, I translated out of his french Harmonie: *But this semeth absurd, that a voice of desperation should escape Christ. The ansvver is easie: that although the flesh apprehended damnation, yet fayth remained firme in his hart.* Where you must note that Caluin hauing discoursed vpon those vvords *my God my God vvhy hast thou forsaken me:* he sayth, that this vvas the greatest agonie that Christ euer suffered, and the reason sayth he was, *because he vvas conuented before his fathers tribunal as culpable, and as one that had God his enemie, and as a man al ready condemned, vvhere vvith he vvas so scarred and affrighted, that it had bene enough to haue svvallovved vp al other men an hundred tymes. So that complaining that he vvas abandoned of his Father, he speaketh not of faintnes nor in iest, for* (sayth he) *the vehemencie of the griefe vvrested out of him this complaint: for as he vvas presented as a pledge for vs, so vvould he susteine verily the Iudgement of God in our name.* And because in these speches he semed to auouch that Christ despared as one forlorne and forsaken of his Father, he sayth that yet his fayth remained firme.

Christ could not despair, neither delibe ratly nor inde deliberately. *Despaire is one of the grefest sinnes.*

7. Is it so Caluin and did Christ as he vvas man so feare the iudgment-seatte, that he despaired? Then either that despaire vvas deliberate, or sodaine and indeliberate. If deliberate then certes did Christ sinne most damnably: for vvhat greater sinne is there then to despare of Gods mercie? For he that despareth, either he thinketh not God able to saue him, or not vvilling, in the one he doth iniurie to Gods omnipotencie, in the other he mispriseth his mercie. If indeliberate, then vvas Christ inconsiderate, and caryed away with Passion like a beast or vnreasonable man, vvhich although Caluin sticketh not to grant

grant (for he sayth that the vehemencie of his agonie wrested out of him feare and despare ere he was aware) yet do al the Fathers and Diuines in this point stand against him, affirming that neuer any Passion in Christ preuented reason and consideration. Yea they conceiue of Christ as of one that was so vigilant ouer his passions, that neuer any arose without consideration, & commandement. For when he would shew zeale he commanded a Passion of anger to arise, yet in that moderation, as it might shew him to be zealous, and yet neither testie nor furious. Likewise vvhen it pleased him to afflict his hart with feare and sorow, he commanded those passions to arise in that vehemencie, which were expedient for him to suffer for vs, or to shew him selfe a man: and yet with that moderation, that they neuer exceded the golden meane of vertue: and he that could command the windes and tempests to cease, could command his passions downe againe. And so when in the garden he feared death, that feare was præuented, and commanded by reason, and so vvas deliberate, and no sinne at al, because it is natural to feare death, and if withal the superior part of the mynd be resolute, and wil not for that feare transgres Gods law or offend conscience, it increaseth the merit of martyrdome, or sufferance of death, because it augmenteth the difficulty. Wherfore Diuines cal Christs passions, *propassions*, because he alvvayes præuented them, and commanded them to arise, and therfore the Euangelist sayth not, that Christ was perturbed or troubled with his passions (as we are) but that *he troubled him selfe*. In like maner vvhen Christ cryed *on the crosse: my God my God why hast thou forsaken me?* that complaint proceded from the sensual part of his soule which feared death, and the panges therof, and was not a complaint indeliberately wrested out by vehemencie of grief, as Caluin auoucheth, but was deliberate, and yet no sinne, because if the superior part be resolute, it is no sinne though the inferior part feare death as contrarie to nature. Neither was that complaint a desperation of saluation, for Christ (as before is declared) was sure of that, but it was a complaint of the sensual part which complained that it receiued no succour from the Diuinitie, but was left as it were to it selfe to suffer feare, grief, and paine for our Redemption, and yet in that complaint (as I sayd) was no sinne, because death is a thing to be feared, and the flesh and sensual part naturally feareth it, and this feare then is a sinne, when it maketh vs only trāsgres the law of God, which effect it could not haue in Christ, because the superior part of his soule was alwayes resolued to dye for mans redemption.

No indeliberate passions in Christ.

Scholastici 3. p. q. 15.

Christ commanded his passions.

Christs passions are propassions.

Augu. tract. 19. in Io.

To feare death is no sinne if the superiour part be resolute.

When feare is a sinne.

Christ lost faith according to Caluī

8. Now wheras Caluin sayth that Christ despaired yet retained faith, I can not see hovv those tvvo things can stand together in his opinion. For if fayth be an assurance of present and future iustice, yea of election and saluation (as Caluin sayth it is) then if Christ despayred of saluation, he lost his fayth, because he lost that assurance, and so by Caluins doctrin, vvas an infidel. Neither vvil Caluins shift be sufficient to hold these tvvo (tovvit assurance and desperation) together: for to say, as he sayth, that this desperation in Christ was indeliberate, and so might stand with fayth, is to vphold one absurditie by an other, for it is most absurde to ascribe vnto Christ any inconsiderate, or indeliberate actions: better vvere it for Caluin to say as Diuines commonly say, that there vvas no fayth in Christ, because fayth, vvhich is an obscure knovvledge, can not stand with the cleare vision of God vvhich Christ had, and vvhich gaue him a greater assurance of saluation, then faith can do.

See the seuēth booke & 5. c.

In Christ vvas not faith but cleare vision.

9. Thus thou seest (gentle reader) how vnlikely it is, vvhich Caluin sayth, that Christ doubted and despaired of saluation, vvho as the Sonne of God, blessed in soule from the first moment of his conception, and so assured of the blisse and glorie, both of soule and body. But because Caluin wil haue it so, let himstil stand to it, that Christ vvas arraigned as guiltie at his Fathers tribunal, and that he so feared the Iudges sentence, that he doubted yea despaired of saluation. But vvhat shal he gaine by this doctrin? he shal declare him selfe to be as he is, a sacrilegious companion, vvho robbeth Christ of his glorie, in vttering such iniurious and opprobrious speaches, and deserueth to be thrust out of the Church and schoole of Christ, for preaching that doctrin from vvhich Christian eares abhorre, and demonstrateth him selfe not to be a Christian, who speaketh so contemptibly of Christ, whom he professeth to honour, and to whom, he sayth (but how truly who seeth not?) that he giueth al homage and glorie.

The conclusiō that Caluin is a sacrilegious companion.

The ele-

The eleuenth Chapter shevveth hovv Caluin bringeth Christ to Hel, and the torments therof, and so maketh him a companion of the damned.

HE sinner when he is once habituated in sinne maketh no scruple of sinne, and when he is plunged in the depth of sinne, he contemneth, and is so farre from seeking meanes to get out of this filthy sinke, that hauing once foyled him selfe, he careth not to vvallow him selfe in filth, and to adde filthines to filthines, and abomination to abomination, without stoppe or stay, ende or measure. So it happeneth to Iohn Caluin, vvho hauing begunne to blaspheme, neuer leaueth blaspheming, but addeth blasphemie to blasphemie, and stil redubleth his blasphemies. For not content to haue despoiled Christ of many noble titles, not thinking it a sufficient disgrace to make him an ignorant and desperate man, he now openeth his mouth to vtter his greatest blasphemie, and to spitte his greatest spite against him, associating him in punishement vvith the diuels, making him a member of the damned crew, and an inhabitant of hel it selfe, and from desperation bringeth him to hel and damnation.

The propertie of a sinner nusled in sinne.

Caluin bringeth Christ to hel

l. 2. c. 16.

2. In his Institutions vvhich T.N. translated into English and Richard Harison imprinted, in the yeare of our Lord 1562. hauing occasion to treate of the descẽsion of Christ into hel, he saith that Christ is sayed to haue descended into hel, not that his soule locally descended (for Caluin acknowledgeth no local Hel) but because in soule he felt the paines of hel: for (sayth he) *not only the body of Christ vvas giuen to be the price of our redemption, but there vvas an other greater and more excellent price payed in this, that in his soule he suffered the terrible tormentes of a damned and forsaken man.* And a litle after, he ansvvereth a question which he supposeth may be moued in this maner: *Novv if a man should aske of me vvhether that Christ vvent dovvne to hel, vvhen he prayed to escape that death? I ansvvere, that then vvas the beginning of it.* And seing that Caluin acknovvledgeth no other hel then the paines of hel, that is, torments of mynd, wherevvith the damned are vexed; it foloweth that Christ in the garden, when

Caluin saith Christ suffered hel paines in his soule.

Sect 12.

Caluĩ denieth local hel.

den, when he feared not only death, as Caluin sayth, but his Fathers tribunal also, begin his hel, and when he despaired (as he sayth) on the crosse, he entered into the depth of hel, and so those vvords: *my God, my God vvhy hast thou forsaken me?* VVere the vvords of a damned man. O blasphemie, and that of one vvho vvil nedes be counted a zealous, and a reformed, and reforming Christian. Thou a Christian Caluin? thou a Ievv and more blasphemous then a diuel. Thinkest thou that Christ vvho redemed vs, could not saue him selfe? If he suffred hel he was damned, because none suffer hel but by sentẽce of damnation, and seing that out of hel there is no redemption, he is stil damned and so no redeemer.

Mat. 27. *Caluins blasphemie.* *Christ according to Caluĩ vvas damned*

3. But to redouble the iniurie vvith a floute, Caluin vvil nedes seme Christs greatest freind in preferring him to hel, for (sayth he) it had bene but a smal matter to haue suffered death of body, yea that death (sayth he) vvould only haue redemed our bodyes, but not our soules: and so to make Christ a complete redemer of bodyes and soules, he bringeth him to hel. Secondly he sayth that this highly commendeth Christs mercie and charitie. And thirdly he sayth, that this also shevved the povver of Christ, vvho not only by death ouercame death but by suffring hel paines ouercame hel also, and by taking the paine vvhich vve deserued, acquitted vs of the same. Thus he shroudeth his impietie and blasphemie vnder the shew of Christs honour, & vvhen he blasphemeth most of al, he vvil seme to honour Christ vvith the title of a complete redeemer, and to commend his charitie, and povver.

Sect 12. *Caluin vvil seeme Christs freind in preferring him to hel.*

4. But to the first I answer that Christ by his death and passion payed a sufficient price and ransome both for soule and body, and therfore S. Paul saith *that in Christ vve haue redemption in his bloud.* And again he sayth that Christ hath *pacified al by the bloud of the crosse both in heauen and earth.* To whom S. Peter subscribing, auoucheth *that vve are redemed not vvith gold nor siluer, but vvith the precious bloud of the immaculate lambe.* And neuer shal Iohn Caluin find either Scripture, or Father, that sayth, Christ suffred the paynes of hel for our redemption, but rather he shal find that they attribute our redemption to the passion and panges of death of Christs body. And therfore if Caluin wil stãd to it, that Christs passion was only able to ransome our bodyes, but not our soule, he detracteth from the dignitie of Christs death, and seing that the Scriptures and Fathers acknowledge no other price to haue bene offred for vs then Christs death and passion, if that were deficient, then according to

Eph. 5. *Col. 1.* *1. Pet. 1.* *Christs Passiõ redeemed soule & body*

Christ according to Caluĩ is no complet Redemer.

ding to Caluin, Christ is no complete Redeemer.

5. But he presseth vs with an argument vvhich he counteth insoluble, for (sayth he) he that satisfieth for an other must pay the debt vvhich the other oweth, and susteine the payne, vvhich he deserued, and therfore because we deserued the paines of hel, and were to suffer them both in soule and body, it was necessarie that Christ in soule should suffer the paynes of hel, else had he bene but halfe a redemer. But by this argument Christ should haue endured in hel perpetual tormentes, and so should neuer haue redemed vs, because he should him selfe haue bene a perpetual prisoner. For if Christ must nedes suffer the selfe same paine which we deserued, thē must he according to Caluins rule haue endured a perpetual hel, because that vvas the punishement prepared for vs, and seing that eternal punishement neuer cōmeth to an end, Christ should neuer haue payed the rāsome dew for sinne, & so we should neuer haue bene redemed. Wherfore I say, that Christs Passion to the sufferance of which, both Christs body and soule cōcurred (for the body by it selfe alone can not suffer paine) vvas a sufficient ransome to redeme both our soules and bodyes from hel and damnation, and therfore to that only, and not to the paynes of hel, the Scriptures and Fathers do attribute our redemption. And this (as I haue proued already) was a most sufficient price, and so sufficient, that in that it was the Passion and death of him, that vvas God and man, it was sufficient to haue redemed a thousand vvorldes, yea the diueles and al the damned. Neither must Caluin be so rigorous as to thinke, that no satisfaction can be sufficient, vnles it be of the same kind with the debt, vvhich is to be payed, or the harme vvhich is to be repaired: for if one of Caluīs brotherhood, had cut of the arme of an other brother, would not a peece of mony haue made satisfactiō for the mayme? or would Caluin haue exacted arme for arme? And if one had owght Caluin an hundred crownes, would not he haue bene content to haue taken the worth or more then worth in corne, shepe, or such like but nedes must haue crowne for crowne, as though there were no other law but *lex talionis*? or if satisfaction for these debtes and losses may be made by other paymentes vvhich are of æqual valew, then might Christ by suffering death, which was of infinite price and valew make a ful satisfaction for the paines of hel: and yet neuer feele the paines therof.

Supra.

Caluins obiection.

An absurditie vvhich folovveth his argument.

The ansvver.

See the third booke and 3.c.

It vvas not cōuenient that Christ should suffer hel paines.

6 And in dede it vvas not conuenient that Christ should suffer the paines of hel. For first those paines are of their nature perpetual: and so

The first reason.

and so if Christ had once permitted those torments to afflict his soule, he should neuer haue bene eased of the same. Secondly it had bene dishonorable to Christ to be felow mate with the damned: and although S. Peter sayth that God raised him from death to life, the sorowes of hel being dissolued, yet he meaneth not therby that Christ once suffred the sorowes of hel, but either that he loosed vs from the sorowes of hel, or that he acquit him selfe from them, because he neuer was tormented with them. Thirdly to haue suffered these paines had bene to no purpose, because that the paynes of hel are not satisfactorie, and therfore after that the damned haue endured them many millions of yeares, they are neuer the nearer an end of their misery.

The second reason.

Act. 2.

The third.

Paines of hel are not satisfactorie.

7. Now as concerning Christs charitie, that vvas sufficiently declared in that he suffred death for vs. For *no man hath greater charitie then to dy for his friend*, and especially for his enemies, and this also extolleth Christs power most highly, who by death ouercame death, yea sinne also, and damnation. But my hand is weary, and my pen seemeth vnwilling to yeld any more inke to a longer discourse vpon these vnchristian, yea diabolical blasphemies, and I doubt not but the Readers eares do burne already to haue heard so much of them. Out of this doctrin peraduenture proceded, that blasphemous speach of one who (as Surius reported) was not afrayed to say that Christ was damned in hel? And for this, as it is very probable, God permitted Iohn Caluin to dye so desperatly. For he that auouched Christ to haue despayred, and to haue suffred hel paynes, at the houre of his death him selfe despayred, and semed euen then to beginne his hel, because then he cursed the day that euer he set pen to paper (which we also may curse) and leauing to cal vpon Christ at his death, vvhom in his life he had so dishonoured, he called vpon the diuel, whose instrument and seruant he had bene, and vnto him rendred his miserable soule, which had deserued as many helles, as were and are the soules which were and stil are, by his doctrine deceiued.

Christes death declared his charitie sufficiently yea and his povver also.

Whence proceded Caluins desperation.

Anno. 1527.

Bolsec in vita Caluini

Geneb li. 4. Cron.

***

The

The tvvelueth Chapter shevveth that the Gospellers can abide nothing that is, or hath bene belonging to Christ: vvhich is an other signe that they are no sincere Christians.

T is a common saying vsual in euery mans mouth, and yet not so common as true: *Loue men loue myn*: which not only the common voice alovveth, but also experience and reason approueth, for such is the nature of loue and frendship, that as it transformeth one freind into an other, and maketh vs to account of our freind as an other our selfe: so doth it engender in vs an affection to our freindes freind, kinsman, alliance, seruant, and whatsoeuer belongeth to him, or is beloued of him. And the reason is manifest: for if frendship be of that nature, that it maketh one soule as it vvere in two bodyes, and causeth vs to esteme of our freind as an other our selfe, then as we first loue our selues, & then others that are linked vnto vs, so we must loue our freind as our selfe, and then his aliance for his sake, and vve must tender his life, his goods, and commodities as our owne. Wherfore we read that *Damon* and *Pithias*, did striue earnestly and contended most louingly who should dy for the other. For as the soule by affection is more vvhere it loueth, then where it liueth, so *Damon* thought him selfe to liue better in Pithias then in him selfe, and therfore to saue him selfe in Pithias, he desired to dy in him selfe. And he that loued Pithias life as his owne, would haue affected Pithias freindes and would for his sake haue tendered his good as his ovvne, we read that Dauid and Ionathas were such louing freinds, *that their soules vvere glevved together*: which loue of Dauid towards Ionathas, could not be stayd in Ionathas his person, but for his sake extended it selfe to his house and familie. King Pharao vvho extolled and loued highly Ioseph the Patriarch, loued not him alone, but for his sake entertained Iacob his father, and al his brethren. For this is the nature and lavve of frendship: *loue me loue myn*. Wherfore we see by experience that, vvhen vve loue a freind sincerly, we loue for his sake his freinds also, and aliances, yea his seruantes, yea his dogge, yea his ring,

The nature of freindship.

Freindship maketh one soule in tvvo bodies.

It maketh vs loue our frēds frend as our ovvne.

The freindship of Damō and Pithias.

Dauid and Ionathas frendship.

1. Reg. 18.

2. Reg. 9.

Gen. 45. 47.

Loue me loue myn.

ring, and image, and vvhatsoeuer hath bene deare to him or appertaining vnto him.

Charitie vvhich is frendship betvvixt God & man vniteth us to God.

2. And lest that any should think that frendship vvorketh this effect betwixt men only, I wil shew how charitie vvhich is the frendship that man hath vvith God, hath the same properties. For charitie maketh vs not only the seruantes of God, but his freinds also, and in a golden chayne so linketh vs vnto him, that we are as S. Paul sayth *one spirit vvith him.* In so much that S. Paul sayd that now he liueth not in him selfe but in Christ, into vvhom by loue he vvas transformed, esteeming of Christ as of an other him selfe, in vvhom he thought he liued better then in him selfe. And therfore he tendered Christs honour aboue his owne commoditie, and would rather dye as in dede he did, then Christ should susteine any dishonour, and rather then he would deny him or forsake him, he denied him selfe and neglected his owne life. The like effect this loue hath euer wrought in the hartes of the Martyrs of the Church, who not only desired to dy for Christ, as Damon did for Fithias, but dyed in dede, and suffered most exquisite tormentes, lest he should susteine the least losse and domage in his honour. And certes they that for loue of Christ tendered his honour more then their owne liues, did no doubt affect and reuerence for his sake his mother: his freinds, his image, his crosse, and whatsoeuer hath beene belonging vnto him: for loue is of this nature that it extēdeth it selfe not only to our freind, but for his sake it tendereth & affecteth his alliance and freindes, yea his seruants: and for his sake it honoureth, and estemeth of his image, ring, & whatsoeuer hath bene apperteining to him. Wherfore the greatest louers and freindes that euer Christ had, to wit the Martyrs who dyed for him, and the first Christians who first receiued his law, and professed his name, did so loue him that for his sake they respected with reuerence his crosse, his image, his wordes, his Sacramentes, his Mother, his Apostles, his seruantes, yea their reliques and images.

Io. 15.
1. Cor 6.
Gal. 2.
S. Paules loue of Christ.
The loue of Martyrs tovvardes Christ.
They that loued Christ, respected for his sake his Mother, and al belonging to him.

The Angels respect to our Lady for Christs sake.
S. Iohns respect to her.

3. The Angel Gabriel for the honour he owed vnto his maister Christ Iesus, speaketh vnto our blessed Lady with great reuerence and respect, because she was to be his mother, knowing that he who honoureth the sonne, must respect the mother: and S. Iohn Euangelist vvhom loue made so bold as to repose him selfe in Christs bosome, had no doubt a great respect vnto his mother, vvho was commended vnto him, and therfore some historiographers write, that he caryed her with him vnto his bishopricke of Ephesus. S. Ignatius writing to the same

same Iohn, sayth that he was desirous to see our Lady of whom Christ was borne. S. Dionisius Areopagita desired to see the body of her, which gaue the beginning of life to him who was *the vvay the veritie & life it selfe. Let Marie be honored,* saith Epiphanius, *and let our Lord be adored. & let vs,* sayth S. Bernard, *cast our selues at her blessed feete.* And againe. *Let vs honor Marie because it is the wil of God, vvho vvould haue vs haue al by Marie. Al the prayse vvhich you can giue this virgin,* sayth S. Austin, *is not so much as her dignitie deserueth. VVhatsoeuer is greater,* sayth Petrus Damianus, *is lesse then this virgin, and only God the vvoorkeman, excelleth this peece of vvoorke.* Sainct Athanasius calleth her his *Mistresse Lady* and *Queene.* S. Bernard is not afraid to cal her *Aduocate,* neither do these Saincts thinke this Queene of Saincts and Mother of God only to be worthie honor: *The honor,* saith S. Basil, *VVhich vve geue euen to other Saincts, redoundeth to our common Lord and Maister. VVhosoeuer,* sayth S. Ambrose, *honoreth Martyrs, honoreth Christ also, and vvho despiseth Saincts, contemneth our Lord.*

S. Bern. ser. 1. super psa Qui habitat. S. Dionisius affectio to her Her 79. Ser in signum magnum. Ser. de aquaeductu. Ser. 35. de Sanctis. Ser. 1. de Nat. Mariæ. Ser. de Annunciatione.

4 And as they honored Saincts as the frendes of God: so did they pray vnto them, to pray for them to Christ, with whom they haue greater credit aboue, then we haue here in this lower world. Of this practise S. Dionisius Areopagita, S. Paules scholar maketh manifest mention and ancient record. This is S. Athanasius prayer: *O Mistresse, Lady, Queene, and Mother of God pray for vs. Euen he that vveareth purple,* sayth S. Chrisostom, *and is crovvned vvith a Diademe vvil visit the sepulchers of the Apostles and laying al pompe aside vvil pray to the tent-maker Paul, and Peter the fisher to be their patrones and protectors. Fare vvel o Paula,* sayth S. Hierom, *and remember Hierom thy VVoorshipper. Thou vvast afraide,* sayth S. Bernard, *to aproch to God the Father, he hath geuen thee* IESVS *for Mediator, but perchance in him also thou mayst feare the Diuine Meiestie: vvilt thou haue an Aduocate also vnto him? haue recourse to Marie. Some Angels,* sayth S. Basil, *are called eyes, because they haue vndertaken the charge to visit vs: some are called eares, because they receiue our prayers.* S. Gregorie Nazianzen speaking of a virgin, whom S. Cyprian then a Magician, endeuored by enchantment, to inflame with loue and lust, auoucheth that she prayed to Marie the virgin, to helpe and ayde a virgin, and so a virgin ouercame, and the diuel was ouercome.

Orat. in 40. mart. Hier. ep. ad Riparium. Ser. 6. Aug. ser. 1. de ss. Pet. & Paulo l. 8. ciuit. c. 28. c. 7. Eccl. Hierarch. Ser. 66 ad po. In vita Paulæ Ser. de nat. Mariæ. orat. in ps. 33. orat in Cypr.

5 And as the ancient Christians honored Christ and his Saints: so did they honor and respect their Images and Reliques. Euagrius, Metaphrastes, and S. Damascen make mention of an Image of Christ, which him selfe imprinted in a linen cloth by the touch of his face, and sent vnto Abagarus. Eusebius also affirmeth that he hath seene

l. 4 hist. c. 26 in vita Const. l. 1, de Imag. Baron. to. 1. l. 7. hist. c. 14

l. 14. hist. c. 2. l. Collectā. l. de pudic. In Liturg. In Iulian. 7. Syn. act. 2. cap. 7. in vita. Hon. 3. in pent. apud Baron. to. 4. pag. 34 Eus. l. 1. c. 20. 21. 22. 23 Prud. l. aduersus Sym. Amb. orat. Funeb. Theod. Seuerus. l. 2. Paul. ep. 11. Socr. l. 1. c. 13. Niceph. l. 8. c. 40. Catec. 10. 13. Tert. l. de corona Mil. l. 2 ad Vxor. Heir. in vita Paulæ. ep. ad Eust. prud. in hym. ante somnum Aug. tract. 118. Ciril. cat. 11. Chry. ho. 55 in Mat & ho quod

the Image of Christ which was made in memorie of the miraculous cure which Christ did vpon the woman afflicted with the bloudy flixe, as also the Image of S. Peter and S. Paul. Nicephorus, and before him Theodorus Lector writ of the Image of our Lady drawne by S. Luke, which to this day are some of them extāt. Tertulian talketh of chalices in which Christ was figured in forme of a shepheard carying a sheepe on his shoulders. *The priest*, sayth S. Chrysostom, *inclineth his head to the Image of Christ. The histories of Images*, saith S. Basil, *I honour and adore*, that is worship. *for this being deliuered vnto vs from the holy Apostles is not to be forbidden.* And S. Ambrose in his booke of our Lords Incarnation: *When in Christ vve adore the Image of God, and vvorship the crosse, do vve diuide him?*

6 S Hierom sayth: that S. Paula *casting her selfe prostrate before the crosse, adored, as if she had seene Christ hanging thereon. Novv*, sayth S. Chrysostom, *Theodosius the father, and his sonne, entering the churches, do lay aside their crounes and do make the signe of the crosse in their forheades.* Gregorius Nissenus recordeth how he found about his sisters necke (she was called Macrina) a crosse and ring of iron, in the knoble wherof was the signe of the crosse, & vnder that, a peece of the holy crosse, by this signe of the crosse Constantine obtained a victorie against Maxentius, as that strange vision and impression in the aire did signifie vnto him: *In hoc vnice. In this ouercome.* This Crosse was odious to al nations almost, til Christ sanctified it with his Passion, but yet amongst the Ægiptiās the crosse was a letter signifiing *life euerlasting*: and since that Christ vsed this crosse as an instrumēt to worke our redemption, Kings & Emperors haue placed it in their crownes, and adored it for Christs sake. S. Helin, our countriwoman & Constantines mother, went to Hierusalem to seke this crosse. And finding there the crosse by a miracle, she adored it, & sent one peece of it to Rome an other to her sonne Constantine. And one of the nayles wherwith Christ was nayled to the crosse she put in a bridle, an other in a crowne, & gaue them both to her said sonne, that Christ in his crowne might rule, and moderate in his bridle. And such deuotion had the ancient christians to the crosse, that as S. Ciril of Hierusalem witnesseth, the whole world was filled as it vvere, vvith peeces of this crosse, vvhich Christians had procured to be cut from the same. With this signe Christians vsed euer to signe their forheades, their mouthes, their breastes, & to blesse the table: vvith this they armed them selues against the diuel, in the morning, in the euening, in the going forth, in entering into the house,

before

before prayer, before meate, before euerie important busines. Without this signe no Sacrament was euer ministred, no Sacrifice offered, no benediction either of Priests or parents was giuen. S. Martin armed vvith this signe, feared not the troupes of his enemies, as Sulpitius vvriteth in his life. And therfore this signe was euer counted the standard and impenetrable armour of Christians. Constantine his Labarum, which was a crosse, wonne many victories. S. Oswald King, by a vvodden crosse put his enemies to flight, and vvrought many miracles. S. Hilarian by the same signe stayed the raging sea, And neuer any miracle was done almost, without the signe of the crosse. Diuels feare this signe, & tremble at the same, knowing that by it they were ouercome And therfore they who hate the crosse may see to vvhom they belong. Yea so Christians vvere euer vvont to be deuoted vnto Christ, that for his sake they haue not only honored his Mother and Saintes nor his image, and crosse only, but al reliques of Christ and his Saints also, euen to their clothes, bones, & dust of their bodyes.

7 And euen in the Apostles time, yea in Christs time also, we haue examples of honor & deuotion to reliques, exhibited by the first Christians. A deuout woman mentioned in the Gospel, beleued, that if she should but touch the hemme of Christs garment, she should be healed: and this her deuotion was so farre from being reprehended, that it was rewarded with the benefite of a miraculous cure, & a great cōmendation. The first Christians also made such esteeme of S. Pauls hand-kerchiefe, and Semicinctia that they caried them to the sicke, & healed therwith miraculously many and sundry diseases, and dispossessed many of euil spirits. Yea such a conceipt had they of S. Peters sanctitie that they ranne to his shadow for soucour and thought that for his sake, it was to be esteemed as soueraine.

8. Let vs now compare these ancient Christians vvith our newe reformers, and if to loue our freinds allianee, be an euident signe of loue towards him, and hatred of them, must nedes argue no good meaning to him, let vs gather by the affection vvhich these men shew towards Christs freindes, vvhat zeale and affection they beare to his Person. And to beginne with the Mother of God, because she was next in dignitie vnto God, and as neare as the mother can be to the Sonne. Let vs see how reuerently they speake of this vvorthy creature. Luther sayth that the Monkes for vvomens sakes, haue extolled the virgin to much, and placed her aboue the Angels: and he is angry with the wo-

Christus sit Deus. *Eus. l. 1. vita Const. c. 20. 22. 23.* *Beda l. 3. hist.* *Aug. c. 2.* *Athan. l. de Incarnat. Domini.* *Aug. l. 83. q. 79.* *Epiph. her 30* *Basil in psal. 115.* *Athan. in vita Ant.* *Bellar. to. 1. l. 2. de Reliq. c. 3.* *Amb. in ser. 93.* *Mat. 9.* *Act. 19.* *Act. 5.*

What loue & respect the reformers beare to Christ vvho can not abide his mother, frends, crosse &c.

Luthers contempt of the mother of God.

man mentioned in the Gospel for calling. *the vvombe of this virgin blessed*: Yea sayth he euery ministers yoke-felow may be as good as she, sauing that she can not be the mother of God, as she was. Caluin sayth that vvhen she put Christ in mynd of vvant of vvine at the mariage, *she kept not her selfe vvith in her boundes*, and an other time vvhen Christ sayed, *vvho is my mother and vvho are my brethren?* He carped (sayth Caluin) *at Maries importunitie, vvho preposterously vvent about to interrupt his preaching*. Yea he also findeth fault with Papistes, for vsing those vvords of the deuout woman in the Gospel *blessed be the vvombe vvhich bare thee*, because (sayth he) the woman vvas checked for so saying. Oecolampadius condemneth her of ambition vvhen she told her sonne at the mariage, that wine vvas vvanting. Brentius sayth, that vvhen she vvith Christs Kinsfolkes, came to speake vvith Christ, she shewed her selfe vnciuil, and exceded the bondes of publike honestie, and therfore by Christ vvas put to publike shame. The same Brentius sayth that vvhen she had lost Christ she fel into these cogitations: *If this vvere the Messias hovv happeneth it, that he is disobedient to his parentes, and so closely stealeth a vvay from them? hovv is he the Messias and author of fœlicitie, by vvhom is yet vve neuer had good fourtune? And vvhen* (sayth he) *this virgin and the disciples savv, that Christ vvas condemned to so shameful a death, then vvere they scandalized, and then appeared their vaine cogitations and impious harts*. Ioannes Agricola suspecteth her maydenly honestie, and maketh the Angel to speake like a lasciuious vvooer to her, and as one that went about to entise her: thus he maketh him to speake: *al Hayle most gratious Lady, vvhose company al men do desire. And thinke you* (sayth he) *vvhat it is to see a trime yong man al alone vvith a mayd in a chamber close shut vp, and vsing svvete vvordes and not obscurely insinuating by vvordes & gesturs hovv much he desired*. O lasciuious companion that could conceue so beastly of the company of an Angel, vvho is chast by nature, and of a virgin, vvho vvas as frie from lust by grace, as an Angel by nature. If now the prouerb be true as reason and experience teacheth it to be most true: *loue me loue myn*: then Iudge gentle reader, by the respect vvhich these men beare to Christs Mother, vvhat their reuerence and affection is, vvhich they beare to her Sonne. Besids this it is a common opinion of theirs, that no honour or religious respect is to be giuen vnto the Mother of God, or the Sainctes of heauen. And Luther seemeth much to enuie at the honour which is giuen to our Lady, saying (but vvith a lye) that papistes make her a goddesse and runne more vnto her then vnto Christ, expecting more grace & fauour of her then of him. Melancthon sayth

Post Dom. 3. Quadr. Luc. 11. Ser. nat Mariæ in Harm. Io. 2. Caluins hate of the virgin. Mother. Hea. Ma. 12. Harm. Luc. 11. Oecolãpadius spite against her. in Io 1. Antid c. 8 Luc. Brẽtius touthe against her. Ha. 19. Luc. Luth. post D. post Epiph. Hom. 17. in Luc. apud Canis. l. 3 c. 11. Calu li. 1. Inst c. 12. 1. 2: l. 3. c. 20. in Post. nat. Mariæ & post Annunciat.

sayth that it is plaine, that amongst papistes the blessed virgin is succeded in Christs place, and that al cal vpon her, and repose confidence in her, as though Christ vvere no propitiator, but only a Iudge and a reuenger. In vvhich as he lyeth lowdly, so he plainly bevvrayeth the enuie vvhich he conceiueth against this virgins honour. Caluin complayneth that vve adorne this virgin vvith the spoiles taken from her Sonne, and that we thinke her not honoured ynough vnlesse *she be made a goddesse.* *Luther and Caluin deny honour to Saintes.* *Apol. conf.* *Harm c.2. lo.* *Rayling against Saintes.*

9. As for other Saintes they so reuile them, and that vvith such bitter scoffes and flowtes, that herin I admire the patience of the diuine Maiestie, vvhich holdeth his reuenging hand. Caluin rayleth at al the Sainctes both of the old and new law. He calleth Abraham a worshipper of Idols & exaggerateth diuers sinnes of Sara & Rebecca, he accuseth Moyses the mildest & meekest man that vvas in his time, of arrogancie and pride. The Saints of the new lavv he calleth longeared creatures vvho can heare so fare of: he nicknameth them by contempt, deadmens shadowes, visards, monsters, beasts. Wherin he foloweth the stepps of his father Wiclefe, vvho calleth the Saints *Scurras principis: the Princes Iesters.* And one Quintine a libertin is so fowle mouthed, that when he nameth S. Paul he calleth him the brokē vessel, S. Iohn he termeth the foolish younker, S. Mathew, the vsurer, S. Peter, the denyer. *l 3 Inst. c. 14. para. 11.* *in cap. 32. Exo* *l 3. Inst. c. 20. 27. de refor. Ecclesiæ.* *ex Th. VVal. to 3. tit. 12. c. 108.* *ex Cal. cont. libert. c. 9.*

10. They take also from al Saints the honour which is giuen them by intercession, and sutes made vnto them. Erasmus to make the way for them, maketh the blessed Virgin to say; that she liketh vvel of Luthers doctrin, vvhich teacheth that Saints are not to be prayd vnto, *for novv* thus he maketh her speake *I may be quiet, vvhere as before al came to me, as though my sonne vvere stil a babe.* Luther sayth that he estemeth no more of the virgings prayers then of an other Christian; yea he denyeth al aduocation of Sainctes. So doth Caluin also in many places of his institutions. And one William Roding, in a booke or libel vvhich he made against the schooles of Iesuits, who (for their teaching and bringing vp of youth especially are disliked of heretikes) bringeth in the blessed virgin speaking in this maner: Leaue of this saluting me, to honour me, leaue of worshipping of Saints, and those that are dead, we detest thy salutations and prayers, vvhere thou art, vvhat thou doest, or whether thou beest aliue or dead, vve know not, and we care not: so farre are we from hearing thy prayers. *They deny prayer to Saints.* *Dial de peregrinatione.* *Ser. nat. virg.* *l. cont. VVal. l. 1. c. 16. 18. l. 3. c. 20 Roding l. cont. Schol. Iesuit.*

11. As for Images and Reliques of Christ, his Mother, and his Saintes, they detest them: and therfore Luther wisheth that al Reli- *Cal. l. de ref. mag. cent. 4. 6. 6. col. 456.*

Ser. de Cruce. *They deny al reuerence to Images and Reliques.* *Ex Cocl. l 3 hist. Hussit.*

ques vvere buried in the earth: yea their breaking and defacing of Images, and their burning of reliques, argueth their mynd and opinion in these matters sufficiently. VVherin they imitate Hierome of Prague, who pulled downe the Crucifix, and defiled and abused it, and yet reteined Wiclefes picture crowned with a diademe: for so these men thinke the best place of their house not good ynough for Luthers and Caluins pictures, and yet deface and defile the Images of Christ, his Mother, and his Saincts.

An obiectiõ. *Deut. 6.* *Mat. 4.* *1. Tim. 1.* *The ansvver.*

12. But they say that this they do for pure loue & honour towards Christ, who should be highly iniuried, if any but he should be honoured, and they haue a warrant for the same out of Gods ovvne vvord: *Thou shalt adore thy Lord God, and him only thou shalt serue.* And againe: *To God only honour and glorie.* But yet because Scripture can not be contrary to reason, and much lesse to it self, they should haue sought meanes to haue expounded those words, rather then to haue fallen into these grosse absurdities: for the same God vvho commandeth to adore and serue him only, commandeth vs to honour our parents and to serue our maisters. And reason teacheth vs that if we honour and loue God, we must respect his frends, and those that he respecteth, for the prouerb must needs be true, *Loue me loue myn*, because it is grounded in reason, and the very nature of frendship. VVherfore I answer that God is a iealous God, and therfore wil haue supreme honour and affection giuen vnto him selfe only, because he only hath supreme souerainitie (which only the alleaged places do proue) but if it be lawful to make this argumēt, God only must haue supreme honour, ergo Saincts must haue none at al. It may also be as wel inferred, that neither our parentes, nor our Princes must be honoured, or affected.

Honour devv to Excellencie *Three Excellēcies.* *The first Diuine.* *The second is moral or ciuil* *The third supernatural.*

13. Let therfore the reformers cal to mynd, that to excellencie and dignitie honour is devv, and therfore seing that there are three kinds of excellencies, vvel haue the Diuines distinguished three kindes of honours or worships. The first excellencie is increate and supreme, which is proper to God, and therfore to him is dew supreme honour, which is called *Latria*, and to giue this honour to any creature is idolatrie. The second is called moral or ciuil excellencie, which consisteth in authoritie, moral vertue, learning, or such like, and to this is dew a ciuil honour, vvhich vve giue to Princes, and superiors, and moral honest, and learned men: for authoritie, vertue, and learning are to be respected. The third excellencie is supernatural which consisteth in grace, sanctitie, and glorie: and to this is dew a religious honour:

nour: yet because this excellencie is infinitely inferior to Gods excellencie, we must giue it a religious, but yet a farre inferior honour. And with this honour our blessed Lady, S. Ihon Baptist, S. Peter S. Paul, aud other Saincts vvhilest they liued, deserued to be respected, and sithence that their Sanctitie is no lesse in heauen then it was in earth, they are no lesse after death to be honoured, then they were liuing. And therfore as ciuile honour giuen to Princes, learned, and mortal men, derogateth not from Gods honour, because it is inferior, so neither doth this religious honour, because it is also inferior.

What honour is devv to Saints.

14. But Caluin sayth that religious honour is only devv to God. This he affirmeth but he can not proue it, and therfore I deny it, and wil proue the contrarie. For religion is a vertue which giueth to God supreme worship, and to Saincts, and holy thinges, inferior honour, and so respecteth euery one in his kind. To God this vertue giueth a supreme honour called *Latria*, to the Saincts an inferior honour called *Dulia* to the blessed virgin because she farre excelleth the other Saincts, it giueth an honour inferior to *Latria* but superior to *Dulia*, which Diuines therfore cal *Hyperdulia*. And I would demande of Caluin, if S. Iohn Baptist were in earth, whether he would honour him or no for his sanctitie? If he say he would, then I aske of him, what honour he vvould giue him? not supreme honour, because that is devv to God, not ciuil honour: because that is giuen to moral vertue only, authoritie, and learning. What honour then shal S. Iohn Baptist haue for his sanctitie? certainly either an inferior religious honour called *Dulia* or none at al. And if Caluin would honour him in earth, & religiously also for his sanctitie, vvhy feareth he to giue him that honour in heauen, sithence that his soule (vvhich is the proper subiect of sanctitie) is no lesse liuing there, then it was here, and is indewed with no lesse sanctitie in heauen, then is was in earth, and besides that, is also there enriched with glorie, which it had not here?

Religiō giueth to God. Latria. to Saints. Dulia. to our Lady Hyperdulia. A question.

15. Now if Caluin wil say, that at least Images and Reliques are not to be honoured, because in them is none of these three excellencies afore mentioned, I wil tel him, that although none of these excelencies be formally in Images or Reliques, yet because these are appertaining vnto them, vvho are honoured, they may and must also be respected and reuerenced (but with a farre inferior respect) and that for their sakes to vvhom they apperteined. For as the Prince and Superior hath only the ciuil excellencie, and yet not he only, but for his sake, his image, his chaire of estate, his ring, and after his death, his dead

What honour is devv to Reliques and Images.

A similitude

dead body also, is to be respected, but yet not vvith that honour wherewith his ovvne person is honoured, so if God and his Saincts may be honoured with religious honour, the for Gods sake his image may be respected, and for Christs sake his name, his worde, his Sacramentes, his Crosse, nayles, and other thinges belonging vnto him, and for the Saincts sake, their images, bodyes, bones, clothes, and such like, may and must be religiously honoured, yet with an inferior honour. And the reason is first because in these things also by a certaine participation and representation, we behold in some sorte their excellencie to whom they pertaine, and therfore we respect them for their sakes. Secondly the nature of frenship wil haue it so, that if vve honour and loue any freind, vve must respect for his sake al belonging vnto him.

The first reasō

the second.

Caluins obiection.

The ansvver.

16. But Caluin wil say, that greater would be the honour of Christ, if vve gaue al honour to him, and none at al to his Saincts: vvhich he affirmeth and I with more reason do deny. For as then I honour and loue my Prince best, when I so repect him, that I honour and loue not him only, but for his sake his alliance, his frends, his officers, his seruantes his image, yea his ring: so do I honour and loue Christ most, when for his sake I respect and honour his Mother, his officers the Apostles, his freindes the Saincts, yea his Crosse and Image. And Princes take it for a dishonour to haue their officers, seruants, and images abused, and count it an honour to be honoured not only in them selues, but also in their adherentes: so no doubt Christ accounteth the honour doone to Saincts (because it is giuen them for his sake, and because they are his freinds and seruants) as giuen to him selfe, and can not but conceiue him selfe to be highly dishonoured, when his Saints, especially his Mother, are reuiled, and his Crosse and Images are defaced and defiled. Wherfore let not the reformers cal vs Idolaters, lest they bewray their ignorance. For Idolatrie is to giue supreme honour dew to God, vnto his creatures, as it is treason to giue supreme ciuil honour dew to the Prince, vnto any of his subiects But as it is no treason nor iniurie, but rather honour to the Prince, to honour his officers and seruants, with an inferior honour for his sake, so is it no Idolatrie but Religion, to honour the Saints of God with an inferior honour for their Maisters sake.

Catholiques no Idolators.

What treason is.

A similitude

17. And if Saincts may be honoured, we may make intercession vnto them, because it is an honour to Princes retainers, to haue sutes made vnto them. And this may be doone also vvithout dishonour to

Christ

Christ, because to him we giue vvhat is dew, to wit the title of a Redemer, and chiefe Aduocate, Mediator, and Intercessor: and we acknowledge Saints as secondarie Mediators and Intercessors, vvhem we desire for the credit vvhich they haue vvith Christ, greater then we haue, to make intercessions to him for our necessities. And so we pray otherwise to Christ, otherwise to Saincts: to him we pray as to our supreme Aduocate, to them as to secondarie Mediators, who haue no accesse to God but by him: to him vve pray as vnto him that bestoweth grace, health, and such other benefits on vs, to them we pray not to bestow those benefites, but to pray to him to bestow them on vs. To him we pray as an Intercessor vnto his Father by him selfe, to them as to Intercessors by him, and therfore al our prayers to Saintes we conclude *by Christ our Lord*. And if some tymes we desire our Lady, and other Saints to send vs health, or to giue vs grace, our meaning is no other, then to desire them to procure of Christ these benefits for vs, by their prayer and intercession. But Saincts, sayth Caluin, can not heare vs so farre of. I grant they can not naturally, nor by corporal eares, for as yet they haue none at al, but I say God vvho reuealed many future thinges to his Prophetes, reuealeth also vnto Saincts al thinges which are belonging vnto them, amōgst which are the prayers vvhich are made vnto them: and I auouch with the Diuines and holy Fathers, that as they see God face to face, so in him they see and know euen our cogitations, prayers, and vvhatsoeuer is belonging vnto them. Wherfore I may iustly suspect our Reformers sinceritie to Christ, vvho cā abide neither his Mother, nor his Saincts, not his Crosse, nor Image, nor any thing belonging vnto him: because the nature of frendship is such, that if they loue and honour him they must loue and honour his frends and seruants.

VVe pray to Saintes vvithout preiudice to Christ.

Hovv we pray to Saints hovv to Christ.

Hovv Saints heare so farre of.

S. Th. 1. p q. 12 a. 8 Aug l. de triplici habit. c. 6 l. 13. conf. c. 15. Greg. l. 4 Dial. c. 33.

18. Here I could demonstrate out of Scripture the honour dew to Saintes, because Scripture auoucheth that Abraham, Loth, Balaam, and Iosue vvorshipped Angels: that Abdias honoured Elias, and the sonnes of the prophetes reuerently respected Elizeus, vvho now are much more worthy honour, then they were in this mortal life, and may accept of it as wel now without preiudice to Christs honour, as then. That Nabuchodonozor adored Daniel, that Cornelius adored Peter not for a God, because he before that was a worshipper of the true God, but as an holy man, and though S. Peter refused that honour yet he did it of modestie as S. Chrisostom affirmeth: and might otherwise haue accepted it. S. Ihon the Euangelist adored an Angel twise,

Gen. 18. 19. Num. 22. Ios. 5. 3. Reg. 18. 2. Reg. 2.

Dan. 2. Act. 10. Chrys. ibidem. Apoc. 19 & 22

 knowing

knowing him to be an Angel, and therfore vnlesse we vvil say that an Apostle, and he that sucked out of Christs bosome such high Diuinitie that for his high soaring in contemplation he is compared to an Egle, knew not vvhat honour to giue to an Angel, we must allow of worship of Angels and consequently of Saincts, vvhose soules are no lesse liuing, and although the Angel refused such honour, yet that was of modestie, and for honour of Priesthood.

Hier. 151. 19. Prayer to Sainctes is also proued by Scripture, as where God sayd, *If Moyses and Samuel should stand before him* (to wit to make intercession for the people) *yet his soule vvould not be vvith that people*, he giueth vs to suppose that they may pray for the people. That vision also of *Iudas Machabeus* in which he savv *Onias* and *Hieremie*, then not liuing, yet praying for him and his armie, doth argue that Saincts pray for vs, and consequently that we may pray vnto them. And this S. Ihon confirmeth by an other vision in vvhich he saw the twentie fowre Seniors prostrated before the throne of God *hauing euery one harpes and golden vials ful of odours vvhich are* (sayth he) *the prayers of Saincts*. Yea the Angel Raphael sayth that he offered vp Tobias prayers vnto God: and an other Angel prayeth for the people, as Zacharie vvitnesseth in the beginning of his Prophecie. The like example of prayer to an Angel we read in Osee: and Iacob blessing the Sonnes of Ioseph prayeth that his Angel who had deliuered him from al dangers would vouchsafe to blesse them: and wisheth that his owne name and the name of Abraham & Isaac may be called vpon for them. To be briefe Angels reioice at the conuersion of a sinner, *Ergo* they know the state of sinners, and consequently their charitie moueth them to pray for them, which also argueth that we may pray to them. And vvhy haue we Angels vvhich are called our Gardians (as Christ him selfe sayth we haue) but to protect and pray for vs? And seing that the soules of the blessed, are immortal as Angels are, see God face to face as they do, and are indewed vvith glorie as they are, they also can heare our prayers, as wel as Angels, and so are to be prayed vnto as wel as they. We haue many examples also of the prayers of Sainctes in this life, and seing that the soules of dead Saintes are liuing, and haue eyes and eares of soule to see our necessities, and to heare our petitions, vvhy may we not pray to them, and that without iniurie to Christ, as vvel as to the liuing Saintes.

2. Mach. 15. This booke is admitted of S. Aug. l. de cura pro mortuis ex l. 8. ciuit. c. 3. Cypr. Exhort. ad Mart. Amb. l. 2. de Iacob c. 9. 11. yea Lut. in prefat. l. 1. Mac. admith this booke. yea Io. 10. mētiō is of a feast instituted by Iudas Mach. Apoc. 5. Tob. 12. Zach. 1 Osee 12. Gen. 48. Mat. 1. See Gen. 48. Io. 5. 29. 33. Exod. 12. Apoc. 8. 1. Reg. 7.

20. Now that their Images and Reliques may be worshipped, it is as manifest in the two Cherubins placed by the Arke, in the brasen

serpent

ſerpent,in the tranſlation of Iacobs and Ioſephs bones & the reuerent *Iob vlt*
and deuout burial of S Stephen. Yea the reſpect vvhich was borne *Rom.15.*
towards the Arke, Manna, the Tables of the law, and Aarons rodde, *Ephes. 6.*
vvhich vvere religiouſly kept in the Arke, argueth no leſſe. And *2.Thes.9.*
Moyſes putting of his ſhovves, becauſe the earth was holy: Chriſts *Col.4.*
hēme of his garment vvhich the woman ſo deuoutly touched, S. Pauls *Heb.3.& vlt.*
napking, Helias clocke,& Helizeus body whoſe touch reuiued a dead *Iac. 5.*
body, vvhat elſe do they inſinuate, but the aforeſayd reaſon groun- *Ex 25. Num.*
ded in the nature of frendſhip which ſayth, *loue me and loue myn, honour* *22. Gen.50.*
me and honour myn, euen to my ſeruant and image, and the abſurditie which *Act. 8*
foloweth contempt of Saintes, Images and Reliques, though we lay *Heb.9.2.Reg.*
aſide Scriptures, Fathers, Tradition, Hiſtories and al monumentes, is *8.Exod. 25.*
an argument ſufficient for the proofe of the worſhip, & reſpect which *Ex. 3.*
is dew vnto them. *Mat. 9*

21. And to make it more manifeſt, I wil propoſe an example, *Act.19.*
vvhich ſhal lay open vnto the vew of any reaſonable man, the abſur- *4 Reg.2.& 3.*
ditie vvhich foloweth contempt of theſe thinges, and the traiterous *the reformers*
meaning towerds Chriſt, vvhich it implyeth. Put the caſe that ſome *traiteurs to*
one in Englād of his Maieſties ſubiects, ſhould profeſſe great loyaltie, *Chriſt.*
loue, and honour vnto him, yet could not abide to heare a good word of his glorious mother, yea would reuile her, and miſcal her, but vnder this pretence that his Maieſtie is now to haue al the honour, and that no honour can be giuen to the mother, but ſo much is taken from the ſonne. Suppoſe he ſhould paſſe by his Lord Chauncelor, & Treaſurer, without mouing cap, and appeare before his honourable counſail without bowing of body, or bending of knee, and being demanded whether his cap were not nayled to his head, or whether his knee wanted not a ioint, he ſhould anſwer them, that his cap is nayled to al but his Maieſtie, and his knee is ſtiffe to al but his owne good ſelfe: Suppoſe alſo he ſhould deſpiſe his fauourites, and hate them as much as he affecteth them, proteſting that he only loueth his Maieſtie, to vvhom he giueth ſo much of his affectiō, that he hath none left for his freinds or welwillers. Suppoſe that vvhen he entereth into the chamber of preſence he ſhould make no more reuerence to his Chaire, then to an alehouſe bench, Suppoſe that vvhenſoeuer he meeteth with his Graces picture, he ſhould deface and defile it, and ſhould caſt into the fiere vvhat ſoeuer he findeth that hath bene vſed by him, and al vnder this pretence that he giueth al reſpect vnto his owne perſon, and wil not giue any at al to any thing elſe, be it neuer ſo nere, or ſo deare vnto

him, lest he should seeme to part stakes, and not to giue al honour and affection to his Highnes: Suppose also that he shoud stop al sutes vvhich are made vnto his Chaunlcer, Treasurer, Counsailers, and other officers, auouching that such suters are traitors to his Maiestie, vvho in that they goe not to him immediatly, do seme not to put that confidence in him, vvhich his goodnes requireth, but rather do imagine that either he is not able of him selfe, or else not so willing as able: would you take this man to be a loyal subiect: or would you not (notwithstanding al these his goodly pretences and solemne protestations) suspect his sinceritie? and might you not iustly feare, lest after contempt of al that are belonging vnto his Maiestie, he would lay violent hands vpon his owne person? Truly I doubt not but that such a one vvould quickly be arested, and apprehended for a traytour.

The applicatiō of the Exāple. 22. The like case is betwixt Christ Iesus, and these new reformers, and zelators. They professe al honour, dutie, and affection to Christ, but they reuile his Mother, and wil haue no honour giuen vnto her, lest that in honouring the Mother they should dishonour the Sonne. They beare no respect vnto Christs chiefest officers the Apostles, to whom he committed his Church at his departue. They fouour not at al the freinds and fauorits of Christ, the Saincts, and Angels: and this they say they do for feare lest they should incurre Christs disfauour, in fauouring them vvhom he him selfe fauoured. When they meete with the image of Christ, or of his Mother, or freindes, they deface and defile it. When they see the Crosse of Christ they swel at the very sight of it, as if they were possessed, and can no more abide it, then can the diuels, vvho because he hateth Christ can not brooke his Crosse. If they should hit vpon any bone of Christs frendes, they would spurne at it, and if any relique of Christ, or his Mother, or his Apostles, and other Saints, should be in their way, if a dunghil were not nere hand, they would cast it into the fier. Al sutes and requestes, vvhich are made to the Mother of God, or any Saint, officer, or freind of Christ, they forbid and condemne as iniurious to Christ as though (say they) Christ were not able or willing ynough of him selfe, but that the vvay must be made by Mediators and Intercessors. These are their goodly pretences, but vvhat litle signe of true meaning towards Christ therby is shewed, the law of frendship shal determine, vvhich telleth vs, that if we loue our freind we must loue his aliance, freinds, and al appertaining vnto him euen vnto his dogge. And if in the other case of case of that braging subiect, vvho pretendeth great honour to his Maiestie, sentence would be pronounced against him as against a traytour, because although he professe great loue and honour towards him, yet he declareth contrarie in the contempt of his Mother, frends and officers, I see not how any indifferent Iudge can condemne him for a traytour to his Maiestie, vnles he pronounce these also traytours vnto Christ his person: because where the case is like, and the cause the same, and only the persons different: if the sentẽce be not the same, the Iudge is partial, and an accepter of persons. *The cõclusion.*

THE FOVRTH BOOKE CONTEINETH A GENERAL SVRVEY OF THEIR RELIGION AND WORSHIP OF GOD. IN WHICH it is proued, that they haue either no Religion at al, or a graceles Religion.

The first Chapter shevveth hovv Priestes and Religion euer vvent together, and that the reformers haue no Priestes, and consequently no Religion.

HE old Lavv being abrogated as able only to shew the way, but not to giue force to walke in the same, to command but not to giue grace to obey: the old Sacraments being antiquated and abolished, as signes only which represented grace, but could not effectuate it: the old Priestes also by good consequēce were turned out of office, as able only to iudge betwixt corporal leprēsies, and to absolue from legal irregularities: because the Law, Sacraments, and Sacrifices, being abolished, there was no vse of the Priests, vvho vvere ordayned only for one of these three offices, that is to preach and interprete the Law, to
Heb. 5. minister Sacraments, or to offer Sacrifice. And in lieu of the old Law, a new Law by Christ being established, which was written not with
Exod. 24. the fingers of an Angel as the old was, but of the Holy Gost, and not in stones as that was, but in the hartes of men: new Sacraments also being instituted not only to signifie grace, but also to sanctifie. New Priests of necessitie were to be appointed, to interprete this Law, and to mi-

to minister these Sacraments: because Law, Religion, & Priestes, euer went together, and therfore as S. Paul sayth the one being altered, the other was to be changed. Three Lavves there are by which God hath ruled his people, to wit, the Law of nature, the written law, & the Law of grace: in al which, as I haue declared in the last chapter of the first booke, were Priestes, and they also diuerse, according to the diuersitie of Lavves. Wherfore if Christ hath planted a Church, and in it established a Law and Religion, certainly he hath also appointed a succession of Priestes, because they euer go together, and haue such a connexion, that the one can not stand without the other. For if there be no Priests to offer Sacrifice, and to minister Sacramentes, and to interpret the Law, no shew or face of Religion can remaine, & as wel may a Kingdom florish without a Prince or magistrate, as Religion vvithout Priests, and Bishops. Wherfore, as I proued before, in the Law of nature the first begotten of euerie familie was a Priest, and in the law written, the tribe of Leuie was deputed, and dedicated vnto Priesthod. In which tribe there were inferior Priests so many that Dauid was fayne to diuide them into twenty fowre rankes, which also conteined a great number. There were also Leuits who had inferior offices. And there were high Priestes which succeeded, one after an others death, to the number of fowre score and odde, and the last High Priest was Finasius, who liued, vntil the Citie of Hierusalem with the Temple, was beseeged and ruined by Titus and Vespasian. These Priestes and Leuites losing their office with the abrogation of the old lavv, Christ IESVS vvho gaue vs a nevv lavv, appointed a nevv Priesthood, of vvhich he him selfe vvas the first Priest, and the principal, and the only High Priest, to vvhom no man succedeth in the same authoritie: and therfore S. Paul putteth a difference herin betvvixt the old & the nevv lavv, that in the old lavv many High Priestes vvho succeeded one an other vvere necessarie, because one dying, an other vvas of necessitie to succede lest the Church should, vvāt an High Priest, but in the nevv lavv there is but one High Priest Christ IESVS, and he is sufficient, because though he dyed, yet he rose again, and neuer gaue ouer the office, but stil offereth Sacrifice, and stil ministreth Sacraments, by the hands of his vnder Priestes. So that he only is the High Priest of the nevv lavv, & none but he, because no man succedeth him in the same authoritie.

Heb. 7

There Lavves.

See the first booke & sixt chapter.

Priests in al lavves necessarie.

The reason.

In the first booke, & 6.c.

Ios. l. 2. cont. App. Tol. in Io. c. 18.

Ios. l. 22. Ant c 8. Tob. in Io. c. 18.

The old Priest put out of office.

Heb. 7

Christ the only High Priest

See the third booke, & 6.c.

2. But here the aduersarie vvil insult, and say vnto me, that I haue affirmed that vvhich he desired. For if Christ be the only High Priest of the

An obiectió.

of the new law, what nede we any Popes, Bishops, and Priests? Thus he argueth: but wih how litle reason a blind man may see. For as it is no good argument, to say that now in England Scotland and Ireland, can be but one King at once, therfore there must be no Viceroyes, nor Deputies, nor Chancelers, nor Treasurers, nor Dukes, nor Noble men, who are the Princes Officers, and Princes in their kind, and vicegerentes also, some in more ample some in lesse ample maner: so it is no good argument to say that Christ is the only High Priest of the nevv law, *Ergo* there are no other Priests but he. For he may haue many vicegerentes, who also are true Priests in their kind. And so the Pope may be his supreme Vicare in earth, and other Bishops an Priests may also be inferior Vicars & Priests subordinate in iurisdiction vnto the Pope. Yea seing that the High Priest Christ IESVS hath vvithdravvne his visible presence from the Church, and executeth not visibly and immediatly by him selfe his priestly function, it vvas necessary that to his visible Church, he should leaue a visible successiõ of Priests, who should rule and minister vnder him & for him, in his absence, not as his successors, but as his vicegerents & ministers: for as no Priest, no Church, so no visible Priest no visible Church. Wherfore when Christ was to bid his Church fare wel he instituted his Apostles Priests, giuing them authoritie to consecrate, & to offer Sacrifice, & after his Resurrection giuing them povver also to absolue from sinnes, and appointing Peter as the High Priest & Vicare vnder him selfe, which to deny were not only to contradict the Councel of Trent defining that in the place alleaged Christ made the Apostles Priests (vvhich Protestants thinks they may boldly do) but also to contemne and condemne the vvhole Schoole of ancient Fathers and interpreters, yea the vvhole Christian world, who haue so interpreted the places alleaged.

The ansvver. — *Visible vnder Priest necessarie* — *Mat. 26. Io. 20. Io. 21.* — *Sess. 23. Can. 2* — *The Apostles Priests*

3. This Priestly function the Apostles in their tyme did exercise in preaching, teaching, baptising, confirming, and offerring Sacrifice also, which is the proper function of a Priest. Yea their Disciples did the same. For S. Luke sayth that they *ministred vnto our Lord*, that is sacrificed as the Greeke word, *Litourgooundon* signifieth, and as Erasmus him selfe translateth it, yea as the maner of speach also importeth. For if they had only preached, or ministred Sacraments, wel might haue bene sayed to haue ministred to the People, but not so properly to our Lord, vnles they had offered Sacrifice, which is proper to him. S. Paul sayth that Timothie was ordained Bishop by imposition of hands of the *Presbyterie*, that is, a company of Bishops, & he affirmeth that

They did the office. — *Act. 13.* — *So did their Disciples.* — *1. Tim. 4. 2. Tim. 1 Hier. in c. 58 Isa.*

that he him selfe imposed his hands vpon him: vvhich imposition of hands is in greeke called *Chirotonia* & as S. Hierome vvitnesseth, signifieth giuing of holy Orders. The same S. Paul writing vnto Titus, sayth that he left him at Creta, that he should *constitute and ordaine Priests in euery citie.* The same S. Paul with Barnabas, ordained *to the people Priests in euery Church,* by imposition of hãds, as the greeke word *Chirotonisantes* importeth. The same S. Paul, as S. Luke reporteth, sent to Ephesus and called the Elders of the Church, that is Priests, for to them he sayd: *Looke to your selues and vnto your flocke.* And of Priests he speaketh vvhen he sayth: *Priests vvhich do rule vvel, are vvorthy duble honour.* And againe: *Against a Priest receiue no accusation vnder tvvo or three vvitnesses.* Of Priests also speaketh S. Iames vvhen he sayth: *If any be diseased among you let them cal for the Priests of the Church.* And because our Gospellers see that by these it is manifest, that in the Apostles tymes Priests were ordeined, they are forced (for other wise they could not cõceale this from the people) to translate *Elders* for *Priestes*, notwithstanding that the greeke word, yea the Latin, Spanish, French and Italian, soundeth as much as Priest in English.

Tit. 1. *Act. 14.* *Act. 26.* *1. Tim. 3.* *Io. 5.* *Presbiter.* *Prestre.* *Prete.* *Priest.*

4. Of Bishops, Priests, and Deacons we haue mention in the Canons of the Apostles, And the Councel of Nice: And Ignatius Bishop of Antioch and scholar of S. Paul, in diuerse of his Epistles speaketh of the same. In his Epistles to the Ephesians this is his admonition: *Endeuour my dearest to be subiect to the Bishops, Priests and Deacons, because he that obeyeth them, obeyeth Christ who appointed them.* And againe in an other Epistle he giueth the reason, vvhy we should obey them: For vvhat (sayth he) *is a Bishop, but one vvho is aboue al principalitie, and is as much (as a man can be) an imitator of Christ? Vvhat is Priesthood but an holy company, counsaylers, and assistants to the Bishop? Vvhat are Deacons but imitators of Angels vvho exhibit a pure and harmeles ministery, as S. Stephen did to S. Iames, S. Timothie and S. Line to S. Paul, Anacletus and Clemens to S. Peter?* And in an other place he reckeneth almost al the inferior Orders of the Clergie: *I salute Subdeacons, Lectors, Singers, Ianitors, Exorcists*: and so forth. By vvhich it is plaine, that in the Church of Christ euen from the beginning, there vvas a Clergie of Bishops, Priests, and inferior Ministers, and that the Church, and they euen from the beginning, went together, and by later writers and histories it is most manifest, that Priesthood vvas an Order vvhich euer florished in the Church of Christ, ruled also in it, and vpholded it. And truly Religion, and Priestood, are so inseparately vnited, that the very Paganes as they practised super-

Canon. Apo. *Couc. Nic.* *Ignat. ep. ad Eph.* *Ep. ad Tral.* *Ep ad Anti.* *Priests & the Church & Religion vvent euer together.*

stition and Idolatrie in steed of Religion: so did they deuise a kind of Clergie and order of Priests, to rule their Church in spiritual matters, to offer their Sacrifices, and to minister their Sacraments, as in the pagane writers is most manifest to be sene.

5. Now that there is no true Priesthood amongst the Gospellers, them selues do confesse, and I shal also proue it: but first let vs take their owne confession. Luther sayth plainly that al are priests alike, and that Christians are not ordained but borne Priests in baptisme. Only (sayth he) this is the difference, that to auoid confusion, the execution of priestly authoritie is committed to some only. And this is the opinion of al the reformers, euen in England, who as they acknowledge no proper and true Sacrifices but only improper, such as prayer is, and a contrite hart: so they acknowledge no other Priests, then those who offer prayer and thankes-giuing, and such like improper sacrifices vnto God. And because al may offer such sacrifices, al with them are priests alike. And so the minister is no more Priest then the minstrel, only the minister by election, or by the Princes lettre, hath the execution of this priestly function committed vnto him. Whence it foloweth that there is no Hierarchie by their opinion amōgst them, nor distinction of the state of Clergie and Laitie in order, dignitie, and power, but only in execution. Wherfore seing that al are not true and proper Priests, there is no true Priestood amongst them at al. This they grant, and by their proofe and argument, by which they proue al to be Priests alike, they declare their meaning. For their principal proofe is taken out of S. Peter and S. Iohn, who say that Christ hath made vs al a *holy nation a Royal Priesthood and Priests to God his Father*: vvhich wordes argue only that we are metaphorical and improper Priests, who in that we are to offer vnto God vpon the Altar of our soule, prayse, thankes-giuing, prayer, contrition, and such like vertues, do in some sorte resemble true Priests, who offer true Sacrifices vpon true Altars: but as our soules are not true Altars, nor our vertues true Sacrifices, so are not al true Priestes. And therfore S. Peter as he calleth vs Priests so he calleth vs Kings, liuing stones, and spiritual houses: and therfore as we are not al proper and true Kinges, as we are not al true stones and houses: so are we not al true Priests. And seing that by this their opiniō vve are al Priests alike, there is no true priesthood amongst them by their opinion, and so no Church nor Religion. For although there is in Christs Church true Priesthood distinct from the state of the Laitie, in caracter, order, consecration, and power, as I haue

L. de abrog. Missa l ad Bragenses de Instit. ministris.

The reformers say that al are priests alike.

1. of Pet. 2. Apoc. 2.

I haue already proued, yet in their opinion there is none, and so amongst them by their owne confession, is no Religion. Because to vphold Religion, not only improper Priests, such as euer were al the faythful, are required, but also proper Priests, such as differed in state from the rest of the multitude, and offered true Sacrifices, were euer in euery law necessarie: and true Priestes and true Religion as yet euer vvent together.

6. And truly as they teach so it is amongest them. For in their Church there can be no true Priests nor Priesthood, as I wil in a word or two demonstrate. And first of al if they haue any true Priests amongst them, let him shew vs a succession of them from the Apostles, else can they not proue them to be true Priests, for if Christ ordained his Apostles Priestes, and in them began the goodly order and ranke of Priests, which by succession he would alvvayes haue to continew in his Church for the vpholding of Religion in the same, then certes they are no true Priests, who can not deriue their pedegree from the Apostles, as Catholique Priests can do, but bastard and apish ministers, vvho cary the name and coate of Priests, and arrogate vnto them selues that office, but are no more Priests in dede, then are their minstrels & coblers. Secondly vvho in Gods name layed hands vpon them? VVhat Bishops ordained them? not Catholique Bishops I am sure, and they them selues vvil think it no credit to fetch their pedegree from them: not their owne Bishops: because before Luther and Caluin, who were no Bishops them selues: neuer any Superintendent of their sect, was seene, felt, or heard of: and before Luther and Caluin, there could be no Lutheranes nor Caluinists, much lesse Lutherane, and Caluinistical Superintendents. Wherfore in the beginning of their new Religion they were enforced to make Superintendentes & ministers of our Apostating Priests such as Parker, Grindal, Sands, Horne, and many others were, who were thought paste fitte to make such superintendents and ministers, without ny other moulding. And vvhere they vvanted Apostataes who were consecrated after the Catholique maner, they tooke laymen of their owne, of vvhich some were base artificers, and vvithout any other consecration or ordination then the Princes or the Superintendents letters, (who them selues were no Bishops) they made them ministers and Bitsheeps with as few ceremonies, and les solennitie, then they make their Aldermen, yea constable, and cryers of the market. And from this stocke procedeth al the rable of their ministers who are no more Priests then they

no true priests in the nevv church.

the first profe *Mat. 29.* *Ephes. 4.*

the second.

were that made them. The like ordination & institution of ministers Tertullian recordeth to haue bene practised by the Heretikes of his tyme: *Their ordinations (sayth he) are light, rash, inconstant: one vvhile they make ministers of Neophits, an other vvhile of lay men, and those vvho are tyed to the vvorld, an other vvhile of our Apostatats, that they may bynd them vnto them by glorie, vvhom they can not by veritie. VVherfore one Bishop they haue to day, an other to morovv, to day he is made a Deacon, vvho to morovv is reader, to day he is a Priest, vvho to morovv is a layman, for to lay men they inioyne priestly functions.* They wil say perchance that our Apostating Bishops could make Bishops, and that so continueth a succession of true Priests amongst them. But then I must tel them, that Luther and Caluin, and many others vvere neuer Bishops amongst vs and so could make no Priests, and those that were Bishops, vsed not the right forme of ordination, and so they also made no true Priests, but only prophane ministers, as I haue proued in the first booke and first chapter. If then they haue no Priests, they haue none who hath authoritie to minister Sacraments, to offer Sacrifice, and to preach to the people, and so can haue no Religion, because Priests & Religion must euer go together. Thus S. Hierom reiecteth & refuteth the Sect of Luciferians: *Hilarius (sayth he) vvho vvas the head of the Luciferians, vvhen being a Deacon he departed from the Church, and he alone vvith his companions, as he thinketh, became the only company and Church of the vvorld, can neither cōsecrate the Eucharist, hauing neither Bishops, nor Priests, neither can he giue baptisme vvithout the Eucharist* (For then Baptisme, the Eucharist, & Confirmation, were giuen together) *& novv he being dead, his Sect & Church is dead vvith him, because he being but a Deacō, could ordaine no Clerk to succede him, & that is no Church vvhich hath no Priest.* Thus he argued against the Luciferians, & the same argument do I make against al the new Sects of this age: You haue no true Priests by your owne doctrin, neither in dede can you haue any, because al your ministers were ordayned without order, that is vvithout consecration & imposition of Bishops hands, & they haue their authoritie from them, who being lay men, could neither haue it them selues, nor giue it to others; and seing that Religion and Priests of necessitie did euer go together, as is already proued, you hauing no true Priests, can haue no true Religion: and so your preachings, Bishopping, and supping, or communicating, and your administrations of other Sacraments (Baptisme only excepted, vvhich in necessitie lay men, yea vvomen may minister) are no more actes of Religion, then if the same vvere done by players vpon the stage, because you haue no more Priestly authoritie then they

l. præsc. vltra med.

l. cont. Lucif.

No true ministerie amōgst the nevv reformers.

A stage play only of Religion.

they haue, and so haue no true Religion amongst you, but only an apish imitation, and a Stage-play of Religion.

The second Chapter proueth that Religion can not stand vvithout a true Sacrifice, and that the reformers haue no true Religion, because they haue no Sacrifice.

MAN being composed of soule and body, is to serue his Creator vvith both, and therfore must not only beleue vvith hart, but must professe also his beleefe with tongue, and must not only prayse God in spirit, but must vse his mouth also as a trompet to sound out his prayse: neither must he pray with soule only, but vvith lippes also: and he ought not only to humble his mynd in prayer, but to bow and bend his knee and body also, and he is not only to mynd and meane wel, but he must also do wel, *to glorifie his Father vvhich is in heauen*, and to edifie his brother in earth. Which thing is so deeply imprinted in the mynds of men, that there were neuer any, either religious or superstitious, whose inward deuotion did not breake forth into some outvvard signes or ceremonies, by which was manifested outwardly, and by some action or gesture of the body, what was inwardly conceiued and concealed in the mynd.

God must be serued vvith soule & body

Mat. 5.

External vvordes necessarie.

2. And amongst al the external worshipps and outvvard signes of inward deuotion & Religion, Sacrifice was euer counted the principal, vvhich therfore, as S. Austin noteth, was neuer offered but either to God, or to some creature, vvhich was esteemed of as God. And therfore al nations of what religion soeuer they vvere, haue euer vsed to offer Sacrifice, as though they thought that they gaue not vnto their God his right honour and vvorship, vnles they should offer vnto him one Sacrifice or other. Plinie reporteth that the people of Sabea offered as sacrifices vnto their Gods al maner of spices but myrhe, wherwith that countrie aboundeth: others haue offered fruites and herbes of the earth, others brute beasts, others haue sacrificed children and men vnto their Gods: vvherin though many superstitions and abominable idolatries vvere cōmitted, yet thereby appeareth that no sooner

Sacrifice the principal.

l.10.cin.c.4.

Al nations vse Sacrifice.

l.10.c.15.20.

Polyd. virg.l. de Inuent. rerum c.8.

 the

the hart of man is possessed vvith religion, true or false, but it thinketh of one Sacrifice or other. In so much that Plutarke sayth: *that a man shal sooner hit vpon cities vvithout vvalles, houses, Kings, lavves, coynes Schooles, and Theatres, then vvithout Temples and Sacrifices*: and therfore, sayth he, Epicure, vvho in deed serued no other God then his belly (and consequētly had no other Church then this kitching, no other Priests then his cookes, and no other Sacrifices then his dishes) offered notvvihstanding Sacrifice vnto the Gods, for feare of the multitude.

Aduersus Colotem.

l. quod nō potest suauiter viui secūdum Epic.

3. And as these because they had the light of nature, offered Sacrifices, but because they wanted light of faith offered them to false Gods, and vvith much superstition: so the true vvorshippers of God who vvere indewed vvith the true light of faith offered Sacrifice to the true God. Adam as I haue already proued was a Priest, and therfore did no doubt offer Sacrifice to appease Gods vvrath conceiued against his fault, although the Scripture maketh no mention of it. Abel, as the Scripture vvitnesseth, being a Priest, was not content to beare a hart ful of reuerence vnto God, but to make manifest the invvard religion of his mynd, he killed the first borne and fatest of his flocke, and offered them to God as a Sacrifice, and God respected Abel and his oblations. Noë also so soone as the fludde was fallen, built an Alter vnto God, and vpon it he sacrificed and offered Holocausts, and burnt offerings of the cleane beasts, aud foules, vvhich he had preserued from the furious vvaues of that vniuersal deluge. The like did Abraham, Melchisedech, Iob and many other Patriarches, and true feruants of God vvho liued vnder the lavv of nature, as is also in the place alleaged, proued and declared. In the Lavv vvritten the vse of offering Sacrifice vvas more frequent, and the Sacrifices, and the ceremonies, vvhervvith they vvere to be offered, vvere determined by Gods ovvne mouth, as appeareth by the booke of Leuiticus and other parts of Scripture. And for this purpose especially God commanded Salomon to build that stately Temple, and would haue no Sacrifice offered but there, which is the cause why the Iewes since the destruction of their Temple, though they exercise other actes of their Religion, yet in no place dare they offer Sacrifice. Wherfore in the nevv Law also, if Christ hath planted a Church, and in this Church Religion, then hath he also amongst the offices of Religion, instituted a Sacrifice.

In the first booke, &c. 6.

Gen. 4.

Sacrifice in the Lavv of nature.

Gen. 8.

See the first booke, last ch.

In the Lavv vvritten.

In the nevv Lavv.

Isa. 53.

Io. 10.

4. And this in part the Gospellers wil not let to confesse, for they grant that Christ offered his owne selfe vpon the Altar of the Crosse as a Sa-

as a Sacrifice vnto his Father, vvhich was the complement of al the old Sacrifices, the veritie of al those shadowes, and the price of our Redemption. But yet because this Sacrifice is not sufficient to vpholde Religion and the worship of God, either they must shew vs some other Sacrifice, or else they can not mantaine any true Religion. For first I haue proued that Religion can not stand vvithout a Sacrifice; vvherfore seing that the Sacrifice of the crosse is past, and neuer to be reiterated, an other Sacrifice is necessarie for the continuance of Religion. Neither wil it suffice for an answer to say, that the effectes and vertue of the Sacrifice of the Crosse remaine, for these effects are no Sacrifices, but only graces vvhich by vertue of the Sacrifice of the crosse are bestowed vpon vs. Much les can it serue for a good answer, to say that Christ stil in heauen presenteth vnto his Father the Sacrifice of the crosse. For that presentation is not a true, nor a new oblation of a Sacrifice, and if it were yet because it is in heauen, it is not sufficient to vphold Religion in earth, because a visible Church and visible worship of God in earth, require a visible Sacrifice in earth. Secondly as S. Austin sayth, neuer as yet did any societie consort together in one Religion but by practise & vse of the same visible signes, and Sacraments, and therfore seing that Sacrifice is the proper, and principal signe of the homage, vvhich we giue to God (because it was neuer offered but to God, or at least to that creature vvhich was esteemed as God, it is impossible that this visible Religion and worship should continew without a Sacrifice and a visible Sacrifice also, that to the oblation of it the people may meete together. And seing that the Sacrifice of the crosse is no more visible, and is not to be reiterated, neither is a visible signe, at the which the people may mete together to worship therby almightie God vniformely and externally, that is not sufficient to vphold Religion in the Church of Christ: for as Religion began with visible Sacrifices, and changed with change of Sacrifices, vvhich is the cause why the Prophets vvhen they complaine of the fal of Religion, they complaine also of the fal of Sacrifices, so doth it continew with Sacrifices, & can not stand without a Sacrifice. For as in England where kneeling is a proper worship dew vnto the Prince, it is not sufficient by cappe or cursye to shew your dutie, because these ceremonyes are giuen to euery noble man or gentleman, yea to al those also who beare any sway in the common welth, and therfore to deny His Maiestie that homage, were to despoile him of honour: so to take away Sacrifice vvhich hitherto hath bene offered vnto

Ephes. 5.

An other sacrifice necessarie besides that of the Crosse.

L. 10. cont. Faust. c. 11.

Aug. sup.

2. Par. 15.
Dan. 3. & 12.

A similitude

vnto God, and neuer vnto any but such as were estemed gods, were were to robbe God of his principal and proper worship, and consequently to ruine religion: vvhich as it principally respecteth God as his proper worship, so can it not stand vvithout the same.

5. And why, I pray you, should we feare to grant a Sacrifice in the new Law? because (say they) Christ abrogated al Sacrifices. True. I grant he abrogated al the old Sacrifices, because they were but shadowes, and figures of future thinges, and therfore the sunne Christ Iesus, rising in the horizon of the new Law, and the light of the verities appearing, the darke figures, and obscure shadowes, vvere to giue place: but yet this is no argument to proue that he hath not instituted a new Sacrifice in the new Law: for so he abrogated al the old Sacraments, as Circumcision vvhich was a Sacrament only and no Sacrifice, and yet as Saint Austin sayth, he hath prescribed new Sacraments for the nevv law, *Greater in vertue, better for profit, easier in vse, and fevver in number.* They wil say peraduenture that the old Sacrifices being abrogated, it is sufficient now to worship God in spirite, or at least by prayse, thankesgiuing, and such other vertuous offices. But then I must tel them that because stil we are composed of soule and & body, it is not sufficient that we honour God in spirit only, and because the Church is a visible congregation it must haue a visible Sacrifice. Neither are the external actes of vertue sufficient, because they (as is proued) are no true Sacrifices but only metaphorical and improper, and therfore as hitherto and in al Lawes, besids those improper Sacrifices, it was necessarie for the maintenance of Religion to haue some proper Sacrifices, such as Abel, Noë and others did offer, so in the nevv lavv besides the metaphorical Sacrifices of prayer, thankesgiuing, contrite hartes and such like, we must haue some proper Sacrifice, because that & religion euer goe together. And if we haue no Sacrifice it foloweth that the Iewes honoured God more then we do, because they offered vnto him Sacrifice vvhich is the greatest honour that can be giuen, and therfore vvas alwayes reserued for God.

l. 19. contra Faust. c. 13.

A true and visible Sacrifice necessarie in the nevv lavv.

6. A Sacrifice then is necessarie in the nevv law. And vvhat more likely to be this Sacrifice then the Sacrifice of the Masse? Melchisedech and his Sacrifice were figures of Christ and his Sacrifice, as before is proued: vvherfore seing that there is no likenes betwixt Melchisedeches Sacrifice and the Sacrifice of the crosse, we must find some other in the new law vvhich doth more resemble it: and what more can resemble it then the Sacrifice of the Masse, which though it be

In the third booke chap 6.

The Sacrifice of the Masse proued. The first profe

it be not bread and wine, yet hath it the accidentes and outward shew of bread and wine. Daniel prophecying of the hauock of Religion vvhich Anti-Christ shal make, affirmeth that he shal take away the dayly Sacrifice. And what Sacrifice I pray you? not the Sacrifice of the crosse because that is past, and vvhich is doone can not be vndoone: not improper Sacrifices of prayer, contrite hartes, and such like, because he speaketh of one Sacrifice, they are many, and of a proper and publique Sacrifice, they are improper and metaphorical. He speaketh therfore of some publique Sacrifice vvhich for reason of persecution shal not be offered any more in publique maner, but very secretly and not so commonly as it was wont to be. And vvhat other Sacrifice is there in the Church for Anti-Christ to take away, then that of the Masse. Let the Gospellers name it, if there be, or euer were any other. Malachie the prophet, or rather God by the mouth of his prophet, sayth that he is *vveary of the Ievves Sacrifices*, that *his vvil is not amongst them*, and that henceforth he wil *receiue no guiftes*, that is no Sacrifice, vvhich is offered by their handes but (sayth he) *From the rising of the sunne to the setting of the same, my name shalbe great amongst the gentils, and in euery place shalbe offered vnto me a cleane oblation*. And vvhat oblation or Sacrifice is that? Not the Iewish Sacrifice: because he sayth this sacrifice shal be offered amongst the gentiles, yea he protesteth that he is weary of al Iewish Sacrifices. Not the Idolatrical Sacrifices of the gentils, because he would neuer haue called them cleane Sacrifices, neither can they be said truly to be offered vnto him, but rather vnto the diuel. Not improper Sacrifices of prayer, thankes giuing, and good workes, because he compareth Sacrifice with Sacrifice, and so promising a new Sacrifice in steed of the old, as he reiecteth proper Sacrifices, so must he in lieu of them, prouide an other proper Sacrifice, which in the dignitie of a Sacrifice surpasseth them al. Yea by this *cleane Sacrifice* according vnto the reformers opinion, it is impossible that he should meane prayer, thankes-giuing, or such like good workes, because the best of these Sacrifices, in their opinion, are so vncleane that they are mortal sinnes, & abominable in the sight of God. Neither can he meane the Sacrifices which Iob & others offered amongst the gentils, because he speaketh of one Sacrifice, those were many, & could be no cleaner then those of the Iewes, yea those were offered but in few places, & so can not be the Sacrifice which Malachie sayth shal be offered in euery place euen from the East to the west. He speaketh therfore of a Sacrifice which in the new law shal be a most cleane & pleasing

The second.

This sacrifice is proued vvith Christs Priesthood in the 3. booke ch. 6.

The third.

Luth. in c. vlt. ad Gal. Cal. l. 3. inst. c. 14. l. 2. c. 5.

Sacri-

The Sacrifice of the Maße is vnbloudy: and that vvhich Malachie fortelleth

Sacrifice, & which in al partes of the Christian world shal be offered vnto God.

7 And vvhat such Sacrifice can the Reformers name, but the Sacrifice of the Masse? what other oblation was euer counted a Sacrifice in the Church? what other Sacrifice is offered euery vvhere, but the Sacrifice of the Masse, vvhich is a most cleane Sacrifice, not only in respect of the outward forme, vvhich is vnblouddy, but also in respect of the most chast, pure, and virginal flesh & bloud of Christ, vvhich it conteineth? and this is the Sacrifice vvhich Christ offered at his last supper, vvhen taking bread and vvine into his handes he *blessed* them, and by blessing, turning them into his sacred body and bloud, he told his disciples that it was his body and bloud vvhich he *gaue for them.* In vvhich vvordes he can meane no other thing then the Sacrifice of his body and bloud, vvhich he offered vnder the formes of bread and wine. For to glosse those vvordes as Caluin doth (as though Christ had sayd: *This is my body*, that is, this is a figure of my body, vvhich shal be geuen for you) is very violent and repugnant to the text, because the greeke text vseth the presentence *Which is geuen for you, vvhich is povvred out for you:* and therfore vnderstandeth some thing vvhich euen then was geuen for them. And seing that Caluins bread & figure could only be said to be geuen to them, but not for them, that vvhich then he gaue for them, was his body & bloud, which vnder the forme of bread and vvine he offered for them. And seing that he bad his Apostles to do as he had done, that is, to offer the same Sacrifice vvhich he did, for so much the latin word (*facite*) in that place and vvith such circumstances importeth, it must needes folow, that he commanded the Apostles, & in them their successors, to offer Sacrifice, & the same Sacrifice vvhich he offered for his Apostles at his last supper, vvhich is the Sacrifice of the Masse. This veritie I could proue more largely by other circũstances of this place, especially according to the greeke, and I could alleage that place of S. Paul, vvhere he compareth table to table, that is Altar to Altar saying *that vve can not be pertakers of the table of our Lord and of the diuel:* that is, we can not participate of that which is offered on the Altars of the gentiles, & of that also which is offered on the Christians Altar, and out of this place I could proue that in S. Paules time there was some thing offered on the Christians Altars, which he opposeth to that which was offered on the Paganes Altars. I could also presse our aduersaries and oppresse them with the authoritie and multitude of Fathers, who al acknovvledge that Christ at his last sup-

Mat. 26. Luc. 22. Mar. 16. 1. Cor. 11. It is proued by Christs vvordes.

Mat. 26.

Luc. 22.

Heb. 13.

Hier. ep. ad Marcellam. Aug. l. 16. ciuit. c. 21. l. 1. cont. aduer

last supper offered a Sacrifice of his owne body and bloud, vnder the forme of bread and vvine, and that therby he was a Priest according to the order of Melchisedech: but this veritie I haue partly proued already in prouing Christ to be an æternal Priest according to the order of Melchisedech, partly I shal herafter proue, when in the last booke vpon occasion I shal demonstrate the real presence of Christs body and bloud in the Sacrament of the Altar. And as for the Fathers authoritie, it were but lost labour to alleage it for any proofe of this veritie, because Luther hath already debarred vs from such proofes, and vvil tel vs plainly that they are not to be credited in this matter, because they were but men. And Caluin also wil tel me, that seing this supper is the supper of the Lord, there is no reason why we should be moued with any auctoritie of men or prescription of yeares. VVherfore let them cary away the bucklers, let them be credited before practise of the Church, which alwayes offered Sacrifice; before reason, which telleth vs that Religion can not stand without a Sacrifice; before the plaine text of Scripture, which in plaine words affirmeth that Christ gaue his body and powred out his bloud at his last supper for his disciples, vvhich vvords can import no lesse then a Sacrifice; before al Fathers also, because they were but men and our reformers as it semeth are godds: let them gaine the gole and gette the victoritie in this controuersie: vvhat shal they gaine therby? truly only this: that amongst them is no Religion.

sarium legis c. 20.
Damasc. l. 4. de fide c. 14.
Theoph. in 1. 5. Heb.
Arnob. in psal. 109.
l. de abrog. Missæ.
l. 4. Inst. c. 18. par. 10.
Vt supra.

8. For if they haue no Sacrifice, as they confesse that they haue not, and in dede they haue not: and if Sacrifice, as being the principal office of Religion and proper vnto God, as is proued, is necessarily required, that without it Religion can in no wise be supported: the conclusion to which my former discourse driueth, must needs folowe, that the reformers haue no Religion, because no Sacrifice no Religion: And seing that in the Catholique and Romain Church only is found a Sacrifice like to Melchisedechs, and correspondent to that of which Daniel and Malachie haue fortold, as the Sacrifice of the nevv Lavv, and the same which Christ offered at his last supper, and commanded to be offered by his Apostles and their successors, it foloweth that the Catholique Church is the true Church of Christ, and that in it only is practised true Faith and true Religion.

The third Chapter shevveth hovv the reformers amongst them haue reiected al the Sacraments, and so can haue no Religion, because Sacraments and Religion euer goe together.

Sacramentes necessarie in respect of our dutie to God.
The first reason herof.
The second.

IT is a common opinion amongst the holy Fathers and Diuines that since the fal of Adam, Sacramentes were alwayes necessary, partly to declare mans duty towards God, and partly for mans owne instruction. For first man being composed of soule and body, was to serue God, not only with inward affections, but also by outward and visible signes. Secondly because he was to receiue grace from Christ against the maladie of sinne, into vvhich he was fallen, he was also to professe his fayth in Christ, from vvhom this grace procedeth, & to acknowledge it as descending from his Passion, by visible signes and figures: such as Abels Sacrifice, and Circumcision were in the law of nature, and such as the Paschal lambe, and other Sacraments were in the law of Moyses, and such as Baptisme, and the Sacrament of the Altar are in the law of grace. Thirdly because he had offended God by vse of corporal thinges, it was conuenient that by corporal and sensible Sacramentes, & by the religious vse of the same, he should restore to God, his honour which sinne had taken from him, and make him satisfaction by such thinges as he had done him iniurie.

The third.

Sacraments necessarie in respect of mās ovvneself.
Gen 3.
The first reasō
Prou. 6.
Rom. 6.

2. For mans behalfe also, Sacraments since Adams sinne, were alwayes requisite. For first, because mans sinne proceded of pride, and a desire to be like to God in knowledge of good and euil, it was conuenient for mans humiliation that he should be set to Schoole, to learne not only of the Ant, diligence, and of other brute beastes, other vertues, but also of these senseles creatures, such as Sacraments are, his faith and religion. Wherfore as the Paschal lambe brought the Iewes into a grateful remembrance of their deliuerie and passage from Egipte, and Circumcision did put them in mynd of a spiritual Circumcision: So Baptisme setteth before our eyes the burial and Resurrection of Christ. For vvhen the infant is dipped into the water, vve thinke of Christes burial, and vvhen he is lifted vp a new creature regenera-

generated to a newe life, we cal to mynd the Resurrection, by vvhich Christ is risen to a new and an immortal life. And in the Sacred Eucharist vvhich by the forme and accidentes of bread and wine, representeth the bodie and bloud of Christ, as separated apart, we commemorate the death and Passion of Christ. Secondly as man by sinne had preferred the creature before the Creator, so was it mete and conuenient, that he should as it were begge grace and seeke his saluation by the meanes of these sensible signes and Sacraments, vvhich are farre inferior vnto him in nature. Lastly as by abuse of corporal creatures he had wounded his soule by sinne, so was it expedient that by vse of the same, his diseases and spiritual sores should be recured. And so it was most requisite that Christ in the new Law should institute sensible signes and Sacraments. And therfore S. Austin sayth that as yet neuer any societie could ioyne in one religion and worship of God, but by the vse of the same Sacramentes. In vvhich point the reformers agree whith vs, for they al auouch (Suenkfeldius only excepted and some other Libertines) that Sacramentes are necessarie, but in the number they vary, not only from the Catholiques but also one from an other.

Mat 26.

The second.

The third.

l. 10. cont. Faust. c. 10.

3. The Catholique Church hath euer vsed seauen Sacramentes, vvhich are, Baptisme, Confirmation, the Sacrament of the Altar, Penance, Order, Mariage, and Extreme vnction. Which number S. Thomas the Diuine explaineth by a very pregnāt reason, or rather similitude, vvhich is betwixt the corporal and spiritual life of man. For in our corporal life, seuen thinges are required to vvhich are correspondent seuen Sacraments in the spiritual life of man. In a corporal life first is necessary generation, vvhich giueth the first being and essence: and to this is answerable Baptisme, which regenerateth vs againe to a new life and spiritual being of a Christian, by vvhich we are new creatures, borne of water and the Spirit, vnto a new life. Wherfore Tertulian calleth Christians spiritual fishes, because though they haue their corporal life from earth by carnal generation, yet their spiritual life and being, like fishes, they receiue from the water, by spiritual regeneration. Secondly in a corporal life is necessarie augmentation by vvhich the litle infant (for al beginnings are litle) waxeth, groweth, and gaineth dew proportion, quantitie and strength, by vvhich he is able to exercise operation and actions belonging to corporal life, as to eate, drinke, talke, walke, laboure, to defend him selfe, and to assault his enemie. And to this is correspondent the Sacrament of Con-

Seuen Sacraments.

3. p. q. 65. a. 1.

A pregnant proofe for 7. Sacramētes by the similitude vvhich is betvvixt a corporal and spiritual life.

Baptisme is our generatiō

 firmation

Confirmation is our augmẽtation. firmation, vvhich perfiteth vs in the ſpiritual life receiued in Baptiſme (vvhich is the cauſe why ſome Fathers ſay, that before this Sacrament we are not perfect Chriſtians) and giueth vs force to defend this our ſpiritual life by confeſſing our fayth before the perſecutor, vvhich faith is the ground of ſpiritual life. Thirdy becauſe this corporal life of ours fadeth and miniſheth continually (for euery houre we loſe ſome part of our ſubſtance, partly by reaſon of the conflict of the contrarie elements which conſume vs whileſt in vs they ſtriue one againſt an other, partly by reaſon of the continual combate vvhich is betwixt natural heate and moyſture, vvhich is as it were the tallowe of our light and liſe (we ſtand in nede of nurriture and nutrition, which reſtoreth that ſubſtance vvhich is dayly loſt, and ſo prolongeth our life. And to this in our ſpiritual life anſwereth the Sacrament of the Altar, vvhich conteining in it the body and bloud of Chriſt (vvho calleth him ſelfe *liuing bread* and ſayth that: *his fleſh is truly meate, and his bloud truly drinke*) nouriſheth the ſoule ſpiritually, and conſerueth our ſpiritual life here, and prepareth vs to an immortal life in heauen. *the Euchariſt our nutrimẽt. Ioh. 6.* Fourthly man hauing a mortal life ſubiect to ſicknes and diſeaſes, vvhich partly come by diſorder in dyet, partly by extrinſecal operation of the Starres, ayre, and wether, to vvhich our bodyes are ſubiect, partly do procede from the complexion and cõſtitution of mans body vvhich is compoſed of contraries: it was neceſſary for preſeruation of corpotal life that God ſhould prouide vs of Phiſitians and corporal Phiſick, vvhich reſtoreth vs to health after ſicknes. In like maner our ſpiritual life vvhich is grace, in this life being not ſo ſtable but that it may be loſt many tymes by mortal ſinne, and our health being not as yet ſo confirmed, but that we may fal into as many diſeaſes, as by our frie wil we may commit ſinnes, it was not only expedient but alſo neceſſary, that Chriſt our ſpiritual Phiſitian ſhould prouide vs of Phiſicke, and of a general ſalue, and medecin, againſt al the ſores and maladies of our ſoules. *1. Tim. 1. 1. Cor. 10. Apoc. 2.* And this is the Sacrament of Penance, vvhich is a remedie againſt ſinne committed after Baptiſme, & vvhich by the Prieſt our ſpiritual Phiſitian, is to be applyed vnto vs. *Penence is our Phiſicke.* For to him as being ſucceſſor to the Apoſtles, Chriſt gaue this power and authoritie vvhen he ſayd to his Apoſtles: *Vvhoſe ſinnes you forgiue are forgiuen.* *Iohn. 20.* Wherfore S. Chriſoſtom ſayth, *l.1. de Sacerd.* that the Prieſts of the new law haue power not only to giue ſentence, whether we be infected with the leprie of ſinne or no (which authoritie only the Prieſts of the old law had concerning the corporal lepreſie) but alſo to cure, clenſe, and purge this

leprie

leprie. Fiftly vvhen man is recured, often tymes there remaine the reliques of his diseases, vvhich kepe him low a great while, and therfore he yet nedeth Phisick not so much for healing as confirming, and perfiting health, vvhich consisteth in some confortatiues or restauratiues. The like happeneth vnto man, after that by the Sacrament of Penance he is recured: for after that, he stil hath a kinde of weaknes and infirmitie, and euil habits and inclinations, yea litle diseases also such as venial sinnes are. And therfore against these Reliques of his disease, Christ hath prouided him the Sacrament of Extreme vnction, which is giuē at the houre of death to purge vs cleane from al reliques of our diseases, to recure the corporal infirmitie if it be expedient for saluation, and to prepare vs to a better health of the next life, vvhich is immortalitie. And these fiue things are requisit in a corporal and spiritual life, for euery man in particular, but besides them, two things also are necessary for the communitie.

Extreme vnctiō is agiinst relikes of our spiritual diseases.

4. The first is coniunction of man and woman, without which mankind can neither be propagated nor preserued, and to make their coniunction lawful, Matrimony was euer necessarie. And to this in the new Law which is a Law of grace, the Sacrament of Matrimonie ansvvereth very fitly, vvhich before Christ, was a ciuil contract but no Sacrament, as now it is. For now as S. Paul sayth, *it is a great Sacrament*, in that it signifieth the coniunction of Christ with his Church, by Incarnation and grace, & giueth grace vnto the maryed, by which they may loue one an other as Christ did his Church, & beare the burdens of vvedlocke more easily. The second thing is constitution of Princes, Gouernors or Magistrats to rule this humaine societie, which Matrimonye hath propagated. For if the confused multitude were left to it selfe, and had not some head to gouerne it, it would like a ship without a Pilot, or a body without a head, by mutual dissension and disorder of members soone ruinate it selfe. To this is answerable the Sacrament of Order, by which Bishops & Priests are ordained to minister Sacraments, to offer Sacrifice, to teach, preach, and instruct, and by Lawes and censures to gouerne this multitude, and to direct it in those thinges, which concerne good life, spiritual peace, and Religion here, and life euerlasting herafter. The seuen Sacraments are those seuen pillers, vvhich as the vviseman sayth, vvisdome it selfe Christ IESVS hath made to support the huge pallace of his Church. And the seuen tymes sprinkling of the bloud of the calfe, prefigured these seuen Sacraments, in which the bloud of Christ is as it were seuen tymes

Propagation of mankinde necessarie. To that ansvvereth the Sacrament of Matrimonie.

Ephes. 5.

Superioritie necessarie in a cōmon vvelth. to this ansvvereth Priesthod and Order.

Prou. 9.

Leuit. 4.

Figures of 7. Sacraments

4. Reg. 5. uen tymes sprinkled, because it giueth them their force, vertue, and efficacie. Yea Naamans seuen washings were a figure of the same Sacramentes, in which the soule of man is seuen tymes washed, and so fried from the leprosie of sinne.

5. But these are but congruences (sayth our aduersarie) let vs see the plaine word of God for seuen Sacramentes, else we are not to admitte them. I grant that these are not plaine demonstrations, because as Diuines say *matters of fact can not be demonstrated*, but yet are they better argumentes, then they can bring for their lesser number of Sacramentes. I could alleage also Fathers for euery one of the Sacramentes before named: but they vvil say that Fathers are men. And are not our aduersaries also men? yes say they, but vve præferre the vvord of God before mens traditions. But then I aske of them, what expresse worde of God they haue against these men? The Fathers auouch seuen Sacraments: where read they in Scripture that there are but tvvo, or three? We haue no such number expressely named (say they) but we gather by good consequence out of Scripture that there are but tvvo or three. Do you so? And did not the Fathers out of Scripture deduce seuen Sacraments? For although they neuer say that there are iust seuen, yet sometimes they name one, sometimes tvvo, sometimes moe, and amongst them al they haue giuen testimonie for euery one of the seuen Sacraments in particular, and none at al deny seuen. Yea for these 500. yeares al the Diuines haue defended seuen Sacraments, who also neuer mentioned this number as any new Article of beleefe, but accepting it from their forfathers, haue approued and defended it, and by Scriptures also do confirme it. Yea the Councels of Florence and Trent haue auouched the same number, and thought them selues backed herin by authoritie of Scripture. But they were al deceiued sayth our aduersarie. Were they so? And how can you warrant vs that you in denying seuen Sacraments are not deceiued? If you say that you deduce your two or three Sacraments out of Scripture, they vvil say that they also out of Scripture deduce their seuen. And so the question is not whether Scriptures or Fathers are to be beleeued, but whether the Church, Councels, and Fathers, vvho proue seuen Sacraments out of Scripture, are to be credited in the exposition of Scripture, or rather your new biblists who began to studie but yester day, and neuer studied so many dayes as they haue done dayes and nightes, who also neither for grauitie nor sanctitie, neither for wit nor learning, were vvorthy to cary their bookes after them. But lest our aduersarie triumphe

Scholastici in 4. dist. 2.

Con. Flor. in decreto. Trid. Sess. 7. can. 1.

triumphe that we can not proue our Sacraments by Scripture, I vvil bring Scriptures for euery one of them.

6. But first I must agree with them vpon certaine conditions. For first of al they must not exact of me to proue that these seuen are expressely called by the name of Sacraments: for so they can not proue their two or three Sacraments, (because Matrimonie only) vvhich yet they deny to be a Sacrament) is expresly called a Sacrament. Secondly they must not demand of me any place of Scripture, vvhich sayth that there are seuen Sacraments, because they can alleage no such place vvhich sayth that there are not seuen, or that there are but two or three. And the reason is because Scripture vseth to treate of many thinges, but not alwayes to number them: For Scripture relateth Christs miracles, & yet numbereth them not, and it setteth downe many articles of faith, as the Trinitie, Incarnation, Passion, Resurrection, Ascension, and many others, yet neuer setteth downe any certaine number. They must be content then that I deduce by as good consequence out of Scripture that there are seuen Sacramentes as they can gather their two or three Sacramentes. And this I can do, and if this I do, I shal refute al their opinions of vvhich some hold one, only, some two, some three, some foure and al conspire in the denial of seuen.

Conditions to be agreede vpon the first.
Ephes. 5.
The second.

7 But before I do this, I must suppose vvhich they wil grant, and can not deny, vnles they wil deny al Sacraments, that to proue seuen Sacraments out of Scripture, shal be sufficient if I can find iu Scripture either in expresse termes, or by good deduction, an external rite, commandment or Institution, and a promise of grace in euery one of the seuen Sacramēts afore named. For by those our aduersaries proue their Sacraments, and because they imagin that some of these conditions requisite to a Sacrament, are deficient in some of the seuen, they deny them to be Sacraments. Wherfore in the Apologie of their confession these vvordes are to be sene: *If vve cal Sacraments, rits, vvhich haue a commandment from God, and to vvhich is annexed a promise of grace, it is easie to iudge, vvhich are properly Sacraments.* And a litle after by this rule they gather that Baptisme, the Supper, and Penance are Sacraments.

VVhat is requisite to a Sacrament.

8 To begin therfore with Baptisme: the external rite we gather out of the third of S. Ihon, and the last of S. Matthew, vvhich is water and vvashing, the commandment and Institution is proued out of these wordes *vnles a man be regenerated of vvater and the Holy Ghost:* The promise of grace hwich is annexed to this Sacramēt, the last chapter of

Baptisme proued to be a Sacrament.
Io. 8.

Mat. 16. S. Marke proposeth in those words: *he that beleueth and shal be baptized shal be saued.* And to go on with the Sacrament of the Altar, the external rite of this Sacrament is bread and vvine, or the formes of bread & wine. The institution and commandement is contained in the words: *Doe this in commemoration of me.* The promise of grace we gather out of S. Iohn *he vvho eateth this bread shal liue for euer.* In Confirmation also vve find an external rite, vvhich is imposition of handes, by vvhich the Apostles, and Apostles and Bishops only, vsed after Baptisme, to giue the Holy Ghost. The promise of grace appeareth by the performance, because al they vpon whom the Apostles layd their handes, receiued the Holy Ghost, and consequently grace. The institution and commandment we may vvel presume to haue proceded from Christ, because Apostles can not institute Sacramentes, nor cause any external ceremonie to giue the Holy Ghost infallibly, and they vvould neuer haue presumed such a thing, without commandement from Christ their maister. Wherfore S. Austin speaking of this Sacrament sayth in plaine termes, *that the Sacrament of Chrisme, is to be numbered amongst the sacred signes, euen as Baptisme is.* The same conditions of a Sacrament, are easily to be found also in the Sacrament of Confession: for Christ sayth vnto his Apostles and in them to al their successors: *VVhose sinnes you shal forgiue, are forgiuen them, and vvhose sinnes you shal retaine, are retained.* In vvhich vvordes he giueth authoritie to Priests as his vnder Iudges, to absolue from sinnes and to detaine sinnes, and because the Priest can not absolue vnles the penitent confesse his sinnes, and the penitent can not know that he is absolued, vnles the Priest pronounce some audible sentence, we gather that the external rite of this Sacrament is an audible confession and absolution, the promise of grace is found also in this Sacrament most euidently, because Christ promiseth that whose sinnes the Priest forgiueth shal be forgiuen, and seing that sinnes can not be forgiuen without grace, if the Priest can forgiue sinnes, he can also giue grace by this Sacrament. The institution and commandement is contained in the same vvords, because Priestes haue commission from Christ to absolue from sinnes, and to hold and detaine our sinnes, and consequently sinners vvho must reconcile them selues to God must do it by confession to the Priest, else can not he absolue, for no iudge can giue sentence vvithout knovvledge of the cause, and othervvise he can not be sayed to detaine our sinnes, for if he detaine our sinnes vve can not be loosed but by his absolution, and seing that al sinners must seeke to frie them selues from the bandes & bondage

The Sacramēt of the Altar a Sacrament.
Mat. 26.
1. Cor. 15.
Io. 6.
Confirmation a Sacrament.
Act. 8. 19.
Dionis. l. c. 11.
Hier. p. 3. c. 2.
Tert. l. de res. carnis & lib. de baptis.
Cip. l. 1. ep. 12.
Aug l. 2. cont lit. Pet c. 384.
Supra.
Confession a sacrament.
Io. 29.
Amb. l. 1. de pon. ca. 7.
Aug. l. 5. de Bap. S. 20.

bondage of sinne, they must come to the Priest, who only vnder God, bindeth and looseth. In the Sacrament of Order vve find also an external rite, to wit imposition of handes, which in Greeke is called *Chirotonia,* vvhich as S. Hierom sayth signifieth ordination of Clerkes. The commandement and institution we gather thus: S. Paul biddeth Timothie not to neglect the grace which he had receiued by imposition of hands, wherfore S. Paul knew that infallibly that external rite gaue grace: but it could not giue grace if Christ had not instituted it to that end, and S. Paul vvould not haue præsumed to haue vsed it to that end if Christ had not commanded and instituted it, *Ergo* this external rite vvas instituted and commanded. The promise of grace we gather by the performance, because S. Paul sayth that Timothie had receiued grace by imposition of hands. That Matrimonie also is a Sacrament S. Paul wil vvitnesse, who because this semed most vnlike a Sacrament or holy signe, calleth it a great Sacrament, because it signifieth the coniunction of Christ vvith his Church. As if he had sayd: Matrimonie to a wordly eye may seme to haue litle sanctitie or mysterie in it, but I say that in this respect that it signifieth the Mariage of Christ whith his Church, it is a Sacrament and a great Sacrament. The external rite of this Sacrament is the contract which by words or signes is made betwixt man and wife, & therfore S. Chrisostom & S. Hierom vpon this place affirme that S. Paul called this contract, a great Sacrament. The Institution we haue in Christs ovvne words: *vvhat God hath conioined let not man separate.* The promise of grace thus we gather: because Christ hath made this Sacrament indissoluble, and consequently he must giue grace by it to beare the burden of perpetual wedlocke easily, else had the Law of Matrimonie pressed more heauilie the necks of Christians then the Law of the Iewes, because they in case of fornication might leaue their old wife, and take a new, and so shake of the burden. Secondly S. Paul sayth that this Sacrament signifieth the Mariage of Christ with his Church, which Mariage was made not only by Incarnation, but also by grace, and therfore the Church is called Christs louing spouse, and S. Paul biddeth men to loue their wiues as Christ loued his Church. Wherfore vnles we wil say that Matrimonie is an idle signe, we must say that it hath a promise of grace annexed, by which man and wife may loue one an other, and beare also more easily the heauy burden of Mariage. Wherfore S. Austin sayth: *in the mariages of Christians, the sanctitie of the Sacrament is of more valevv then the frutefulnes of the vvombe.* Last of al, that

Order a Sacrament. *1. Tim. 4.* *2. Tim. 1.* *Supra.*

Aug. l. 2. cont. ep. Parn c, 13. l 1. de bap. c. 1. *Ephes. 5.*

Matrimonie a Sacrament.

Mat. 19.

2. Cor. 10.

l de bono coniug. c. 19. vide etiam cap. 24.

Extreme vnction is also a Sacrament, it is plaine by the vvords of S.
cap. 5. Iames: *Is any sicke amongst you? let him bring in the Priests of the Church, and let them pray vpon him, anointing him vvith oyle in the name of our Lord, and the prayer of fayth shal saue the sick-man, and our Lord shal alleuiate him, and if he be in sinnes, they shal be forgiuen him.* In vvhich vvords who seeth not the external rite, to vvit prayer, that is the forme of vvordes vsed in this Sacrament, & the anointing with oile? The promise is alleuiation and forgiuenes of sinnes, which are neuer remitted without grace. The institution and commandment is easily deduced: because an Apostle who may promulgate & minister Sacramētes, but not institute them, would neuer haue so bouldly promised forgiuenes of sinnes by an external rite and ceremonies, had he not bene assured that Christ had instituted it to that effect. VVherfore S. Bernard in the life of S. Malachias affirmeth, that he *anointed a vvhoman, knovving that in this Sacrament sinnes are forgiuen.* And thus much for proofe of seuen Sacraments. Novv let vs see vvhat Sacramentes the reformers haue.

Extreme vnction a Sacrament.

Ber. in vita Mal.

Innocentius ep. 1. ad Decentium c. 8.

9. Luther very peremptorily auoucheth that *he must deny seuen Sacramentes, & alovv of three only for the tyme.* He sayth for the tyme, because he was not sure how long he should remaine in that mynd. And what are those three Sacramentes which for a tyme he is content to allovv vs; *Baptisme* (sayth he) *Penance, and Bread.* Zuinglius aloweth also of three, but not the same vvhich his Maister Luther admitteth, vvhich are Baptisme, the Supper, and Matrimonie. Caluin admitteth also thre Sacraments, but not the same vvhich Zuinglius granteth, Baptisme, the Supper, and Ordination. Melancton is more liberal for he affordeth vs foure, to wit, Baptisme, the Supper, Penance, and Order. The softer Lutherans in their conuenticle at Lipsia, alowed of seuen Sacraments, for so Sleidan the Historiographer, relateth.

l. de cap. Bab.

Disagreemēt of heretikes about the nūber of Sacramēts.

l. de vera & falsa rel. c. de matr.

l. 4. Inst. 6. c. 19. 32.

Mol. in locis.

l. 20. hist. an. 48

10 Out of this diuersitie of opinions I gather, first that they haue amongst them denyed almost al the Sacraments; and so can haue no Religion, or a verie graceles Religion, because Religion and Sacraments euer went together. Secondly I gather that if any man wil forsake the Catholique Church and her beleefe of seuen Sacraments, that he hath no moral nor probable assurance of any Sacramentes, for seing that he hath no more reason to credit Luther when he sayd once that there was but one Sacrament, an other tyme that there were but two Sacramentes, then when he admitted three for the tyme, he is not to credit him at al. And seing that he can alleage no more for him selfe then others (that is Scripture interpreted as he pleaseth) and they

Collectiōs the first.

The second.

l. de cap. Bab. initio.

in fine

no more

no more then he, no man can haue iust cause to beleeue any of them, and so if he leaue the Catholique Church, he may doubt of al the Sacramentes. Lastly seing that the reformers can not bring expresse Scripture for any of the Sacramẽtes but Matrimonie, which not with standing almost al of them deny, and seing that by deduction (as I haue declared) we may gather out of Scripture as probably seuen Sacramentes, as one, though the reformers leaue the authoritie of the Church and Fathers, and trust only to their owne wittes in gathering by deduction, and consequence, their Sacramentes out of Scripture, then as one distrusteth an others deduction, so may he distrust his owne, and so they haue no certaintie of any Sacramentes at al, and consequently haue no probable assurance of their Religion, because Sacramentes and Religion go together: vvhich Luther him selfe vvil confesse, who affirmeth, that consent in doctrin of the Sacramentes, is a note of the true Church and Religion.

The last.

l. de not. Bab.

The fourth Chapter shevveth of vvhat litle importance they make the Sacraments to be.

THE reformers, as by the former chapter appeareth, are very sparing in their Sacramentes, some and the most of them not affording vs aboue two or three, but these also they seme to grant vs with an euil wil, because they so detract from their dignitie, and attribute so litle vnto them, that they might as wel with Suenkfeldius haue denyed these also, because as good neuer a whit as neuer the better.

2. For they deny with common voice, that Sacramẽtes giue grace, or effectuate any iotte of sanctification in our soules. To vvhat purpose then serue they, or vvhat necessitie was there of them? Melancthon sayth that they serue for badges to distinguish vs from Infidels. But for this effect we neded no Sacraments at al, because the yelow cap of the Iew in Rome, or some noble mans cognisance would haue bene more fitting for this purpose. For seing that Baptisme according to Melancthons opinion giueth no caracter, after the childe is washed in baptisme, and the water dryed vp, vvhat signe remaineth I pray you to distin-

Hovv heretikes detract from Sacraments.

l. de loc. c. de signis.

Melancthons opinion of them.

to distinguish a Christian from an infidel? And wil not profession of our fayth, vvhich is no Sacrament, distinguish vs better? Zuinglius maketh Sacramentes no better then souldioars markes, by vvhich they are admitted and distinguished, but this is refuted by the same argument by vvhich we haue reiected Melancthons badges Luther granteth a litle more vnto Sacramentes: for he sayth that Sacramentes are external signes, ordained to no other purpose then to stirre vp fayth vvhich only iustifieth, and therfore vvhen he & his Lutheranes sometymes saye that Sacramentes do sanctifie vs, and that baptisme doth regenerate vs, they meane not as Catholiques do that Sacramentes immediately giue vs grace, but only that they stirr vp faith vvhich sanctifieth: wherfore somtymes they cal Sacraments pictures vvhich put vs in mind of Christ & his Passion. But then it foloweth that they who haue pictures of Christ or his Passion, or bookes of the same subiect, stand in nede of no Sacraments, because these thinges are more apte to stirre vp faith then sacraments. Secondly Baptisme is to no purpose in children, because it can not stirre vp their faith at al, who haue no vse of reason at al:

l. de vera & falsa rel. c. de Sacramentis. *Bucers opiniō.* *l. capt. Bab. c. de bap c. vl.* *Luthers liberalitie.*

3 This so presseth Luther that it had made him an Anabaptist, had he not had a shift in store vvhich also is a very pore one. He sayth therfore that infants at the time of Baptisme haue vse of reason, and that they vnderstand what Baptisme signifieth, & so beleue also in Christ. And this he proueth by the example of S. Iohn Baptist who reioyced and acknowleged Christ in his mothers wombe: but by the same argument he might haue proued that al asses can speake, because Balaams Asse by miracle once spake to the Prophet. For as it was a priuiledge that S. Iohn had vse of reason in his mothers wombe, so was it that Balaams Asse did speake, and therfore if this be a good argument: S. Ihon had vse of reason, when he was an infant *Ergo* al childrē haue: this also is a good argument: Balaams Asse could speake *ergo* al asses can speake. At lestwise by this argument of Luther, we may experience in him, vvhat an asse can speake, and is not ashamed to vtter. And truly if children at that age were as wise as Luther wil make them, we must condemne them of hainous sacriledge who by their crying, and resistance vvhich such litle ones can make, shew how vnwillingly and with what litle respect they receiue this sacrament. Caluin sayth that Sacramentes are but seales vvhich outwardly signe the grace, vvhich we receiue by the promise of God, and therfore he sayth flatly: that Sacramentes giue no grace and that the Sacramentes of the new lawe are

Luth. pressed. *l. cont. Coelenum.* *Luc. 1.* *Num. 22.* *Aug ep. 57.* *l 4 Inst. c. 14. 1. 5. 14.* *Caluins opinion.*

are no better in this respecte then were the Sacramentes of the old law. Yea he addeth that as S. Paul sayed, that Circumcision is nothing, so he might haue sayd, that Baptisme in this respect is nothing vvorth. *1. Cor. 5.*

4 And their reasons vvhy they wil giue no vertue vnto Sacramentes are two especially. First say they if we grant that Sacramentes giue grace, then foloweth it, that we must put our trust in Sarcamentes, and seke for saluation else where, then at the handes of Christ, vvhich can not but derogate much from the Passion and Person of Christ. But this reason semeth to haue litle reason. For as the sicke patient principally after God, putteth his trust in his Phisitian, yet expecteth health also by the medicins vvhich he prescribeth, and so putteth his trust in the Phisitian as in the principal causes of his health, and in the instrumental causes, and yet doth no iniurie to the Phisitian, yea rather in allowing of his medicins doth him great honour: so may we put our hope and confidence principally in Christ as our spiritual Phisitian, and yet hope also for health by the Sacramentes, as by his medicins and instrumental causes of spiritual health. Secondly they are of opinion as shal be herafter related and refuted, that only Fayth iustifieth,: wherfore they must consequently say that Sacramentes giue no grace, they should also iustifie and sanctifie, and so only Faith should not iustifie. And so folovving this doctrin some of them say that Sacraments are only badges to make vs knowne to be Christians, others say they only stirre vp faith; others make them seales and signes of former iustice, and al deny that they sanctifie vs.

The first reason, vvhy they diny that Saments giue grace.

The second reason

5 Against al these opinions might suffice that place of S. Paul, vvhere to put a difference betwixt our Sacraments and the old, he calleth the old, naked elements, that is, bare figures and of no force nor vertue to giue grace. But we vvant not many other places of Scripture vvhich may also proue this veritie. S. Ihon sayth that if a man be not regenerated of water and the Holy Ghost, he can not enter into heauen, *ergo* not only the Holy Ghost, but vvater also regenerateth, and consequently not only the Holy Ghost as a principal Agent, but also the water as an instrument, vvorketh grace in vs by vvhich we are regenerated. The Sacrament of the Altar Christ him selfe calleth true meate vvhich geueth life and nourisheth. The Sacrament of Penance remitteth sinnes, because Christ geueth power to his Apostles, and in them to their successors to remit sinnes: by the sentence of absolution. And S. Paul wil vvitnes that Order geueth grace to Priests, and

Gal 4. *Sacraments giue grace.* *Io. 8.* *Io. 6.* *Io. 22.* *1. Tim. 4.* *2. Tim. 1.* *& 8. 19.*

Act. 8. 19. and the actes of the Apostles auouch, that the Apostles vvhen they confirmed the first Christians, gaue the Holy Ghost by imposition of handes. The like profes I could bring and haue before brought in the

The coclusion. former chapter for the other Sacramentes. But be it so that Sacramentes giue no grace, then doth it folow that they are to no purpose, because other thinges we haue more fitte to distinguish Christians from Infidels, and to stirre vp fayth, vvhich are by our aduersaries opinion, the only effectes of Sacramentes: and so it foloweth that if Sacramentes giue no grace, that they are of no vertue and altogether superfluous, and so as good it were to haue no Sacramentes as Sacramentes, because as good neuer a whit as neuer the better: and no Sacramentes no Religion, because as before, Sacramentes and Religion euer went together.

The fift Chapter shevveth hovv in effect the reformers take avvay from vs those fevv Sacramentes vvhich they seme to alovv of.

Heretikes liberalitie. OVR Reformers are so liberal as to afforde vs two Sacramentes, to wit Baptisme and the Eucharist, or the Sacrament of the Altar vvhich they cal the Supper. For though some of them alowe vs also Order, and some, Penance, yet in these Sacramentes as is before declared, they do not agree. But yet if we consider the estimation vvhich they make of these two Sacramentes vvhich al of them alowe vs, we shal see that herein we are not much beholden vnto them.

in Synop. Cal. c. 27. & in c. 3. Gal. 2. And as concerning Baptisme, Luther is of opinion that no forme of words is necessary, yea he thinketh it sufficient, if you baptize the children in the name of the Lord. And being demanded once

Luthers opinion of Baptisme. vvhether it was lawful to baptise in milke or beare, he answered that any liqeour that is apte to bath or wash, is sufficient. And so you see how he taketh away the matter and forme of Baptisme, or at least

l. 4 Inst. c. 17 bringeth them both in doubt: And as touching the vsual forme of words Caluin iumpeth with him in the same opinion, and addeth that such formes of words are mere magical charmes and enchantementes.

mentes. Brentius sayth that if the minister after that the Crede is read, say only, In this fayth I wash thee, depart in peace, it wil serue wel ynough. And Bucere denyeth that words are necessarie in the Eucharist, and would say no doubt the same in Baptisme. The same Luther as is before related, is of opinion that actual fayth euen in children is necessarie, and that Sacramentes haue no other effect then to stirre vp this fayth. VVherfore seing that Baptisme can not stirre vp childrens faith, because they haue no knowledge of the signification of such mysteries, it must nedes folow that to Baptise children is but *laterem lauare to vvash a tile*, and to loose labour. *in c.26. Mat.*

3. Caluin also is neither a frayd nor ashamed to say, that S. Iohn Baptists Baptisme was as good as Christs Baptisme. And yet S. Paul rebaptized them vvith Christs Baptism whom S. Ihon before had baptized, vvhich argued his Baptisme of insufficiencie, and proueth Christs Baptisme to be of more perfection, which suplyed that vvhich was wanting in S. Iohns Baptisme. The same Caluin sayth that in necessitie women may not baptise, and that if the child dye without Baptisme, he may be saued if either he be predestinated, or be the child of faithful parenres, yea he sayth that few do marcke how much harme that doctrin hath done, which teacheth that Baptisme is necessary to saluation. And if you vrge him with those wordes of our Sauiour: *vnles a man be borne againe of vvater and the Holy Ghost, &c.* He wil rather glosse the text most grossely, then yeld to you that Baptisme is necessary to saluation. The meaning is not (sayth he) that material water is necessary, but this is the sense: *vnles a man be borne againe of the Holy Ghost, vvhich like vvater vvasheth, he can not enter into heauen.* And so by this exposition water is not necessary, only the regeneration and washing of the spirit is necessary, and this Baptisme according to Caluins opinion, children may haue without water, euen in their mothers wombe, if they be predestinate, or children of faithful parentes. This is Caluins doctrin, I say Caluins, for it is his singular opinion contrarie to opinion of the Church and al the ancient Fathers and Councels, yea contrarie to Scripture it selfe. For Scripture telleth vs plainly that vve are al *borne children* of wrath, and that *vve al sinned in Adam*, and consequently are conceued and borne in original sinne: wherfore Iob who was predestinate curseth the day of his natiuitie and night of his conception, and Dauid not only predestinate but borne also of faithful parentes confesseth *that he is conceiued in sinnes*, that is in original sinne, for the hebrevv vvord signifieth *sinne* in the singular number,

l.4. Inst.c.17. 32. *Act. 19.* *Caluin maketh Baptisme vnnecessarie.* *Io.3.* *l.4. Inst. c.16 17.18.* *A violent exposition of Caluin.* *Al borne in original sinne.* *Ephes. 2.* *Rom. 3.* *Iob. 5* *Psal. 501.*

which not withstanding the Translatour translated *sinnes*, because original sinne is the roote of al sinnes.

Gen. 17.

The benedictiō of Abrahams posteritie saueth none frō original sinne.

4. And wheras Caluin alleageth the blessing of God to Abraham and al his seed and posteritie, that serueth only to bewray his ignorance. For first after that God had made that promise, yet he commanded Circumcision, and threatned that those that had it not, should perish. And so although Caluin were of Abrahams seed and his parentes also, yet doth it not folow that he shal be partaker of that benediction without Baptisme. Secondly that promise and benediction is now to be vnderstood carnally or spiritually: if carnally, then are none but Iewes capable of the benediction, because they only are the carnal children of Abraham, and so Caluin hath no part in it at al. If spiritually then they only are partakers of the benediction, who as S. Paul sayth, do imitate the faith and workes of Abraham. VVherfore seing that children euen of faithful parentes, do in no wise imitate either Abrahams faith or workes, they can not be partakers of his benediction vntil they be baptised, and so by receuing the Sacrament of fayth, do in some sorte imitate Abrahams faith. And if Caluin say that at lest by predestination children may be saued without baptisme, he shal but discouer herein how blockish a Diuine he is. For none are predestinate but by the Passion and merites of Christ, which first are applyed by Baptisme, and not without Baptisme at least in desire, and therfore Christ threateneth damnation to al that are not baptised. Wherfore although al children that are predestinate shalbe saued, yet not without Baptisme, and they which dye without Baptisme as by Christs owne sentence they are excluded from heauen, so are they not predestinate.

Rom. 9.
Gal. 5.
Aug. ep. 23. ad Bonif.
Neither doth predestinatō.
Io. 3.
Io. 3.

l. 4. Inst. c. 19.
Caluī denyeth baptisme to the reprobate.
ibid.
He saith that it is not necessarie for the predestinate and children of the faithful.

5. But let vs see more of Caluins doctrin, not to folovv it, but to beware of it, not to imbrace it, but to detest it. The same man affirmeth that the reprobate, or the children of infidels not predestinate, are not to be baptized lest Baptisme be contaminated and be made a false seale, because (sayth he) Baptisme is a seale of former iustice, and therfore if defiled infidels be baptised, the vvater is contaminated, and the seale is falsified. He addeth that the children of the faithful or the predestinate, nede not Baptisme as a necessarie meanes vnto saluation, & therfore if they dye without it they may be saued. Yet (sayth he) Baptisme is not to be contēned, because it is commanded as a ceremonie to incorporate vs members of the Church. Now put al this together, to wit, that Christs Baptisme is no better then S. Ihons, that it is not neces-

necessarie for the predestinate, or children of faithful parentes, because they may be saued without it, and that it can not be ministred vnto the children of infidels, lest it be contaminated; and it foloweth euidently that Baptisme is not necessarie, yea that it is superfluous, because to the children of the faithful and the predestinate it is not necessarie, and to the children of the faithles (notwithstanding that Christ bad his Apostles to baptise al nations which then were infidels) it is not to be giuen, then is there no necessarie vse of Baptisme, because it serueth to no other purpose, but to seale former iustice, which sealing is not necessarie, because saluation is sure ynough without it, or to bring vs into the Church by an external ceremonie, which is altogether nedeles, because if it be omitted, children if they be of faithful parentes, or predestinate are sanctified in their mothers wemb, and so before God are members of the Church, and capable of saluation, before and without Baptisme. And thus Baptisme is gone.

Mat. vlt.

Caluin in effect taketh Baptisme avvay l. cont. Luth.

6. Now as concerning the blessed Sacrament of the Altar, Luther semeth very liberal in this point, affirming that Christs body is really and substantially in this Sacrament not by consecration but by *Vbiquitie*. For he is of opinion that as Christs body is vnited to the Diuinitie, so it is in euery place where the Diuinitie is, and consequently in the bread and wine. But whilest Luther thinketh to fil our mouthes in giuing vs bread with Christs flesh, he taketh away al true eating of Christs body, and drinking of his bloud. For eating is a conveighance of meate from the mouth into the stomake, and therfore if Christs body be euery where with his Diuinitie, it can not be eaten, because it was before in the stomake and euery where, and so can not be conveyghed by eating into the stomake, because conveighance importeth a motion of a thing to some place where before it was not.

Luthers opinion of the B. Sacrament.

Luther taketh avvay al true eating of Christs body.

7. Caluin giueth vs a bare figure and an emptie signe, auouching that Christ hath giuen vs a figure of his body, which in substāce is but common bread, yet because Christ hath made it a signe and figure of his body, it is called Christs body, as Cæsars image is called Cæsar. Which opinion of Caluin maketh Christ a niggard, and his Sacrament of litle or no importance. For Christ although he made a great shew of a magnifical supper, yet according to Caluin, his supper was not only inferior to Assuerus his banquet, but also to the meanest that euer was. This supper Christ would haue to be præfigured by the heauenly Manna, wherewith he fed the Iewes in the desert: by the Pas-

Caluī maketh the Eucharist a bare figure.

Figures of the Eucharist. Exod. 16. Io. 4. Sap. 6. Psal. 77.

Exod. 12. ſchal lambe, which the Iewes were commanded to eate in remembrance of their deliueráce out of Ægypt: *Gen.* 14. by Melchiſedeches Sacrifice *Mal.* 1. and diuerſe others: he would alſo haue it fortold by Malachie the Prophet, *Prophecies of it.* ſaying that a cleane oblation ſhal be offered vnto him euery vvhere: by the Patriarch *Iacob*, vvho fortold that the Meſſias ſhould *vvash his ſtole*, that is his humaine nature with which the Diuinitie was *Gen.* 49. clothed *in the bloud of grapes*, that is in his owne bloud: vvhich he called the bloud of grapes, because it was to be vealed vnder the formes of *6. Mac.* wine, vvhich is called in Scripture the bloud of the grape. *Inuitations to it.* He would inuite alſo al the world to this banquet, exhorting them to *eate the bread and to drinke the vvine, vvhich he hath mingled for them.* *Prou.* 9. he made this banquet alſo a litle before his death, for a farewel to his louing and beloued *The tyme.* ſpouſe the Church, and yet after al this oſtentation, after this ſolemne inuitation, notwithſtanding alſo that the tyme of farewel, the dignitie of Chriſts perſon, and the preeminence of the new Law aboue the olde, required a moſt ſumptuous banquet, vvhen the ſupper was prepared, it proued but bread and wine, and after al this boſte, the gueſtes vvho were bidden, had no roſte at al, but only an odour and ſmel of good chere, that is a bare ſigne and figure of Chriſts body and bloud.

The Eucharist by Caluin is but a ſmel of good cheare. And wheras Chriſt promiſed a twelue moneth before that he would giue them an other maner of meate, and more excellent then *Manna* was: for (ſayth he) notwithſtanding that your forfathers were fed with manna yet they dyed, but vvho ſoeuer eateth of the bread which *Io.* 6. I ſhal giue, ſhal liue for euer: yet if we beleeue Caluin, he performed nothing leſſe. For if Chriſts bread be but common bread in ſubſtance, *Ibidem.* and only a ſigne of Chriſts fleſh, vvhich is *the true foode*, then vvas not only Manna, but the Paſchal lambe alſo farre more precious then the *Not ſo good as Manna or the Paſchal lambe.* bread of Chriſt. For the Paſchal lambe was fleſh, Chriſts banquet is but bread and wine in ſubſtance, and as this is a figure of Chriſt, ſo was that and a more apte figure. Manna alſo was made by Angels handes, and in the aire, Chriſts bread or rather Caluins cake, was moulded and *Sap.* 6. baked by mens handes, and in no better place, then the backhouſe; Manna had al taſtes and delightes, Chriſts bread if it be no better then Caluin maketh it, hath but one taſte and that not very delicate. And as Caluin ſayth, that Chriſts breade is a ſigne and figure of Chriſt, ſo was Manna alſo, as Chriſts bread ſtirreth vp faith becauſe it is a ſigne, ſo was manna as fitte for that purpoſe, becauſe it was a ſigne, and as good a ſigne, becauſe it ſignified the ſame thing, vvhich giueth perfection vnto both ſignes. Wherfore vnles this Sacrament contayne Chriſts

body

body and bloud in an other maner then the signe containeth the thing vvhich it signifieth, Christs banquet is no better, yea it is not so good as Manna vvas, and so the veritie shal be inferior to the figure.

8. But Caluin sayth, that this Sacrament is not a bare figure, but such as bringeth with it the body and bloud of Christ: and if he did meane as he speaketh, I would not dispute with him, but would shake hands with him as with a Catholique. These are his wordes: *I say that in the mystery of the Supper by the signes of bread and vvine, is Christ truly deliuered, yea and his body and his bloud.* And a litle before those wordes he giueth the reason, *because* (sayth he) *Christs vvordes: This is my body, are so plaine, that vnles a man vvil cal God a deceiuer, he can neuer be so bold as to say that he setteth before vs an emptie signe.* And yet againe he repeateth this his assertion: *In his holy Supper Christ commandeth me vnder the signes of bread, and vvine, to eate his body and drinke his bloud, and I nothing doubt but that both he doth truly deliuer them, and I do receiue them.* And lest you should thinke that he talketh only of eating and receiuing Christ spiritually by faith, he hath preuented you by saying, that he meaneth really, and alleageth S. Chrysostom, vvho sayth that Christ mingleth his substance with ours, in this Sacrament, not only by faith, but in very dede. What thinke you now of this man? is he not a Catholique? doth he not really auouch the real presence? But if you vnmaske this vvily felow, you shal see a wolfe vnder a sheepes skinne. For the same Caluin in the same chapter in plaine wordes telleth you, that Christ is not really in this Sacrament, nor any vvhere else out of heauen, but yet (sayth he) the bread and vvine is called the body and bloud of Christ by a figure, vvhich calleth the signe by the name of the thing it selfe, as the Arke or rocke may be called Christ, because it was a figure of Christ. What meaneth he then vvhen he sayth that with the signe we receiue the body and bloud of Christ verelie? his meaning is, that although Christs substance be as far from this Sacrament, as heauen is from earth, yet because this signe stirreth vp faith, and faith apprehendeth Christ by this signe and with it we receiue the body & bloud of Christ. But here Caluin seemeth to go from him selfe, for as you haue heard he sayd before, that we eate not Christ only by faith, but also in very dede; yet to saue him selfe from contradiction, he hath deuised a subtile dinstinction. I grant (sayth he) that there be that in one word define, that to eate the body of Christ, and to drinke his bloud, is nothing else but to beleue in Christ, but I say that the flesh of Christ is eaten by beleuing, because by faith it is made ours. So that Caluin is

l. 4. Inst. c. 17. 15.

Eodem cap. 6.

Hom 61. 61. ad pop.

Caluī seemeth a Catholique but is not.

Sect. 20. 21. 22

Caluins meaning.

Sect. 16.

Supra.

Sect. 5.

of opinion that this Sacrament is but a signe and conteineth not really the body and bloud of Christ, but yet because this signe stirreth vp faith vvhich apprehendeth Christs body, we receiue verily the body and bloud of Christ vvith this signe, and by it, because faith apprehending Christ, vniteth him vnto vs & maketh him verily our owne. This is Caluins opinion.

9. Out of vvhich let vs take as granted that Christs body and bloud are not really conteined in the Sacrament, & consequently that this Sacrament is no better, yea nor so good as *Manna* vvas, vvhich was as good a signe of Christ, as this Sacrament is, if this containe not Christ really, and vvas as apte to stirre vp faith. Secondly it is cleare that if Christ be not really in this Sacrament, then faith can not really vnite him vnto vs, and consequently that in and by this Sacrament, we can in nowise really be pertakers of Christs body and bloud. For proofe whereof I demand of Caluin, how faith can really conioine vs with Christ? either this fayth really plucketh Christ out of heauen, vvhich Caluin neither can say, because faith is but an apprehension, neither wil say, because he sayth that Christs body since his ascension was neuer out of heauen: or else it really lifteth vs vp to heauen, vvhich is against experience, and so can not really vnite Christ vnto vs, because it neither bringeth him really vnto vs, nor vs vnto him. And so in beleuing in Christ by faith vvhich is but an apprehension of the vnderstanding, we do no more really eate the body of Christ, then doth the hungrye man his dinner, vvhen he apprehendeth, and desireth it, but can not haue it. And so Caluins boste is greater then his roste, and his promise is more ample then his performance, and Christs supper is but a bare signe, and no meate at al, but only a sauour and signe of good cheare, and our eating is no real eating, but only a naked apprehension. And seing that preaching, and pictures, can better stir vp faith then bread and wine can do, this Sacrament of Christ is altogether nedles, because as good neuer a whit as neuer the better. And so my intended conclusion foloweth to witte, that amongst our reformers there is no Religion because, fiue or six, of seuen Sacramentes they haue quite taken away, and the other in vvhich al of them agree, to wit Baptisme and the Eucharist, they haue so disgraced and defaced, that they are to litle purpose, and so they haue no Religion, because no Sacramentes no Religion.

By faith only vve can really receiue Christ.

Caluins bost greater then coste.

The cõclusion.

The Sixt

The Sixt Chapter shevveth, that according to their doctrin they can haue no prayer, and consequently no Religion.

ONE of the greatest benefits, which God hath bestovved on man is prayer, by which man hath accesse vnto God, and the creature is admitted to the speach of his Creator, and flesh and bloud conuerseth familiarly with the Diuinitie. For as S. Austin saith, when vve read Scriptures which are the word of God, then God speaketh to vs, but when we occupie our selues in prayer, then do we speake familiarly to God. Which is so great a thing, that Angels dare not do it, without couering their faces with their immortal vvinges, blushing to appeare before such Maiestie, and trembling to speake to a Prince so mightie. Prayer is honourable to God, honourable also and profitable to our selues. It is honourable to God because it is an act of Religion, by which we prostrate euen our soules and spirits vnto God, acknowledging him the supreme essence, fountaine, and autour of al goodnes, and our selues his needy and naked creatures, vvho haue nothing of our selues, yea nothing but from him, not so much as our selues, because he gaue vs our selues, and being for nothing, and of nothing. It is honourable to our selues, first because it æqualizeth vs with Angels, making vs Queresters of their chappel, where by prayer we ioine voices with them, in praysing God as they do, and praying vnto him. Secondly because it procureth familiar conuersation with God, vvhich is so honourable a thing, and so rayseth vs in state and dignitie, as almost nothing more. For as S. Chrysostom sayth if it be such an honour to conuerse familiarly with Cæsar, that such men though otherwise neuer so base and poore, can not whilest they are in this credit with him, be any more either base or poore: how can they who in prayer conuerse dayly and familiarly vvith the Diuine Maiestie, be of base or low condition? It is profitable also vnto vs, because by it we obtaine at Gods handes what is expedient for vs. For God is the source and fountaine of al goodnes, and perfection, sufficient of him selfe, and within him selfe, needing

in Psal. 75. Vvhat a benefit prayer is.

It is honourable to God.

It is honourable to our selues

Orat. 1. de orando Deo.

It is also profitable.

Psal. 15. *God is to him selfe sufficiēt.* needing not in any thing the helpe of any. To whom vvhen we haue giuen al the prayses, and offered al the Hecatombes and Sacrifices in the world, we haue not abettered his state or his person, and when we haue reuiled him and blasphemed him to the vttermost of our malice, we haue not made him a iotte the worse: but man in that he is a creature is depēdent of his Creator, no lesse yea more, then the riuers of the fountaine, the branches of the tree, or the sunne beames of the Sunne: who of him selfe hath nothing, yea is nothing, but is to liue by begging and praying.

Man liueth by begging. 2. And wel he may so obteine those thinges vvhich he wanteth. For if any Prince would promise his subiect, that vvhat soeuer he asketh he should obtein, might not that subiect thinke that Prince very bountiful, and him selfe a most happie subiect? Thus God dealeth with vs; he biddeth vs *aske and vve shal haue*: *Mat. 7.* and seing that God is so faithful that he can as soone deny him selfe as go from his word, because his *Prayer obtayneth.* Word is him selfe, he can not, but performe, vvhat soeuer he promiseth: and seing that prayer is the thing by vvhich man obtaineth at Gods hand what soeuer he iustly desireth, what an inestimable gemme and precious pearle is prayer, vvhich procureth our hartes desires in al thinges, because it is the price of al? And if we some tymes pray, and obtaine not, either it is because our prayer is not such as it ought to be, or that the thing vvhich we pray for, is not conuenient for vs. For if he that prayeth, beleueth that God can helpe him, and hopeth also that he wil helpe him, if he him selfe vvho prayth, or he for whom he prayeth, be not odious to God by reason of sinne, if he pray with humilitie, and without a doubting mynd, if he adione to his prayer, attention, to his attention, deuotion, and to both perseuerance, and if the thing for vvhich he prayth be necessarie or expedient (for otherwise God is a greater benefactour in dnying then granting our petition) then certainly, such is the vertue of prayer, that vvhat we aske we haue, and vvhat we pray for, we obtaine. Prayer certes is better *Prayer better then the Philosophes stone.* then the Philosophers stone, although it were of that vertue vvhich it is fayned to be of: for as fooles haue fained it was able to turne al into gold, but prayer turneth al to our good be it gold or siluer, riches or pouertie, health or sicknes, grace or glorie. Yea it is better then Fortunatus hatt is fained to haue bene, because that procured al wishes good or bad indifferently, but prayer then only obteineth vvhat vve vvish for, vvhen our wishes are expedient or conuenient for vs.

Prayer satisfieth. 3. Besides this vnspeakable vertue vvhich prayer hath, to obteine vvhat we aske for, it satisfieth for sinne also, especially vvhen it is ioined with almes dedes and fasting, vvhich are the vvinges of prayer, by vvhich it soreth spedily euen to the throne of God. It meriteth glorie as other good vvorkes do, and that more especially also, in that it is a prayer. It giueth vs great confidence also if it be frequent and vsual, because as before I haue sayd, prayer causeth familiaritie, and familiaritie imboldeneth, and boldnesse breedeth confidence. It is a great motiue also vnto humilitie, and peraduenture you shal not fynd a greater, because it putteth vs alwayes in mynd that we are but beggars. And lastly (if I may say so of prayers commodities vvhich are without end) it maketh vs to fal out of loue with this deceiteful world because it maketh vs to conuerse in heauen, & admitteth vs to familiaritie with God & his Angels. In the Church triumphant prayer is vsed, because the Saintes & Angels pray to God for vs. In the Chucrh militant prayer also is practised, as shal be proued, only in hel and hellish Synagogues prayer is abandoned.

Tob. 12. *It meriteth.* *It maketh vs confident.* *Humble.* *Out of loue vvith the vvorld.* *Prayer is in heauen.* *In hel it is not*

4. Wherfore in the law of nature, as they vsed Sacrifice, so did they practise prayer, and although Seth and Enos be called the first of them who by prayer, most especially and frequently called vpon God, yet no doubt Adam and Eue amongst other actes of penance, omitted not prayer as one of the best dispositions vnto reconciliation with almightie God. Abel their sonne also, as he was religious in his Sacrifices, so was he not slothful in prayer. Noê also taught his posteririe prayer, Abraham was much giuen to prayer. Isaac his sonne in his diligence in prayer and meditation also declared him selfe worthily to haue bene the sonne of such a father. Dauid prayed seuen tymes a day, and rose at midnight often tymes, shortning his sleepe to lengthen his prayer: and Daniel three tymes a day called vpon his God. By prayer, Moyses made the Sea to diuide it selfe, & procured victorie to the Israelits so long as in prayer he held vp his handes, yea by prayer he obtained pardon often times for the people & bond as it were the hands of the omnipotent. By prayer Anne the wife of Helcan obteined Samuel. Ezechias by prayer prolonged his life fiftene yeares. Tobias by the same exercise was restored to his sight. Elias after a great drought by prayer obtained raine.

It vvas in the lavv of nature *Gen. 24.* *Psal. 118.* *Dan. 4.* *Exod. 16.* *1. Reg. 2.* *4. Reg. 26.* *Tob. 11.* *3. Reg 16.* *Mat. 14.* *Luc. 4.* *Mat. 26.*

5. In the new law Christ our High Priest prayed oftentymes al the night long, and a litle before his departure out of this vvorld, he prayed three tymes in the garden: yea he him selfe taught vs the prayer vvhich in Inglish we cal our Lords prayer. And no sooner was Christ depar-

Prayer very frequent in the lavv of grace.

departed, but his Apostles and disciples assembled them selues together, and in prayer attended the Holy Ghosts descension. S. Peter and S. Ihon ascended into the Temple to pray. S. Peter furrowed his face with the streames of teares, which trickled yea streamed from his eyes in prayer. S. Bartholomew is sayd to haue prayed on his knees an hundred tymes in the day and as ofthen in the night. S. Iames knees by prayer became as hard as camels knees. Whose examples the first Christians after the Apostles folowing, met together dayly at prayer, euen before they had Churches, in so much that Traian the Emperour forbid such flocking together. And Plinie prefect of this Emperour, informed him of the assemblies of Christianes to prayer before day. To be briefe, the Ecclesiastical histories are ful of the Churches, and monasteries vvhich haue bene builded for prayer, & speake almost of nothing else but of Christiās prayers, Masses, Liturgies canonical howers, as nocturnes, lauds, the prime hower of prayer, third, sixt, ninth hower, Euensong, and Complete: yea so is prayer diuided in diuers Churches and monasteries, that in euery vigil of the night in one place or other, prayers and prayses are songue to God: yea seing that our Church is dispersed through out the vvorld, and that the hower vvhich is to one countrie, one, to an other is two, to an other, is three a clocke, and so forth, there is no hower in the day or night in vvhich prayer is not exercised publickely in the Church. So that wel is the Catholique Church called the *house of God, because it is the house of prayer.*

Act. 2. Act. 3. Clem. Rom. Bar. to. 2. an. 100. l 10. ep. 971. Tert. Apol. c. 2. Hieron. ep. ad Eustoch. Athan. l. de Virg. Basi 37. Clem l. 8. Const c. 4. Tho. VVald. to 3. de Sacramental. c. 20. Isa. 56. Luc. 19.

6. Now let vs see how like vnto this house of God, which is the house of prayer, our Reformers Sinagogue is. In most places they haue no prayer at al on working dayes, and on holy dayes (vvhich now they haue brought to a lesse number, because they celebrate few Saintes dayes) they spēd almost al the tyme that they are in the Church in yelling out a Geneua Psalme, to vvhich they adde a Sermon: and generally in England now adayes, you shal find few that vse any priuate prayer in their chambers, but as dogges go to their kennel, so they go to bed, and so they rise in the morning, shaking or stretching them selues out, neuer bowing knee, no nor opening mouth nor hart in prayer. In so much that vvhen one of our Catholiques in his Inne in London vvas found by the chamberlaine, kneeling by his bed side, to say his deuotions, proclamation vvas by and by made, that he was a Priest and a traitour (for then in England they were al one) as if theyr owne consciences had accused them, that prayer is no signe of a man of their religion.

Litle vse of prayer amōgst the reformers.

A Priest apprehended vpon suspicion because he prayed.

7. And

7. And truly this contempt of prayer amongst them is not to be blamed by their preachers, because it is most conformable to their doctrin. For first they say that prayer meriteth no reward at Gods hands. Secondly they auouch that it can not make the least satisfaction, for the least sinne in the world. Why then should we weare our hose out in the knees with praying, if prayer neither satisfieth, nor meriteth, any thing at Gods hands? Truly if we weare our hose out, we lose more then we gette, if this doctrin be true. Thirdly Caluin auoucheth that the iustifying faith is a firme and ful assurance that we are elect and iust by Christs iustice; and seing that faith is a necessarie disposition to prayer (for as S. Paul sayth how shal they pray and cal vpon him, in whom they beleue not? it foloweth that before we settle our selues to prayer, vve must firmely beleue that we are iust and that our sinnes are forgiuen VVhence I gather these conclusions. First that in vaine the faithful man praeyth for iustification or remission of sinnes, because before he prayeth, his sinnes are forgiuen, and he is iustified, or else his ful assured faith is a lying and deceiptful faith. The second is that no faithful man can pray for iustification or remission of sinnes, vnles he vvil be an infidel and forsake his faith by praying. For he is bound by Caluin to beleue assuredly that his sinnes are forgiuen, because this is his iustifying faith, and if he stagger or doubt he is an infidel, because he hath not the right faith; vvhence it foloweth that in praying for remission of sinnes, he loseth faith, because in that he prayeth, he shevveth that he hath not that assurance: for who wil pray for that vvhich he is assured of already? Or if he pray it is an argument that either he thinketh that he hath not the thing for vvhich he prayeth, or that he doubteth therof, or that he feareth, of which euery one is sufficient to make a man an infidel in Caluins opinion, because they despoile him of that assured faith. The third conclusion is that he can not pray at al for remission of sinnes, would he neuer so faine euen with losse of his faith. For as if I be in good health, and assure my selfe of the same, I can not pray for health, though I may pray for continuance of it, so if before I pray, I be assured that my sinnes be forgiuen, though I may vvith lippes, yet vvith hart I can not pray, that God would forgiue me: and if I could in vaine should I pray for that which I haue already. The fourth is that no faithful man can pray for eternal blisse in heauen: for if before I pray I must haue faith (as S. Paul saith I must) and if faith be a ful assurance that I am not only iust, but also elected, and chosen to be one of the

Gal. l. 3. Inst. c. 70.

Melanct. tit. de peccat.

Contemp of prayer conformable to the nevv Religiō.

See the seuenth booke.

l. 3. Inst. c. 2. 6. 7. 9. 10. 16. 19

Rom. 10.

Caluī maketh prayer for remissiō of sinne a vaine thing.

yea pernicious to faith.

yea impossible

An example.

Rom. 10.

No man by Caluin can pray for aeternal blisse.

Citizens of heauen, I can not vvith hart pray that I may be receiued into heauen. VVel I may pray that speedilie God wil take me to him, and his glorie, because I am not sure when shal be the time, at vvhich he vvil cal me, but to pray absolutely to be admitted vnto God his glorie and Kingdom, I can not possibly, because by Caluins faith, I am already assured of this kingdom and glorie. But Caluin vvil obiect against vs that S. Iames biddeth vs pray in faith and confidence, nothing doubting or staggering. I grant that vve must beleue that God can helpe, and hope also that he wil helpe, and so vve must not pray doubting, but yet vve may and must pray betvvixt feare & hope. For if I hope not, but despaire of obtaining, I haue no cause to pray, and if I doubt of Gods mercie, I do him iniurie, yet if I be sure, I can not pray, and therfore I must feare the worst and yet pray for the best. Moreouer Caluin telleth vs that the iustifying faith assureth vs not only of present, but also of future iustice, that is, acertaineth vs not only that we are now at this present iust, but also that we shal perseuer vnto the end: whence it foloweth that we can not pray to God for perseuerance in grace, or that he wil so assist vs, that no tentation of the diuel, insurrection of the flesh, or allurement of the world, giue vs the foyle or fal: because by faith we are assured of our standing. He auoucheth also that sinne hath so weakened mans nature, that he can not vvith al the grace that Christ hath giuen, resist any tentation. Whence enseweth also that he can not pray, not to be ledde into tentation, that is not to be permitted to yeld to tentation, because he is assured by Caluins doctrin, that he can not but yeld if he once be tempted. And although these tvvo last points seeme contradictorie, because the one saith, that a faithful man can not fal from iustice, the other saith, that he can not but yeld to sinne and tentation, which is the fal of the soule: yet Caluin hath a way to auoide this cōtradiction, because (saith he) though a faithful man yeld to tentation, yet God imputeth it not as sinne, because he is faithful, and so saith he, a faithful man is assured that he can not fal: and then say I, that I am assured that he can not pray that he may stand, and not fal by tentation. He is also of opinion that the best workes of a iust man are so vncleane that they are mortal sinnes: which if it be true, then can vve not pray that Gods name be halowed and sanctified in vs, that is in our workes, because neither in vs, not in our actions, is any one iotte of true sanctitie. He denyeth also freevvil and al voluntarie cooperation with Gods vvil and grace. And so vve can not pray that Gods vvil be doone

Iac. 5.
Caluins obiection.
The ansvver.
See the seuēth booke.
l. 3. Inst. c. 2. 8. 18.
Nor for perseuerance.
See the same booke.
Nor for ayd against tentation.
l 2 Inst. c. 5 l. 3 c. 14.
nor that Gods name be halloued vs.
Al the opinions of Cal-

doone in vs: for a prayer argueth ſome dependence of Gods wil on ours, which ſo would haue vs to do wel, as it wil leaue it in our powre to reſiſt the wil and grace of God. And if Caluin obiect thoſe vvords of Scripture: *Who reſiſteth his vvil?* I anſwer that no man can reſiſt Gods wil, when he wil abſolutely haue it fulfilled and independently of vs, but yet we may reſiſt Gods wil, when he willeth dependently of our willes, elſe vvould he not haue ſayd: *hovv often vvould I haue gathered thee as a henne gathereth her chickins together and thou vvouldeſt not.* Now put al this together and you ſhal ſee that the *Pater noſter*, or our Lords prayer, muſt be cut out of the Catichiſme, and blotted out of the Reformers Goſpel. For although Chriſt taught his Apoſtles that prayer, yet according to Caluins doctrin no faithful man, that is, no Caluiniſt, can in conſcience recite that prayer. And ſo either Chriſt is deceiued or Caluin teacheth falſe doctrin: but Caluin wil ſvveare that he teacheth the truth and that he is ſure that a faithful man is ſure of his iuſtice, remiſſion of ſinnes, and election: & therfore you know what foloweth. But leſt you thinke that I do iniurie to Caluin in affirming that he taketh away the Lords prayer, as vnlawful & quite repugnant to Chriſtian faith, I wil proue it manifeſtly and by no other argument, then by calling to mynd that vvhich is already ſayed.

uin ſee in the ſeuenth booke. *l.1. Inſt.c.8.* *Rom. 9.* *Mat. 27.* *Caluin taketh avvay our lords prayer.*

8. In the firſt petition of our Lordes prayer we deſire that his name be halowed in vs, vvhich is a prayer cleane appoſit to Caluins opinion, vvhich teacheth that there is no ſanctitie in vs or our workes, and ſo holding his opinion, we muſt omit the firſt petition. In the ſecond, vve pray that his Kingdom may come, and that we may be receiued into it, vvhich petition we can not make from our hart, if before we pray, we are aſſured by faith (as Caluin ſaith) that we are elect and predeſtinate to that kingdom, as before is proued. The third is that Gods wil be done in heauen as in earth, vvhich petition alſo according to Caluin is friuolous, for if we cooperate not with God by our friewil, in vayne do we pray that his wil be doone in earth, becauſe that argueth ſome dependence of Gods wil on ours, as is before demonſtrated. The fourth is that God wil giue vs our daylye bread, that is al thoſe benefites either of Nature or Grace, vvhich are belonging either to ſoule or bodye: vvhich petition alſo can not ſtand with Caluins faith: becauſe if faith aſſureth me of preſent & future iuſtice, yea and of glorie alſo, and as Caluin ſaith it doth, then I can not pray either for iuſtification, or remiſſion of ſinnes, or perſeuerance in grace, or final glorie, becauſe no man can pray for that vvhich he is aſſured

Hovv he taketh avvay the firſt petition. *l.2. Inſt.c.5. l. 3.c.14.* *Hovv the ſecond.* *l.3.Inſt.c.2.* *Hovv the 3.* *l.1.Inſt c.8.* *Hovv the third.* *Hovv the fourth.* *l.3. Inſt.c.2.*

of, as is before declared. And so we can only pray for health, riches, fayre wether, or such like corporal benefites: yea if it be true that al these thinges come by fatal necessitie (as Caluin must say that they do) because he affirmeth that Gods foresight and decree imposeth a necessitie vpon al thinges, and consequently on these thinges also, because he foreseeth and decreeth these thinges no lesse then he doth mens actions: then in vayne also do we pray for health, or vvelth, or faire weather, because these thinges of necessitie shal be or not be whether we wil or no, and as vaine it is to pray for health or welth, as for the sunne rising vvhich of necessitie riseth vvhether vve pray or no. In the fifth petition vve demande that God, wil forgiue vs our trespasses and offences, vvhich as is before proued, we can not pray for without losse of our fayth, vvhich if it be right, assureth vs without al doubt that they are already forgiuen. The sixt and seuenth are that God wil not permit vs to fal into temptation, and by tentation, but deliuer vs from al euil, especially of sinne: vvhich petitions also are vaine, yea impossible if Caluins faith be true. For if by faith I be assured of future iustice, I can not pray with hart that God wil assist me that I fal not from iustice, because I am (as Caluin sayth) ful wel assured that I shal not fal, and so I can no more pray, that I may not fal by tentation, then that the heauens may not fal vpon me, being as sure of the one, as the other, and if sinne and other euils befal vs of necessitie (as Caluin saith they do) in vaine do we pray to be deliuered from al euil. And so our Lordes prayer can not stand if Caluins doctrin do go for currant: and seing that this prayer was made by Christ, if we wil folow Caluin we must forsake Christ: and for as much, as this prayer conteineth in a briefe summe, and methode, al thinges vvhich we are to pray for, if by Caluins doctrin we can not say this prayer, vvhich is a *Compendium* of al prayers and petitions, we can not pray at al, and so no prayer can be vsed in Caluins Church according to Caluins doctrin.

l. 1. Inst. c. 15. 8.

Hovv the fifth

Hovv the sixt and seuenth.

Hovv he taketh avvay al prayer.

9. VVherfore I meruaile not that so litle prayer is practised amongst them, I vvonder not that they build no nevv Churches, but pul dovvne the old vvhich vvere builded for prayer: rather I meruaile that they sometimes exhort men to prayer, seing that their doctrin and prayer can not stand together. And I like better of Luther and of his plaine dealing in this matter, for he hauing once pronounced sentēce that faith only iustifieth, affirmeth consequently that prayer is not necessarie, these are his vvordes: *Euery hart hovv much the more perfect knovvledge*

knovvledge (he meaneth the knovvledge of faith) *it hath of it selfe, so much, more ready is the vvay for God vnto it, although in the meane tyme a man should drinke nothing but malmesey and vvalke vpon roses, and neuer pray one vvorde.* And so if Caluin vvould deale as plainly as Luther doth, as he agreeth vvith him in the premises, to vvit, that only faith sufficeth, so should he also agree vvith him in the conclusion, vvhich is, that prayer is not necessary.

Ser. de Dom. 4. Aduent. edit. an. 1525.

Luth. plainly saith that no prayer is necessarie.

10. But it is time now that I also come to my conclusion, to vvit that amongst our reformers is no Religion, because by their doctrine they can haue no prayer: vvhich conclusion if the premises be called to mynd doth folovv easily, and euidently. Because prayer in al lawes vvas euer necessarie to the vpholding of Religion, as I haue proued by induction, and the reason also is, because it is one of the most principal actes of Religion, by vvhich vve acknovvledge Gods soueraintie, and our ovvne basenes and beggerie, but amongst the reformers no prayer, not so much as the Lords prayer, can be vsed, as is also proued, *ergo* amongst them there is no Religion: because prayer and Religion must of necessitie go together. And so our reformers haue no seruice to vse in their Churches but onlie a sermon: vvhich also I see not to vvhat purpose it is amongst them if men haue no frie vvil: for then as vvel may their ministers preach to a flocke of sheep, as to a Church ful of faithful people, because these haue no more frie vvil (if vve beleue Caluin) then they haue: and so are as absurdely exhorted by a Sermon as they. And if Caluin vvould laugh at a Minister that should persvvade shepe and asses to abstinence, labour, and such like, vve may laugh at him and his ministers vvhen by a laboured Sermon, they go about to perswade men to vertue, or to dissvvade from vice, vvho haue no more frie vvil to folow such persvvasions then shepe or asses haue.

Hovv Luther and Caluin take avvay sermons also.

THE

THE FIFTE BOOKE CONTAINETH A SVRVEY OF THEIR DOCTRIN CONCERNING GOD, IN WHICH is declaied, hovv impious the Reformers are, and hovv iniurious their doctrin is to the Diuine Maiestie.

The first Chapter shevveth hovv they make God the autour of al sinne and vvickednes.

IMON Magus the first Arch-heretike of fame, was the first man that opened his mouth to the vtterance of this blasphemie, but he had no sooner broken the yse, but by and by Florinus, Blastus, Cerdon, Marcion, and Manicheus, vvith open mouth, & common voice, applauded to his blasphemie, agreing vvith him that God is the autor of al sinne and euil. Yea because this doctrin semed to offensiue to Christian eares, they deuised a kind of moderation, to make their doctrin more sailable. VVherfore Simon Magus sayd, that God was the autor of sinne, not that he immediately moueth vs to sinne, but because he hath giuen vs such a nature, which of necessitie sinneth, and so by a certaine consequence, he sayd God was the the autor of sinne. Cerdon and Manicheus also were ashamed to father sinne vpon the good God, and therfore they affirmed, that there were tvvo Gods, the one good, the other bad: and that the euil God vvas the autor of sinne and euil.

Tert. l. præsc. c. 13.

Heretikes vvho sayd God vvas the autor of sinne

2. But

2. But Caluin and his folovvers (as it is easier to adde then to inuent) haue farre exceded and ouerreached them in malice, auouching that God immediately and directely, is the author of al vvickednes, vvhich Simon Magus durst not say, yea the good and the only God vvorketh and effectuateth this malice, vvhich those ancient heretikes were ashamed to say. These are Caluins vvordes, or rather blasphemies: *God not only forseeth mans sinnes, but also hath created him of determinate purpose to that end.* And a litle after: *God not only permitteth sinne but vvilleth it.* Yea sayth he: *It is not likely that man by him selfe by the only permission of God, vvithout any ordinance, brought destruction to himselfe.* And therfore, *vvhen Absalon abused his Fathers vviues, it vvas Gods vvil* (sayth he) *so to punish Dauids adulterie, and God commanded him to do it to that end,* Again he sayth that *God blindeth and hardneth the reprobate not only by not illuminating them nor mollifying them by grace, but because he stirreth vp their vvilles: And not only suffereth sinners, but bovveth and turneth their hartes.* So that according to Caluins opinion God not only forseeth that vve vvil sinne, but ordayneth vs to sinne, not only permitteth vs to sinne, but willeth and commandeth, yea boweth our hartes to sinne. And lest you should thinke, that at least God hath no part in those sinnes, to which the Diuel and vvicked men prouoke vs, or that the iniuries, vvhich they do vs, procede not at al from him, he auoucheth that Satan and euil men in these euil offices, are but the instrumentes of God, and that God setteth them on, and is the principal agent and author. *I grant* (sayth he) *that theues and murderers and other euil doers are the instrumentes of Gods prouidence, vvhom the Lord doth vse to execute those iudgementes, vvhich he hath himselfe determined.* Yea he sayth, *that vvhat our enemy mischeuously doth against vs, he doth as suffred and sent by God*: And he is not afrayed to say *that God armeth as vvel diuiles as vvicked men against vs.* And that *Sennacherib vvas an axe and instrument of God directed and driuen by his hand to cutte. Finally* sayth he: *the vncleane spirit is called the spirit of the Lord, because he ansvvereth his commandement and povver, being rather his instrument in doing, then an author of himselfe.* By vvhich speaches who seeth not, that Caluin maketh God a greater Patrone of sinne, then the diuil, because the diuil is but his instrument and minister in al the euil he doth, God is the printipal Agent and commander. The like saying hath Melancthon, *vvho auoucheth that Dauids adulterie and Iudas treachery, vvere as much the vvorke of God, as S. Paules vocation.* The like hath Beza and diuers others, vvhose blasphemies I list no more to relate, neither can Christian eares desire to heare them.

Caluin vvorse in this then they.

l.4.Inst.c.19. 6.

his blaspemies.

l.2.c.18. 4.

l.2.c.4.2.3 4.

Ibidem.

l.37.2.3.

l.2.c.4 sect.1.

Sect.4.

Sect.6.

In c. 8.ep. Rom.

Catholiques opinions in this point.

3. Much more honourably doth the Catholique Church speake of the Diuine Maiestie, which auerreth that God is the authour of the paine of sinne, because in that is no sinne, but iustice; but not of the malice of sinne: likvvise confesseth that God permitteth al sinnes that are, because he wil not force mens libertie; yea suffereth also the diuil and his ministers to prouoke vs to sinne, but neither willeth, nor commandeth them so to doe; Catholiques also teach that God is so the authour of al essence and goodnes, that he concurreth with our wil to the substance of the act of sinne, but hath no part in the malice of the sinne. And vvhere Scripture semeth to say, that God is the autour of euil or commandeth euil men, or sayth that the wicked are his instrumentes: the Catholique Church sayth that this is to be vnderstood by permission only. Yea this Church teacheth vs, that God neuer vseth euil persons as instruments moued by him to sinne, but only permitteth them to sinne, and afterwards vseth this their sinne, either to the iust punishement of them selues or of others, or to the glorie of his seruantes, whose patience by euil persons is tryed, or to a greater repentance of the sinner, who being fallen into such abomininatiom, thinketh of a greater repentance: as king Dauid, Mary Magdalen, and some others did.

The first reasõ vvhy God can not be the autor of sinne.

4. And certainly it is as euident that God can not be the authour of sinne, as that he can not but be God. For first of al, God is goodnes it selfe, and therfore as euil frutes can not proced from a good tree, because they are contrarie to the good nature and disposition of the tree, so from so good a nature as God is, who is *summum bonum* and goodnes it selfe, we must not looke for so euil frutes as sinnes are, in vvhich is no goodnes at al: and therfore to say that he is the autour of sinne, is to make him an euil God, and of a malitious nature, as Cerdon and Manicheus did, and so no God at al. For God and Good must of necessitie go together. Secõdly sinne is as opposite to Gods goodnes as false hood is to his *Veritie*, but God can not lye, nor authorize a lie, because he is the *first Veritie: ergo* he can not be the autour of sinne, because he is the chiefest goodnes: or if such goodnes can do euil, such veritie and truth may lye, and so the Scriptures loose their credit. For if God can lye, peraduenture in Scriptures he hath lyed: and to say that God can be the autour of sinne, is to say consequently that he may be the autour of lyes, vvhich is to open the gap to Atheistes and misprisers of Scriptures. For as wel may he moue the writers of Scriptures to write lyes, as he may moue them to sinne and wickednes. Thirdly if God be authour

Mat. 7.

The second.

The third.

authour of sinne, then by his wil, vvhich is the cause of al thinges, he worketh sinne, vvhich if it be so, then sinne is according to Gods wil, and so no sinne because that vvhich is according to the Princes wil, can neither displease his wil, nor impeach his commandement, and consequently is neither offence nor preuarication. Fourthly euerie error is a sweruing from the rule which is prescribed, and therfore the artificer erreth vvhen he worketh not according to his platforme, or *idea*, and the singer erreth vvhen he singeth not according to his Gamma vt, and the writer scribleth, vvhen he foloweth not his example, and the subiect transgresseth, vvhen he liueth not according to the Princes good law, and the moral man offendeth, when he foloweth not reason, vvhich is the lore, rule, and square of al his actions. And because al these workers are distinct from their rule, they may swerue from the same, and so commit a fault in their art: but God (sayth S. Thomas) is to him selfe a rule, and foloweth no other law or rule then his æternal reason and law, which is him selfe, and so can no more sinne (vvhich is to swerue from his reason) then he can deny him selfe, or goe from him selfe. Lastly sinne is an auersion from God, and an offence vvhich highly displeaseth him, and so by consequence, if God could sinne: he should as it were turne him selfe from him selfe, and be auerted from him selfe, and displeased with him selfe, and so he should be so farre from endewing others with felicitie, that he should want it him selfe, and liue in a continual miserie, as he must neds doe, who hath an auersion from him selfe, and is displeased with him selfe.

Psal. 113.
Th. 1. p q. 19 a. 4.
The fourth.
Th. 1 p. q. 62. ar. 1. in Cor.
The fifth.

5. But Caluin sayth that although God be the authour of sinne, yet he is no sinner, because he worketh it for a good end. As for example (sayth he) of the same sinne vvhich the Chaldees committed in vniustly affiicting Iob, God was the autour, Sathan was the autour, and the wil of man was the autour: but because God was the autour of it for a good end, to wit, for the exercising of Iobs patience, he sinned not in that action, but did wel and iustly in the same action, in vvhich they sinned, and trasgressed. But this is no good ansvver. For first, if God may be the autour of sinne to exercise the patience of the iust, or to chastice the wicked, he may also be the autour of a lye, for the punishment of sinnes, and so Scriptures must lose their credit, because peraduenture they are lyes, which God hath put in the tongue and penne of Moyses, other Prophets, and the Euangelists, for a good end: that is to shew his iustice in the Iewes and Gentils, whom for a

l. 2. 6. 4. sect. 2
Caluins answer refuted.

iust punishment he hath seduced, and deceiued with a false writen law, because they would not folow the law of nature, vvhich he had grauen in their hartes. Secondly to make a sinner, it is sufficient if he be the author of sinne, and a good end or intention wil not excuse, vvhen the meanes and election are naught. Wherfore if God be the author of sinne he sinneth what soeuer his intention be. And if a good intention may excuse, it may also excuse vs, and so a man may steale to helpe his parentes, or to offer Sacrifice and oblations of his theftes vnto God, and yet God condemneth such offrings and S. Paul sayth plainly, that *euil things are not to be doone that good therby happen.*

Sinne is not excused bying dour to good end

Rom. 3.

6. But now it is more then tyme to draw nere our conclusion, and therfore out of Caluins blasphemies I wil deduce these illations. The first is, that such men if they had liued in Platoes tyme (who by law banished those that would father their sinnes vpon God) they should not haue bene permitted to haue liued in any citie or common welth. And if that learned Iew Philo had bene appointed their Iudge, he would haue adiudged them to be stoned to death. Secondly I gather hereby, that these men are not led by the Spirit of God, and their doctrin can not be of God, because it is vnlikely, yea impossible, that the Spirit of God should dictate such doctrin, vvhich is so iniurious to God, and so opposite to his goodnes: but rather this doctrin doth proced from him who sayd *that he vvould be a lying spirit in the mouthes of al false Prophets.* Thirdly I gather vvhat litle credit is to be giuen vnto them in other matters, who erre grossely in this opinion, vvhich the light of reason argueth of falsitie, and is as euidently false, as it is euident, that tehre is a God.

The first illation.
l. 2. de Repub.
l. de Agricult.

The second.

1. Reg. 12.
2. Paral. 18.
The third.

The second Chapter shevveth, hovv their doctrin maketh God not only a sinner, but also the only sinner.

l. 3 Inst. c. 23. 6

T is the opinion of Iohn Caluin and of Caluinists that God is not only the authour of sinne, but that his wil & power also doth so dominere ouer the wil of a sinner, that he can not resist Gods motion, which eggeth and vrgeth him to sinne, but must of necessitie sinne. Yea, I (saith Caluin) *vvil not doubt to confesse l*

simpy

simply vvith Austin (he should haue sayd vvithout Austin, for S. Augustin hath no such thing in the palce alleaged) *that the vvil of God is a necessitie of things, and that vvhat he vvilleth, must of necessitie come to passe.* Sitnence then God vvilleth al our sinnes, as Caluin hath in the former chapter confessed, it foloweth that we of necessitie sinne, because *Gods vvil is a necessity of things.* He affirmeth also (as is already declared in the last chapter) that the diuil in soliciting and tempting vs, is the instrument of God, and the executor of his wil and determination, and consequently it is Gods wil that he should tempt vs, and seing that as Caluin sayth his wil is a *necessitie of things*, it foloweth also that the diuel of necessitie tempteth vs. Sect. 1.

2. Out of vvhich premises foloweth euidently my intended conclusion, to wit, that God only is the sinner. For if God so forcebly moueth the diuil by his owne wil and ordinance that the diuil can not choose but tempt vs, and if the wil of God doth so ouerrule and presse the wil of man, that vvhen God wil haue him sinne (as Caluin sayth he wil) he can not resist, it must neds folow that God is the only sinner, and that man and the diuil are to be excused. For, as Caluin affirmeth, God is the authour of al sinnes, and consequently is a sinner, because his good intention can not excuse him, as is already proued in the last chapter: neither can God alleage necessitie for an excuse, because there is none vvhich boweth his vvil by force, but he him selfe most frankely & friely willeth & worketh our sinnes: & seing that the diuil as Gods instrument is violently, at least necessarily moued to tempt vs, he can not sinne, because he can not iustly be blamed, for that vvhich he could not auoide: and for as much as mans wil is compelled to sinne by the ouerruling wil of God, he also for the same reason can not sinne, and so God is the only sinner, & man and the diuil are innocentes, worthily to be excused, & in no wise to be counted sinners.

Caluī maketh God the only sinner.

And mā & the diuel no sinners.

The third Chapter shevveth, hovv their doctrin, that the commandementes are impossible, maketh God an vnreasonable Prince.

T is a common Maxime amongst the Gospellers, that the commandementes of God are impossible, and that a man can as soone touch the heauens with his finger, as fulfil the least commandement. Luther sayth that when the Scripture vseth these vvords or the like: *If thou vvilt keepe the commandementes*; or, *kepe the commandementes*, God dealeth vvith vs as the mother dalyeth with her infant. For as she calleth her child to her, not in earnest, because she knoweth wel that he can not walke, but to make him to see his owne imbecilitie, and to shevv his desire to come vnto her: so when God biddeth vs kepe the commandementes, according to Luther, he iesteth with vs, and biddeth vs obserue the law, not for that he thinketh we are able, but because he wil make vs know our owne impotencie, and yet to shew our good vvil and desire to kepe his lawes, if we were able. But this a strange iesting and dalying, vvhen God wil command vs things impossible, to make vs know our insufficiencie, and yet wil damne vs eternally if vve obserue not these his commandementes. Caluin sayth plainly, that the lavv is impossible, and therfore was neuer fulfilled by any; and he giueth a reason, because (sayth he) *it is hindred by the ordinance and decree of God, that it shal not be fulfilled.* And if you obiect that Christ sayed vnto the young man: *If thou vvilt enter into life kepe the commandementes:* Caluin vvil answere, that Christ sayd so, not that he thought he could kepe them, but because he would represse his pride in proposing a thing which he could not do. As if Caluin should vaunte that he is a new Apostle, and one should say vnto him to represse his vanitie, if thou art an Apostle, worke I pray thee some miracles, for proofe of thy Apostleship, which he can not do. And if you againe reply that the young man sayed that he *had obserued the commandements from his youth.* Caluin wil be so bold as to tel him that he lyed: which Christ him selfe would not say, though he knevv better then Caluin, how truly he auouched that he had

l. de seruo arbitrio.
Luther sayth the commandements are impossible.
A strange iesting.
l. 2. Inst. c. 7. sect. 2.
So doth Caluin.
Mat. 19.
Caluin in har
Ibidem.
Ibidem.

had kept the commandementes: and S. Marke sayth, that our Sauiour *loued him*, which is at least some argument, that Caluin lyeth in saying that he lyed, because Christ loueth neither lyes nor lyers: *For to God is odious the impious and his impietie.* Sap. 18.

2. I could here vse many arguments to *proue that the commandementes are not impossible.* And might beginne with the old Testament, & thence proue that the Iewes were able to kepe the commandementes, and consequently that much more Christians are able, because that on them God bestoweth his grace more liberally. For after that God had giuen vnto that people the law and *Decalogue* he in diuerse places telleth them, that he commandeth them not to do more then they are able. *The commandement* (sayth God) *vvhich this day I command thee, is not aboue thee, nor placed farre from thee*, not in heauen nor beyond sea, that thou mayest pretend an excuse: *but my speach is very nere thee, in thy mouth, in thy hart, that thou mayst do it.* To this subscribeth our Sauiour Christ the lawgiuer of the new law, telling vs that *if vve vvil enter into life, vve must kepe the commandementes.* And lest we should excuse our selues by a pretence that his commandements are impossible, he preuenteth vs saying, that his *yoke is svvete and his burden light.* And S. Iohn his louing and beloued Disciple auoucheth that *his commandementes are not heauy.* Now if the commandements be impossible then are they as farre out of our reach and power, as if they were in *heauen or beyond sea*, then are they not *nere vs*, then are they not so at hand, that God may say, that they *are in our mouth, and hart, to do and fulfil them.* For what is farther of then that which is cleane out of our reach and power? If the law be impossible, then it is not a *light burden.* For what can be more heauy, then that which we can not beare at al. But to me this only argument semeth sufficient to stoppe Caluins mouth: that if the commandements vvere impossible, God should be the most vnreasonable Prince in the world.

The commādments proued to be possible. Exod. 20. Deut. 30. Rom. 10. Mat. 19. Mat. 11. 1. Io. 5.

3. Neither sufficeth it, vvhich Caluin alleageth, that although the commandements be impossible, yet God hath reason to command them, to shew vs our infirmitie, and to prouoke vs to shevv our vvilling mynd to do what we can: for this vvould not excuse God from being vnreasonable, because at least in that ouerplus which excedeth our power, he should shewe him selfe vnreasonable. As for exāple, if a king would commād a creeple to folow him, though therby he might make him see his ovvne impotencie, & geue him occasion by motion of his body, to declare his desire to folow, yet if he cōmād him in dede to folow,

Caluins ansvver reiected.

to folow, he is very vnreasonable. Or if Caluin wil say that God wil seme only to command vs, because he would make vs to see our imbecilitie, and to do vvhat vve can, at least to shew our desire, then foloweth it, that there are no commandments, because God doth not verily command them, but semeth only to command, to make vs see our owne infirmitie, and to shew our desire. Or if Caluin wil not be so bold as to deny al commandements, then must he grant that God is vnreasonable, in commanding vs more then we are able to performe. As for example, if the master would command his seruant not only to runne, but also to fly on his arrand, and for a shorter cut to leape ouer a riuer, ouer vvhich he can scarsely see: would you not thinke him vnreasonable, and quite beside him selfe? The like doth Almightie God, if we beleeue Caluin, for he commandeth vs to loue him aboue al, and our neighbour as our selues, he biddeth vs not to steale, not to kil, yea not to couet our neighbours wife, or goods, vvhich is as if he should command vs to fly, or to moue mountaines, or to leape ouer the sea: because these thinges in Caluins opinion, are no more impossible, then are the commandements, and therfore in these commandementes God sheweth him selfe as vnreasonable, as man should do in the other.

An other example.

4. Yea if once we grant, that God may command impossibilities, then is there no reason why brute beastes may not be commanded not to kil one an other, not to liue of spoile, to faste sometymes, and to honour yea loue their Creatour: because God commandeth man to do these thinges, who yet is no more able to do them, then beastes are. And if beastes could speake and would tel Almightie God, that he hath no reason to command them to do these thinges, because they are not in their power, then may men make the same exception, and accuse their Creator as a Prince most vnreasonable, who commandeth them to execute those lawes, which they no more can fulfil then oxen, and asses can do. And if God wil condemne them as guiltie of offence, for not obeying his commandments they may answer with S. Chrisostome: *Si impotentes nos fecit & deinde imperat, culpa eius est: If he hath made vs impotent* (as Caluin sayth he hath, because by his decree and ordinance he hindreth vs or at least, if we be already by Adams sinne made impotent) *and yet he commandeth vs, the* fault is his, and not ours if we trasgresse his commandement.

Hovv. 16. in ep. Heb. Sepra l. 2. Instit. c. 7. sect. 5

The

The fourth Chapter shevveth, hovv the former doctrin maketh God a most cruel tyrant.

ERDON that infamous heretike, and diuers of his folowers, reading in the old testament, vvhat seueritie in that law God had sometymes vsed, and not considering that the enormitie of sinne is such, that it deserueth not only temporal, but also æternal death, and imagining that such seueritie could not procede from the good God, who is goodnes it selfe (as though God vvere merciful, and not iust also) they affirmed, that there were two Gods the one good, the other cruel, the one the author of the old testamēt, the other of the new, the one Creator only of superior substances, the other of this inferior vvorld. Against these men S. Austin wrote a booke entitled *Against the aduersarie of the lavv and Prophetes*, in vvhich he proueth that in the new law God hath shewed as great seueritie, to wit, in the death of Ananias & Saphira, in threatening ęternal damnation (which passeth al temporal punishement) against those that shal not giue almes, and not only against those that shal kil, but also against them that shalbe angrie, and shal cal contumeliously their brother foole. Whence it foloweth that one and the selfe same God is seuere and sweete, iust and merciful. And good reason, for as the king must not only be gentle but iust also, & therfore the Ægiptians Hierogliffe of a King, was a Bee, vvhose hony signifieth the swetnes vvhich ought to be in a Prince, and his sting importeth, that he must be withal seuere: & iust also, where mercie and faire meanes wil not serue: so God the king of kinges offereth his grace most frankely and bestoweth benefites on vs bountifully, & many tymes winketh at our faultes & expecteth patiently amendment and repentance: but if we contemne his benefites and abuse his patience, then doth he lay his hand seuerely vpon vs, because as he is good so is he iust, and must be iust, else were he not God.

Ex Ter. li. præsc. c. 12.

Cerdons tvvo Gods the one good the other euil.

Act. 3.

Mat. 25. & 5.

Gost is iust & merciful.

A similitude

2. And although some, respecting only the shortenes of the pleasure vvhich they haue taken in sinne, thinke it hard to be punished eternally for a momentarie pleasure; yet if they consider what it is to

offend so great a Maiestie, and how when we sinne, we do in affection desire eternally to perseuer in that sinne, and pleasure or commoditie, we wil thinke with S. Gregorie that the sinner who hath sinned in his eternitie, should be punished in Gods eternitie? Yea if Princes for a momentarie transgression may iustly punish their subiectes with perpetual exile and death it selfe, vvhich of it selfe is perpetual, because resurrection is supernatural: why may not God iustly punish vs with eternal paines, for our temporal faultes, especially seing that they vvhich dye in mortal sinne, neuer thinke of repentance, but remaine perpetually obstinate in their malice, and so deserue to be perpetually punished, because sinne as long as it remaineth, is vvorthy paine, and therfore remaining for euer it may iustly be punished for euer and euer? But although it be so that there are not two gods as Cerdon sayd, the one meeke and mylde, the other cruel and churlish: and although the selfe same God, and the good and the only God, be and must be, because he is God, merciful and iust, and consequently gentle and seuere without al crueltie, because iustice is no crueltie: yet if we wil auouch Luthers and Caluins doctrin for currant, we must of necessitie confesse, that God is the cruellest tyrant that euer vvas or can be.

l. 4. dial. c. 66.

3. For they affirme, as we haue related in the former chapter, that God commandeth vs thinges altogether impossible: and they can not deny but that for transgressing these commandementes, the wicked are tormented in hel perpetually (for Christ biddeth *them goe accursed in to euerlasting fyre*, who clothed him not in his members, vvhen he was in them naked, and who fed him not vvhen in them he was hungrie) vvhich if it be so, then is God most cruel and barbarous. Luther once wel perceiued, that this consequence, to wit, that God is cruel, folowed euidently out of their said premises, that the commandmentes are impossible: and vvhat thinke you doth he answer, or how doth he frie Gods goodnes from crueltie? he saith *that by light of nature and grace, it is vnsoluble. hovv God damneth him vvho can not chose but sinne and transgresse, and* here (sayth he) *both the light of nature and grace do tel vs, that the fault is in God only, and not in miserable man*: *but by the light of glorie* (vvhich the blessed enioy) *Gods iustice herrin is manifested, vvhich novv seemeth iniustice.* Yea (sayth he) *Gods iustice in this point is novv incomprehensible.* So that Luther sayth that now neither by light of nature nor of grace, that is fayth (for so I thinke is his meaning in his obscure distinction) we can excuse God from iniustice and crueltie, who commandeth

Mat. 25.

l. de seruo arbitrio.

Ibidem.

thinges impossible vvhich we can not performe, and yet punisheth offenders æternally.

4. And truly if it be so as they say, that God commandeth impossibilities and yet punisheth and damneth the transgressors, then not only by the light of nature and grace, but by al light and reason imaginable it is manifest that God is most cruel and tyrannical. For if that maister be cruel and barbarous, who commandeth his seruant that is lame to runne or leape, and because he doth not so, beateth him blacke and blew, breaketh his bones, and in fine killeth him also, then certes God him selfe who commandeth vs impossibilites, and for not doing them doth not only punish temporally, but also damneth men perpetually, and condemneth to those æternal flames of hel, vvhere they shal euer feele the panges of death and yet neuer dye, where they shal alwayes be dying & neuer dead, vvhere after millions of yeares of imprisonment & torment, they shalbe neuer awhit the nearer an end of their miserie: he I say must neds be most cruel and inhumain, more barbarous then any Scithian and so tyrannical, that in respect of him, Nero, Domitian, and Dionisius, were no tyrants but rather clement Princes.

An example of a Tirant.

God according to Luth. & Caluī is the most cruel Tyrant that euer vvas.

The fift chapter maketh it manifest, that the reformers pul the true God out of his throne, & place an Idol in the same, of their ovvne imagination.

Ertullian that ancient and learned writer when he was best disposed (that is vvhen he was a Catholique and a writer against heretikes, in defence of the Catholique and Romain Church and Religion) was of opinion that al heresies are idolatries, and al heretikes idolaters. Which opinion though at the first sight, it may seeme to rigorous, yea erronious, yet if it be wel wayed and considered, it may very truly be verified of the heretikes of his tyme, and of this our vnhappy age, and in some sorte of al heretikes vvhat soeuer. But before we come to the proofe of this his opinion, we wil first set it downe in his ovvne vvords, vvhich are these: *Either they faine an other God to the Creator* (as the Marcionistes did)

Heretikes are Idolaters.

l præsc.c. 42.

or if they confesse the only Creator, they declare him othervvise then in dede he is: so euery error concerning God is in somesorte a variation of Idolatrie. By vvhich appeareth, that in his opinion euery heresie is a kind of Idolatrie.

2. And truly there is no heresie but either directly or indirectly it denyeth the true God. For either it denyeth some thing in God, and then it directly denyeth God, or it denyeth some thing vvhich pertaineth vnto God, and so indirectly and by a certain consequence, it taketh away the true God. As for example: the Marcionites affirmed that God vvas cruel, and that the good God was not Creator of this inferior world, vvhich conteineth the fowre elementes, and al those thinges vvhich are compounded of them: and seing that there is no such God who is cruel, or who is not the Creator of the whole world, they denyed the true God and confessed an Idol of their own imagination. In like maner the Arians denied, that God the Father had a Sonne coequal and consubstantial vnto him, & seing that the true God is one God, vvhich is the Father the Sonne and the Holy Ghost, the Arrians in denying the second Person to be God coequal with the Father, denyed the true God: because the true God is not distinct in nature from God the Sonne, and they adored an Idol of their owne imagination, that is, a God who hath no Sonne, or not coequal and consubstantial vnto him. Wherfore Athanasius complaineth that the Arrians vnder pretence of religion, had brought in Idolatrie, and abandoned Baptisme, vvhich can not be equally ministred in the name of the Father the Sonne and the Holy Ghost, if those three Persons be not al equal in Deitie and dignitie.

Some heresies deny God directly.

Examples.

Ser. 1. & 4. cõt. Arianos.

3. Other heretikes there were vvhich held no error concerning the Diuinitie or any Diuine Person, & so could not be sayed, directly to deny the true God, but yet indirectly they denyed him by denying some veritie which hath a cõiunction with him. As for example, Nouatianus, who sayd that there was no remedie against sinne after Baptisme, directly only denyed the Sacrament of Penance, but yet indirectly and by a certain consequence he denyed God, because he is not a true God, vvhich wil not accept of penance after Baptisme, and therfore seing that he confessed only such a God, he adored a false God, and so was an Idolater. Nestorius also who sayd, that in Christ besides the Diuine Person, there vvas also an humane person, and consequently two persons, directly denyed the vnitie of Christs Person, and affirmed two persons in Christ: but indirectly he denyed Christ and consequently God, because Christ is God and man in one and the selfe same,

Other indirectly.

Examples.

same Person, & therfore he denying Christ consisting of two persons, adored a false Christ, and consequently a false God, and so was in Idolater. S. Thomas giueth the reason of this: because (sayth he, and he alleageth Aristotle for authoritie) God is a thing infinit in perfection, yet so simple and void of composition, that in him is no distinction but of Persons, vvhich also are one indiuisible God, and therfore as an indiuisible point is altogether touched, or not at al, because it hath no partes, so our vnderstanding either rightly attaineth vnto the knowledge of God, or not at al, and if it erre in one perfection of God it erreth in al, because al is one. And so if an heretique denieth any thing of God, he denyeth al. *22 q. 2. a 2. ad 1. l. 9 met.* *The reason.*

4. But although al heretikes are in some sorte Idolaters, yet I wil not deny but that there is a difference betwixt them, and paganes. For these men deny the true God in expresse termes, and adore some creature for God, as Iupiter, or the planetes, or some such like: but heretikes only affirme some thing of God, vvhich implyeth a denyal of the true God, yet they professe in wordes religion vnto the true God. Now therfore if al heretikes be in some sorte Idolaters, then certainly the heretikes of this tyme are especially Idolaters. For they (as is already proued) say that God is the author of sinne, and their doctrin implieth that he is of a bad nature, vnreasonable, and cruel, wherfore seing that there is no such God, they confesse & adore not a true God, but an Idol of their owne coceipt and fiction, and so are Idolaters, who pul the true God, vvhich is a good God, not cruel, nor vnreasonable, nor author of sinne, out of his throne, and place therin a false God, an Idol of their owne imagination.

 THE

THE SIXT BOOKE CONTAINETH A SVRVEY OF THEIR DOCTRIN CONCERNING PRINCES AVTHORITIE and their lavves, in vvhich is proued, that the doctrin of the reformers, despoileth princes of authoritie, and bringeth their lavves in contempt.

The first chapter shevveth hovv in that they say, that no Prince can bynd a man in conscience to obey his lavv and commandment, they despoile princes of authoritie and superioritie, and giue the subiects good leaue to rebel and reuolte.

Eccl. 13.

BY experience vve see, and holy Scripture teacheth, that like of nature do easily sorte them selues together. Shepe do flocke to one fold, deere meet together in one parke, bees in one svvarme, and fovles of one fether do flye together, and fishes of one finne, do swime together. The reason may be, because like of nature are like in conditions, and so do more easily symbolize and agree together, and one alone hath no helpe but of him selfe, and therfore for mutual aide and comforte, they accompanie them selues with others. But amongst al liuing creatures man especially is ciuil and compaignable, and therfore is called *animal sociabile, a sociable creature.* For first man is apt to language, by which

Th de Regim princip. l. 4. c. 2. 4.

Man especially is sociable.

The first reasō

by vvhich he desireth to expresse his mynd to others, and therfore if he vvil haue any vse of his tongue and facultie of speaking, he must liue in company. Secondly man especially is disciplinable, desirous to learne of others, and by discoursing and deuising, to knovv vvhat other men thinke and conceaue. For as he is vvilling to impart his owne conceites, so is he desirous to be partaker of the knowledge and cogitation of others, which his desire he can not satisfie vnles he repaire to company. Thirdly man only amongst al liuing creatures is apt to frendship, that is to loue and to be beloued, and because loue cometh by sight, and sure frendship is not gotten but by much familiaritie, and long experience, he can not attaine to this also, but in company and societie. Lastly man only is borne naked, where as in other liuing creatures, garmentes do grow with them, destitute of al weapons of defence, vvhere as the bul hath his horne, the bucke his head, the horse his hoofe, the bore his tuske, and euery one hath one vveapon or other to defend and offend. Wherfore seing that man is so destitute, that being alone he wanteth many commodities, he must fly to societie vvhere one helpeth an other, and because euery countrie beareth not al thinges, one countrie must trafique with an other, and hence procedeth societie. Wherfore no sooner were men created, but they assembled them selues together, first in families, then in townes and cities, & afterwards as their number increased, in common weales and kingdomes. And although the Poets fayne that Orpheus was the first vvho with his melodious tunes called men together, yet certain it is, that euen from the beginning men liued in societie, induced thervnto by no other Orpheus, then Nature, and God the author of nature.

The second.

The third.

The fourth.

Vvho assembled men together, at the first.

2. Now as the natural body of man is framed by God and nature of diuers members vnited together, and hath from God and Nature authoritie to defend it selfe against al, that shal vniustly seeke to molest or iniurie the same: so the ciuil body of a societie of men, be it a Kingdom ro other comonwelth, receiued from god and nature authoritie and power to conserue it selfe, and to vvithstand al foreiners, who shal iniuriously inuade it. For if nature did not geue men authoritie to defend and preserue them selues in societie, in vaine, yea not in vaine only, but also perniciously, and to mans great preiudice, had God and nature enclined him to liue in companie. Wherfore al societies lawfully assembled, haue from God and nature, power and authoritie to rule and defend them selues: and because the confused multitude is

Euerie lavvful societie hath authoritie to defend it selfe.

The reason vvhy.

tude is vnfit to gouerne, becauſe it is *bellua multorum capitum, a beaſt of many heades*, wauering, inconſtant, and mutinous (yea hard it is for the multitude to mete always together to determine vpon ſtate, matters, and vvhen they are met they can as hardly agree) it was neceſſarie that this multitude ſhould haue authoritie, to chooſe ſome head or heades, by vvhich this ciuil body might be directed, ruled, and defended. Hence it is that diuines yea Scriptures affirme, that al lawful authoritie vvhich Princes and Superiors haue ouer others, is of God; because it procedeth from the peoples election, who as they were by God and nature inclined to liue in ſocietie, ſo they receiued authoritie to rule, and defend them ſelues, vvhich becauſe they could not do by them ſelues, they receiued alſo authoritie from God and nature to appointe rulers and gouerners; and ſo al lawful gouerners are appointed by God, by meanes of election, and therfore they *vvho reſiſt them, reſiſt Gods ordinance* And although now for the moſt part Princes come to authoritie by ſucceſſion, yet the origen alſo of this procedeth from election, becauſe the people, to auoyed inconueniences vvhich might happen, if after the death of their Prince, they ſhould be to ſeeke for an other, were content vvhen they choſe the firſt Prince, that al his lawful heires, ſhould after him ſucceed in the ſame authority.

Rom. 13. Vicerelec. de poteſt. ciuili. Hovv al authoritie is of God. Rom. 16.

3 Now if the Prince haue not authoritie to command and bynd his ſubiectes alſo in conſcience to obey his commandment, then in vaine is he head and Prince of the people, becauſe if he command and yet the ſubiectes may chooſe whether they wil obey or not, then no order can be eſtabliſhed, and as good no head at al as ſuch a head. Wherfore holy Scripture telleth vs that Princes may command and ſubiectes in conſcience muſt obey, and *giue to Cæſar vvhat is devv to Cæſar.* S. Paul ſayth that *euerie ſoule muſt be ſubiect to higher povvers*: and he giueth the reaſon, becauſe (ſayth he) *there is no povver but of God, and therfore they vvho reſiſt povver, reſiſt Gods ordinance and purchaſe to them ſelues damnation.* Yea ſayth he: *of neceſſitie be you ſubiect not only for diſpleaſure, but alſo for conſcience.* And afterwards he biddeth vs to pay tributes, and ſubſidies vnto Princes, becauſe they are the miniſters of God appointed by him. S. Peter alſo biddeth vs to *be ſubiect to euery humaine creature for God*, that is to euery magiſtrate and temporal ſuperior; vvhom he calleth humaine creatures, becauſe their authoritie is in temporal and humain thinges. And therfore he addeth, as it were to ſpecifie vvhat he meaneth by the humain creature: *vvhether it be to the King, as excelling, or the Rulers ſent from him. &c.* Yea he biddeth vs obey not only gentle and courteous

Mat. 22. Rom. 13. Ibidem. 1. Pet. 2.

maiſters.

maisters, but euen those vvhich are *hard to please*. And this obedience these Apostles command vs to giue to Princes although they be Infidels, if otherwise they be lawful, for vvhen the Apostles wrote, there were no Christian Princes, and faith is not necessarie to iurisdiction, neither is authoritie lost by the only losse of faith. But yet this must be vnderstood, vvhen Princes command within the limits of their iurisdiction: for otherwise, if they command vs any thing against God or conscience, we must answer them, as the Apostles answered the Iewes, *vve must obey God before men*. Because Princes are appointed by God, and so can command nothing, vvhich is against God: or if they do, we must obey the supreme Prince before the inferior, and the King before his viceroy. Wherfore S. Policarpe although he refused to obey the Proconsul who commanded him to do that vvhich was against God, Religion, and conscience, yet he sayd: *Vve are taught to giue to principalities and Potentates ordained by God, that honour vvhich is devv to them, and not hurtful to vs*. This being so, that Princes haue authoritie to command, and to bynd also in conscience to obedience & that from God vvhose ministers they are, and *by vvhom* (as the wise man sayth) *Kinges do raigne, and the lavv makers deterne vvhat is iust*: it remaineth that we examin our aduersaries doctrin in this point, that we may see vvhat they giue to superioritie, authoritie, and higher powers. *Ex Euseb.* *Prou. 8.*

4. But peraduenture some wil thinke that this is a vaine examination, because they are so farre from suspicion of detracting from Princes authoritie, that rather they seme to grant them to much. Luther affirmeth that Bishops and Prelates are subiect to the Emperour euen in Ecclesiastical causes, and that Ecclesiastical iurisdiction is deriued from temporal. And vvhen Catholiques in England refuse to go the Church, because profession is made there of a religion contrarie to theirs, the reformers vrge nothing so much as that we must obey Princes, and their Iniunctions. But this they do only vvhen Ecclesiastical power calleth them to an account, or when the Princes lawes do fauorize their doctrin: for then they flatter Princes, and preferre their authoritie before the Church; not because in hart they reuerence their authoritie, but because by their power, they would establish their heresie So Arius by the meanes of Eusebius Bishop of Nicomedia, first insinuated him selfe to Constantia the Sister of Constantin the great: and by him he got audience of Constantin him selfe, and by flattery and dissimulation he procured a commandment from the Emperour to Athanasius, to receiue him againe into the Church. And *Ar. 27.* *Vvhen heretikes acknovvlege authoritie.* *To vvhat end.* *Arius flatterie of Princes.* *Ruff. l. 1. 6. 11.*

afterwards he crept by this meanes into credit with Constantius the Arian Emperour, and sonne to Constantin, by vvhom he banished Catholique Bishops, called many Councels, & propagated his heresie: in so much that S. Hierom sayth *Arrius vt orbem deciperet, sororem principis ante decepit Arrius that he might deceiue the vvorld first deceiued the sister of the Prince.* They curried fauour also with Iulian the Apostata, and they offered their seruice to Iouinian the Emperour, but he vvould none of their proferd seruice, knowing that they vsed to flatter Princes for promotion of their heresies. So that one Themistius a Philosopher vvas wont to say, that heretikes adore the Purple, not God: and are as mutable as Euripus. Luther backed also by the Duke of Saxonie contemned the Popes legate, who sought to reclaime him, and preached confidently those heresies which oterwise he durst not haue done, and perseuered obstinately in them also, vvhich otherwise peraduenture he would not haue done. Caluin sought by a flattering epistle to procure fauour and credit with the French King: and our English Protestantes by the fauour of the late Quene got credit amongst the people, and graced heresie with her crowne. And to winne this fauour they wil not sticke to flatter Princes, yea to adore them and to giue them higher Titles and greater power, then euer God bestowed vpon them. In king Edwards tyme vvhen the state fauoured them, they acknowledged him Supreme head not only in temporal, but also in Ecclesiastical causes. In Quene Maries tyme because that Princesse vvas not for them, then women could not gouerne: but in Quene Elizabeth tyme, because they had insinuated them selues into her protection, women might gouerne as wel as men: and so they are the best temporizers in the vvorld.

Ep. ad Ctesiph *Theod. l. 4, c. 3* *The Arians flattrie.* *Vvhat temporizers they are* *Luth. bakled.* *Præfat. Inst. ad Reg. Gall.* *Caluins flatterie.* *Protestantes flatterie of Princes.*

5 But if you marke their procedings, or doctrin, you shal see that they honor not authoritie, but loue their heresies: which if Princes wil not like, then they contemne and despise al authoritie, & wil not let to make a mutinie, and stirre vp the subiects to rebellion. Luther exhorteth the Germanes not to take armes against the Turke, *because the Turke for pollicie, consaile, integritie and moderation excelleth al our Princes.* And in the same place he calleth the Emperour Charles the fifte, *a rotten and fraile carcase.* And in his booke against the king of England, he calleth him blocke heade, foole, and by manie other worse names. In an other booke he not only inueigheth against Princely authoritie, but also calleth them al fooles, knaues, tirãtes. In an other booke which he wrote against the two Edicts of the Emperour, he calleth the Princes of the

to. 2. post duo Edicta Cæsar. *Luthers contempt of authoritie.* *l. cont. Reg. Angliæ.*

of the Empire fooles, madmen, furious, tenne tymes worse then the Turke. Of which doctrin and example Thomas Munster taking hold, with an hundred thousand rustickes, trubled al Germanie, and in one Franconie he destroied two hundred nyntie three Monasteries. The Lutheran Princes also armed with this example of Luther, tooke armes against the Emperour, and therby were the cause that the Turke surprised many townes, and strong fortes of the Christians. And vvhat stirres the Caluinistes and other sectes haue made in France, Scotland, and the lovve countries, al the vvorld knovveth, and Flanders to this day feeleth.

l de potestate seculari.
Sur. an. 1525.
Munsters saccage.
The Lutheran Princes cause of the Turkes entrance.
Sur. 1530. & 1566.
Caluinistes garboiles.

6. And truly this contempt of lavvful Princes, this disloyaltie & rebellion, is altogether according to their doctrin. Luther in his comment vpon the first Epistle of S. Peter sayth plainly, that he vvil not be compelled, nor bond to obey any prophane magistrate, because he vvil not loose his libertie, which is to be fried in conscience from al Princes authoritie: yet he sayth he vvil obey them friely and frankely, but not of any obligation. And afterwards explicating those words: *Honour the Kinge*: sayth, that if the Pope as a temporal Prince should command any to weare a friers hood, to shaue his crovvne, or to fast certaine dayes (as Luther did before his apostasie) that he should obey him, but yet of frie choyse, as a temporal Prince (which yet I doubt whether Luther would do but (sayth he) if he command thee in the name of God, vnder paine of excommunication and mortal sinne: *Tum dicas, bona verba, sitis mihi propitius domine Papa, equidem quod mandatis nullus fecero. Then say, Be good in your office, be good vnto vs Sir Pope, vvhat you command I vvil not doe.* And he giueth you a reason in the next words: *To higher povvers it behoueth vs to be subiect, so long as they bind not our consciences* So that Luther is of opinion that though we must for order sake obey Princes & magistrates, yet we are frie in conscience, & can not in conscience vnder paine of sinne be bond to any temporal or Ecclesiastical authoritie. Caluin subscribeth to him in al pointes touching this matter, for hauing made a long discourse about Christian libertie, he concludeth in this maner: *Vve conclude that they are exempted from al povver of men.* And lest this might seme to haue escaped him vnaduisedly, in the next booke he repeateth it again diuerse tymes: *Our consciences haue not to doe vvith men but God only.* And again: *Paul in novvise suffereth faithful consciences to be brought into bondage of men.* Yet Caluin in the same places fearing to displease Princes, exhorteth vs to do as they shal command vs, not of any obligation because Christ (sayth he) hath fried

Luther taketh avvay obediēce to Princes.
Luther absolueth vs in cōscience from obedience to Princes.
l. 3 6. 29. 10.
So doth Caluī.
Caluī cōtrarie to himselfe.

vs from al the lawes of men but of frie choice and libertie; so not for conscience, but for common peace. In which wordes he is cleane opposit to S. Paul, vvho sayth that of necessitie we must be subiect not only for fear of displeasure, but for conscience.

Rom. 13.

The first conclusion deduced out of the former doctrin.

7. Out of this doctrin I inferre as a most euident conclusion, that in vaine Princes haue authoritie ouer their subiectes: for if the subiect may chuse whether he wil obey or no, then the prince may command and he may answer, that as he is not bond to obey because by Christian libertie he is fried from al mens lawes, so he vvil not at this tyme obey, and so in vayne shal the Prince command. Secondly I conclude out of Luthers and Caluins premises, that there are no Princes nor Superiors ouer Christians, and consequently that al Christian Princes are vsurpers, because they chalenge Superioritie and authoritie ouer Christians, vvhich in dede they haue not, and wil nedes be Princes and Superiors, vvho are but priuate men. For if they can not so command vs as to bynd vs to obedience, then are we not subiect to them, and consequently they are no Superiors: and although we may obey them, of frie choise, yet that maketh them not our Superiors, because so we may obey our equal and inferior if we wil: yet because he can not bynd vs in conscience to obey, he hath not authoritie ouer vs, and we in that we are frie are not subiect to him. And wheras they affirme, that yet we must frankelie and friely, not for conscience but for order sake, and for auoiding scandale, obey our Kinges and Princes: I demand of them, what they meane by that (must)? If they meane an obligation in conscience, then in that case lawes bynd in conscience, and their doctrin is false. If they meane only a congruitie, then neither for keping order, nor for auoiding scandal are we bond in conscience to obey Princes authoritie: whence foloweth, that to disoby Princes is no sinne, but an incongruitie, & so in conscience we are not subiect to their authoritie, and consequently they are no Snperiors. Which that it may the more plainly appeare, we must note that a Superior and subiect are correlatiues, as are the father and the sonne, the maister and the seruant: because as the father is the sonnes father, and the maister the seruātes maister, so a Superior is the subiectes superior. And as no sonne no father, no seruant no maister, so no subiect no Superior, because correlatiues are of that nature that one inferreth an other, and one can not be vvithout an other.

The second. No Princes by Luthers and Caluins doctrin.

8. Wherfore if al Christians be set at such libertie, that they are not bond in conscience to obey any Princes lawes, then are they not subiect

subiect to them, but as frie as he that hath no maister: and seing that vvhere is no subiect, there can not be any Superior, it foloweth, that if Princes can not bynd vs to obey them, we are no subiectes, they no Superiors. Is not this gentle reader, to contemne & deny al authoritie and superioritie? And consequently, is not this to open the gate vnto al mutinie and rebellion? For vvhen the subiectes are taught that by Christ and Christian faith, they are fried in conscience from men, and mens authoritie: if the Prince command, they may deny obedience: if he exact tributes, taxes, and subsidies, they may chuse whether they wil pay a peny: and if they like not his gouernment, they may by rebellion frie them selues from him, to whom in conscience and before God they are not subiect: because they are frie men, vvho in that they are frie can acknowledge no Maister.

Princes are no Princes nor Superiors by the former doctrin.

9. Who wil now blame the subiectes in France, Flanders and Germanie, for making rebellion? They did but according to their doctrin, and in refusing to obey men, they did but vse that friedom, vvhich Christ hath giuen them, which is to be subiect to none. Yea who now can do otherwise then to commend rebelles for rebellion, and discommend al loyal subiects? Because in disobeing and rebelling they shew them selues to be frie men, and acknowledge Christ their Redemer, and in obeying, they make them selues subiect to men, they vse not their libertie, and they do iniurie to Christ, as though he had not redemed them from al seruitude of men. If Princes considered wel this doctrin, they would be so farre from fauouring these new Christians, that they vvould banish them their countries. For what assurance hath a Prince of subiectes so perswaded? or how can he but alwayes stād in feare of their rebellion: who by their religion are warranted, that they can not sinne in rebellion, because they are not bond in conscience to obey any humaine authoritie.

The second Chapter shevveth hovv by their precedent doctrin, Iudges and tribunal seates are brought in contempt.

AS the Moral vertue Iustice was euer highly estemed, as the strength of al common welthes: so Iudges who are the ministers of iustice (whose office is to condēne the nocent, and absolue the innocente) were euer had in such reuerence, that their sentence was counted an oracle, and their Seate and Tribunal where they vsed to pronunce sentence, was respected as a sacred place. Wherfore in Scripture it selfe Iudges are called gods, because like litle gods, vnder God they giue sentence as his vnder Iudges, and if the sentence be iust, then what they adiudge in earth God ratifieth in heauen. This honourable conceite of Iudges and Tribunals, the doctrin of our reformers alleaged in the former chapter, diminisheth very much, yea it bringeth them into plaine contempt and condemneth them al of Tyrannie and open iniustice. For if Princes haue no authoritie as by the doctrin of these nouellantes I haue proued they haue not, then can they giue none vnto their Iudges, and consequently neither the Prince nor the Iudge hath authoritie, to giue sentence or to punish any malefactors, because if they haue no authoritie they are but priuate men. For although priuate men may *vim vi repellere, repelle force by force*, and stand in their ovvne defence, that is warde a blow, when it is offered, and strike rather then be stricken, yea kil rather then be killed, because this is but to defend them selues, and to repel iniurie: yet after that the iniurie is receiued, and quite past, they can not them selues requite the euil receiued, with a like euil, because that vvere not to defend, but to reuenge them selues, vvhich God hath reserued to him selfe, and to them to whom he hath giuen authoritie, and wil not in anywise that priuate men be their ovvne Iudges and reuengers, because that were to open the way to al outrages, much lesse vvil he permit them to punish those that haue done iniuries vnto others.

Psal. 83.

The reformers doctrin taketh avvay al Tribunals.

Rom. 12.

VVherfore if Princes haue no authoritie to command as in the last chapter, by this new doctrin I haue proued they haue not, then are they

they priuate men, and so can neither reuenge their ovvne nor others iniuries, and consequently vniustly they condemne malefactors to prison, to death, and other paines and penalties.

2. And truly if it be true vvhich Luther and Caluin and their folovvers also affirme, that no man can bynde vs in conscience by law and commandement, yea if it be good doctrin, vvhich is their doctrin, as in the next booke shal be related, that by Christ and Christian fayth we are fried from al obligation of Diuine lawes also, then the malefactor hath great scope giuen him to auoyd the Iudges sentence, although the offence be manifest. For suppose the Iudge condemne him for transgression of the Princes law, he may confesse the fault, & contemne the sentence. And first he may say, that his sentence can not bynd him in conscience to accept of it, because by Christ he is made a frie man, subiect in conscience neither to man, nor mans lavv nor sentence. Secondly he may confesse that he hath done contrarie to the kinges law, and yet plead not guiltie: alleaging that the Princes lavv can not bynd him in conscience, because he is exempted by Christ, from al humaine lavves and commandements. And then he may say that vvhere no lavv byndeth in conscience, there is no obligation, vvhere no oblihation, there is no sinne, and so he may confesse the fact and yet plead not guiltie, because he sinned not. And he may also refuse the punishement by sentence decreed, because where no sinne is, there no payne is due. Or if the Iudge condemne him for breaking Gods lavv in stealing, murdering, or such like, he may confesse likevvise the fact, and yet deny the fault, because he is so frie, that God his lavv also can not bynd him, and seing that vvhere no obligation is, there can be no fault (because euerye sinne is against some bond or obligation) he may claime absolution from the payne by the title of innocencie, because vvhere no sinne is, there no paine can be dew. Yea although he confesse that he hath sinned (which yet he nede not) in transgressing Gods law, yet he may escape the sentence by appeale. For he may say, I confesse the fault for vvhich I am condemned, but I refuse to stand to your sentence, I appeale to God, let him punish me if he wil (vvhich I knovv not how he can do iustly if I be frie from his lavves in conscience) but of your sentence I vvil not accept, and if you vrge me vvith conscience, and alleage that I am bond in conscience, to stand to your arbitrement, because you are appointed to do iustice, I chalenge Christian friedom, by which I am so frie, that in conscience I am not bond to mans law, nor sentence.

See the first chap.

Chap.

Hovv a condemned man is taught by Caluin to auoid the sentence.

The first vvay to auoid.

The second.

The third.

So sayth Luth. in c. 2. & 4. ad Gal. l. de libert. Christ. Calul. 2. Inst. c. 2.

The fourth.

3. And

3. And if this wil not serue to frie him from the sentence (as I see no reason why it should not serue) then he may defend him selfe by other opinions of the new reformers. He may say, that by Luthers and Caluins opinions, which are the Patriarches of the reformed Church, he is taught that he hath no frie wil, nor choise in any action, vvhich he doth, vvhether it be good or bad, and that therfore the Iudge is vnreasonable, cruel, and barbarous, in condemning him for theft, murder, or adultrie, vvhich was not in his power to auoyd. And as iustly might he condemne him for not flying at the Kinges commandment, as for not absteining from murder, vvhen either by anger or desire of money he was moued therunto. He might alleage also for his defence, that God moued him vnto those offences, vvhich he committed and so forcibly also, that he could not resist him, for this is Caluins opinion, as before is declared: yea he might say and haue Caluin also for his authour, that God was the author and principal agent of the theft or murder, for vvhich he is condemned, and that therfore by good consequence he can not iustly be condemned for that, in vvhich God hath more part then he hath, and to vvhich he moued him so forcibly that he could not resist. What is this then (gentle reader) but to condemne al Iudges and tribunal seates, to stoppe the Iudges mouth from pronouncing any sentence, & to loose the bridle vnto al malefactors? Who may commit what outrage they wil, because there is no tribunal vvhich can iustly condemne them, and no sentence can be pronounced against them, vvhich they may not auoid by Luthers and Caluins doctrin.

The fift. See the next booke, chap. 6 Luth. l. de seruo arb. Calu. l. 1. Inst. c. 8. l. 2. c. 2.

The sixt.

In the fift booke chap. 1.

Caluin condēneth Iudges & Tribunals.

The third Chapter shevveth hovv the former doctrin bringeth al Princes lavvs in contempt.

A Kingdom is commonly called a body, not natural but ciuil and political, vvhose head is the King, vvhose eyes are the Kinges counsaylers, vvhose body and members are the People, and vvhose soule is the Law. For as the natural body of man, so soone as the soule hath left it, looseth al vital operation, becometh gast, vgly, and deformed, deuoid of colour and beautie, and subiect to dissolu-

A kingdom is a ciuil body. Vvhose life is the Lavv.

to dissolution of al the members by putrifaction: So the body of a Kingdome destitute of law hath no reasonable action or motion, because it wanteth the rule of the law, vvhich squareth out al such operations, it looseth al beautie, because it wanteth law to set downe an vniforme order, vvhich is the beautie of al common welthes, and it tendeth to a dissolution of al the partes and members, because it is destitute of lawe, which is the soule and sinew that vniteth and knitteth these diuerse partes together. Wherfore Plato sayd that if men were lawles & destitute of lawes, they would litle differ from brute beastes; and the reason is because, as I haue sayd, without lawes there would be no reasonable operations, nor order amongst men, by vvhich especially a societie of men differeth from a heard of beastes. *l. 9. de leg.*

2. And because the old and ancient sages knew wel how much it imported to haue lawes in a common welth, they deuised meanes to moue the people to a great and high conceite of lawes, that they might the more vvillingly embrace them, and more diligently put them in execution. Zoroastes vvho prescribed lawes to the Bactrianes and Persians, made Oromasis the authour of them. Trismegistus who gaue lawes to the Ægiptians, sayd that a God enacted them: Minos, of vvhom the people of Crete receiued their lawes, told them that Iupiter was the inuentor of them. Charondas, to bring the Carthaginians to a reuerent conceit of his lawes, auouched that he was taught them by Saturnus: Licurgus who ruled the Lacedemonians fathered his lawes vvherewith he ruled them vpon Apollo: Solon who deuised lawes for the Athenians, affirmed that they proceded from Mineruas brayne: Plato who set downe lawes for the Sicilians and Magnesians protested, that Iupiter and Appollo had inspired him. Moyses; vvho promulgated the law vnto the Iewes told them (vvhich was true in dede) that God vvas the author thereof, and shewed them a table, wherin the tenne commandments were written. And Christ Iesus the author of the new Law professed, that he was sent by his Father, and that *the lavv and doctrin, vvhich he preached, vvas not his, but his fathers, vvho sent him.*

Lavv giuers fathred their lavves on God.

Christ the author of the nevv lavv.

3. And truly good reason had they to imprint in their subiectes myndes a reuerent conceite of lawes, because nothing is more soueraine, nothing more necessarie in common welths then law. Lawes are certaine conclusions of the æternal law of God and nature, they are like sinevves, vvhich bynd and knit the subiectes together, they are the life & soule of a ciuil body, they are rules and squares of humaine

Commendation of lawes.

 actions,

actions, they are bridles and curbes of humaine appetites, they are silent Magistrates. vvhich looke to good orders, they teach the subiectes their dutie, kepe them in aw and order, mainte in peace, vphold iustice, reuenge iniuries, defend the innocent, chastice the offenders, preserue good subiectes from receiuing euil, and hunder the bad from offering euil; vvithout vvhich no discipline can be kept, no good order obserued, no peace established, no iustice mainteined.

Heretikes say the lavves bynd not. 4 Now let vs see vvhat esteme the reformers make of lawes, and vvhat good counsaile their doctrin affordeth vs, to excite and stirre vs vp to the obseruation of lawes. Caluin pronounceth thus: *the lavves of men vvhether they be made by the Magistrate, or by the Church, although they be necessary to be kept, yet therfore do they not by themselues bynd in conscience.* And for an example he affirmeth, *that the Apostles neither did, nor could make any lavv in their first Councel, but only promulgated the libertie that Christ had giuen: and added, not as a lavv that byndeth, but as an admonition, that of charitie to their vveake brethren, they should abstayne from thinges offered to Idols, from strangled and from bloud.* And he repeateth, *that although it be necessary for gouernment to haue lavves humain and Ecclesiastical in the Church, yet they must not be though to bynd vs in conscience.* So that Caluin is of opinion that although the lawes of the Church and of Princes, & magistrates ought to be kept, for order sake, or for feare of offence and scandal, yet they bind vs not in conscience. And he giueth his reason: *because* (sayth he) *if vve once grant, that men can bynd our consciences by their vvil and lavv, Christ loseth the thankes for his so great liberalitie,* (to wit in redeming vs from the bondage of the law) *and our consciences lose their profit.* The same is Luthers opinion, as is related before in the first Chapter of this booke.

l. 4 Inst c. 10. 27.

Act. 15.

par. 27.

l. 5. c. 19 sect. 14.

5. And therfore I wil not stand now to refute this paradox, partly because I haue proued already that we are bond in conscience to obey al lawful superiors, and consequently that their lawes do bynd our consciences: partly because the absurde sequele of this doctrin, vvhich by and by shal appeare, sufficiently confuteth it: neither wil I repeate vvhich I haue already declared, that obligation of lawes is nothing repugnant to Christian libertie, because we are not therfore sayd to be fried from the yoke of the law, because the law bindeth vs not, but because we are fried from the old law, and haue receiued grace from Christ, to fulfil the new law, so that it can no more tyranize ouer vs, in commanding more then we are able to performe. I wil therfore draw towards my conclusion, vvhich is that the alleaged doctrin of

Chap 1.

In the 3. booke chap. 2. Hovv vve are fried from the lavv.

Caluin

Caluin bringeth al lawes in contempt, and looseth the bridle to al malefactors.

6. And first of al I must tel Ihon Caluin that in denying lavves to bynd in conscience he taketh away al lawes, because it is the essence of a lavv to be able to bynd the subiect, and in this only it differeth from counsaile, exhortation, and admonition. Secondly Caluin by this doctrin abrogateth al promises, and contractes, euen of matrimonie, which are particular lawes. And therfore, if to say that lawes bynd in conscience, be to despoile Christ of the honour of a Redemer, and man of Christian libertie, then is it also iniurious to Christ and mans libertie, to be bond in conscience to kepe promises, and to obserue contractes, even with wiues. Thirdly the commandements also of parentes, and maisters are particular lawes, and consequently we are not bond in conscience to obey our maisters, or parentes, and so one of the tenne commandements must be blotted out, because if we be not bond to obey our parentes, which is one of the chiefest honours we can giue them, we are not bond to honour our parentes. Yea, by this doctrin it folovveth that the tenne commandementes bynd vs not in conscience: which though our aduersaries wil not stick to grant, as we shal see in the next booke, yet vvho seeth not vvith vvhat absurditie?

The first illation.

The second.

The third.

The fourth.

See the fifte booke chap. 3. and the 7.

7. Lastly, at the least, which yet is not the least absurditie, this doctrin bringeth al lawes in contempt. For as the wild and vmbroken colt litle careth, if you should tye him with heares or threedes, because he knoweth that such bandes are not of force to hold him: so when men are once perswaded that lawes of Princes bynd them not in conscience, they wil make litle scruple to transgres them, and so lawes are brought into contempt. And although feare of the penaltie or punishement, which the law layth on them, may make them sometymes to kepe them, for feare of punishement, yet when they can escape the ministers of iustice eyes, or handes, or auoid by subtile shift, or open force, the payne of the law, they wil make no scruple of transgressing the law. For why should they make conscience of that which toucheth not conscience?

a similitude.

8. But Caluin wil say, that they ought notwithstanding to kepe lawes for order sake, and for auoiding of offence. But then I aske Caluin what he meaneth, when he sayth that they ought to kepe the law? either he meaneth by those wordes an obligation in conscience, vnder payne of sinne, and then it foloweth (which Caluin wil not

grant)

grant) that lawes bynd in conscience: or else he meaneth only a congruitie or decencie, and then it foloweth stil that lavves are brought in contempt. For if once a man be perswaded, that it is only conuenient but not necessarie to kepe the law, he nedeth to make no scruple to transgres the lavv, because the transgression is no sinne, but only an incongruitie.

Caluin giueth libertie to al Rebelles.

9. And so if this doctrin be true, men wil not care a straw for the Princes lavves. Rebellious subiectes, mutinous souldiars, stubborne children, crooked seruantes, may be disobedient by Caluin because no law, nor commandement can bynd them in conscience to loyal obedience. And then lawes lose their force, authoritie is not to be esteemed, rebellion and mutinie are allowed, the way is open to al malefectors, al outrages are lawful, because where no law bindeth, no sinne can be committed, no man is subiect, euery man is lavvles, and as frie as the king, subiect to no lavv nor authoritie of God or man. VVhat securitie hath a Prince amongst such lavvles subiects? How can he choose but feare reuolt and rebellion of those, vvho are persvvaded by religion, that no lavv can bynd them in conscience, to order and obedience? Is this religion like to be of God, vvhich is so opposit to humaine authoritie, vvhich is of God: yea vvhich also despoileth God of al authoritie to command his creatures? If our noble Prince and graue Counsellers in England considered wel this doctrin, then certes the first Parlament they called, should be to banish this lavvles and licentious Religion, which bringeth lawes in contempt, Princes in danger, and openeth the gap to outrages of malefactors.

litle securitie for a prince giuen by this doctrin.

Rom. 13.

⁂

The

The fourth Chapter shevveth hovv according to their doctrin, no Prince can rely on his subiects, no subiects on their Prince, nor on felovv subiects, and consequenly al Societie, and ciuil conuersation is taken avvay.

AN, as I haue vpon an other occasion declared, is of nature bent and inclined to company and conuersation in some Societie or other: vvhere if he be a Superior he ruleth, if he be an inferior he is ruled, and learneth to comply with his felowe subiects. And of these three parts consisteth ciuil conuersation. For if the Prince rule not as he should do, or the inferior obey not his superior, or comply not with his felow subiect as he ought to do, gouernment degenerateth into tyranne, obedience turneth to rebellion, and conuersation to ciuil dissension. *Man ciuile.* *3. partes of ciuil societie.*

2. These three partes are mainteined by one thing, vvhich is trust or confidence of one in an other. For seing that the Prince can not do al alone, but must expect aide & assistance of his subiects, he shal neuer rule wel vnles he may rely vpon the fidelitie and correspondence of his subiects. And if the subiect put not a confidence in his Superior, as in one that tendreth the common good of al, and particular of euery one, he wil neuer obey willingly, nor rely on him securely, but shal euer liue in feare and distrust of him. And if one subiect trust not an other, euerie one shal liue in suspicion of an other, and so mens words wilbe taken but for wind, promises contractes and bargaines wil not hold assuredly, frendship breaketh, familiaritie decaieth, and conuersation is ruined. For who wil make bargaines, or strike a league of frendship, or familiaritie with them, on whose secrecie, fidelitie, and other correspondence he hath not any probable assurance, because he putteth no trust nor confidence in them: rather hath he cause to fly al company, and like a *Misanthropos* an hater of men, to liue in woods and wildernes, then in townes cities and societies. Now, if the reformers doctrin (which teacheth that lawes bynd not in conscience) may goe for currant, the three partes of ciuil conuersation are taken *Vvhich are maintai ned by Confidēce.* *Calu. l. 4. Inst. c. 10. Luth. in c. 2. Gal.*

 away,

away, and so Societies must breake vp, and euerie one must liue alone, like an Anachorite or Heremite, because in company is no securitie, vvhere according to this doctrin, neither the Prince can rely, on his subiects, nor they on him, nor one subiect on an other.

See the first booke 3. chap.

3. And to begin with the Prince, vvhat confidence can he put in his subiects, who are persvvaded in religion, that neither his lawes can bynd them to obedience, nor the law of God or nature hinder them from rebellion, mutinie, or other outrages? hath he not iust cause thus to discourse with him selfe? This people is persvvaded by religion, that no law byndeth them in conscience, and consequently they make no scruple, nor conscience of Rebellion, for vvhere no law byndeth in conscience, there no conscience is to be made: I must therfore stand continually on my gard, and rely vpon no subiects fidelitie. And how shal I stand on my garde, vvhen euen my garde according to Caluins opinion, is bond by no law, to be true and faithful vnto me. And so he shal liue alwayes in feare of his subiects.

The prince can not rely on Caluinist fidelitie.

4. And on the otherside, vvhat confidence can the subiects haue in their Prince? For if no law bynd him in conscience, he hauing al in his owne hands, may vse vvhat extorsion and tyrannie he pleaseth. For vvhat should withhold him from it? feare of god? God can not iustly punish vvhere no lawes bynd in conscience, and so he is not to be feared. Conscience? Where no lawe byndeth, conscience nedeth to make no scruple. Vvhy then is not al lawful for the Prince vvhich he liketh? And so the subiect shal euer haue his Superior in suspicion.

Subiects by Caluins doctrin must not trust their princes.

5. And vvhat good felowship, amitie, or conuersation can there be amongst the subiectes, vvho must nedes, by this doctrin liue in a continual feare and distrust one of an other, because no man is bond to kepe touch and correspondence vvith an other. For if lawes bynd not, promises and contractes, not only in lending and borowing, buying and selling, but also in marying, are not of force to bynd our consciences, because they are but particular lawes. or if they are more forcible in bynding then lawes, then according to Caluin, Christ is no perfect Redemer, because he hath not fried vs from the bondage of promises, & bargaines, which notwithstanding are no lawes of Princes, but particular lawes of particular men, made betwixt man and man, for more assured conuersation. And so the wife may iustly feare lest her husband when he is weary of her, or liketh better of an other, may shake her of, and diuorse him selfe from her. For why may he not? If lawes of Princes bynd not in conscience, then the contract of

Nor one another.

Nor the vvife her husband.

matrimo-

matrimonie (which according to Caluin is but a particular law & no Sacrament) can take no hold on consciēce, & so by the libertie vvhich Caluin giueth him, to be frie in cōscience from al lawes, he may leaue his wife, as often as he wil, and as often take an other. And if his wife compl aine that he kepeth not promise with her: he may answer her easily, that if he be not bond in conscience to keepe Gods lawe, he is not bond to kepe the law of matrimonie; vvhich is but a particular law. And if she reply that God also commandeth vs to kepe this particular law and contract, he may tel her that he confesseth it to be true, but Caluin hath assured him that Christ hath fried him in conscience, from al obligation of al lawes, whether they be humaine or diuine: and so he is not bond to kepe the law of matrimonie: and therfore chalenging his libertie, he may leaue his wife as lawfully and as friely, as if he had neuer made her promise, because no law, much lesse anye promise, is able to bynd in conscience.

6. In like maner let merchantes who vse to lend money, or to sel of trust and credit, looke better about them, then hitherto they haue doone. For if no lawes bind in conscience, then contractes also bynd not, & so their debters may chalenge the libertie, which Caluin hath giuen them, vvhich is not to be bond in conscience to pay them a peny. We must henceforth also take hede not only of knowen theeues and murderers, but of them also that go for honest men, yea euen of our neerest and dearest freinds: for vvhat should withhold them, from doing vs a mischiefe, if no law neither of God, nor man, nor nature, bynd them in conscience? And so the parentes may distrust their children, and the children their parentès, because according to Caluins opinion, the one is not bond to the other, neither by the law of God nor nature. The husband must liue alwayes in iealousie of his vvife, and she of him, because the lavv of matrimonie according to this opinion, bindeth not one partie in conscience, to kepe touch vvith the other.

Merchants by Caluins opinion must trust no debters.

Nor the parēts their children.

Nor the husband his vvife.

7. And so by this doctrin no man in any thing can trust or rely on an other, but al must liue in feare, iealousie, and suspicion of others: and so they must forsake societies and flye to mountaines, and trust rather to beasts, vvhom nature vvithholdeth from iniuries, then vnto men, vvhom, according to Caluins doctrin, no lavv, & consequently no conscience stayeth, or vvitholdeth from mischief. By this let the reader take a scantling of this doctrin, & iudge vvhether it be like to be of God, that is so opposit to al societie, vvhich is of God.

Societie ruined by Caluin.

THE

THE SEVENTH BOOKE CONTAINETH A SVRVEY OF THE NEVV DOCTRIN CONCERNING MANERS, IN which is declared, hovv by diuers of their opinions they open the gappe vnto al vice.

The first Chapter shevveth hovv the reformers take avvay hope of heauen and feare of hel, and consequently open the gap to al vice.

TWo thinges there are which as firme and constant pillers do vphold and sustaine al common welthes from falling, and præserue wel ordered societies from dissoluing: to wit, hope of reward, and feare of punishment. Hope like a spurre pricketh and eggeth onvvard vnto vertue, feare pulleth backe from vice: hope inciteth vs to obserue the law, feare maketh vs not to transgresse the law. VVherfore Solon the graue lawgiuer, vvas vvont to say, that payne and revvard are the things, which kepe al Societies in avv and order. And wel in dede might he say so, for take away hope of reward, & men wilbe slouthful and sluggish in the exercise of vertue, and laudable actions: and take away feare of punishment, and the euil disposed vvil be as forward in attempting of theftes, murders, treasons, treacheries, and whatsoeuer villanies.

Hope and feare are stayes of common welthes.

Solons saying.

Hope and feare necessary in the church.

2. These tvvo things so necessarie in a common welth, Christ would not haue to be wanting in his Church, which is the best ordered

ordered common wealth that euer was on earth, and therfore he proposeth vnto vs a heauen to hope for, & an hel to feare; the one to stirre vs vp to al vertuous actions, the other to deterre vs from al wicked attempts. For although vertue (as the Philosopher sayth) be so amiable & so beseeming mans reasonable nature, that if there were no heauen nor no other reward of vertue, but vertue, yet we should imbrace it for it selfe, & liue chastly for the loue of chastitie, iustly for the loue of iustice, and temperatly for the loue of temperance: and although vice be a thing so detestable, filthie, abominable, and repugnant to the reasonable part of man, that if there were no hel nor punishment for it, yet we should detest it for it selfe, & flye it for the dishonestie vvhich it implyeth: yet on the one side, because vertue is repugnant to sensualitie, & placed amid many difficulties, like a rose amongst thornes, man would neuer long liue vertuously, if there were no other reward for vertuous actions, then vertues honestie: and on the other side, vice is so pleasing to sensualitie, and so sutable to our corrupt nature, that if there were no other punishment to deterre men from it, then the dishonestie, vvhich is ioyned with it, few or none vvould flye and eschew it. Wherfore God hath proposed a heauen to allure vs to vertue, and a hel to deterre vs from vice: *Come* (sayth Christ to the good, vvhose reward is heauen) *yee blessed of my Father, enioye the Kingdom præpared for you, from the beginning of the vvorld.* And in terrible words he thundreth out the sentence against the reprobate, vvhose punishement is the fier of hel: *Depart from me yee accursed into euerlasting fier, vvhich is præpared for the deuil and his angels.*

Heauen and Hel.

The reason.

Th. 1.2. q. 11. art. 2.

vertue is a rose amidst thornes.

Mat. 25.

Heauen allureth.

Ibidem.

Hel terrifieth.

3. And that this heauen, and the hope of it, may the more forcibly moue to good life, and obseruation of the commandmentes, the holy Scripture setteth it forth with al the glorious titles in the vvorld, and euen with the names of those things vvhich men most desire: If you desire life, heauen is called *æternal life.* If you couet rest, heauen is a repose after labour. If light be grateful, heauen is a perpetual light shining in the faces of the Saincts. If mariage like you, heauen is a perpetual mariage. If pleasure please you, heauen is a riuer of pleasure. If banquetting be thy desire, heauen is a supper & a great supper, where with Angels we shal by fruition and cleare vision, satiate our selues in feeding vpon the Diuinitie: If home be grateful vnto thee, heauen is thy countrie, from vvhence according to thy soule thou fetchest thy race and origin, and whither thou trauelest so long as in this vvorld thou liuest, vvhich is but a way or Inne, no home nor mansion place.

Heauẽs titles.

Io. 6 & 10.

Apoc. 4.

Sap. 18.

Apoc. 22.

Luc. 12.

Psal. 15.

Luc. 14.

Psal. 130.

If a Paradiſe, vvhoſe name importeth a place of al honeſt pleaſure and felicitie, delighteth, heauen is called ſo, and vvas by Chriſt him ſelfe
Luc. 23. promiſed to the good theefe by no other name. Briefly if thou deſire a
Mat. 20. reward of al thy paines and trauels, heauen is the common wage of al
1. Cor. 9. Gods ſeruants, a gole to runne at, and a crowne to fight for.

Hels names. 4. In like maner to make vs to refrain from ſinne for feare of hel,
Vide Bel to. 1. holy Scripture giueth hel very terrible names, and painteth it forth in
l. 4 de Chriſto. terrible formes. It is called in Greeke and Latin by names vvhich ſig-
c. 10. & Au- nifie a lowe and deepe place vnder the ground, in Hebrew by a name
thorem Reſol. vvhich ſignifieth a great goulfe. The Prophet Malachie calleth it a
Angl. l. 1. p. 1. fornace, for the kindling of vvhich the vvicked muſt be the ſtraw and
Mal. c. 4. fewel. S. Ihon calleth it the lake of Gods ire, becauſe the anger of God
Apoc. 14. 19. is as it were al gathered to that place, and there eſpecially is manifeſted in thoſe exceeding torments, yea he termeth it alſo a ſtanding poole, repleniſhed with fier & brimſton. Chriſt him ſelfe giueth it the name
Mat. 22. of *vtter darkenes, vvhere ſhal be vveeping and gnaſhing of teeth.* Iob ſayth that in that place *is no order, but ſempiternal horror.* And vvhy doth Scripture ſo liuely ſet forth theſe two things, heauen and hel, but becauſe God the author of Scripture, vvould haue vs hope for the one, and feare the other, knowing that nothing beareth greater ſway in the rule and good diſcipline of a common welth, then hope of reward, and feare of puniſhment.

The force of hope. 5. For if the hope of temporal honors, fame, and riches giueth ſuch courage to the harts of men, that they wil runne through fier and water for the attaining of the ſame; how ſhal the hope of heauen and the immortal crownes, vvhich there are layed vp for vs in ſtore, incite
Aug. l. 4. de vs and egge vs forward vnto al laudable actions? If Mutius could haue
ciuit. c. 20. the courage to hold his hand in the fier for hope of tẽporal renowme and glorie for ſuch fortitude: vvhat fiers and waters, heat and cold, ſhal not a Chriſtian, armed with hope of heauen, be able to endure couragiouſly? Shal the ſouldiar runne through the pikes & paſſe by the cannon mouth, for hope of a ſpoile or victorie, & ſhal not Chriſtians de-
The force of feare. uoure al difficulties for hope of heauen? And looke how much hope eggeth forward to laudable actions, ſo much and no leſſe doth feare reſtraine vs from euil, and is no leſſe neceſſarie to bridle the licentious, then hope to animate the vertuous. Wherefore the ancient ſo eſteemed feare, that the citie of Spartha made it a God, and dedicated a Temple vnto it, as to the preſeruer of their common welth.

6. But becauſe there are diuers kindes of feare, it ſhal be neceſſarie

to diſtinto distinguish them, that we may see which is that feare, which is so commendable. First therfore there is a wordly and humain feare, which is conceiued for some temporal euil, or humaine respect, and this sometymes is good, and sometymes also bad. As for example, if for feare of the princes displeasure, or torment, or death which he threateneth, we offend God in transgressing his law, or doing against our conscieuce, this feare is euil, and no lesse euil then the sinne of which it is the cause. This feare made S. Peter to deny his Maister: which also our Sauiour forbiddeth saying: *feare not them who kil the body*, that is, offend not God for feare of them, that can only kil the body, but rather feare God who can cast both body and soule in to the fier of hel. But if for feare of the magistrate we abstaine from sinne, this feare is not euil, and therfore S. Paul biddeth vs feare the magistrate, because (sayth he) *not without cause he caryeth the sword, for he is the minister of God*. The second feare is called a reuerential feare, which proceedeth from a high conceite of the Diuine Maiestie, and remaineth (as Dauid sayth) and that for euer also, euen in the blessed. For although they be assured that they shal neuer suffer any euil, and therfore feare no euil at Gods hands: yet when they behold the soueraigne Maiestie of God, who punisheth the damned, & could annihilate the blessed if he would, they conceiue a great reuerence, which is called reuerential feare, much like as children who are assured that their father wil not touch them, yet conceiue a reuerential feare at the very sight of him, especially if they see him sharpe and seuere with his seruants. The third feare is called filial or childrens feare, which maketh vs afrayed to sinne, not for feare of punishment, but for feare of offending; and this feare they haue who though they were sure neuer to suffer punishment, neither in this life nor the next, yet would not commit a sinne because it is an offence of God Which feare is called filial, because good children are afrayed to do any thing, which shal offend their parentes, though they were sure they should not be punished. Of which feare S. Austin discoursing sayth, that otherwise doth the adulteresse feare her husband, otherwise the chaste spouse: she feareth lest he come and punish, but the other feareth lest he be offended and forsake her. The fourth is called seruile feare, which maketh vs to abstaine from sinne, for feare of hel and damnation: which is called seruile, because it is proper to seruants to do their dutie for feare of punishment. And this feare in expresse termes the reformers condemne as I shal relate: the other feares then do they

Humain feare.

Mat. 26. c. 10.

Rom. 15.

Th. 2. 2. q. 19.

Psal. 18.

Reuerential feare.

Filial feare.

In Psal. 18.

Seruile feare.

disalowveth. But lest I may seeme to charge them with more then they say, I wil make them speake, in their owne wordes, their opinion of hope and feare.

7. And first of Hope Caluin sayth plainly, that God is not delighted with that obedience, which the hope of reward in heauen beateth out of vs: *for God* sayth he, *loueth a chearful giuer, and forbiddeth any thing to be giuen as it vvere of heauines or necessitie.* So that according to Caluin, it is sinne to giue almes or to fulfil the commandements for hope of revvard in heauen. But Caluins reason is as bad as his doctrin. For he proueth it to be vnlawful to be obedient to God, for hope of revvard, because that is to giue God his dew with heauines: and yet we see that hope is so farre from making vs to do thinges heauily, and with an euil wil, that it encourageth vs, and pricketh vs forward vvith a vvilling mynd, as is already proued, and experience may vvitnes.

l.3. Inst. c. 15. par. 1.

in Antid. Sess. 6. Can. 31.

Caluin condēneth hope of heauen.

8. And as for feare of hel, Luther condemneth it euen vnto hel, saying that it maketh a man an hypocrite and a greater sinner. And as concerning the other kindes of feare, their doctrin in a maner abolisheth them al. They affirme as is before mentioned, that no lavves bynd in conscience: whence folow these conclusions. First that neither Princes nor Iudges haue authoritie to condemne vs to any paine, as is before proued, because where no law byndeth, no Prince can iustly punish the transgression, and so humaine feare is taken away. Secondly this doctrin abolisheth al filial feare: for where no law byndeth in conscience, no sinne can be committed, and so we need not to feare theftes and murders, for feare of offending God, because where no sinne is, no offence is to be feared. Reuerential feare also they abandone, because as is before proued, in denying lavves to bynd they take away al authoritie euen from God, and where no authoritie is, no reuerence is devv.

a.6. apud Roff & ser 3 pœn.

Luther condēneth feare of Hel.

They take avvay feare of lavves and magistrates.

They take avvay filial feare.

Yea reuerētial feare also.

9. As for seruile feare, they condemne it in expresse termes. And Luthers wordes we haue heard already: let vs heare also Caluin speake. He affirmeth that a sinner can not be iust, vnles he beleue assuredly that he is elect, prædestinate and vndoubtedly to be saued: whence folovveth that no man must feare hel, yea that no man can feare hel, and retaine his fayth. For if he be by fayth sure of saluation, he can not feare hel and damnation, because he is as assured of escaping hel, as of attaning heauen, & no man can feare that euil which he is assured to escape. As for exāple, no man feareth lest the heauens fal vpon him

l.3. Inst. c. 26. par. 6. 7. 8.

Seruile feare also.

Feare of Hel standeth not vvith Caluins faith.

him. Or if Caluin feare hel, he looseth his faith, because he is not assured to escape hel, and to attaine to heauen. And because Caluin savv vvel ynough that feare of hel is taken avvay by this his doctrin; he checketh S. Gregorie the great, saying that *he teacheth pestilently* vvhen he sayth in a certain homelie: that *vve knovv only our calling, but are vncertain of our election:* vvherby (sayth Caluin) he moueth al men to feare and trembling, because vve knovv vvhat vve be to day, but vvhat vve shal be, vve knovv not. Luther also as he holdeth the same opinion of assurednes of saluation, so he biddeth vs to take hede lest vve feare hel or iudgement, because that vvere to loose our fayth. These are his vvords: *VVherfore if thou be a sinner as verily vve al are, do not propose vnto thy selfe Christ as a Iudge in a rayn-bovve, for then thou vvill be afrayed and despaire, but apprehend the definition of Christ, that he is no exactor of the lavv, but a propitiator.* So that Luther thinketh that Christ vvil exacte no lavv at the handes of a faithful man, and therfore he nedeth not to feare hel, in vvhich transgressors of the lavv are punished. Wherfore as they take avvay al hope of revvard, so they take avvay al feare, and especially the feare of hel, vvhich is the greatest bridle that is, to restraine men from sinne.

Hom. 38. in Mat euang.

Luther and Caluin vvil not haue men feare Hel.

in to. 2. c. 1. ad Gal.

Luthers counsel.

10 But first I wil aske them, why holie Scripture setteth forth heauen and hel with such names and titles, if it be a sinne to hope for the one, or to feare the other? Truly if it be sinne, then hath God in setting forth heauen and hel so liuely, layed baytes to catch vs, and to allure vs to sinne. And why then doth Scripture in so many places command vs to hope, and to feare? And how are those two thinges vnlawful, vvhich are so necessarie in al common welthes? Why may the plowghman trauel al the day in hope of his wages, the husbandman sow his sede in hope of a haruest, the soldiar folow the warres in hope of honour, and yet a Christian man may not fulfil the commandementes in hope of a reward in heauen? For if it be lawful to hope for heauen, vvhy is it not lawful also to giue almes in hope of heauen, as Dauid inclined his hart to *keepe the lavv for revvard and retribution*? They answer that we must serue God purely for his loue and glorie, but not for reward. True, that must be the principal end, but yet thence it followeth not, but that we may also serue for reward, as for a secondarie end and motiue. But say they, he that serueth for reward, would not serue God if reward were not, vvhich argueth an euil mynd. I answer that al men are not so affected. And if hope of heauen be of that force as to moue them to kepe the law, why may it not also

Hope & feare

Psal. 118.

2. fond answers reiected

 be suffi-

be sufficient to moue them to lay aside that euil affection, vvhich is also against the law: In like manner if I may lawfully feare death and other euils of the body, why may I not feare hel, vvhich is the greatest punishement that is both of soule and body? and if I may feare hel, why may I not absteine from sinne or fulfil the law, for feare of hel? They say, the reason is, because he that fulfilleth the law for feare of hel, vvould sinne with al his hart, if hel were not. Be it so: yet this argueth feare to be good rather then euil, because it is a cause why we absteine at least from the outward act of sinne: and if the mynd be euil disposed, that procedeth not from the feare of hel, but from an euil disposition. Yea if feare of hel be sufficient to kepe vs frō the act of sinne, it is sufficient also to restraine vs from the euil desire of the mynd, because against that also hel is prepared.

A difference betvvixt feare of hel & feare of other paines

11. And in this is a plaine difference betwixt feare of hel and temporal punishments: because Princes by temporal paines punish only the outward act, of which only they can iudge; and therfore the theefe may absteine from theft for feare of hanging, and yet haue an inward desire to steale: but God punisheth in hel not only outward act, but also the inward affection and desire of sinne: and therfore, if feare of hel kepe a man from theft, it wil restraine him also from the desire. And consequently feare of hel can not be il, but rather good, vvhich is no cause of il, but rather a cause why we absteine from euil. And although some peraduenture, yea and without peraduenture, vvould sinne and neglect the commandements, if hope of heauen and feare of hel were not, yet that is no argument that therin they sinne, if they haue no present il affection or consent to sinne. For so many vvould sinne if they should liue longer, or if they had this or that ocasion, or if God gaue them not this and that grace, and yet, that they vvould sinne, is no sinne, if they haue no present affection or desire to sinne. Yea this is an argument that hope of heauen and feare of hel are very laudable and good, because they are bridles to restraine men from sinning. Wherfore to draw nere a conclusion, vvhich is, that our Reformers in taking away hope of heauen and feare of hel, open the dore to al vice: I report me to the indifferent reader, how the Church is like to flourish in vertue without hope of heauen, and feare of hel, seing that as is proued, no commonwelth can enioy temporal and ciuil peace and discipline without them.

12 Take away hope of heauen, & take away prayer, almes deeds, erecting of Churches, founding of Colleges and hospitals: then fasting and

sting and penance, vvorkes of iustice, mercy and charitie, wil decay: in briefe men wil be negligent, and slouthful in exercise of vertue and obseruation of the law. For vvho wil runne that seeth no gole? vvho vvil fight that hopeth for no victorie? who wil vvorke that looketh for no rewarde. I know that the very loue of God, yea of vertue should moue vs to good, but yet so dul we are, and so backward, that these motiues litle moue vs, and so natural vnto vs it is, to be moued with hope of reward, that if men hoped not for heauen, few vvould striue to ouercome their passions, and the difficultie in exercise of vertue, and obseruation of the commandements. *Vvhat foloweth vvhen hope is taken avvay.*

13. Likewise if feare be the keper, preseruer, and conseruer of al cōmonwelthes, how shal we imagin that the Church of God can stand vvithout it? I grant that sinne is so fowle a thing, that euen for the hatred of sinne, we should abandone sinne, but seing that sinne is so agreable to our corrupt nature, & neuer appeareth in her owne likenes, but is alwayes masked and disguised with a shew of commoditie, pleasure, or profit; few there are who vvould absteine from sinne for the turpitude therof and dishonestie vvhich it implyeth. For vvhat should restraine a man from sinne? shame of the vvorld? I suppose he hath a secret place. Feare of temporal punishment? I supose the fault be vnknowen? Feare of God? VVho wil feare God that feareth not hel, vvhich he hath prepared? *The necessitie of feare of hel.* VVherfore if notwithstanding the hope of heauen and feare of hel (vvhich for al Caluins heresie possesseth the hartes of most men) yet so few liue vprightly and so many go awry, vvhat vvould they do, if hope of heauen, and feare of hel were quite rooted out of their myndes? Truly the narrow path of vertue vvould be ouergrowne with vveeds, for vvant of treading, and the broad way of vice vvould become so smoth, that none vvould imbrace vertue, al vvould tumble head-longe into the depth of vice, and pleasure: and so the way to vertue vvould be hedged vp, & the gate and vvay to vice would alwayes lie open, heauen vvould be a place inaccessible, and hel our common home. *The conclusion.*

***

The

The second Chapter shevveth hovv in teaching that only faith iustifieth, they open the vvay to al vice.

SATAN the common enemy of mankind, knowing hovv easily he might entise and allure vs to sinne (to vvhich thing his malicious mynd is alvvayes bent & inclined) if he could persvvade the vvorld, that only faith sufficeth for mans iustification; hath long since gone about to beate this doctrin into mens heades, and to bevvitch their vnderstandings vvith it. And because he knoweth that when he speaketh in his owne person and likenes, he findeth litle audience, he hath gone about, and that euen in the Apostles tyme, by certaine of his ministers, who went vnder the name of Christians, to intrude vpon vs this his pestilent doctrin. For they not vnderstanding (as S. Peter sayth) what S. Paul sayd, would make him speake as fooles make belles to sound, to wit, as they imagined: and so auouched that only faith vvas sufficient to iustification and saluation, and that S. Paul so warranted vs. Wherfore S. Austin affirmeth that S. Peter, S. Ihon, S. Iames, and S. Iude wrote their Epistles to refel and refute this heresie, and to expound S Paules meaning. After these companions, Simon Magus imbraced the same opinion, and after him Eunomius, who bragged that the faith which they preached, vvas sufficient to saue their folovvers, vvhat sinnes soeuer they committed.

2. Pet. 1.

l. de fide & operibus.

2. This damnable heresie long since dead in the mynds of men, & buried also in hel, Luther not by miracle, but mere madnes hath called to life again: who in diuers places affirmeth that only faith iustifieth, before, and without charitie and good workes. And because he saw that in thus saying, he semed to open the way to al wickednes, he addeth an other heresie, to wit, that true faith and good workes can not be seuered, and therfore (sayth he) although only faith iustifie, yet that argueth not that good workes are not necessary, because a true faith alwayes bringeth with it good vvorkes. Caluin ioyneth vvith Luther in this opinion, affirming that faith only iustifieth, and that good workes are only signes and effectes of this faith. Yea Luther and he both,

Ar. 10. 18. l. de Christiana libertate. Com. in c. 2. Gal.

The solafidians opinion.

l. 3. c. 14 par. 17. c. 18 par. 8

he both, auouch, as shal be afterwards declared, that good vvorkes are so farre from iustifying, that they are al mortal sinnes, and by faith only obteyne this fauour of God, as not to be reputed nor imputed to the faithful man. And this faith (sayth Caluin) iustifieth not a vvorke of ours, because vvhatsoeuer procedeth from our corrupt nature, he counteth sinne, but as it is an instrument by which we apprehend Christs iustice, & apply it to our selues, and make it so our owne, that no sinne is imputed vnto vs. These are his words: *The povver of iustifying, vvhich faith hath, consisteth not in the vvorthines of the vvorke: our iustification standeth vpon the only mercie of God, and the deseruing or merit of Christ, vvhich iustification vvhen faith taketh hold on, it is sayd to iustifie*: So that faith also according to Caluin, is a sinne, because it is a kind of vvorke of ours, yet it iustifieth, because it apprehendeth Christs iustice, and so by a sinne as by an instrument vvhich apprehendeth Christs iustice, we are made or rather reputed iust.

Caluin sayth that only faith iustifieth, and yet that it is a sinne.

3. But before I come to inferre my intẽded conclusion out of this doctrin, I wil be so bold as to aske them, vvhere they read in Scripture that only faith iustifieth? S. Paul (say they) affirmeth *that a man is iustified by faith*: True, but he sayth not, by only faith; neither doth any place of Scripture auouch so much. Wherfore Luther seing that this place was not plain inough to proue, that only faith iustifieth, in his Germaine translation, he foysted in (only) into the text, making S. Paul to say: *vve thinke a man to be iustified by faith only.* And being warned of this his corruption of scripture by a certain freind of his, he answered, that that vvas the meaning: vvherin yet he shewed him self a false translator, vvhose office is to translate faithfully as the words lye, and not as he vvould haue them interpreted, for that is the office of an interpretor: and if this be lawful for Luther, heretiques haue scope inough to make scriptures speake, as they vvil imagin that they should speake. But Luther wil say that Sainct Paul sayth that a man is iustified by fayth, and not by the vvorks of the law, vhich is al one as if he had sayd, that a man is iustified by faith only, and not by good vvorks. But to this I answere that if Sainct Paul had sayd, that a man is iust by faith and not by vvorks, adding no more, then Luther had had some argument; but he sayth not so, but only, that a man is iust by faith and not by the vvorks of the law, excluding only the Iudaical Sacramentes and ceremonies, vvhich he calleth vvorks of the lavv: and vvhen in other places he excludeth vvorks, he meaneth the selfe same vvorks, or else those vvorks

Rom. 3.

Luth. corrupteth the text, to proue that only faith iustifieth.

In Resp. ad duos art. ad amicum.

Ex Bel to 3 l. 1 de iust. c. 16.

Luth answer to his freinds admonition.

His obiection answered.

Vvhat vvorks S. Paul excludeth.

Rom. 6.

Gal. 2. 3.

vvhich proceed not from faith and grace, such as were the vvorkes of the Gentils.

How faith iustifieth. 4. Neither is faith sayd to iustifie, because that only iustifieth, but because it is the beginning, and ground vvorke of iustification, or because it concurreth to iustification, or because by that faith which iustifieth, is vnderstood, not a naked faith but a faith ioyned with charitie & good vvorkes, such as S. Paul speaketh of, vvhen writing to the
Gal. 5. Galathians, he excludeth the workes of the law, saying that *in Christ Iesu neither Circumcision is of any vvorth, nor the Prepuce, but faith vvhich vvorketh by charitie.* Wherfore S. Paul is so farre from thinking that only fayth iu-
1. Cor. 13. stifieth, that he auoucheth that if he *had al the faith in the vvorld & so great a faith that he could moue mountaines, yet if he had not charitie, he vvere nothing.* And if Luther and Caluin, because scripture sometymes sayth, that faith iustifieth, wil therfore inferre, that faith only iustifieth: then be-
Rom. 8. cause scripture saith that *by hope vve are saued,* & that *blessed is the man that*
Psal. 83. *hopeth in God,* I wil inferre that only hope iustifieth: and because scrip-
Psal. 111. ture also affirmeth that *the man is happie that feareth our lord,* I wil conclude that feare only iustifieth. Or if they wil answere that hope and feare are sayd to iustifie, and to make man happie, because they dispose or concurre to iustification and happines, the same I wil say of faith, to wit, that it is sayd to iustifie, not because it only iustifieth, but because it disposeth with charitie, it concurreth to our iustification. For
Iustification ascribed to charitie especially. to charitie also is attributed our iustification, and more then vnto faith. For as Christ told S. Marie Magdalen, that her faith had saued her, so he sayd that *many sinnes vvere forgiuen her, because she loued much*: and Scripture attributeth those effects to charitie, vvhich are necessarilie
Luc. 7. linked with iustification. As for example, charitie is called *the fulnes of*
Mat. 22. *the lavv,* the *end of the lavv,* the *obseruation of the lavv,* and the *bond or knot of*
Rom. 13. Col. 3 *perfection.* Charitie also is sayd to make vs *children of God,* by it the *holy*
1. Tim. 1. *ghost is sayd to be diffused in our hartes*: charitie is sayd to *hide and couer our*
1. Io. 3. Rom. *sinnes,* and to *make God do dvvel in our hartes.* S. Ihon pronounceth boldly
4. 1. Pet. 5. 1. that vvho *loueth his brother by charitie, is in the light,* & that we are *translated*
Io. 4. *from the darkenes,* that is of sinne, to *the light,* that is of iustication, *because*
1. Io. 2. *vve loue our brethren.* yea he sayth that *vvhosoeuer loueth not, remaineth in death.*
Ibidem. And againe: *Euerie one that loueth, is borne of God.* By which it is plaine, that
Th 1. 2. q. 110. either charitie is alwayes ioyned with the grace of iustification (as S.
a. 3. 4. Thomas sayth) or that it is al one with the sayd grace, as others say:
Scot. 2. d. 26. and so is the formal cause of iustification, and then faith only concur-
Dur. ibidem. reth as a disposition, as hope also and feare do. At least hence it followeth

loweth that only faith iustifieth not, because he that hath not charitie, as S. Ihon sayth, remaineth in death, and if a man haue al the faith in the vvorld (as S. Paul sayth) vvithout charitie, he is so farre from being iust, that he is nothing, and no body. *Supra.*

5. Now, vvheras they say, that faith only iustifieth, but not vvithout charitie and good vvorkes, because it can not be vvithout them, it is an other absurd heresie. For S. Paul vvhen he sayth, that if he had al the faith in the vvorld, and yet haue no charitie, he is nothing, supposeth that faith may be separated from charitie. And S. Iames supposing that it may be vvithout good vvorkes, sayth, that *faith vvithout good vvorkes is dead*, and diuers parables as of the corne, and cockle in the same barne, of good and bad fishes in the same nette, of good and bad guestes at the same supper, yea of the sheep and goates also, argue that men may be in the Church by faith, and yet be bad Christians for vvant of charitie and good vvorkes, vvhich the good Christians haue. Yea reason teacheth, that it is one thing to beleue and to know our dutie by faith, and an other thing to do our dutie. Yea if there were no other argument, then the euil life of Lutherans and Caluinists, who bragge that they haue true faith, and yet liue most viciously, it vvould conuince them, that faith (if there be any in them) may be seuered from good vvorkes, and ioyned with euil. *1. Cor. 13.* *Faith vvithout good vvorkes.* *Iac. 2.* *Caluin in praefat. recepit hunc lib.* *Mat. 13.* *Ibidem.* *Mat. 22. & 25*

6. But to come to a conclusion, if faith only iustifie, then it followeth that the way is opened vnto al vice and villanie. For vvhen they come to the definition of this faith which only iustifieth, they say that it is an assurance by vvhich we are fully persvvaded that Christs iustice is ours, by vvhich faith also they say, Christs iustice is so applyed vnto vs, that it is ours, and couereth our sinnes, and maketh vs appeare iust in the sight of God. Out of vvhich doctrin I deduce this argument: If faith only iustifie, then if we retaine that faith, though we commit al the villanies in the world, they can not hurt vs, because so long as we hold that faith, we are iuste, and so the way is opened to al vice. For if a man be once perswaded, that faith only iustifieth, and that this faith is no other thing, but an apprehension that Christs iustice is ours, if he persvvade him self that Christs iustice is his (as he must, because Caluin & Luther affirme that euery man must beleue so if he wil be a Christian) then needs he only care to retaine that faith and apprehension. For if that only iustifie, then retaining that, he is assured that he is stil iust, though he commit al the sinnes in the world, and so by this doctrin he hath good leaue to sinne. *Supra.* *The opinion of only faith, openeth the vvay to al vice.*

Luth. in c. 2. Gal. Calu. l. 3. Inst. c. 11.

7. And for more confirmation of this argument it must be noted, that Luther and Caluin affirme that Christs iustice is the iustice of al men, and that if al men be not iust by it, the reason is because by faith they do not apprehende it. If then the greatest sinner in the world do vpon a sodain apprehend that Christs iustice is his, then is he iustified without any other pænance from al his former sinnes, and if he hold fast this apprehension, he need not care for amendement of life, but he many lance into a sea of sinne and iniquitie, and neuer feare drowning, because whilst he apprehendeth Christs iustice to be his, he is iust in the sight of God, euen then when he is in the act of sinne, and so as Luther sayth, he need not respect what he him self hath done or doth, but what Christ hath done, because, sayth Luther, faith respecteth not *vvhat I haue done, vvhat I haue sinned, vvhat I haue deserued, but vvhat Christ hath done and deserued*: which is to loose the bridle to al vice. Because if we respect only what Christ hath done, we need not care whath we our selues do. VVherfore although Luther sometimes for very shame of the vvorld, affirmeth that good workes are necessarie, aad that true faith can not be vvithout them; yet because he seeth that in thus saying he speaketh with no consequence, sometymes he granteth in plaine vvords the conclusion vvhich I haue inferred, to wit, that if faith only iustifieth, good vvorks are not necessarie, and euil vvorks are not to be feared: These are his vvords vvhich shal be my conclusion: *Sola fides Christi necessaria est ad salutem, cetera omnia liberrima, neque præcepta amplius neque probibita: Only the faith of Christ* (to wit that Christs iustice is ours) *is necessarie vnto saluation, al other things are most free, neither commaunded any more, nor prohibited.*

Comment. in c. 3. Gal.

in c. 2. Gal.

8. So that if a man beleue that Christs iustice is his, he needeth not to care for fulfilling the commandments, because nothing is commanded him, neither need he to feare fornications, adulteries, murdes, and such like treacheries, for none of al these villanies are forbidden him. But let the indifferent reader be iudge, vvhether this doctrin be of God or the deuil, vvhich so fauoureth sinne, vvhich God forbideth and the deuil alloweth, & whether that this faith of theirs be like to be our iustification, which looseth the bridle to al licentious liuing.

The

The third Chapter shevveth hovv Caluin and Luther in assuring men by an assured faith of election, remission of sinnes, iustice, and perseuerance in the same, loose the bridle vnto al iniquitie.

L is not gold that glistereth, as the common prouerb wil witnes, and al is not true that seemeth true, as the Philosopher doth tel vs, because (sayth he) many falsities, many times are more plausible and probable, then truthes and verities. And not to go far for an example: to say with Luther and Caluin that by faith we are assured of our saluation, and acertained that Christs iustice is ours, and that consequently vvhat soeuer our ovvne life be, we may boldly rely on him as children on their father crying *Abba Pater*, because by his iustice and not by our owne, we must looke for saluation; hath a goodly shew and lustre, and seemeth a doctrin most pious and plausible. But who so wel examineth the same, shal find, that this is the doctrin especially, vvhich lulleth men a sleep in al impietie, and like popple-seed or cold poison, casteth them into such a deepe and dead lethargie, that they heare no clamors, and feele no remorses of conscience.

2. Martin Luther in a certain booke which he made of the works of the first commandment, preferreth faith as the principal vvorship of God, and defineth it to be an assured confidence, and confident assurance, by vvhich vve are assured that vve are iust. And in an other place thus he pronounceth: *Crede eum tibi fore salutem & misericordiam, & ita erit sine dubio: Beleue that Christ vvil be thy saluation and mercie, and so it shal be vndoubtedly.* See what a compendious & neere way to heauen Luther hath found out. If you be clogged with al the sinnes in the world, beleue that you are iust (which is easie to do) and that you shal be saued, and then vndoubtedly, Luthers soule for yours, you shal be saued: & because so long as you beleue that you are iust, you are in deed iust, you can not be damned so long as you can beleue, how il soeuer you liue in the mean time. VVherfore the same Luther auoucheth that a Christian man is so rich & on so sure a ground, that he can not damne him

Comment. in c. 2. Gal.

l. de captiuit. Babil.

him self though he would, vnles he wil not beleue; and what must he beleue? that he is iust, or that he shal be saued. These are his words: *Tam diues est homo Christianus vt se damnare non poterit quantumuis velit, nisi sola incredulitate. So rich is a Christian man that he can not damne him self though he vvould, but only by incredulitie.* And what is the incredulitie vvhich only damneth him? not incredulitie of the Incarnation, Trinitie, Passion, or Resurrection; but of his owne saluation. So that liue he how il soeuer he wil, and be he neuer so incredulous in the articles of his beleefe, yet if he beleue that he shal be saued, it shal be so. And beleue he the mysteries of our faith neuer so firmely, liue he neuer so regularly, yet if he feare his owne saluation, he shal be dãned, because only this assured faith of saluation saueth, and only want of this fayth damneth, if Luther may be beleued.

Luthers faith vvhich saueth, and is infidelitie vvhich damneth.

3. Caluin in this doctrin subscribeth to Luther, and shaketh hands very freindly: these are his words: *Vve shal haue a perfect definition of faith, if vve say that it is a stedfast and assured knovvledg of Gods vvil tovvards vs.* And this only assured knovvledge of saluation and Gods good vvil towards vs, he calleth the iustifying faith: for (saith he) the vngodly may beleue that there is a God, and that the historie of the Gospel and other partes of Scripture are true, *But this is but an image or shadovv of faith, not vvorthy the name of faith: but ther is none truly faithful, but he that being persuaded vvith a sound assurednes that God is his merciful and louing father, doth promise him self al things vpon trust of Gods goodnes. And although* (sayth Caluin) *vve see Gods good vvil tovvards vs afarre of, yet vvith so sure light, that vve knovv vve are not deceiued.* At length to make the matter yet more sure, he concludeth that we are not only sure of present iustice and fauour, but also of future, and so are sure that vve shal not be damned. These are his words: *It is against order to limit the assurednes of faith to a moment of tyme, vvhose propertie is to passe beyond the spaces of this life, and to extend farther to immortalitie to come.* So that according to Caluin, beleue you the Trinitie, Incarnation, Passion, Death and Resurrection of Christ neuer so firmely, yet if you beleue not vndoubtedly that you are iust and shal remaine iust to the end, that God not only for the present time fauoureth you, but also vvil fauour you to the end, you can not be saued: and if you beleue only that you are iust, and shal remaine iust, and at length shal be also vndoubtedly saued, Caluins soule for yours, you can not be damned. And how can Caluin assure him self or vs, that we are iust and shal be iust? hath he had any special reuelation? no, but sayth he I am warranted out of

L.3. Inst. c. 2. par. 1.
Caluins faith.
par. 9.
par. 10.
par. 16.
par. 19.
The assurance of his faith.
Ibidem.

Scripture

Scripture that Christs iustice is ours, & so if I wil beleue vndoubtedly
that it is mine, and vvil be mine, then am I sure that I am iust, and shal
be iust, and can not fal *so long as I kepe this standing.* *par. 17.*

4. Against this phantastical faith of theirs, I might bring many *Arguments*
arguments, but that, as in other matters, so in this, I couet to be *against Cal-*
short. First, if this faith of theirs be so necessarie, how commeth *uins assured*
it to passe that Christ neuer exacted it of them, vvhom he cured? For *faith*
it is an opinion of some Fathers and Diuines, that vvhom soeuer *The first.*
Christ cured in body, he healed also and iustified in soule. VVhen he *Mat. 9.*
cured the blind men that came vnto him, he exacted faith of them,
and asked them vvhether they beleued; vvhat? not vvhether they
beleued that they were iust or elect, but vvhether they beleued, that
he could restore them to sight. If this stedfast faith and assurednes of *Second.*
our ovvne saluation be so necessarie, how came the Publicane to be a
iust man, who was so farre from assuring him self of Gods fauour, *Luc. 18.*
and his ovvne iustice, that he durst not looke vp to heauen. And yet
he retourned home iust, and the Pharisee who gloried like a Thrasonical Caluinist in his owne iustice, and assured him self that he was not
a sinner as the Publicane and other men are, vvas condemned and reiected. If this vndoubted faith of our ovvne saluation be so necessarie
to saluation, surely the Apostles were much ouerseen, vvho inculcated
so often the faith of the Incarnation, Resurrection, and such other *Act. 1. 2. 3. 4.*
mysteries, which is but an image and shadow (as Caluin sayth) of the *8. 10. 13. 17.*
true faith, and make no mention of that vvhich is the only iustifying
faith, and al in al neuer exacting of their auditors to beleue that they
are iust and elect, but only to beleue that Christ is God and man, that
he dyed, that he rose again, and such like. Truly either this faith is not
necessarie, or they vvere very negligent & incircumspect, vvho neuer
mentioned the same, and yet so often inculcate the faith of the mysteries of our faith, vvhich is but a shadow of the true faith, if Caluin lye
not, and is not sufficient to saluation vvithout Caluins assured faith.
Likewise when they made a Creed, as a breefe abridgemēt of al which
was necessarie to be beleued, vvhere was their mynd and memorie,
who omitted Caluins article of assurednes of our saluation, and election, vvhich is so necessarie to be beleued, that the faith of other articles is but a shadow in comparison of this? If Caluin say that this *Caluins an-*
his article is included in the article of *remission of sinnes*, he is much de- *svvers reiected*
ceiued: because in that article we only beleue that in the Church is
remission of sinnes, bnt that Caluins sinnes or any of our sinnes in
particu-

particular are forgiuen, is not there expressed.

5. Now if Scriptures and the Apostles had only omitted this assured faith vvhich Caluin sayth is so necessarie, it were sufficient to make vs not so assured of Caluins doctrin. For if it were necessarie, it is not like that the Apostles, vvhose preachings, trauels, life and death vvere ordained to the saluation of others, vvould haue omitted that vvhich only saueth, and without vvhich no other faith or works can possibly saue vs. But scripture not only omitteth assured faith of our owne iustice and saluation, but also condemneth it, and exhorteth vs to feare of our owne state and saluation; and therfore assureth vs as much that this faith of Caluin is false, as Caluin assureth it to be necessarie. Caluin sayth, that by faith we are assured of Gods good wil towards vs: Scripture saith that a *man can not tel vvhether he be vvorthy hatred or loue*: Caluin sayth, that a iust man is sure that he is iust: Iob sayth, *although I be simple*, that is, iust, *yet this my soule shal not knovv*. And S Paul sayth, that although *his conscience accuse him not of any sinne, yet in that he is not iustified*, to wit, before his owne eyes, because he knew he might haue secret sinnes, from vvhich Dauid desired to be clensed. Caluin sayth, that a man may be sure and consequently secure of the forgiuenes of his sinnes: and yet Scripture biddeth vs not to be *vvithout feare of our sinnes forgiuen*, or as the Greeke text hath, *of the forgiuenes or propitiation of our sinnes*. Caluin saith, that a man may be assured not only of present, but also of future fauour and iustice: & yet Scripture sayth that *a man knovveth not vvhat vvil be his end*, because al are reserued as vncertain for the tyme to come. Caluin, sayth that a faithful man must not feare to fal, but rather assure him self that he shal keep his ground and standing: and yet S. Paul speaking to a faithful man sayth: *thou standest by faith, thinke not highly, but feare: and thou that standest* (sayth he) *take heed lest thou fal*. And againe, *he biddeth vs vvorke our saluation vvith feare and trembling*. So that either we must leaue Caluin, or renounce Scripture, because they are contrarie, and stande in plain termes one against an other.

Scripture is quite cōtrarie to Caluin.
Iob. 9.
Psal. 18.
Eccl. 5.
Eccl. 9.
Rom. 11.
Philip. 2.

6. Neither is this doctrin opposit only to scripture, but also to reason. For first there are many corners in a mans conscience, vvhich we seldom or neuer looke into: For as Hieremie sayth, *the hart of man is vnsearchable*, and lyeth open only to God. How then can Caluin by faith be assured that his sinnes are forgiuen, that he is iust and elect? or if he know, God only is not the searcher of harts. And if ther be many corners in mans hart, to vvhich the hart it selfe is not priuie, perad-

The first reasō against Caluins assured faith.
Hierem. c. 17.

uenture

uenture after al our seeking, some sinne may lurke in a corner which we know not of. Secondly by Caluins owne confession, we must beleue nothing but what we find in scripture: and where fyndeth he, that Caluin is iust, or that his sinnes are forgiuen: If he find it not, he rashly beleueth it. If he sayth that Christ is our redemption and propitiation: I answere that so he is the redemption and propitiation of al, and yet Pagans & Infidels, and many of the reprobate are not iust, and therfore must not beleue assuredly that they are iust or elect, and if they should, they should beleue that vvhich is not so. Christ therfore is our propitiation, because he hath payed by his passion a sufficient price for our iustification and redemption, but yet if that price by faith in Christ, together with hope, charitie, Sacraments, and obseruation of the law (for al these are cōmanded) be not applyed to vs, we are neuer a whit the better. Thirdly suppose only Caluins faith by vvhich he beleueth Christs iustice to be his (vvhich notwithstanding is already refuted) were sufficient to applie this propitiation, yet for as much as Caluin sayth, that good vvorks do necessarily followe a sound faith, I demand of him, vvhether that he and his haue not iust cause to doubt, or at least to feare their owne iustice, and faith also, vvhose euil deeds are so many, and so manifest. Fourthly, euerie one of them sayth, he is assured that he is iust and shal be saued: & yet some of them are deceiued, because some of them haue contrarie faithes: why then may not Caluin also feare lest he be deceiued, seing that Christ dyed for al, and yet al are not iust nor elect, though they assure them selues of the same. Lastly this doctrin openeth the way to al maner of vice and vvickednes. For if it be sufficient to iustification to beleue vndoubtedly that I am iust, or that Christs iustice is mine, then doth it follow, that as after I haue sinned I may apprehend Christs iustice to be mine and my selfe to be iustified by the same: so vvhen I am moued to sinne by the deuil or my owne cōcupiscence, yea euen then when I am in the act of sinne, I may apprehend that though there is no goodnes in me of mine owne, yet Christs iustice is mine, of which, if euen in the act of sinne, I assure my selfe, I may assure my selfe also, that no sinne can hurt me, because that assurance iustifieth me. And so the fornicator may thus discourse with him selfe: I confesse (ô Lord) that there is no goodnes in me, and that this act to which I am now tempted, is a sinne, but Christs iustice is mine if I wil apprehend it so, I am iust if I wil beleue so, and from this faith I wil neuer be disswaded, but wil hold it fast euen in the act of sinne, and so I need not

Second.

Hovv Christ is our propitiation.

Third.

Supra.

Fourth.

Fifth.

feare this ſinne, becauſe if I hold faſt by this faith, no ſinne can hurt me, becauſe by this faith I am iuſtified. And ſo the way is open to al vice and vvickednes, becauſe if a man wil beleue that he is iuſt, and hold faſt by this faith, no ſinne can hurt him, becauſe that aſſurance of iuſtice doth iuſtifie him.

The fourth chapter ſhevveth hovv in ſaying that faith maketh no ſinne to be imputed to a faithful man, they giue good leave to al faithful men, to commit al ſinne and vvickednes.

Luth. in c. vlt. ad Gal. & Calu. l. 2. Inſt. c. 5. l. 3. c. 14. Supra c. 2.

HE reformers are of opinion, as anone I ſhal relate, in the next chapter, that al our workes are ſinnes. In which leſt they may ſeeme to contradict them ſelues (for they ſay alſo that true faith can not be ſeparated from good works, which ſeemeth to alowe of al the works of a faithful man) they haue found out this way to eſcape a contradiction. True, ſay they, al the workes euen of faithful men are ſinnes, and yet true it is, that faith can not be ſeparated from good workes, becauſe faith maketh God to impute nothing as ſinne, but rather to eſteme of al the actions of a faithful man, as good and laudable. Wherfore Luther in a certain ſermon vttered theſe wordes: *Vbi fides eſt, nullum peccatum nocere poteſt: VVhere faith is, no ſinne can hurt. And ſo* (ſayth he) *a Chriſtian man is ſo rich, that he can not damne him ſelfe, but only by incredulitie.* Caluin alſo ſayth plainly, that al iuſt and faithful mens works are of them ſelues ſinnes, but are by faith reputed as good. VVhich doctrin if it be true, then nedeth not a faithful man feare any ſinne, be it neuer ſo great, becauſe God wil neuer impute it vnto him: and conſequently it ſhal neuer be brought to examination at the latter day, nor puniſhed in hel, becauſe God imputeth it not as ſinne, and conſequently maketh no reckening of it.

Ser. ſuper, Sic Deus dilexit. Sup. l. de capt. l. 3 Inſt. c. 14. ſect 17. & c. 18. ſect. 8.

Pſal. 50.

2. Wherfore Dauid vvho was a faithful man, in vaine cryed God mercie for his aduoutrie and murder, becauſe if he was faithful (as certes he was) thoſe ſinnes could not be imputed as ſinnes vnto him. In vaine alſo do preachers threaten vnto Chriſtians judgement and damnation, and in vaine do faithful men feare ſuch bugbears. For if God im-

The cōcluſion.

God impute no sinne vnto them, he wil exact no punishment for sinne at the latter day. And so there is no iugdement for faithful people, but only for infidels, of whom notwithstanding it is sayd: *He vvho beleueth not, is already iudged*: and so shal neede no iudgement at the latter day. And false it must be which S. Paul and Christ him self sayd: that vve *shal receiue according to our vvorks*, and *as vve haue done*. For after the reformers doctrin we shal receiue only according to our faith. And so if Christians wil hold fast by Caluins faith, and beleue that Christs iustice is theirs, they shal not need to feare either theftes or adulteries, because Luther and Caluin haue giuen them a warrant, sealed and signed with their owne handes, that if they hold their faith, no sinne can hurt them, because it is not imputed vnto them. And why then make we scruple any longer of sinne? let euery man, if this doctrin be true, follow his concupiscences. For although he commit al the sinnes which either the diuel putteth into his mynd, or the flesh and world suggest, he is assured that they can not hurt him, because they are not imputed.

Ioan. 3. Aug. ser. 38. de Sanctis. Mald. in c. 3. Ioan. Mat. 16. 2. Cor. 5. The cōclusion.

The fifth Chapter shevveth hovv the reformers auouch that al our actions are of them selues mortal sinnes, and hovv this doctrin looseth the bridle to al vice.

Vo be to them (sayth God) *vvho affirme bad to be good, and good to be bad, light to be darknes, and darknes to be light.* VVhich curse must nedes light vpon our Gospellers, who condemne the iust mans good dedes as mortal sinnes, and account the faithful mans euil dedes as good and honest, or as such, that are not reputed euil, but rather good. Luther sayth, that the best works which infidels do, are sinnes. these are his words: *VVhosoeuer out of Christ vvorketh, prayeth, suffereth, doth vvorke, pray and suffer in vaine: because vvhatsoeuer is not of faith, is sinne.* And in his confutation of Latomus reason, thus he speaketh: *Omne opus bonum peccatum est, nisi ignoscat Dei misericordia: euery good vvorke is a sinne, vnles Gods mercie forgiue it.* And in the same place he sayth, that God pardoneth it, in that he imputeth it not to the faithful. And a

Isai. 5. in c. vlt. ad. Gal.

Luther sayth that S. Paul neuer did good vvork. litle before that, he sayth that S. Paul neuer did good worke in his life, and that the best which euer he did, was a sinne, though God imputed it not to him, because he was faithful. And yet again before that, he sayth that euen our iustice is vncleanes, and al our good works are sinnes. Likewise in one of his propositions collected and condemned by the famous vniuersitie of Paris, he hath these very words: *Omnes virtutes morales, & scientiæ speculatiua, non sunt veræ virtutes & scientiæ, sed peccata & errores: al moral vertues and speculatiue sciences, are not true vertues and sciences, but sinnes and errors.*

l.3. Inst. c. 14. par. 2. 2. Ihon Caluin although he wil seeme to make a differēce betwixt the moral vertues, and vices of the heathens (for otherwise, sayth he, *if these be confounded, there shal remaine no order in the common vvelth*) and although he calleth the pagans moral works, the *guiftes of God*, yet presently after, either forgetting or correcting his former speaches, he *Sect. 3.* sayth plainly, *that they are no more to be counted vertues, then those vices vvhich are vvont to deceiue by reason of nerenes and likenes to vertue.* And he pronounceth this sentence against Scipio, Cato, and other moral men amongst the Romaines, that al their moral vertues were vices. Then he setteth downe this general conclusion as a final sentence, from which no man *Sect. 6.* must appeale: *VVhatsoeuer man thinketh, purposeth, or doth before he be reconciled vnto God by faith, is accursed, and not only of no valevv to rightuousnes, but of certain deseruing to damnation.* And he giueth this reason: because for-*Sect. 5.* sooth, our nature by original sinne is so *corrupted and soked in the poison of* *& l. 2. c. 5. in fine.* *sinne, that it can breath out nothing but corruption*: and therfore, sayth he, *oyle shal sooner be vvrong out of a stone, then any good vvorke from vs.* Yea the *l. 3. c. 14. sect. 7. 9. 11.* same sentence he pronounceth not only against the sinful, but also the iust and faithful Christian: that no good procedeth from either of them, but that the best worke which the iustest man doth, deserueth *The ground of their doctrin.* shame and damnation. The reason and ground of this their doctrin is, because they thinke that original sinne hath so defaced our nature, that it hath blotted out the image of God, bereaued vs of free-wil, inclined our nature wholly to sinne, vnabled it to vertue, in so much that whatsoeuer procedeth from this infected nature, is filthy, abominable, and odious in the sight of God.

The iniurie this doctrin doth to mans nature. 3. But thus they first of al do mightie iniurie vnto mans nature, which by this doctrin is rather brutish then reasonable. For if mans vnderstanding be so metamorphized, that al his science & knowledge either speculatiue or practical is error and deceit, as Luther sayth, I see not why man should be counted reasonable, more then a brute beast.

And

And if he be wholly bent to sensualitie and sinne, and hath no inclination to vertue, no power, nor facultie to do the least act of vertue, or to resist the least tentation, then is his nature no more noble, then the nature of a beast, because he is altogether sensual as a beast is, and no more inclined to vertue or able to do a vertuous action then an oxe or an asse. And so the old definition by which Philosophers vse to define man, must be corrected, because they define a man to be *animal rationale, a reasonable creature.* Which definition by this doctrin agreeth no more to a man, then to a beast, because man is as vnable to the works and operations of reason as a beast is, and so is no more man but a beast by Caluins definition. Secondly, this doctrin condemneth al Philosophers and Philosophie, which teach vs, that in the most vicious man that is, there are some inclinations and seedes of vertue, which is the cause that the most wicked man that is, loueth vertue at least in others, hath a remorse of conscience when he hath done euil, blusheth at his euil dedes as not beseeming his nature, and some times doth some good worke or other. For you shal hardly find a man giuen to al vice, and inclined to no vertue. From hence proceeded the moral vvorks of the Romaines, for vvhich S. Austin sayth, almightie God bestowed on them, so ample an empire, and honoured them with so many victories Hence proceeded also the lawes of Licurgus, Solon, Plato, and the rest, and al the moral precepts and vertues of the ancients. From hence also proceed the speculatiue sciences of natural Philosophie, Metaphysike, Mathematique, Astrologie, and such like: which to condemne of error, as Luther doth, is mere madnes: against whom I wil vse the same argument, which Philosophers vsed against the Academikes who denyed al science. Either Luther knoweth that al speculatiue and practical sciences are errors, or he knoweth not: if he knowe not, he is rash to deny sciences: if he knowe them, in denying science he granteth science.

Man is no mā by this doctrin.

This doctrine ruineth Philosophie.

Natures good inclinations.

l. 5. ciu. c. 15.

Hence the lavves of old Sages.

Hence Philosophie.

An argumēt against Luth.

4. And although I wil not deny but that the vertues of pagans are many times vice, because their end or scope is often times vain glorie, or else some other euil circumstance is annexed: yet to say that al their actions are of necessitie sinnes, is to make man no man, as I haue proued. I wil grant also that sinners good works, as prayer, almes deedes, and such like, are *opera mortua* dead workes, as Diuines say, because in that they proceed not from the life of grace, they are not condignely meritorious, yet they may be morally good, and if they proceed from a good intention, and motion of God, which is called

D. Th. 3. p.

grace præuenient, and which is neuer wanting, they dispose a man to penance, and penance disposeth to iustification. Wherfore although Nabuchodonosor was in mortal sinne, yet Daniel counsayled him to redeme his sinnes by almes deedes. Which counsail he would neuer haue giuen, if to giue almes, had bene a mortal sinne. Thirdly, this is to condemne Scripture, yea and God him-self, who forbid certain actions as euil, and counsail and command others as good: which is absurdely done, if al be sinnes and euil actions. Fourthly, hence it followeth that al sinnes are æqual, because if our actions be euil for that they proceed from an euil and corrupted nature, they must be (at least in this respect) equally euil, euen as the fruites of a crab-tree are of like sournes, because they proceed from the same tree, and take their sournes from the same sappe.

Dan. 4.

This doctrine is opposit to Scripture.

It maketh al sinnes æqual.

It openeth the vvay to al vice

5 Lastly, thus the way is open vnto al vice. For if whatsoeuer man doth, is sinne, then if he be tempted to fornication, to what purpose should he refrayne? For if he resist the temptation, he must do it either by chastising his body, or by prayer, or by a contrary resolution of the mind and wil, vvhich if it be sinne also (as by this doctrin is aboue proued) he auoydeth one sinne by an other, and so might as wel haue yeelded to the temptation. And if he haue an other mans vvife in keeping, or his landes, or goodes in possession, he can not get out of this sinne but by restoring, because the sinne is not forgiuen, vnles the thing vvhich is wrongfully holden, be restored. And yet to vvhat purpose should he restore, if restoring also be a sinne, as it must be, if al our actions be sinnes? truly he hath litle reason, because in restoring he auoydeth not sinne, but changeth one sinne for an other. Yea if this doctrin may take place, the Prince may as wel vse oppression of his subiects, as bountie & magnificence: subiects may as wel rebel as obey; souldiors need not to feare murder, pillage, luxurie; courtiours need not to make scruple of vanitie, flattery, dissimulation, ambition: merchants need not to forbeate vsurie, nor vniust selling and buying: Iudges may take bribes, & pronounce partial sentences: and the Iurie may as wel giue vvrong, as right informations: the rich may as wel bestow blowes, as almes on the poore, and beggers may as wel steale, as begge: because as these are sinnes, so are the contrarie vertues, vvhich are no more vertues (as Caluin sayth) *then are those vices, vvhich for their likenes and shovve of vertue, do goe for vertues:* And so no man shal need to make bones of any sinne, because some thing he must do, and vvhatsoeuer he doth, is sinnne, and vvhen he thinketh that he doth best, his

beſt, his doings deſerue no leſſe then æternal damnation.

6. But they wil ſay that although al actions be ſinnes, yet God imputeth not al as ſinnes, and therfore we muſt do almes-deedes and abſteine from iniuries, becauſe God imputeth theſe as ſinnes, but not the other. Thus they ſay, but yet thus they take not a way the abſurditie. For yet it followeth, that an infidel may do vvhat he wil, and make no more ſcruple of one action then of an other, becauſe God imputeth al his actions as they are, that is, ſinnes and vices. And if the faithful and iuſt mans actions be al ſinnes, either God muſt impute al as ſinnes, or none at al, becauſe al are alike, neither hath God any reaſon to repute his almes deedes as good vvorks, rather then his theftes, if thoſe be ſinnes, and deſerue damnation as wel as theſe. Whence it followeth, that we muſt put no difference betwixte our actions, but may as freely and as boldly aduenture vpon theftes and murders, as any vvorks of charitie, iuſtice, mercie, or any other vertue.

The Sixth Chapter shevveth hovv they deny fre vvil and ſo alſo open the vvay to ſinne.

AINT Auſtin ſayth that it is a thing ſo commonly receiued, that man hath free wil, and that he is not to be blamed for that vvhich is not in his power, that the ſhepheards ſing it on the mountaines, Poets in theaters, the vnlearned in circles, the learned in libraries, maiſters in ſchooles, Biſhops in ſacred places, and mankind throughout the vvorld. And Cicero throught it vvould be counted ſuch a paradox to deny free wil, that he choſe rather to deny Gods preſcience, vvhich ſeemed repugnant to it, then to deny free-wil vvhich vvas ſo commonly receiued. And ſo ſayth S. Auſtin, he vvas iniurious to God, leſt he ſhould be iniurious to the common welth, vvhich could not ſtand vvithout free wil. And yet the Stoikes denyed free-wil as vvitneſſeth S. Auſtin, and after them Simon Magus, Manicheus, and Wicleph, and laſt of al our late Reformers, a bad broode of as bad breeders.

Ep. 11. l. de duabus animabus c. 1.

Aug. l. 5. ciu. c. 19.

l. 5. ciu c. 8. 9.

Aug. ſer. 35.

2. Luther therfore vvriting againſt Eraſmus, and againſt free wil alſo, vvhich Eraſmus had proued both learnedly and eloquently, entitleth

titleth

Lut. l. de seruo arbitrio. titleth his booke, *of Seruile Arbitrament.* In vvhich booke he disputeth with al might and main against free wil. And to set before our eyes more plainly our seruile condition, he calleth mans vvil a hackney, vpon vvhich if Gods spirit chance to sit and settle it selfe, it goeth necessarilie that way to which the spirit spurreth it: but if the deuil bestride this hackney, it runneth vvhether Satan vrgeth it, and hath no power either to resist the one, or the other. And a litle after he sayth, that free-wil is a diuine name which agreeth only to God, but not to man: yea in an other place he sayth that freewil in man is *a title only, and name vvithout the thing it self.* Caluin in this point agreeth with Luther. For he in his first booke of Institutions, granteth that Adam had free-wil before his fal (which I see not how he can grant, because he sayth that Gods prouidence and predestination taketh away free-wil, yea that Adams first sinne vvas committed by the ineuitable decree of God) but after his fal, he in him self, and we in him, lost free-wil: and therfore Caluin rebuketh the Philosophers, who auerre that man hath free-wil, and that else al difference betwixte vice and vertue is taken avvay: for (sayth he) they say true, if they take man before his fal. And in his second booke, hauing giuen a sharpe censure and sentence against both Philosophers and Fathers, because they absolutely affirme that man hath free-wil, these giue free-wil his part together with the grace of God: he vvisheth that this name *freevvil* should no more be spoken of, and he vvould wish others, if they vvould aske his counsaile, to forbeare it also, lest that therby they take occasion of pride, and of a proud conceit of their owne force. And so if vvishers might be woulders, we should neither haue freewil, nor the name of freewil. By vvhich it is plaine, that Caluin absolutely denyeth freewil, as Luther & Melancthon once did, although afterward they gr $\bar{a}$ ted it in external and ciuil actions, as buying and selling, talking and vvalking, and such like: but in moral actions of vice and vertue, yea in supernatural actions, to vvhich the grace of God is necessarie, as the loue of God, conuersion, and repentance of a sinner, they grant no free-wil not choise at al. The vvhich opinion is so absurd, that by this a man may see vvhat credit is to be giuen them in greater matters, and higher mysteries, vvho haue erred so grossely in a matter so euident, that not only reason, but also experience proueth it.

Luth maketh free-vvil an hackney.

c. 8.

l. 1. c. 15. sect. 1.

l. 3. c. 14.

Caluins opinion.

l. 2. c. 8.

c. 2. sect. 8.

Bellar. to. 3. l. 4. de grat. & lib. arb. c. 5.

Experiences of freevvil. 3 For first we deliberate and consult concerning some actions & not others; as vvhether we shal take phisicke or no, and yet we consult not vvhether we shal dye or no, fly or no, and such like, which is

a signe

a ſigne that the former actions are in our power, elſe as wel might we conſult vvhether we ſhould fly or no in the ayre, when by running or riding we can not eſcape our enemie. And why haue Princes their counſailers to conſult and deliberate, if al things follow the ſvvay of neceſſitie? VVe command alſo our ſeruants or ſubiects to runne or go, but not to fly, or to ſtay the courſe of the ſunne, becauſe thoſe actions are in their power, not theſe. VVe exhort men alſo to leaue this vice, to follow that vertue, and we counſaile the ſicke to take this not that medicine, becauſe al theſe thinges are in his power and free choiſe, and yet we exhort him not to put awaye his ague, to be ſicke no more, and if we would, he would count vs but fooles for our labours, becauſe theſe thinges, are not in his choiſe. We are alſo wary in our actions and heedful, leſt we erre or banger: vvhich argueth that vve may do il or vvel, and conſequently are not enforced by neceſſitie either to the one or the other. We are angry alſo with our ſubiects for doing certain things, and they meruaile not; and yet if vve vvould be angrie vvith them for not mouing a mountayne, or not carying a greater burden then a man is able to beare, they would think vs mad, if we be but angrie. VVe are angrie with our ſelues alſo, and blame and repent our ſelues, for ouerſhooting our ſelues in vvords, for making an euil bargaine, for eating or drinking to much, for ſtealing, or ſuch like actions, which is a ſigne that we might haue done other wiſe: elſe I demand a reaſon why we repent not our ſelues, that vve did not ſoare vp into the ayre vvhen our enemye purſued vs, or the theefe robbed vs? we prayſe and diſprayſe men for vertuous or vitious actions, as for liberalitie, and nigardnes; and yet we praiſe them not for growing and waxing tal & big, neither do we diſprayſe them for litle ſtature, or for not putting forth their limmes. And why, but becauſe thoſe thinges are in their power, theſe are not, and therfore worthy neither prayſe nor diſpraiſe? we aske alſo and enquire of men, why they did this, why they did not that. As God asked Cain, vvhy his countanance was fallen? Which argueth that they might haue done othervviſe. Or if Caluin wil ſay, that we make enquirie of neceſſarie things, then let him demand of the lion vvhy he roareth, of the aſſe why he brayeth, of the ſheep vvhy he bleateth, and of the ſick man why he wil be ſicke, and the blinde man why he ſeeth not? But to leaue experience (which commonly is called the miſtreſſe of fooles, becauſe it teacheth euen fooles to be wiſer, and might perſwade Luther and Caluin alſo that man hath freewil, were they not worſe then

Gen. 4.

fooles, and as witles in this point as mad men) I vvil demonstrate the same by reason also. And first of al I demande, why rewards are proposed not only by Princes, but by God also for them that embrace vertuous and heroical actions? Certes, no Godamercie to him that doth wel, if he could not do otherwise. And why do they prescribe punishments against transgressors of their lawes, if there be no free-wil? Certainly he that necessarilie is euil, is rather worthy compassion then paine or punishment. Or why do God and Princes set downe lawes and precepts, for their subiects to obserue? If they haue no free-vvil, they may as vvel prescribe lavves to sheepe that they grase not vpon other mens groundes: or to horses that they breake not their maisters hedges, to runne into their neighbors corne: or wolues that they worrye not the innocent lambs: or to foxes that they liue not vpon the spoile of the poulterers hens and capons. VVhy are not mad men punished for the euil vvords, vvhich they speake, or euil deeds which they do in their madnes, seeing that thy haue as much free vvil as men haue, when their wittes are freshest? Secondly, man is endewed with reason to vnderstand not only what the end is, but also what are the meanes to attaine vnto the same; he seeth, that there are many particular ends to which he may apply him self: he seeth also many meanes to attaine vnto the end which he proposeth to him self; as if he propose health, he perceiueth that this he may attaine either by purging, or letting blood, or exercise, or diet. And seeing that the wil followeth the vnderstanding which is her eye, & without which she is blinde, and can neither loue nor hate, neither desire nor feare, it must needs follow, that as the vnderstanding proposeth many meanes, and apprehendeth none of them in particular necessarie, (because if one be not vsed, an other wil serue) so the wil hath freedom to vse which meanes she wil, because the vnderstanding iudgeth none in particular necessarie, and therfore by preiudicate opinion enforceth her to none. And in this may be seen a difference betwixt men and brute beasts, because though they change their imaginations, and imagin one while water to be conuenient, an other while meate, yet that which they first apprehend, caryeth away their appetites by a svvaye of necessitie. Lastly, ther was neuer yet any nation so barbarous, which confessed not vertue to be in some of our actions, vice in others: and therfore they prayse the one and dispraise the other: and yet if we haue no free-wil, it must needs follow, that there is no more vice and vertue in our actions, then in operations of beasts, as I shal in an other chapter

The first reason for free-vvil.

The second.

The third.

chapter proue most manifestly.

4. But they wil say (as commonly they say when they knew not what to say) that in reasons may be sophistrie and deceite, and that therfore against al the experience and reason alleaged for free-wil, we must beleue the holy word of Scripture, which reiecteth free-wil. Is it so? and are scriptures contrarie to reason? I wil not deny but scripture teacheth many things aboue reason, but that it teacheth any thinge against reason, is most vntrue. For as grace perfiteth nature in eleuating it to a higher beeing, & to more heroical actions then of it self it can attain vnto, and in no wise destroyeth it: so scripture which is the booke of faith, leadeth reason farther then of her self she could go, but induceth her not to any thing which is against reason. For so God, vvhich is the author of reason and faith, in ruinating reason by faith and scripture, should deny him self, because he should be contrary to him self. Yea if Scripture should deny free-wil, it should be contrarie to it self, because it giueth as plaine testimony for it, as for any thing. *An obiection answered.*

5. Doth not Ecclesiasticus affirme, that *God from the beginning created man, and lefte him in the hand of his ovvn counsail?* doth he not say in the same place, *If thou vvilt keep the commandements they shal keepe thee?* doth he not again inculcate free-wil vnto vs, saying: *God hath set before thee vvater and fier, to vvhich thou vvilt put thy hand?* To vvhat end doth God say to man, *if thou vvilt*, if man haue no free wil? were it not ridiculous, if one should say to a blind man that can not see: if thou wilt, looke and thou shalte finde: or to a lame man, if thou wilt follow me, thou shalt not loose thy paynes? The like words to the former hath Esaie the Prophet: *If you vvil and shal heare me, you shal eate the goods of the earth.* And againe: *This sayth our Lord God of Israel, If you returne & ceasse from sinne, you shal be saued.* The like speeches vseth almightie God by his Prophet Hieremie: *If thou vvilt be conuerted, I vvil conuert thee.* And how often doth scripture exhort and command vs to conuert our selues to God? Which were ridiculously spoken, if it were not in our free-wil by the assistance of Gods grace to tourne vnto God. And in the new Testament sayth Christ: *If thou vvilt enter into life, kepe the commandements.* And again he complaineth vvith teares of Hierusalems ingratitude, saying: *Hierusalem, Hierusalem, hovv often vvould I haue gathered thee as a hen gathereth her chikins vnder her vvings, and thou vvouldst not?* VVhat man in his vvittes vvould speake thus, vnles he thought that Hierusalem had free-wil? else might Hierusalem haue answered Christ in *Eccl. c. 15. Is. c. 1. c. 30. c. 15. Ezech. 18. 33. Mat. 19. Mat. 23.*

this maner. VVhy complainest thou so pitifullie of my slouth and ingratitude? knovvest not thou that I can not? vvhy sayst thou to me, *and thou vvouldst not*, knovving that I haue no vvil, and that thine only is the vvil, myne is seruile necessitie? So that it is manifest by experience, reason, and scripture, that man hath free-vvil. And seeing that ther is no page of scripture, but it conteineth either commandement, or counsail, or exhortation, or some one or other of the signes of free-vvil, vvhich are before alledged, I may be bold to say that there is no page in holy Scripture, out of vvhich may not euidently be deduced a pregnant proofe and argument for free-wil.

6. VVherfore although some fevv places are in Scripture, vvhich, til they be vvel vnderstood, may seeme to disproue free-wil, yet rather should the heretike confesse his vvant of skil to interpret those places, then to deny free-vvil, vvhich al scripture almost so euidently auoucheth. Let them not therfore obiect, *that God VVorketh al in vs*, that *mans vvay is not in man*: that *it is not of the vviller, nor of the runner, but of God that taketh mercie on vs*: that *God calleth and knocketh at the dore of our soule*: that *God the father dravveth vs*; For I can easily ansvver, and haue al the Fathers and Diuines to backe me in it, that God only operateth in vs by his antecedent grace, but vve also by vertue of it cooperate vnto his motion: that mans vvay, that is, the vvay of saluation, is not in mans povver in respect of the beginning, because God only putteth vs in the vvay by his vocation, and præcedent grace, but yet by vertue of this grace it is in our power to vvalke in this way; that it is God only, that beginneth al good wils and courses, but supposing his precedent grace, vve also vvil, and runne, but not vve only, but his grace vvith vs, and vve vvith it: That God only calleth and knocketh by his præuenient grace, but we also by consent do open the dore vnto him; that God the father draweth by his motions, but sweetly, without violence, by persvvasion and allurement, not by compulsion.

1. Cor. 12. Ier 10. Rom. 9. Eph 5. Apoc. 3. Io. 6.

Places of Scripture expounded.

7. But to labour no farther in so euident and plaine a matter: by a great absurditie vvhich followeth this doctrine, I wil demonstrate it to be absurd, because one absurditie followeth an other. If man haue no free-wil, al vice and vvickednes must go for currant, and no man must endeuour to auoid sinne, because he hath no power to auoid it. Be it then that Maister Minister dehorte me from vice with al the Rhetorick vvhich he hath, let him lay before myne eyes filthines of

sinne,

sinne, the dishonestie vvhich it implyeth, the offence of God, the scandal of my neighbor vvhich followeth it, therby to dissvvade me from it: yet if I haue no free-wil nor power to auoid sinne, I may answer him that his perswasions are but lippe-labour vvhich he might as wel vse to a beast as to a man. For, vvhat I shal do, that of necessitie I shal do: and as he disswadeth me from vice, so the pleasure or temporal profit vvhich vice bringeth, doth so allure me, and the deuil so vrgeth me, that I can not resist, because I haue no free-wil, but must behaue my self passiuely, permitting concupiscence and the deuil to vvorke in me vvhat they wil, because I haue no power to resist them. For as a man that is perswaded that he hath no force to resist his enemie, or the ministers of iustice, layth downe his armes and vveapons, and permitteth them to do their pleasure, knowing that resistance is vaine, vvhen, wil he nil he, their pleasure must be done: so vvhen a man is perswaded that he hath no free-wil nor power to auoide sinne, he must yeeld him self as a slaue to al vice, and vvhen he feeleth the temptation, he must yeeld presently, and acknowledge his own impotencie. And if any man rebuke him for his sinnes, or if God herafter at the day of Iudgement accuse him or condemne him, he hath an excuse ready for such an accusation, and a tricke in store to auoid such a condemnation, to vvit, that he could do no othervvise, because he had no free-wil. And so he may commit what sinnes he wil, and no man, yea not God him self can iustly finde fault with him, vnles they first finde a fault in Luthers and Caluins doctrin, vvhich teacheth him that he can not do otherwise.

To deny free-vvil, openeth vvay to al vice.

***

The seuenth Chapter proueth that the reformers in auouching the lavves and commandements of God to be impossible, giue occasion also of al impiety.

Luth. l. de ser. arbit. Calu. l. 2. Inst. c. 7. & in harm. Mat. 19.

I SHAL not need to dwel long on this point, nor to vse any long discourse to come vnto my intended conclusion, because I haue already in the fifth booke set downe Luthers and Caluins words, in vvhich they affirme the commandements to be impossible: vvhere also I haue disproued this doctrin, and proued the contrarie, to wit, that man hath power with the grace of God to fulfil his commandements. Only now out of those premises, as in that booke I inferred God to be vnreasonable by Luthers and Caluins doctrin, so now out of the same I wil conclude, that the gap is opened to al vice and vvickednes. For if a man be once perswaded, that he can not fulfil the commandement of keeping the Saboth day, if desire of gaine, or lucre moue him to seruile vvorks and labours, he wil easilie be perswaded to labour, vvho is already perswaded that he can not keepe the Saboth, as he should do. And if he once giue credit to Caluin that he can not obserue the law, vvhich forbiddeth him to couet his neighbors wife or goods, if he be tempted or moued with such obiects, he wil neuer vrge him self to withstand such temptations, because he is perswaded that he can not fulfil this law, but must needs transgresse it, and not only couet & desire, but also inordinatly vse his neighbors wise, and vsurpe his goods also, vvhensoeuer they crosse the vvay of his desire. Breefly seeing that there is no sinne, but it is a transgression of one law or other, he that is perswaded that he can not fulfil any law of God (as al Lutherans and Caluinists are) is perswaded also that he can auoid no sinne, and consequently if any sinne moue or allure him either by profit or pleasure vvhich it implyeth, he can not, being so perswaded, endeuour to withstand the temptation, because that were to shewe him self able to resist sinne, and to fulfil the commandments, and consequently to condemne Ihon Caluins doctrin. And although in so doing he openeth the gap to al maner of iniquitie, yet therin he sheweth him self a true Caluinist, who being perswaded by reli-

To say the commandements are impossible is to open the vvay to al vice.

by religion and conscience, that he hath neither force nor wil to resist any sinne, or to fulfil any commandement, must not, yea can not without offence of conscience and hazard of faith, go about to fulfil any law: for so though not in vvords, yet in fact and deed he should deny his religion.

The eigth Chapter shevvveth hovv in affirming that Christ hath freed vs from al lavves, they loose the bridle to al vice.

HE reformers, as is recounted partly in the third booke and second chapter, partly in the fifth chapter of the same booke, are of opinion that Christ was no lawgiuer, but rather that he came to free vs from al lawes: vvhich doctrin although I haue in the former places alleaged, yet to ease the reader, it shal not be amisse here also to set downe the same doctrin in other their owne vvords Luther in a comment of his one holy scripture, often tymes inculcateth that by Christ we are so freed from al lawes, that none of them can bynd vs, or touch vs in conscience. These are his vvords: *Discat igitur pius legem & Christum, duo contraria esse prorsus incompatibilia: præsente Christo lex nullo modo dominari debet, sed cedere debet é conscientia, & relinquere cubile (quod angustius est, quam vt duos capere poßit) soli Christo: Let therfore the godly man learn to knovv, that Christ and the lavv, are tvvo contraries altogether incompatible: Christ being present, the lavv must in no vvise rule, but must depart from conscience, and leaue the bed (vvhich is to narrovv for tvvo) to Christ alone.* Where you see, that he maketh Christ and al lawes, euen his owne lawes, so contrarie, that if Christ stand, no law can stand, nor haue any force ouer conscience. And in an other place of the same Comment, thus he defineth: *quatenus est Christianus, est supra omnem legem: as he is Christian, or in that he is a Christian, he is aboue al lavv.* And yet again in an other vvorke of his, he speaketh more boldly and plainly: *nullo opere, nulla lege homini Christiano opus est, cum per fidem sit liber ab omni lege: for a Christian no lavv nor vvorke is needful, seing that by faith he is free from al lavv.* The same opinion holdeth Ihon Caluin, as in the former, and many other places is plainly to be seene.

in cap. 4. Gal

in c. 2. Gal.

l. de libertate Christiana.

Supra, & l. 2. Inst. c. 2. par. 9. 14.

2. By

2. By vvhich doctrin although they wil seeme to make Christ a more perfect Redemer as before is noted, yet in deed they make him a fauourer and patron of al vice and vvickednes. For if we be freed from al obligation of lawes, then do they no more bynd vs then lawes abrogated: if they bynde not in conscience, then no man is bound in conscience to obserue them: If he be not bound in conscience to obserue them, then he sinneth not in trăsgressing them, no more then in doing contrarie to a law vvhich is abrogated, because euery sinne is against the obligation of one law or other, yea then he trăsgresseth not, because where is no obligation, there can be no trăsgression. If it be no sinne to transgresse lavves (as Luther and Caluin say, that to a Christian such transgressions are not imputed as sinnes) then need not any Christian make any scruple of any action by vvhat law soeuer it be forbidden, and so he may as freely steale as giue almes, and as boldly he may follow his lust and sensualitie, as liue chastly, and moderate his appetites: for where no law byndeth in conscience, al is lawful that liketh, and so the way is open to al maner of vice.

The ninth Chapter proueth, that in affirming God to be the author of sinne, the Reformers open the vvay to al vice.

See the fifth booke chap. 1

HAVE already related the blasphemies of our new Christians against the goodnes of God, and I haue demonstrated that they are sensles, absurd, & impious, in making God the author of our sinnes, vvhose mercie pardoneth, and vvhose iustice punisheth sinnes, but can not vvorke, or commit the least sinne vvithout preiudice of his goodnes & Deitie also, vvhich is goodnes it selfe. So that now I wil suppose for my premises, that they are of that opinion, and I wil deduce for my intended conclusion, that this doctrin looseth the bridle vnto al iniquitie.

1. For if a man be once perswaded as al Caluinists are, that God is the author and vvorker of his sinnes, vvhat is ther remaining to restrayn and vvithhold him from sinne? he may and wil easily discourse thus with him self vvhensoeuer the deuil vrgeth, or the flesh allureth, or the vvorld entiseth him to sinne. This act to vvhich I am tempted

and vvhich

and vvhich commonly is called a sinne, is the worke of God as wel as mine, and more his then mine, because as my oracle, (that is Ihon Caluin) telleth me, he vvorketh it in me, and vrgeth me vnto it. VVhy then should I either be afrayd or ashamed to do that vvhich God not only doth vvith me, but also so forcibly moueth me vnto it, that (as M. Caluin telleth me) I can not possibly resist him? Am I better then he? or can any sinne be so vglye, as not to beseeme me, vvhich beseemeth him, vvho is goodnes it self? But paraduenture God dispenseth vvith him self, but not vvith me, and therfore vvil not haue me to sinne. VVil he not? VVhy then doth he vrge and egge me to sinne? where I am vrged, certes I am willed, and vvilled by him by whom I am vrged. Yea if sinne be the worke of God (as it is vnles Caluin lye) then is it the effect of his vvil (for, as Dauid sayth, *he doth al by his vvil*, and as Diuines say, *his povver is his vvil*) and so Psal. 113.
I in sinning shal do his pleasure, and conforme my self to his wil. Let 1. p. q. 19. a.
vs sinne then freely, we do but Gods wil, and let vs not make scruple 4.
of that, of vvhich he is the willer and vvorker: let vs not blush at the turpitude of sinne, of vvhich God him self is not ashamed, neither let vs feare offence vvhere we do our maisters wil and pleasure: rather let vs perswade our selues that al sinnes are lawful and pleasing to God, because they are the vvorkes of his wil, and consequently according to his wil. But sye rather vpon this impious and licentious doctrin. God forbiddeth sinne by his law, & therfore would not haue it done: and punisheth sinne most seuerly, and therfore is no author of it: and he is goodnes it self & deuoid of al malice, and therfore can not worke sinne, vvhich is deuoid of al goodnes, & nothing but malice.

***

The tenth Chapter by many points of their doctrin proueth, that they take avvay al vice and vertue from mens actions, and so giue them leaue to sinne, and to do vvhat they vvil.

T is a thing so manifest, that vertue and vice, honestie and dishonestie, is to be found in the actions of man, that there was neuer any people so barbarous or vitious, vvhich hath not commended many of mens actions, and hath not dispraised many others, and blushed at them euen in them selues, as not beseeming mans nature, vvhich as it is reasonable, so it should be ruled by reason. VVherfore to certain actions, honors and rewards haue been proposed, and to others seuere punishments and chastisments. The vvisest of the Gentils, vvhose reason by sinne and superstition was least obscured, were of opinion, that some actions were sinnes, and offences of God, and that others were grateful and pleasing vnto him. For they knew that God the author of nature, as he had ordained al things to their end, and giuen them faculties to exercise those actions, vvhich should bring them to their end; so he hath ordained man vnto his end, vvhich is to liue vertuously, and by vertuous life so to serue God here, that he may enioy him herafter: and therfore he hath endewed him with reason, by vvhich he may know vertue from vice, and good from euil, and a wil also to execute that vvhich reason shal command: so that vvhen he liueth according to reason, he followeth his nature, and Gods ordinance, and exerciseth those actions vvhich beseeme his reasonable nature, and are pleasing vnto God: and when he followeth sensualitie and leaueth reason, then doth he that vvhich is not beseeming his nature, then doth he breake Gods ordinance, and swerue from the end to vvhich he is ordained, and consequently sinneth and offendeth God. Wherfore Aristotle sayth, that wise and vertuous men vvhich liue according to reason, are most deare vnto God. Plato affirmeth that God is the reuenger of sinne and dishonestie: and in an other place he distinguisheth three kindes and states of men: The first of those that liue vertuously, and they sayth he, are sent to the happy

Al men grāt vice and vertue.

Mans end.

VVhy man some tymes sinneth.

l. 1. Eth c. 8. Ex Clement. Alex. orat. hortator. ad gentes. in Phædone.

the happy Ilands, vvhich we vvould cal heauen: the ſecond ſtate is of them vvho commit leſſer faultes, vvhich we vvould cal venial ſinnes, & ſuch ſayth he, are purged for a time (the ſame do Catholiques ſay of them that dy out of mortal ſinne, yet are defiled ſo with venial ſinnes, that they need ſome purging in Purgatorie) and then with the firſt ſort, are admitted to the happy Ilands. The laſt are they vvhich commit enormious and hainous crimes: and ſuch ſayth Plato, are tormented perpetually, becauſe their paines do them no good, vvhich is as much to ſay, as Catholiques ſay of them, who for greater offences, of vvhich they repent not before death, are condemned to a præmunire and perpetual impriſonment in hel By vvhich it may appeare, that not only Chriſtians, but alſo pagans & thoſe that vvant the light of faith, haue yet by light of reaſon eſpyed vice in ſome of our actions, and vertue in other ſome, and haue deemed thoſe vvorthy puniſhement, theſe worthy ſome reward.

Plato his three ſtates or places

2. And yet if we giue credit to our new Chriſtians, we muſt acknowledge no more vertue or vice in the actions of men, then in the operations of brutiſh and vnreaſonable creatures. For firſt if it be true vvhich Luther and Caluin teache vs, that no lawes can bynde a Chriſtian, then doth it follow that a Chriſtian can not ſinne, and conſequently that there can be no vice in any of his actions. For wher no law byndeth, there is no lawe: vvhere no law is, there is no tranſgreſſion of law: vvhere is no [illegible]greſſion, no ſinne can be, becauſe euery ſinne is a tranſgreſſion of one law or other. Wherfore S. Paul ſayth that without law ſinne is dead and of no malice. And S. Ihon ſayth, that vvhoſoeuer ſinneth committeth iniquitie, and that ſinne is iniquitie, that is, tranſgreſſion: for ſo the Greeke word ανομία vvhich he vſeth, importeth: and therfore the Grecians commonly cal ſinne by the ſelfe ſame name. And although ſome actions vvhich are of them ſelues euil, are not ſinnes, becauſe the law forbiddeth them, but therfore are by the law forbidden becauſe of thẽ ſelues they are ſinnes: yet certain it is, that there is no ſinne but it is forbidden, either by the law of God, or of nature, or of man: & therfore wel might S. Auſtin ſay, that no ſinne ſhould be, if no law did forbid it. And although S. Paul ſayth that the Gentils ſinned without a law, and therfore ſhal be puniſhed vvithout a law: yet he excludeth only a vvritten law ſuch as the Iewes had, and vvithout that (ſayth he) the Gentils do ſinne, but yet not vvithout al law: for at leaſt they tranſgreſſed the law of nature, otherwiſe they could not haue ſinned, becauſe euery ſinne is againſt one

Luth. in cap. 2. Gal & in c. 4 Gal. & l. de libertate Chriſtiana.
Calu. l. 2. Inſt. c. 2. par. 9. & 14. See aboue c. 8.
No ſinne in a Chriſtian by this doctrin.
Rom. 7.
1. Ioan. 3.
l. 2. de pec. mer. c. 16.
Rom. 2.

 law or

law or others: and so if no law bynd vs in conscience, no sinne at al can be found in our actions, be they neuer so crossing and contrarie to reason. Secondly they denye free wil, and consequently take away al vice and vertue. For if vvhen I do that action vvhich is counted a sinne, I haue no free-wil, then I can do no otherwise: if I can do no otherwise, I am not to be blamed for that, vvhich I could not auoyd, but rather to be pityed that I am so constrained. And if vvhen I pray to God, or giue almes to the poore, I can do no otherwise, (as I can not if I haue no free-wil) I am not prayse vvorthy, because no God-a-mercie to him that doth wel vnawares, or vvhether he wil or no. Wherfore we commend those most vvhich do wel freely and of their owne choise, & vvhere we see men by feare or cõpulsion are driuen to wel doing, we commend them the lesse, by how much greater was the constrainte: which is a signe that free choise, more or lesse, is necessary to the making of a vertuous action. Thirdly they say that God imputeth no sinne vnto a faithful man: vvhence it follovveth that there is no sinne in their actions, or that God is deceiued, or is no right esteemer of things. But this they wil not say, and therfore must auouch, that there is no sinne in Christians actions. Fourthly (although herin they speake not with that consequence vvhich might haue been expected of men of reason) they affirme that al our actions, euen those that go for best, are of them selues mortal sinnes, vvhich deserue no better reward then eternal damnation: vvhich if it be true, thence must needs follow, that there is not any vertue in our actions, because vvhere vice is, vertue can not be: and so vertue vvhich proceedeth not but *ex integra causa, from an intier cause*, is cleane taken away. Fifthly they affirme that God is the author of al our sinnes, and seeing that his wil is his povver, by vvhich he causeth al things, sinne is according to his wil: yea they affirme that he moueth vs and eggeth vs to sinne, vvhich is a signe that he wil haue vs sinne. If sinne then be according to Gods wil, it can not offend him; but rather please him, because then we are pleased vvhen things do fal out according to our wil and desire: & seeing that vvhere no offence is, there can be no sinne, it followeth, that if God be the author of sinne, then sinne is no sinne at al.

Luth. l. de seruo arb. & in aßert. art 36. Calu l. 1. Inst. c. 15. par 8 l. 2. c 2. See aboue chap 6.

No vertue, no merit in our actions by this doctrin.

Luth ser super Sic Deus dilexit. Calu. l. 2. Inst. c. 14. & 18. See aboue chap. 4.

No sinne by this doctrin.

Luth. in c. vlt. Gal. Calu l. 2. Inst c. 5 l 3. c. 14. See aboue chap. 5.

Calu. l 4. Inst. c. 23 l. 2. c. 4. l. 1. c. 17. See aboue, booke 5. chap. 1.

Sinne pleaseth God by this doctrin.

3. Out of these opinions I gather, that neither sinne nor vertue is remaining in mens actions, and consequently if this doctrin be true, no man needeth to feare sinne or to care for vertue, because this word, *Vertue*, is but a word vvhich hath no thinge answerable vnto it: and this name, *sinne*, is but a bullibag or bugbear, deuised and inuented to

scarre

ſcarre fooles with al, becauſe according to the new religion, there is no more ſinne in the actions of men, then of brutiſh beaſtes.

The eleuenth Chapter shevveth, hovv they take avvay al conſcience, and ſo alſo open the vvay to al vice.

SO careful is our heauenly father, leſt we ſhould commit any ſinne, that he hath prouided, not one or twoe, but many and ſundry meanes to reſtrayn vs from it, as being the only thing vvhich diſpleaſeth and preiudiceth vs. He hath engrauen in our harts a law of nature and reaſon, vvhich dictateth vnto vs vvhat is good and vvhat is euil, and commandeth vs to embrace the one, and to auoid the other: by reaſon of vvhich law the Gentils (as S. Paul ſayth) could not plead ignorance for an excuſe for their ſinnes, becauſe they had a law written in their hartes, by vvhich they might haue ſquared their actions, and directed their liues according vnto reaſon, and within the bonds of nature. To this law before Chriſts comming, he added a vvritten law for our better direction in the way of vertue, not only natural, but alſo ſupernatural. And vvhen the fulnes of tyme, that is, the tyme of Chriſt and the new law, was come, he gaue vs an other law more perfect then the old, vvhich therfore leadeth vs to greater perfection And becauſe lawes are mute, vvhich can not ſpeake nor interprete them ſelues, and if they be not put in execution, they are eaſily contemned: he hath appointed interpretors, ſuch as are our Paſtors and Doctors, to expound this law vnto vs, and Magiſtrats alſo to ſee it put in execution, and to puniſh the tranſgreſſors. But leſt that we ſhould take our libertie in ſinning, vvhen we can auoide the rigour of the law, & the eye of the Magiſtrate, he hath lodged in our boſoms, a ſeuere iudge and monitor, called Conſcience, vvhich keepeth vs in awe, and maketh vs feare to ſinne, euen then, vvhen ſecrecie promiſeth ſecuritie. Wherfore Origen calleth conſcience a corrector & correcting ſpirit, becauſe it puniſheth and amendeth our faults and diſorders yea he calleth it alſo a Pedagoge and Schoolmaiſter, becauſe it inſtructeth vs and teacheth vs our duties, & kepeth vs in no leſſe awe then doth the Schoolmaiſter his ſchollers

Meanes to auoid ſinne.

The lavv of nature and reaſon.

Rom. 1.

The lavv of Moyſes.

The lavv of Grace.

Paſtors.

Magiſtrats.

Conſcience.

l.2. in c 1. Ep. ad Rom.

Ex Th 1. p.q. 71.a. 11. S. Damascen calleth conscience the eye of the soule, because it layeth al our actions open vnto the vew of the soule, and ruleth our vvhole life, as the eye doth the body.

Conscience is a lavv. 2. This conscience like a lawe telleth vs what in euery particular circumstance is lawful, what vnlavvful; like a witnes it accuseth vs, and bringeth in euidence against vs: like a Iudge it condemneth vs as guiltie, when we haue committed a fault, and declareth vs innocent of the fact when we haue not done it: & like an executioner or minister of iustice, it tormenteth vs, and layth vpon vs our dew paine and punishment. That conscience is a law, we easily perceiue, and knovv by daily experience in our selues. For when natural reason and our *Synderesis.* Synderesis telleth vs, that vice is to be eschewed, and that fornication is a vice, conscience concludeth, *ergo* thou mayst not commit it: and if notwithstanding consciences prohibition, we do commit the same, we do against conscience, & transgresse the law of conscience, which always in particular doth dictate vnto vs, what is to be embraced, and what is to be eschewed. When the lasciuious man is moued vnto lust, conscience like a law forbiddeth him, and when the theefe is tempted vnto thefte, conscience sayth he must not commit it, because he must not do that to an other, which he would not haue done to him selfe. And if a friend leaue a iewel with his friend, to which none but they two are priuie, conscience wil vrge him to restitution, and command him to restore that, to which the Princes law can not compel him, because it medleth not vvith secrets. And so conscience is a lavv, and so rigorous a lavv, that it admitteth no excuse, no cloake, nor dispensation.

Conscience is also a vvitnes 3. It is a witnes also, vvhich accuseth vs euen of our secret sinnes, and works of darkenes, and proueth vs guiltie before the Diuine tribunal. And whether thou be in bed or at borde, at home or abroad, in company or alone, it stil cryeth against the, *guiltie*. And if thou seekest by silence to put this vvitnes to silence, or by stopping the eares of thy soule, not to giue eare vnto him, he wil always busse in thy eares, that vvhich thou wouldst not heare, and wil so plainly conuict the, that thou canst not deny the fault. *Gen. 3.* When Adam and Eue had eaten of the forbidden fruite, before God accused them or tooke notice of the matter, their owne conscience accused them, and so plainly conuicted them, that they went & hid their heads in a bush for shame. *Gen. 4.* Cain also their vnto-ward sonne, had no sooner made oblation of his niggardly sacrifice, but conscience accused him, and brought in such

euidence

euidence against him, that he changed countenance like a guiltie person, and hong down his head like a sheep-biter. And he had no sooner butchered his innocent brother Abel, but Abels blood cryed vengeance against him. And thinke you that conscience held his peace? No, no, this witnes cryed out so shrilly against him, that he cryed *peccaui*, and acknowledged his fault to be so great, that Gods mercie was not able to forgiue it. Likewise the brethern of Ioseph after that they had most traiterously sold him, and vvith a bloody coat had couered al the matter, and cleared them selues also before their father: yet stil, (especially vvhen any aduersitie crossed them) their conscience accused them, and made them to confesse, that iustly their designements vvere crossed for the vnkind part vvhich they had played vvith their brother. So that the old prouerb herin is verified: *conscientia mille testes, conscience is a thousand vvitnesses.*

Gen. 4.

Gen. 42. 44.

4. Neither is conscience a lavv and vvitnes only: it is a Iudge also, vvhich condemneth vs if we be guiltie, and absolueth vs also, if vve be innocent and guiltles. Cain you see hangeth down his head like a condemned man, and confesseth the sentence iust: only his error was that he appealed not from the tribunal of conscience, to the high Iudge God him self, who vvould haue shewed mercie, if he had not dispayred of mercie. Conscience condemned Manasses, Dauid, Marie Magdalen, and al those pænitent sinners vvhich scripture hath recorded, and that vvith such euidence, that they confessed them selues guiltie, and the sentence iust. And vve see by experience, that vvhen vve seeke to excuse and flatter our selues, conscience vvil not be flattred, but like an incorrupt Iudge pronounceth sentence against vs, euen then vvhen before Princes tribunals vve be freed and absolued.

Conscience is a iudge also.

Gen. 4.

2. Paral. 33. Psal. 50. Luc. 7.

5. Conscience hauing pronounced sentence like a Iudge, executeth the sentence, and punisheth vs like an executioner, and minister of Iustice, causing in our mynds, vvher the sinne vvas contriued and conceiued, a certain remorse and vvorme of conscience, vvhose gnavving tormenteth vs. So that vvhen the soule hath conceiued sinne, and borne it also, and brought it to light by external action, farre othervvise doth this impious impe torment her, then doth the litle infant the vvoman great vvith child. For the vvoman conceiueth vvith pleasure, and though she beare vvith paine, yet after that she is deliuered and brought to bed, she reioiceth, and vvith so ioyful a hart, that she forgetteth her paines in bearing. But the soule, though in con-

Conscience is also an executioner.

The torment of an euil conscience.

in conceiuing sinne she finde some pleasure, yet not without some murmuring and grudging of conscience, and when she is deliuered of this bastardly Impe, then beginneth her torment. Iudas was so inwardly vexed and tormented after he had conceiued and contriued his treason against his louing and innocent Maister, that for an ease he went and hanged him self, counting that a lesse punishment then the torment of conscience. And true it is which the scripture sayth: *Semper præsumit sæua perturbata conscientia: a troubled conscience alvvays imagineth cruel and terrible things.* True it is also which S. Austin affirmeth, *that euery inordinate mynd is a paine vnto it self.* And true it is which Iuuenal the Poet sayth,

Mat. 27.

Sap. 17.

l. 1. Conf. c. 12.

Prima est hæc vltio, quod se
Iudice, nemo nocens, absoluitur.
The guilties first torment, is this:
That neuer he absolued is,
If he him self pronounce sentence,
VVhich is decreed by conscience.

Satyr. 13.

6. But to go no farther, experience wil witnes, that conscience wil neuer let a sinner be quiet, til by penance he hath ridde him self of his sinne, but waking it tormenteth him with remorse, sleeping with fearful dreames: and wher soeuer he goeth, it putteth hel before his eyes, and the seuere iudgement of God, the abomination of the sinne, and the greatnes of the offence. For as the dronken man, drinketh at the first with pleasure, but when he is dronke, his head aketh, his stomake is oppressed, and al his body is distempered: so although in the committing of the sinne we take some pleasure, yet when the sinne is committed, we feele the smart. And as the aduouterer, theefe, or murderer, after that the fact is cōmitted, hath always the seuere lawes and punishments before his eyes, and feareth the rumour of the people, and censure of the Iudge, thinketh euery man that looketh on him, ready to arrest him, and where men are not, is afrayd of trees, bushes and shadowes: so a man whose conscience condemneth him of sinne, feareth his owne shadowe and the darkenes of the night, imagineth that in euery thunder-clappe God leueleth at him, that euery old hovvse by which he passeth, or into which he entreth, staieth to make a fal on him, and surmiseth that in euery bush, one lyeth in wayt to kil him. King Richard the third may beare witnes of the torments, wherwith conscience vseth to afflict al transgressors: for he after that he had

A similitude

An other.

The feares of an euil conscience.

Sir. Th. More in his life.

he had most vnkindly and traiterously butchered his innocent Nephewes, vvhom he should haue protected, was always so troubled in mind, that after the fact he looked euer like a madman, sometimes laying his hand on his dagger, sometymes starting, sometymes soodainly looking back, as if he vvould vvarde some deadly blovv, vvhich always seemed prepared for him. Besides al this, sinne always breedeth a vvorme in conscience, which is fed by sinne, and neuer leaueth gryping and gnawing, til sinne vvhich is this vvormes food, by penance is taken avvay, that so the gnavving vvorme may dy for vvant of food, and conscience receiue ease, and be freed from such a torment.

The vvorme of Conscience. The food on vvhich it feedeth.

7. Novv contrarywise if conscience finde vs guiltles, she absolueth vs like a Iudge by sentence, and cleareth vs euen then, vvhen men condemne vs, and declaring invvardly our innocencie before God and our owne soule, recreateth the minde and feasteth it vvith a banquet of contentment, according vnto that saying: *Secura mens iuge conuiuium: a minde vvithout care is a continual banquet.* This peace foloweth a good conscience, which like a good iudge declareth vs before God not guiltie. So S. Ihon sayth that *if our hart* (that is our conscience) *reprehend vs not, vve haue a great confidence in God.* And S. Paul sayth, *that our glory is the testimonie of our conscience.* For although men think euil of vs, and condemne vs as guiltie, yet if conscience cleare vs, that is our contentment of mind, and glory before God. Wherfore S. Austin biddeth thee to think what thou wilt of Austin, only (sayth he) let not my conscience accuse me before God. By vvhich good offices of conscience it appeareth most manifestly, vvhat a sway conscience beareth in the rule and ordering of mans life, and actions.

The state of a good conscience. *Prou. 15.* *1. Io. 3.* *1. Cor. 1.* *l. cont. Secũd. Man. 6. 1.*

8. The Prince and magistrate ruleth only the outward man, punisheth only our external actions, because of them only he is able to iudge, but conscience gouerneth both the outward and inward man, iudgeth of our inward actions, condemneth them & correcteth them most seuerely as is already declared. So that he that taketh avvay conscience out of the world, openeth e wider gap to al vice and disorder, then if he should put al Princes and Magistrates out of office, & take the sword from them, because these being taken away, yet conscience being left, we shoul haue some guide and stay of our moral life: but if conscience be abandoned, then haue we no ruler nor gouernor of our inward man, yea nor of the outward man, when either secrecie promiseth securitie, or power dareth warrãt vs to go harmles.

Conscience ruleth the invvard man. *The svvay of conscience in the life of mã.*

And this the heathen Philosophers could see, yea could not but see; in so much that Cicero sayth: *Orat. pro. Milone.* *Magna vis est conscientiæ in vtramque partem, vt neque timeant qui nihil commiserunt, & pænam semper ante oculos versari putent qui peccauerunt: great force hath conscience in both partes* (that is in good and euil life) *in so much that they feare not, vvho haue committed no fault, and they, vvho haue offended haue alvvayes the punishemet before their eyes.* *l. 2. legib.* And in an other place he proueth by experience, how necessarie conscience is to restraine vs from sinne. For (sayth he) take away conscience, and what wil he do in the darke, that feareth nothing but the vvitnes or iudge? VVhat wil he do in the desert, vvhen he meeteth with a man loden vvith gold, and weaker then him selfe? Truly if conscience be taken avvay, vve vvil neuer make scruple of secret sinnes, no nor of publique transgressions, if either by power or bribe we can escape the penalties of the lawe. If conscience be once banished the vvorld, bargaines wil seldom holde, and promises wil as seldom be kepte, chastitie wil always be in danger, riches and treasures wil not be secure, Princes liues wil be subiect to hazard, false dealing vvil be rife in buying and selling, theeues, cooseners, cutpurses and conicatchers haue good leaue and libertie to exercise their artes, and the gap willy open vnto al vice. *The Reformers take avvay conscience by many points of their doctrin.* How pernicious then vnto vertue and how fauourable vnto vice is our Reformers doctrin, which (as I shal euidently proue, and therfore briefly, because euidently) despoileth the world of conscience, more necessarie to mans life, then the verie sunne it selfe.

9. They say as is already related, that to a faithful man and true Christian, God imputeth no sinne: *Aboue in the 4. c.* why then should a Christian make conscience of sinne, which if it be not imputed either is no sinne at al or else not to be cared for? *Calu. l. 3. Inst. c. 14.* They auouch, that since Adams fal, man neuer had frievvil and libertie, *Aboue ch. 6.* and seeing that where no libertie is no sinne can be, for no man deserueth euil for that vvhich he could not auoid, it folovveth that vvhosoeuer is perswaded, as al must be by their opinion, that he hath no frievvil, must make neither conscience nor scruple of any sinne. *Aboue ch. 8. Luth l. de lib. Christ. & in c. 2. & 4 ad Gal. Calu. l. 2. Inst. c. 2.* They affirme also, that by Christ we are fried from al obligation of lawes, in so much that no law can binde or touch our conscience: we nede not then make scruple of any transgression of sinne, which in that it is sinne, is against the obligation of one law or other, because where no law bindeth there is no obligation, where no obligation is, no breach or transgression can be found and where no transgression, there is no sinne, and where no sinne is, no

is, no conſcience of ſinne is to be made. It is an article alſo of faith amongſt them, or at leaſt a thing neceſſary to be beleued, that the commandements are impoſſible, vvho then wil be ſo mad as to make conſcience for not fulfilling the lawe which is impoſſible to be fulfilled? as wel truly may the priſoner make a conſcience that he goeth not to the Church or ſermon on the holy day, when he is faſt chained to a blocke in priſon, and the dores are faſt locked and bolted. Becauſe it is as impoſſible, if Caluin lye not, to kepe the commandements, as for that priſoner to go to the Church. They are of opinion, that God is the author of al our ſinnes, as vvel yea more then vve our ſelues, because he is the principal cauſe, we are only his inſtruments; which if it be true, no man nedeth to be ſo ſcrupulous as to make bones of that, of which God him ſelfe maketh no conſcience? And if conſcience be taken avvay, the law, witnes, Iudge and Executioner are taken a way: & ſo good leaue is giuen to play what euil parts you wil, if either we can by ſecrecie auoid the Magiſtrats eye, or by violence and force reſiſt his povver: for then, conſcience being taken a way, nothing is remaining to kepe vs in awe.

Aboue ch. 7. Luth. l. de ſeruo arb. & Calu. l. 2. Inſt. ch. 7. & in Harm. Mat. 19.

Aboue in the 5. booke, cha. 3. Calu. l. 1. Inſt. c. 17. l. 2. c. 4.

The tvvelfth Chapter shevveth hovv they open the gap to pride.

I Haue already declared how the Reformers by many points of their doctrin open the gap to al vices in general: now it ſhal not be amiſſe to ſhew, hovv they fauourize ſome eſpecially & in particular And firſt I wil beginne with pride, becauſe that vvas the firſt ſinne, and the firſt cauſe of al ſinnes, becauſe the diuel ſinned before man, and his firſt ſinne was ſwelling pride, by which he coueted to be as great, and as high in perfection as the higheſt. Yea many are of opinion, that Adams firſt ſinne alſo was pride, which moued him to eate of the forbidden fruite maugre the commandement of God imagining that ſo (for ſo the diuel had promiſed) he ſhould become like vnto God in knowing good and euil. And this is the cauſe why proud men eſpecially are called the children of the diuel, becauſe by pride they eſpecially reſemble him. Wherfore that doctrin which

Eccl. 10. Pride the firſt ſinne.

Gen. 3. Ioan. 8 The proud are children of the deuil.

stirreth vp a proude conceit in vs, can not be of God, because it moueth to pride which is of the diuel; and therfore if I shal proue that our reformers doctrin puffeth vp with pride al those which folowe it, I shal proue it not to be of God, but of the diuel.

Pride is a faut of al heretikes.

2. For although pride be a common disease of al heretikes (for who so preferreth his owne iudgement before the whole Church as al heretikes do in that they are heretikes, must nedes condemne him selfe of an extraordinarie pride) yet some heretikes by some points of their doctrin, haue giuen more especial cause of this sinne of pride. The Gnostikes were of opinion, that as gold though cast into the mire, neuer looseth his natiue colour and perfection: so a iust man (such as they counted them selues) can neuer be soyled, neuer loose his perfection, in what actions soeuer he intermedleth him selfe, though in aduouteries and fornications. VVhich doctrin moued them to such a conceit of them selues, that they thought them selues to knovv al things, and to be so perfect, that no sinne could contaminate them. The like was the pride of the Nouatians, vvho therfore called them selues, pure and cleane. And to omit the personal pride of Arius, Nestorius, Luther, and Caluin, which in the first booke I haue set downe, let vs see how their doctrin puffeth men vp vvith pride.

The Pride of the Gnostikes ex Iren. l. 1. c. 1

Olde heretikes pride.

Ex Amb. l. 1 de pœnit. c. 3.

aboue chap 6.

The reformers pride.

3. They are of opinion, as is already related, that we are iust by no other iustice then Christs own iustice, vvhich doctrin who soeuer embraceth, he must nedes be perswaded that he is as iust as Christ him selfe, because in his opinion they haue both one and the same iustice: vvhich persuasion is ynough to stirre vs vp to Luciferiã pride, as is already in an other place demonstrated. They assure their Schollars also, that the iustifying faith is a ful assurance of election iustice and saluation, as may appeare by their owne words, vvhich I haue in this seuenth booke already set downe vvhich also giueth great occasion of an insolent pride. For if vvhen we perswade our selues (as Catholiques do) that we are nether sure vvhat now we are before God, nor vvhat shal become of vs hereafter, we haue occasion to humiliate our selues, *and to vvorke our saluation in feare:* then certes he that perswadeth him selfe, that he is most sure of his saluation, hath great occasion to become careles, arrogant, hautie, and highmynded. VVe haue an example of a noble woman called Gregoria maide of honour to the Empresse, who hauing conceiued highly of S. Gregories sanctitie, wrote vnto him to imparte vnto her a secret, to wit, whether her sinnes were forgiuen or no: but S. Gregorie answered her that she demanded

Aboue booke 3. Chap. c. 3. 8.

Aboue in the 3. chap.

Calu l. 3. Inst. c. 2. par. 7. 9. 10. 16. 19.

Philip. 2.

Greg l. 6. Reg. c. 186.

manded

manded of him a hard and vnprofitable question: harde, because his sanctitie was not such as to deserue a reuelation from God of so secret a matter: vnprofitable, because (sayth he) such a reuelation vnto you were not expedient: better it is that you should be ignorant of that til the last day, vvhich must alwayes be feared and suspected, that in the meane tyme you may vvash avvay your sinnes, by teares of contrition.

4. They affirme also that euery man hath a priuate spirite, by vvhich he is sure vvhich is true Scripture, and vvhat is the true meaning therof: who therfore, be he man or vvoman, clerke or cobler, is supreme iudge of religion, and is to rely neither on Pope nor Church nor Councel, for faith and religion. Which doctrin hovv high it is able to enhance the spirites of men that are so perswaded, a blind man may see. And this is the very cause why Luther wil iudge both of Churches & Councels & preferre his owne iudgemẽt before them al. For although he sayth only that by Scripture he wil iudge Fathers, Churches, Apostles, and Angels also, yet seing that the controuersie is not whether Fathers or Scriptures are to beleued, because they were neuer contrarie, but rather whether Luther or they better vnderstood the Scriptures, he maketh him selfe in effect iudge of Church, Pope Counceles, Fathers and Angels: vvherin how brauely he playeth the part of Lucifer, is as euident, as that Luther and Lucifer begin vvith a letter.

See the first booke, chap. 2.

see the first booke, chap. 3.

The thirtenth Chapter shevveth hovv their doctrin induceth men to idlenes, yea hovv idlenes, according to their doctrin, is the perfection of a Christian life.

L creatures are created to vvorke and labour, and so they must attaine vnto their end and perfection, because God and nature hath so ordained it. The angelical spirits like birds in the spring tyme (for heauen is a continual spring tyde) sing prayses vnto their Creatour, and attend continually vpon the diuine Maiestie on high, yet so that they haue also an eye vnto our affayres and necessities in this lower vvorld. For the supreme Angels receiue illumina-

Al creatures labour, as Angels.

tions from God, vvhich they impart vnto the inferiour, vvhich are alwayes occupied in garding and defending vs and menaging our affaires: and so ether mediately or immediately they are *administratorij* *Heb.1.* *spiritus, administring spirits.* The heauens moue continually, for the better *The heauens.* and more equal bestowing of their light and influences vpon this inferiour vvorld. The Sunne leaueth our hemisphere at night, not to *The sunne.* slepe or to rest him selfe, but to runne an other course in the other hemisphere for the illuminating of those that are Antipodes to vs, vvhich course being runne, he returneth to vs in the morning, and so is neuer idle. The moone euery moneth endeth her course, and euery *The moone.* starre and planet hath his taske appointed him, vvhich in a certain tyme he must accomplish. The earth vvhen she is out of her place *The earth.* moueth dowhward to the center, and vvhen by force she is deteined, she sheweth by her weight what an inclinatiō she hath vnto her proper motion. The fire mounteth aboue al towards the concauitie of *The fire.* the Moone, vvhich is his natural place: the water and ayre take vp the midle roomes, where and vvhither they moue continually. Trees, *The aire and vvater.* plantes, and herbes seeme in winter to take their rest after their former labours, and in the spring tyme they fal to worke again, and first *Plantes.* they bring forth leaues, then bloomes and blossomes, and lastly the sweete fruites of their labours. Brute beasts besides the labours, to vvhich by man they are appointed, haue their owne proper exercises in vvhich they occupie them selues. The Bee is not so bigge in body, *The Bee.* as busie in operation, in so much that vvhen we wil describe a laborious man, we say that he is as busie as a bee. These litle creatures what paynes take they in gathering their hony, in making their combes, in disposing & vvorking their hony, & whilest some are working abroad to bring home the matter of hony, some stay at home to order it, some vvatche for the securitie of them that laboure, and al are incensed against the idle drones, and do not only expel them out of their company, but punish them also seuerly euen vnto death it selfe. The ante *Prou. 6* also, of whom the scripture biddeth the idle person to lerne his lesson, *The Ante.* laboreth in the sommer to make prouision for that on vvhich he is to liue in winter. So laborious are these litle creatures, that often they *Plin. l. 11. c. 3.* carie burdens bigger then them selues, and that with such diligence, *Horat. l. 1.* that with passing often times one way, their litle feete do make a path *Satyr. 1.* to appeare euen in the flinte And vvhen amongst other prouision they haue brought home their corne to their barnes, they are not idle after haruest is done, but sometymes they are occupied in nibling vpon the

the endes of the corne, and graines, lest they should growe afreshe; and lest that the moysture of the earth corrupt their corne, they bring it forth in a sunnie day to drying, and afterwards they carie it again into their granaries. Birdes builde their owne nestes and fly farre and often for the tymber & morter vvhich is belonging vnto the making of such a pallace. Conyes worke their burrowes out of the ground, and there is no creature vvhich is not deputed to vvorke in one kind or other. *Byrdes.*

2. And shal we think that mans felicitie consisteth in idlenes? No no, as *the birde is bread to fly, so man is borne to vvorke and labour*: in so much that God appointed Adam his taske in Paradise, which was to labour and til the grounde; vvhich labour notwithstanding should haue been no paine but rather a pleasure and recreation vnto him. For if Cyrus King of the Persians tooke such delight in gardening, that he cast the beddes and knottes of his owne gardens, set his owne herbes, and planted, and pruned also his trees with his owne hands; if the Romaine dictators taken from tillage and husbandry, returned againe to the same exercise after the tyme of bearing office vvas fully expired, much more might Adam in the state of innocencie and the garden of pleasure haue laboured, and vvorked for his recreation and pleasure. Thus God delt with Adam to signifie by this corporal exercise vvhich he appointed him, the taske and labour vvhich is necessarie for the soule in the exercise of moral & supernatural vertue, vvhose operations are called vvorkes. *Iob. 5. Adams labour in Paradise. Perier. l. 4. in Gen. Vvhat Adams labour signified.*

3. And truly vvhoso considereth the end of man and his felicitie, vvhich consisteth in the perpetual vision and contemplation of God, vvhich is the most noble operation that man hath, wil not meruail that the meanes to attaine to this end should be good vvorks and operations. Wherfore Scripture almost in euery place exhorteth vs to the obseruation of the commandements, to vvorks of charitie, iustice, mercie, temperance, fortitude, patience and such other vvorks of vertue. And for this cause our life is some tymes compared to a warfare, in vvhich we must alwayes be fighting, or arming, or fortifying our selues, or obseruing the enemie, as souldiars do; some tymes we are compared to labourers in the vinyeard, who vvorke for wages: some tymes to runners, and wrastlers, who runne and striue for a gole, crowne, or reward. So that our perfection also consisteth in action, labour and operation. *Th. 1. 2. q. 3. a. 2. & 4. Felicitie is in action, so are the meanes.*

4. And truly who considereth how vnfitting idlenes is, so a man

wil

Idlenes, hovv pernicious it is

wil neuer dreame, that in it should consist a Christians perfection. For idlenes is the mother of al vice, and the very bane of vertue, and no lesse pernicious to mans soule and body also, then it is to the grounde of the gardener or husband man. For as the earth not tilled nor laboured, bringeth forth nothing but weedes, as the tree not pruned beareth nought but leaues, and at the length not so much as leaues: so if by continual exercise of vertue, and good vvorks, the seedplotte of our soule be not continually manured and tilled, the seede of Gods inspirations and inclinations to vertue, vvhich are neuer wanting in our soule, bring forth no frute of good vvorks and vertuous actions, but only the breres, brambles and vvedes of vice do ouergrow the soule. And as the poole that standeth and moueth with no streame stinketh, and engendreth nothing else but frogges, snakes and serpents, so the soule of man which is alwayes idle and vnoccupied, and neuer moued with the erercise of vertue, putrifieth in her owne corruption, and bringeth forth nothing but monstrous vices. Truly when man is idle, he is vnarmed and exposed to al danger. Then the diuel taketh his tyme, the flesh assaulteth him, the vvorld molesteth him, and he becometh slaue and captiue to them al, because by operation he maketh no resistance. And vvhereas much hurt cometh of, idlenes neuer any exploit or entreprise vvorthy a man proceeded from it. Hence procede fornications, adulteries, robberies: for vvhen the minde is not occupied in good cogitations, it is occupied in euil, because it can not be altogether idle, but either it is wel or il occupied. Wherfore the Poete demandeth vvhy Aegistus became an adulter, and he answereth thus. *In promptu causa est, desidiosus erat: The cause is easily to be told, he vvas an idle person.* When a man is idle and not exercised in vertuous actions, vvhich produce good habits vvherby our sensualitie is bridled, and our passions are moderated, then the flesh waxeth wanton, sensualitie becometh effeminat, the passions are vnruly, and the man impotent to al vertue. Wherfore Scipio in one thing was vviser then Cato, because Cato vvould haue had Carthage destroyed, that Rome might enioy a freer peace and libertie: but Scipio counted it more profitable for Rome to haue Cathage stand, that Rome might so haue an enemie to exercise her: which opinion of Scipio time proued truest: for when Carthage was afterwards ruined, Rome thinking her sel e secure, became carcles and idle, and Romaines by idlenes lost their former force & prowes, & became altogether effeminat, impotent & slaues to sensualitie, who before had bene Lords of the world.

A similitude — *An other.* — *To vvhat danger an idle mā is exposed.* — *Effectes of Idlenes.* — *Scipio his Counsel.*

5. And

5 And yet according to our new reformers doctrin, idlenes is the accomplishment and perfection of moral, and Christian life. For they first of al wil make vs to beleue that a naked faith, by vvhich we aprehend Christs iustice to be ours, is that vvhich iustifieth. and vvhich is sufficient to saluation, vvithout good vvorks, or obseruatton of the lawe. VVhich if it be true, Christian perfection shal consist in an abstracted and idle apprehension of Christs iustice, but in no practise nor exercise of vertue, in no labour or good vvorke at al: and so wheras al other creatures attain to their end by action, motion, & labour, man only by idlenes, that is by apprehending only, & doing nothing, shal purchase his felicitie. The artifier shal come to perfection in his art by labour, exercise, and operation, not of one or two but many dayes, yea of his vvhole life, because by continual practise he augmenteth his skil: but the art of a Christian shal require no practice at al, no labnur, no vvorking, because according to this opinion, one only act of faith before a man dyeh, is sufficient to iustifie him from al his former sinnes, and to make him as iust and as holy as Christ him selfe, who is the *holy of holyes*: and so eternal felicitie, vvhich is an operation, by vvhich vve see God face to face and enioie our *summum bonum*, shal be gotten vvithout operation, and we shal vvinne our gole vvithout runuing, at cheue our victorie vvithout fighting, and gaine our vvages vvithout vvorking; that is by an idle fayth, vvhich apprehendeth only, but doeth nothing.

Hovv the reformers fauour idlenes. *Aboue in the 2. chap.* *Luth. l. de lib. Christ. & com. in c. 2. Gal. & in assert. ar. 36. Calu. l. 3. Inst. c. 18.*

6. They teach vs also, that since Adams fal our nature is so corrupt, that al our actions, euen those that go for best, are mortal, and damnable sinnes, in so much that you may as wel and as soone get oyle out of a marble stone, as wring one good vvorke from the nature of man. Which if it be true, then certes sleeping and idlense is our greatest perfection. For if in euery act we sinne mortally, better were it to sleepe, then to vvatch and pray, better to sit idle and to do nothing, then something, because in doing nothing we do no harme, in doing something vvhatsoeuer it be (be it prayer and almes dedes) we sinne mortally, and so idlenes is our perfection, because better it is to be idle them il occupied. Whence foloweth my intended conclusion, that according to the reformers doctrin idlenes is the perfection of a Christian mans life, and the best and surest meanes to attaine vnto his felicitie and to purchase his saluation.

Aboue in the 5. chap. *Luth in c. vlt. ad Gal. l. confut. Rat. Lat. Calu. l. 2. Inst. c. 5. l. 3. c. 14.*

The cōclusion.

The fourtenth Chapter shevveth vvhat an enimie the reformers doctrin is to Chastitie, euen that vvhich is required betvvixt man and vvife.

Chastitie cōmended.

Lucretia.

CHASTITIE is a vertue vvhich always hath bene prized at an high rate, & valewed as one of the most precious iewels of moral vertues: in so much that euen the heathens, though destitute of the light of faith, beholding the beautie of this vertue, fel into admiration of it, and from admiration came to be in loue with the same. Lucretia a noble matrone of Rome is famous for this vertue, who being violently oppressed by Tarquinius Superbus sonne, tooke the matter for such a disgrace, that with her owne handes she killed her selfe, counting lesse of death then of life ioined with such a blemish. And the pagane Poets vvere so moued with the splendour of this her vertue, that they could not see the fowle fault vvhich she
l. 1. ciu. c. 19.
comitted in killing her selfe. For as S. Austin sayth, if it was no dishonestie to be oppressed vnwillingly, it was no iustice to punish her selfe
In the Vestal virgins.
with death, who had not bene dishonest. The Vestal virgins also were much admired for this vertue, or at least for a shew of the same, and seuerly were they punished vvhen professing chastitie, they liued
Liu. dec. 1. l 8. Dec. 3. l. 2.
loosely: vvhich yet they did so seldome, that when such a fault hapned, the yeare was counted vnluckie, and the citie of Rome was pur-
Ex Gorg. in orat. pro Hel.
ged, and the Gods appeased with extraordinarie sacrifices. The lawe of Areopagus punished no lesse him, that by importunitie entised, then
In the lavv of Areopagus.
him that enforced, because the first abused both soule and body, the second the body only. By vvhich it may wel appeare, of vvhat valew this vertue is, because the diuel as by pagans he desired to be honoured for God in their sacrifices, so vvould he be serued of them, by his Vestals, as God is by his Virgins.

2. And not only pagans haue estemed of chastitie: but brute beasts also, although they be not capable of true vertue, haue affected an
Epiph. hær. 7. In the Liones.
image of this vertue. The Lionesse permitteth the Lion but once, and propagateth her kinde but once only, to kepe chastitie, so much as may be vvithout iniury to her kind. The birde called Porphyrion

vvil

vvil sorte her selfe with no mo mates then one, and so abhorreth womanish dishonestie, that if she see the wife commit adulterie, she wil bewray it to the husband by hanging her selfe. Yea if this bird perceiue any maide to play the harlot, she wil pine her selfe away to death. The like is the nature of the Turtle, who vvhen her mate is dead, mourneth in solitarie places, and neuer wil admit any other to her company, much lesse wil she do it vvhilest her mate liueth, and so (sayth S. Gregorie Nazianzene) she giueth vs to vnderstand, at what a price virginitie is to be valewed. The Storke is such a louer of chastitie, that (as Ælian reporteth) vvhen on a tyme a certain vvoman of the citie Ceres in Thessalia vvas false to her husband, in being to familiar with her man, this bird so abhorred the fact that she pulled out the adulterers eyes. Bees also are so delighted with chastitie that besides that they conceiue vvithout carnal copulation, they wil not stay in their hiues, if their keper be blasphemous, slouenlyke, greasie, vnchast, or impure of body.

Ælian l 14. 8.c.35. Plin. l. 10.c. 56. In byrdes. Cirillius. Carm. ad Virg l. 8. c. 27. Georg. Pictorius Villinganus med & Pelladius.

3. And be a man neuer so much giuen to luxurie, yet he experienceth how nature reuerenceth this vertue of chastitie. For vvho is so impudent, that is not ashamed of his owne lustes, & therfore euerie one desireth darkenes, or obscuritie and secrecie to hide them, euen then vvhen he taketh but his lawful pleasure with his wife. And why sayth S. Austin are we more ashamed of our lustes, then other vices or passions? The reason is (sayth he) because the rebellion of the flesh, is farre different from other vices and passions, because these we can vvhen we wil especially if we adde force to our wil, represse and moderate, but the flesh hath gotten (since Adams fal) such an hand ouer the spirit and wil, that though we may deny consent vnto her lustes and desires, yet we can not alwayes quite represse them, be we as holy and perfect as S. Paul was. And this maketh the spirit ashamed, to take so fowle a foyle of the flesh, vvhich as she is inferior to the spirit, so should she be at the spirits becke and commandement. Out of these premises Cicero gathereth this conclusion, that seing man is ashamed of pleasure, it is an argument, that it is vnworthy the excellencie of mans nature, and I wil adde an other conclusion, vvhich is this, that if lust and corporal pleasure be a thing to blush at, then chastitie vvhich is an abstinence from pleasure, is a vertue most honourable, gracing and beseming mans nature.

In Bees. Aug l. 14. ciu c. 17. 18. 19 In man. c. 19. Th 2. 2. q. 151. a. 1. VVhy vve are most ashamed of lust. l. 1. Offic. l. 3. Tusc quest.

4. And although in the beginning of the vvorld, when mankind vvas not yet fully propagated, and again after Noes flud, vvhen it was

VVhy matrimonie vvas

commanded at first. Gen. 2. almost ruinated, God commanded matrimonie, yet did he euen then by many signes and tokens, but afterwards more especially, commend also perpetual chastitie as a vertue most commendable. For although he him selfe made the mariage betwixt Adam and Eue, and bad them increase and multiplie, yet he created them of virgins earth, vvhich as yet had not lost her integritie, and he preserued them virgins so long as they kept their inocencie; and so virginitie and innocencie vvere companions in paradise, and the vse of matrimonie began with miserie. And if antiquitie may procure credit, virginitie must take the precedence of matrimonie, because the vvoman is a virgin before a wife, and a mayd before a mother. Yea although both in the law of nature, & in the law vvritten, the greatest part imbraced matrimonie, and few then did settle their cogitations vpon virginitie, partly because men were as yet carnal and imperfect, partly because mankind was not much propagated, partly because the Messias vvas not yet borne, & therfore euery one desired to mary, hoping that the Messias might chance to descend from their race (vvhich was the cause why barrennes was then so ignominous) yet euen then virginitie had her folowers, & wel vvillers. Abel, the first Priest we read of after Adam, & the first martyr, was a virgin: Helias, Helizeus, Hieremie, and S. Ihon Baptist, as the Scripture insinuateth, and S. Hierom affirmeth, were al chaste and vndefiled virgins. The high Priest of Moyses law, although he might marry (because that people vvas carnal and their sacrifices vvere carnal & so required no virgin Priests) yet he commanded to mary a virgin, and to absteine from her also vvhen he vvas to offer Sacrifice.

Virginitie & Innocencie companions. Matrimonie began vvith miserie. Virginitie is before Matrimonie The reason of mariage before Christ. Abel, Helias &c virgins. li. 1. cont. Iou.

5. But in the new law, vvhich brought more grace and greater perfection with it, and therfore is called the fulnes of tyme, virgins were more frequent. For after that the authour of this law Christ Iesus vvas borne of a virgin mother, then al the world semed to be inamoured with virginitie. The Apostles vvhich were Christes first Priests, and Bishops, were either virgins, or liued chast like virgins, after pristhood. S. Philip had fowre daughters, vvhich liued and dyed virgins. S. Mathew the Apostle in Æthiopia instituted an angelical college of virgins, to vvhich he appointed Iphegenia the Kings daughter for the Abbesse, which afterward cost him his life, but got him the crowne of martyrdome. Philo the Iew maketh mention of diuers societies, vvhich in the primatiue Church liued chastly. Iustinus martyr affirmeth, that no people was so giuen vnto chastitie, as were the

Virginitie florisheth in the nevv lavv especially. The Apostles virg. Hier. lib. con. Iou. Act. 21. S. Philippes daughters.

Christ-

Christians of his tyme, vvhen (as he sayth) both men and vvomen kept virginitie to the end, and caryed it with them to their graue, yea to heauen for a iewel. The like report giueth Tertullian of the Christians of his tyme: S. Ignatius S. Paules scholar in one of his epistles, saluteth a College of virgins, and a societie of vvidowes, and vvhen he was going to martyrdome, the cogitation of his death, & the lions vvhich were to deuour him, could not put them out of his mynd, but euen then he commended them to his Deacon and successors, as the *precious Ievvels of Christ.* Ruffinus also and other Historiographers in commendation of Quene Helena Constantines mother, our countrie woman, telleth how she coming to Hierusalem being the Emperesse of the vvorld, vouchsaffed to serue the virgins at table, as a wayting maide. And Eusebius putteth amongst the prayses of Constantine her sonne, that he caryed alwayes a great respect to virgins, perswading him self, that God him selfe, dwelled in such chaste myndes. Neither can our Reformers answer with any probalitie, that this was the abuse & corruption of that tyme, because it vvas the vse and custome of the prime Christians, in vvhose memories the life, vvorkes, words, and examples of Christ and his Apostles vvere fresh, and in whose harts the bloud of Christ as yet was vvarme.

Euseb. l. 3. c. 30.
In vita eius.
S. Matthevvs Nunrie.
l. de vit. contempl.
Apol. 2.
Virgins of the primatiue Church.
Apol c. 2.
Ep ad Philad.
Ep. ad Herc. Dec.
Q. Helens respect to virgins
Ruff l. 1. c. 8.
Theod. l. 1. 6. 18.
l 4. vita Cōst. c 28.
Constantins respect also.

6. And if this were an abuse, holy Scripture is the cause of it, which in many places commendeth chastitie and virginitie. The Prophete Isaie or rather God by his mouth, biddeth Eunuches, that is, chast virgins, not to complain that they haue no posteritie in vvhich their name may continewe, for sayth he, I wil giue them a *place in my hovvse and a better name*, then they could haue in sonnes and daughters, for I giue them *an æternal name* vvhich shal neuer perish. Where he can not meane Ennuches by nature, for there is no reason to promise more to them then to others, because their chastitie is forced, but he must nedes be vnderstood of those Eunuches, of vvhich Christ speaketh, vvhen he sayth there are some that haue *gelded them selues*, that is haue depriued them selues of carnal pleasures by frie election. S. Paul also auoucheth, that *it is good* not to touch a woman, And againe he counsayleth them that are *frie from a vvife not to seeke a vvife* Yea, sayth he, *I vvould haue al like my selfe*, that is chast and continent as al the Interpreters expound. And although (sayth he) *I haue no lavv, yet I counsail al to be virgins.*

c. 56. Aug. l. de san Virg. l. 19 proof out of Scripture for Virginitie.
Mat. 19.
1 Cor. 7.
Ibidem.
Aug l. de Sanct. Virg.
Ibidem.

7. Yea reason also giueth virginal chastitie the precedence of Matrimonie. For first as I haue sayd already, in that we are ashamed of al

Reasons to proue Chastitie. carnal copulation, euen of that which by mariage is made lawful, it is an argument that such chastitie is more beseming the nature of man. *The first.* *The second.* Secondly, man is reasonable and sensual, spiritual and carnal, by reason of his compound nature, and by the reasonable part, he agreeth vvith Angels, by the sensual part with beastes: and seing that the reasonable part, is the best and noblest portion in him, abstinence from corporal pleasures maketh him most like to him selfe, yea to Angels, because by that he liueth a reasonable life, yea and Augelical, & more then Angelical, who in flesh, and bloud liueth chastly like an Angel. *The third.* Thirdly oure goods are diuided into three partes, to wit, the goods of fortune, which are riches, honours, offices, and such like: the goods *Our goods are three fold.* of the body, which are health and pleasure: the goods of the mynd, which are vertues, and our owne willes, and desires: if then it be a thing highly pleasing God, when by voluntarie pouertie, or almesdedes, we despoile our selues of our goods of fortune, for his sake, or his members the poore: if it pleaseth him also, when by obedience we resigne our willes and desires, which are the goods of our mynd, into the handes of our Superiors, and consequently into the handes of God, from vvhom they haue their authoritie: vvhy shal it not be laudable to weane our selues, euen in the flowre of our yeares, from those goods of the body, which are called pleasutes, but yet so are goods and pleasures of the body, that commonly they do the soule the *The fourth.* greatest domages and displeasures. Lastly if to vse moderation in eating and drinking be a vertue called temperance, why shal not a mo- *An obiectiō.* deration in pleasurs of the flesh and sensualitie (which we cal chastitie) be esteemed also as a vertue?

8. But our Epicures wil say, that a moderation in pleasurs is good, but yet as it is vnlawful to absteine altogether from meate, so is it a *The ansvver.* sinne to renounce al pleasurs of the kody. To this vve haue an easy answer, that the first abstinence is vnlawful, because it killeth the body which can not liue without meate, but the second is lavvful and laudable, because corporal pleasures are not necessary for the bodyes maintenance, and commonly are preiudicial to the soule, and some- *An other obiection.* tymes to the body also. But yet they haue not doone, it is against nature as they say, and preiudicial to mankind to liue chastly. I answer *The ansvver.* that chastitie is against or aboue the nature of the flesh and sensualitie, by which we agree with beastes, but it is most beseming our reasonable nature, which is the principal part of man, and so is absolutely agreable vnto man, because the reasonable part is that vvhich maketh him a

him a man. And although if al men should liue chaste it would be preiudicial to mankind, yet for some to be chast, it is not any vvise derogating: and vve nede not feare lest al men be chast, because it is not a thing so easie, but is an harde and heroical vertue, vvhose difficultie deterreth the most part of men. Such an obiection Vigilantius once made, *If al be virgins* (sayd he) *mariages shal not be, children shal not cry in cradles, and mankind shal perish.* But S. Hierom ansvvereth him: *rara est virtus, nec à pluribus appetitur: the vertue is rare, and not desired of many*, and so it is not to be feared lest al be virgins. S. Austin also ansvvereth, that he could vvish vvith S. Paul that al vvould abstain from the vse of mariage (vvhich yet is not to be feared) for so (sayth he) the Citie of God vvould be accomplished, and the vvorld should sovvner haue an end, and Christes Church more speedily be translated from hence to heauen.

Hier. l. 2. contra Vigil. *Ibidem.* *l. de bono cõiugali c. 10.* *1. Cor. 7.*

9. Novv therfore it being proued, that virginitie and chastitie is laudable, and more beseming man then Matrimonie, because it is agreable to man as he is reasonable, it remaineth that we declare how our aduersaries by their doctrin do misprice this vertue. But first it shal not be amisse to distinguish three kinds of chastitie, that so it may appeare the better vvhat enemies they are to al the three kinds. The first chastitie is neuer to haue experienced carnal pleasurs, which is called virginitie. The second, is to haue experienced them in Matrimonie, but neuer after, and this is widowes chastitie. The third is a moderate vse of this pleasure in Matrimonie betvvixt man and vvife. The last is lavvful and honest, because as Matrimonie is lavvful so is the vse of it, and consequently the delight which folovveth the vse is also lavvful. The second is more perfect, because it abstaineth at least from future pleasurs. The first is perfectest of al, because it is a perpetual abstinence from al carnal pleasure.

3. Kindes of Chastitie. *Virginitie.* *VVidual Chastitie.* *Coniugal chastitie.*

10 To come therfore more nere our purpose, let vs see vvhat is the conceit of our reformers concerning this goodly vertue. Luther semeth to be of Rabbi Salomons opinion, vvho condemned al those as guiltie of homicide, vvho endeuoured not to beget children: because he labourreth by al meanes for multiplication: and to make matrimonie more frequent, and to giue sensualitie a greater scope, he taketh avvay al impediments, and obstacles, vvhich the Church had layd in the vvay of sensualitie, partly for the loue she hath of chastitie, partly for the greater honour and decencie of Matrimonie.

in c. 9. Gen. *Hovv Luther laboureth for multiplicatiõ.*

11. And first to begin with consanguinitie, he permitteth and ad-

mitteth

To. 5. ser. de Mat. Vitteb. 1522. l. de cap. Bab. c. de matrim.

mitteth matrimonie betwixt brothers and sisters children, betvvixt the sonne and mother in law, yea (sayth he) if the vvife can do it secretly, she may ly vvith her husbands brother, if she experience that she can haue no issue by him. In briefe he taketh away al impedimẽts of consanguinitie, vvhich are not set downe in the old law. In affinitie, he maketh very few impediments: for, sayth he, a man may mary with his vvifes sister, with his wifes mothers daughter, with the daughter of his wifes vncle, with any cousin germaines of his wifes cousins. In spiritual cognation, which is contracted by Baptisme, he acknowledgeth no impediment at al, but alloweth of Mariage euen betwixt the godfather, and goddaughter. In adoption also he findeth as few impediments, permitting the father to mary with his adopted daughter. Infidelitie with this man of faith, is no obstacle, for, sayth he, it is lavvful to mary with a Turke, or Iew, as to eate and drinke with them. Vow of virginitie is no hinderance vvith him, and therfore he being a Freyr maryed a Nonne. The like is his opinion of Priesthood. And thus he maketh the way broader to al sensualitie and consequently to hel it selfe. Caluin in part subscribeth to Luther, for he misliketh much that the Church hath made *spiritual cognation* an impediment, and hath made mo restraintes from mariage then either Moyses or the policie of many countries haue euer dreamed of. And thus they giue greater libertie to Mariage, and endeuour by al meanes to bring virginitie, which is the noblest and worthiest kind of chastitie into disgrace. Luther and al the reformers so highly esteme, and prayse matrimonie, coldy commending, yea by odious comparisons iniuriously despising virginitie.

He taketh a vvay al impediments of Matrimonie.

l. 4. Inst. c. 15. Caluin giueth great scope to mariage.

12. Luther sayth that virginitie only in this excelleth matrimonie, that it is not combred with cares, and trubles, which are incident to mariage, and therfore is a lesse hindrance to preaching and prayer, but as for merite before God, he sayth, that matrimonie is as good as virginitie: yea so was this mans mynd sotted vpon mariage, that he was not ashamed to say, that *matrimonium est velut aurum, status vero spiritualis veluti stercus: matrimonie is like gold, but the spiritual state of life is like an homly thing.* See hovv carnal this man of God is, hovv sensual he is and beastly, that taketh vpon him to reforme the world, and auoucheth him selfe the only man that hath the spirit of God. See how opposit Luther is to S. Paul, he counsayleth virginitie as better, then Matrimonie, Luther sayth it is no better then an homly thing, wherwith it had bene better that his mouth had bene filled, then that he

Serm. cit. de matrim. to. 5. in 1. Cor. 7. S. Austin. l. de Sact. Virg. c. 13 teacheth otherwyse. Ibidem. Hovv Carnal a Prophet is this? 1. Cor. 7.

should

should haue vttered such beastly doctrin. But he wil say that it is not virginitie, vvhich with so fowle a mouth he thus mispriceth, but the vow of virginitie, vvhich is a state of life: but if virginitie be good lawful, and commendable, why may not a man vow that life vvhich he may laudably lead, especially seing that holie Scriptures allow of vovves, cōmanding al to kepe them that make them. Secondly Luther auoucheth that if one wife wil not content sensualitie, one may haue mo then one at once, for (sayth he) this was permitted in the old law, and in the new I find it left indifferent, neither forbidden nor commanded. And seing the vvomans sensualitie is as hardly satisfied as the mans, she also by the same reason may haue many husbandes at once (vvhich was neuer permitted to the Iewes) and seing that no iust number can be set downe (for if two vviues content one man, three wil not satisfie an other) it foloweth that a man haue a *tot quot* of wiues, and so may contend with Salomon in the number of concubines.

Psal. 75 Ecc. 5. In propositionibus de bigamia 62. 65 66.

Luther permitteth many Wiues at once. l. de captiu. Bab. c. de matrim.

He permitteth often diuorce, in the very bōde of vvedlock.

13. Thirdly this spiritual father permitteth diuorsement in many cases, not only for bed or cohabitation, but also euen in the bond of mariage, and alloweth of them who not only separate them selues from the company of their wiues or husbandes, but who also take others in their places. In vvhich point Caluin and al the new confrerrie agreeth. And first in case of fornication they al affirme that the partie innocent may mary an other, not vvithstanding that Christ sayth, *Vvhat God hath conioyned let not man seperate, and againe: vvhosoeuer shal dimisse his vvife and mary an other, committeth aduoutrie.* And S. Paul not in his owne, but in Gods name commandeth, that the wife leaue not her husband, and if she leaue him, he biddeth her remaine vnmaried, or to be reconciled to her husband. And therfore seing that Scripture can not be contrarie to Scripture, vvhen Christ sayd: *Vvhosoeuer dimisseth his vvife, but for fornication, & shal mary an other doth cōmit aduoutrie*: the sense is not, that in case of fornication a man may take an other wife, but only that he may leaue his wife, and therfore (saith our Sauiour) *if he leaue her* (vvhich he may not do but in case of fornication) *and marie an other, he committeth aduoutrie*: vvhence it foloweth not, that for fornication, he may both leaue & marie an other for. S. Paul sayth plainly, that if the wife leaue her husbād, she must remaine vnmaried. Luther yet addeth an other case in vvhich the husband may take an other wife, that is vvhen the first wife wil be gadding, and not stay with her husband, in which case (sayth he) I see no reason

Cal. l. 4. Inst. c. 1.

Mat. 19. Mar 10. 1. Cor 7. Se the English Test.

Cases in vvhich Luth. permitteth to take a nevv vvife.

why the man may not take an other. So that if the wife of stubbernes, or the man for some long iourney vvhich he hath to make, wil leaue home for a tyme, the partie abiding according to Luther, is not bond to stay the others coming, but may take an other mate. He addeth yet an other case, that wiues are some tymes so crabbed, that although they see their husbandes fal into aduoutries, yet they wil not seke to giue them satisfaction: and then (sayth) he, the husband may say: *Si tu nolueris, alia volet. Si domina nolit, adueniat ancilla: If thou vvilt not, an other vvil: If the mistresse vvil not, let the mayd come.* Fourthly he yet findeth out an other case in vvhich the man may leaue the old wife, and mary a new: to wit, if the wife sollicit him to sinne, or be litigious, and so he may vpon such occasions, take ten new wiues one after an other. And lest he may seme to speake vvithout reason, he yeldeth this reason: *neminem enim vult Deus in incontinentiæ discrimen esse coniectum. For God vvil not haue any man to be cast into danger of incontinencie.* So that because according to this mans doctrin, a man can not liue chaste vvithout a wife, if one wil leaue her husband, or be stubborne, or litigious, or giue not satisfaction, the husband may take an other, as often as he wil, lest for vvant of a wife he should be incontinent. Wherfore Bucer speaking conformably to this doctrin, auoucheth, that as often as the wife semeth not fit for the mans purpose, he may take an other, and she so often as she is weary of one husband, may take an other. And good reason also, if Luthers and Caluins doctrin be true: for if man hath no freewil, he hath no force to resist the assaultes of the flesh, if he be tempted: and seing that he is not sure how long he shalbe vvithout a temptation, to make al sure, if one wife satisfie not his lust, he must take an other, lest he cast him selfe into danger of incontinencie. Lastly Luther affirmeth that man is so bent & prone vnto lust, that he can no more be without a woman, then it is in his power, not to be a man: these are his wordes: *Vt non est in meis viribus situm, vt vir non sim, tam non est etiam mei iuris, vt absque muliere sim. Rursum, vt in tua potestate non est, vt fœmina non sis, sic neque in te est, vt absque viro degas: As it is not in my povver, not to be a man, so is it not in my povver, to be vvithout a vvoman. Againe, as it is not in thy povver, not to be a vvoman, so is it not in thy povver, to liue vvithout a man.*

To. 5. ser 5. Matr. — *Luth. com. in 1. Cor. 7.* — *in c. 19. Mat.* — *Ser. cit. de Matr.* — *Hovv carnal an Apostata is this?*

14 Which doctrin if it be true, then euery one must mary, and so virginitie & widowes chastitie is exiled the world, or else he must take a queane, and so honestie is gone. For if it be as impossible for a man to liue without a woman, or for a woman to be without a man, as for a man not

Vvhat folovveth this doctrin.

man not to be a man, or a vvoman not to be a woman, then must the case often tymes happen, that the man must nedes take a queane, or that the vvoman must nedes haue a man besides her husband. For first if the man or vvife be long from home, seing that neither partie can liue any tyme vvithout a mate, it foloweth that the vvoman must vse the helpe of her man or some other, and the man must vse his mayd as Luther sayth, or some other mans wife, mayd or daughter: else Luthers and Caluins doctrin is false, vvhich teacheth that a man can not liue without a woman, nor a woman without a man. If they answer that he may liue some tyme vvithout a woman, then say I, that it is not as impossible to be without a vvoman, as not to be a man, because in no tyme is it possible for a man not to be a man. And I suppose that a temptation may happen, as wel in an hower, as in a yeare: what then shal the partie tempted doe? if he resist, Luther and Caluins doctrin is false: if he can not resist, then if he can not mary (as cōmonly there is some tyme required to get a wife) he must nedes haue a queane. Whence it foloweth, that not only merchant venturers must take hede how they go from home, but noblemen also must not aduenture to go so much as a hunting, vnles they locke vp their wiues, or take them along vvith them. Hence it foloweth also, that when the wife is sicke, especially any tyme, or when she lieth in, the man may take a new vvife, if he be betempted to lust. For if he be tēpted, he can not absolutely ouercome that temptation, *ergo* he must haue a vvoman: but in these cases his wife wil not serue his turne, *ergo* he must haue an other wife; and if he can not get a wife, he must haue a queane. And this also in this case of such a great necessitie, must be lawful for him, because no man sinneth in that vvhich he can not auoid, neither is he to be blamed, but rather pitied for doing that, to vvhich necessitie compelled him. And seing the vvoman in this point is as fraile yea frayler then the man, being the vveaker sexe, she may as often take a new husband, as the man a vvife. Which doctrin vvhat a vvide gate it openeth to al dishonestie, I leaue to the gentle readers iudgement.

Fornication many tymes must be lavvful according to this doctrin.

Vvhat a gap Luther openeth to dishonestie.

15. Wherfore very wel doth a certain frenchman in a booke of his, that treateth of the Synode holden by the reformers at Monpeliar, bring in a vvoman deputed for the femal sex of the Reformed, complayning of this doctrin of Luther and Caluin, vvhich holdeth, that we haue no power to liue chast, nor no force nor freewil to resist the violence of the flesh: for (sayth she) if we haue no force nor free-

Les Actes du Synode de la saincte Reformation.

a vvomans iust cōplaint of this doctrin.

wil to resist our owne fleshlie temptations, it foloweth that we and our daughthers are al queanes, and our husbandes cuckoldes, and not only cuckoldes but horemasters. For if the flesh assault vs (sayth she) vvhen our husbandes are abroad, or if vvhen they are at home, we take greater liking of an other man, either we can resist the temptation, or we can not. If we can, then haue we free wil, which is countrarie to that vvhich Luther and Caluin teach vs: if we can not resist, then are we al queanes, and our husbandes cuckoldes, vvhich is the greatest disgrace to our sexe that can be. Wherfore she demandeth that this doctrin may be changed, else the vvomanish sex is defamed. For either the vvoman to shew her selfe a Caluinist or Lutherane, must yeld to the temptations acknowledging her vveaknes, or if she resist, she doth not like a Caluinist, and so either she must deny her selfe to be a Caluinist, or confesse her selfe a queane.

The conclusiõ. 16. But I am ashamed to deduce any mo of these beastly consequences out of these fowle premises of Lutheranisme and Caluinisme, and peraduenture I haue offended the reader, in raking in these dunghilles, and haue iniured my pen, and paper, in fowling that, and blurring this, with so filthie ordures; yet as it is good to set forth vertue, to allure men vnto it, so is it not amisse to lay open the filth of vice and heresie, to make men detest it. This I am sure was my intention & proiect, and I hope, yea I perswad my selfe, that I haue brought to passe my intended purpose. For what man of a chast and honest mynd, can allovve of this doctrin as the pure, immaculate, and chast worde of God, from which procede and folow so beastly consequences, or who can thinke the tree good that beareth so bad frutes? Yea vvhat wise man can be perswaded, that the authors of this doctrin vvere men of God, indevved vvith his spirit, that haue no taste of things belonging to the spirit, such as chastitie, and virginitie are, in which we folow the spirit not the flesh, and resemble Angels, nor carnal men: but apply them selues wholly to the fleshes desires, and therfore haue taken away al impediments, wherwith the Church in fauour of virginitie, and for the decencie of Matrimonie, had crossed the way of sensualitie, and haue giuen libertie to haue many vviues at once, and to take a new, as often as the old displeaseth, or is not present, and when a wife can not be gotten, by their doctrin they permit euery one that wil to take a quean. Wherfore I meruaile not that their clergie is so dissolute, that vviuing and revviuing, and chopping and changing of vviues is so rife amongst them: neither is it strange that where

vvhy such vviuing is

vvhereas amongst Catholiques we haue euer seene many thousandes of societies that haue professed virginitie, amongst the reformers you shal find none such, but in lieu of them, Colleges of maryed ministers filled vvith their brattes, because such flowers as virginitie and chastitie are, grow not vpon such dunghilles, and such pretious margarites are not to be cast before such filthy hogges.

amongst the reformers, & no Nunries at al.

The fifteenth Chapter proueth that the reformers doctrin, holdeth a sinner so fast in sinne, that after he is once fallen, he can not rise again.

VVE haue seen in the former Chapters of this booke, how easily the reformers doctrin leadeth vnto al vice in general, & diuers also in particular: now if it did shevv as easie a vvay to penance and iustification, as to sinne and iniquitie, and did as speedily helpe vs, it should make some recompence, but in dede as their doctrin tumbleth men headlong into the depth of sinne, so it holdeth them captiues with an impossibilitie of rising vp again, and so is worthy duble detestation. And how shal I proue this conclusion, which semeth such a paradox? Truly very easily and that without running farre for an argument.

2. If you remember they are of opinion that the only vvay for a sinner to arise vp again after he is fallen by sinne, is to beleue assuredly without al doubt or staggering, that he is iust and elect, and that Christs iustice is his: which if I proue to be impossible for a sinner to beleue, I shal proue also that by their doctrin, it is impossible for a sinner to be iustified, or to arise from the fal of sinne, to the high and eminent state of grace. To proue this I wil only suppose one principle and Maxime of Philosophie, to wit that truth and veritie, or at least some probable apparance therof, is the obiect at which our vnderstanding aymeth, and that therfore, as the vvil can not imbrace any obiect vnles it be good, or at least haue some apparance of good (for no man can like of euil as euil) so the vnderstanding can not yeld her assent to any thing, vnles it be a veritie, or haue at least some probable shew of veritie. And this is the cause vvhy we can not beleue and say

aboue chap. 3. Luth. in c. 2. Gal. Cal. l. 3. Inst. c. 2. p. 7. 9. & seq. See the preface to the Reader.

with hart, that black is white, or that a known falsitie is a veritie, as I haue declared in my Epistle to the reader more at large.

3. Out of these premisses I gather this conclusion: that it is impossible for a sinner, to frame on a sodayne this assent, that he is iust: and consequently, if this be the only vvay for a sinner to rise vnto iustification, it is impossible for him after he is fallen by sinne, to rise againe by iustification, & so vvhere he falleth, there he must nedes lye. For as it is impossible for a sicke man (if he be in his vvittes) to beleue verily that he is vvhole, vnles he see some alteration in him selfe, and find some ease of his disease, so is it as impossible for a sinner who is spiritually sicke, yea dead, vpon a sodaine to beleue (especialy so assuredly as Caluin vvil haue him) that he is iust, vvhole, and sound, and fully recouered of his spiritual disease, vnles he see some alteration in him selfe before he frame so firme an assent. For I vvil aske of Caluin vvhen he commeth fresh from his vilanie, vvhat moueth him to this assent and beleefe, that he is iust and elect? hath he a reuelation? or hath euerie one of his folovvers vvhom he vvil haue to beleue the same, any illumination from God by which they are acertained? He must nedes say no, because they experience in them selues that they haue no such euidence: find they any contrition, or loue of God, or haue they any inherent grace in them, which hath altered them and made them of sinners iust and holy? They vvil say no, for then faith should not iustifie, but that which goeth before this faith. And this they must nedes say, because faith is the first goodnes in vs, and with them it is the first and only thing which iustifieth: yea in their opinion, contrition which is inherent in vs, can not be our iustification, because they say that there is no inherent grace nor iustice. And if before this faith of theirs, God should by infusion of grace iustifie them, yet vnles they had a reuelation, they could not, especially with such assurance beleue it, because the vnderstanding can not giue assent without some apparance of truth.

Impossible for a sinner to rise, by caluins doctrin.

aboue chap. 2

4. They vvil say that Christs iustice is theirs, so that they wil apprehend it by faith, and so they are iust by that iustice, if they vvil beleue so. But neither wil this shift serue their turne. For before they beleue this, Christs iustice must be theirs, and by it they must be iust, because that is the obiect of their beleefe, and the vnderstanding must see it to be so, before she beleue so: wherfore seing that before this faith of theirs, Christs iustice is not theirs, and they also are not yet iust, it foloweth that they can not, so long as they are in their wittes, beleue

Caluins faith impossible.

beleue that they are iust, because this veritie must appeare to the vnderstanding before she can beleue it: and therfore if before faith they be not iust, they can neuer beleue so. For as the sicke man must be whole and sound before he can beleue that he is so, because it is not in his povver to beleue that which is not, or which at least appeareth not, so a sinner can not on a sodaine (vnles he haue some reason for it) beleue assuredly that he is iust. And therfore if this assured faith be necessarie to arise after our fal taken by sinne, it is impossible to rise again, after that vve are fallen. And to make the matter yet more plaine: as if the only remedie for a sicke man to recouer his health, were to beleue that he is wel, it were impossible for him to recouer, because whilest his disease remaineth, he can not beleue that he is recouered, hauing no reason to thinke so, but rather the contrarie: so if the only meanes for a sinner to recouer, be to beleue in the middest of his sinnes, that he is iust, it is impossible for him to recouer, because he can not with hart thinke so, hauing no reason for it, but rather to the contrarie.

a similitude.

a similitude.

5. Hence I gather two thinges to be noted. First that if a sinner be iustified by beleeuing that he is iust, then is he iustified by a lying faith, because he beleueth that vvhich is not: and if you say that so soone as he hath beleeued so, he shal be so: that is not sufficient, for yet it foloweth that he beleueth that he is iust before he is iust, because iustice folovveth faith, and so he is iustified by a false and lying faith. The second thing which I note is how malitiously, and yet how couertly the diuel by his members seeketh our damnation. For not content by their doctrin to haue induced men to al sinne, he taketh away the meanes of rising again from the state of sinne, denying penance to be necessarie, yea affirming in Luther that contrition is a mortal sinne, and auouching in Luther and Caluin both, yea and in al their Scholars, that the only meanes for a sinner to be iustified, is to beleue without al staggering, and with al possible assurance, that his sinnes are forgiuen: vvhich beleefe being impossible, as is already proued (because it is not in the vnderstandings power to beleue white to be blacke, or that a man is iust vvhen no probabilitie of it appeareth) it foloweth that vvhen a sinner is fallen, it is impossible for him to rise againe, because it is as impossible for him to beleue that he is iust, before he see some apparance of the same, as for a sicke man to beleue that he is recouered and vvel at ease, when he is in the middest of the fitte of an hoate ague, or in the

Caluins faith is a lying faith.

the malice of the deuil.

Sup a c 1.
Supra. c. 3.

in the panges of death. And so our reformers do not only tumble men headlong into the very depth of sinne, but hold them there in perpetual durance, vvithout hope of libertie, because they require an impossibilitie, which is, in the midst of sinnes to beleue that we are iust, and elect, hauing no probabilitie of the same, but rather great euidence to the contrarie: which is as impossible to beleue with hart, as it is for the sicke man to assure him selfe that he is vvel, vvhen he is in the middest of his fitte.

The conclusiō.

***

THE EIGTH BOKE CONTAINETH A SVRVEY OF THE NEVV DOCTRIN which leadeth vnto Atheiſme and contempt of Religion.

A SHORT PRÆFACE.

RELAND Is famous for that it breedeth no toades, nor venimous ſerpents, and England hath bene of long tyme eſtemed happie, becauſe it hath no wolues: but in ſteed of wolues, it hath bene of late yeares vnfortunate for engendring of certaine monſters called Atheiſts begotten by hereſie, which haue more vvaſted & depopulated the countrie, then al the beares and vvolues of the deſert, or monſters of Africa could haue done, if they had bene al turned looſe into the land. For they could only haue made their pray vpon the bodies of men and beaſtes, but theſe monſtrous Atheiſtes haue made hauocke of mens ſoules. They could only haue diſturbed the temporal ſtate and ciuil peace, theſe haue ruined Chriſtianitie, and brought Religion into contempt, vvhich is the principal bliſſe of the ſoule in this life. Of theſe monſters there are two kindes both feirce and cruel, but the one more ſauage then the other. The firſt denyeth flatly the Diuinitie, and therfore moſt properly is called an Atheiſt, that is vvithout a God. The ſecond confeſſeth God and Godhead, but yet is of opinion, that it litle skilleth what honour you giue him, or with vvhat vvorſhip of Religion you ſerue him. Of this kinde are our Macheuellians, who ſquare out Religion according to ſtate, & make no more account of Scripture then of Æſops fables, and ſo they may liue and eſtabliſh a temporal ſtate, care not vvhat Religion

The monſter Atheiſts.

The firſt kind of Atheiſts.

The Second.

ligion florisheth: because they count it but a peece of pollicie to keepe men in awe and order. Against these monsters I must arme my selfe, and change my vveapons as I change my aduersarie, and by reason only I wil confound these, as I haue by Scriptures, reason, authoritie, and al maner of argumentes refuted Heretikes. And for as much as my general drift and proiect in al these bookes is, to shew how odious, heresie ought to be, I wil shew in this last booke, how Atheisme is engendred of heresie, that by this viperous and mostrous brood we may haue a greater guesse of the breeder.

The first Chapter declareth hovv certaine points of the Reformers doctrin, make vvay to a denial of the Diuine Maiestie and his Godhead.

Vvhat God is, is not knovven in this life.

Trismegistus opinion of God.

IT is so hard to Know, vvhat God is, that neither the light of reason, nor of faith, nor both lights ioined together, are able to discouer this veritie. Wherfore Trimegistus being demanded this obscure question, gaue as obscure an answer: to wit, that God is a thing vvhose center is euerie vvhere, and his circle or circumference no vvhere: signifying therby, that the least thing in God (if a man may say so of God, in vvhom al things are so great, that they are no lesse then God) is so great, that it farre surpasseth the sphere of our capacitie, much more doth the circumference of his infinite perfection excede the compasse of humane vvitte. Simonides being asked the same question, required tyme to consider, after which tyme he being demanded to giue his censure, required longer tyme: At the length being vrged to make no mo delayes, he answered only this, that God vvas such a thing that the more we consider him, the lesse we conceue him, and the more we conceue of him the lesse we can say of him. Aristotle the Prince of Philosophers could only say of God, that he is *Ens entium*, *the thing of thinges*, that is the thing, from vvhich al things procede as from the fountaine and first cause of al things, and a thing vvhich is al thinges, because eminently (as Diuines say) & compendiously, he containeth in him selfe al thinges. Not that in God, they be liuing and not liuing, corruptible and incorruptible,

Simonides opinion.

Aristotles opinion of God.

1. p. q. 4. 2.

Hovv al thinges are in God.

tible, great and smal, agreable and diuers, perfect and imperfect, as they are in them selues: because al in God is liuing, al incorruptible, al great, increat, and infinite, al one, al perfect vvithout imperfection: to be briefe in God al is God. For as the cause conteineth diuerse effectes vvithout diuision and imperfection of the cause, and as the artificers peece of vvorke, hath a more noble being in the artificers Idea and mental platforme, then in it selfe; so al thinges are in God, in more eminent maner, then in them selues; because in him, they are as in their cause, & fountaine, yea as in their idea: & therfore though in them selues, some of these creatures, be corporal, some be spiritual, yet in God al are spiritual, though in them selues some be liuing creatures, some deuoid of life, yet in God al are liuing *and life it selfe*: though in them selues they be create, yet in God they be increat, though in them selues they be imperfect, yet in God they be perfect: though in them selues they be diuerse, yet in God they are al one: though in them selues they be creatures, yet in God they are God. This the learned scholar of S. Paul Dionisius Areopagita, explicateth by a fitte similitude. As the lines (saith he) vvhich are drawen from the center, are diuided from them selues, and diuerse in them selues, but in the center, they are vnited in one without any distinction: so al creatures, as they procede from God, who is the center and resting of al things, are diuers and different, but as they are in God, they are al one. And as the forsaid lines in the center, are nothing else but the center: so al creatures vvhich are but so many lines drawne from Gods indiuisible nature, in God are God, vvithout al diuision and imperfection.

a similitude.

Io. 1.

Aug. trac. 1. in Io.

c. 5. de diuinis nominibus.

2. But as vvhat God is we know not, so that there is a God, is so manifest, that though the toungue may deny him, the hart can not, if it be not caryed avvay with passion, for inconsideration. True it is that Protagoras and Diagoras were so godlesse, as to doubt, yea to deny that there vvas a God: yet these men vvere long since hissed out of the schooles of al Philosophers, and could not haue denied God in hart, vvhere the light of reason discouereth him, had not some blinding passion ouerruled them. And therfore if it vvere not, that heresie had countenanced Atheisme, and giuen it authoritie to passe amongst Chistians vvithout blushing, yea with honour and credit: I vvould haue contented my selfe to haue hissed also at these companions, and vvould neuer haue gone about to ouerthrow that by reason, vvhich standeth with no reason. But lest that the authoritie and sway, vvhich atheisme novv a dayes beareth in the vvorld, may ouer

That there is a God is euident.

ex Cicer. l. 1. de nat. deor. plut. l. 1. de plac. c. 7.

rule the vviser, & seeme reason ynough to the simple, I wil by certain pregnant reasons, cōuince these godles Atheistes, that there is a God, and a Diuine povver. And first of al this world semeth to me to be a booke wherin vve may read this veritie. For, as the booke vvhich we read (if we vnderstand the wordes) teacheth vs the veritie or science vvhich it conteineth so if we read with diligence the booke of this world, in which euery creature is a worde, we shal by it lerne, that there is a God. For as S. Paul sayth, *the inuisible things of God.* (that is his diuine attributes and perfections) *are knovvne by these things that are created.* Vvherfore that couragious mother in the Machabees, vvhich was as forward to prefer her sonnes to Martyrdome, as others would be to detain thē, biddeth her sonne to read this booke of creatures, & *to looke vpon heauen & earth & al vvhich is in thē contained, and therby to lerne, that it was God that made them al of nothing.* This booke S. Antonie studied, & proficed therin so much, that he could cōfute Philosophers, and conuince a Godhead & Diuinitie. Yea these creatures are not only so many wordes in vvhich we may read this veritie, but they are also so many preachers vvhich cry out with a voice most lowd, and shril, and in a language intelligible of al men, that *God it vvas that made them and not they them selues.* And so a Godhead is taught vs not only by the vniuersitie of Athens, Paris, Oxford, but also of al the creatures in the vvorld. For first I demand of vvhom this vvorld (vvhich Philosophers do cal Al because it containeth al) tooke his beginning, being, and existing? If thou say with Epicure or Democritus, that it vvas made *Fortuito causarum, atomorum concursu, by a chancing concurse of causes, motes or indiuisible bodies:* I aske who made these causes and indiuisible bodyes? If thou ansvver that a creature made them, I aske again vvho made that creature & so at length I wil bring thee to a thing exempt from creation, vvhich created al things, and this I cal God. If thou sayst that the world framed it selfe, I must nedes tel thee that that is impossible because nothing can operate or worke before it hath a being as the Phisopher sayth, *prius est esse quam agere.* And so if the world made it selfe it vvas before it selfe, which implyeth a contradiction. If thou say that it was neither framed by it selfe, nor by any other cause, but was euer of it selfe, vvithout any making, then thou makest the vvorld a God and so vvhilest thou seekest to deny a God, thou grantest a God. For if it be of it selfe, it is independent of any other, and so hath a necessarie being which euer was and euer shalbe: because if it be of it selfe, it can not by any cause be brought from nothing to something, and so

The first argument to proue a God, is the vvorld.

Ro. 1.

Sap. 13.

Act. 14.

1. Mac. 2.

The vvorld vvas S. Antonies booke.

Creatures preach God.

Psal. 99.

The vvorld an vniuersitie in which a Godhead is taught.

The force of the first argument.

The vvorld is not by chaunce.

euer was of necessitie, neither can it be brought from something to nothing, & so euer shal be, and that of necessitie. If it haue a necessarie & indedendent being, it hath an infinite essence, because it is not limited by any, and so excedeth the bonds of a creature: & therfote if the vvorld was of it selfe, it is a God: which perfection notwithstanding it can not haue, because the worlds material substance, mutabilitie, visibilitie, and determinate quantitie, argueth a creature, not a God, vvho is immaterial, inuisible and infinite in his immensitie. Vvho then was it that created this goodly palace and so huge a building as is this world? Not it selfe, as is proued, not any Angel, or other cseature, because creation of nothing argueth infinit power, and vvhere is infinite power, there is an infinite essence, and so God only was he that could create it. And if thou vvilt obstinatly defend, that an Angel, or some other creature created it, I wil thus argue against thee. Either that creature vvhich thou imaginest to haue created the vvorld, vvas of it selfe, or it vvas created of an other? If it vvas of it selfe, it vvas God, and so thou grantest, which I endeuour to drowe from thee by force of argumẽt? if it was created of an other creature, I aske who created that other, and so at the length I vvil leade thee to the first cause, vvhich created al, and vvas cteated of none, vvhich is the God vvhom vve seekefor,

The vvorld made not it selfe.

No Angel made it.

4 Secondly not only the vvhole vvorld but also euery part of it, wil make a plain remonstrance of a Godhead. And to begin with man, vvho though he be a litle vvorld, yet is but a part of the great vvorld: who I pray you was it, that gaue the first man his being? Vve see by experience that men breede not as flyes & wormes do of the corruption of other liuing creatures, neither do they spring out of the earth like herbes or toadstooles, as Iulius Cæsar said of the first inhabitants of England, neither are they begotten of beastes of any other kind, as mules are, but rather as we see by experience, man only begetteth man, and of no other liuing creature, no not of an Angel can he be begotten. Who then was it that gauethe first man his being? of him selfe man could not be, for then had he bene a God: of an other man he could not be begotten, beause no man could be before the first man, no other creature could beget him, as is already proued, *ergô* some thing that was no creature created him. And vvhat is that but God?

The second argument. The litle vvorld, man, proueth a God.

5 An other part of the world, and that the most noble, is an Angel. And vvho I pray you created those spirits and immaterial substances? one Angel could not beget an other, because that vvould ar-

The creatiō of Angels proueth a God. gue them to be material substances, and corruptible creatures and so no spirits. To say that men can produce Angels, or that any other creature extant could do the same, is farre lesse probable, because they are the highest creatures in perfection, and so could not be produced of their inferiors. It foloweth therfore that some cause not included *Angels proued.* vvithin the ranke of creatures created them: and what can that be but the Creatour. To deny al Angels and spirits, is against Philosophie, & al the best Philosophers. For Aristotle the Prince of Philosophers affir-*l. 12. met. c. 70. 1. l. c. de cato c. 9. In Plut. ad Tyrannum, & in Symposio Zenocl. de morte Marusc. in Pymondro.* meth, that the heauens are not moued by rheir owne proper formes & faculties, but by Angels, which he calleth intelligences. Plato and the Platonists make often mention both of good and euil Angels So doth Plutarch also, and diuers others, aud who hath not read of Socrates familiar, which was called *demonium*, that is a good or euil spirit. Yea experience proueth that there are diuels, vvhich are spirits and differ only from the good Angels in malice. For if vve behold the strange effectes which are to be sene in possessed persons, we can not with any probabilitie ascribe al to a melancholike humonr: for those pullings and conuulsions, strange motions and operations can not procede *Diuels proued.* from any humour or natural cause. For we see them some tymes lifted vp from the ground, some tymes they howle like dogges, some tymes they yel like wolues, sometymes they tel secrets, & speake in strange *Read Martinus de Rio, and Springer.* languages. The manifold & strange operations of witches, their meetinges and voyages which they make in the ayre, the strange appatiōs, which al the world talketh of, and therfore can not lye, demonstrate that there are Angels and immaterial spirits. And seing these creatures can neither produce one an other, nor be produced of *The heauens proue a God.* any create cause, we must nedes confesse a God and an increated spirit, who created them. The like proofe for a diuine povver rhe heauens do also yeld vs, for seing that no creature, nor second cause, could create those huge and incorruptible bodyes, vve must nedes confesse a God and first cause, vvho extended and framed them.

The third argument, is order and disposition. .6 Thirdly the goodly order & disposition of things which we see, argueth a nature of intelligence not contained within the ranke of cre-*The order of the 4. elements.* tures wich ruleth, guideth, and directeth al, and appointeth euerie creature his taske and place. We see how the elements are disposed of, and appointed euerie one to his natural place. The fire as most noble and of a most light and aspiring nature, taketh the highest place, the aire and water take the middle roome, because they participate of two extremes, the one agreeing with the fire in heat and ligth-

nes

nes, the other with the earth in cold & heauines: and the earth being of a heauy & lumpish nature, is vvorthilie thrust downe to the lowest place. We see how the heauens and planets moue in order, and distinguish the times & seasons, neuer altering their course since they were created, in so much that by their vniforme motion the Astrologers can tel most certainly, the time yea minute of the change of the mone, of the sunnes setting and rising, and of the sunnes & moones Eclipes. We see the order & diuersitie of partes & members in planets, beasts, and men, vvhich are so furnished of al parts and faculties belonging vnto nature, that there is no part vvanting, none superfluous not so much as a vaine, sinew, or litle bone, as we see by experience when we want the least of them. The eyes are placed in the head, vvhich are also made to turne about, that we may looke about vs, and therfore are called the guides of the body. The eares are the organes of discipline, because by them we heare what others say, vvithout the which mans life were no life at al, for it should be deuoid of conuersation. The nose smelleth a farre of al odours, vvhich are good or bad for the bodies health, and besides it is the trumpet of the voice. The sence of feeling is dispersed through out al partes of the body, whose office is to feele vvhatsoeuer approcheth or toucheth the body, therby to flye it, if it be hurtful, or to take commoditie of it, if it be conuenient. The mouth receaueth the sustenance and meate, vvhich is necessarie for the body, the tongue besides that it is the instrumeut of speaking, and the interpreter of the mind, is to taste his meate and to iudge of it before it passe any farther, which iudgemẽt being geuen, the throte swaloweth it downe. The stomake boyleth & disgesteth it, the liuer maketh blood of it, the vaines conueigh this bloud to al partes of the body, and nothing there is not necessarie or expediẽt, not so much as the guttes whose office as it is base, because they are as it were the sinkes of the kitchin to passe the filth and excrementes, so are they so necessarie, that otherwise the body would be poisoned and infected. Tel me novv, ô godles Atheist, vvho it is that hath set dovvne this order? who is he that so ruleth the motion of the heauens, that they moue at the same tyme from East to west and backward againe, and one within an other, and yet so, that they hinder not one an other? Vvho hath established a perpetual peace amongst the fowre elementes, vvhich yet by reason of their contrarie qualities, are of a iarring nature. And who hath so placed them as they may best agree? for the aire agreeth vvith the fier in heat, and therfore is placed next vnto him: the vvater in moy-

The orderly motion of the heauens.

The order of the parts of mans body.

The offices.

The disposition of al.

in moysture agreeth with the ayre, and in could vvith the earth, and therfore is lodged betvvixt them, vvheras if the vvater vvere placed next the fire, & the ayre next to the earth, they vvould make vvarre continually one vpon an other, and neuer vvould be satisfied vvithout the ruine of one an other, because they disagree in both qualities, the fire being hote and drye the vvater cold and moyst, the ayre hote and moyst and the earth cold and drye. Who hath so ordered the partes of the bodyes of liuing & mouing creatures as they may best serue their turnes, and by their proportion and disposition be the greatest ornament. Who sorteth al beasts vvith their kind, and placeth them in roomes fittest for their nature? some in the vvater, as fishes? some in the aire, as brids? some on the earth as beastes and plants? some in the fire, is there crekit and salamandre. Who setteth the plants & herbes, & giueth them a roote as a mouth to receiue their conuenient nurtriture, and veines to conueigh it euen from the roote, to the highest bovves, yea leaues and frutes, and giue to euery one of them a seed, or some other thing in steed of seed, by vvhich they propagate them selues & retain a posteritie? vvho I pray thee, ô vngodly Impe (cōsidering this goodly order & disposition, vvho I pray thee beholding this goodly palace of God & men, in which is al this forniture, prouision, order, & disposition, wil not think of an artificer of intelligence, who builded it, and of a hovvskeper most vvise & prouident, vvho ruleth and disposeth of al in the same? Thou wilt say vvith Epicure, & such graceles, godles, & vvitles cōpanions, that al this goodly order happened by chance, and that by the like chance, this goodlye palace vvith al the partes and vvorkmanship therof, vvas framed and effectuated. By chance, sayest thou (o man) or rather no man, but some monster of mankind considerest thou vvel vvhat it is, vvhich thou auerrest to haue ben effectuated by chance? The printer shal neuer be able to set his print by casting his letters together at al aduētures. The painter by a careles casting of his colours vpon a cloth or table, shal neuer draw his intended picture. The mason by throwing of stones one at an other, shal neuer build his goodly palace. And canst thou thinke that al this goodly order, vvhich is set dovvne in the vvorld, at vvhich men and Angels stand astonished, vvas framed and established by chance medlie? If thou shouldest enter into a Westminster halle, a Non such, or Royal exchange in England, into a Louvver in Paris, or a Scurial in Spaine, where thou shouldst see statelie building, aspiring turrets, loftie roofes, vvittie conueighance of roomes, and chambers,

Amb. l. 3. Hexam. c. 8. Basil. ho. 5. in Hex.

Epicures opinion.

The vvorld vvas not by chance.

Examples.

chambers, and orderly disposition of windowes, pillers, chimnies? vvouldest thou, or couldest thou imagim these artificial vvorkes and buildinges, to haue bene vvrought by a chancing flight of stones frō the quarrie? & not rather by the art & skil of some ingenious artificer, & canst thou entering into the sumptous building and palace of the world, whose pauement is the earth, paued vvith so rich stones, & metals & rushed with the greenes of al herbes & plants, whose fundation is the center which stayeth al, vvhose roofe are the heauens, siled so richely, with so many bright and glittering starres vvhose vvalles are the same heauens, vvhich do not only couer but also compasse al about, vvhose diuers roomes and lodgings are the fowre elements, in which diuers creatures according to their diuers nature are diuersly lodged, vvhose indweller & inhabitant is man, vvho vnder God also is Lord ouer al, vvhose prouisiōs & moueables are the goods and fruite of the sea & land, layd vp in store for mans prouision: who I say entering into this Princely palace, so vvel ordered, & gouerned, can imagin al this to procede from chance, & not rather from an intelligent artificer, vvho worketh these vvonders & miracles of nature, & a prouident prince vvho gouerneth and ruleth al so vvisely, and like a pilot sitteth at the sterne, guiding and directing the course of this world, & of euery creatures actiōs. For as Cicero that famous Orator and Philosopher auoucheth, nothing is so open and so euident, vvhen we looke vpon the heauens, and the celestial bodies, as that there is some Diuine power of most excellent vnderstanding, by vvhom these tings as they vvere first framed, so are they stil conserued and gouerned.

Description of the World.

l. 2. de natura deorum.

The fourth argument taken from brute beasts so ingenious operations.

4 Fourthly against these vvitles Atheistes, the very brute beastes shal argue for their Creatour, vvhose operations are so witty and agreable to the end, which is to them by God and nature prescribed, as if they had discours, and were indewed with reason. They feare those things which are contrarie to their good, and distinguish the good from bad, as if they had the science of good and bad. The shepe, yea the young lamb, euen at the first, discerneth the vvoolfe from the dogge, and quaketh at the very sight of him, although he differeth litle from the dogge, vvhich he feareth not. The chicken can put a difference betwixt the kite and te Peacocke, and feareth one, litle caring for the other although in body bigget The smal byrdes feare the sparhauke, the duck the faucon, and do tremble at the very noise of their belles & yet they care not for the swanne, nor crane, though in body much bigger.

Sheep feare the vvoolfe.

Chickins the kite.

Smal birdes the hauke.

bigger. Vvho teacheth them thus to discerne their enemies, vvho putteth in thẽ such a feare of that, which in dede is to be feared? Thou vvilt say, the instinct of nature, but vvho put such an instinct in nature by vvhich they fly their foes, as if they had reason, but he that is the author of nature & reason? Vvho teacheth brute beastes, in a medovv or garden, vvhere there are so many herbs one like an other, to choose the good, and to refuse the bad, and so coningly, as if they vvere Phisitiās, or herbistes, & knew the nature of simples? in so much that wheras men, many tymes are poisonned in taking one drug, or herbe for an other; such an error neuer hapneth amongest them. Vve see hovv artificially byrdes do build their nestes, vvherin they make such a defence against the vvether, that no mason can correct their vvorke. The spider spinneth the threde out of his ovvne substance, which aftervvard he vveaueth so artificially, that he maketh a formal nette, which also he putteth in those places, vvhere flyes are likest to passe. And he like a byrdcatcher, lyeth lurking in a corner of the same, without any motion: but no sooner doth the fly touch his nette, but he vvith al spede maketh hast vnto it. I haue already described the trauels of the Antes in making their haruest, and carying in their corne, and hovv they eate the end of it, lest it grovv in the earth, and bring it forth to drying in a sunny day, lest moysture corrupt it. And I haue in part described the cōmon welth of bees, which is so wel ordered, that a statist & cōmon welth man may lerne policie & gouernement of them. The hare vvhat slight vseth she to eschape the houndes, how many leapes maketh she, how many bywayes taketh she, and if she come nere a vvater she wil passe it, if nere a heard of catel, she entreth amōgst thẽ, to deceue the houndes, and to make them loose the sent. How subtile and craftie the Foxe is, I report me to huntsmen: and what deuises he vseth to attain to his pray, few there are which know not. On a tyme (as a man of credit told me vvho was an eye vvitnes) the Foxe espying duckes in a riuer, deuised this stratagem to deceue them: he taketh a bush of ferne, which he caryeth in his mouth to the water, and putteth it into the water, farre aboue them, lest he should be espyed, and aboue the streame also, that it might descend dovvne vnto thẽ, and passe also thorovv them: and this he did tvvise, or thrise. The duckes suspecting nothing, let the ferne passe by them: at the length the foxe him selfe cometh svviming down the streame, with a ferne bush in his mouth, and that so couertly, that nothing appeared aboue the vvater, but the bush: the duckes suspecting no more deceit, then was before, & imagining

Beasts seme to be herbistes.

The artificial building of birdes.

The spiders vveauing.

In the seueth booke. chap. 15.

The prouision of Antes and bees.

The slight of the hare.

The crafte of the foxe.

ning that it was but a ferne bush which came downe the streame, fled not for the matter, because they feared nothing: but when the Fox came amongst them, he shevved him selfe to be a fox, for leauing the bush, he snatcheth at a ducke, & changeth his bush for the same. Hence I deduce this argument: These creatures are witles & deuoid of reason, and yet do they procede in their actions most wittily and reasonably, as if they had discours & reason, & some tymes they shew more witte in their actions, then do men them selues, who are reasonable and discoursing creatures. And seing that so orderly and so reasonable actions, can not procede from any reason, vvhich is in them, because they are vnreasonable, I do inferre that there is some one of reason aboue al these creatures, who thus directeth and gouerneth their actions. Neither wil it suffice to say, that they do al this by the instinct of nature, which is nothing else but a natural inclination: because seing that this natural instinct is not reason, and yet directeth them so reasonably, it must nedes procede from one of reason, who could imprint in them such an inclination, which being not reason, doth direct them notwithstāding, and gouern them in their actions, as if they had reason. VVherfore as vvhen thou seest the arrovv fly directly to the marke, thou streightvvayes imaginest an Archer, though thou seest him not, because so direct a motion, could not procede from the arrovv, had not the Archer, vvho is indevved vvith reason, giuen it his direction, and imprinted in it a force also, which carrieth it directly to the marcke, at which he aymed: so whē thou seest vnreasonable creatures to procede in their actions so vvittily, and so orderly, thou must thinke of some one of intelligence, who hath imprinted in them a natural instinct vvhich directeth them in their actions, as if they had reason.

The force of this argumēt.

A fit example and similitude.

5 Fifthly, what soeuer is in this world, either it is of it selfe, or of an other. If of it selfe, then is it God, because, as before is proued, to be independent, is to haue a necessarie & infinite essence, vvhich is no other thing then God. If it be of an other, I aske againe of whom dependeth that other: & so at length I wil bring thee to a thing, of vvhich al thinges are depending & that is depending of none: which is the God we seeke for. To this argument may be reduced that argument of Aristotle by vvhich he proueth the first Moouer, vvhich S. Thomas also vseth. VVhat soeuer (sayth Aristotle) is moued, is moued by an other. The inferiour creatures are moued by the heauens, and their influēces, which reach euen to the bovvelles of the earth, where

The fifth argument is dependance of al creatures of one Independent.

1. p. q. 2. 63. l. 2. met.

 by verby vertue of them, gold & siluer are engendred, the inferior heauens are moued by the first heauen, vvhich is *primum mobile*, because al the other heauens folovv the sway of that. The first heauen then, ether it moueth it selfe, or it is moued of an other? it can not moue it selfe, because it is a creature, and so as in essence and being, so in motion & operatiõ, it dependeth of an other? If it be moued of an other, then I demand, vvhether that moueth of it selfe, or by the motion of an other? if you say of an other, I aske againe vvhether that is moued by it selfe, or by an other, And so ether we must ascend *in infinitum* (which is impossible) because an infinite distance can neuer be passed, and so the inferiour cause which receiueth vertue from the superiour, should neuer be able to moue, because it should expect an infinite tyme, to receiue motion from a superiour cause, vvhose motion must passe through infinite inferior causes, before it come to the lowest, or else at length we must stay in a supreme cause, which moueth al, & it selfe is moued of none. And what is that but God.

The first mouer proued

Vide Greg. de Valentia, Gabrielem Vasques. 1. p. q. 2. Nolmia ibidem.

The Sixt argument taken from the revvard of Vertue.

6. Sixtly I wil bring a moral argument, which also conuinceth this veritie. It is the opinion euen of the Paganes, to vvhich the light of reason hath induced them, that there is vice and vertue in our actiõs, and that the one deserueth punishment, the other reward, as in the last booke is related: and seing that in this life, nether vice hath his dew punishement (because the vicious liue in prosperitie and enioy most commonly the felicitie of this life in more ample maner then the vertuous) nor vertue her reward, because the vertous are misprized, it foloweth that there is an other life, in vvhich God, vvho hath an equal prouidence ouer al, shal giue to euerie action his iust and dew reward.

Supra.

The seuenth argument is taken from the common opinion euen, of Atheists in extreamtie.

7 Seuenthly (as Cicero sayth) neuer any nation vvas so barbarous, whom the light of reason, indewed vvith an opinion of God or Gods, yea euen the Atheistes them selues, if they fal into any extremitie, are forced by nature to cry and cal vpon a God. For if a man by shipwrake were in danger of drovvning, then so long as he seeth humaine meanes to saue him, he vvil snatch at a cord that is cast vnto him, or he vvil reach for a borde, or seeke to get hold of a boate, rocke, or tree, to helpe him selfe by, and if he be an Atheist, then so long as these meanes faile not, he seeketh for no other, but if he perceue, that by no creatures he can be holpen, then be he Christian or Pagane, Ievv or Atheist, he thinketh vpon some higher povver, and vvhen al creatures forsake him, and his owne force wil no more serue him, na-

ture

ture biddeth him to seeke farther, & to demand that helpe of the Creatour, vvhich no creature can yeeld him.

The 8. argument is take from the remorse of conscience.

8 Lastly the greatest sinners that are, vvho vvould vvith al their hartes that there vvere no God, that they might sinne the more freely, in the middest of their vices, & pleasures haue many tymes remorses of conscience, and feare euen naturally, by natures instinct and instruction, some diuine power, that vvil cal thẽ to an account. Hence procede their melancholike moodes by day, & fearful dreames by night, as in the former booke, & in the chapter of conscience may appeare. And truly we see that nothing hath so much force in the rule of mens actions, and direction of their life, as the cogitation of a Diuine Maiestie, to vvhom they must yeeld and render a strict account. For thus some tymes the greatest sinners are enforced to discourse. I let the bridle loose to al vice and pleasure, I bridle no passions, I refraine from iniustice, vvhen by iniuring others I can profit my selfe: I liue according as I wil, & as freely as he that hath no master, & if there vvere no Diuinitie, to vvhom I am to yeeld an account for euery action, I might take my hartes ease amidst al my pleasures: but if there be a God, as I feare there is, & as me thinke there is (for else why doth this cogitation of a Diuinitie so often crosse the vvays of my pleasures) then haue I cause to looke to my actions, and to make my account before hand, lest I be taken in the lurch. But vvhat if there be no God, then had I lesse cause to care. But because peraduẽture there is a God, in the middest of my pleasure I haue not my hartes desire, and ful repose. Many other argmentes I could alleage for Diuine power, but these are the principal. who desireth more, let him read S. Thomas in his Theological Summe, & in his worke which he wrot against the Gentiles, as also Granado in the beginning of his Catechisme, and the English Resolution or Directorie: and he shal find that al say the same in substance. Now let vs draw nerer to our cõclusion, & intended purpose: which is to shew hovv our reformers doctrin leadeth vs vnto the denial of a Godhead. VVhich I wil do briefly and yet so plainly, as the reader shal confesse, that to haue vsed mo vvordes in a matter so plaine, had bene prolixitie and superfluitie. If you remember, they are not afraid to auouch that God is the author of al sinne and wickednes, that he hath ordained vs to sinne from al eternitie, that vve sinne not only by his permission, but also by his wil & cõmandement, yea that he vrgeth vs and compelleth vs to sinne: vvhence it folovveth that he is of a malicious nature, bent to al euil, because so bad frutes

A sinners discourse.

See also Greg de Valentin & Vasques. 1. p. q. 2. Molmia ibidem.

See the fifth booke. chap. 1.

can not procede from a good tree: he cōmandeth vs also vnder payne of damnation to refraine from al sinne & vice, which notwithstāding by the reformers doctrin we can not do, because we haue no freez wil: & if vve sinne and dye in sinne, he punisheth vs vvith a perpetual & hellishfire, for that fault vvhich vve could not auoid, and in which he him self had as much part as we our selues: whence it folovveth that he is not only malicious, but cruel also & tyrannical, as vpon an other occasion, is before demonstrated. If therfore a Christian be once perswaded that this doctrin is true, he wil easily be induced, to thinke as Atheistes do, that there is no God at al. For seing that the common conceit of God hitherto hath bene very hononrable, euery one deeming that which is most perfect, best, and most amiable, to be God: men wil more easilie be perswaded with Diagoras andd Protagoras, that there is no God at al, then that he is of so bad, cruel, and malicious a nature.

See the 5. booke. chap. 3. 4.

The conclusion.

The second Chapter shevveth hovv the nevv religion by the same doctrin ruineth religion and vvorship of God.

ELIGION is a moral vertue, and one of the principal vertues of that kind, whose office is to offer vnto God supreme honour, homage, and worship, as vnto the highest: vvhich although she haue not the Diuinitie for her immediate obiect, as the Theological vertues haue, yet cometh she as nere as may be, because she hath the worship of this Diuinitie for her obiect, and attendeth vpon the diuinitie so faithfully, that no sooner is a God acknowledged, but Religion adoreth him, and yeldeth him his homage for a tribute.

Religion folowyeth knovvledge of God.

2. Wherfore euer since there vvas a reasonable creature, able to knovv God, the vvorld vvas neuer vvithout Religion. In Paradise our first parentes vvorshipped a God for the tyme, and if that state had continued, there should haue bene a publike practise of Religion, and by Sacrifice also, as some diuines teach. And vvhat vvorship of God by Sacrifices, and Sacramentes vvas vsed in the lavv of nature, and of Moyses

Religion vvas euer.

Svvarez 3. p. de sacrificio Missæ.

Moyses I haue already declared. Yea neuer as yet vvas there any nation, vvho acknowledged a Diuinitie, but it also vvorshipped the same with some kind of Religion. For men easily perceiued, that to Maiestie, povver, and excellencie, honour vvas a dew tribute, and by good consequence, that to supreme Maiestie, power and excellencie, vvas dew also supreme homage and religion. Which is the cause, as Liuie reporteth, that Rome vvas no sooner built, but a religion also vvas established, and temples dedicated vnto the Gods. For vvhich deuotion, Valerius Maximus commendeth the Romaines, saying, that they thought nothing vvas to be peferred before religion, but that rather as the Gods vvere estemed aboue their Senators, Dictators, and Emperours, so religion should take place before their ciuil lawes and customes. Of vvhich opinion Plato also sheweth him selfe to haue bene, vvho in his vvorke vvhich he made of lawes, decreed some for gouernment and policie, others for religion, and these he counted the principal and fundamental lawes: vvel knovving that to be true, which Cicero after him obserued, that if once pietie and religion tovvards God, be taken a way, fidelitie and iustice amongst men, can not long continevv. And Plutarch affirmeth that you shal sooner find a citie vvithout coyne, walles, lawes, and lernig, then without temples and vvorship of Gods. And although this religion of the paganes, vvas no religion but superstition, yet this superstition proceded by abuse, from a natural inclination, vvhich man hath to vvorship & honour a God. Because superstition and religion do only differ in this, that superstition ether worshippeth a false God, or at least giueth not a right honour vnto the true God, but religion worshippeth the true God, & not whith a vaine & phantastical, but with a true, sincere, & reasonable worship. So that mā by nature is inclined to religiō, only he faileth ethet in the thing which is to be worshipped, or in the maner of worhip, & therfore if a man be of any discourse able to know, that there is a God, you shal not nede to persuade him that God is to be worshipped, only in this he shal nede your help, vvhat is this God, & with what worship & religion he is to be serued. And herein cōsisteth the principal point of the cōtrouersie which to this day euen frō the beginning, hath trubled the world, and the greatest vvittes of the vvorld, to vvit, with vvhat vvorship and religion God is to be serued for although al almost agree in this, that God is religiously to be honoured & respected, as the diuersitie of religions vvhich possesse the vvorld, wil testifie. Yet in the other point, to vvit, vvith vvhat reli-

Supra. l. 1. c. b & l. 4. c. 2 & 6.

l. 1.

l. 1. c. 1.

l. 4.

l. 1. de natura deorum.

Aduersus Colotem.

Hovv superstition and religion differ.

The controuersie vvhich troubleth the vvorld.

religion he is to be reuerenced, men are as diuerse, as there are diuers religions in the vvorld.

3. Wherfore here might I take occasion to refute the religion of the Iewes, Turkes, Paganes, and old Heretiques by many argumentes, and by as many argumentes I could demonstrate the Catholique and Romaine faith and worship of God, to be the only true religion, which I haue done in my commentaries vpon Secunda Secundæ: but this were a thing to long, and besides my purpose, vvhich vvas only to make a general suruey and examination of the nevv religion. Wherfore I leaue that to others, and peraduenture to some other booke, vvich, if this be vvel accepted, I may herafter set forth: only here, in a world or tvvo, I wil direct the reader to certaine places of this Suruey, in which vpon occasion I haue disproued the nevv religion, and
l. 1. established the old, by pregnant reasons. For first of al my first booke demonstrateth that vve can not admit nether the Reformers nor their religion, for good and lavvful, vnles vve bynd our selues by the same reason to receiue al heretikes and heresies that euer vvere hertofore, or shalbe herafter: yea in the fifth chapter of the sayd booke I haue proued the Catholicque Religion to be the only religion, because it is conformable to that vvhich was so strangely planted by the Apostles, and in the same place I haue proued manifestly that the reformers haue no probable meanes or motiues to induce a reasonable man to be of their profession. In the second booke I haue declared
Proofes of the catholique, and disproofes, of the nevv religion.
l. 2. how the markes of heretikes agree vnto them, & that therfore they must be taken for heretikes, & their doctrin for heresie, if Arianisme or any other such like doctrin be iustly so to de censured. In the third booke I declare hovv their doctrin disgraceth Christ, and so can
l. 3. not be Christian religion, & in the bookes folowing I shevv how it repugneth to ciuile state and policie, hovv iniurious it is to God, how it openeth the gap vnto al vice and Atheisme, and so can not be of God. Yea in the fourth booke I proue that they haue no religion, be-
l. 4. cause they haue no Priestes nor Sacrifices, nor prayer, & scarsely any Sacramentes, notvvithanding that these things & religion euer vvent
l. 1. c. 5. together. Secondly in the alleaged fifth chapter I haue compared our ancient Pastors of vvhom vve receiued our Religon vvith their nevv ministers of vvhom they receiued theirs, and I haue proued that our Pastors in al pointes are to be preferred, & consequently our religion.
l. 2. c. 5. Thirdly in the second booke and fifth Chapter, I proue that once Christian religion was planted in the world, & Pastors were appointed. I

ted, I haue proued alſo that this Religion and ſucceſſion of Paſtors are neuer to be changed, & conſequently, that is the true Church & Religion, vvhich can deriue it ſelfe by a continual ſucceſſion from the firſt Paſtors & the firſt faith that was planted and practiſed. I haue proued alſo that the reformers haue not this ſucceſſion, and that Catholiques haue: whence it foloweth euidently, that their religion is not the true Chriſtian religion, and that ours is the true and only Religion. In the Sixth Chapter I proue that in Chriſts Church and religion is peace & vnitie in faith and doctrin, which Chriſt at his departure bequeathed to his Chrurh, and I haue demonſtrated that his peace and vnitie is not to be found amongſt the reformers, but only amongſt Catholiques, and conſequently that the Catholique Religion is the only Chriſtian Religion. In the Seuenth chapter I proue that the Religion of true Chriſttans is no particular ſect, but Catholique and vniuerſal, and one & the ſame in al countties and ages, & ſeing that only the Catholique Religion hath this propertie, it foloweth that that is the true Chriſtian Religion. So that I ſhal not nede to vſe any other argument, to proue that the Catholique Religion only is the true Religion and worſhip of God.

l. 2. c 6.

l. 2. c. 7.

4 It remaineth therfore only, that I now declare how the reformers open the gappe to a certaine kind of Atheiſme, which is irreligioſitie & contempt of al religion, & becauſe this concluſion is often tymes to be inferred out of other pointes of their doctrin in the Chapters folowing, I content my ſelfe in this Chapter with their doctrin alleaged in the former Chapter, and out of that only I wil deduce my intended concluſion, which I may do with as much breuitie as facilitie. For if God be the author of al ſinne, then if we may gather what the tree is by the frute, he is of a malicious nature as is before proued: and if he command vs impoſſibilities and puniſh vs with hel fyer for not fulfilling them, then is he vnreaſonable, cruel, and barbarous. And if we once make this conceit of God (as we muſt nedes if we beleue the aduerſaries opinion) then muſt our harts of neceſſitie be cuold in Religiō, & worſhip of God. For who can be induced to worſhip, loue, & honour ſuch a God, in whom is nothing that is amiable, nothing worthy honour, wel we may feare him for his cruelrie, bur loue him, and honour him from the hart we can nor. And ſo Religion falleth.

Hovv the Reformers bring in contempt of Religion.

Caluin ſaith ſo as is related aboue in the 5. booke chap. 1. See the ſame booke chap. 4.

The third Chapter shevveth that in contempt of the Churches authoritie they bring al religion in contempt.

Cal. l. 4. inſt. c. 2. Monſieur du Pleſſis en ſon traicte de l'Eeglise. See the ſecond booke & firſt chap.

IT is a Maxime and almoſt an article of faith receiued amongſt the reformers, that the true Church which once vvas, hath erred groſſely, & in no leſſer matters then faith, iuſtification, purgatorie, prayer to Saincts, worſhip of images, number and vertue of Sacramentes, Sacrifice, and ſuch like. Yea they confeſſe that the Romain Church vvas once the true Church, but they adde vvithal that afterwardes it erred, and fel, & novv of the Church of Chriſt is become the Synagogue of the diuel. This is the cauſe vvhy vvhen vve vrge the authoritie of the ancient and preſent Church, for the proofe of pointes, of Religion they anſwer vs that the Church, was but a congregation of men, which hath erred in manie things. And therfore Luther careth not for a thouſand Churches, & Caluin, Beza, & others deſpiſe al the Coũcels, & anciẽt Fathers, as appeareth by their wordes which are related in the firſt booke, and the third, & fourth chapters. So that vpon the bare authoritie of the Church they wil not hang their ſoules: becauſe the Church as it may be deceiued, ſay they ſo it may deceiue. But I demand of them vvhat aſſurance they haue of Scripture, and by vvhat meanes they come to the knovvledge of it.

See the firſt booke chap. 3. 4.

Vvhat a Catholique can ſay for Scripture.

1. Tim. 3. Io. 14. 15. l. cont epiſt. fund. c. 5. See aboue booke 1. chap. l. 2. c. 23. 4. l. præfa. de expoſ. Symb. l. 2 c 4. 5. 46. l. 4. c. 11.

2 A Catholique vvould ſay that he beleueth theſe bookes to be the word of God, becauſe the Catholique Church, vvhich is the piller of truth, to vvhich by the Sonne of God was promiſed *a ſpirit vvhich should teach her al veritie*, hath euer ſo beleued & defined. Vvherfore S. Auſtin ſayth, that he vvould *not beleue the Goſpel vnles the Churches authoritie moued him*: not that the Church maketh Scriptures, or giueth them their truth and veritie (for that they haue of God vvho vvas the inditer of them) but becauſe vve can not knovv vvhich is Scripture, vvhich is not, but by the voice of the Church, to vvhich only in this matter the ancient Fathers were vvont to harken, as Ireneus, Tertullian, S. Hierom, S. Leo the firſt, and diuers others, of vvhom Nicephorus maketh mention. Wherfore the firſt Toletan Councel, in the one

one and tvventith canon, accurseth them vvho accept of any other Scriptures then those vvhich the Catholique Church receiueth. He vvould alleage for an argument that Christ made Peter, & his successour the Pope, supreme pastor of the Church, and commanded him to *feed his shepe*: and seing that a principal office of the shepheard, is to shew them such pastures as are most holsome for them: it perteineth to the supreme Pastors of the Church, to tel vs infallibly, vvhich are the true Scriptures: for when he declareth vvhich are the true Scripturs, he shevveth vs our pasture, & the place wher vve are to graze, and vvhen he expoundeth them, he feedeth vs. And seing that the Pope of Rome is this Pastor (as is proued in the sixth chapter of the first booke) it foloweth that we must receiue that for Scripture which he alovveth of as Scripture. He vvould alleage also the antiquitie of Scriptures for a profe of their sinceritie: because Moyses vvho vvas the vvriter of a great part of the old testament (as Iosephus, Tertullian, and Eusebius affirme) by many hundred yeares, vvas more ancient then al the vvriters of the Romains and Grecians also, vvhich therfore deserue great credit and reuerence, because, as Cicero sayth in his Tusculans questions, to Antiquitie no lesse is devv. He vvould confirme this argument by an other of no lesse efficacie, to vvit, that these bookes haue bene conserued so many thousand yeares, notvvithstanding so many captiuities of the Iewes, and persecutions of the Christians, vvhich argueth that God who vvas the Author of them, had a special care of them, and a vigilant eye vnto them, as vnto his ovvne vvord and writing. He might alleage also the confomitie of these bookes, vvhich vvere indigted of diuers, & at diuers tymes, and yet haue in them no contrarieties, and vvere translated out of Hebrevv into Greke by 72 Interpreters, diuersly disposed, vvho yet notvvithstanding so agreed, as if al their translations had bene copied out of one. For vvhich causes euen the Gentils and Pagans them selues, haue borne great respect vnto these vvritings, not daring to mingle them vvith their prophane writinges, because (as Iosephus and Eusebius affirme) some that haue attempted it, by the diuine and secret povver, haue bene sharpely and seuerly punished: al vvhich is warranted by historie and tradition. This a Catholique may say vvith great confidenc and no lesse probabilitie, for the authoritie of holy Scripture.

Io.

S. Peters successour telleth vvhich is Scripture.

Antiquitie of Scripture.

l. 2. cont. Ap. l. 19 prapar. Euangelii Apolog. c. 19. 20. 24. 1. Tusc.

The strange conseruation of Scripture.

Conformitie of Script.

Iustins orat. paræn ad gentes.

l. 18. Ant. c. 1. præpar. c. 1.

3 But what vvould, or what could, our reformers say? vvould they say with the Catholique, that they beleue them to be holy Scri-

ex Hosio. l. 3. cont. Brent. ture, because the Church sayth so? Luther in dede sayth that he in this point beleueth the Church and Pope, & good reason hath he: because of whom did he receiue the Scriptures when he began first to preach his new doctrin, but of the Romain Church, who euer had the custodie of them, euen since the time of the Apostles? And how could he *Euseb. l. 1. 2. c. 25.* know that the Gospel of the Nazarens, of S. Barnabas, & S. Thomas, were not as true Scripture as the Gospel of S. Matthevv, and other Euangelistes, but that the Romain Church alowed of these, and not of those? For this cause some of them do say, that in this point they must nedes beleue the Pope, and Romain Church, because they can not in dede haue any probable knowledge of Scripture, but by this meanes, as shal appeare by the refutation of al other meanes vvhich they can faine or imagin. But I wil be so bold as to take this meanes from them, and then I wil aske them, how they know that the new and old Testament are not mere fables, and fictions, as the Atheistes *Supra. Calu. l. 4. inst c. 1. 2.* say that they are? For they are of opinion, that the Romain Church may deceiue, and be deceiued, and therfore they wil not beleue her for the number of canonical bookes, nor for the meaning of Scripture; *Heretiques can not credit the Romain church for Scriptures.* how then can they credit her vvhen she defineth that the old and new testament are holy Scripture: their authoritie is one & the same in the affirmation of this, and of other thinges: if then they beleue her not in those things, they can not beleue her in this. For as if the Astrologer say that to morow shal be rayne, and vvithin three monethes there shal be rayne, I can not beleue this to be true, for his assertion, vnlesse I also beleue that, because his authoritie is the same: and yet may I beleue rather that within three monethes & we shal haue raine, then that to morow we shal haue rayne, because that in it selfe is more likely: so if we beleue one thing vvhich the Romain Church affirmeth, & not an other, we beleue not any thing because she sayth so, but either for the probabilitie of the thing, or for some other reason vvhich pleaseth vs. Wherfore seing that our reformers beleue not the Romain Church in al pointes, it must needes folow, that they can not beleue that the old & new Testament are holy Scriptures, because she sayth so, but for some other imaginations, which they haue: for if they beleued this because she sayth so, they would beleue other things also which she auoucheth, because her authoritie being the same, deserueth the same credit in the one, and in the other. But let vs suppose that they beleue that the old & new testament are holy Scripture because the Romain Church sayth so, yet because they affirme that the

Romain Church may lye, and hath also lyed loudly in many important matters: it foloweth that they haue hereby no assurãce of Scripture, because as the Church, in their opinion, hath erred in othe, things, so may she in this, and if she may, peraduenture she hath erred and so they haue no assurance of Scripture.

Supra.

by the Romain church heretikes can haue no assurance of Scripture.

4. They wil say peraduenture that they are assured by tradition from tyme out of mynde vnto this present, that those bookes are holy Scripture, because our forfathers euer esteemed them so. But neither can this be a sufficient vvarrant, because they are vvont to say, that al thinges necessarie to be beleued, are conteined in scripture, and that therfore they wil beleue no tradition. And if they beleue that these bookes are holy scripture, because by tradition so it is deliuered vnto them, vvhy do they not beleue the real presence, & the Sacrifice of the Masse? Vvhy contemne they, the Fast of Lent, Images, holy vvater, the signe of the Crosse, and such like, vvhich we haue by the same tradition, by vvhich we haue the Scriptures. Yea seing that Tradition is nothing else but an opinion or custom of the Church, not written in holy writte, but yet deliuered by the handes of the Church from tyme to time, and from Christians to Christians, euen vnto the last age; if the Church can erre, she may allow of euil traditions, and so traditions also may be erroneous, and consequently can be no sufficient vvarrant vnto the Reformers, for the authoritie of holy Scripture. They wil say peraduenture, that they beleue most voices, and therfore seing that al the vvorld allovveth these bookes for holy Scripture, they wil ioine with them in this opinion, because the voice of the people, is the voice of God. But neither can this voice assure them. For either they vnderstand by this common voice, the voice of the vvhole world, or the voice of the Christian vvorld. If they meane the voice of the vvhole vvorld, then haue they mo voices against them, then for thẽ, because the greatest part of the world was euer Pagan: if they meane the Christian world, then in dede the most voices are for Scripture, because the Catholique Church, vvhich aloweth of Scripture, vvas, is, & shalbe the greatest part of Christianitie, but because they say that this Church may erre, they can haue no assurance of Scripture by this voice.

tradition can not help them.

Most voices helpe them not.

Se the 2. booke chap. 7.

Heretikes haue no assurance by their ovvne church.

5. Yet they wil say perhaps that they beleeue that Scripture is the vvord of God, because their ovvne Church, vvhich is the true Church, affirmeth it to be so. But niether vvil this shift serue their turne. For first of al they can not proue their Church to be the true

Church nor their Pastors to be the true Pastors. Because their Church hath not the markes of the true Church, hauing neither succession from the Church planted by the Apostles, vvhich should make it Apostolique, neither hauing euer possessed the greatest part of the knovvne vvorld, vvhich should make it Catholique, and being so farre from being one, that it is diuided into cōtrarie sectes, & so farre also from being holy, that it leadeth to al vice & Atheisme, yea hauing al the markes of heresie, as my second booke demonstrateth. As for their Pastors, they can not proue their mission, as also is proued *in the first booke. chap. 1.* But if I should grant that their Church is the true Church, yet by their Churches warrant, they can haue no assurance of Scripture, because they are of opinion that the true Church may erre, and cōsequently their Church also may erre, and if it may erre in other thinges, it may erre in this, & if it may erre in this, peraduēture it hath erred in this, and so they haue no assurance of Scripture. Wherfore laying aside the Churches authoritie as insufficient in their opinion, I demand vvhat assurance they haue of Scripture?

Scripture can giue no testimonie of her selfe.

6. They can not alleage Scipture to proue scripture, because no part of Scripture affirmeth that the Bookes called Scripture, are the word of God, dictated & indighted by his holy Spirit. And if Scripture did affirme it selfe to be holy Scripture, yet were not that a sufficient warrant, for as I may doubt whether the bookes called Scripture be the vvord of God, so may I doubt of that testimonie vvhich Scripture geueth of her selfe, vnles by some other meanes I be assured, that these writings are the word of God. They wil say peraduēture that the very maiestie of the phrase of Scripture, and the diuine matters and mysteries which it conteineth do argue, that it is the word of God. But this answer is also insufficient, because to a worldly man or prophane Philosopher, the stile of Scripture semeth base & barbarous, and the mysteries seeme to be nothing els but dreames and imaginations, the histories seeme tales, & the matters seeme either follies or impossibilities, and so they would seeme vnto vs also, vvere it not that we haue a reuerent conceite of them, because we beleue them to be the word of God. Vvherfore Iulian the Apostata. Celsus, Porphirius, Apion, and others, contemned Scripture, both for the phrase and matter, and estemed no more of them, then we do of Æsops fables.

Phrase of Scrip. no argument.

7 They may ansvver me peraduēture (& now I know not what else they can answer) that the spirit assureth them that these bookes and no other, are the holy Scripture. But against this spirit, I haue disputed

puted at large in the first booke and third chapter, and so I might referre the reformer, and the reader vnto my arguments, vvherVVith in the aforesayd place, I haue refuted this phantastical spirit. Yea to ease them both of that labour, I wil in a word reiect this answer, by reiecting this spirit. I vvil aske of him that thinketh him selfe most deeply inspired, why he beleueth this his owne priuate spirit, rather then the common spirit of the Church? Especially seing that it is more like that God vvil more amplv communicate his Spirit to his Church then to a priuate man, & if the Church may be deceiued (as they say she may) notwithstanding that Christ promised her a *spirit vvhich should teach her al veritie*, vvhy may not euery priuate man doubt at least, lest his ovvne priuate spirit be a lying and deceiuing spirit. He ansvvereth that his spirit assureth him, that it is a true spirit. But how doth it assure him, by vvhat reasons, miracles, or reuelations, by no such meanes (saith he) it doth assure me, but yet I am sure. Vvhy art thou sure, if nether for reasons, nor miracles, nor reuelations, then art thou sure only because thou thinkest thy selfe sure. And so did Suenlkfeldius thinke him selfe sure of a right spirit, when he denyed al Scriptures, & vvould be ruled only by the invvard spirit, & yet he for al his surenes, was deceiued, & consequently so mayst thou be, though thou thinkest thy selfe assured And do not al heretikes thinke them selues to be inspired vvith the right spirit? As they therfore are deceiued, so mayst thou be, vnles thou haue some certaine rule and iudge, such as the Church is, to acertain thee of thy spirit. If now some Infidel or Atheist vvould deny the old and nevv testament to be holy Scripture, hovv vvouldst thou conuince them? vvhat a Catholique could say for the proofe of Scripture, I haue allready declared. I demand therfore what thou who takest vpon thee to be a reformed Christian, couldest alleage for the authoritie of Scripture?

The spirit is no assarance l. 1. c. 3.

Io. 14. 15.

8. Wouldst thou alleage the Churches definition or tradition, or cōmon cōsent? he vvould say, tush, tel me not of Church, Tradition, Fathers, Councels, al these by your ovvne confession may erre and haue erred in other as great matters as this, & therfore this can be no sufficient warrant. Vvouldst thou say that Scripture giueth testimony of her selfe that she is Scripture; he Would aske thee vvhere, and thou shouldst not be able, to quote the place, and if thou couldst, yet he whould say that Scripture is not to be beleued in her owne cause, and that as he doubteth of Scripture, so he doubteth, vvhether it be Scripture, which affirmeth these bookes to be Scripture. Wouldst thou say that

The Reformers can not proue scripture against painims.

that the phrase of Scripture argueth it to be Gods owne word? He would tel thee that he wil shew thee as good phrases in Tullie, Liuie, and other prophane writers. And if thou shouldest say that thy spirit assureth thee, that these bookes are of Gods owne indighting, he would laugh at thee, and tel thee, that Suenkfeldius by his spirit denyed al Scripture, and that he hath no more assurance of thy spirit then thou hast of his. Yea he wil come vpon thee with the common spirit of the Romain Church, & tel thee, that if that spirit may deceiue, as thou sayst it may, much more may thy priuate spirit deceiue thee, & al that wil be so mad as to beleue thee. And so if thou cōtemne the authoritie of the Romain Church, thou shalt be able to assure him no more of Scripture, then of a Robin Hoods tale.

9. If the Churches authoritie then be reiected as insufficient, we haue no probable assurance of Scripture, & so we may iustly doubt lest it be but some Apocriphal writing, which hath hetherto bene called the word of God, to keepe fooles in awe. And if we may doubt of the bookes of Scipture, we may as iustly doubt of the contentes, & so the mysteries of the Trinitie, & Incarnation, Christs life, Doctrin, Passion, Death and Resurrection, may be called in question, & so Christian religion falleth; and seing that after an Apostasie from Christianitie, we haue no reason to imbrace Turcisme, or the Iudaical ceremonies, much lesse the superstitions of Pagans, & Idolaters, adew al Religion, and welcome Atheisme. And thus thou seest, gentle reader, how contempt of Scripture must nedes folow the contempt of the Churches authorieie, which being layd aside, we haue not so much as probable assurance of Scripture or Christian Religion. Wherfore hold fast let vs with the Catholique Apostolique & Romain Church, & neuer linke our selues in Religion, with the pretended reformers, who like Chammes contemne their mother the Church, lest we be inforced to shake handes with Atheistes, whose frendship we can not refuse, if we breake amitie and league with the Romain Church, as is most euidenrly demonstrated.

The conclusion. How contempt of the Romain church bringeth in Atheisme.

***

The

The fourth Chapter shevveth that in admitting some bookes of Scripture and reiecting others, they open the gap to contempt of al Scripture and religion.

VE say commonly that a lyer had nede to haue a good memorie: for otherwise he being alwayes ready to speake, not as the truth requireth, but as he may best for the present serue his owne turne, wil be in danger to contradict himselfe, and to vary in his owne tale. For want of which memorie, the reformers do often eate their vvordes, and go from that vvhich before they stood vnto. And amongst many other examples this may serue for one, that they wil nedes receiue Scripture at the Romain Churches hand, and for this point account her authoritie sufficient, but their memorie is so short, that forgetting them selues, they vvil not accept of the number of the bookes of Scripture, vvhich she hath deliuered vnto them: although they haue not any other vvarrant of Scripture, then they haue of the number of the bookes of Scripture, vvhich is the Romain Churches authoritie. I must therfore desire them better to remember them selues. For if the Romain Church be of sufficient credit, to vvarrant vs of Scripture, vvhy is not her authoritie a sufficient vvarrant also, for the nũber of the bookes of Scripture. Or if she may erre in the nũber of the bookes of Scriptute, she may erre also in Scripture and so if they vvculd remember them selues better, and rubbe their brovves harder, they vvould see plainy, that ether they should take al or none of her, because her authoritie is as sufficient being one & the same to vvarrant vs for the bcokes of Scripture, as for Scripture. If they beleue then that there is Scripture, because she sayth so, they must beleue that there are so many bookes of Scriptures, because she also sayth so: her vvord being as good for the one as for the other. But as they are lyers, so are they forgetful, and therfore so cotrarie in their tale, that they vvil say that they beleue her in that, but not in this, vvhere as rather it folovveth, that they beleue her nether in the one nor in the other: but only do giue credit to their priuat spirit and imaginations, affirming that to be Scripture vvhich they imagin, and

a lyer must haue a good memorie.

The reformers vvant such a memorie.

an example therof.

They take scripture at the Romain Churches hand, but not the number of bookes.

Vvhat bookes they reiect.

in ser. can. tit de libris vet. & noui test.

those bookes only to be Scripture, vvhich their spirit liketh of.

2. Wherfore Luther affirmeth that the booke of Iob is but a tale, deuised to set forth an example of patience before our eyes; he iesteth at the author of Ecclesiastes, saying that he wanteth bootes & spurres, and therfore rideth in his sockes, as he did vvhen he vvas a fryar. Yea he spareth not the new Testament, affirming that he liketh not of the common opinion, which aloweth of fower Gospels: & he addeth, that S. Ihons is the only true and principal Gospel: vvhence it foloweth that the other three are not authentical. For if they vvere, then vvere al fovver of equal authoritie, and so S. Ihons Gospel were not the principal. He denyeth that the Epistle to the Hebrewes is Apostolical, the like is his censure of the Epistles of S. Iude, & S. Iames. Caluin reiecteth the bookes of Wisdom, of Ecclesiasticus, of Iudith, of the Machabees, of Tobie. And vvhy? truly for no other reason, then that these bookes seme most contrarie to diuers points of their doctrin. For otherwise, seing that they can not discerne Scripture from other vvritings, but by the censure of the Romain Church, as is proued in the last Chapter, they haue no reason to receiue some bookes on her vvord & not al, seing that she giueth the same testimonie of al.

Pref. in nouum Test. *Prafat. in Heb.* *Præfat. li. 1. Inst c 11 8. l. 2. c. 5. 18. l. 8 c 5. 8. Ant. sess. 14.*

Vvhat an Atheist may say to this.

3. But giue an Atheist this aduantage, and vvhat wil he say? he wil tel the Reformers, that he seeth no other warrant which they haue for the Epistle to the Romains, then for the Epistle to the Hebrewes, and the Epistle of S. Iames: nor for S. Iohns Gospel, more then for the other three? nor for Genesis more then the first and second booke of the Machabees, Tobie, Iudith, and Iob: and that therfore if the reformers deny these, he wil deny al the other, because if the Romain Churches vvarrant (for they haue no other vvarrant as in the former Chapter is proued) be not sufficient for some of these bookes, it can be no sufficient vvarrant for any. And so he wil say, that you may as wel deny al scripture, as some bookes of scripture, or if you vvil not, he wil deny it for you, and ground him selfe in your owne doctrin.

Hovv this bringes contempt of religion.

4. And he wil yet go farther and auouch that if he may doubt of Scripture, as vvhy not, because there is no other vvarrant for it but the Romain Churches vvord, he wil doubt also of the contentes of Scripture, and so he wil cal in question Moyses, Christ, the Apostles, the Trinitie, the Incarnation, the Passion of Christ and Resurrection, and al the Mysteries of Chrstian Religion. Wherfore as you credit the Romain Church for Scripture, so giue her credit for the number of the bookes of Scripture, because her word and warrant is as good for this as for

as for that; or if you vvil not beleue her in this, you can haue no assurance of any part of Scripture, & so you may bring al into question; vvhence foloweth contempt of al Religion, as is before proued.

The fifth Chapter proueth, that their dissension in Religion openeth the gap to contempt of al Religion.

The force of Religion.

OTHING is of more force then Religion, vvhich kepeth vs in awe, bridleth our appetites, ruleth our actions, gouerneth our life, and inculcateth vnto vs our dutie towards God & man. And if there vvere no other argumēt, then the example of so many thousand Martyrs, vvho haue endured so exquisite torments and so horrible deathes rather then they would deny their Religion, it were sufficient to beare witnes for Religoni, that it is of greater force then al the violence of the Tyrantes, then al their engines and instrumentes of crueltie, yea then death it selfe. But as the force of a riuer is great, and so great, that sometymes it ouerthroweth houses, and bridges, and beareth downe al vvhich standeth in the way of his streame, but yet diuide it into many litle brookes, and a childe vvil resist his force: euen so religion is of great force & efficacie, and beareth a great svvay in the life of man, but yet if it be diuided into diuers sectes, it looseth force and vigour, and vvheras vvhilest it remaineth vnited, it vvil not be resisted, vvhen it is diuided it is easily cōtemned. I haue already described the iarres, and dissensions of the Reformers in matters of religion, and by this marke I haue descried them to be heretikes. Hovv let vs see vvhat an aduantage this their dissention giueth to an Atheist, and what a wide gap it openeth vnto Atheisme.

The force of a riuer vnited, and hovv vveake it is, deuided.
So religion.
See the second booke chap. 6.
Dissension of heretikes.

An Atheists argument grounded in diuersitie of Sectes.

2 An Atheist, out of these their diuersities of opinions may easily draw this discourse. I see sayth he (or at least he may say) diuers sects and opinions, diuers Synagogues, and Religions, diuers conuenticles and congregations amongst you: vvhich as they haue diuers names, so professe they diuers doctrins, and folovv diuers Authors. For some of them are called Lutherans, some Caluinists, vvhich are by a subdiuision parted into softe and rigorous Lutherans, and into Protestants and Puritans, others are called Zuinglians, others Bezits,

others Anabaptists, others Libertins, others Brovvnists, others Martinists, others are of the Familie of loue, others of the damned crew. And although al these agree against the Romain Catholique & Apostolique Church, yet they disagree amongst them selues, and although they hold many, and those also contrarie opinions, yet they al vse one argument to proue their opinions, to vvit Scripture sensed by their priuate spirit. And so vvil this Atheist say, if I beleue one of these sectes, I must beleue al, because they alleage one proofe for their religion; but seing that I can not beleue al, because they teach contrarieties, lest I do any partial vvrong in preferring one before an other, al hauing the same reason I wil beleeue none of them al, nor none of their opinions. And seing that they contemne the Catholique Romain religion, for a fardel of superstitions (which notvvithstanding was euer counted the true Christian religion euen by the Pagans them selues, who therfore presequuted it) and haue no reason to bynd me to any of their religiõs, vnlesse I wil be bond to an impossibilitie, that is to be of al their religions, and nether can with any reason perswade me to be ether Turke or Iewe, I may by authoritie be of no religion. And thus Atheisme must nedes folow diuision in religion & cõtempt of the Romain Church.

The Conclusion.

Hovv Atheisme entereth.

The sixth Chapter shevveth, hovv their vvant of a visible head geueth a great aduantage to Atheists, and such as mocke at al religion.

N the first booke and Sixt chapter, I haue declared at large, how necessarie a visible head is in al societies, and especially in the Church of Christ, & I haue also demonstrated, that there is no such visible head in the Synagogue of the reformers. whence I haue inferred, that amõgst them it is lawful, for euery heretike to preach what doctrin he wil, and no man shal controle him. Now I am to deduce an other conclusion, to wit, that thus also the vvay is opened vnto Atheistes, godlesse, and irreligious persons: which I can do easily, and wil do in a word. For if a visible head be vvanting, euery man may preach and imbrace what Religion he

vvil

wil (as in the alleaged place I haue proued) & seing, that if this head be wanting, there is no certaintie of any religion, but only the priuate spirit, and bare Scripture, which are altogether vncertaine, as before is proued, it wil folow that a man shal haue no more reason to imbrace one religion then an other, yea he shal haue no probable reason to induce him to any religion at al, and consequenty he may take good leaue to be of no religion. And thus he may argue in forme and figure.

In the first booke, ch. 2. 3.

1. If there be no visible head to determine by authoritie vvhat religion is to be imbraced, euery man may be of vvhat religion he wil, & no mā can cōtrole him, & so I also may vse my libertie in choosing my religiō, as wel as an other. And seing that if the authoritie of a visible head be layd aside, I haue no more reason to be of one religion then an other (because al religions alleage the same reason which is no reason, to wit, bare Scripture sēsed by the priuate spirit) and I can not possibly be of al, because they be contrarie one to an other I may by good reason refuse to be of any religion, and no man can controle me for it, if there be no visible head, who can proue that he hath authoritie to determine of religion. And so he that forsaketh the Catholique Church, where only this visible head is to be found, hath leaue and licence to be of what religion he wil, yea to be of no religiō at al, because leauing that, he hath no more reason to be of one religion then an other, because he hath no other reason then bare Scripture sensed by a priuate spirit, which is not sufficient, as is proued in my first booke & third chapter, yea leauing the Catholique Church, he cā not haue any probable reason to induce him to any of these new religions, as I haue proued in my first booke, and fifth chapter, and seing that God nether can, nor wil cōmand him to be of a religion, for which he seeth no reason, nor motiue vvhich is sufficient to induce a reasonable man, as in the same place is proued, he may vvith reason, after he hath left the Catholique Church, ioyne vvith Atheistes vvho are of no religiō.

Hovv vvant of a visible head bringeth in atheisme.

The Conclusion.

***

The seuenth Chapter shevveth hovv the Reformers, in denial of the real præsence, do ruine Christian Religion, & cal al the other Mysteries of Faith in question.

Acrifice is a thing so highly pleasing and acceptable to God, that he wil haue none to be partakers vvith him in such honour, but reserueth it as an homage dew only to him selfe, & proper to a Diuine Maiestie. Yet obedience is more grateful vnto him then al the Hecatombs and Sacrifices in the vvorld, because by the old Sacrifices were consecrated to his seruice the liues & substance of brute beasts, but by obedience we make a burnt offering, & Holocaust of our owne soules, resigning our desires & vvils, yea our owne selues, vvholly vnto his wil and pleasure. But vvhilest this obedience resteth in the vvil, though it be very meritorious, yet hath it not the ful complement of perfection, because so long as the wil hath reason to perswade her, the lesse thanks she deserueth for obeying: but vvhen this vertue reacheth to the vnderstanding, and maketh reason against sence and aboue reason, to yeld to more then reason can reach vnto, then hath this vertue her perfection. And this perfection she hath not of her selfe, because of her selfe she can only submit the vvil vnto the commaundment of the Superior, but she is fayne to borrow so much of the Theoligical vertue, called Faith, vvhose propertie is to make the verie vnderstanding to stoupe, and vvithout any reason to yeld to things, for vvhich there is no reason, because they are aboue reason.

1. Reg 15.

Obedience more pleasing then sacrifice.

The perfection of obedience.

borrovved of faith.

2. Many such things there are in Christian faith vvhich seeme to sense senseles, to reason vnreasonable, and to humain faith incredible, & (as mans reason can see) euen to Diuine power impossible. Amōgst vvhich these three are principal, and to humain reason seme incredible, to vvit, the Trinitie, in vvhich we beleue that three are one, that is that three Persons are one God. The Incarnatiō, in vvhich we confesse, that two are one, that is two natures in Christ, the one Diuine, the other Humaine, are one & the same Person. The blessed Sacramēt of the Altar, in which we acknowledge that bread & vvine by the

The 3. hardest articles of faith.

by the vertue of Christs vvord, are changed into his body & bloud, and that one body is not only in one but in diuers places at one and the selfe same time. But as these three are the hardest to conceiue of al the mysteries of Christian fayth, so hath our blessed Sauiour giuen vs more plaine and euident testimonies of them in his holy vvritte, then of any other, which are more easily to be cōceiued. For the blessed Trinitie vvhat more pregnant proofes can we desire, then we haue in S. Matthew? *Going therfore teach you al nations in the name of the Father, & of the Sonne, & of the Holy Ghost.* Where the anciēt Fathers note that three are named, to signifie three distinct persons, and yet Christ biddeth his Apostles to baptise, in the name, not names of these three, to signifie that these three are one God. And that the Father is God, euery leafe almost of Scripture doth testifie: that the Sonne is God, many places most manifestly do beare vvitnes, & testimonie: that the Holy Ghost is God, S. Peter auerreth, vvho hauing demanded of Ananias the reason vvhy he vvould lye vnto the Holy Ghost, auoucheth that he lyed not to men but to God. Wherfore S. Paul sayth, that we are the Temple of the Holy Ghost, & seing that to God only Temples are erected, if we be his Temple he is our God. Now that these three are one God, S. Iohn wil acertaine vs, for (sayth he) *three there are vvhich giue testimonie in heauen, the Father, the Vvord, & the Holy Ghost, & these three are one.* No lesse pregnant proofes doth holy vvrit afforde vs for the Incarnition, in which mysterie we confesse one Diuine Person, Christ Iesus, to be true God and man. And first let the Father speake for his Sonne. *This is my beloued Sonne, in vvhom I haue taken great pleasure.* Secondly let the disciple speake for his maister: *Thou art the Sonne of the liuing God.* Let an other disciple, & no other then he vvhom Iesus loued, because he loued, tel vs his opinion in this point: he sayth, that *in the beginning vvas the Word, and that the vvord vvas vvith God, yea vvas God.* And afterward he sayth, that this word was made flesh, that is, became man. Let Christ him selfe be credited also in this matter because he is the truth: vvhen the Iewes told him that he had not yet 50. yeares of age, and therfore could not see Abraham: he āswered *that he vvas before Abraham,* and yet the same Christ is called by S. Mathew, the sonne of Abraham, vvhich must nedes argue two natures in one person of Christ, the one Diuine, in respect of vvhich he vvas before Abraham, the other Humaine, by vvhich he vvas after Abraham, as the sonne is after the father: and so the selfe same Person is God and man, and that man Iesus that liued in earth and conuersed amongst vs, is

proofe of the Trinitie. *cap. vlt.*

Rom 1. 3. *Tit.* 1. 3. *Iuda.* 2. *Mat.* 16. *Act.* 5.

1. *Io.* 5. *Proofes of the Incarnation.*

Mat. 3. *cap.* 16.

Io. 1.

Io. 8.

Mat. 1.

the nathe natural Sonne of God, & the word of God, is the word Incarnate, who in respect of his Diuinitie was before Abraham, but in respect of his Humain nature, was long after him.

The Euch arist.

3. Now as cōcerning the third Mysterie, if I bring not as plaine text for it, as can be brought for the others, I vvil grant the victorie to myn aduersarie. But to auoid multitude of allegations, I wil make choise of two places only, vvhich seme to me to be the plainest. And the first shalbe taken out of the sixt of S. Iohn, vvhich chapter although of some it be expounded only of spiritual eating of Christ, yet by the common consent of interpreters speaketh not only of a spiritual, but also of a Sacramental and real eating, as shal be made most manifest. For first our Sauiour Christ to dispose them to a firme beleefe of this Mysterie, made such a multiplication and increase of fiue barley loaues and two fishes, that he fed and filled aboue fiue thousand persons therwith, and that so sufficiently, that the fragments of the banquet vvere as much as the vvhole feast. For if he could make so much of a litle, vvhy can he not turne bread and vvine into his body, and if he could vvithout diminution of the feast satisfie so many, vvhy may he not fede vs al vvith his body, vvithout diuision or diminution of the same? And if after that fiue thousand had eaten their fil of the loaues and fishes, the fragments and reliques, vvhich they left, vvere as much as the feast vvith vvhich they vvere filled, vvhy should it seme impossible, that Christs body should be eaten of vs, and yet remaine in the pix or altar, or that after the communicants haue receiued it, the reliques vvhich they leaue, should remaine stil as great as the vvhole banquet vvas Secondly after that miracle vvas vvrought, because there vvas a great agrement, betwixt it and the blessed Sacrament, thus he taketh the occasion to discourse with them of it, and to induce them to the beleefe of the same, *Amen amen I say to you, you seke me not because you haue sene signes, but because you did eate of the loaues, and vvere filled*: so svvete a tast had that miraculous banquet, and such contentment it gaue, though of it selfe it vvas meane, that they folowed him for the good cheare he made them. but saith Christ, *vvorke not the meat that perisheth, but that vvhich endureth to life euer lasting, vvhich the Sonne of man vvil giue you.* They answered, *vvhat shal vve do, that vve may vvorke the vvorkes of God? This is the vvorke of God* (sayth Christ) *that you beleue in him vvhom he hath sent. VVhat signe* (say they) *doest thou, for which we should beleue thee? Our fathers did eate Manna in the desert, and God gaue them bread from heauen to eate.* Here Christ beginneth to close

Io 6. proued out of S. Ihon. c. 6.

Vvhy Christ multiplied loaues.

This miracle applied to the Eucharist.

Secondly. Christs discourse.

to close with them, & to enter into his intended discourse of the blessed Sacramẽt. *True* (sayth Christ) *but Moyses gaue you not the bread from heauen but my father geueth you the true bread from heauen. Lord* (sayd they) *giue vs alvvayes this bread.* Iesus answered, *I am the bread of life.* At which the Iewes murmured, because they vnderstood him not. And yet most fitly is he called the bread of life. For first in Scripture al that nourisheth is called bread: wherfore seing that Christ is the food of our soule, wel is he called bread, & not whatsoeuer bread, but the bread of life, to distinguish him frõ cõmon bread. Secõdly in Scriptures when one thing is changed into an other, that into which the chãge is made, taketh the name of the thing changed. So the serpẽt into which Aarons rod was changed is called a rod, because it was made of a rod: & because bread was to be changed into Christs body, wel he is called bread. Thirdly because his body was to be couered with the formes of bread, it is called bread, for that it hath the shew & forme of bread, & for this cause his bloud is called *vvine,* and the *bloud of the grape,* because it vvas to be inuested as it vvere, vvith the accidentes of vvine in the same blessed Sacrament. And notwithsting the Iewes murmuration Christ wil not eate his vvord, but againe he repeteth it: *I am the bread of life, your fathers did eate manna in the desert, and they dyed, this is the bread that descended from heauen, that if a man eate of it he dyeth not. And I* (sayth he) *am this liuing bread that came frõ heauen, of vvhich he that eateth shal liue for euer, and the bread that I vvil giue, is my flesh for the life of the VVorld.* Now he speaketh his mynd plainly, and so plainly that he compareth the figure with the veritie, *manna* vvith his bread of the blessed Sacrament, and giueth the preeminence to the veritie: for (sayth he) *your fathers did eate of manna and yet dyed,* but *my manna is a more soueraine viand* because vvhosoeuer eateth of it shal liue for euer.

The first reason vvhy Christ is called bread. *Second.* *Exod. 7.* *Third.* *Gen. 46.*

3. Now if it be true, that the blessed Eucharist is only a signe of Christs body and bloud, then I demand of our aduersaries vvith what shew of truth Christ could preferre it before *mãna?* Why should Christs bread giue life rather then *manna,* seing that *manna* signified Christ, who is this bread, as wel as the Eucharist? Yea vnlesse the Eucharist contain Christs flesh and bloud really, *manna* must nedes take the precedence in dignitie, as it hath in antiquitie. For first *manna* was better in substance, as being made by Angels handes, and in the ayre, hauing also al tastes, as is before declared, and so in substance *manna* is more excellent in figure and signification, *manna* is as good if not better. for if the Eucharist contain not really Christs body and bloud, it is but a

Sap. 16. *Psal. 77.* *See the fourth booke chap. 6.* *The real presence proued by the figure Manna.*

signe, and consequently no better then *manna*, because it signified the same Christ, and so vvas as noble a signe, and it vvas more apt to signifie, and so vvas a fitter figure. for as *Manna* vvas framed by Angels handes, and neuer passed the heate of the fyer: so Christ our bread of life vvas framed by the King of Angels fingers, vvithout al helpe of man, and vvas baked in the ouen of the Virgins vvomb, vvithout al heate of concupiscence. As vvhen God rayned downe *Manna*, the Iewes cried *Manhu!* that is, *VVhat is this*! So vvhen Christ promised his *Manna* the Capharnaites murmured. That *Manna* vvas giuen to the Iewes in the desert, this to Christians in the vvildernes of this vvorld only, for in the next vvorld, I meane in heauen, our only home and land of promise, we shal not fede any more of Christs body by eating or cōmunicating, but we shal tast of the swetnes of his Diuinitie by fruition. *Manna* vvas vvhite, but yet vvas no common bread, and it vvas like a coriander sede, but yet was not of any such substance. and this *Manna* in externe forme and colour seemeth bread, but in dede is the body of Christ. That vvhen it vvas measured was found to be of one measure in al the gatherers hands, and this *Manna* although some haue great hostes some litle ones, although some receaue whole hostes some but a peece, some many hostes some one only, yet when by faith it is measured, we find as much in the litle hoste as in the great, as much in the pece as in the whole hoste, and as much in few yea in one as in many. That *manna had al tastes*, and those most delicate, according to the eaters desire, and this it had not of his owne nature but of God, vvho gaue it such a supernatural vertue: So hath this *Manna* also, because it tasteth to our soules, according to our deuotion & desire, & though it be but flesh, yet it feedeth the soule, not by the vertue of common flesh, for to the soule flesh of it selfe *non prodest quicquam, profiteth nothing*, but by a supernatural vertue, vvhich it receueth by the strange coniunction that it hath vvith the diuinitie, euen as the hote iron burneth, not as iron but as it is vnited to the fire. And seing that such conuenience, and agreement can not be found betwixt bare bread & Christs body, it foloweth, that if the Eucharist be but bread in substance, that *Manna* vvas a better signe then it, and so the figure shal excel the veritie, and the shadow shal surpasse the body, and the promise the performance.

Ex. 16. Ioan. 6 *The application of Manna to the b. Sacr.*

Sa. 16.

4 But let vs go on. After that our Sauiour had told the Iewes, that he was the bread of life, which descended from heauen, and giueth life euerlasting, which manna could not do, because it only extinguished

tinguished hunger, and prolonged life for a tyme, the Iewes murmured once again, and grombled at the matter, yea, as the text sayth, *they stroue amongest them selues saying, how can he giue vs his flesh to eate?* But Christ wil not goe from his former words, rather now he threatneth, that *vnlesse they eate his flesh, and drinke his bloud, they shal haue no life in them.* And he inculcateth again and again, that *his flesh is meat in dede and that his bloud is drinke in dede, that he that eateth him shal liue by him*; that his bread *is the bread that came dovvne from heauen, and so forth.* Wherfore, now many of his disciples begin to stagger, saying that *this is a hard speach not to be endured.* But yet Christ for al this their scandal, changeth not his tune nor tenour of wordes. Only because he knew, that the matter was hard and high of which he spake, he seeketh to induce them to beleue this Mysterie, by an other of as great difficultie. Doth this, sayth he, scandalize you, that I say you must eate my flesh and drinke my bloud? if then you shal see me ascend, from vvhence I descended, you wil much more be scandalized. But yet to take away as much scandal as I may, & to ease your vnderstanding as much as the Mysterie wherof I talke wil permit: *It is the spirit that quickneth, the flesh profiteth nothing, the vvordes vvhich I haue spoken vnto you be spirit and life.* That is, you must not conceue any horrour in that I tel you, that you must eate my flesh, for you must not imagin, that I wil giue it you raw or rosted, as the meate which commeth from the shambles or kitchin, I wil giue it you after a spiritual maner, hiding it from your eyes, vnder the veale of a Sacrament, and in this spiritual maner it shal profit you, for as for that carnal maner in which you do imagin, that I wil giue you my flesh, it profiteth nothing. Or if you thinke it impossible that flesh should giue life, it is not flesh only that can do it, because flesh alone profiteth nothing, but it is the spirit of the Diuinitie and flesh vnited to this spirit that quikneth, for as (S. Austin sayth) if flesh could profite nothing, *Verbum caro non fieret vt habitaret in nobis, the Word vvould not haue bene made flesh to dvvel amongst vs.* So that Christ meaneth that they must eate his flesh, not only in a figure (for so they had eaten it in the paschal lambe) nor only by faith (for so their forfathers and al that euer beleued in Christ had eaten Christ, & therfore at this eating they could not haue bene scandalized) but he speaketh of a real eating though in a spiritual and sacramental maner, and yet the Iewes, after the explication mentioned vnderstood him not, and therfore stil they murmured, yea after this (as the text sayth) *many of his disciples vvent backe and novv they vvalked not vvith him.* Blessed Sauiour, thou that

Christ notwithstanding they vnderstood him really, yet speaketh of no figure.

Aug. tract. 7 Io.

Ibidem.

Ibidem.

Christes meaning.

cammest

camest not to deceue, but to saue soules, if thou haue any easier meaning then that is, in which these men do take thee, tel it them out of hand, to helpe their vnderstanding. If thou meanest only an eating of thee in a figure, or by faith only, as Caluin & Zuinglius do interprete thee, do but say so, and thou shalt take away from these men al cause of scandal, and murmuration: because they are wel accustomed to figures, vvhose vvhole law was figuratiue, and they can easily conceue how they may eate thee spiritually by faith, because that is only to beleue in Christ & the Messias, vvhich thy disciples, that stagger at these thy words, do already beleue, and al their forfathers haue long since beleued. But Christ wil giue them no such easie answer: vvhich sheweth that he spoke nether of figuratiue eating only, nor spiritual only, but of real eating of his flesh, though in a spiritual maner. What then answereth our Sauiour to these afflicted people, nothing at al more, then vvhich already he hath answered, but now he turneth to the twelue Apostles, saying. *Vvhat vvil you also depart?* As if he had sayd: I haue told you a high Mysterie, at which many murmure, many are scandalized, & for vvhich many haue left me, but I haue no other thing to say, faith is here required, vvithout vvhich none can come to me or my Father, none can beleeue this Mysterie: And they that wil not captiuate their vnderstanding to the obedience of faith, let them goe, but wil you my twelue vvho are vsed to my Mysteries be gone also? S. Peter answereth for al twelue (not knowing Iudas infidelitie, vvhom notvvithstanding Christ calleth a diuel for the same) *Lord, to vvhom shal vve goe? thou hast the vvordes of eternal life.*

5. Out of this discourse I gather two thinges for my purpose first that the Iewes vnderstood Christ, not of a figuratiue or spiritual eating by faith, because such eating could not haue scandalized them, vvho were accustomed to spiritual eating, neither would such meates haue gone against their stomake, because figuratiue dishes vvere their ordinarie fare. Secondly I gather that Christ meant not figuratiue or spiritual eating only, but sacramental and real eating. For if he had meant so, he no doubt vvould haue explicated himselfe, to take away al occasion of offence & scandal, vvhich they conceued, because they vnderstood him of real eating, as is proued: or if Caluin wil nedes haue it, that Christ meant only figuratiue and spiritual eating, he must nedes say withal, that Christ vvas most cruel, and peremptorie, and that he endeuoured rather to deceue soules, then to saue them, and to blind them rather then to illuminate them: who, though he perceiued that

2. Annotations out of Christes discourse. The first.

The second.

that they vnderstood him of his flesh, vvhich scandalized them, yet would not voutsafe to tel them, that he meant only a figuratiue and spiritual eating, that so with a word he might haue taken away the scandal, taught them the truth, and geuen the deceiued soules satisfaction.

6. My second argument shal be deduced out of the words of our Sauiour, vvhich he vsed, in the institution of this Sacrament: *This is my body, this is my bloud*: or, *this is the Chalice of my bloud.* What could he haue sayd more plainly? Tel me Caluin, if Christ vvould haue giuen vs to vnderstand, that he meant to giue vs no bare figure but his true body, vvhat playner vvords could he haue vsed? he might haue sayd (sayth Caluin) This is my true body: but might not yet Caluin haue vsed his ordinarie glosse and haue sayd, that he ment only to say that it is the true figure of his body, or the figure of his true body? And I demand of Caluin, vvhether Christ vvas able to turne bread in to his body, as before he turned vvater into vvine, and multiplied the loaues & fishes? If he say he could not, I aske vvhy? If he answer, it semeth impossible: I must nedes tel him, that he taketh much vpon him, in confining Gods power within the narrow compasse of his shalow head: as though God could do iust as much as Caluin can conceiue, but no more. Al the ancient Fathers, though they could not conceiue this Mysterie, yet because Christ calleth that vvhich was in his hands, his body, do confesse that Christ vvas able to do it, because they knew he could do more then they could conceiue. And why could he not do this as vvel as he hath done the like? speake Caluin, and tel vs vvhere lyeth the difficultie, vvhich maketh thee with Iudas and the Capharnaites, to thinke that Christ can not giue vs his body really? either thy reason is because he can not turne bread into a mans body: and vvhy I pray thee can he not as wel turne one thing into an other, as create a thing of nothing? Vvhy can he not turne bread into his body, and vvine into his bloud, who turned water into wine, a rod into a serpent, and a serpent into a rod, and a rocke into vvater. Yea he that turned water into bloud, can he not turne wine into bloud? Or else the reason is, because a mans body can not be in so litle a roome, as is a litle hoste or a litle peece of the same: And vvhy can he not make a great body to be in a litle roome, as he can make two bodyes, by penetratiõ to be in one roome, vvithout enlarging the place: which he did vvhen by penetration he issued out of the virgins vvomb, vvithout breaking her virginal closet, & whẽ he came out of the graue without remouing the stone,

The second argument.
Mat. 26. Mar. 14. Luk 22. 1. Cor. 11.
Io. 2. Io 6.
Caluin a Capharnaite.
Io. 2. Exod 2. Psal. 77. Exod. 7.
that God can turne bread into his body.
Mat. 1. 2. Mar. 16. Luc. 24.
that a great body may be in a litle roome.

ſtone, entered into his diſciples the dore being ſhut, & paſſed through al the heauens in his Aſcenſion, vvithout diuiſion of thoſe incorruptible bodyes? or elſe the reaſon is, becauſe one body can not be in diuerſe places. And vvhy may not one body be in diuers places, as wel as diuerſe bodyes by penetration vvere in one place in his natiuitie, and reſurrection, in his entrance into the houſe, vvhere his diſciples vvere, and in his Aſcenſion into heauen, and aboue al the heauens? Briefly it is no more repugnant, for a body to be in a litle roome or in diuerſe places at once, then for a mans body to ſtand vpright vpon the vvater and not to ſinke, as Chriſts and S. Peters bodyes did: or for a heauy body to aſcend in the vvater as the head of a hachet did, neither is it more impoſſible for a body to occupie more place then his owne quantitie is, then for a body to liue a longer age then nature wil afforde, and yet Ezechias liued longer, and Elias and Henoch are as yet liuing.

and in diuers places.

Mat. 14.
4. Reg. 6.

Caluins obiection.

7. But Caluin vvil ſay, that it is no more neceſſarie to vnderſtand Chriſt really in theſe vvordes *this is my body*, then in diuerſe others, in vvhich he ſayth *I am the dore, I am the Vine*: or in thoſe, *Chriſt vvas the rocke*, or in thoſe, *behold the lambe of God.* But by Caluins leaue there is much more reaſon, vvhy we ſhould vnderſtād Chriſt really in thoſe vvords, *This is my body*, then in the other wordes alleaged. For when Chriſt ſayd, *This is my body*, he made his laſt vvil and teſtament, at vvhich tyme men ſpeake plainly, & not in parables or figures, leſt that the heyres ſhould take occaſion to vvrangle, and to ſew ech other in the law, about the meaning of the vvil: then alſo he enacted a law and inſtituted a Sacrament, in vvhich proper and plain vvordes are required. he ſpoke alſo thoſe vvordes to his Apoſtles, to vvhom he vſed not to ſpeake in *parables* but in plaine wordes, or if he chanced to ſpeake obſcurely to them, they vſed to deſire him to explicate him ſelfe, vvhich here they did not, or elſe ſome one of the Euangeliſtes vvould haue explicated this figuratiue ſpech, as they vſed in other matters to do: yea vvhen Chriſt ſpoke theſe vvordes, he lifted vp his eyes to heauen, and bleſſed the bread vvhich he neuer did, but ſome great miracle folowed, as appeareth by the miracles of the multiplication of loaues and fiſhes, and ſuch like, vvhich argeweth ſome real change in the ſubſtance of bread: which can be no other then trāſubſtantiation, the very vvords, *this is my body*, importing no leſſe. Secondly he ſayd in the preſent tenſe *this is my body vvhich is giuen for you: This is my bloud vvhich is shed for you.* For ſo the Greek text teacheth vs: vvhich addition alſo argueth

The anſwer. firſt.

Mat. 13.
Mat. 15.
Io. 2. 12. 15.
Mat. 16.

Io. 6.

Secondly.

gueth some thing, that then vvas offred for them: and seing that bread and v vine could only be offered to them, but not for them, nor for remission of their sinnes, it folovveth, that Christ then made an oblation & Sacrifice vnbloudy, of his body and bloud, as is before, vpon an other occasion, proued. Which S. Paul confirmeth saying that Christ sayd *This is my body vvhich is broken for you* (for so the greek vvord signifieth) to signifie that Christs body vvas really vnder the accidentes of bread and vvine, else it could not haue bene sayd, to haue bene broken, in respect of the accidents of bread vvhich are broken: vvherfore S. Chrisostom saith, that Christ vvho vvould suffer no bones to be broken on the crosse, vvas broken in the Sacrament. Thirdly if Christ had geuen them but bare bread, or a bare signe of his body, he vvould neuer haue added *this is my body vvhich is giuen for you*, because that argueth a real geuing of his real body, and therfore vvhen he sayd I am the vine, he added not, vvho suffred on the crosse, nor any such like wordes: and although pointing to the image of Cesar vve say sometymes, behold Cesar, or, this is Cesar, yet not so aptly can vve say of the image, this is Cesar that ouercame Pompey, because that addition argueth Cesar in person. Fourthly when we speake metaphorically, we name and expresse the thing, so Christ expressed him selfe, vvhen he sayd I am a vine, so S. Paul named him expressely, vvhen he sayd, Christ vvas a rocke, so S. Ihon pointed at him, vhen he sayd *behold the Lambe of God*, and seing that Christ remaining Christ, can not be truly a vine, a rocke, or a lambe, we easily perceue that such speches are to be taken metaphorically. And so if Christ had sayd, this bread is my body, we must haue vnderstood him figuratiuely, and metaphorically, because bread remaining bread can not be really his body: but for as much as Christ sayd only, *in confuso, confusedly*, this is my body, we must vnderstand him really, & so the sense of these vvordes must be: this vvhich I haue in my handes, is truly & really my body.

1. Cor. 11.

Thirdly.

Fourthly.

8. Lastly the greeke text in S. Luke is sufficient to demonstrate this veritie, vvhere speaking of the chalice he hath these wordes, τȣ̃το τὸ ϖοτήριον κκαινὴ διαθήκη ἐν, τῷ αἵματι μȣ, το ὑπὲρ ἡμων ἐκχυνόμενον: This chalice the new Testament in my bloud, which is shed for you. Wherby it is plaine, that the pronoune (*vvhich*) is referred vnto the noue *chalice*, vvith vvhich word it only agreeth in concord of Grammar, and not vvith the vvord *bloud*. So that this is the clere sense of those vvordes: *This is the chalice the nevv Testament in my bloud*,

Which

vvhich *chalice is shed for you.* Where the continent is taken for the contained, the material chalice or cup can not be shed, & seing that vvine can not be sayd to be shed for vs, it must nedes folow that Christs bloud was in the chalice, because that only was shed for vs. Vvhich text is so plaine, that Beza confesseth, that it must nedes be translated *quod poculum funditur, vvhich chalice is shed for you,* if vve vvil folow the Grammatical construction, yet because thus he maketh an argument against him selfe, he translateth it *qui pro vobis funditur, vvhich blood is shed for you,* saying that thus it should be, & that either the Euangelist made a sollecisme, or that the text is corrupred. But in the one he is very saucie to correct the Euangelist, in the other he lyeth, because al the greeke copies haue it as I haue set it downe. By this it is manifest, that as Christ promised, that he vvould geue his body and bloud to be eaten and drouken really, as is proued in the first argument, so he gaue really his body and bloud to his Apostles at his last supper, vnder the formes and accidents of bread and vvine. And so the text and letter of Scripture is plain for the real presence: & that the letter is to be vnderstood really as it soundeth, and not metaphorically, tropically, or figuratiuely, I haue proued by many arguments, and plaine discourse of Christ vvith his disciples, in the first argument, and by many circumstances and euident signes in the second argument.

In Annot. The text is for the real presence.

The interpreters also.

9. Yet because euery man must be beleued in his Art, espcially vvhen there is no suspicion of partialitie, I vvil proue the meaning of Christs vvordes to be real & literal, & not figuratiue or spiritual only, by the authoritie of the ancient Fathers, whose art & profession vvas to interprete Scripture: in which also they vvere so conning, that for the same, they are as famous amongst Christians, as Aristotle for Philosophie, or Cicero for eloquence, Homer, Virgil, and Ouid, for poetrie, Liuie and Salust for historie, vvho also can not be suspected to fauour partially one side, rather then an other, because they are more ancient then either the Catholiques or the Reformers of this tyme. And hauing these men on my side, I vvil not feare to shew my selfe in the field against al the pretending reformers in the vvorld, because hauing them on my side, I shal haue many moe to fight for me, then against me. And as hauing them on my side I may take courage, so my aduersaries if they had any forhead, vvould be ashamed, so few to stand in field against so many: so young vpstartes against so ancient Captaines (who most of them haue vanquished one Archheretike and sectmaster or other, by their learned vvritings) so vnlearned

he may be bold that is so backed.

against

against so learned? so vicious against so renowmed Saintes, & so light ministers against so graue Pastors and Prelates. But because a Chapter is not a field large and spacious ynough, to muster al these souldiars of Christ together, I wil only bring forth a fewe of them, and those that speake very plainly, and consequently do strike most forcibly: & for the others I vvil refere the Reader to Cardinal Allen, Bellarmin, Suarez, Gregorius de Valentia, and others, vvho haue brought them al into the field, and placed euery one of them in his ranke and station, that is, in the tyme & age, in vvhich they liued. And because al these Fathers, ether expresly do interpret the vvords aforesayed, *This is my body*, or at least do ground them selues vpon them, or allude vnto them, their sayings may wel serue for interpretations of the text alleaged. *Vide Ioan. Garet. de præsentia corp. xpi.* *Fathers teach the real presence.*

10 S Ignatius, S Paules Scholar hath these vvords: *non gaudeo corruptibili nutrimento, panem Dei volo, panem cælestem, qui est caro Christi & Filij Dei viui, & potum volo sanguinem eius: I reioice not in corruptible nutriment, I vvil haue the bread of God)* he alludeth to Christ vvords in S. Iohn, vvhere he calleth him selfe bread *the(heauenly bread, vvhich is the flesh of Christ & the Sonne of the liuing God, & I vvil haue the drinke vvhich is his bloud* To vvhich vvords Caluin can not shape any reasonable answer, vnles he vse much violence, in vvresting the text: for he calleth the Eucharist incorruptible nutrimēt, Caluins Supper is as corruptible as bread, he calleth it the bread of God and bread celestial, alluding to Christs vvordes, vvho of his owne flesh and not of common bread, pronounced those vvordes *I am the liuing bread, vvhich descended from heauen*, Caluins bread hath no higher source and origin from vvhich it is descended, then the backhouse or ouen. This bread he calleth the flesh of Christ the Sonne of God, & this drinke he auoucheth to be the bloud of Christ, vvheras Caluins bread and vvine is but bread and vvine, or but a signe of the flesh & bloud of Christ, but in dede it is no signe at al, because Christ instituted that bread for a signe & Sacrament, which is consecrated by a Priest, vvhich consecration Caluins bread hath not, because his Ministers are no Priestes as I haue demonstrated But because Caluin might by a violent glosse affirme that Ignatius calleth the Eucharist incorruptible meate, celestial, and the bread of God, because it is a signe of Christs flesh, which is incorruptible, & celestial, and the bread of God, I vvil bring places, that can admit no glossing. And first of al I wil bring some Fathers, vvho say that this Sacrament is not a bare figure, but is the true flesh of Christ. S. Chrysostome, that *Ep. ad Rom.* *Io. 6.* *Io. 6.* *Caluins bread not so much as a signe.* *See the fourth booke chap. 1.*

golden Mouth of the Church of Christ, stoppeth Caluins mouth, with these words: *Semetipsum nobis commiscet & non fide tantum, verum & reipsa nos suum corpus efficit; he doth mingle him selfe with vs, & not only by faith, but also in very dede he maketh vs his body.* Caluin sayth that we eate Christ only by faith, & consequently that his substance is not really vnited to our sub stance, because according to his opinion, they are distant as farre as heauen and earth, but S. Chrisostom sayth, that Christs substance in this Sacrament is mingled with ours, not only by faith, but also in very dede, *ergo* in very dede Christs body is in the Sacrament, & by meanes of the Sacrament, in the receuers also & communicantes.

Fathers that calit really Christes body.

Ho 61 ad. pop.

Theophilactus vvriting vpon the sixt of S. Iohn speaketh, if it be possible, more plainly: *Attende autem quod panis qui a nobis in mysterijs manducatur, non est tantum figuratio quadam carnis Domini, sed est ipsa caro Domini: Marke, that the bread vvhich is eaten of vs in the mysteries, is not a figuration* (that is an expression or figure) *of the flesh of our Lord, but it is the very flesh of our Lord.* how is it possible for the greatest Papist that is, to speake more plainly: Hilarius speaketh as plainly, as if he stroue, who should speake most plainly: *De veritate carnis, & sanguinis non est relictus ambigendi locus, nunc enim & ipsius Domini professione, & fide nostra, vere caro est &, vere sanguis est: Of the veritie of the flesh and bloud, there is no place left to doubt. For now, both by our Lords profession,* and *by our faith, it is truly flesh and truly bloud.* Where the vvordes, *veritie*, & *truly* are cleane opposite to Caluins figures, and spiritual manducation. S. Ciril of Hierusalem hath these vvordes: *Hoc sciens & pro certissimo habens panem hunc qui videtur a nobis, non esse panem, etiam si gustus panem esse sentiat, sed esse corpus Christi. &c Knovving this, and holding it for most certain, that this bread, vvhich is sene of vs, is not bread, although the taste iudgeth it to be bread, but the body of Christ: &* who vvould say so of a bare figure? yea who could? Can a man pointing to Cæsars picture say this which you see, is not paper, Inke, and colours layd proportionally, although the eye iudgeth so, but it is Cæsar him selfe? Can we say, pointing to baptisme, the water vvhich thou seest is not vvater, though to touche, tast, and eye, it seemeth so, but it is the holy Spirit or some other thing? I grant the same S Ciril saith the oile of Confirmation is not common oyle, but the chrisme of Christ: but he sayth not, that it is not oile, nor that it is any other natural thing, but that it is not cōmon oile, because it is a Sacrament. Secondly the Fathers admire how Christs body remaining in heauen, is notvvithstanding receued of vs in the blessed Sacrament. S. Chrysostom as a man astonished, exclameth in this sorte. *O miraculum, ô Dei benignitatem,*

in c. 6. Io.

l. 8. Trin.

Catech. 4. Mystagog.

Fathers admiration proueth the real prayers.

Catech. 3.

atem, qui cum Patre sursum sedet, in illo ipso temporis momento omnium manibus contrectatur: O Miracle, ô Gods benignitie; he that sitteth aboue vvith his Father in that very moment (that is in tyme of Consecration and Communion) *is handled in euery ones handes!* Now if Christ be only in the Sacrament as in a signe or figure, vvhat miracle is here, vvorthy such an exclamation? For so Christ were only really and in his owne person in heauen, and in earth he were but as in his Image, and consequently it were no greater a miracle, then that the King at the same tyme should be really in his chamber of presence, and yet figuratly in as many other places as he hath coynes or images. Yea this miracle the vintner maketh dayly, vvhose vvine is really in the caue, and at the same tyme in the Iuie bush, which is without the dore, for in it the wine is as in a signe. S. Austin vvondreth, how Christ caryed him selfe in his owne handes vvhen he sayd *this is my body*, vvhich is no vvonder if the Sacrament be a figure and signe of him, for so he caryeth him selfe, who caryeth his owne image. Thirdly the Fathers compare this Sacrament with strange and miraculous mutations. Ireneus and Cirillus compare it with the Incarnation, S. Ambrose with the Creation of the vvorld, and the Natiuitie of Christ of the Virgin Mother. The same Ireneus, and S. Ambrose count it like to the conuersion of the rod into a serpent, of water into bloud, and of the rocke into water, which strange mutations were vvrought by Moyses in Ægipt and in the desert. Againe S. Ciril of Hierusalem cōpareth it vvith the turning of water into vvine at the mariage in Cana Galilea: Christ once changed (saith he) *by his only vvil vvater into vvine, in Cana of Galilee, vvhich vvine is neere to bloud, and shal he not be vvorthy to be beleued, that he hath changed vvine into his bloud?* Which comparisons were very foolish, if the bread & wine had no other mutation, then that of bare bread and wine, they are made a signe, and as wel might they compare an Iuie bush vnto the same mutations, because the Iuie bush vvhen it is hanged before the Inne, of no signe is made a signe. Fourthly as in these alleaged conuersions and mutations, the aforenamed Fathers make recourse vnto Gods omnipotencie, so do they in the mutation of this Sacrament, prouing that it vvas possible, because God is omnipotent. S. Ambrose sayth: *he that of nothing could make something, can he* not turne one thing into an other? And S. Ciprian sayth, that by the omnipotencie of the vvord, the bread is made flesh. And vvere not these Fathers madde, to endeuour to explicate by so hard examples, how Gods omnipotencie vvas able to change bread into Christs body, vvine into his bloud, if

l. 3. de Sacerdot.

Con. 1. in Ps. 33.

Fathers comparison to strange mutations.

Li. 4. c. 14. Cat. 4. 5. l. de iis qui initiantur c. 9. Iren l. 3. c. 12. Amb. l. 4. de sacr c. 4. 9. Catech. 4. mystag.

Fathers to explicate this Sacr. rune.

Gods omnipotencie.

l. de iis qui initiantur c. 9. Cipr ser de Cana Domini.

 the mu-

the mutation vvere figuratiue only, seing that the vintner vvithout omnipotencie can do the like, in making an Iuie bush, of no signe a signe? Fiftly they admire herein our Sauiours great charitie & bou͂tie, who is so liberal, as to feast & fede vs, with his owne flesh & bloud.

Ho 45. in Io. *VVhat shepheard* (sayth S. Chrisostom) *feedeth his shepe vvith his ovvne bloud? And vvhat say I, shepheard? many mothers there are, vvhich vvil not bestovv their milke vpon their suckling babes, but rather do put them forth to nourcing, but Christ dealeth not so niggardly, but feedeth vs vvith his ovvne flesh and bloud, and mingleth his substance vvith ours.* Now if Christ hath giuen vs only a bare signe of a his flesh & bloud, I see no such extraordinarie loue and charitie: at least herein he sheweth no more, yea not so much charitie, as he shevved to the Iewes, to vvhom he gaue manna from heauen in their extremitie, vvhich vvas a more noble substance, and a

Fathers vvonder that christ is not consumed. better figure then Caluins bread is. Lastly the Fathers note for a strãge thing, that Christ is eaten of vs in the blessed Sacrament, and yet neither diuided, nor diminished, nor consumed. This S. Andrew told Ægeas the Proconsul for a great miracle. I (sayth he) *do offer dayly to the omnipotent God the Immaculate lambe, of vvhom vvhen al the people haue eaten, the lambe remaineth vvhole and entiere.* S. Ciprin calleth this Sacrament, *inconsumptibilem cibum, meate inconsumptible.* S. Austin speaking of this Sacrament, and of the murmuration of the Iewes, who imagined that they should teare Christs flesh carnally vvith their teeth, sayth thus: *sic reficeris, vt non deficiat vnde reficeris: so thou art refreshed, that it is not deficient, of vvhich thou art refreshed.* And the reason is, because Christs body is glorious, and is receiued vvhole of euery one, and so is not diuided, and vvhen the formes of bread and vvine perish, Christs body leaueth them, and though one man receueth Christs body whole, yet there is neuer the lesse for an other, for he also receueth it vvhole, neither in this is there any greater difficultie, then that 5000. men should be fed with fiue barly loaues, and two fishes, and yet the reliques to be as great or more, then vvas the feast. now if Christ be not really present in this Sacrament, but only as in signe and figure, it is no more meruaile, that he is not consumed, then that a mans picture should be burnt or broken, and he receue no harme: and if we eate him only spiritually by faith, vvhat vvonder is it, that his substance is not diuided, seing that faith hath no teeth to rent or teare him.

in vita apud Sur. — *Ser de Cœna Domini* — *Hom 1. de Verb. Apost.* — *Io. 6.*

Chr 4. practise. 11 I could adde to these Fathers (vvho as I haue proued in the first booke, euer vvent vvith the Chruch) the practise of the Christian vvorld, which for reuerence of this Sacrament (as Cardinal Allen noteth)

l. 1. de Eucharist. c. 20.

noteth) hath builded so goodly Chruches, erected so stately Altars prepared so rich vessels of gold and siluer, to containe this Sacrament, hath caryed it in Procession, and adored it: vvhich honour and homage Christians vvould neuer haue giuen it, had they thought that it vvere but bread and vvine, or a bare signe, or figure of Christs body. So that if euer there were any truth in the Church, this of the real presence is a truth, because the Scriptures are as plaine for it, as for any other mysterie of our faith, the Fathers agree in the exposition of the Scripture for the real presence, as they do in the exposition of Scriptures against the Arrians for the defence of the Trinitie, or against the Nestorians or Eutichians for the Incarnation: the practise of the ancient Chruch argueth no lesse: miracles (vnles al bookes and recordes lye) vvere alvvayes as frequent for this Mysterie, as for any. The consent of al Christians conspireth in this article, as wel as in the Trinitie, and this the Paganes knew ful vvel, vvho therfore called vs *Anthropophagos* and *Infanticidas* as vvitnesseth Tertulian. And so if we haue any truth of any Article of our faith, this is an assured veritie: & if euer there were any heresie, Caluins opinion, vvhich denyeth the real presence, is an heresie, because the autors of this opinion, were euer noted for Heretikes, as Berengarius, Wicleph, and others before them: & their folowers had particular names, as the Arians haue, they were condemned by Councels, and by that Chruch vvhich was commonly called Christian, and they haue al other markes of heretikes, set downe in the second booke, as wil easily appeare, by application of them to Caluin & his felowes. When this opinion vvas first taught the world vvondred at it, and the Pastors and Fathers of the Chruch vvrote against it, and they alleaged as plaine Scriptures against this heresie, as euer they did against Arianisme. And so, if euer there vvere any heresie in the vvorld, the denial of the real presence is an heresie.

If any truth the real presence is true.

In Apol. c. 1. 7. Pamel ibid. Euseb. l. 5. c.

If any hersie. Caluins opiniõ is heresie.

12. Conferre now (gentle reader) the testimonies vvhich Catholiques haue for the real presence, with those vvhich the reformers alleage against it, and tel me vvhere is likest to be the truth? Catholiques haue plainer Scripture for it, then they haue against it: the Fathers also vvho are interpreters of Scripture stand for it, the reformers stand against it. Which are to be beleeued, thinkest thou? Whether al the Fathers, or al the Reformers, yea or euery one of the Reformers, because they agree not, and euery one wil be supreme Iudge, by his priuate spirit. They wil say Scripture must be beleued before Fathers. But this is not the question; for Scriptures are plainer for the real presence,

greater probabilitie of the real presence. then of the contrarie.

Scripture plaine for it.

Fathers also.

sence; then those are, vvhich the reformers bring against it. And Fathers bring Scriptures to proue it, as wel as they do to disproue it: so that the question is, vvhether the Fathers are liker, to vnderstand the Scripturs rightly, rather then the reformers, yea, rather then any one of the reformers in particular. But to draw to my intended conclusion, out of al this discourse I gather, that we haue as plaine Scriptures for the real presence of Christs body & bloud in the blessed Sacrament, as we haue for the blessed Trinitie, & we are as sure of the meaning of the textes, vvhich are alleaged for the real presence, as of them, vvhich were vsed for proofe of the Trinitie or Incarnation: because the text is as plaine, and the Interpreters as many and as plaine also, that the texts make as much for the real presēce, as for those other two mysteries. The real presence is no more impossible, nor incredible to mans conceite, then those Mysteries are, yea those are of greater difficultie. Why then do the reformers deny the Real presence, rather then the Trinitie or Incarnation? If we haue as good proofes for this as for those verities, we can not beleue those, but we must beleue this, or if these testimonies be not sufficient for the real presence, they are not sufficient for those verities, & so if notvvithstanding plaine text, circunstances of the texte, Interpreters of the texte, and practise of the Church, we deny the real presence, or doubt of it, we must necessarily doubt of the Trinitie and Incarnation, and cal them; and al the other Mysteries of Christian faith in question, for vvhich we haue no greater, nor no other profe, because one proofe is for al: and as good for the Eucharist as for any. And if al the Mysteries of christian faith be called in question, then seing that we haue no reason to ioyne with Turck or Iew in their Religiō, we may bid adew to al Religion, and sorte our selues with Atheistes, who are of no Religion.

Theconclusion.

If the real prensence be denyed, al Christian faith is shaked.

Hovv Atheisme entereth.

***

The

The eight Chapter first teacheth the Reader hovv to make his profit of this Suruey. Secondly it shevveth hovv deformed and deforming the nevv Church is. Thirdly it shevveth the euidence of the Catholique & Romain Church. And lastly it proueth that out of this Church is no saluation, and so exhorteth the Reader to continevv if he be already, or to make him selfe speedily, if as yet he be not, a member of this Church.

T is a pleasure certes to bring a stranger vnacquanted, into a S. Peters palace in Rome, or an Escuryel in Spain, or a Louer in Paris, or a Nonsuch, or Richmond, or Roial Exchange in England, and there to shew him the gorgeous building, witty conueyghances, and varietie of roomes and chambers, the rich seeling, curious caruing, and painting, and vvhat soeuer is worthy sight or admiration. But it is no lesse displeasure, if you lead not this your stranger out againe: who many tymes is so intentiue in his gazing, and so wistly admireth euery thing vvhich he seeth, that he marketh not how he entred, and so is as ignorant how to get out, as he was at first to get in. This is the fault of worldlinges, vvhom the almightie by Creatiō hath brought as by the hand into the goodly palace of this vvorld, of vvhich he him selfe is not only Lord, but the Architectt also and builder: but they are so occupied in gazing vpon the beautie order, disposition and richesse of the same, and do so admire the loftie roofe of this building, seled so richly with so glittering starres, and are so distracted with the sight of such varietie of thinges most admirable, vvhich in this Palace are contained: that they neuer marcke how they came into this vvorld, nether know they, nether care they how to get out: but here setting as much as they can both their hartes & desires, make that their home, which is but a place of exile & a passage to their home, & neuer thinck of the end to which they were created, and to vvhich they are to passe by this vvorld, as by an

by an Inne in the high vvay: but ether with Epicure imagin that they are created to no other end, then here to take their pleasure; or thinke
Lactant l. 3. de vera & falsa Rel. c. 4. with Auaxagoras that they were borne only to speculate the heauens and starres, and not by them to make a farther step to the knowledge of God, the autour and Creatour. The like is the fault of many curious wittes in England, vvho desire to peruse and read al bookes of controuersies, and to enter into euerie such discourse: and being entred they admire this, delight in that, and so they may acquaint them selues with varietie of opinions and fynde matter of dispute, argument, and table talke, for the rest they care not: and so they neuer marke how they entred in, nor that God it was, vvho by his grace leadeth them into such discourses, to bring them therby vnto the knowledge of him selfe, his Church, true faith, and true Religion: nether do know nether care they how to get out of such discourses, vvith making therby their soules profit, and vvorking their owne saluation.

2. Wherfore (gentle reader) hauing brought thee by the reading of this booke to see and suruey the great difference betwen the Catholique Religion, and the new doctrines vvhich certayne pretended reformes haue brought into the world, I haue thought it good by this last chapter, as by an Epiloque, to shew thee how to make thy
Mat. 16. profite, and spiritual commoditie therof, vvhich vvas the end and proiect of my laboures. For this Suruey hath not only deciphered and detected the fowle and detestable absurdities of the new Religion, but also hath shewed thee the goodlie Palace of the Catholique Church, builded by our Sauiour vpon the rock of S. Peters Seat, so firmly that
Mat. 5. not al the heresies that euer haue yet bene, nor schismes, nor persecutions that haue bene raised against it, could beate it downe, & placed like a citie on a hil, a tabernacle in the sune, so hiegh, great and eminent, that it hath continually bene conspicuous and visible, yea and glorious euen in the eyes of her enimies. And I perswade my selfe thou admirest the order and discipline therof, the varietie of offices and functions, the goodlie Seruice and vvorship of God, consisting in Prayer. Sacraments, and Sacrifice, vvhich in this Iererchie thou seest: and that thou art delighted with the swetenes, & truth of the Catholique Churches doctrin vvhich is taught in her. And I hope the euident markes of the true Christian Church, Which here I haue noted, are not only motiues to draw thee thither, but also bandes to hold thee there, being once entred. But because my principal drift, and intention

intention was, to geue thee a view of the absurdities of the new Church, I haue bene longer in the suruey of their new doctrin, then in declaration of the ancient true Religion. Neuertheles because I counted it not sufficient to shew thee what to flye, vnles I told thee also what to folow, in disprouing the new Church and religion, I haue proued the old, setting forth one contrarie by an other: and if thou marke, before I shew the absurditie of the heretical doctrin, I proue commonly the Catholique veritie, to make thee so to flye that, that thou forget not to flye to this: So that thou hast seen both that the Catholique Romain Church is the onlie true Christian Church, and that the new Synagogue, called by them the reformed Church, is the most deformed and deforming congregation that can be.

3. And first how deformed it is thou couldst not but see, & seeing thou couldst not but detest & abhorre. For first this congregatiō hath a very weake foundation, which is either the only pretense of the bare letter of Scripture, where according to their priuate spirite it semeth to make for them, though both the expositiōs of the ancient Fathers, & other Scriptures be plaine against them; or the bare assertiō of their preachers without proofe of their mission: which hath bene the fundation of al heresies, but so sandie, and vnstable, that though on it there hath bene some shew of standing for a time, yet in time also they haue fallen, as these late heresies in part are fallen already, and for the rest, do, by their shaking & tottering also prognostigate, a speedie fal, Secōdly in this congregatiō there is no one head, to decide matters of faith, as the sixth chapter of the first booke maketh manifest: for which defect it is a monstrous bodie. Thirdly it is yet more monstrous for that it hath manie heades, for al are such heades, as wil not subiect their priuate spirites to anie other priuate, or common: but wil be iudges them selues in al things, & so in effect make no distinction of members, no subordination, no Hierarchie, nor order. Fourthly this bodie like some *Centaurus* is compacted & compounded of contrarie and disagreeing parts. For some are Lutherans, some Demilutheranes, some softe, some hard and rigorous Lutheranes, some Antilutheranes, that is, direct opposit to Luther, & yet of his broode, Some Zuinglians, some Caluinistes, some Protestantes, some Puritanes, some Brownistes, some Barowistes, and the like. Fifthly it hath al the fowle spottes, and vglie markes of heresie: As I haue declared in the second booke, & is compacted and patched vp of manie old heresies

The nevv congregation is al deformed

See the first booke. c. 12.

Li. 2.

raked & assẽbled together. And that with such Ægyptiacal darknes, such filthines and ordures of vices, such horrible blasphemies, and such a sinck of lothsome stuffe, as rather sheweth it to be a stable of beastes, then a Church of Christianes.

The new congregation also maketh al deformed so much as in it lieth.

4. Neither is it deformed only but also the most deforming companie that euer heresie brought forth. It deformeth and defaceth God so much as in it lyeth: making him the author of sinne, the onlie sinner, cruel, and tyrannical, as appeareth in the fifth booke. It deformeth and disableth Christ: making him not the sonne of God, no Redemer, no spiritual Phisition, no Lawmaker, no eternal Priest, no Iudge of the quick and dead, but rather metamorphozeth him into an ignorant, passionat, desperate and damned man: as the third booke sheweth. It deformeth & defaceth the Church as in the fourthe booke is shewed, auouching that she hath doted almost euer from her infancie, making her an Idolatresse, affirming that she maintaineth manie errors: sometimes making her inuisible sometimes starke dead, & exẽpt of being. It depriueth her of Pristhood, of Order or Hierchie, making her headles in earth, without a visible chiefe Pastor. It hath taken frõ her fiue of the seuen Sacraments, & maketh the two it hath left her, of smal valew and vertue. It depriueth her of a visible and proper Sacrifice, and hath taken away the ancient solemne and deuout forme of Seruice, and left almost no essential part of Religion. It hath ruined, vvhere it reigneth, al Ecclesiastical disciplin and gouernment. It hath vtterly ouerthrowen vvhere it ruleth, the State of vowed Religious, condemning it as superstitious, yea pernicious: vvhich yet vvas in part begune by the Apostles, and propagated by so manie Paules, Antonies, Hilaries, Basiles, Benedictes, and others. It deformeth and despoyleth Princes depriuing them of authoritie, and their Lawes of al force and vigore, their tribunals of iust terrour and estimation, as the sixth booke declareth. It deformeth and turmoyleth al commonwelthes: as is proued in the same booke, teaching dissensious & mutenous doctrin, which breedeth ielousies distrustes, oppressiõs of people, and rebellion against officers & Superiors. It hath deformed, and derogated from mans nature: despoyling vs, in their doctrin, of Gods Image, of freewil, & al inclinatiõ to vertue, making it a dunghil, that vaporeth nothing els but mortal sinne & al iniquitie: supposing it so feeble and impotent, that it can not, though sturred vp and ayded by Gods grace, merite anie thing at Gods hande: nor satisfie for the least, offence, nor yet resist the least tentation, as in diuers chapters of the seuenth

Act. 4.

seuenth booke is made manifest. Finally it hath deformed Religion and moral life, by bringing in dissolution of maners, irreligiositie, Atheisme, & contempt of al Religion. Of al vvhich let our countrie be iudge whether before this new doctrin came in place of the former Catholique Religion, the Iudges had euer so manie theeues and murderers brought to be tried and condemned, as since Zuinglius and Caluins opinions were embraced. And let the voice of the people geue sentence, vvhether so manie fornications, adulteries baudries, deuorcements, & rewiuing, were so rife as now in England. Let the lawyers of ancient standing tel vs plainly, vvhether vvhen the vvhole Realme professed the Catholique Religion, there was so much packing, cosening, falsifying of testaments, Indentures, obligations and other vvritings as now? And vvhether then, yea and now also, a Catholiques word were not surer then any Protestants or Puritanes obligation? By which and other their general knowen fruites, iudge discrete reader, vvhich is the good tree. *For by their fruites, our Sauiour saith, you shal knovv them.* Here I omitte to repete, what hauock they haue made of al Church ornaments, especially of siluer and gold Chalices, Crosses, Pixes, Paxes, Candlestickes, Censars, rich shrines of Reliques, Copes, vestments, yea in manie places of lead, glasse and the like, robing spoyling and wasting those holie things, vvhich deuout Catholiques thought no vvhere so wel bestowed, as vpon Gods house to Gods honour. The soules in Purgatorie are by these men, and these meanes depriued of relife, vvhich vvas vvont to be in euerie Church imperted vnto them. Yea if these new doctors could do as they say, they would depriue al penitent poore soules of the very place it selfe, by which at last they should be saued, & would thrust al those that are not fully prepared for Heauen, presently and desperatly into Hel. Yea they derogate also from the glorious Saintes in Heauen, making them vnable to heare or vnderstand our prayers, and of so litle charitie, that they care for vs, of so smal credit with their Lord and Maister, that they may not presume to promote anie suites, or requests for their dearest freinds in the world, and vvould not haue them honored in anie religious sorte. Only this new doctrin fauoureth Hel, teaching that it is not so as vglie, commonly it is imagined, yea that is no circumscripte place, but only a remorse of conscience, and so preferreth as manie as it can thither, to amplifie the diuels dominion, assuring so manie as vvil beleue it, that al vvorkes, euen those that

as appeareth by the 8. booke

Mat. 7.

Li. 3. cap. 12.

go for best, deserue hel fire, & that no man can resist the diuel, in anie tentation, but must nedes yeld vnto him, and further more it leadeth to al heresies vices and atheisme, which are the very pathes, yea the gates and directest entrance into hel. So you see what a deformed and deforming congregation this new Synagogue is: and consequently how iust cause you that are in it, haue to hasten your selues out of it.

5. But I know what some wil say: that for sooth you see & confesse, this new Church hath manie grosse absurdities, yet because it beleueth in Christ, and the B. Trinitie, you hope in this Church and faith you may be saued. Which flatring conceipt, I haue refuted in the second booke. Where I haue shewed, that anie one heresie cutteth of from the true Church, & is cause of eternal damnation. Here only I remit you to S. Augustin: who speaking of the Pelagianes, pronounceth this sentence of them. *Neither* (saith he) *are these Pelagian heretikes such as thou wouldest easily contemne, because they liue continently, and are laudable in good workes, neither do they beleue in a false Christ, as the Maniches and other heretikes do, but they beleue in the same true Christ that we do, confessing him to be equal and coeternal to his Father, beleuing him to be truly man, that he came from heauen, and that he is to returne againe at* the last day, *but because they, not knowing the iustice of God, would establish their ovvne iustice*: the holie Doctor concludeth, that for this one error wherin they were like to the foolish virgins, though in manie other things they were like to wise virgins, *if they slept in that one, and so avvaking that is rising from death, should be found without they should worthely remaine without, because in the meane time*, before they slept *they entred not in*. And the same would he say to anie Protestant Puritane or the like, notwithstanding he beleueth in Christ, seing he doth not wholly and inuiolably beleue the Catholique Christian faith. Wherfore if you wil be in the state and possibilitie of saluation, returne to the Catholique Church the only house of saluation, because it is the only true Church: as I haue shewed in the second booke & in the Epistle to the honorable priuie counsel: where & in manie other places of this booke you may see how the markes of the true christian Church agree al vnto it, & to no other. Why then doubtest thou, why differrest thou to enter into so secure an hauen, and to repose thy selfe vpon this pillar of truth? *Shal we doubt saith* S. Augustin, *to repose our selues in that Churches lappe, which euen from the Apostles sitting & ruling therin by succession of Bishops (heretikes in vaine barking against it, &*

[Margin notes: *4. chap.* — *To. 2. ep. 120. chap. 37.* — *merito foris erunt.* — *Symb. Athan.* — *li. de vtil. credēdi. c. 18.*]

it, & partly by the common iudgement of the people, partly by the grauitie of councels, partly by the maiestie of miracles being condemned) hath obtayned the top and height of authoritie? Three things held the same great Doctor in this Church, Succession of Priests in S. Peters Seate, Consent of nations, and the name Catholique: al which I haue shewed in the said second booke to remaine stil in the same Catholique Romain Church. And why then fearest thou, where so lerned a Father found him selfe so secure? and where els canst thou settle thy selfe securly, but where only al ancient Christians haue hoped for saluation? Certes if in this Church thou canst not be saued, al thy foresathers, though neuer so religious and vertuous, were damned, for there was neuer anie other commonly knowen & receued for the true Christian Church.

lib. cont. ep. Fund.

6. Those Neroes, Domitians, Diocletians, Maximinians, against this Church, as the only true Church of Christ, which they therfore especially hated, armed their furie, and whetted their instruments of crueltie. And as Iustinus Martyr noted, they neuer persecuted the heretikes of their time, *because* (saith he) *the diuel knovving his ovvne incensed them only against the true Church, the only enemie of his Kingdom.* And if they were now liuing, and saw the state of the present Romane Church, they would sweare by their crownes and scepters, it is the same with that, against which they were so enraged. And if they saw this new Sinagogue of our deformed deformers, the would auouch by their honours, that they neuer stricke blow against it, neither could, because it was not. Al the ancient and worthie Christian Kinges of France, England, Spaine, Scotland, Pooland, Beamland, and such others were baptised, sacred, and crowned in our Religion, and by the handes of our so graue and holie Bishops. And they promised by solemne oath to defend our Religion & Clergie, as I haue briefly shewed in myn Epistle to the honourable Counsel, yea this is so an approued & knowen a Tradition, that the new Superintendents of England were to seek and knew not where to begin, nor what Ceremonies to vse in the coronation of our worthy King, bicause nether they nor any of their proper predecessours had been accustomed vnto such an office: it hauing euer been the office of our bishops, as to consecrate preestes with holy oyle, so to anoint and sacre Kinges. And not only the Popes, Patriarches, and Primates, but all other Bishops also euen of our great Britannie, were consecrated in, and by our Church and ruled in the same. Al the lerned Doctors & Fathers,

in prefat. desens. ad Anton. pium.

annointing of Kings by a Bishop.

S. Clement, Dyonisius Areopagita, Ignatius, Martialis the Apostles owne scholars, and others succeding, as S. Cyprian Ambrose, Augustin, Ierome, Gregorie, Leo, Ciril, Basil, Chrysostome, and manie moe taught and defended our Religion with tongue and penne. Al those General and venerable Concels of Nice, Ephesus, Chalcedon, Constantinople, and the rest were called by our Popes and consisted of our Bishops. The canonical Scriptures are ours, & haue euer bene in our possession, and had neuer come to Luthers handes had not our Church conserued them. Al Diuine Seruice, as Masse Canonical houres & the rest be ours. Al Ecclesiastical gouuerment & discipline is ours. As for new Iniunctions & lately made Canons they are only imitations of ours. The Canon Law is nothing els but Decrees, and Decretal Epistles of Popes, & Bishops, especially assembled in Councels. The ciuil & cōmon Lawes are ful of constitutions made for the mantenance of our Church, and expresly against heretikes her deadlie enemies. The schoole diuines, who for lerning haue the next place after the Fathers, explicate and defend our Religion against Turkes, & al Infidels, as Petrus Lombardus, Albertus, Hales, Aquinas, Scotus, Bonauenrura & such like. Al the Abbots, Mounkes Eremites, Friars, and other Religious men were Papistes in the highest degree by our aduersaries confession; yet were they Paules, Antonies, Macarius, Basiles, Gregories, Ieromes, Augustins, Benedicts, Bernards, Dominikes, Franceses, & such like. Yea al the order, or Hiererchie of the Ecclesiastical state is onlie ours, for that which now they haue in England, is but an imitation, or rather a corruption of the same. Yea al ciuil and temporal dignitie in the Church, of Kings Dukes, Earles, Barons, knights is ours, & procedeth from our Church touching the ceremonies vsed in their creation. For example M. Camden testifyeth that in ancient time, when a knigth was to be dubbed, he was to watch the night before in prayer, and after confession to heare Masse, & communicate in the same: then the swoord was blessed and deliuered vnto him. Thus knights were made in the time of the Saxons. Al conuersions of countries to Christian Religion were made by our Church, & to our Religion, as Bosius in his histories of euerie countrie hath clerly shewed. For example, our King Lucius receiued Christian faith from Pope Eleutherius, as M. Camden and al our late chroniclers confesse. And againe, Pope Gregorie the first, restored our Religion, which by the Saxons entrie was extinguished in most partes of England; & that he did by Monkes. And

The nerma of making knights in England in old time.

li. 4. de signis Eccl.

now

now in this last age by diuers Orders of Religious men, especially by Iesuites, the new found landes are cõuerted to the same Religion. And neuer yet could Heretikes conuert anie countrie from Paganisme to Christianitie. But after their conuersion haue peruerted some, that is, after the good corne was sowed, they haue scatered their cockle. Al the Saintes in heauen had their sanctitie from Christ in our Church. And if they should now speake with an audible voice, you should heare thẽ al auouch, that they were Apostles, Martyrs, Doctors, Virgins, and Confessors of our Church militant in earth, and were from hence trãsported to the Church triumphant in heauen. And therfore by our Chucrh only their liues, actes, and passions are recorded, their memories and feastes celebrated, by vs they are honoured, by the pretended reformers much debased, & by some reuiled. Lastly because I would not be tedious, al Churches, Abbeys, Nunries, Vniuersities, most Colleges, & Hospitals were founded by our Catholique Kings, Bishops, & others of our Religion. And namely our vniuersities of Oxford and Cambridge by M. Cãdens owne confession, are to thank the Church of Rome, for making them of Colleges Vniuersities. So that al good & special things in the Christian world, came from our Church, or be only to be fond of ancient time in our Churches, & al waste, ruine, & deformitie from the new Synagogue, as I haue proued: and al ancient monuments, euen to tombes, walles, and windowes shew only our Chnrch, and Religion: and demonstrate that the Church, commonly coũted Christian, was euer permanent, visible, & conspicuous & neuer died, nor so decayed, that it became inuisible, neuer lurked, nor lay hid in corners. And where then was this present Church of England? what Church alwayes florished but ours?

Heretikes diminish Christianitie, but increase it not.

Our Vniuersities ordayned by the Pope.

7. They answer that our Church was once the true Church, but after wards (they say) it degenerated. But when, how, by whom, and by what occasion it was thus metamorphized, they know not. But I haue proued, in the second booke, and in myn Epistle, to the Coũsel that the true Church can not degenerate in matters of faith & Religion. And consequently if our Church once was the true Church, stil it is. And if once it was pure, and free from errors, stil it is, & the deformers departing from this Church are herettikes, & their opiniõs, which they hold against her, are heresies. And seing that one heresie cutteth from the Chnrch (as in the aforsaid places is proued) they are out of the true Church, and so long as they so remaine, they are out of al possibilitie of saluation.

the true Church faileth not. ca. 5.

8. by

8. Why then lingrest thou to leaue this so deformed and deforming a companie? Why doubtest thou to incorporate thy selfe to that Church, for which al ancient monumẽts do make so manifestly: & in which al ancient Christianes haue reposed them selues so securely? More secure certes it is (though there were no certaintie of the church) to aduenture saluation with them, thẽn with the Protestãtes of this so new and so improbable a Religion. But manie other arguments for this Church I haue vsed in this booke, then I nede here repete, & those so pregnant & conuincing, that vnles thou be negligent in pondering, or wilful in resisting the clere truth, thou canst not but acknowledge the Romaine Church to be the only true Christian Church, it being so visible, that as S. Augustin saith, *they are stark blind, which see not this citie situated on a mountaine, this tabernacle placed in the sunne, and this light set vpon a candlestike, not couered vnder a bushel.* And acknowledging this Church I hope thou wilt not differ thy incorporation. For although thou maist be damned in this Church, if thou liuest not accordingly, because the bodie hath dead members, and the tree hath rotten bowes, yet if thou be seuered from this bodie by heresie or schisme, thou canst not possibly be saued, because thou canst not be partaker of the grace, the soule, and life of this bodie, except thou be an inherent member ther of.

Tract. 2. in Ep. 10.
Mat. 5.
Psal. 18.

9. For, as the same S. Augustin saith, the Church being a mystical bodie not vnlike to the natural bodie of man, as the soule is the life of mans bodie, so the spirit of God is the soule that animateth, & geueth life to the mystical bodie of Christs Church. And as the soule though it impert life equally to al partes, yet imperteth not al offices vnto them, for the eye only seeth, and the eare only heareth; so the spirite of God communicateth not the same functions to al members of the Church, but to some it imperteth virginitie, & religious life, to some wedlock chastitie, & some are Doctors, some Pastores, some Euangelistes, some worke miracles, some haue the gift of prophecie. But as the members cut of, do presently lose life and feeling, because the soule foloweth not the partes cut of, but remaineth with the whole, and with the partes vnited: so (saith this great Doctor) if by heresie or schisme thou be seuered from the bodie of the Church, there is no more life remayning in thee: *If therfore* (saith this Father) *thou wilt liue of Gods holie Spirite, hold charitie, loue veritie, secke vnitie, that thou maist come to eternitie.* The same Doctor with S. Cyprian auoucheth that heretikes are beames seperated from the sunne, riuers cut of from

Ser. 186. de tempore.

Ro. 12.
1. Cor. 12.

ibidem.

the fountayne, and boughes riuen of from the tree. And consequently their light goeth out, their water drieth vp, and they are quite deuoide of sappe and life. Wherfore saith he out of the Church thou maist haue honour, & dignitie, thou maist haue the Sacraments also, thou maist sing *Alleluia*, and answer, *Amen*. Thou maist haue the Gospel, thou maist preach Christ, and beleue in the name of the Father, the Sonne, and the Holie Ghost. Finally thou maist haue al but saluation out of the Catholique Church. but a poore al it is, Which comprehendeth not saluation. Which is al in al.

Tomo 10. ser. 181 & 10.7. li. cont. Cresc. ca. 33. Cypri. de simplicit. Prelat.

10. Come then (gentle reader) come al ye that are cut of from this bodie, vnite your selues vnto it, if you wil be partakers of life. *Venite fratres* (saith the same Doctor) *si vultis vt inseramini in vite. dolor est cum vos videmus precisos ita iacere, numerate Sacerdotes vel ab ipsa petri Sede, & in ordine illo Patrum, quis cui successit videte, Ipsa est petra, quam non vincunt superba inferorum portæ.* Come bretheren that ye may be ingraffed in the vine. It is a grief when we see you lie cut of in this maner: number the Priestes euen from Peters seate, and see who succeded to whom in that order of Fathers: that is the rock, Which the prowde gates of hel do not ouercome. And againe in an other place: *Firmiter tene, & nullatenus dubita, quemlibet hereticum vel schismaticum, in nomine Patris & Filij & Spiritus sancti baptizatum, si Ecclesiæ Catholicæ non fuerit aggregatus, quantascumque eleemosinas fecerit, & si pro Christi nomine sanguinem fuderit, nullatenus posse saluari.* Hold firmely, and doubt not at al, that no heretike nor schismatike (a sore saying for those in England, who being Catholiques in hart, but by communicating externally with heretikes, make them selues externally members of their Church, and so cut them selues of from ours) although baptized in the name of the Father and the Sonne and the Holie Ghost, can be saued, how great almes soeuer he geueth, yea although he shede his bloud for Christs name.

To. 7. Psal. contra partem Donati.

Tomo. 3. de fide ad Petrum. c. 3. 8. 39.

The state of an heretike, or schismatike.

11. Wherfore once againe, gentle reader, I desire thee, as thou tenderest thy saluation (and marke what I say, when I say saluation) vnite thy self vnto this bodie of the Catholique Church, from vvhich euerie heresie cutteth of, and out of which thou canst not worke thy saluation. And therfore neither to gaine a world (which if thou hadest thou couldest not long possesse) neither for feare of losse of landes, liuings, or life, seperate thy self from this Church. For what wil it pleasure thee to gaine a world, with losse of thy soule, which is worth tenne thousand worldes? And What shouldest thou

Saluation importeth more then manie vvorldes.

feare so much, as to be seuered from that Church, which separation importeth a losse no lesse then of soule and bodie, the damnation of soule and bodie euerlasting? Wherfore yet once againe (because thy saluation can not be to often inculcated) feare nothing so much as to be seuered from this bodie, out of which who liueth is dead, & whosoeuer dieth is certaynly damned. And let this sentence of S. Augustin
Tract. 27. in Ioan. (with whom as I haue begunne, so wil I end) alwayes be printed in thy hart. *Nihil sic formidare debet Christianus, quam seperari a corpore Christi, quod est Ecclesia, vtique Vna Catholica: si enim separatur a corpore Christi non est membrum eius, si non est membrum eius, non vegetatur spiritu eius: quisquis autem spiritum Christi non habet, hic non est eius.*
Rom. 8. Nothing ought a Christian to feare so much, as to be separated frō the bodie of Christ, which is the Church: One and Catholique: for if he be separated from the bodie of Christ, he is no member of his, if he be not his member he is not quickned with his spirite: and whosoeuer hath not the spirite of Christ, that man is not his. And I wil adde, that he that is not partaker of Christs grace and spirite in his Church militant in earth, shal haue no part with him in the glorie of his Church triumphant in heauen. And therfore I besech our Lord Iesus Christ, in whose name dwelleth grace, geue thee so much grace, as may make thee desirous, and careful of thy saluation, and this Sune of iustice send thee some beames of his light, to illuminate thyne eyes, to see the right way, that leadeth to saluation. And because this way is true Religion, and true Religio bringeth to eternal life: I besech this *dore* to open thyne hart and direct thee into this way: I besech this *vvay* guide thee in the truth, I besech this *truth* leade thee to the life of thy soule, I besech this *life* to protect thee and bring thee to life euerlasting. Amen.

FINIS.

A TABLE

A TABLE OF THE *principal things proued or disproued in this booke.*

A

C

It neuer

Here-

T.

FINIS.

THE PRINTER TO THE CVRTEOVS READER.

SOME faultes are here escaped in printing, though nothing nere so manie as in the former Edition. The greatest part seme to be in the marginal annotations: and perhaps some few in the quotations. I can not here set downe the errors, for that he who hath bestowed great diligence and paines, to auoide manie greater, hath not leysure to reade the whole once againe, for correcting of the smaller. But the iudicial reader wil easily vnderstand, how it should haue bene; and so of his curtesie amend and pardon that is amisse.

Deo gratias.